# Principles of the criminal law of Scotland.

## Archibald Alison

*The Making of Modern Law* collection of legal archives constitutes a genuine revolution in historical legal research because it opens up a wealth of rare and previously inaccessible sources in legal, constitutional, administrative, political, cultural, intellectual, and social history. This unique collection consists of three extensive archives that provide insight into more than 300 years of American and British history. These collections include:

Legal Treatises, 1800-1926: over 20,000 legal treatises provide a comprehensive collection in legal history, business and economics, politics and government.

Trials, 1600-1926: nearly 10,000 titles reveal the drama of famous, infamous, and obscure courtroom cases in America and the British Empire across three centuries.

Primary Sources, 1620-1926: includes reports, statutes and regulations in American history, including early state codes, municipal ordinances, constitutional conventions and compilations, and law dictionaries.

These archives provide a unique research tool for tracking the development of our modern legal system and how it has affected our culture, government, business – nearly every aspect of our everyday life. For the first time, these high-quality digital scans of original works are available via print-on-demand, making them readily accessible to libraries, students, independent scholars, and readers of all ages.

**The BiblioLife Network**

This project was made possible in part by the BiblioLife Network (BLN), a project aimed at addressing some of the huge challenges facing book preservationists around the world. The BLN includes libraries, library networks, archives, subject matter experts, online communities and library service providers. We believe every book ever published should be available as a high-quality print reproduction; printed on-demand anywhere in the world. This insures the ongoing accessibility of the content and helps generate sustainable revenue for the libraries and organizations that work to preserve these important materials.

The following book is in the "public domain" and represents an authentic reproduction of the text as printed by the original publisher. While we have attempted to accurately maintain the integrity of the original work, there are sometimes problems with the original work or the micro-film from which the books were digitized. This can result in minor errors in reproduction. Possible imperfections include missing and blurred pages, poor pictures, markings and other reproduction issues beyond our control. Because this work is culturally important, we have made it available as part of our commitment to protecting, preserving, and promoting the world's literature.

**GUIDE TO FOLD-OUTS MAPS and OVERSIZED IMAGES**

The book you are reading was digitized from microfilm captured over the past thirty to forty years. Years after the creation of the original microfilm, the book was converted to digital files and made available in an online database.

In an online database, page images do not need to conform to the size restrictions found in a printed book. When converting these images back into a printed bound book, the page sizes are standardized in ways that maintain the detail of the original. For large images, such as fold-out maps, the original page image is split into two or more pages

Guidelines used to determine how to split the page image follows:

• Some images are split vertically; large images require vertical and horizontal splits.
• For horizontal splits, the content is split left to right.
• For vertical splits, the content is split from top to bottom.
• For both vertical and horizontal splits, the image is processed from top left to bottom right.

# PRINCIPLES

## OF THE

# CRIMINAL LAW OF SCOTLAND.

## BY ARCHIBALD ALISON,

### ADVOCATE.

o

8·

WILLIAM BLACKWOOD, EDINBURGH; AND

T. CADELL, STRAND, LONDON.

MDCCCXXXII.

PRINTED BY NEILL & CO. OLD FISHMARKET.

TO

Sɪʀ **WILLIAM RAE,** Bᴀʀᴏɴᴇᴛ.

LATE LORD ADVOCATE OF SCOTLAND,

TO WHOSE LEGISLATIVE IMPROVEMENTS

ITS CRIMINAL LAW IS SO GREATLY INDEBTED,

AND

BY WHOSE ABLE AND UNWEARIED EXERTIONS

ITS PRACTICE HAS BEEN SO MUCH IMPROVED,

THIS TREATISE IS INSCRIBED,

WITH THE WARMEST FEELINGS OF REGARD AND ESTEEM,

BY THE AUTHOR.

# PREFACE.

NOTWITHSTANDING the great and acknowledged ability of Baron HUME's work, which must always form the foundation of our Criminal Jurisprudence, it must have occurred to every one practically engaged in Justiciary Practice that a treatise was much wanted of more immediate application to the business which actually comes before the Court. The change of manners has consigned to oblivion a great variety of crimes and cases which occupy a conspicuous place in his elaborate Commentaries; while the same cause, joined to the vast increase of criminal business, has brought prominently forward a complete new set of delinquencies, of which little is to be found in the records prior to the last twenty years. In truth, such has been the extraordinary increase of crime of late years, that probably a greater number of cases have been tried since the Peace in 1814 than from the institution of the Court of Justiciary down to that time.

To remedy this defect, and render the law, as explained in books, applicable to the daily practice of the Court, is the object of the following work.

It was originally my intention to have condensed the whole into one volume, after the manner of Mr BELL's admirable Principles of the Scotch Municipal Law, but I soon found, notwithstanding the utmost efforts at condensation, that this was impossible. This will not appear surprizing when it is considered that, besides embodying every decision in HUME and BURNETT on the subjects on which it treats of practical application at this time, this Volume contains above a thousand unreported cases, which, of course, could not be referred to without some account of them being given, and above five hundred decisions upon the analogous points in English practice.

The present volume, therefore, which is complete within itself, contains the subject of Crimes; and the second volume, which also will be a separate work, will embrace the important subjects of Indictment, Trial, and Evidence.

By this arrangement the second volume, which is in a state of great forwardness, will become accessible to that numerous class of practitioners who wish to render themselves familiar with the system of pleading, and the rules of evidence, adopted in a court of such extensive practice, without being embarrassed with the details of criminal delinquencies; while both together will form a complete Treatise on Scotch Criminal Law.

I have to express my obligations to my valued friends the DEAN OF FACULTY, Mr D. MACNEIL, Mr ALEXANDER WOOD, Mr ROBERT DUNDAS, and Mr GEORGE SMYTHE, for the ready access which they have afforded me to their valuable collections, the importance of which will chiefly appear in the next part of the subject. Mr MACONOCHIE has also most obligingly given me many valuable documents, for which I take this opportunity of returning my best thanks. The unreported cases contained in this volume are almost all those in which I myself was Counsel, and the account of them is taken from the indictments which I drew, or the notes of evidence taken at the time of their trial.

A. ALISON.

WOODVILLE, *October* 27 1831

## ERRATA.

Page 94, line 8 from bottom, *for* culpable homicide, *read* assault,
Page 483, line 15 from top, *for* Session ; *read* Justiciary ;

# CONTENTS.

# CHAPTER I.

## ON THE DIFFERENT KINDS OF HOMICIDE WITH REFERENCE TO THE INTENTION OF THE KILLER.

HOMICIDE is the act which, either directly, or by natural consequence, takes away the life of another.[1] It consists of four kinds,—that which is inexcusable, that which is blameable, that which is justifiable, and that which is casual. Hence the division into Murder, and Culpable, Justifiable, and Casual Homicide.

The act producing homicide may be considered in two lights: with reference to the intention of the killer, and the circumstances under which the fatal injury is inflicted; and with reference to the effects upon the sufferer, and the circumstances under which it is received. Hence, the first branch of the subject relates to the distinctions between the different degrees of the crime, with reference to the person who committed the injury; the second, to the different effects which it produces in regard to the person who suffers from it.

### SECT. I.—OF MURDER.

1. Murder, the greatest crime known in the law, consists in the act which produces death, in consequence either of a deliberate intention to kill, or to inflict a minor injury of such a kind as indicates an utter recklessness as to the life of the sufferer, whether he live or die.

IN this essential particular, the law of Scotland coincides with that of England. "Our practice," says Hume, "does

[1] Hume, ɪ. 179.

A

not distinguish between an absolute purpose to kill and a purpose to do any excessive and grievous injury to the person, so that, if the pannel assault his neighbour, meaning to hamstring him, or to cut out his tongue, or break his bones, or beat him severely, or within an inch of his life; and if, in the prosecution of this outrageous purpose, he has actually destroyed his victim, he shall equally die for it as if he had run him through the body with a sword. This corrupt disregard of the person, and life of another, is precisely the dole or malice, the depraved and wicked purpose, which the law requires and is content with."[1] "The malice prepense," says Blackstone, "essential in murder, is not so properly spite or malevolence to the deceased in particular, as an evil design in general, the dictate of a wicked, depraved, and malignant heart, and it may be either express or implied in law. Express, as when one, even upon a sudden provocation, beats another in a cruel and unusual manner, so that he dies, though he did not intend his death, or when a park-keeper tied a boy that was stealing wood to a horse's tail and dragged him along the park, and a schoolmaster stamped on his scholar's belly, so that each of the sufferers died; these were justly held to be murders, because the correction being excessive, and such as could not proceed but from a bad heart, it was equivalent to a deliberate act of slaughter."[2] Implied, as where one wilfully administers some poison to another, or a man gives a woman medicine to procure abortion, and she die, this is nothing less than murder in both cases, though in neither the life of the sufferer was intended to be taken[3]. Dolosum homicidium est, quod vel animo et proposito occidendi, vel *solum vulnerandi voluntate* committitur[4]. *Malice*, in the English law, does not signify hatred, nor is it used in its ordinary signification when applied to the matter of homicide; it is a term of law importing directly wickedness, and excluding any just cause of excuse."[5]

The deliberate intention to kill, so clearly constitutes the crime murder, that a few illustrations will be sufficient on that subject. Thus it is equally murder, whether the fatal violence be committed by blows with a hatchet on the head, or by ad-

---

[1] Hume, ii. 254-256, Burnett, 5.—[2] Blackstone, iv. 199, Hale, i. 454, 472-4, Hawkins, i 74, Foster, 291 —[3] Hale, 466, Blackstone, iv. 200.— [4] Carps, Quest. xxvii No. 5.—[5] Coke, ii Inst 384, Russell, i 615

ministering poison to the stomach, or by lying over the victim and impeding respiration, as in the noted case of Burke and Hare.[1]  Whatever means, in short, the ingenuity and depravity of the human heart may adopt for the completion of the crime, it is equally murder, if death ensue from a deliberate intention to effect it.

But it is equally settled, by a long train of decisions, that the crime of murder is committed, if death ensue from an intention to commit an inferior bodily injury, provided it be of such a kind, as plainly, and, in the ordinary course of events, puts the life of the sufferer in hazard.  Thus, in the case of Brown, tried by Lords Kilkerran and Elchies at Perth, in May 1753, it turned out in evidence, that a father and son were both concerned in an assault, and the father having seized the deceased, and holding him fast, called to his son " to come and pay well, *but spare the life.*"  The son, with a cudgel, having beat the man so severely that he died.  the father had sentence of death.[2]  So also, in the case of Griffith Williams, 27th January 1800, it appeared that the accused had discovered an abstraction by the deceased of a sum of money, with which she had been entrusted; and he had declared his resolution to " beat her *so as just to leave life in her.*"  He beat her at intervals accordingly, and the woman died next day, for which he was condemned and executed [3]  At Glasgow, on February 27. 1815, Colin Telfer was tried on an indictment, which charged him with having struck the deceased with a bone, in a butcher's stall, such a blow on the temple, that he fell to the ground, and died within a week.  The external appearances of the wound were not considerable, and then the question emerged whether the crime of murder was committed, in consequence of death consequent upon such an injury.  Lord Meadowbank observed, " That there was here a merciless blow struck on the temple of the deceased, certainly with an aim for that purpose.  Death might in all probability not have been intended, but indifference whether it should follow or not must have been experienced by the pannel, otherwise the force exerted would have been less, and the weapon used less violent.  Now, it is *this indifference*, this recklessness, as our books term it, of another's life, from which the law, when so indicated, pre-

[1] December 24. 1828 , High Court —[2] Burnett, 4.—[3] Hume. L 257.

sumes a degree of malignity against the individual, or disregard
to the safety of the innocent, as imply the crime of murder." [1]
So also in the case of Joseph Rae, 22d July 1817, the libel
stated that the deceased, a chimney-sweep boy of eleven years
of age, having stuck fast in a vent, the accused fastened ropes
to his legs, " and did pull and draw the said ropes so fastened
with great force, notwithstanding the cries of the said John
Fraser (the deceased) and the remonstrances of several persons
present, and until the said John Fraser died, in consequence
of the force so applied, and was thereby murdered." The presiding Judge, Lord Justice-Clerk, with the concurrence of the
whole Court, laid it down as clear law, " That this was an instance of absolute recklessness and utter indifference about the
life of the sufferer ; and that the law knew no difference between
the guilt of such a case, and that of an intention to destroy." [2]  In
the case of John Cowie, November 29. 1803, the accused was
convicted of having killed the deceased by beating her with a
stick, and trampling on her with his feet.  He had used expressions proving that he was willing to run the risk of the
event, whatever it should prove, to satisfy his rage  He received sentence of death [3].  James Anderson and David Glen,
5th November 1823, had sentence of death, and were executed
for the murder of a man on the road near Ayr, by blows on the
head with *the fist* only, which produced concussion of the brain,
and death in a few hours after.  Lastly, in the case of Mary
Horn or Mackstraffick, tried at Glasgow in autumn 1826, the
libel charged her with murder, in consequence of having beat
the deceased, a boy of twelve years of age, with a hammer on
the head, " *with intent to murder* ·" the Jury found the pannel
" guilty, but the *intent* to murder not proven."  The case being
certified for the consideration of the whole Court, upon this
verdict, it was pleaded for the prosecutor, that, as the jury had
found the pannel guilty of murder, but without the intention
to commit that crime, the case resolved into one of death following an injury committed with an utter recklessness as to
consequences.  The Court were clearly of opinion, that *such
recklessness was a sufficient ingredient in intention to constitute the
crime of murder ;* but, in that particular case, as the express intention to murder had been libelled, however unnecessarily,

[1] Hume, 1 257.—[2] Ibid. 1 258.—[3] Ibid 1. 257.

they held that no capital sentence could follow on the verdict, and the accused had sentence of transportation for life [1].

2. In considering the intention of the accused in this matter, many different circumstances must be taken into view. Special consideration is to be had of the age, sex, and strength of the sufferer; the same degree of violence, which is justly held to amount to utter recklessness in a person of tender years or delicate health, being indicative of a very different intention if applied to one of a stronger habit of body.

This principle cannot receive a stronger illustration than occurs every day in the case of child-murder, where the slightest application of violence is justly held to indicate a murderous intention, though, if applied to a person of stronger years, it could not amount to an offence of any sort. To expose the infant to cold, even for a short time to put a finger on the windpipe, to place the hand for a few minutes, on the mouth, may as effectually extinguish the feeble spark of life in infancy, as if the victim in maturer years were strangled with ropes, or thrown into the sea [2]. One who smites, says Hume, a woman, a boy, or an infant, or an aged or infirm person, with his hand, and with all his might, takes a mode of assault as likely to be fatal as if he strike with a stone or a club one of his own years."

Thus, in the case of Malcolm Brown, July 29. 1664, a libel was found relevant for killing a boy by a *blow on the ear with a fist* [3]; whereas it seems extremely doubtful whether, in modern practice, [4] such a degree of violence would be held to infer a murderous or reckless intent, if applied to a grown person, unless the blow were extremely severe, or repeated with merciless severity. Again, in the case of Macraw, Perth, April 1806, the accused was charged with having seized a girl of ten years of age by the vagina, which was lacerated so much in consequence that she died. He was convicted of murder, under the direction of Lords Justice-Clerk Hope and Meadowbank, although the intention to kill could not have been inferred from

[1] Unreported. High Court. See many more cases to the same purpose; Hume, i. 253; Burnett, p 4.—[2] Burnett, 7, Hume, i. 260.—[3] Hume, i 262 —[4] It was otherwise in former times where the blows were very severe; Lindsay, Feb. 29. 1748, Hume, i. 262.

the act, nor even utter recklessness, if applied to one of maturer years.[1]  On July 28. 1735, James Brown was convicted
of murder, and suffered death, for striking his mother *with the
hand,* and treading her under foot.[2]  To the same purpose a
libel was found relevant for murder against James Stewart, at
Perth, autumn 1824, which charged him with having killed
his wife, by beating her repeatedly on various parts of the
body with his fist, though none of the injuries, taken singly,
had produced very serious effects; but, when applied to a woman, and repeated to a great extent, they were justly held by
Lord Justice-Clerk Boyle to amount to the crime of murder,
though the pannel had the good fortune to escape with a verdict of culpable homicide.[3]

The law was the same in the Roman and English practice.
" Unde et ex lege Cornelia de sicariis merito dixeris teneri eum,
qui cujuscunque conditionis hominem, *et quocunque instrumenti
genere* dolo malo occidit, vel etiam sine ullo instrumento extrin-
secus assumpto, *dum vel pugnis vel capitis, impetu* aut calci-
bus ictis et conculcationibus dolo malo homicidium factum
probetur."[4]  If a man in England does an act, of which the
probable effect may be, and eventually is death, such killing is
murder, though no stroke be struck by himself, and no killing
may have been primarily intended.[5]  Thus, where a person carried his sick father, against his wish, in a severe season, from
one town to another, by reason whereof he died;[6] or where a
harlot left her infant child in an orchard, covered only with
leaves, in which condition it was killed by a kite; or where a
child was placed in a hog-stye, where it was devoured;[7] or
where a master refuses his apprentice necessary food or sustenance, or treats him with continued harshness and severity,
and his death is occasioned thereby;[8] or where the parish-offi-
cers shifted a child from parish to parish, till it died for want
of care and sustenance.[9]  Great doubt was even entertained on
the case, where a step-mother killed a step-child, a girl of ten
years of age, by throwing a four-legged stool, of sufficient size
to kill, at her, which hit her on the temple,[10] though no intention to kill existed.

[1] Burnett, 4 —[2] Hume, 1 262.—[3] Unreported.—[4] Voet ad L. Corneliam
De Sicariis, § 1.—[5] Blackstone, iv. 196.—[6] Hale, 431.—[7] Hawkins, c 31. § 5;
Russell, 1. 619; Ibid 1. 619.—[8] Leach, 127 —[9] Blackstone, iv 197.—[10] Leach,
.. 371, 4th edit.

3. It is material, in estimating the intention of the accused, to consider the instrument with which the injury is inflicted; the taking of ponderous or lethal weapons being as material a circumstance against, as laying them aside before the violence commences is in favour, of the accused.

Cases of murder *in rixa*, generally occur from the use of a lethal weapon, as an axe, a hammer, a pair of tongs, or a knife, these being the instruments which most readily present themselves to the infuriated hands of passion; and, in general, it has been adjudged, that the assumption of such weapons, if followed by death, is a material, if not a fatal circumstance against the accused.[1] Thus, in the case of James Macara, 21st January 1811, it appeared that the accused had a verbal altercation with his brother Alexander, in consequence of some work which had gone wrong at one of the furnaces in which they were engaged. In the course of the strife the deceased hit the accused a sharp slap on the face with the *open hand*, which made him bleed a little at the mouth. The accused did not resent the injury *at the moment*, but, after walking about for *some minutes* with his hands in his pockets, suddenly seized a pair of *heavy furnace tongs*, and struck his brother violently with them on the belly, saying, " Sandie, you have struck me, and now, by God, you shall account for it;" and, upon the deceased laying hold of him by the collar, he shortened them in his hand, and struck him a fatal blow between the eyes, which occasioned death Lord Justice-Clerk Hope laid it down that this was murder, though the accused had met with severe provocation, and his opinion is supported by Baron Hume, who bestows unusual censure on the jury for bringing in a verdict of culpable homicide.[2] Again, in the case of Peter Scott, Aberdeen, spring 1829, it appeared that an altercation had taken place between the accused and another lad, in the course of which the accused had been struck more than once : the deceased interfered apparently to separate them, and the accused immediately *drew a knife from his pocket*, and stabbed him in the side, of which he soon after died. Lord Justice-Clerk Boyle held that this was murder, and the pannel was con-

---

[1] Hume, i. 252 — [2] Ibid i 253.

victed and sentenced to death.  In like manner, in the case
of Pyper, 4th January 1802, it was proved that an altercation
took place between the accused and the deceased, who was
his fellow-servant, in the course of which the deceased threw
the accused on the ground, but without striking him with his
hand : on getting up, the prisoner laid hold of a pair of tongs,
and the parties prepared to fight; but the deceased was standing on the floor, *with his back to the prisoner*, the latter struck
him a violent blow on the back of the head with the tongs, in
consequence of which he died a few days after.  The Court
were of opinion that this was murder, but the jury found it
culpable homicide only.[1]  Thus it appears, that even in cases
of homicide *in rixa*, it is an established principle, that the assumption of a lethal weapon is always a material circumstance
against the pannel; and unless when done immediately after
the provocation, or in circumstances of strong and justifiable
excitement, it will aggravate the case to murder[2]

As much as the assumption of such lethal weapons aggra-
vates the case against the accused, is it alleviated if they be
laid aside before the mortal injury is inflicted.[3]  If the pannel,
having a drawn sword in his hand, lay it aside and strike with
a staff only; or having a loaded pistol, he fires it off and strikes
with the butt end; or if, having a hammer, he throw it away, and
strike with the fist only, he shall hardly, except on the clearest
case of subsequent violence, be convicted of murder.[4]  Thus,
in the case of Richard Hamilton, July 1807, the accused had
killed an infirm old woman by several blows on the head with
his fist; but before doing so, he had thrown aside a mell or hammer which he had used in breaking into the room, and he was
accordingly found guilty of culpable homicide only, though of
the most aggravated kind.[5]


4. The defence of provocation will not avail the accused, if the fatal acts are done at such a distance of time
after the injury received as should have allowed the mortal resentment to subside, or with such weapons, or in
such a manner, as indicates a desire of unmeasured revenge.

[1] Burnett, 16.—[2] Hume, 1. 260.—[3] Ibid. 1. 256.—[4] Ibid.—[5] Ibid. 1. 256.

Though the law will in some cases make allowance for injuries done on strong and immediate provocation, it never can tolerate the feeling of cold-blooded revenge. Thus, if a husband, who finds an adulterer in the act, instead of killing him on the spot, confine him till next day, and then kill him, or force him to swallow a dose of poison, he shall be held guilty of murder.[1] So also, if a schoolmaster, instead of chastising his pupil in the usual way, shall send for some unusual and cruel instrument of discipline, or shall bind his pupil neck and heel, and in that position scourge him, or shall lock him up for an hour and then scourge him, and in any of these cases death shall ensue, he shall answer for the acts with his life. All these are acts of deliberate and inventive cruelty, which is always held as murder.[2] Accordingly, in the case of Andrew Burt, 12th September 1804, before Lords Justice-Clerk Hope and Cullen, a man was charged with having killed his apprentice by a stroke on the head with a heavy iron rod, an inch in diameter. He pleaded provocation by neglect of work, and that he meant only to chastise, but the court held it murder; and, in this opinion, both Hume and Burnett coincide.[3] So also in the case of David Peter, 5th October 1807, a party of young men had insulted and disturbed a man in his house, by knocking at the door and breaking the windows, upon which, instead of resenting the injury *at the moment,* he walked to a neighbour's house and procured a gun, and having followed them to some distance, fired at the party and killed one. He was convicted of murder and executed.[4] And again, in the case of Walter Redpath, 26th November 1810, the accused and the deceased having had a quarrel, had struck one another; *after* which, the former brought out a musket which he presented to the breast of the latter, and it immediately was discharged and killed the deceased. Baron Hume states this as a case of murder, "as he had laid aside two stones, the ready instruments of vengeance, and brought into the field a loaded gun, which began a new and far more serious strife, in which he was the aggressor."[5] Francis Cockburn was severely struck by a lad on the face. Half an hour *after* he armed himself with a knife, and having met him, and a scuffle ensued, he stabbed him in the eye, and

[1] Hume, i. 252, Burnett, 17, 18; Foster, 296; East. c. 5. § 20.—[2] Hume, i. 252.—[3] Hume, i. 252; Burnett.—[4] Hume, i. 253; Burnett, 18.—[5] Hume, i. 252.

death followed. Lord Justice-Clerk Boyle held that the previous provocation was no alleviation of this revenge *ex intervallo,* and he was condemned and executed at Stirling, April 1828.

In this particular, the law of Scotland agrees with that of England. " In all possible cases," says Foster, " homicide, upon a principle of revenge, is murder." [1] In cases of this kind, the material object of inquiry is, whether the suspension of reason, arising from sudden passion, continued from the time of the provocation received to the very instant of the mortal stroke given, or whether, from any circumstances whatever, it appeared, that the party reflected, deliberated, or cooled before the fatal stroke was given; or if, in legal presumption, there was time or opportunity for cooling, the killing will amount to murder, as being attributable to malice and revenge rather than human frailty.[2] And malice will also be presumed, even though the act be perpetrated recently after the provocation received, if the instrument or manner of retaliation be greatly inadequate to the offence given, and cruel and dangerous in its nature.[3] Thus, in the case of Richard Mason, it appeared in evidence that the prisoner and the deceased, his brother, had wrestled in a drunken bout, and afterwards began to play at cudgels, in the course of which the prisoner received a smart blow with a cudgel, and the parties for some time fought in good earnest, but were afterwards separated by their friends. The prisoner then left the room, threatening to bring something to *stick him,* or run him through the body; and in *about half an hour* returned and looked into the room where the deceased was, who invited him to come in and play at cudgels again. They did so accordingly; and after the prisoner had got two blows with the cudgel on the shoulder, he drew a sword from his bosom, and, after one ineffectual pass, stabbed his brother to the heart. This case was reserved for the opinion of all the Judges, and the case was unanimously adjudged to be murder.[4]

5. In judging of the intention of the accused, expressions indicating a mortal purpose, or a resolution to be avenged, be the consequences what they may, are matc-

[1] Foster, 296.—[2] Lord Raymond, ii. 1496.—[3] 1 East. P Crown. 252.—[4] 1 East. L 239, Russell, i. 640-642.

rial, provided they are uttered recently before the fatal injury is inflicted.

Trials for murder seldom occur without such expressions being proved, so reckless are the abandoned among the lower orders in their sentiments of vengeance, and so careless of the expressions they use when under the influence of strong passion. They always form a strong and frequently decisive indication of the *animus* under which the fatal violence was perpetrated. Thus, in the case of John Cowie, 29th November 1803, the accused, who had killed his wife with a stick, was proved to have gone to the door and declared " he would beat her, though he should *hang at the west end for it*," alluding to the west end of the Tolbooth, where executions in Edinburgh then took place. This was justly considered as a most important circumstance.[1] In like manner, in the case of Jean Humphreys, Aberdeen, autumn 1830, who was convicted of murdering her husband by pouring sulphuric acid down his throat as he lay asleep in bed, it was proved that, on the day before the fatal act, she swore she would be avenged, " *though she should face Marischal Street for it*," alluding to the place of public execution in that city, which is opposite to that street.[2] The expression used among the populace in Glasgow is, that they will be revenged " though they should *face the Monument for it*," in allusion to the place of execution there, which looks to the Monument in the Green. Such an expression was proved in the case of Divine, convicted of the murder of his wife, June 16. 1824, High Court.

But such expressions can be admitted to proof only when uttered *recently* before the murder is committed, it being incompetent to prove mortal purpose at a remote period before the commission of the crime. In the case of Archibald Maclellan, accused of murder, Inverness, autumn 1830, Lords Mackenzie and Meadowbank refused to allow such expressions to be proved prior to the time specified in the indictment, for the commencement of the malice, which was there limited to twelve months from the date of the deed[3] In the case of Divine, June 16. 1824, High Court, the Judges held that the latitude, where no previous malice was libelled, could not go beyond a

[1] Hume, i. 257.—[2] Unreported; before Lord Mackenzie.—[3] Unreported

fortnight before the commission of the crime, because previous expressions only proved general malignity of temper, or former malice to the individual, but could not be taken as indications of the animus with which the particular act before them had been perpetrated.

Where the prosecutor proposes to prove expressions of malice for a long period before it is usual and indeed necessary to libel previous malice and ill will.—Such a part of a libel for murder is now matter of daily practice,[1] and was sustained by the court, after a full argument, in the case of Joseph Rae, July 22. 1817.[2]

6. In cases of previous strife or provocation, words or contumely will form no vindication of blows, nor blows with the hand, for the assumption of a lethal weapon.

In this delicate and important department of the law, the practice of Scotland is at variance with that of the sister kingdom.

It is no excuse, strictly speaking, in our law, that the pannel is in a rage and heat of blood, though excited by some rude or contemptuous freedom taken with the person. This passion must be occasioned by *some adequate and serious cause;* some severe and continued assault, such as is attended with trepidation and a dread of farther harm and pain of body, so that the sufferer is *excusable* for the loss of his presence of mind, and excess of the just measure of retaliation.[3] Thus in the case of William Aird, September 9. 1693, who was tried for the murder of Agnes Bayne, the defence was repelled as irrelevant, that she had tossed the contents of a chamber-pot in his face.[4] The defence pleaded there was provocation; but the answer of the Lord Advocate was sustained by the court, "Though our law did of old distinguish between afore-thought, felony, and chaude melle, the first being *ex proposito,* and the second *ex calore iracundiæ,* yet the act 1661 has cleared the case, setting down all the situations in which homicide falls under an arbitrary punishment, viz. homicide in defence, *sed cum excessu,* and homicide casual, where there may be some

[1] Jean Humphreys, Aberdeen, autumn 1830; A M'Lelland, Inverness, autumn 1830.—[2] Hume, ii. 397.—[3] Hume, i. 247, Burnett, 13.—[4] Hume, i. 249.

intermixture of *culpa*, but *in no other case* is an arbitrary punishment admissible by our law."[1] So also in the case of Davies, 18th December 1712, which was a case of killing in a scuffle in the street, the court, in their interlocutor of relevancy, expressly required, as a ground of mitigation, that the prisoner, though attacked by more than one person, beat with staves, and mutilated in the hand, ought to have retired and called for assistance, before giving the mortal wound.[2] Again, in the case of Lindsay and Brock, 15th November 1717, the defence pleaded was, that the killing was *in rixa*, and fell under the exception of the act 1661; but this the court repelled.[3] In the noted case of Carnegie of Finhaven, August 1728, the provocation given was of the grossest kind. The deceased had been grievously injured by rude behaviour, and injurious words and gestures, followed by an assault on the person, by throwing him into a deep and offensive puddle; yet all these circumstances were found by the court insufficient to liberate from the pains of murder[4] In the also noted case of Mungo Campbell, December 1769, which was pleaded by the greatest lawyers of the day, an equally decisive judgment was given. The facts there were, that Lord Eglinton, who had forbid all unqualified persons to come upon his estate, was informed that two persons, of whom the prisoner was one, with a gun in his hands, had been trespassing on his grounds. On his approaching them, they went off his property, where they had just been, into the adjacent lands, and the Earl desired the prisoner to deliver up his gun, which he refused, and presented the gun to him. Some words then passed between the parties, during which the Earl dismounted, and walked towards the prisoner, who earnestly begged his Lordship to keep off, or he would shoot him. The prisoner was at this time retiring backwards, and he tripped and fell; and the Earl having paused for a moment, at the distance of two or three yards from him, the prisoner raised himself upon his elbow, discharged the gun, and killed the deceased. This case was argued with great ability, and the opinion of English counsel taken;[5] but, in the end, the Court found the accused guilty of murder, upon the ground chiefly, that homicide, to

[1] Burnett, Appendix, p. 8.—[2] Ibid.—[3] Ibid.—[4] Hume, i 244.—[5] Maclaurin, 510

prevent an *anticipated* invasion of property, except in cases of
robbery or housebreaking, is without excuse.[1]   " This case,"
says Baron Hume, " was judged in strict conformity to the
entire series of our precedents, as well those in later as in earlier times.   On the whole circumstances of the situation, even
those Judges who were most favourable to the pannel, and
along with them the jury, had been of opinion that the injury
to the person was not of that degree, nor had been prosecuted
that length, which could excuse his anger, or materially extenuate his guilt : so that the deed was rather to be held a wilful and *resentful* deed than in any excusable perturbation, or
terror, or immediate distress of body.   If, in pursuance of his
unlawful purpose of seizing the piece, Lord Eglinton had advanced and seized Campbell, the case would have been one of
culpable homicide.[2]

Several cases have occurred in later times, which prove that
these principles still maintain a firm footing in our practice.
Thus, in the case of Mrs Mackinnon, March 13. 1823, it appeared that the deceased, along with some other young men,
had gone at night to a brothel in the South Bridge of Edinburgh, where a disturbance and quarrel arose, in consequence
of the women of the house barring the door to prevent them
from getting out until they had satisfied their demands for
money.   The evidence was very contradictory as to the amount
of the violence offered by the men to the inmates of the house;
but it appeared distinctly that the accused, who was in a room
below, came up upon hearing a violent altercation, and on entering found every thing in confusion, the men striving with
the women, and was informed that the latter had suffered
great violence from the former.   In a moment of ungovernable
passion, she seized a table knife, and stabbed the deceased with
it, who died in a few days after.   Mr Jeffrey, her counsel, in
a powerful speech, strongly insisted upon the excusable circumstances of perturbation in which the accused was placed,
at seeing her house the scene of such a tumult, as lowering the
case to one of culpable homicide; but the Court was clearly of
opinion that it was murder, and she was condemned and executed.[3]   In like manner, in the case of Andrew Ewart, February 1828, it was proved that the pannel, along with seven

---

[1] Maclaurin, 521.—[2] Hume, l 244 —[3] Unreported

other persons, had assembled in the Churchyard of Libberton to defend the graves from the depredations of resurrection men, which had recently been very frequent in that church-yard for some time past. The accused went out a little after eleven, to make his rounds, with a gun in his hand, and met the deceased at a corner of the churchyard, who had also a gun in his hand, and was one of the party watching the graves. In the dark he took him for a resurrection man, and at the dis-tance of two or three yards levelled his gun and fired. There was no evidence of the deceased having levelled at the accused. It was unanimously held by the Bench that this was a case of murder. Lord Gillies, the presiding judge, after observing that the fact of the mistake made no difference, and that the case must be judged of as if the deceased had really been a resurrection man, as the accused had imagined, laid it down as clear law, that it was clearly illegal to shoot a resurrection man, even where caught *in flagrante delicto*, and that the plea of self-defence was out of the question, as the accused was as well armed as the deceased, as there was no appearance of an assault upon him, and if there had, he might have fallen back on his friends in the watch-house. He was condemned to death; but the Crown, in pursuance of an earnest and most appropriate recommendation to mercy in so melancholy a case, commuted the punishment to imprisonment for twelve months.[1] Again, in the case of Peter Scott, Aberdeen, spring 1823, it was held by Lord Justice-Clerk Boyle, that the accused was guilty of murder, he having in the heat of passion stabbed the deceased with a penknife, who was striving, as a peace-maker, to separate him from a boy with whom he was fighting, and from whom he had suffered such severe blows as was am-ply sufficient to excite the passions. He was found guilty, and sentenced to death.[2] The same was held in the case of Edward Armstrong, Stirling, autumn 1826. The facts were, that the accused and the deceased had a quarrel, and got into grips, when coming from the fair at Falkirk in the evening. Blows were exchanged, but the accused, who was upon the whole the aggressor, after grappling some time with his antagonist, drew a knife from his pocket and stabbed him in the side, of which wound he soon afterwards died. The Lord Justice-Clerk Boyle

---

[1] Syme, 321 —[2] Unreported, Edward Armstrong, Sept. 15. 1826

laid it down that this was murder; but the jury, in the face of clear evidence, found the libel not proven. Another case of a similar complexion, however, had a different issue, also tried at Stirling, April 5. 1828. It there appeared that the deceased had struck the accused a severe blow on the face; and he, in consequence, armed himself with a tableknife for his defence. In half an hour *after*, the parties met at the door of a public-house, and a scuffle ensued, in the course of which the accused struck at the deceased with the knife over the head of a third person, who intervened to stop the affray, and having pierced him on the eye, occasioned his death. Lord Justice-Clerk Boyle considered it as clear law, that this was murder, and that a blow with the fist was no alleviation of a homicide committed with a lethal weapon, even if done at the moment, much more if an interval had elapsed before the injury and the subsequent fatal affray.[1] The accused was condemned and executed.

The law on this head has undergone a material change in the progress of time, which it is important to attend to whenever reference is made to the older authorities on the subject. In Catholic times, the distinction between deliberate murder and " slaughter on suddenty," or *chaude melle*, as it was termed, was fully established.[2] The origin of this was, that the privilege of the sanctuary was extended to manslayers *in rixa*, which was not the law when the homicide was of a forethought felony.[3] The practical effect of this was, that, in the former case, the life of the accused was generally saved. But, on the abolition of the Catholic faith, with the privilege of sanctuary in criminal cases which it had introduced, some legislative provision was found necessary to distinguish the cases where homicide was capital from those where it was punished with an arbitrary pain. In consequence, the act 1661, c. 22, was passed. This statute is entitled, " Concerning the several degrees of *casual* homicide," and proceeds on the narrative of being intended to remove all doubt that may arise hereafter in criminal pursuits for slaughter. It then enacts, " That the cases of homicide after following, viz. casual homicide, homicide in lawful defence, and homicide committed upon thieves and robbers breaking houses in the night; or in case of homicide the time of masterful depredation, or in the pursuit of de-

---

[1] Francis Cockburn, April 5. 1828, Stirling.—[2] Hume, i 240.—[3] Burnett, 12.

nounced and declared rebels for capital crimes, or of such who assist and defend the rebels and masterful depredators by arms, and by force oppose the pursuit and apprehending of them, shall not be punished with death, and that notwithstanding of any laws or acts of Parliament, or any practice made heretofore or observed in the punishing of slaughter."[1]

Upon this statute, a vehement debate was maintained in former times. Upon the one hand, it was urged, that being made for the settlement of all controversies concerning slaughter, and bearing a full enumeration of all those cases of homicide which shall *not* be punished capitally, without mentioning homicide in *chaude melle*, it necessarily *excluded* this latter species from the benefit of the privilege therein declared. On the other hand, it was argued that the case of homicide in *chaude melle* was properly included under the description of *casual* homicide, with which the statute sets out; that the phrase " casual homicide" was not only in common, but in legal, language applied to slaughter committed in *chaude melle*, where the meeting is usually casual and accidental; and that the legislature itself had demonstrated that they used the word casual in the larger sense, from the concluding clause of the statute, which declared, " that all cases to be decided by any judges of the realm, in relation to *casual homicide in defence*, committed at any time heretofore, shall be decided as is above expressed."[2]

Where the enactments of the legislature were so ambiguously expressed, it is not surprising that the course of decisions should have fluctuated in interpreting it, more especially where, as in this instance, the stern sentence of the law, founded on a sense of experienced necessity, was struggling with the humane and equitable feeling which deems the shedding of blood worthy of a very different pain when committed in the heat of passion or on gross provocation, and when perpetrated under circumstances of premeditation or revenge. " In omni injustitia permultum interest utrum perturbatione aliqua animi, quæ plerumque brevis est, et ad tempus, an consulto et cogita fiat injuria; leviora enim sunt ea quæ repentino aliquo motu accidunt quam quæ meditata et præparata inferuntur."[3] The course of precedents accordingly varied extremely with the complexion of each particular case, and the temper of the times

[1] 1661, c. 22.—[2] Ibid.—[3] Cicero.

B

in which it occurred; but at length the milder construction
became firmly established, and the legality of construing cases
of homicide on gross and excessive provocation, as a lesser
crime than murder, has been firmly established.[1]  These cases
fall under the denomination of CULPABLE HOMICIDE; the consideration of which, in all its branches, belongs to a subsequent
part of this chapter.[2]  The cases which belong to this inferior
class are those where the homicide has arisen from the heat of
passion, occasioned not from mere verbal irritation, or inconsiderable violence, but strong and immediate provocation of
real injury, sufficient to put the mind in that perturbed and
agitated state, as in a certain sense to be not master of itself.[3]

Every charge of murder is now held to include under it,
though not expressed, an inferior charge of culpable homicide,
and thus the determination of the nature of the crime, and of
course the life of the prisoner, is left in the hands of the jury,
under the direction of those legal principles which may be un-
folded to them by the court.

It only remains to observe, that, in judging of the intentions
of the accused, it is always a most important circumstance to
consider who struck the first blow.[4]  Thus if John strike
James a blow with the hand, and James returns it with severe
blows of a staff, whereupon John draws, but gives James time
to do the like, and thus they fight, and James is killed, this is
murder in the Scottish practice.[5]  The person who commences
violence must answer in law for its consequences; and if one
of these consequences is the compelling the aggressor, even in
self-defence, to slay the original object of his violence, he is
still answerable for having feloniously *imposed upon himself the
necessity* of taking away the life of another.  So the Court
found in the case of Ensign Hardie, where it is sustained as
relevant to restrict the pains of law to an arbitrary punishment,
that is, to lower the case to culpable homicide, that the deceased was the first aggressor, and laid hold of the horse's
bridle, and struck Hardie on the face with a rung; but that it
is relevant to elide this defence *simpliciter*, that the pannel beat
the deceased on the face with a rod before he struck him with
the rung.[6]

[1] Hume, i. 245, 246; Burnett, 13, 14.—[2] See Sect. II. Chap. I.—[3] Burnett, 14.—[4] Hume, i. 248.—[5] Ibid.  So in England, Mawgridge's case, Russell, i. 647.—[6] Hume, i. 248; Burnett, 42, 43, 48.

In the several particulars above mentioned, the law of England has adopted different principles from that of Scotland.

In the English equally as the Scotch law, the most grievous reproaches by words, or insulting or menacing gestures, will not free the party from the guilt of murder, if, upon such provocation, a lethal weapon was used, or an intention to kill, or do some grievous bodily injury was manifested.[1] Farther, even in the case of provocation by a slight degree of bodily injury, the law will not, in all cases, hold the case as any thing short of murder, if the acts of resentment are violent, bearing no proportion to the injury received, or indicating brutal malignity rather than human frailty.[2] Thus it was ruled by Chief-Justice Holt, that it was murder if a man, upon receiving a single box on the ear, *from a woman*, slew her;[3] but if she had struck him with an iron patten, and drawn blood, it would be manslaughter.[4] And it is stated, as the result of all the cases on the subject, that, in all cases of *slight provocation*, if it may reasonably be collected, from the weapon made use of, or any other circumstances, that the party intended to kill, or do some great bodily harm, such homicide will be murder.[5]

But while this is the law with them, in cases of slight provocation, followed by the use of lethal weapons, or barbarous usage, the rule is different where the injury is more serious, or the violence used such as not decidedly to indicate a murderous or highly injurious tendency. Whenever death ensues from a sudden transport of passion, or heat of blood, upon a reasonable provocation, and without malice, it is considered as manslaughter. Where an assault is made with violence, or circumstances of indignity upon a man's person, as by pulling him by the nose, and an assault is made immediately after, it has been adjudged manslaughter.[6] So also where A was riding on the road, B whipped the horse of A out of the road, and A alighted and killed B, this was held to be manslaughter.[7] So, when the prisoner had employed the deceased to tend some sheep, and he suffered them to escape, and the prisoner took up a stake and threw it at the deceased, and killed him, this was considered as manslaughter[8] But, notwithstanding this lenity, all cases of provocation are with them adjudged as mur-

---

[1] Russell, i. 701 ; Foster, 290 , Hawkins, c. 31. § 33 ; Hale, i. 455 —[2] Lord Holt, Comb. 408, Russell, i 634.—[3] Foster, 292.—[4] Ibid —[5] Russell, i. 639 —[6] Blackstone, iv 191.—[7] Hale, i. 455.—[8] Leach, i 378.

der. 1. Where the provocation was sought for and induced by the *act of the party* accused, in order to afford him a pretence for wreaking his vengeance. 2. Where there was *sufficient time* to let the passion cool, how great soever the provocation may have been, for revenge is never excused by the law.[1]

7. Though it is lawful to kill in defence of one's own life, or in resistance of a violent and dangerous assault on the person; yet the use of lethal weapons is not justifiable in such a case without a reasonable necessity; and, if death ensue from their precipitate or unnecessary use, it will be murder.

The general notion of homicide in self-defence is, that it is committed from *necessity*, in the just apprehension on the part of the manslayer, that he cannot otherwise save his own life, and without any allowance of less excusable motives.[2] But this must be taken under the due limitation; for mere personal violence will not justify, nor even excuse, the immediate use of lethal weapons: it must be personal violence of such a kind as may reasonably seem to endanger life.[3] Matters must have come to the situation *morti proximum*, in which the sufferer has an immediate and reasonable dread of death, before he can justifiably shed the blood of the aggressor, and put an end to the outrage.

Thus, in the case of John Macmillan, July 24. 1690, sentence of death passed o a verdict, which implied that the deceased had received several strokes with a rung, though not sufficient to draw blood.[4] Again, in the case of Peter Maclean, March 1. 1710, it was only found relevant to restrict the libel to an arbitrary punishment, that is to reduce the crime to culpable homicide; that the pannel, who was a soldier, had been abused with words, her Majesty reviled in his presence, and an attempt made to wrest his piece from him.[5] So also, in the case of Ensign Hardie, June 9 1701, the defence pleaded was, that the deceased was the aggressor, had stopped his horse by seizing his bridle, struck him on the face, to the

---

[1] Russell, i. 707 —[2] Hume, i. 223.—[3] Ibid. i. 223; Burnett, 53, 54 —
[4] Hume, i. 218.—[5] Ibid.

effusion of blood, with a stick, and brought him to the ground from his horse. All these injuries, how great soever, were only sustained to the effect of restricting the libel to an ordinary punishment.[1] The illustration of the cases on this head will come to be considered more fully under the head of Culpable Homicide, into which questions of this nature usually resolve; but one general remark may be made, which appears generally applicable, viz. that it is the undue and precipitate assumption of *lethal weapons*, in circumstances neither of assault with such, nor of overpowering odds, nor of manifest peril to life, which most frequently constitutes guilt in the estimation of law. Certainly, if the pannel only oppose force to force, and resist with the *kind of weapons* with which he is assailed, his conduct, be the consequences what they may, can never be made the subject of criminal punishment

8. It is murder to inflict death upon a person trespassing or *stealing*, or attempting to trespass or steal property, whether from the person, the house, or the estate, if it be done or attempted without housebreaking or personal violence.

On no subject is misapprehension on the law more common than on this; and therefore it is fortunate that the English authorities are agreed with our own on the point. " Our law," says Baron Hume, " agrees with the English in this particular, that it makes no account of provocation by trespass on lands or goods, if unaccompanied with violence to the person; so that if John find James breaking down his fence, or entering his enclosure, to search for game without his leave, or pasturing cattle on his grounds, or poinding his cattle on his own grounds, in none of these cases is it *any thing less than murder*, if John shall be so far transported with rage at the trivial and reparable offence as to knock the trespasser on the head." [2] It may be a high crime, and even a capital one, to pick a person's pocket of a large sum of money, or to steal his linen to a great value from his hedge; but certainly the owner shall not be justified, if, instead of seizing, he instantly stab the pickpocket, or, without any sort of warning, shoot the thief from behind the

---

[1] Hume, i. 223.—[2] Ibid. i. 247

4

hedge.[1]   In like manner, if a rabble of boys assemble before a man's door, not to break into it, but to throw mud against it, or break his windows; he is not justifiable, it may be, will not be excusable, if, in resentment of this indignity, he straightway sally out on the aggressors, to kill them with a lethal weapon.[2]

Accordingly, in the case of Andrew Ewart, February 11. 1828, it was laid down as clear law by Lord Gillies, with the concurrence of the Court of Justiciary, that it is murder to shoot a resurrection-man in the very act of lifting a body, though that is the act, perhaps, of all others most revolting to the feelings of our nature.[3]   And, in the case of James Craw, 18th June 1827, it was unanimously found by the Court, after great consideration, that it is murder to lay a spring-gun in a preserve, if death thereby ensue to a poacher, though in the very act of destroying the game.[4]   " If the most desperate poacher," said Lord Mackenzie in that case, " coming up to the owner of the ground, on being desired by him to stop instantly, should persist in advancing; and if the owner, after having exhibited fire-arms, and threatened to fire, should discharge his piece and shoot the poacher, that is murder.   The law of Scotland is peculiarly tender of life, and, except in some very particular cases, does not allow it to be taken, except in defence of life."[5]   " The lowest provocation," said Lord Justice-Clerk Boyle, " or species of invasion, which, in our law, *at all excuses* homicide, is that of a person breaking in to steal by night; yet even there, so tender of life is our law, that it does not, without hesitation, admit even of that plea in justification.[6]

Such being the principles of our law, there seems to be no sufficient ground for the opinion of Mr Burnett, even though supported by Mr Hume, " That the right of defending our property may justify our killing a thief, or predonious invader, in the act of running away with our property, if he cannot otherwise be taken, or the goods secured."[7]   Certainly, the consideration seems invincible on the other side, that the law cannot permit a man to inflict a severer pain with his *own hand*, than it would judge adequate to a *conviction* for the offence; or to take away life, in circumstances where a few

<hr>

[1] Hume, l. 219.—[2] Ibid.—[3] Syme, 321.—[4] Ibid. 214.—[5] Ibid.—[6] Ibid. 219.—[7] Burnett, 57; Hume, l. 222.

months imprisonment would possibly be the utmost extent of the punishment. A gardener, for example, whose orchard has been frequently broken, and at last sees a number of boys descending from the trees, and fires, to make them abandon the fruit, with which their pockets are filled, would hardly be deemed guilty of any lesser crime than murder, if death were to ensue. Such a question occurred in the case of Kennedy, November 7. 1829, where the accused was charged, on the recent statute against discharging loaded fire-arms, with having fired a gun at a boy, with intent to murder, when in the act of scrambling over the wall of an orchard which he had been plundering. The trial went off on an error in the citation, but the opinion of the Court was understood to have been, that if death had ensued, it would have been nothing less than murder.[1]

Upon this important point the English authorities are completely agreed with our practice. " No trespass," says Foster, " either on lands or goods, though accompanied with the most provoking circumstances, will free the party killing from the guilt of murder, if he make use of a mortal weapon, or otherwise an intention to kill, or do some great bodily harm." [2] " The right of killing in defence," says Blackstone, " *reaches not* to any crime unaccompanied with force, as picking of pockets, or the breaking open of any house in the daytime, unless it carries with it an attempt of robbery also." [3] A melancholy instance of the law in this respect lately occurred in the case of Lieutenant Moir, who having been much annoyed by a person trespassing on his farm near the Thames, and repeatedly given notice that he would shoot any one who did so, at length did discharge his gun at a person who was trespassing, and wounded him in the thigh, which led to erysipelas, and proved fatal. He had *gone home for a gun on seeing the intruder,* but no personal contact had ensued. He was condemned and executed, April 1830.

The important branches of the law, regarding the right of killing in defence of property, life, or female honour, when *violently* assailed, with the limitations under which that right must be received, will be considered under the heads of Culpable and Justifiable Homicide.

---

[1] Unreported.—[2] Foster, 290, 291 ; Hawkins, c. 31. § 33, Hale, L 455.— [3] Blackstone, iv. 180.

9. Officers of the law, whether civil or criminal, are under its special protection, while in the execution of their duty; and if they are killed in such execution, without gross illegality on their part, it will be murder.

The difference between an officer of justice employed in the execution of any warrant, civil or criminal, and a private individual, lies here—that he is bound *to advance* and discharge his duty, while the person against whom his warrant is directed is bound *to yield obedience,* and therefore, resistance to an officer terminating fatally for him, will be murder in many cases, where it might be justifiable, or at the worst, culpable homicide, if he had been an ordinary individual. If an individual be assaulted, or seized by an unauthorized person, he is entitled to resist, and if fatal consequences ensue, it must always be an important feature in the case that he was not the aggressor, but acting in self-defence; but if the assailant be an officer of the law, acting in execution of a legal warrant, the case is inverted: his commission justifies, his duty commands, him continually to press forward towards the attainment of his object, and law regards the *prisoner as the aggressor,* if he resist an authority to which he was bound to have yielded obedience.[1] It is no extenuation, therefore, of a homicide, that it was committed on an officer of the law when acting in the execution of his duty; it is, on the contrary, an aggravation that it has occurred in wilful resistance to legal authority.

What is true of homicide committed on ministers of the law, is equally true of homicide committed on their assailants or concurrents, as they are legally termed, if they have been lawfully commanded to assist them, were known as such to the party resisting, and are chargeable with no undue precipitation or excess in their proceedings. Resistance to all such will be deemed aggression, not less than to the officer himself; and death, inflicted in such circumstances, nothing less than murder.[2]

Upon this essential point the law of England agrees with our practice. Ministers of justice, as bailiffs, constables, watchmen, while in the execution of their office, are, in an especial manner, under the protection of the law, " a principle," says

[1] Hume, i. 198; Burnett, 62-64.—[2] Burnett, 64, 65; Hume i. 200.

Hale, "founded in wisdom, equity, and every principle of political justice, for without it the public tranquillity cannot be maintained, or private property secured, nor offenders brought to justice."[1] For these reasons, the killing of persons so employed has been deemed murder of malice prepense, as being an outrage wilfully committed against the justice of the kingdom. And this will apply, though he be killed, not in the actual execution of his office, but going to or coming from it, if it appear in evidence that the resistance in the first case was intended to prevent, in the last to deter from or revenge the execution of his duty.[2] This protection extends not only to the actual ministers of the law but every one attending at the time, and lending their aid whether commanded or not, for law will support all who are injured in striving to support it.[3] Nay, it extends, under certain limitations, to private persons interfering to prevent an affray, or apprehend a felon, for law is their warrant, and they are its ministers, though no actual officer have as yet come forward.[4]

10. In resisting irregular or defective warrants, or warrants executed in an irregular way, or upon the wrong person, it is murder, if death ensue to the officer, by the assumption of lethal weapons, where no great personal violence has been sustained.

" A messenger," says Baron Hume, " by mistake arrests John instead of James, or he arrests John on a warrant against him, without announcing his mission and character, or on a warrant containing an erroneous description, or defective in point of form,—in all these situations there is a wrong or trespass on the part of the officer; but it is not the disposition of our law to hold that this is such an error as shall excuse the party thus molested, if he shall straightway kill the officer with a mortal weapon, though no personal violence have thus ensued.[5] If, instead of submitting for the time, and looking for redress to the law, he shall take the advantage of the mistake to stab or shoot the officer when no great struggle has yet ensued, and no grievous harm of body has been sustained, certainly he cannot be found guilty of any lower crime than

---

[1] Hale, L 456–460.—[2] Foster, 308, 309; Russell, i. 650.—[3] Hale, L 463; Foster, 309.—[4] Foster, 309; Russell, i. 651.—[5] Hume, i. 250

murder.[1] In like manner, if a sheriff-officer, bearing a warrant against a criminal, inadvertently follow him beyond his jurisdiction, and there lay hold of him, and the latter draw a knife and stab him, he cannot be justified nor even excused.[2] If a struggle or beating ensue in consequence of the illegal detention, it will depend upon the degree of the violence, as in other cases, whether the death shall be considered as culpable or justifiable homicide.

Thus, in the well-known case of John and Arthur O'Neal, February 4. 1796, it appeared that the pannels, who were father and son, were aware that a warrant had been issued to apprehend them as disorderly persons, in order to their being sent off under a temporary statute as soldiers. On arriving at the house, the officers, who were accompanied by a large body of the militia, found the doors locked; they notified their business, but *without attempting to break in*, whereupon the accused fired several shots from the house, one of which killed a man. It afterwards was discovered that there was an irregularity in the warrant; it bore a *blank* day of examination, instead of the " next lawful day of meeting," in terms of the statute, and it was not under the *seal* as well as the hand of the magistrate, which, being an English statute, it was contended was necessary. Lord Justice-Clerk Macqueen was clearly of opinion that the case was one of murder, and that the irregularity of the warrant, which was utterly unknown to the pannels, was no excuse; and the father, who had fired the fatal shot, was in consequence sentenced to death. But different views were entertained in another quarter, probably from the ideas of English law, for a royal pardon was obtained for the criminal.[3]

In this matter three things seem material for consideration : 1*st*, The nature of the error in the warrant, and, in particular, whether it occurs in the writing in the officer's hand, which he is bound to look into, or in those previous steps of procedure which he has no opportunity of discovering. 2*d*, The fact whether the error was known to the pannel, or he saw or asked to see the warrant, or justified his resistance upon the allegation of the formality in that important instrument. 3*d*, The degree of violence offered by the officer, or the amount of the struggle which had ensued before the fatal wound was

[1] Hume, i. 250; Burnett, 19.—[2] Hume, i. 250; Burnett, 20.—[3] Hume, i. 251.

given. All these points are of importance, and, in fact, essential to the question, whether the homicide be murder, culpable or justifiable. If the irregularity be unknown to the pannel, it can afford no vindication of his resistance, nor any extenuation, morally speaking, of the consequences which followed; and if the error be in a part of the process inaccessible to the messenger, he is nowise blameable for not having discovered it.[1] On the other hand, if the messenger, in pursuance of a warrant, *ex facie* incomplete or informal, proceeds to execute what he knows, or is bound to have known, was an illegal instrument; if the prisoner discovers the informality, points it out to the officer, and insists upon his right of resistance, his case stands in a very different situation. He is *entitled* to resist by *ordinary* means; and if he *only* have recourse to lethal weapons when the personal struggle has proceeded a considerable length, and his liberty then illegally invaded, cannot otherwise be maintained, it is difficult to affirm that the homicide is not justifiable. In every case, however, where a disposition to revenge, or a preparation of lethal weapons occurs preparatory to the contemplated resistance to warrants, if death ensue on such resistance, it will be considered as murder; even though there was an informality in the writ.[2] Even in the English law, which is much more favourable than ours to the execution of irregular warrants, it is held extremely doubtful whether premeditated malice or cruelty would not make the law murder, even where the officer killed was executing an irregular warrant.[3]

In this particular, the English law is at variance with our practice.

With them, if the process be defective in the frame, or, as we would say, the body of the warrant, as if there be a mistake in the name or address of the person on whom it is to be executed, or if the name of the officer or the party be inserted without authority, and after the issuing of the process, and the officer endeavouring to execute it is killed, this will amount to no more than manslaughter.[4] Thus, where a blank warrant was issued, which is justly deemed illegal by their practice, and a notorious offender was arrested on such a warrant, and one of the officers was killed in the scuffle, it was held to be manslaughter

---

[1] Hume, i. 200, Burnett, 17, 19, 20.—[2] Burnett, 20, 26.—[3] East, l. 310, 311.—[4] Hale, i. 457; Hawkins, c. 31. § 64; Foster, 312; Russell, l. 734.

only.[1]  So also in the case of Cook, where a bailiff, having a
warrant to arrest a person upon a *capias ad satisfaciendum,*
came to his house and gave him notice, upon which the person
menaced to shoot him if he did not depart; the bailiff did not
depart, but *illegally* broke open the windows to make the
arrest: this was held to be not murder, but manslaughter.[2]
And again, in the case of Hugget, it appeared that a man had
been pressed without any warrant by a press-master and his
friend, and a friend of the impressed man having interfered to
rescue him from the violence, and killed the press-master's
friend, this was held to be manslaughter.[3]  But, on the other
hand, the crime with them will not amount to any thing less
than murder, if the error in the warrant be not in the frame
of it, or if it have issued in the ordinary course of justice from
a court or magistrate having jurisdiction in the law.[4]  Though,
therefore, there may have been an error or irregularity in the
*proceeding previous to issuing the warrant,* it will be murder if
the officer be killed in the execution of it, for the officer must
at his peril pay obedience to it.[5]  So, though the warrant of a
justice of the peace be not strictly speaking lawful, as if it do
not express the cause with sufficient particularity, yet if the
matter be within his jurisdiction, the killing of the officer executing the warrant will be murder; for it is not lawful in the
officer to dispute the validity of the warrant, if it be under the
seal of justice.[6]  And in all kinds of process, both civil and
criminal, the falsehood of the charge contained in such warrant will afford no alleviation to the guilt of the person killing
the officer, and this will hold though the warrant have been
obtained by false information or gross imposition on the magistrates.[7]

Thus the distinction appears to be, that the Scotch law re-
probates the *immediate* assumption of lethal weapons in resisting an illegal warrant, and will hold it as murder if death
ensue by such immediate use of them, the more especially if
the informality or error was not known to the party resisting;
whereas the English practice makes such allowance for the
irritation consequent upon the irregular interference with liberty, that it accounts death inflicted under such circumstances
as manslaughter only.

[1] Russell, i. 735; East. i. p. 310, 311.—[2] Hale, i. 458.—[3] Ibid. i. 465.—
[4] Foster, 311; Russell, i. 733.—[5] Foster, 311; Hale, i. 457.—[6] Hale, i. 449,
460; Russell, i. 733.—[7] East. i. 310; Foster, 135, 312; Russell, i. 734.

10. In the execution of civil warrants, the officer is bound to *advance* and perform his duty; but if, in the execution of that duty, he shall kill unnecessarily, or by the prior and precipitate use of lethal weapons, he shall be held guilty of murder.

In like manner, as one may kill in defence of one's life, if it cannot otherwise be saved, so an officer of the law may kill in defence of his office and warrant, if it cannot otherwise bo carried into execution.[1] But, in judging of the *degree* of resistance which shall justify the assumption of lethal weapons, the rule is, that none is sufficient which does not give the officer reason to conclude that his life shall *come* to be in hazard, if he shall persist in the execution of his warrant. The fear of a wrestling bout, or *even of a beating or bruising,* is not a relevant defence, nor indeed any thing short of a preparation of lethal weapons against the officer, or of such an overpowering force as plainly indicates that, but with the peril of his life, he *cannot* advance and discharge his duty.[2] The same degree of offence or aggression which will not justify the private party in killing the officer, will justify the officer in putting to death the private party.[3]

But, on the other hand, it is equally clear, that, if the officer shall *hastily,* and without any sufficient cause, make use of lethal weapons to enforce his warrant, and death shall ensue, the crime will not be construed any thing less than murder.[4] This will be more especially the case, if there be any appearance of premeditation or malice on the officer's part, or reason to believe that he has made use of his office, and his commission, to give a colour to, and obtain impunity for, private vengeance.[5] Thus in the case of James Gordon and others, July 31. 1691, a messenger, and his assistants, were indicted capitally for the murder of Alexander Jack, whom they had shot while resisting a caption on law-burrows. They pleaded in defence, 1*st,* The danger of their lives, they having been invaded and fired on; and, 2*d,* The execution of duty. Now, these particulars were required by the Court to render the last defence relevant, viz. " That the said James Gordon, messenger, having his blazon displayed, was, by force of arms, hindered to enter the house

---

[1] Hume, L 204; Mackenzie *voce* Murder, No. 19.—[2] Ibid. L 204.—[3] Burnett, 20.—[4] Hume, L 201 —[5] Burnett, 70

of Longmay, and that they did threaten and menace the messenger, and that threats were used to raise the country, and that thereafter the country did rise, and beset the house, and surround the messenger, armed with guns, swords, or invasive weapons, relevant to elide the libel *simpliciter*." [1]  From the *extent* of the violence required in this case, to justify the use of lethal weapons, some opinion may be formed of the reluctance of the Scottish practice to extenuate homicide in such situations.  So also, in the case of William Fife, June 30. 1691, the pannel was charged with the murder of Andrew Wilson, an infirm old man, who had interposed to rescue his son-in-law, their prisoner, under letters of caption, the Court sustained this defence, " That William Fife, the messenger, and his assistants, had Peoch their prisoner, by an execute caption, and that the defunct did, by violence, try to rescue him, and actually *drew a dagger* upon William Fife the pannel, invading him therewith."  It was found relevant to elide this defence, that the pannel had killed the deceased when he was rescuing his son-in-law from a mastiff who had thrown him on the ground.  On the proof, it appeared that the accused had wounded the deceased severely with a sword on his first coming to the spot, and evinced a disposition to resist *before* the dagger was drawn; and he accordingly had sentence of death [2] Farther, in the case of Archibald Beath, June 14. 1672, the pannel was charged with the murder of two of the crew of a boat, which, in violation of the Privy Council's order, had come to Lamlash in Arran.  It appeared that these persons, who were authorized by the Privy Council to seize such a vessel had taken possession of it; but, after doing so, the crew recovered the boat, and made out to sea.  Beath and an armed party pursued in another boat, and, *on refusal to surrender*, fired and killed two of the crew.  The excess was here apparent, and Beath had sentence of death, though his life was saved by the Royal mercy. [3]  Again, in the case of Malloch, July 13. 1750, it appeared that the deceased, who was a notorious smuggler, had, on the prisoner, who was an excise officer, coming up to him and his companion, agreed to surrender the spirits, notwithstanding which the prisoner had fired his gun, and mortally wounded the deceased.  The prisoner was found

---

[1] Hume, i. 202.—[2] Ibid. i. 202.—[3] Ibid. i. 204.

guilty, and had sentence of death; but he was pardoned, probably on the ground that the proof on the part of the deceased was of a doubtful character.[1] Farther, in the case of Joseph Tough and Alexander Fortag, the libel charged the accused with having fallen in with a boat belonging to the Isle of Man, " and, without hailing the said boat, or giving any signal by which they might be known to be in the service of the Customs, repeatedly discharging muskets loaded with ball at the said boat, and killing one of the crew;" and concluded for the pain of murder. It appeared on the proof that the revenue cutter had espied a boat making toward the land; they *hailed* her at the distance of 150 yards, but as she did not heave to, they fired several shots to bring her to, one of which killed a man. The boat was laden with contraband salt; and the cutter had no pendant or other distinguishing mark flying. The Court, holding it proved that the revenue officers had hailed before firing, directed an acquittal;[2] but the fact of a charge of murder having *been found relevant* on such a *species facti*, demonstrates how the law stands on the subject. Again, in the case of Alexander Maclean, Inverness, September 23. 1827, the opinion of the Court was expressed as to the use of lethal weapons in such circumstances, though no death actually followed. The accused, who was an excise officer, was there indicted under the late statute for discharging loaded fire-arms with intent to murder. It appeared on the proof that he had gone out on the sea-shore of Ross-shire to shoot ducks, and saw a smuggler proceeding along with two ankers of whisky. He made up to him, and desired him to give up the smuggled goods, which was refused, and some altercation ensued, in the course of which the smuggler, who was armed with a stick, threatened to strike the pannel, and raised his stick for that purpose, but without doing so; upon which the latter discharged his piece, and wounded him severely in his side. Lords Pitmilly and Alloway held the firing here unjustifiable, and the pannel was convicted; though, in consideration of his good character, he received a lenient punishment.[3] Lastly, in the case of Peter Macintyre, Inverness, September 24. 1827, the accused was one of the revenue cutter Atalanta, stationed at Inverness to prevent smuggling, and had gone with a party to

[1] Burnett, 71.—[2] Ibid. 70.—[3] Unreported.

a moor in the neighbourhood of Beauly to seize a still. In the
course of doing so he got into a violent struggle with one of
the smugglers, was seized by the middle, and seriously hurt
in the privy parts; and in the course of the contest he discharged his pistol, and killed the aggressor. It did not very
clearly appear whether the pistol went off by design or accident; but Lord Pitmilly held the homicide justifiable in either
case.

Thus, upon the whole, it appears that though the law is justly sensible of the difficult and delicate situation in which its
officers are placed in enforcing its warrant against men, often
desperate and lawless, and although, for that reason, it looks
upon violence used in such circumstances with a very different
eye from that with which it regards it in ordinary cases, yet it
can neither justify nor excuse the infliction of death in circumstances where it is not called for by risk to the officer's life,
nor manifest peril to the discharge of his duty; and that, in
aggravated cases of that description, the offence will be deemed
nothing short of murder.

In cases of this description, the fatal consequences almost
always arise from the use of lethal weapons, and it is the precipitate and unnecessary use of such perilous weapons that
constitutes the chief element in the officer's guilt. It is of the
last importance, therefore, to know in what circumstances the
use of such lethal weapons is permitted by the law   On this
point there is one general rule laid down in our statute law,
which seems so reasonable in itself, and agreeable to justice,
that an officer walking by it will seldom deviate far from his
duty, and certainly never involve himself in a charge of murder. It is to be found in the 9th Geo. II. c. 35, which authorizes the officers of customs and excise, and their assistants,
when resisted in seizing or searching for goods, by persons who
are passing with the same, armed with offensive weapons, " to
oppose force to force, and to endeavour, by the *same methods*
that are violently used against them, and by which their lives
are endangered, to *defend themselves,* and *execute the duty of
their office.*" [1]  " This rule," as Mr Hume justly remarks, " is
only declaratory of our common law on the subject; for if
they are *bound to advance* towards the discharge of their duty,

[1] Geo. II. c. 35.

they are entitled, by the ordinary rule, to defend their lives *when so advancing,* by the same means by which they are assailed "[1]  If, in doing this, any person shall be killed, the common law, not less than the statute, may be pleaded in defence.[2]  Their criminality begins, when, in the course of their advance, they commence the strife of *lethal weapons,* either when none such are in the possession of the adverse party, or when, if they are, the situation of the parties is such, that the object of their duty might, to all appearance, have been accomplished, without having recourse to such fatal instruments.

Cases of this sort usually resolve themselves into culpable or justifiable homicide ; and, therefore, a fuller discussion of the numerous precedents which have occurred upon them, will be found under these heads of the subject.

The law of England upon this head is somewhat different from our practice.  They hold that the party cannot be lawfully killed in flying from *civil* process, but on *resistance* only.[3]  But it is not every resistance which will justify such violent methods ; for, though an officer may repel force by force, where his authority to arrest or imprison is resisted, yet he ought not to have come to extremities upon every slight interruption, nor without reasonable necessity.[4]  And if he should kill where *no* resistance is made, it will be murder, and the offence would be the same if he slew after the resistance had ceased, provided sufficient time had elapsed for the blood to cool[5]  And in *civil* suits, or in arrests on a *misdemeanour,* if the party fly, and the officer make use of a lethal weapon from inability otherwise to arrest him, or if he fly after arrest actually made, and the officer pursue and kill him, it will amount to murder.[6]  And, in some cases, it would be murder to kill a seaman flying from an impressment, and in all manslaughter ;[7] so that the law of Scotland and of England are the same on this important point, except in that single matter which regards the *degree* of resistance which will justify or extenuate homicide by the officer ; their practice holding any, or at least a much smaller resistance, sufficient to extenuate, than we should do ; a distinction which runs through the two laws, in all the branches of homicide on resistance whatever.

[1] Hume, i. 214.—[2] Ibid. i. 214.—[3] Foster, 271, Hale, i. 481.—[4] Blackstone, iv. 180, Russell, i. 652.—[5] East. i 297 ; Russell, i. 665.—[6] Hale, i. 481, East. i. 306, 307.—[7] East i 308, Russell, i. 666

12. If the warrant, whether civil or criminal, on which the officer proceeds be erroneous, he loses his privilege, and will be judged of as an ordinary man, if death ensue in its execution, provided the error be in such a part of the process as he had in his custody, and is of such a kind as should have attracted the notice of a person of ordinary attention and skill.

The effect of the possession of a warrant by an officer of the law, is to justify him in the use of violence, provided it be unavoidable towards the discharge of his duty; but what if the warrant be irregular, as if it be not signed, or signed by one who is not a magistrate, or not so in the district where it is executed, or if it does not contain the name of the accused; or if the officer lays hold of a wrong person, or illegally forces his way into a house, when not possessed of letters of caption which imply such a power, and death ensue to the prisoner, or those with him, in any of these cases. In such a case the officer loses his privilege, he is regarded as a mere ordinary individual, nowise authorised to commit violence of any sort, and his guilt shall be judged of according to the rules of homicide between man and man.[1]

But this rule must be taken with the proper limitations. The officer's privilege, in such a case, is much broader than that of an ordinary individual, in resisting such irregular process of the law. In other words, the former will be justified in killing, under circumstances which would not even extenuate the guilt of the latter.[2] Farther, the officer shall lose his privilege in the case of such vices *only*, as are in the immediate frame or texture of the warrant; and he is not affected by those more remote and extrinsic, and to him unsearchable irregularities which have happened in the way of applying for the warrant, or in the proceedings which have been the grounds of obtaining it.[3] According to this rule, if an officer shall slay, in pursuance of a warrant which does not bear the magistrate's signature, or the name of the accused; or, if he shall execute it upon a person whom he knows, or should have known, was not the one designed, or in a place notoriously *extra terri-*

---

[2] Hume, i. 200; Burnett, 66.—[2] Burnett, 66.—[3] Hume, i. 200; Burnett, 67.

*torium* of the judge signing, he shall be held as without his privilege; but if the error consist not in the warrant put into the messenger's hand, but in the previous proceedings, as in the petition on which it proceeds, or the process which preceded it, or the decree that was its warrant; then the officer remains protected with the full privilege of his character, as if the proceedings had been altogether unexceptionable. This will hold with a warrant originally obtained in England, or any other foreign country, and indorsed in this country; the officer is bound to look to the regularity of the indorsation, which is his warrant, but not to the form of the English or foreign warrant, concerning which he is not bound to have any information; or which, at all events, rather lies upon the indorsing judge to inquire into.[1] Nay, the same will hold, though the warrant be issued culpably or maliciously by the magistrate or judge; for still the officer is bound to execute the warrant put into his hand, and cannot inquire into the motives of the judge who granted it.[2]

The officer's privilege, however, will be far weaker, indeed in gross cases it will be entirely destroyed, where the irregularity consists, not in any defect in his warrant, or the proceedings which led to it, but in his *own conduct* in its execution, as in breaking open doors upon a warrant of poinding only, or without letters of open doors; or in carrying off poinded goods, instead of leaving a schedule with the debtor, and reporting the proceedings to the judge. In these and similar cases, if death ensue in consequence of the resistance offered to such illegal acts, it is difficult to see any ground on which it can be held to be any thing short of murder. For the officer is unquestionably bound to know his *own duty* in the execution of warrants; and the law can make no greater allowance for homicide committed by its officers in illegal stretches of power, than for similar crimes in ordinary individuals.

In England, accordingly, the rule is, that where persons having authority to arrest or imprison use improper means for that purpose, they are not entitled to the special protection of the law; and if they purposely kill the party for not submitting to such arrest, it will be murder in all cases, at least where an indifferent person acting in the like manner without

---

[1] Hume, 1. 200.—[2] Ibid

any such pretence would be guilty to that extent.[1]   Thus where a warrant had been addressed by the Admiralty to Lord Danby to arrest seamen, and his servant, without any written warrant, which their practice requires in such a case,[2] impressed a person who was no seaman, and, on his trying to escape, killed him, this was adjudged murder.[3]   In like manner, if a person in jail die in consequence of cruel or oppressive usage on the part of the jailor, or, in the language of the law, of duress of imprisonment, it is viewed in the same light[4] And where a jailor knowingly confined a prisoner in the room with another prisoner who had the smallpox, and he died in consequence, this was held to be murder.[5]

13. In the execution of *criminal* warrants, a broader privilege is conferred on the officer, or his assistants, than in civil process, in consideration of the superior danger which they incur, and higher interest of the public in the apprehension of criminals ; and their killing will be justified, if resistance be made to the warrant with such weapons, or in such a manner, as affords a probability of the criminal's escape.

The decided cases in Scotland will not permit the law on this important point to be laid down in clearer terms than in the above proposition; nor does it seem consistent with the principle of our practice to adopt the peremptory rule on the subject which is admitted in the English law.

" The books of Adjournal," says Mr Hume, " do not enable me to say that we should in all cases warrant the killing of the fellow who is barely *flying* from justice."[6]   The public interest, however, is more deeply affected where high and atrocious crimes have been committed, and where the private party has so strong an interest to fly to the uttermost, than in cases of less urgency and importance   In the case of one charged with a *capital* crime, and flying from the pursuit, the officer pursuing, or even private persons specially delegated for that purpose, may proceed to the last extremity, though direct resistance is not made, if it distinctly appear from the circumstance of the case, as from his being fully armed, or supported

[1] East i 312; Russell, i. 666.—[2] Douglas, 207.—[3] East i 312.—[4] Hale, i. 465 ; Foster, 321.—[5] Foster, 322, Russell, i. 668.—[6] Hume, i 193.

by desperate associates, that he cannot be taken alive.[1] "The difference between a warrant to apprehend for a civil and criminal (capital) case is this," says Royston, " that it is not lawful in the first case to kill, unless the prisoner invade, or attempt to deforce, the officer; but, in the second, he may be lawfully killed *if he fly*, or cannot otherwise be taken, even though he neither invade nor resist the officer; which agrees with the law of England."[2]

But this extraordinary privilege of killing on mere flight is confined, even if it be there established, to *capital* cases: there seems no ground for holding that it would extend to the case of those flying from apprehension for *inferior* criminal delinquincies[3] That the officers charged with the apprehension of such criminals would be justified, or at least their case extenuated, in killing on much *less* resistance than in case of a quarrel ensuing on civil process, seems indeed certain; for the greater danger of the officer in dealing with such desperadoes justifies the use of lethal weapons on smaller violence than would warrant it in apprehending more peaceable characters; but still, to inflict death on the first resistance in such cases, or to shoot the criminal when flying from arrest on such a charge, seems wholly unwarranted by our law, and would amount to nothing short of murder.[4] Certainly nothing can be found in the consideration of public interest or state necessity, urged on the other side in such a case, to counterbalance the consideration that the officer has here taken upon himself to kill a person *suspected* of an offence, for which, if *convicted*, the law would have inflicted a milder punishment. But this is to be observed, on the other side, that in the case of an atrocious assault *morti proximum*, or with lethal weapons, and where the future consequences of the wound are uncertain, the officers or their assistants are clothed with nearly the same privilege as if death had actually ensued.[5]

In the case of John Gillespie[6] and others, indicted for the murder of Major Menzies, December 4. 1694, it appeared that the pannels were *private persons* dispatched on a verbal order from the Magistrates of Glasgow in pursuit of Menzies, who had killed the town-clerk a few hours before: they found him in a garden enclosed with high walls, and he *advanced* to resist

[1] Burnett, 62.—[2] Royston's Notes on Mackenzie, Tit Murder; Burnett, 64.—[3] Burnett, 64.—[4] Ibid.—[5] Ibid. 65.—[6] Maclaurin, No 8.

them with a drawn sword in his hand. Upon his doing so they fired and killed him; and the prisoner, under the direction of the Court, was acquitted. This case was a case of death on *threatened resistance* with a *lethal* weapon: it is not, therefore, decisive of any thing but the principle, that threatened resistance with lethal weapons will justify killing by the officer.[1] Again, in the case of Samuel Burch, July 1748, it appeared that the accused, who was a recruiting sergeant, had a quarrel with a man in the burgh; and the matter having been brought before a magistrate, he granted warrant for the imprisonment of the man, and Burch was ordered to assist in conveying him to jail. In the course of carrying him there, Burch and his party were struck with staves and stones, and at length a drummer was seized by the hair and thrown on the ground; whereupon the accused drew his sword, and after striking more than once with the flat of his sword, and making feigned passes to keep off the multitude, he ran one Aitken through the body, and killed him. He was indicted for murder, but the jury found it proved that what he did was *in self-defence*, and in the execution of his office.[2] The accused was there placed in circumstances where he could not *continue* to execute his duty, or prevent the liberation of the criminal, without using violence; and the nature of the assault with which he was threatened clearly justified the use of lethal weapons.

In England, the rule is laid down in a much more unqualified way in favour of officers executing criminal warrants than is yet to be found in our practice. With them, if a *felony* has been committed, or a dangerous wound given, and the party fly from justice, he may be killed in the pursuit if he cannot otherwise be taken.[3] But if the criminal fly from an arrest for a *misdemeanour* only, the officer must not kill him, though there be a warrant to apprehend, and the criminal cannot otherwise be overtaken; and if he kill him it will be murder.[4] Their right to kill in apprehending a criminal accused of a misdemeanour rests on the same basis as in civil cases, viz. that he is authorized to repel force by force, and will be justified in so doing though death should be the consequence, provided he have not proceeded to extremities without a reasonable necessity.[5] Thus the law of the two countries practically leads

---

[1] Hume, i. 198.—[2] Ibid. 199.—[3] Russell, i. 761; Hale, i. 481; Foster, 271. —[4] Foster, 271; Hale, i. 481.—[5] Russell, i. 652; Blackstone, iv. 180.

to nearly the same result, with this difference, that the English law justifies death in the case of a flying *felon* who cannot otherwise be apprehended, while the Scotch declines to make any such marked distinction between the pursuit of a felon and any inferior criminal or civil debtor, and is rather disposed to judge of the criminality of homicide in such a case by the degree of resistance which is offered, and the amount of risk which the officer incurs in proceeding to enforce his commission.

14. A soldier or sailor on duty shall be excused from homicide, if committed in obedience to orders from his officer, or in defence of his post or arms, if they cannot otherwise be maintained; but not for the precipitate use of his arms, or orders to fire, without such a necessity; and his privilege ceases with the termination of his duty.

A soldier stands in a more favourable situation, when opposed in the execution of his duty, than even an officer of justice. He is entrusted with arms for the especial purpose of repressing disorder, trained to a nice and punctilious sense of honour, and bound under the severest pains to obey the orders of his commanders. These important considerations require a higher allowance for his forwardness in maintaining his service, whatever it is for the time; and they are, moreover, a warning to every one not to molest or meddle with him.[1] An invasion with mortal weapons, or an actual and immediate danger of life, is not required to entitle him to use his weapons in maintaining his post, and defending his arms, for he is liable to death, by the mutiny act, if he lose his arms, or quit his post, without doing his utmost to defend them. Not only any invasion on him with hostile arms, therefore, but any violent attack on him with other weapons, or any outrageous or violent tumult raised against him when on duty, shall justify the use of his arms.[2]

Thus in the case of Wallace, 3d August 1692, it appeared that there had been a tumult in the city, and that the populace had assembled in numbers, armed with swords and firearms, against the post occupied by the pannel, who was a soldier on duty; whereupon, after warning the people not to ad-

[1] Hume, i. 205, Burnett, 71.—[2] Ibid.

vance, and their continuing to do so, he gave orders to fire, and killed a man. He was acquitted, although the violence being only such as was in preparation, and might be anticipated, would not have justified the use of arms by a private person, or civil officer of justice.[1] Again, in the case of William Hunt, February 19. 1711, the pannel was charged with murder, and it was found relevant to assoilzie that the deceased was one of a rabble in the street, who had insulted, abused, and beaten some soldiers on the street; and that the pannel was one of the guard ordered out to relieve them, and that they were assaulted with poles, clubs, and shovels, before he fired.[2] So also, in the case of John Willhouse, Thomas Turner, and others, June 15. 1730, the facts were, that the pannels had been called out to protect a cargo of contraband spirits, just seized by a revenue-officer: while posted at the house, and in the absence of the revenue-officer, the soldiers were assaulted with stones and clubs by a mob of men and women, who broke in upon the party, knocked down one of the soldiers, and struck him when down; whereupon the serjeant in command gave orders to fire, which killed one of the crowd. They were most justly assoilzied.[3] Farther, in the noted case of Macadam and Long, 25th September 1735, it was pleaded in defence, that the pannels were quartered at Inverness, and were called by a revenue officer to assist him in the discharge of his duty. They came up with a boat with ten men, and a cargo of smuggled goods on board, armed with cudgels only: words ensued between the parties, the officer was knocked down, and thrown into the sea, the men seized and thrown down, in the attempt to wrest their arms from them, when they drew their bayonets, and a man was killed. The judge-admiral repelled the plea of duty, but the Court *suspended* that interlocutor, and the pannels were never again brought to trial.[4] So in the case of Henry Hawkins, July 24. 1769, the mob had broken in upon the guard with staves and stones, and knocked down and cut Hawkins, one of their number, who thereupon drew his bayonet, and stabbed the assailants. He was acquitted.[5] Again, in the case of Woodwert, April 1792, the accused was a soldier on duty, as sentinel, at Glasgow, when a mob began to assail him. He advised them to keep off, or he would discharge his piece,

[1] Hume, i. 205.—[2] Ibid. i. 206.—[3] Ibid.—[4] Ibid. i. 207.—[5] Ibid.

but they continued to throw stones for some minutes, during which he made preparations as if to charge them. Several stones had struck his musket, but none his person, and, when the mob were about a musket's length off, he fired and killed a boy. It was proved that the sentinel had orders to keep his post clear, and defend his arms from the risk of seizure; and the Court being of opinion, " that a sentinel who kills in defence of his post, where he is assaulted unlawfully, and without provocation, and which he cannot leave without orders, was a case of justifiable homicide," directed an acquittal.[1]

The same rule has been fully exemplified in later times, in which, indeed, the disposition to protect the military, when acting in defence of their posts, duty, or arms, has been carried even farther than in our earlier practice  Thus in the case of Henry Lloyd, 3d December 1810, it appeared, that the pannel, who was a midshipman on board the guardship at Leith, was sent with a party in a row-boat to *bring to* a Danish galliot, which was making for the harbour. Agreeably to usage on such occasions, he fired a shot a-head of the vessel, and she, not having come to, he soon after, from the distance of half a mile or so, fired a second shot, intended, as it was said, to pass over her, but which unfortunately took effect, and killed a man. It appeared in evidence, that the pannel had acted according to the known rules of the service, and rather *within* than without his commission, and he was honourably acquitted.[2] It is settled law that it is *resistance*, in the sense of the law, if a smuggling boat do not *bring to*, after being hailed by a revenue cutter, known to them as such.[3] So it was found in the case of Joseph Tough and Alexander Fortay, February 29. 1808.

But while this is true on the one hand, it is equally necessary to observe on the other, that there must be a *reasonable and well founded apprehension* of being impeded in the discharge of their duty, or deprived of their arms, or forced in their post, before soldiers or sailors on duty will be justified in proceeding to fatal extremities. Certainly there is no authority for asserting, that a sentinel on duty is warranted in discharging his piece, or stabbing with his bayonet, the moment that he sees a crowd collecting, or that he is assailed with abusive epithets, or even struck with mud or slight missiles.[4] In

[1] Hume, i. 208.—[2] Ibid. i. 209.—[3] Hume, i 214.—[4] Hume, i. 205.

judging of the *degree* of violence, real or threatened, which
will justify the use of arms, the same principle is adopted
which runs through the other branches of our practice, name-
ly, that he is justified in using his arms, not merely in defence
of his *life* against extreme danger, but in maintaining his *post*
and *arms* against such odds as seriously threaten them.  Thus
in the case of Captain Porteous, July 19. 1736, it appeared,
that, as captain of the City Guard, he was called to attend the
execution of one Wilson, a smuggler, who was a favourite
with the people.  A violent tumult took place when the body
was hanging on the gibbet, and the City Guard were assailed
with stones, upon which Porteous gave orders to fire, and
seventeen persons were killed or wounded.  The jury, by a
special verdict, found, that at the time of the firing, " the pannel and his guard were attacked and beat by several stones, of
considerable bigness, whereby several of the soldiers were
bruised and wounded."  Upon this verdict Porteous had sentence of death, and afterwards became the victim of the well
known popular tumult called the Porteous Mob.  Whether
this was a case of murder may be doubted, seeing that considerable violence had been used towards the soldiers, and more
might reasonably have been anticipated; but that it was a case
of culpable homicide cannot be questioned, seeing that the assembly of the people was at first at least for a lawful object,
and therefore very different from a mob, which is convened for
a tumultuous and illegal object; and that the danger, whatever it might have become, was not, at least when the order to
fire was given, of that pressing kind, as to threaten serious
danger to the considerable armed force by which the scaffold
was surrounded.[1]  So also, in the case of Lieutenant-Colonel
Mackenzie and others, 6th January 1803, it turned out, that
the Ross and Cromarty Rangers were stationed at Aberdeen,
and that some of the officers and of the soldiers on guard had
garbage thrown at them; but the guard was not forced, nor
had the mob any intention of doing so.  Colonel Mackenzie
upon this gave orders to bring a detachment from the barrack,
and on their arrival retired, upon which the mob became riotous.  Stones were thrown at the soldiers, and several of them
struck; on which Macdonaught, the officer, gave orders to load

[1] Hume, I. 210, 211.

with ball. Soon after the men marched back to the barracks, during which the mob renewed their *insults* by hooting or hissing, but without throwing stones, or using any other personal violence. The men, on being so insulted, of their own accord wheeled round, and commenced an irregular fire against the people, by which some men were killed.[1] The persons concerned in this fatal result were brought to trial on different grounds · the officers with having unnecessarily ordered out the guard, and directed them to load with ball; the sergeants with having aided and abetted the private soldiers in actually firing. The officers were found not guilty, and the libel not proven against the sergeants.[2] It does not appear that the *privates* were put to the bar, though there could be no doubt *they* had been guilty of culpable homicide. In reviewing this decision, it seems impossible to doubt, that, considering the violence going on at the time the guard was *called out*, the officers were justified in taking that step; but the act of the soldiers, or the sergeants, in *firing*, when only assailed by *verbal* abuse, seems to have been precipitate, and deserving of punishment.

In the case of Ensign Maxwell, 15th June 1807, it appeared that the prisoner was commander of a guard of thirty-six men stationed at Greenlaw to watch the French prisoners. The soldiers had orders to fire on any prisoner attempting to make his escape, and to be particularly careful to prevent the walls being undermined. On the night in question a light was observed in the prisoner's room about an hour after the time when it should have been extinguished, and some noise was heard within. This being reported to the prisoner, he went to the window where the light appeared and knocked, and repeatedly ordered those within to put out the light, to which they paid no attention. He then ordered the sentinel to *advance and fire*, which not having been immediately obeyed, he repeated the order *twice* to fire *straight through the window*. This was at length done, and one of the prisoners killed. The officer was indicted for murder. It appeared on the proof that the prisoners had formerly been extremely riotous, and that, on a former occasion, an attempt to escape had required to be checked by firing. The Court were of opinion that the or-

[1] Burnett, 76.—[2] Ibid

ders issued did not warrant the orders to fire, and that the duty of the pannel to guard the prisoners did not in the circumstances warrant his doing so. He was found guilty of culpable homicide, and sentenced to nine months' imprisonment.[1] So also in the case of James Henry, 12th July 1813, the pannel, a midshipman, had been ordered ashore with a boat's crew at Campbeltown, and one of the crew was interrupted by a mob: stones were thrown at the boat as it returned to rescue him, and, after firing four times over the heads of the mob, Henry shot one of them. This was deemed by the Court culpable homicide, though the jury acquitted the pannel.[2]

Further, in the case of William Inglis, it was proved that the orders to the soldiers on duty at the prison at Greenlaw were to fire, if the prisoners were *escaping*, and, if attempting to do so, to report the case instantly to the commanding officer. The prisoners were confined in a room three stories high, so that escape was hardly possible; but the pannel Inglis, who was on duty as a sentinel, was insulted by the throwing of stones and wood from the windows, upon which he sent the turnkey up to inquire what was going on above, and, in his absence, without waiting for his answer, fired and killed a man. The Court viewed the case as little better than murder, and he was convicted of culpable homicide, and transported for fourteen years.[3] Again, in the case of Thomas White, 13th July 1814, it appeared that the prisoner, a midshipman, had been sent ashore, in command of a boat, to bring off a party of six who had been working in the dockyard. Jones, one of the six, behaved absurdly, and, when ordered to come on board, ran off, and was afterwards seen lying on the pier, where he continued to lie, though ordered to rise, and swore at the pannel. Upon this the pannel drew his hanger and struck the deceased, who was still lounging on the pier, several blows with it, which immediately killed him. The Court considered this case as nearly approaching to murder, and Baron Hume has added his high authority to the same view. He was convicted of culpable homicide, and transported for fourteen years.[4]

To entitle a soldier or seaman to these high privileges, they must be *on duty* at the time of committing the homicide. They will not belong to him if he takes upon himself, without orders,

[1] Burnett, 78, 79.—[2] Hume, i. 209.—[3] Burnett, 80.—[4] Ibid. i. 210, 211.

to act as a civil officer, or to seize contraband goods without being summoned by the proper officer to do so. In no case would a homicide, in such circumstances, be considered as justifiable; in many it would amount to murder.[1] Thus, in the case of Davies and Wiltshire, March 1740, it appeared that these two persons, who belonged to a corporal's guard, were returning *from* conveying a deserter in a cart. They met the deceased on the road, who was driving a cart, which they supposed contained smuggled spirits; upon which they stopped the cart, screwed on their bayonets, and loaded their pieces, insisting that the cart should remain where it was till an excise officer was sent for. Some wrangling ensued, in the course of which the deceased and Wiltshire approached each other, and the latter presented his musket and bayonet to the former's breast, who laid hold of the musket and wrenched it out of Wiltshire's hand, who fell into the ditch. At that instant he called to Davies to fire, who did so, after taking a deliberate aim. The corporal with the party had given no orders to fire, and the goods turned out to be not smuggled. The Court were of opinion that there was neither here duty nor personal danger to justify or alleviate the homicide; and that the mere suspicion of the deceased being *versans in illicito*, even if it had been well-founded, would not authorize soldiers off duty of their own accord to interfere. They had both sentence of death, though they received a crown pardon.[2] In like manner, in the case of William Dreghorn, 16th February 1807, the pannel, during a scuffle, was under the orders of a sergeant who commanded him *not* to fire, but leave his post and make off as he best could, which he accordingly did. During his retreat he was sharply pursued by the crowd, and especially by three men armed with bayonets, which they had previously shown a disposition to use against him. After being chased about fifty or sixty yards he turned and fired, by which one boy was killed. The Lord Justice-Clerk Hope laid it down that the pannel, being *off duty*, his peculiar privilege *had ceased;* and he left it to the jury to consider whether he was an ordinary individual put in such fear of his life as justified the use of his weapons. The jury found the pannel not guilty, moved by the long-continued assault and the circumstances of danger

[1] Burnett, 80, 81.—[2] Ibid. 82.

in which he was placed at the moment;[1] but Baron Hume inclines to the opinion that the case was one of culpable homicide, though in a very slight degree.[2]  The only situations, therefore, in which a soldier is privileged above an ordinary citizen is when *on duty* he acts by the orders of his officer, or of a magistrate or regular peace-officer, or on his own responsibility from immediate risk to his post, arms, or life.[3]

As to homicides committed by soldiers with their bayonets, or otherwise, when altogether off duty, they are so far from being privileged, that the law rather regards as peculiarly culpable those who make such use of the weapons which the state has entrusted to them for very different purposes, and whom the habit of facing danger should have trained to more than ordinary coolness in moments of peril or irritation.[4]

It is not true, however, in every possible case, that a soldier's privilege terminates with the cessation of the duty for which he was called out,[5] or does not commence till the duty has, strictly speaking, begun.  Thus, it may happen that an officer and his guard are called out to assist the civil magistrate in repressing a tumult, and that, *before* he orders them to fire, they are assailed by a tumultuary mob, so as to be in danger of being driven from their post, or losing their arms : in such a case they will be justified in using their arms, or rather, the officer in command of the detachment will be justified in commanding them to do so, on the same principle on which a single sentinel on duty would be justified in doing the same when exposed to a similar necessity.  Being *brought out* to aid the civil power, the detachment are to be regarded as on duty till they are *dismissed* by the magistrate.[6]  Nay, the same privilege will hold though they are retiring towards their barracks *after* being dismissed, provided their *arms* or their lives are brought into peril; for, having been brought out on the requisition of the civil powers to preserve the peace, they are not only entitled to defend their lives, but to maintain the arms which the state has given them till they have altogether concluded the expedition on which they have been called out.[7]  It was on this principle that the case of William Dreghorn, already noticed, 16th February 1807, was decided; for he was then off duty, and was retiring to his barracks when the second

---

[1] Burnett, 84.—[2] Hume, i. 208.—[3] Burnett, 82.—[4] Ibid 85.—[5] Hume, i 213.—[6] Ibid.—[7] Ibid

assault was committed which led to his firing; and it was the peril to his arms and life when so retiring which was held to justify the homicide which ensued.[1]

It is hardly necessary to add that, in every law, the distinct command of the officer will liberate the soldier, or of the civil magistrate the officer, unless he command some thing plainly illegal. This is implied in all the cases on the subject.[2]

15. Magistrates are protected in the discharge of their duty; and the homicide resulting from their orders will be justified, if the lives or properties of the lieges within their jurisdiction are seriously endangered by riot or tumult.

The magistrate is bound, by the nature of his office, to keep the peace within his bounds; and if he kill when attempting to do so, and when forcibly resisted, or give orders to use the means entrusted to him for the preservation of the public peace, and these end in death, he will be justified in so doing.[3] Generally speaking, the conduct of the magistrate will be viewed in a favourable light, if the riot and tumult be once proved; and it is to be understood, that it is not only his own personal danger which will justify such a step, but any highly outrageous conduct of the riotous assembly in breach of the peace, and resistance of his authority.[4] In the case of the Tranent Riots in 1797, the mob, in great numbers, surrounded the house where the deputy-lieutenants were assembled, assaulted it with stones, and tried to break open the doors; and when the deputy-lieutenants went to the door they were pelted with stones, and forcibly driven back. The military were then called out, and several of them were severely wounded by the mob; upon which orders to fire were given, and several persons were killed. This was deemed fully justifiable in the assembled magistrates.[5] This also is to be observed of a magistrate, within his jurisdiction, that his duty *never ceases;* being invested with a permanent office, and required at all times to maintain the public peace, he is bound to quell disturbance the moment he sees it, and so far from waiting for orders from others, to give it to them.

[1] Hume, i 213.—[2] Ibid.—[3] Burnett, 61.—[4] Ibid.—[5] Ibid.

It is not to be supposed, however, that it is every appearance of riot or violence which will authorize a magistrate to proceed to such fatal extremities. The same rule applies here which obtains in the other branches of our practice, viz. that the violence and danger must have arisen to such a height as seriously to endanger the lives or properties of the lieges, and warranted the magistrate in entertaining reasonable apprehensions that, if not speedily repressed, the tumult will endanger the authority of the law. To justify a private individual in using lethal weapons, his life must be put in that danger which lawyers call *morti proximum :* to justify a magistrate in adopting or ordering the same measures, his *authority* must be *morti proximum ;* in other words, matters have come to that crisis when, without the use of lethal weapons, the authority of the magistrate is likely to be suspended, and the lives or property of the people exposed to the risk of a licentious multitude.[1]

The law of England stands on the same footing. In the case of a riot or rebellious assembly, the peace-officer and their assistants, endeavouring to disperse the mob, are justified both at common law and by the riot act in proceeding to the last extremity, if the riot cannot otherwise be repressed.[2] And even in the case of private persons, it has been resolved that they may kill such rioters as are evidently dangerous, inasmuch as the law authorizes all its subjects to arm themselves for the repression of extreme disorder.[3] But as the peril of such a proceeding is manifest, it is more prudent for such private persons to wait, if the case will admit of any delay, and put themselves under the guidance of some of the constituted authorities.[4] This is totally distinct from homicide in resistance of a *violent* attack on the lives, houses, or property of the lieges, in which case the use of lethal weapons is clearly admitted[5] both by the English and Scotch law.

16. Every homicide is presumed to be murder, unless the contrary appear from the evidence which proves the death ; and this presumption it lies on the pannel to rebut, by showing that it was justifiable or culpable only.

[1] See below, of the Riot Acts, Chap. on Mobbing.—[2] Hale, l. 53, 494, 495; East. i 304; 1st Geo I § 2. c 5; Russell, i. 787.—[3] Hawkins, c 28. § 14; Foster, 272.—[4] Russell, i 788.—[5] Ibid. i. 789

" The malice necessary to the crime of murder," says Baron
Hume, " is implied *prima facie* in the act of intentional killing,
which is the highest possible injury; and thus it lies with the
pannel to overcome, by evidence on his part, of some of those
circumstances of necessity or excusable infirmity which may
serve him for his defence." [1]  " Non enim," says Malthæus,
" eam defensionem proposuisse, satis est, nisi eadem idoneis ar-
gumentis probetur.  In dubio enim cædes, sicut quævis injuria,
præsumitur dolo malo facta." [2]  The commentator has rightly
said " *sicut quævis injuria*;" for this is not any strained or peculiar rule out of aversion to blood, but the ordinary rule
which applies equally in any other case of bodily harm.[3]
Judgment has accordingly been given in a great variety of
cases, overruling the plea, that malice or deadly hatred must
be proved by the prosecutor.  In all, the answer was sustained
as good law, that the malice was necessarily inferred from the
act of intentional killing, and that the prosecutor, *prima facie*,
was required to do no more than establish that the death
arose in that way, leaving it to the pannel to prove the innocent motive which led him to take away the life of another.
William Aird, September 8. 1693; George Cuming, November 20. 1695; Lindsay and Brock, November 15. 1717; George
Donald, August 4. 1730.[4]  No such plea has ever been advanced in later times; and, accordingly, no indictment for
murder now libels on previous malice or deadly hatred, unless
it is intended to prove previous expressions of ill-will as a separate article of charge.

The law of England has adopted the same rule.  " All homicide," says Blackstone, " is presumed to be malicious, until
the contrary appears from circumstances of alleviation, excuse
or justification; and it lies upon the prisoner to make out such
circumstances to the satisfaction of the Court and jury, unless
they arise out of the evidence against them." [5]

But though this principle is thus so completely established
in law, that previous malice is never alleged in a charge of
murder, except as a separate article of indictment, and nowise
essential to the principal crime, yet in practice the rule is of
little importance.  The circumstances of the case usually, and
indeed almost necessarily, come out in the course of establish-

[1] Hume, i 254.—[2] De sicarus, c. 3, No. 14.—[3] Hume, i 255.—[4] Ibid. i 254,
255 —[5] Blackstone, iv 201 ; Foster, L. 255

ing the fact of death having been intentionally inflicted; so that the prosecutor generally is obliged to prove that the death arose either from intention, or such recklessness as law deems equivalent to it, before the prisoner comes to substantiate any thing whatever in his defence.

17. It is murder if the pannel shoot or aim at one person, and by mistake kill another, if it would have been murder had the person aimed at died, or if he inflict death by such acts as may reasonably be expected to kill some person or another.

If there be such an intention to kill as law deems essential to the crime of murder, and death follow, it matters not whether it take effect on the person intended, or whether there be any particular person in the contemplation of the killer, seeing " the killing a man, not any particular man, is murder." [1] This is constantly illustrated in the case of soldiers firing on a mob, where no particular individual is selected for vengeance, or if there is, it generally occurs that the shot takes effect on a person at a distance, and comparatively innocent. Nay the same shall, though the fatal stroke, missing the person for whom it was intended, shall take effect upon an indifferent spectator, or on the dearest friend of the pannel, and whom at the hazard of his life he would have protected from any injury.[2] In the case of Peter Robertson, 18th April 1818, it appeared that the pannel had, in a fit of passion, thrown a pair of tongs at his servant, which missed her and killed his own child: he was found guilty of culpable homicide;[3] because the instrument used, as applied to the person against whom it was directed, did indicate a reckless intent. But, in the case of Andrew Ewart, already noticed, February 11. 1828, the pannel shot a companion of his own in the Churchyard of Libberton, whom he mistook for a resurrection man; and as the case would have been murder as against the resurrection man, it was adjudged nothing less though the shot had taken effect on the pannel's friend; and he had sentence of death.[4] Judgment was long ago given to the same effect in the case of Carnegie of Finhaven, who hastily thrusting at Lyon of Bridgeton,

---

[1] Burnett, 5.—[2] Hume, i 22, 23.—[3] Ibid i. 23.—[4] Syme, 321

killed the Earl of Strathmore, to whom he bore the highest re-gard.[1] In general, therefore, the rule is, that the law recog-nises no distinction between the case of the person killed ha-ving been intended or any other individual, but judges of the criminality of the accused precisely as it would have done had the fatal act taken effect where it was intended.

The law of England is the same on this head. If it appear from circumstances that the injury intended to A, whether by poison, blow, or any other means of death, would have amount-ed to murder if he had been killed by it, it will amount to the same offence if B happen to fall by it.[2] So, where A gave a poisoned apple to wife, intending to kill her, and she gave it to her child, or died in consequence, this was held to be murder, though he husband being present, tried to dis-suade the wife from so doing.[3] And the same was held where a woman mixed poison with some medicine received from an apothecary to kill her husband; and the poison not having proved fatal, the apothecary, to vindicate his reputation, tasted it himself, and it proved fatal to him.[4]

The crime will also be murder if death ensue in consequence of such acts, though directed against no particular person, as necessarily, or by reasonable probability, may be presumed to kill some one or other. Thus if a person fire from a window into a crowded street, or discharge a cannon loaded with small shot up a crowded alley, and death ensue, this seems to be no-thing short of murder.[5] Thus, in the case of James Niven, March 1796, it appeared that the pannel having loaded a small cannon with powder and a bit of iron, and pointed it up a lane or street of common passage, and fired it off there, when two persons were standing in the direction of the piece, and several others were passing at the time, this was held by the Court to be murder; though the accused, from defect of evidence, was acquitted by the jury.[6]

18. It is murder if death ensue from an intention not to kill, but to do some other highly wicked and felonious act.

[1] Hume, 1 22.—[2] Hale, 1 441.—[3] Hale, 1 436, Russell, 1. 659.—[4] Hale, 1. 436, Russell, 1 659.—[5] Hume, 1 23.—[6] Ibid

If a person give a potion to a woman to produce abortion, and she die in consequence, this will be murder in the person giving, if the potion given was of that powerful kind which evidently put the woman's life in hazard.[1]  Thus, in the case of Robert Dalrymple and Robert Joiner, 10th May 1785, it was found a relevant charge of murder to state that the pannels gave a violent drug to two young women without their knowledge to procure abortion, and that they died in consequence in the same night.[2]  In like manner, if one wilfully set fire to a house with intent merely to destroy a building, but the fire kill an individual, this will be held as murder, though the raiser had no reason to believe that any person was in the house;[3] or if he set fire to a stack-yard, and the flames spread to a dwelling-house, and kill any of the inmates, this is nothing less than murder.[4]  So also if a person proceed to the highway with intent to rob, and he attack a passenger, who resists, and in the struggle the passenger is killed, this also is murder; and this will hold though the robber has carried out no lethal weapon, and the fatal result ensue from the passenger falling in the struggle and breaking his neck[5]  In like manner, if one from the desire of lucre set fire to a house of his own which is insured, and a life is lost in consequence in that house, or in his neighbour's, to which the flames have spread, this appears to be no lesser crime;[6] for here equally, as in the other cases, death has ensued in consequence of the commission or attempt to commit a highly criminal act.   The same would hold if a man, in attempting to ravish a woman, should kill her; or occasion the death of a child by indecent and libidinous practices.

But it is not to be understood that in every case it will be held murder if a person be *versans in illicito*, and death ensue. Thus, if a person be poaching, and, while shooting at game, he kill a person, this will be only culpable homicide; and in like manner if he shoot a fowl, intending to steal it, this will amount to no higher crime.[7]  Perhaps the safest rule that can be stated on this subject is, that homicide, though not originally intended, will be held as murder which is committed during the commission, or in the attempt to commit, a capital crime,

---

[1] Hume, i. 204; Burnett, 5.—[2] Burnett, 5; Hume, i 263.—[3] Burnett, 6; Hume, i. 24.—[4] Hume, i 24.—[5] Ibid.—[6] Ibid. i. 25.—[7] Burnett, 6

or one obviously hazardous to life; but that, where it ensues, without being intended, during the course of an inferior delinquency, and from which no peril to life could reasonably have been anticipated, it will amount to culpable homicide only.

The law of England on this subject recognises a variety of distinctions, which do not appear to have obtained a footing in our practice. Wherever an unlawful act, or an act *malum in se*, is done in prosecution of a felonious intent, and death ensue, it will be murder: as, if A shoot at the poultry of B, intending to steal the poultry, and by accident kill a man, this will be murder, by reason of the felonious intention of stealing; and if trespassers in deer parks kill the keeper, it is murder, even though the keeper had assaulted them first, and they fled and did not turn, till one of their party had been wounded.[1] But if the death has ensued from the mere design to commit a trespass, it will be manslaughter only; as if a man kill another in firing at a fowl *wantonly*, and without the intent to steal.[2] Generally, if any one voluntarily, knowingly, and unlawfully, intends to hurt the person of another, and produce death, his crime will be construed manslaughter or murder, according to the circumstances of the instrument used, and the manner of using it.[3] So, throwing stones wantonly in play will, if it produce death, be construed manslaughter, or if fatal consequences follow any unlawful sport.[4]

19. Deliberate duelling, or fighting with lethal weapons, if death ensue, is murder; if with weapons not lethal, culpable homicide.

Nothing is better established in law, how much at variance soever it may be with prevailing opinions or prejudices, than that where death ensues in a duel, it is murder, how fair and honourable soever the conduct of the parties may have been; and this equally in the receiver as the giver of the challenge.[5] For the *deliberate* intention to kill, or put the life of a fellow creature in hazard, can never be either justified or alleviated, on the ground of any provocation[6] There is an essential dis-

---

[1] Foster, 258, 259, Fast. 1 256, Russell, 1 661 —[2] Hale, 1. 475; Foster, 259.—[3] East. 1 256.—[4] Hawkins, 1 c 29, § 5 —[5] Hume, 1 230, Burnett, 50 [6] Hume, i 239.

tinction between the case of fighting deliberately and *ex inter-vallo* in a duel, and that of combating, in the heat of resentment, for an immediate injury, or in defence of life or property against violent aggression. To give or receive a challenge, intended to produce a *subsequent* combat with mortal weapons, in cool blood, savours of the principle of *revenge*, which is always an ingredient in murder, by the laws of all civilized states,[1] and never can be vindicated on the principle of self-defence, because the peril was of the parties' own seeking. In Scotland, in addition to the common law, there is an express statute against duelling. This is the act 1600, c. 12, " Anent Singular Combats," which enacts, " That no person, in tyme cumming, without his Highness's licence, fight any singular combats, under the paine of death, and his moveable gear escheat to his Majesty's use; and the provoker to be punished with a more ignominious death nor the defender, at the pleasure of his Majesty."[2] This statute, therefore, makes it capital to *fight a duel,* even though no fatal consequences ensue, and that equally in the receiver as the giver of the challenge, with this difference only in favour of the former, that he is to suffer a *less ignominious* death. And truly there seems much need of a strong legislative provision against this inhuman and savage custom, which permits individuals to take upon themselves, by the most violent means, the redressing of their own wrongs, which entrusts the punishment of injuries to the chance of combat, or the coolness of premeditation, and exposes the person who has suffered an injury to the *additional and greater evil* of becoming a murderer, or being murdered.

But though this is unquestionably the law in all cases of duelling, and although nothing is better established than that the most scrupulous observance of the laws of honour will form no defence against a charge of murder, if fatal consequences ensue; yet such has been the natural and humane sympathy both of courts and juries, with the alternative to which the best men are often reduced, of fighting a duel, or losing their place in society, that there is hardly an instance, for a long period, on our records, of a capital sentence being pronounced on such a charge, if there was nothing unusually

---

[1] Hume, i 230–231.—[2] 1600, c 12

savage or dishonourable in the conduct of the accused. Thus in the case of Lieutenant George Rae, 18th June 1798, who had in a duel killed Lieutenant Macvicar of the same regiment; it appeared that Rae gave the challenge, but the deceased was the aggressor; that he had given the prisoner the lie, and called him a scoundrel, which led to a challenge from the prisoner. He was acquitted by the Jury.[1] Again, in the case of Macdonnell of Glengary, 6th August 1798, it was proved that the pannel took offence, without the least reason, at the deceased, for some observations about a lady in a ball-room: from high words he came to blows, and he struck the deceased with a cane and his fist on the face. The deceased sent the challenge, and was killed. The Court strongly expressed their opinion that the case was one of murder, and that the plea of self-defence was inadmissible in a case of killing in a duel. The jury, however, found the pannel not guilty.[2] In like manner, in the cases of Alexander Cahill, 2d and 3d January 1811;[3] of Stewart of Dunearn, June 4. 1821; and of Landale, Perth, September 1828, successive verdicts of not guilty were delivered by juries, although the law was expressly laid down, as above stated, by the Court.

But although such, for a long period, has been the result of such trials, when every thing appeared fair and honourable on both sides, yet cases frequently occurred in our older practice, of sentence of death being pronounced on charges of murder arising out of appointments to fight. Thus, in the case of William Douglas, June 4. 1667, it appeared that a dispute had arisen in a tavern in Leith, and the accused and deceased, and their two seconds, set out in a coach together from the tavern to the sea-shore, where they all four set to fight, and one of the principals was killed. He was condemned and beheaded.[4] Again, in the case of William Mackay, June 17. 1670, it turned out that the pannel, a tailor, came to the barracks in Edinburgh Castle, where he had a quarrel with a soldier: they got swords, and went to the fields to fight, and the soldier was killed after a fair fight. He was condemned to die.[5] Lastly, in the case of James Gray, June 11. 1678, the parties had quarrelled in a tavern, and they left the house straightway

---

[1] Burnett, 50.—[2] Ibid 51 —[3] Hume, 1 232 —[4] Ibid. 1. 231 —[5] Ibid

with the purpose to the fight, and they fought accordingly hard by the house till one was killed. He was sentenced to be beheaded.[1]

Between these three cases, and the preceding class which terminated favourably, there is this distinction, that in all of them the appointment or argument to fight took place *in heat of blood*, and *de recenti* after the quarrel had taken place; whereas in the former the challenge was given *ex intervallo*, and in cool blood. And, certainly, there is this ground of *expedience* for visiting with far heavier pains the survivor in a duel, which terminates fatally, fought *de recenti*, that it tends to discourage such rash and hasty combats, in which the parties, generally under the influence of wine, rush on their own destruction before their passions have got time to cool. But, in point of *principle*, or on the grounds of justice, it is impossible to consider duels in cool blood, as any thing else than the *worst species* of homicide of that description; or to reconcile the acquittal of the high ranks, in cases of mortal combat of that deliberate description, with the just severity of the law towards murder committed *ex intervallo*, and on a principle of revenge, in the lower classes of society. If it were law, indeed, that duelling is in *no case* murder, where the proceedings are fair, in respect of the means of defence allowed to the suffering party, the principle of the distinction would be clear; but this being not the case, the wit of man will search in vain for a reason why such combats, taking place in cool blood, and when the passions have had time to subside, should be viewed in a different light from those which take place immediately after the injury has been sustained.

All seconds in duels, which end in death, are art and part in the murder; but they are entitled to the benefit of all the pleas which go to exculpate or alleviate the guilt of the principals.[2] Mackenzie even extends this to those who knowingly carry the challenge, though not present at the combat.[3]

In the law of England it is fixed, that where a party kills another in a deliberate duel, it is murder; for if two persons in cool blood meet, and fight on a precedent quarrel, and one of them is killed, the other is guilty of murder, and cannot defend himself by alleging that he was first struck by the deceased, or that he had often declined to meet him, or that he meant not to kill but to disarm his adversary.[1]  " Deliberate duelling," says Foster, " if death ensue, is murder in the eye of law, for duels are generally founded in deep revenge ; and though a person should be drawn into a duel, not upon a motive so criminal, but on the punctilio of honour, it will make no excuse."[2]  But if, upon a sudden quarrel, two persons fight, and one kill the other, this is only manslaughter, and so if they, upon such an occasion, go out and fight in the field, for this is one continued act of passion, and the law pays such regard to human frailty as not to put a hasty and deliberate act upon the same footing with regard to guilt.  But if there be a sufficient cooling time for passion to subside, then it is deliberate revenge, and amounts to murder.[3]

In Scotland, if two persons go out to fight with their fists, and death ensues, it is considered culpable homicide only ; not in general, in consideration of the provocation that may have been received, for to that the law in this country pays little regard, but because the means of combat are not such as usually prove a mortal, and, consequently, a murderous or reckless intent is not to be inferred from going out upon such an adventure.

20. If several go out, or conspire together, on a purpose to commit murder, or any other felony, and death ensue in pursuance of their common design, they are all guilty art and part of the murder; and they may be implicated as accessaries, by previous advice or command, presence at the crime, or such subsequent co-operation, as infers previous participation.

1. Counsel or instigation, *consilium sine ope,* must be urgent and deliberate, shewing a clear and undoubted purpose of the instigation ; and it must be *direct and special,* pointing out the particular act, and exhorting to the commission of it, before it can so connect the adviser with the after deed, as to make him art and part in the crime.[4]  If, beside advising in general the commission of a crime, the adviser also instructs as to the way

[1] Hawkins, c 31, § 21.—[2] Foster, 297.—[3] Blackstone, iv 19 —[4] Burnett, 263, Hume, i. 279

and manner in which it is to be done, *si instruat et perficiendi sceleris viam ostendat*, his accession becomes stronger, and may be truly said to become an instar a towards the execution of the deed.[1] The advice must be that which has been followed, and which was one of the main inducements to the commission of the act.[2]

What will infer advice, instigation, or order, in such cases, must depend on the terms used, the consideration or promise given, and the other circumstances of the case, joined to the relative situation of the parties. Less counsel will implicate a party, who has any authority or control over the person to whom it is addressed, than if addressed to an indifferent person.[3] Thus a mandate or counsel from a husband to a wife, a parent to a child, or a master to a servant, will implicate him as art and part in any murder which may follow, when the same expressions would not have that effect if addressed to an indifferent person.[4] By stronger reason, orders given by a commanding officer to his soldiers, will unquestionably implicate the officer, though they may liberate those who are bound by their duty to obey them.[5]

But, to render the person giving the order or advice answerable in such a case, the consequences must be such as necessarily and directly flow from the mandate or counsel given.[6] Thus if an officer order his soldiers to fire, there can be no doubt that he is responsible for the consequences; but if he only order out a detachment to protect the guard, and even order them to load with ball-cartridge, and they afterwards, in a fit of irritation, discharge their pieces at the people, he cannot be implicated at least in the charge of murder; because their act was a remote result, not the necessary consequence of the order previously given, which, as a measure of precaution, may have been highly proper.[7] So it was found in the case of Lieutenant-Colonel Mackenzie and others, tried for the Aberdeen riots, already noticed.[8] But if the mandate or counsel clearly point to the commission of murder against some one, it will be immaterial, in the question of his guilt, though by accident the fatal measures take effect upon another person

[1] Burnett, 264.—[2] Ibid.; Hume, i. 278.—[3] Burnett, 265; Hume, i. 277.—[4] Burnett, 265; Hume, i. 277.—[5] Burnett, 265, Hume, i. 277.—[6] Burnett, 265.—[7] Ibid.—[8] Ibid. 264.

from the one intended.[1]  And, in like manner, if the mandant
direct a person to do some highly wicked and felonious act,
and death ensue in consequence, as to give a person an outrageous beating, or to go out on the highway and rob, or to set
fire to a house, or to give a woman medicine to procure abortion, and death ensue in any of these cases, from the consequence of the act thus enjoined, the mandant will be held
guilty of murder.[2]

Nay, it matters not though the mandate be not executed by
the person who first received it.  If he transfer the execution
to another, the original party who gave the orders is answerable for the whole.[3]  Thus in the case of Robertson and Bachelor, July 1806, it appeared that a surgeon, who had been applied to for medicines to procure abortion, employed another
person, which other employed the prisoner Robertson.  Bachelor, the first surgeon, was charged as art and part, though he
had no direct communication with the prisoner who committed
it, and he was transported in consequence.  Had death ensued
from the medicines given, he would, on the same principle,
have been implicated in the murder.[4]

Accession before the fact may also and generally is founded
on *actual assistance* given to the perpetration of the deed, as by
furnishing the materials for its execution, laying and devising
the plan, or pointing out the most expedient mode of carrying
it into effect.[5]  This is so much more immediate co-operation
than simply giving counsel, that it has almost uniformly been
held to implicate the party accused in the pains of murder.[6]
Thus, if one furnish a highwayman with pistols, or a housebreaker with picklocks, knowing what they are about to commit, and death ensue from the perpetration of such felonies,
the furnisher shall clearly be held guilty of murder.[7]  In like
manner, an apothecary who furnishes poison to be administered
to another, knowing the purpose to which it is to be applied,
is just as guilty, and perhaps more so, as the person who administers the fatal draught.[8]  Thus, in the case of Thomson,
16th March 1692, the person who furnished the poison, knowing its destination, was convicted and had sentence of death

[1] Burnett, 266, 267.—[2] Burnett, 367; Hume, i. 278.—[3] Burnett, 266.—
[4] Ibid. 267.—[5] Hume, i. 278; Burnett, 268.—[6] Ibid.—[7] Burnett, 268.—
[8] Ibid.

along with the actual administrator; and the same result took place in the noted case of Nairn and Ogilvy, August 1765, where the latter sent the poison which the former administered.[1]

But it is to be observed in regard to this species of accession before the fact, that the acts done, or the assistance rendered, must be material to the ultimate issue of the enterprize, such as substantially forwards and encourages the actor to persevere in his wicked designs. Thus, if one lend the assassin his watch, that he may be sure of the hour when he is to lie in wait for his victim, or tell him the nearest road to the place of rendezvous, or furnish him with victuals on his way thither, certainly in none of these cases, even though the assistance was given in the full knowledge of the crime intended, is the proof of accession complete  They are strong articles of evidence to infer participation, but, standing alone, do not decisively prove it.[2] But, on the other hand, if the aid given be such as materially aids the ultimate accomplishment of the object, it will implicate the party even when standing alone. Thus, in the case of Muir of Auchindragne, July 17. 1611, it appeared that he had received a letter from the tutor of Cassillis, informing him of his intention to travel next day to Edinburgh, and requesting Muir to meet him at a certain place, whereupon Muir immediately gave information of his intended journey to Kennedy of Drummurchy, in order that he might waylay and kill him, which was accordingly done. For this foul act he most justly had sentence of death.[3] In like manner, in the case of Patrick Kinninmonth, a libel was found relevant, which bore a charge of furnishing swords and lighted candles for a combat, which terminated fatally for one of the parties.[4]

2. " Art and part " is the Scotch legal phrase, which signifies accession to a crime, and many may thus be involved in the guilt of murder by presence at the spot, besides the one who strikes the fatal blow. If a number conspire and lie in wait to kill a certain person, " si plures non per rixæ occasionem, sed præmeditato consilio, in necem alicujus conjuraverint," it signifies nothing who gives the mortal blow, or how few blows are given.[5] Though but one of the party strike, he is but the executioner of their common design; and they, by

---

[1] Burnett, 268.—[2] Hume, l 279, 280.—[3] Ibid. l 275 —[4] Ibid.—[5] Ibid. l 264, Burnett, 263, 264

their presence, aiding and abetting, are ready to support him
in its execution. Their *mere presence* is an assistance; it adds
to the terror and danger of the person assaulted, and, for aught
that they know, may prevent others coming to his assistance.[1]
Thus, in the case of James Shaw, February 10. 1673, the
pannel had sentence of death on a verdict which specifies his
presence at the murder as the main ground of conviction.[2] In
like manner, in the noted case of Burke and Macdougal, 24th
December 1828, the court were of opinion that the pannel
Macdougal was guilty, art and part, of the murder of the old
woman Docherty, though she was *lying in bed* when Burke
smothered the deceased by lying across her mouth, and it was
proved that she turned her face aside not to witness her dying
struggles; in respect, it appeared from the evidence that she was
aware that she had been inveigled into the house with a view
to her destruction, and that she had had some hand in that
nefarious persuasion herself.[3] The rule of law is, that being
present at the commission of the crime, and doing nothing to
prevent it, will always be a strong circumstance against the
deceased; and if accompanied by evidence of previous knowledge or consent to the design, will infer an accession to the
offence.[4] And in this matter it will be of no moment though
the design was to give a beating only with sticks, without the
use of lethal weapons, for that is the recklessness of life which
is deemed equivalent to an actual design to extinguish life.[5]
Thus, in the case of Macintosh, Macdonald, and Sutherland,
20th March 1812, it was proved that there had been a confederacy among some desperate characters in Edinburgh to beat
and disable the police, and commit robberies on the street by
open depredation, and, in pursuance of this design, one of the
police-officers was killed. The Court were of opinion that they
were all art and part of the murder, even although they had
not all struck with the cudgels, or joined in the assault, upon
the ground of previous reckless intent and co-operation by
presence at the time of the murder.[6] So also in the case of
Taylor and Smith, 2d February 1807, it appeared that the deceased, an infant child, had been murdered by Smith *in presence of Taylor*. Taylor had been previously informed that he

[1] Hume, i 264; Burnett, 269 — [2] Hume, i 264 — [3] Syme, 345. — [4] Burnett, 269. — [5] Hume, i. 266. — [6] Ibid

I

was to get a child, but without saying whether dead or alive, and he had accompanied Smith to the spot where the child was, and heard it cry, and saw it killed, and afterwards got the body away with him. The Court were of opinion that presence at a murder joined to after concealment of the body, and being in possession of it, were circumstances sufficient to infer art and and part; but that the only doubt in the case was, whether from the instantaneous nature of the act, previous knowledge or accession could be inferred. The jury found Smith, who actually killed, alone guilty; but there seems reason to think that Taylor also was art and part in the crime.[1]

Every person shall be deemed to be present who in any shape co-operates in, facilitates, or protects the actual execution of the homicide. One, for instance, gives notice of the person's approach by a signal from a distance, a second dispatches him at a spot agreed on, and a third takes post at a convenient place to prevent interruption, or favour their escape; all are in one degree of guilt  By the construction of law they are all present, and partakers of the murder, because each of them is in his place, and at the time, lending effectual aid to the perpetration of the deed, and but for this mutual assistance and encouragement, the attempt might not be made.[2]  Thus, in the case of Brown and Wilson, 28th June 1773, it appeared that both having gone out to commit the robbery and entered the dwelling-house of the deceased, one of them assaulted, beat, and wounded him, in consequence of which he died, while the other beat his wife. Both were convicted of the *murder* as well as the robbery, though it was pleaded that the person who beat the *wife* could not be accessory to the murder of the husband.[3]  In like manner, in the case of Lindsay and Brock, July 1717, which was a scuffle betwixt two persons, and a third, who was killed in the scuffle by a wound in the neck with a knife, but by which of the two was uncertain, the Court pronounced an interlocutor finding " That the said pannels, or *either of them*, having, at the time and place libelled, given the defunct a wound with a knife, whereof he died; or that the said pannels, both or *either of them*, were art and part therein, relevant to infer the pains of .eath." [4]  So also in the

---

[1] Burnett, 271, 272 —[2] Hume, i 265.—[3] Burnett, 282.—[4] Burnett, 279

2

case of Andrew Brown, Perth, May 1773, the facts were, that the father, having been provoked by some boys, called out to his son to come up and pay well, but spare the life, on which the son coming up struck the boy as he was held several blows on the head, of which he died a few hours after. The jury found that the father held the deceased till the son came up and gave the fatal strokes, on which the former, as art and part, had sentence of death.[1]

But while this is true on the one hand, it is not the less material to observe on the other, that the mere circumstance of presence at the commission of the crime will not render a person art and part, if in the whole circumstances of the case it appears that there was not a mortal or reckless purpose in the whole party *previous* to the commission of the fatal act, but that it arose from a sudden gust of passion or ebullition of malice on the part of one, independent of or unknown to the others. Thus in the case of Ross and Roberts, 9th July 1716, the charge against Roberts was, that, in a scuffle with the deceased, he held his hands, while Ross stabbed him with a knife. The defence was, that he knew not that Ross had a drawn knife, and that he held the man's hands to hinder him from striking in his passion. The Court found " Roberts holding the deceased's hands when the wound was given him by an *occult weapon* relevant only to infer an arbitrary punishment."[2] Nothing could be clearer than that, if the fatal weapon was *occult*, the party who did not use it could not be implicated in the murder, whatever he might be in the simple assault, if no previous concert or intention was proved. So also in the case of Kennedy, July 1706, where a father and son were engaged in a scuffle with a third person, and the latter received a thrust with a sword from the hand of the son, which killed him, the Court found that the father, who struck with the cane only, was liable only to an arbitrary punishment.[3] In like manner, in the case of Crieff and Lordie, March 1719, where one of two soldiers, who had quarrelled with the deceased and his companions, stabbed the former with his bayonet, the Court, on the verdict that the one had stabbed and the other given abusive language only, assoilzied the last.[4] So in the case of Mac-

---

[1] Burnett, 277.—[2] Ibid. 279, Hume, i. 267.—[3] Hume, i. 267, Burnett, 280.—[4] Burnett, 280

pherson and others, 11th January 1808, it appeared that the
prisoners, three in number, had gone to a house of bad fame,
where a Negro happened to be.    Several of them called to put
out the " black buggar," and the door being opened, he was
struck down with a stone, and lay for some time insensible:
upon which several of the soldiers ran through the house with
their bayonets, and at length having discovered the Negro,
stabbed him.    The Court did not consider the *mere presence* as
sufficient to fix the guilt of murder upon them all; there not
being deemed evidence of an *unity of purpose in all* to murder,
and as the jury could not fix with certainty on the real murderer, they were all acquitted [1]   To the same purpose, in the
case of Thomas Marshall, George Scott, and James White,
Perth, September 1824, it appeared that a number of apprentices and lads in Dundee had got into an affray, apparently without any foundation, with some masons from the
country: blows were freely exchanged on both sides, in the
course of which one of the masons was killed.    There was
clear evidence to fix the mobbing and assault on all the pannels, but great uncertainty as to who struck the fatal blow;
and Lord Justice-Clerk Boyle laid it down, that in such a
case, where there was no evidence of a previous concert, and
where the quarrel had been taken up at the moment, the crime
of murder could not be fixed on any of the pannels, unless the
jury were satisfied that he struck the fatal, or one of the fatal,
blows   They were all acquitted of the murder accordingly,
and convicted and transported for the assault and riot.[2]   A
still stronger case occurred at Inverness in September 21. 1830,
where William Durrand, George Jamieson, and John Henderson, were brought to trial for the murder of William Small in
December 1825   It appeared that Small had gone to Durrand's public house in Wick to drink, and met the prisoners
there.    According to the story told by the witnesses for the
prosecution, a quarrel arose betwixt Small and Durrand about
some dead bodies which Durrand had been accused of sending
by sea to Edinburgh.   Durrand took Small by the neck, twisted
his neckcloth round, and threw him on the ground, striking
him at the same time on the head with a bottle, of which he
died immediately after.   Henderson put out the light the mo-

---

[1] Burnett, 281.—[2] Unreported

ment the scuffle began, and Jamieson took no hand in the business at that time; but none lent any assistance to the deceased They then all carried the dead body down to a cellar below the room, where the money in the pockets, amounting to £ 20, was divided among the whole party equally; and then they all took the body out, and threw it over the pier into the sea. where it was found on the following morning. Upon this evidence, Lord Mackenzie was of opinion that there were not sufficient grounds to implicate Henderson and Jamieson in the charge of murder, considering that the slaughter appeared to have arisen out of a *sudden quarrel*, in which Durrand alone was concerned; and that the subsequent division of the spoil and removal of the body were not evidence of a previous concert or accession, but only of a determination *subsequently* taken up to make the best they could of the slaughter thus perpetrated by another.ᐧ The pannels were found not guilty, in consequence of a mass of contradictory evidence, which the jury thought threw suspicion over the witnesses for the crown. It is evident that the putting out the candle at the moment of the murder, dividing the money found in the pockets, and assisting in getting quit of the dead body, were to the last degree suspicious, and, coupled with the slightest indications of *previous* concert, would have implicated all the accused as art and part in the whole crimes.

Persons may be implicated in a charge of murder, not only in consequence of a concert to kill, or to do some grievous bodily harm, but to commit *any other felony*, provided the nature of the attempt imply, or the behaviour of the parties indicate, a unity of purpose in all concerned, and a resolution to control resistance by numbers and force.[2] Thus, if several go out to rob on the highway armed, and one is killed in the assault, it is murder in all those who are aiding and abetting in the robbery, whether present or not. or, if some members of a party break into a house, and one of them kills, either in forcing an entry, or in effecting their escape, it is murder in all those who are aiding and abetting the original felony.[3] Or if a large party set out on a smuggling expedition, or to rescue a cargo of smuggled goods, and if, in the prosecution of this felonious enterprize, the revenue-officer or any of his party be killed. all the smug-

[1] Unreported.—[2] Hume, i 268.—[3] Ibid

glers shall answer for it with their own lives.[1]   The principle
in all these cases is the same, that the fatal act is committed
by the actual murderer in pursuance of the common object of
the enterprize ; that he is emboldened to kill by the numbers
who support him in it; and that, were it not for their company,
he would not have been on the expedition.

But while this is true, on the one hand, where the *unity of
purpose* is clearly substantiated in evidence, it is not the less
material to observe on the other, that if the assembly be of
that kind where numerous persons meet together without any
common design, or with the design of committing riot only,
without engaging in felony, then justice requires that, if a homicide is committed by one of the party, it should be visited
on himself or his immediate abettors only.[2]   In arbitrary
times, indeed, the mere presence in an unlawful assembly was
frequently held sufficient to convict all concerned in the pains
of homicide committed by one of the party; but these precedents it is hoped will never again be followed.   In all questions of this description, the material point to be looked to is,
whether the homicide is committed in pursuance of the common enterprize, and if that enterprize was of such a kind as
might on reasonable probability be supposed to lead to a fatal
issue.   Unless this be the case, it would be highly unjust to
visit the fatal consequences upon all who were engaged in the
unlawful proceedings.   On this principle, where three soldiers
went together to rob an orchard, and two got upon a pear-tree,
and the third stood at the gate with a drawn sword in his
hand, and the owner's son having come by and collared the
soldier with the sword, and been killed by him, it was ruled
by Holt that this was murder in him who stabbed, but that
those on the tree were innocent; for they came to commit an
inconsiderable trespass, and the man was killed on a sudden
quarrel without their knowledge.   " It would," says Holt,
" have been otherwise had they come thither with a general
resolution against all opposers."[3]

One thing, however, is to be observed, that much less accession will suffice to convict a person as art and part of a
crime committed by a large assembly of persons, where the
guilty purpose is proved to have been known or communicated
previously, than where the numbers are more scanty   The

---

[1] Hume, 1 268.—[2] Ibid.—[3] Foster, 313, Hume, 1 268

reason, which is founded in substantial justice, is this, that where a number are leagued together for the commission of a particular outrage, the share falling to each is necessarily diminished from the number of his associates. In such a case, the material things to be proved are, 1. The original felonious design; 2. The pannel's knowledge of it; 3. His presence at the time of its execution. If these three points be established, it is difficult to see how he can shake himself loose of the consequences, how small soever his share in the actual perpetration may have been.[1] But, on the other hand, it is to be observed that *mere presence* in a mob or assembly, where fatal acts are perpetrated, will not be sufficient to convict a party, unless it be established either by his dress, arms, deportment, or the like, that he came with the design of supporting the outrageous proceedings of the meeting.[2] The great point to be considered in all such cases is, whether the fatal acts have arisen from an intention taken up at the moment, and only known to the actual perpetrators of the outrage, or from a previous design communicated or common to all. In the former case, the rule applies, *culpa tenet suos auctores ;* in the latter, the fatal acts will be visited upon all present at their commission. Thus, in the case of John Penny, John Allan and others, Gloucester, 9th April 1816, it appeared that the prisoners, *eleven in number,* were part of a gang of fourteen or fifteen who had gone out to poach. They were all armed, some with guns, others with sticks, their faces were blackened, their hats chalked, and they were proved to have adopted the resolution to quell all resistance. They were drawn up in line before going out, and on falling in with the gamekeepers they drew up in line, and advanced regularly two deep, and Penny fired and killed Ingram; after which several more of the poachers fired and wounded some of the keeper's party. Mr Justice Holroyd laid it down that they were *all accessary to the murder,* as they had all partaken in the design, and stood by armed and saw it executed; and they were all convicted accordingly.[3] But, in general, it may be observed as to all cases of accession to murder, that, as its pains are so severe, and its guilt so clearly distinguishable from almost all other offences, so the tendency both of judges and juries is to discover the *actual perpetrator,* and visit him with the capital sentence, leaving the others to be punished with those inferior pains which, except in cases of peculiar atrocity, is generally commensurate to the share they have had in the transaction.

3. The Scotch law, different in this particular from that of England, recognises no accession *after* the fact, except by such conduct as infers, by legal evidence, previous knowledge, counsel, or co-operation.[1] If one, at no great distance from the scene of murder, should immediately harbour the murderer, or conceal the dead body, such conduct, though highly suspicious, would not be held *per se* decisive of previous knowledge, which is essential to implicate a pannel in the guilt of murder.[2] But it is evident that these circumstances, joined to slender proof of previous participation, and any evidence of subsequent participation in the profit of the crime, would be sufficient to infer accession, not less on the principles of law than the rules of justice.[3] Thus, in the case of Robert Walker and David Graham, July 15. 1642, who were tried for the murder of Isobel Walker, whom they strangled in a solitary place, it was proved that the pannels, who had no hand in the actual murder, had *contrived the occasion of the deed*, by sending her that way on a pretended errand in the night, and afterwards expressed their joy at the event, and threw the body into a salmon cruive  They were all justly condemned to die.[4] So also in the case of James Stewart, September 1752, the pannel was charged as art and part in the murder of Colin Campbell of Glenure  The chief circumstances which appeared were indicative of accession *after* the fact; and it was admitted by the counsel for the prosecution, that, " if the jury were satisfied that the prisoner was ignorant of the intended murder, and aided the escape of the pannel from motives of compassion merely, and in consequence of a resolution *then first taken up by him;* this, though punishable, would not infer art and part in the murder." But it turned out upon the proof that these circumstances were accompanied by others, which showed *previous* knowledge and communication on the part of the pannel; in particular, he was the person who had felt the real enmity against the deceased, and he had expressed his ill-will towards him; and before intelligence of the slaughter could

have reached him, he had procured money for the actual perpetrator, and had sent clothes to him, which were returned
after the murder by a mutual friend. These circumstances,
as indicating a fore-knowledge of the act, were justly held sufficient to implicate the pannel in the murder.[1]

If this be true of such accession after the fact as may seem
nearly allied to assistance in its perpetration, much more will
the same hold where all that is proved against the pannel is an
attempt to screen the pannel from justice, or furnish him with
the means of escape.[2] Thus, in the case of Barbara Coutts,
July 1746, her assisting to conceal the corpse of a murdered
person, was only found relevant to infer an arbitrary punishment.[3] And, in the case of Thomas Bryce, where a person was
indicted as accessary to a murder, in respect he gave shelter to
his son, who was taken red hand, and resisted a constable who
was in pursuit, the plea that this did not amount to accession
had the effect of extinguishing the prosecution.[4] And, of
course, all expressions of mere approbation, or satisfaction at
the commission of the crime, how strong or pointed soever,
will not *per se* involve the parties uttering them as accessaries
to the principal offence, however important they may be when
coupled with circumstances indicating previous knowledge or
co-operation, as articles of evidence to infer legal accession.[5]

It only remains to add that, by our law differing in this particular from that of England, it is settled that the principal and
accessaries may be tried on one and the same libel, and at one
and the same time;[6] or the trial of the accessary may take
place, though the principal has neither been charged, fugitated,
nor is in custody, and, though not brought to trial, if he is accessible.[7] Thus, in the case of James Edmonston, July 29.
1695, the pannel objected that he was brought to trial alone on
a libel which stated that he was accessary to a murder committed by another; and it was strongly urged that the accessary could not be tried till the principal were convicted, or at
least outlawed for non-appearance. The objection, after a full
debate preserved in the record, was repelled.[8] The like judgment had long before been given in the case of Mure of Auchindragne, July 1611, who objected without success, that Ken-

[1] Hume, i 262, Burnett, 286.— Burnett, 267 Hume, i 282.—[2] Maclaurin, No 97.—[4] Hume, i 282.—[5] Burnett 288 Hume, i 282.—[6] Hume, i
283, Burnett, 289.—[7] Hume, i 264.—[8] Ibid

nedy, the actor, had not been discussed.[1] And the law was
settled in the same way by the opinion of all the judges, delivered after great consideration in the case of Mackenzie *v*
Johnson and Jameso , 14. 1817.[2] The *species facti* there was
that Johnston was brought to the bar of the Court of Session
for breach of interdict, committed by him as accessary to Mrs
Taaffe, against whom the interdict had been directed. He
pleaded that the accessary could not be tried till the principal
had been discussed ; but this plea, after being remitted for the
opinion of all the judges, was overruled. The case was ultimately not pressed to a decision, on account of a compromise
betwixt the parties ; but the opinions of the whole judges were
delivered on this point, and they were unanimous that this objection was ill-founded. When Burnett therefore asserts that
the accessary cannot be tried till the principal is put to the
bar, if the latter is in custody and can be tried, he is delivering
what is not law.

According to the law of England, where divers persons resolve generally to resist *all opposers* in the commission of any
breach of the peace, and to execute it in such a manner as naturally tends to raise tumults and affrays, as by going to beat
a man, or rob a park, or standing in opposition to the sheriff's
posse, they must, when they engage in such bold disturbances
of the public peace, at their peril abide the event; and if, in
doing any of these acts, they happen to kill, they will all be
held guilty of murder.[5] But in order to render the killing
murder in all concerned, it must happen *on account* of the unlawful act in contemplation, and *during* the strife for its accomplishment, or within such a time thereafter as may leave
it probable that no fresh provocation has intervened.[4] Therefore, if divers persons be engaged in an unlawful act, and one
of them with malice prepense kills a person, it shall not be
construed murder in the rest, because it had no connexion with
the crime in which they were engaged.[5] so, where two men
were beating another in the street, and a stranger made some
observation upon the cruelty of the act, and one of the two
drew a knife and stabbed the stranger, the other party was acquitted.[6] Again, where a party of smugglers were met and

[1] Hume, i. 283 —[2] Unreported, First Division.—[5] Hawkins, i c. 31, § 51 ,
Hale, i. 439 ; Blackstone, iv 200 ; East. i. 257.—[4] East. i 259.—[5] Hawkins,
c 31, § 52.—[6] Ibid

opposed by an officer of the crown, and during the scuffle a gun was discharged by a smuggler, which, by mistake, killed one of his own gang, it was agreed by the Court, that if this had taken effect on one of the King's party, or if the shot had been discharged in prosecution of the purpose for which the party was assembled, it would have been murder in the whole smugglers; but as it did not appear that the gun was discharged in prosecution of the common purpose, it was held to affect the person who fired it only.[1]

So far the English cases are analogous to our practice, and being obviously founded in reason and justice, they may fitly be quoted as authority in the Scotch courts. But in another particular the laws of the two countries vary, and this distinction must be attended to in this matter. They distinguish accessaries *before* the fact and *after* the fact, while aiding and abetting *a' the fact* are considered as principals[2] An accessary before the fact is he who, being absent at the time the offence was committed, has yet procured, counselled, or abetted it. An accessary after the fact is one who, knowing that a felony has been committed by another, receives, relieves, comforts, or assists the felon.[3] Any assistance given to one known to be a felon, in order to his being apprehended, tried, or suffering the punishment to which he is condemned, is sufficient to make a man an accessary of this description.[4] Persons aiding and abetting at the commission of the crime, as by standing by or within sight or hearing of the fact, or keeping guard at a convenient distance, are not with them termed accessaries, but *principals in the second degree.*[5] These principles have given rise to a multitude of nice and subtile distinctions in this matter, which it would be useless to notice, as the difference of the two systems of law in this particular renders the precedents inapplicable to our practice.

22. The crime of murder can only be committed on an existing human creature; but if it be alive, it is immaterial for how short a period life has to endure, or how worthless the being that is destroyed.

[1] Foster, 352, and Marsell and Storbert s case, Hale, 1 440 —[2] Blackstone, iv. 34-37, Hale, 1 529, Foster, 356.—[3] Hale, 1 618 —[4] Ibid, Blackstone, iv 38 —[5] Blackstone, iv 34, 35

A child, though it has become quick, is regarded as *pars viscerum matris*, and not a separate being; and it cannot with any certainty be said whether it would have been *born* alive or not. The destruction of an unborn infant, therefore, though an atrocious crime, and severely punishable under a different denomination, is not murder.[1] But if breathing once has begun, it is immaterial how frail may be the tenure by which life is held,[2] or how worthless the existence which is terminated; and whether the person killed is an alien, a rebel at the horn, or a native Scotchman. A child which is only a minute old, or an old man on the brink of the grave, are equally entitled to have their lives protected by the pains of murder; for it belongs to the Supreme Disposer of events, not any human hand, to determine the duration of life, or prolong its thread.[3]

23. Murder may be committed not only by actual violence, or the administration of poison, but by such cruel and unnatural treatment as proves, though slowly and indirectly, fatal to life.

The law knows no distinction as to the mode in which human life is destroyed. It is equally murder, whether the deed be done by the hand of the pannel, as by shooting or stabbing, or by mingling poison with the food, which the intended victim takes of his own accord, or by exposing him to the wasting operation of some destructive power.[4] Thus it is equally murder, if death ensue, to expose a new born infant, in a solitary place, and rigorous weather, as to squeeze its throat, or put a hand on its mouth.[5] Nay, the same will hold with an infant or child, of maturer years, if exposed in such way, or in such circumstances, as to render the loss of life a matter of reasonable probability, and indicate an utter indifference as to the life of the sufferer, whether it live or die. Thus Elizabeth Key was indicted, and the charge found relevant, for the murder of her apprentice, a girl of eleven years of age, by carrying her out in the night, when sick and ailing, and exposing her in the open air, whereby she died of cold and hunger, though it was in the streets of a considerable town.[6] The same would

---

[1] Hume, 1 186 —[2] Ibid 1 183.—[3] Ibid 1 190 —[4] Ibid —[5] Ibid —[6] April 10 1699, Hume, 1 190

hold if a parent or master were to confine his child or servant
in a damp or unwholesome room, so that the victim of this
cruelty at length sunk under its sufferings; or if a jailor should
confine a prisoner in a cell with a maniac, or in one where the
seeds of a contagious disorder are lurking, and should refuse
to remove him, though he observe his dying condition,[1] and,
in consequence of such conduct, death should ensue

By the Roman law, the like penalty was affixed to the case
of one bearing false testimony against another, if a capital conviction follow.[2]  In England, however, it seems to be settled
in the modern practice,[3] different in that respect from the ancient common law,[1] that this offence is not cognizable as murder.[5]  And, in Scotland, there seems to be no authority for
holding that such an offence, how great soever, and however
punishable as perjury or a conspiracy, could be made the subject of capital punishment.

24.  Legal evidence in murder, is founded either on the
direct testimony of two witnesses, or of one witness with
a train of circumstances, or of such a train of circumstances by themselves, as leave no reasonable doubt in
the mind that the pannel was guilty.

Perhaps the most important branch of criminal law in practice, is one upon which little or no information is to be found
in books, viz. the *amount of evidence* which is requisite to convict a criminal.  This is, in an especial manner, the case in
trials for murder, as the stake of the pannel is there so great,
that the utmost exertions are rightly made by his counsel to
screen him from punishment, and juries are perpetually misled by erroneous statements of what is really necessary to constitute legal proof.

It is matter of common observation, that legal evidence is
*something more* than what produces moral conviction, and nothing is more usual than to hear jurymen say, when they have
acquitted a prisoner who was clearly guilty, that they have no
doubt of his guilt, but that they did not think it was legally
proved.  What, then, is it, which fills up that important mea-

[1] Hume, 1 190 —[2] Dig. lib. 46. tit 8. l. 1 —[3] Russell, 1 621 —[4] Hawkins, 1
c 31, § 7, Blackstone, iv 196 —  Leach 1 44  Foster 132 —[5] Hume, 1 186

sure, so constantly referred to, and yet so little understood?
To illustrate this matter, the evidence shall be recapitulated
which has prevailed in all the most important trials which
have occurred for murder of late years.

In the noted case of Burke and Macdougall, December 24.
1828, the pannels were charged with having murdered an old
woman of the name of Doherty, in Burke's house in Portsburgh.   To support the libel, it was proved that the deceased
had come to a shop in Portsburgh, where Burke happened to
be at the time, begging, on the day preceding the murder;
that he spoke to her, and took her away with him, offering to
give her lodgings in his house; that she was then in perfect health; that she remained there during the day, and
that both pannels urged the deceased not to leave the house;
that, at eleven at night, she was alive, and merry, dancing,
and drunk; that, at two in the morning, Burke went to a
medical student, and told him he had a subject to dispose of,
and that he came and saw the body among some straw, under a bed, but without removing it on that occasion; that, on
the following day, Burke was seen by the neighbours frequently to sprinkle spirits on and under the bed, which stood
in the room; that an old woman being left there alone, peeped
under the bed, and saw the body, and went for the police, but,
in the interval, it was removed by Burke to Dr Knox's, in
Surgeons' Square, and Burke himself went and got the money
for the subject in the evening.   This was the chief *circumstantial* evidence against the accused; but it was proved by
Hare, the infamous associate of his crimes, that he was present,
along with Mrs Macdougall and his own wife Mrs Hare, when
Burke smothered the deceased, and that he himself had held
her feet.   Mrs Hare corroborated this statement, adding, that
she and Macdougall were together in bed, and that, when
the violence began, they ran out of the room, and staid behind
the door till all was over.   Upon this evidence, it was strongly
contended by Sir James Moncrieff, then Dean of Faculty, that
the whole *circumstances* amounted only to such as would necessarily attach to a person who made a trade of selling dead
bodies, and had one to dispose of, being that of a person who
had died of intoxication in his house; and, therefore, that the
charge of *murder* rested solely on the evidence of the *socius*
Hare, and his wife, the former of whom was plainly implicated

in this as well as other murders, and totally unworthy of credit; while the latter, from being out of the room, could not tell whether the crime was committed by her husband or the pannel. The jury, by a great majority, convicted Burke, but acquitted Macdougall; but the opinion of the bench was, that both were proved guilty of the crime.[1]

In the case of Jean Aitken or Humphreys, Aberdeen, September 1830, the pannel was indicted for the murder of her husband, by pouring sulphuric acid down his throat, as he lay asleep in bed. It appeared that the pannel and her deceased husband were both much addicted to habits of intoxication, and had frequent quarrels in that state; and that she had frequently threatened to murder him, and, on one occasion, actually d - sired a person to buy some laudanum for her for that purpose. On the night in question they had a severe struggle in the room with some company, and the deceased struck his wife, and was struck by her. After the company went away, about twelve at night, he went to bed, and soon after was seen asleep, there being no person in the house but the pannel and a servant-maid. The pannel then left the servant's room on her *stocking soles*, a thing unusual to her, and was absent about twenty minutes, at which time the door was locked, and no other person was in the house; when she returned, she said *smiling* that her husband was roaring mad with drink, and the servant, upon descending, found him lying on his back in the utmost agony, exclaiming that he was all roasting She at first shewed an unwillingness to send for a doctor, but at length did so. When she left the guests at twelve, there were only two glasses on the table in the room; but, when the neighbours came in, after the alarm, there were *three*, and the third was proved to have come from a room above stairs, of which she had the key. A child, which was brought in by one of the neighbours, seized hold of this third glass, and put it to its lips, upon which it screamed aloud, and all the persons around put it to their lips, and felt a sharp pain. The pannel came in shortly after, and, upon their inquiring what was in the glass, she replied it was *alum water*, a taste which they did not think it at all resembled. In the room where the deceased was lying, a vial, containing three teaspoonfuls of sulphuric acid, had been standing for some weeks.

[1] Syme's Cases, 315

it had contained the usual quantity the day before, but, on the morning after the catastrophe, there was only as much as covered the bottom of the vial. The deceased lived two days, but never could give any farther account of the matter, than that he went to sleep quite well, and wakened all roasting, and had suffered the utmost agony ever since. Sometimes he used expressions tending to criminate his wife, at others the reverse; and, on one occasion, before a clergyman, he absolved her altogether His death, which took place in two days, was clearly owing to a corrosive acid; and sulphuric acid, in considerable quantities, was detected on his shirt, and on the blankets and bedcover, and a little on the pannel's bedgown and handkerchief, but none was discovered in his stomach and intestines. The defence pleaded, with great ability by Mr Neaves, was suicide, and want of evidence; but the jury, under the direction of Lord Mackenzie, unanimously found the pannel guilty, and on the next day she confessed the crime.[1]

In the case of Robert Emond, February 6. 1830, the pannel was accused of having murdered Mrs Franks and her daughter, in a lonely cottage, near the village of Abbey, in the county of Haddington It appeared on the proof, that the daughter had come, on the morning of the day libelled, to get milk at the door of a neighbour, and that the windows were seen open, and the smoke ascending from the chimney on that, but not on the following day. Two days afterwards, the neighbours, alarmed at the deserted appearance of the cottage, entered over the wall of the garden, and found the mother and daughter both murdered, the one in the room of the house, the other near the door of the garden. The pannel, who was a relation of the deceased, had been heard previously to use threatening expressions towards her, and, some days before the murder, had been at her cottage, inquiring concerning her, and had then spoke and used suspicious expressions to one of her neighbours. On the night libelled he had a violent quarrel with his own wife, in the village of North Berwick, seven miles distant, and he had locked himself into his own room at night, apart from his family Owing to some family connexions he imputed the animosity of his wife to Mrs Franks' machinations, and was irritated at her after domestic dissension From his room it was possible to descend, by a water-cask, to the garden behind, and, on the night in question, there were marks of his having let himself down, and left the house. On the following morning the door of the room was still locked, and the bed standing in it bore no marks of having been slept on. He was not seen at all that night, but, on the following morning, he was seen coming on the road from Haddington to North Berwick, at five o'clock, at the distance of *two miles* from Mrs Franks' cottage; and a number of other persons saw him on the road, walking in a disturbed manner, and with a wild expression of countenance, until he reached his own house at eight o'clock. His feet and stockings were then steaming with moisture, although the morning was dry and the roads dusty. His stockings and pantaloons bore the appearance of having been steeped in water, or imperfectly washed. He had t   t out a *second coat* with him when he went away, but he had it not when he returned, and he never could produce it, or point out where it was. Some small spots of blood were found on his shirt and hat: the shoes, which were on his feet when he returned, bore a dark mark on the sole, and were of a very peculiar construction, with iron nails and double iron heels, and marks precisely similar appeared on the floor of the room where the girl was lying murdered, as if some person had stampt in blood, and left the marks of the most prominent parts of the sole on the floor. When taken to the scene of the murder, he evinced a repugnance to enter the room with the bodies, and, when questioned concerning the offence, evaded the question, but never directly asserted his innocence. This was the unexceptionable part of the evidence; but, in addition to this, he was proved, by two young men, the companions of his cell in Edinburgh Jail, to have voluntarily made a sort of confession to them during the night, of his guilt; but this evidence could not be relied on, as they stood charged with a most serious theft and embezzlement committed upon their employers at Glasgow, and had received a free pardon, to enable them to be received as witnesses The pannel was ably defended by Mr Macneil, but the Court were of opinion that the case was sufficiently proved, and he was convicted and executed Shortly before his conviction he made a full confession of his guilt.[1]

At the Perth circuit, September 8 1830, James Henderson was accused of the murder of an old man of the name of Millie,

[1] Unreported

who lived in a lonely cottage near the gate of Melville Park, in the county of Fife. It appeared that the accused was an apprentice of the deceased, and had in consequence ample means of knowing where his money and valuables were placed. He had considerable property in linen and other articles of household plenishing, and also a deposit-receipt for L. 40 of a bank, in the house. A few days before the day libelled the deceased was seen alive and well; but the pannel the day following ordered the girl who brought him milk in the morning not to bring it any longer for some time, as his master was going from home. Neither the pannel nor the deceased were seen for several weeks; but at length, alarmed at the deserted aspect of the cottage, the neighbours entered and made a search, and discovered the body buried under the ground in the garden, bearing distinct marks of violence and wounds in many places. There were marks of an attempt to make an excavation in the interior of the cottage, which appear to have failed. The pannel was proved, some days after the night libelled, to have brought a carter in the night to the cottage of the deceased, and taken a variety of articles from the house; and large quantities of his moveables were traced to his possession and sold by him in Dunfermline and elsewhere, whither he had retired after the death of the deceased. He was repeatedly asked by the neighbours what had become of Millie, before the discovery of the murder, and he gave contradictory accounts concerning him. He presented the deposit-receipt at the bank for payment, with a forged signature of the deceased indorsed on it. The washerwoman who washed his clothes discovered some marks of blood on them shortly after the disappearance of the deceased. In these circumstances, there could be no doubt of the guilt of the accused : the defence pleaded, that the theft only, and not the murder, was proved against him, was overruled both by Lord Meadowbank and the jury; he was convicted, and shortly after confessed his guilt.[1]

Mrs Mackinnon was tried on March 13. 1823, for the murder of a young man in a brothel, which she kept in the South Bridge of Edinburgh. The deceased was proved by several witnesses to have gone to the house of the pannel in company with some other young men, and a quarrel arose between them and the girls there concerning the payment of the reckoning,

---

[1] Unreported

in the course of which they chained the door in the inside. During the struggle, the pannel, alarmed by the noise, came up with a table-knife in her hand; and one witness, a friend of the deceased, of the name of Kerr, swore that he saw her strike him, or at least strike in the direction of his breast. The deceased in his dying declaration identified the pannel as the woman who struck him. There was no other direct evidence, and little circumstantial. She was defended in an eloquent manner by Mr Jeffrey, but the jury by a plurality found her guilty, and she was condemned and executed.[1]

Much of the same sort was the case of J. Devine, 14th June 1824. The pannel was there charged with the murder of his wife, who was found with her throat cut in her own house. The principal evidence against him consisted of the *declaration* of a boy of eleven years of age, who was playing at ball in the court where the house was situated, and, happening to look through a hole in the window, saw the pannel come behind his wife, seize her by the head, and cut her throat with a razor. This boy was the only witness who spoke to the actual fact; but he was corroborated by other witnesses, who deponed to concurring circumstances. He was convicted, and executed.[2]

Again, in the case of Robert Macleod, March 1. 1821, it appeared that the accused had been in company with the deceased in Glentanner, leading from the valley of the Dee to Angusshire over the Grampian Hills, on the day preceding her death, both on the road and in several houses by its side. On the day libelled he was seen with her ascending the Firmouth, and also sitting by her side near Lochmaven, at its summit. Her death appeared to have been occasioned by blows from a small iron anvil, which belonged to the pannel, and was found near her body, within a few yards of the place where he had been seen sitting by her side, and some articles belonging to her were found in his possession. The chain of evidence was considered complete both by the Court and jury, and the accused was condemned and executed.

In the case of James Allan, December 27. 1825, it appeared that the deceased was a drover returning from Angusshire to Aberdeenshire, and the pannel, who was returning in the same direction, joined company with him two days before his death, and they travelled together. It was proved that the pannel knew the road, while the deceased did not, and that he repeatedly took him by short and unfrequented paths. In the course of the journey he saw the money which the deceased was possessed of, consisting of £1, 16s and a dollar He was seen walking with the deceased on the day of his death across the Garioch, to within half a mile of the place where the murder was committed and his body was found, which was about two hundred yards to the south of the toll-bar of Fyvie, in Aberdeenshire. He was again seen walking alone farther on in the same line of road, on a subsequent part of the same day. He bore a loaded hunting-whip, with which it was supposed the fatal blows had been inflicted. Some articles belonging to the deceased, and, in particular, a crown-piece and the snuff-box which he bore, were found in the pannel's possession. He was condemned, and executed

In the case of Margaret Wishart, Perth, 14th April 1827, the pannel was charged with murdering Jane Wishart, her sister, by mixing up arsenic with the food which she administered to her. It appeared on the proof that the deceased, who was blind, had eaten some porridge on the night libelled; that she was seized in twenty minutes with vomiting and pains in her stomach, which continued with slight intermissions for five days, when she died. This occurred in the pannel's house, with whom she lived, who usually prepared an administered the food, and who was present when the supper was taken The deceased bore a child in the interval between receiving the poison and her death, which also died. The prisoner evinced a repugnance to sending for a doctor, and repeatedly said a doctor could do her sister no good The father of the child of the deceased had been seen in suspicious circumstances with the pannel; and the deceased had repeatedly complained of the miserable life which she had between that father and her sister. The pannel evinced no sorrow for her sister's sufferings, but rather irritation when spoken to on the subject. When in jail, she sent for a witness, and asked her to say that she had gone with the deceased to a particular shop to get arsenic, which she declined to do, having never been there with her. Her declarations contained contradictions to the evidence in several particulars, but there was no evidence of her having purchased arsenic Arsenic was found in considerable quantities in the stomach of the deceased mother, but none in that of the child. The Lord Justice-Clerk Boyle charged the jury to convict, and the pannel was condemned and executed.[1]

John Lovie was indicted for the murder of Margaret Mackessar, by administering arsenic at Aberdeen in September 1827. It appeared in evidence that the pannel, who was a small farmer near Fraserburgh, in Aberdeenshire, had hired the deceased as his female servant, and that she was pregnant by him. The family consisted of the prisoner, his mother, the deceased, and a servant lad. To this servant lad the pannel had repeatedly spoken concerning the effect of different poisons, and in particular arsenic and laudanum, in procuring abortion, about a week before the death of the deceased; and asked him if a particular doctor in Fraserburgh was likely to have it. The evening before she received the poison the deceased was in her usual health and spirits, and rose in the morning to go to her work; but, shortly after her breakfast, she was taken violently ill with retching and vomiting, which continued for two days, when she died in great agony. The pannel was seen coming from the house after breakfast, and he went to work with his servant lad in the field hoeing turnips. This lad told him the deceased was unwell, on which his face turned red, and he went to the house; when he returned he said he had heard her vomiting, and that if she continued in that way she could not long survive During the course of the day her mother three times passed within hail of the pannel, when at his work, but he never told her that her daughter was ailing. Some days before he had purchased arsenic from a shopkeeper in Fraserburgh, professedly to kill rats, but it was proved there were no rats about the place. No medical man was sent for during the illness of the deceased, though her pain and symptoms of distress were most violent; but at length, upon the mother of the deceased reproaching them with this neglect, the pannel went for one, who did not arrive till after death After death, he objected to the body being opened, on the ground that she was with child, and that it would thereby become known, and testified a great desire to have the funeral over as quickly as possible Arsenic was found in large quantities in the stomach and intestines of the deceased, and she was six months gone

---

[1] Syme, App. No 1

r

with child. The accused, in his declaration, denied that he
had bought any arsenic from the druggist, but admitted having
purchased some stuff to rub on the back of his cows and heifers;
after doing which he washed the saucer, and threw the contents on the dunghil. But the dunghil was searched, and
nothing of the kind found there; and it was proved the cattle
had no complaint which required a similar application. The
pannel denied to a sister of the deceased that he had ever
bought poison, and said some one must have got it in his name,
without his authority. The jury, misled by the eloquence of
Mr Cockburn, found the libel not proven; but the Court were
of opinion the case was clearly made out,—an opinion with
which, it is probable, no man of sense who considers the evidence will be disposed to differ.[1]

James Glen was charged, on 10th November 1827, with having murdered his illegitimate child, by throwing it into a
canal near Glasgow. It was proved that the mother of the
infant, being unable to maintain it, delivered it to the pannel
in good health, two days before it was found drowned; when
she returned, two days after, to inquire for the child, he could
not produce it, and laughed at her when she wanted to get it
back. She saw the child disinterred, which was found in the
canal, and knew it to be her own. In this statement she was
supported by another witness. When apprehended, before any
thing was said of the charge against him, he said it was not
him who drowned the child, and added soon after, if they
would allow him twenty minutes, he would produce the child;
but this he never could do. He afterwards said he had given
it to a woman, and varied repeatedly in his account of what
sort of a woman she was. In his declaration, he said he took
out the child after he got it from its mother, and wrapped it in
a grey mantle, in which he carried it to Cowcaddens, and there
gave it to a poor woman, whom he did not know, with twelve
shillings for its board; and that, previous to his apprehension,
he had not heard that he was accused of the murder of the
child. The Court considered the case as proved, and the pannel was convicted and executed.[2]

In the case of Archibald Maclennan, Inverness, September
1830, the pannel was indicted for the murder of his wife, by

[1] Syme, App. p. 30; but chiefly from my own Notes.—[2] Syme, 264.

strangling her on the sea-shore and throwing her over a rock into the ocean. On the proof it appeared that the body of the deceased, who was a maniac, and for some years had wandered through the country apart from her husband, was found on the shore on a Friday night with evident marks of compression and violence on the throat, and contusions and wounds on the head. The pannel had frequently been heard to express ill-will towards her, and used her in a violent and cruel manner, having on one occasion pitched her on her head among some stones, and on another, only two days before the death, forced her head under water in a burn near his house, after sunset, till the eyes almost started out of their sockets. On the morning of the day on which the body was found, the deceased left the house of a neighbour where she had passed the night, and which was situated at a short distance from the sea-shore; and, shortly after she set out, the pannel called, inquiring for her, and being told which way she had gone, set out to follow in the same direction. He was seen following her, by two witnesses, towards the sea-shore, where they were both lost sight of. She was at the distance of about twenty yards from the place where her body was afterwards discovered, and he was cutting across by a shorter path through some potatoes in the same direction. At the top of a rock at a short distance from the place where the body was found, were discovered the marks of a desperate struggle; the track of something heavy having been drawn for some yards over the grass to the very edge of the rock, was quite evident, and the tufts of bent and projecting eminences on this line were torn up as if caught hold of by some creature, when endeavouring to resist the violence and save itself from being pushed over. Human excrement was found on this spot, which bore the appearance of having been voided when the person was in the act of being dragged; and fragments of the bed-gown and handkerchief which the deceased wore that morning were found lying on the spot close to the marks. A sharp stone of three pounds weight was found there also, which had been newly taken out of its bed, the appearance of which was quite fresh; and the footmarks were those of two persons, one with, and the other without, shoes. The pannel, on the morning in question, had on shoes, his wife none. Two hours *after* they had been seen going towards and so near this fatal spot the pannel returned home, and was seen with *his shoes wet,*

though there was no dew on the grass, and the weather was
fine. It was nearly full tide at this time, and the person who
pushed the body into the water would probably, in such a state
of the tide, have wet his shoes. The jury found the libel not
proven; a result not at all surprising, considering the class
from whom the persons intrusted with that important duty are
drawn in that remote and uncivilized district; but Lords
Meadowbank and Mackenzie thought the case proved, and the
verdict would probably have been different in any other city
of the kingdom.[1]

—Another case occurred at the same circuit, terminating in
the same result, in consequence of the most extraordinary and
unprecedented contradiction of evidence. This was the case
of William Durrand, John Henderson, and George Jamieson,
Inverness, September 1830. The *species facti* there was that
the body of Small, a mariner, was found stiff, with the fists
clenched and the elbows akimbo, at the back of the pier of Wick,
on 2d September 1825. The body was interred; but no suspicion having fallen on any particular person at that time, no
legal proceedings were commenced. Five years afterwards, in
consequence of information received, the prisoners were apprehended, and the body was raised from the grave. It was found
with the bones of the arms and hands still in the same posture
in which they were when first discovered, and it was proved
that they could not be straighted by the utmost exertion of
strength at the time when the body was first interred, and that
this effect usually takes place when death ensues in the midst
of great struggling. On the trial it was sworn to by a girl
who was at the time servant in the house, that the deceased
and his captain came to drink in the evening, and were shown
into a room below, where the prisoners were sitting; that after
they had been there some hours, the landlady, wife of the
pannel Durrand, came into the room where she was lying, and
looked in her face with her candle to see if she was sleeping, and
that her suspicions being excited, she followed her and saw the
three prisoners, Mrs Durrand, and seven or eight other persons,
surrounding Small's dead body: *that the arms were akimbo*, as if
death had taken place during a desperate struggle: that the
whole party took the body down a stair to a cellar, and that she

[1] Unreported.

the witness followed them, and saw through the keyhole that Mrs Durrand took £20 in bank notes out of the pocket of the deceased, and divided it among the three prisoners: that the body was taken out about three in the morning, carried to the back of the pier, and there thrown over. Farqul, who was present at the murder, deponed that the three prisoners and Small, the deceased, were in the room together, when a quarrel ensued between Durrand and Small about some dead bodies which Small said had been sent from his house to the doctors in Edinburgh: that Durrand rose up, seized Small, threw him down, twisted his neckcloth round, and struck him violently on the head with a bottle, which immediately occasioned his death: that neither of the other prisoners took a hand in the affray except Henderson, who, when the struggle began, put out the candle: that the body was taken down to the cellar, and the money divided, and the corpse afterwards thrown over the pier. So far the case was distinctly proved, and Lords Meadowbank and Mackenzie considered the guilt of Durrand established, though, as there was no clear evidence of the murder having been preconcerted, they held there was no sufficient case against the other prisoners. Six witnesses also swore that Emily Sutherland, the girl who saw the servant, was in Durrand's service at that time: on the other hand, eight witnesses swore that she was *not* there at that time, and did not come for a twelvemonth afterwards; and four witnesses who, however, were all relations of Mrs Durrand, deponed that she was also absent from home on the night in question. To complete the embarrassment, the pannel Jamieson, in his declaration, *confessed the crime*, and told the story in nearly the same terms as Farquhar. The pannel Durrand confessed in his declaration that Emily Sutherland was his servant at the time libelled; and the pannel Henderson declared Mrs Durrand *was* in the house at that time With such contradictory evidence the prosecutor declined to ask for a conviction; but the impression of the Court was that Durrand was really guilty, and that the alibi was got up by fixing real occurrences at another time on the day of the murder; and, in this opinion, they were supported by the great authority of Baron Hume on reading the evidence.[1]

John Stuart and Catherine Wright were indicted, July 13.

----

[1] Unreported.

1829, for the murder of Robert Lamont, a passenger on board a steam-boat on the river Clyde, on its way from Tarbert to Glasgow, and robbing him, after he was insensible, of £17, and a black silver purse, and also for administering laudanum to John Lamont, and some other persons, his relations, with intent to murder. It appeared in evidence that the prisoners were, with the deceased and his relations, in the cabin of the vessel, for some hours, during its voyage up the river Clyde, in the course of which they called repeatedly for porter; which was drunk by all present, and the pannels treated them with officious attention. Catherine Wright was seen to make motions as if putting something into a mug of the porter, and, before this both she and Stuart had an opportunity of seeing the money the deceased was possessed of, and had gone out of the cabin more than once at the same time. The deceased drank largely of the contents of the mug, at the request of the pannels; and his relations John Lamont, Catharine Macphail, and Margaret Macphail, also took some, but in a smaller quantity. Shortly after they were all seized with sickness and vomiting, and went on deck to relieve themselves, leaving the pannel Stuart and the deceased alone in the cabin together. John Lamont having returned unexpectedly, found the deceased lying on the bench in the cabin, and Stuart bending over his body. The deceased was taken to Glasgow insensible, and died on the following day; but the others, after suffering severely, recovered. His purse and all his money were gone, when he was searched upon being put to bed at night, and the prisoners had disappeared hastily, when the vessel arrived at the Broomielaw, but were apprehended together next day, and some notes, which could not be identified, and the purse of the deceased, which was distinctly recognised by the person who made it, found upon Stuart. They were both found guilty and executed.[1]

At Glasgow, September 1831, James Byres, and Mary Steel his wife, were also indicted for murder, by poisoning, and stealing from the deceased four pounds in money, after he was insensible. On evidence, it appeared, that an old man, of the name of John Martin, lodged in the same house at Glasgow, with the prisoners, and they went about the town, to which he

---

[1] Unreported.

was a stranger, with him. In the course of their rambles they entered several public-houses, where they drank porter and spirits. After leaving one, Mrs Byres asked one of the witnesses if a doctor's shop was near, and went away in search of one. When returning from it, her husband went to meet her, and they talked a little together apart from the rest of the company : on returning they proposed to go and get some more drink, which was agreed to, and they all adjourned to a tap-room in the High Street. There Mrs Byres called for a tankard of porter, and went to the counter to get it, returned with it in her hand, and poured some into a tumbler, which she also had; but, before the porter was put into the tumbler, something dark was observed by one of the witnesses in the bottom of the glass. At this time all the party were in good health: the deceased, at the request of both prisoners, drank it off; but the prisoners did not partake of it. Soon after drinking, the deceased became drowsy, and was taken home. During the whole time, in this public-house, the deceased was served by Mrs Byres, and not by the people of the house. Upon arriving home he got rapidly worse; insomuch that the suspicion of the people who had been with them was strongly excited, which was increased by the two prisoners going out together. A man went out after them, and got hold of Mrs Byres, but the husband could not be found. On being charged with having put something into the tumbler, she said they had all drunk of it, which was false. It was proved that the deceased had some large notes, and four small ones, in the morning of that day : his friend, who saw them in his possession at that time, searched him after he became insensible, but the smaller notes were gone. He died that night in a state of stupor: on the body being opened there were no appearances of apoplexy, and the appearances were those of perfect health, but laudanum was found in the stomach and intestines. The doctor, who sold the laudanum, identified Mrs Byres as the person who bought it; and some notes, but which could not be identified as those belonging to the deceased, were found on Byres himself. They were both condemned and executed, after having confessed their guilt.

Lastly, in the case of Mrs Smith, February 19. 1827, the pannel was indicted for the murder of a servant maid in her house, by means of arsenic. It appeared in evidence that, on the day libelled, which was a Tuesday, the deceased was working in the fields as usual, and that, in the evening, a glass of something was administered to her by the pannel, which left a white sediment, and that on the following morning she was taken ill: that on the Wednesday and Thursday she continued to be violently affected with vomiting and purging, and complained of violent pain in her inside, accompanied by a burning feeling. that the pannel all this time objected to the mother of the deceased being sent for, though she had expressed a wish for that purpose: that the deceased said that the pannel had burnt her inside with whisky, and was frequently giving her drink. Her mother came on the Friday morning, and the deceased then said that those who had hurt her would get their reward, and used other expressions clearly indicating an opinion that some poisonous matter had been given her by her mistress. She died in great agony on Friday night. The deceased was with child to the pannel's son, and the pannel had repeatedly given her drinks apparently for the purpose of procuring abortion. On the Wednesday she was better and she ate some milk and oat-cake to dinner. The pannel said that she had given her castor-oil on the Tuesday evening, and that the doctor told her she had died of water in the chest; but the liquid in the glass did not resemble castor-oil, and had white sediment, and the doctor had never given her such an opinion. No drugs nor appearance of any kind were found in the deceased's chest to countenance the opinion that she had destroyed herself by poison. The pannel had bought arsenic from a druggist in Dundee, asking for poison for rats, five days before the death, and had bought no castor-oil. There were no rats about the place during the whole summer, though there had been in great numbers eighteen months before; no dead rats were found in the neighbourhood of the farm-steading, nor was there any evidence of arsenic having been laid for them Arsenic was found in the stomach of the deceased, and the symptoms of her illness were such as would have been produced by that poison. In her first declarations the pannel admitted having given the deceased some castor-oil on the Tuesday evening, but denied having got any poison or arsenic, or had any in the house; but, in her second, she admitted having bought arsenic five days before the death of the deceased. which she said she gave to rats, and that she mixed it with meal and gave it to the rats in the presence of the deceased, but of no one else.

On the other hand, it was proved by the witnesses in exculpation, and by the cross-examination of some of those in chief, that the deceased was subject to occasional depression of spirits, and on these occasions let fall expressions of an intention to destroy herself; that rats had infested the farm-buildings to a great degree on former occasions, though at the time libelled nothing but their dung was discovered; and that on one occasion, two or three weeks before the deceased died, she had expressed herself in serious terms to an old beggar-woman, who came there to lodge for the night, in regard to her unfortunate situation, from being pregnant, and ill-used on that account by her relations, and of her wish to commit suicide. Some attempt also was made to prove that arsenic had been bought by a boy; but there was nothing to connect it with the deceased. The jury found the libel not proven; which is not surprising, considering the doubt thrown over the case by the evidence in exculpation; but the Court were unanimous that the case was proved, and it is probable no person who considers the evidence with attention will form an opposite opinion.[1]

From these cases it must be evident that the measure of legal evidence can be determined by no other rule than that it must be such a chain of circumstances or such direct proof, as appears inconsistent with the prisoner's innocence, and leaves no reasonable doubt in any intelligent mind that the prisoner is guilty of the murder in question. Unquestionably the evidence of one witness will not in any case be sufficient; that is to say, it will not do for the prosecutor to examine one witness and close his case. But, on the other hand, the evidence of one witness, accompanied by a train of circumstances, each link of which is established by a single unexceptionable testimony, is unquestionably sufficient; nay, a chain of circumstantial evidence alone, proved in the same manner, of itself often amounts to the most conclusive legal proof. No more specific rule can be laid down for the weighing of such testimony, but that it must be such as produces conviction of guilt in a reasonable mind; and that, if any serious doubts are entertained by the jury, it is their duty to acquit the prisoner. It is to be re-

---

[1] Syme, 92, and my own Notes.

gretted that the composition and habits of our juries, under the
late act of Parliament, is such as, in many parts of the country, to render them in a great measure incapable of exercising
the important duty of weighing any long chain of evidence,
and that, when the trial has endured a considerable time, the
merits of the evidence too often enters but little into the formation of their verdicts.

25. The punishment of murder is death, and confiscation of moveables; to which, by special statute, feeding
on bread and water up to the time of execution, and dissection after that event, is superadded.

By the common law of Scotland agreeing in this particular
with the Jewish law, and that of all civilized nations, the punishment of murder is death and confiscation of moveables.
In cases of great atrocity it has been usual to superadd some
other indignity, the more strongly to express the public indignation, as hanging in chains, or quartering the limbs and affixing them in different places.[1]   In modern practice, however,
the only peculiarities are that the sentence is frequently ordered
to be carried into execution at the place where the crime was
committed; and, in very aggravated cases, the body is hung in
chains on the spot.   This course was adopted by Lord Justice-
Clerk Hope at Inverness, in autumn 1810, on occasion of the
conviction of a prisoner for a very aggravated murder of a
young woman in a lonely moor in that desolate district; and
in the case of John Scott, for the murder of two men in a
moor, tried at Jedburgh, autumn 1817.

By the statute 25th Geo. II. c. 37, entitled " An Act for
better preventing the horrid crime of murder," it is enacted
that, previous to execution, the convict shall be confined apart
without access of any person to him, except by permission of
the sheriff or of the court where he was convicted, and that he
shall be fed, except in case of violent illness, with bread and
water only.   It is also enacted, that the sentence shall be for
delivery of the body to surgeons to be dissected, unless ordered
to be hung in chains, and that in no case shall the body be
buried until it be dissected.[2]   In practice, however, it is usual

---

[1] Hume, i. 284.—[2] 25th Geo. II. c. 37.

to allow them such wine or other restoratives as the medical attendant deems proper during this melancholy interval.

26. In cases of culpable homicide, or of the pannel convicted of murder escaping execution, he becomes liable to an assythment to the widow and next of kin of the deceased.

When the pannel is convicted only of culpable homicide, or execution of the sentence is prevented by an act of indemnity, or he escape execution of the capital sentence, through the interposition of the royal mercy, he becomes liable to an *assythment* to the widow and children, or other next of kin of the deceased.[1] So firmly is this right accruing to the private sufferers established in our practice, that the King has never pretended to any power to interfere with it; but, on the contrary, by the ordinary style of remissions, they bear a special clause obliging to assyth the party.[2] Formerly, the usual course for ascertaining or taxing the assythment was by the Barons of Exchequer, who were entrusted with the remission; but, in later times, the practice has been to make the remit to the Court of Session, where process was raised to have the amount ascertained, and decree issued against the guilty party.[3] On pleading of a remission in the Court of Justiciary, the judges of that tribunal seem to be as competent to tax the assythment among themselves as to remit to any other judicatory.[4]

In the case of a conviction for culpable homicide in a process at the instance of the next of kin, concluding for assythment, it is a regular and legitimate part of the sentence to tax and award the amount.[5] Further, in any case where this interest has not been settled by the decree of some other competent tribunal, the Court of Session, independent of any remit, have the undoubted jurisdiction in ascertaining it.[6] Under the present form of process, it would of course be fixed as any other question of damages by a jury trial.

In the distribution of the assythment, the widow is entitled to a share along with her issue; the heir along with the other children, and the immediate issue to the exclusion of the more remote.[7]

---

[1] Hume, i. 234.—[2] Ibid. i. 285.—[3] Ibid—[4] Ibid. i. 286.—[5] Ibid.—[6] Maclaurin, 98, 99; Hume, i. 286.—[7] Balfour, 517; Hume, i. 286.

### SECTION II.— CULPABLE HOMICIDE.

CULPABLE HOMICIDE may be committed in three ways:—1. By the intentional infliction of death, in circumstances which law deems blameable, though not so much so as to amount to murder; 2. By the unintentional deprivation of life, in pursuance of an intention not to kill, but to do some inferior bodily injury, from which it was not probable that death would follow; 3. By undue negligence, or want of attention, in the performance of a lawful act. Of the first sort are the cases approaching to murder, where death is blameably inflicted under circumstances of severe provocation; of the second, those where death has ensued from illegal acts, as boxing matches, throwing stones, &c. where so fatal an event could not reasonably have been expected; of the third, the numerous cases where, from negligence in driving, riding, or conducting steam-boats, fatal consequences ensue.

1. It is the duty of every person, when provoked, or placed in circumstances of real or supposed danger, to exercise a due control over his passions, and if death ensue, where that control has not been exerted, or the belief of danger was not real, the homicide will be deemed culpable, even though the circumstances were not such as to render it murder.

Though men, like other animals, are subject to the feeling of resentment for injuries which have been received or are anticipated, yet law, as well as reason, require that this instinctive feeling should be placed under due control; and human life not extinguished upon every received insult or supposed danger. To gain this state of self-command is a part of every man's duty; and any undue excess requires to be chastized, as the only means of preventing the angry passions from becoming the source of perpetual contention.[1] It follows, that the degree of culpability of such excess must depend on the circumstances of each particular case, and its punishment may in con-

---

[1] Hume, 1. 239.

sequence vary, from a day's imprisonment, or a fine of a shilling, to transportation for life.

The general description of this species of culpable homicide is, that it is homicide on high provocation. It originates, in general, in those quarrels arising from intemperance, which are so frequent among the people of this country; and it generally turns out, that both parties were at first to blame, although the sufferer has received more than his due chastisement from the intemperate revenge of the survivor.

Thus in the case of George White, August 4, 1788, the libel bore a narrative, that he had killed the deceased, by striking him on the head with a candlestick, and afterwards with a bottle, which wounded him severely. He was charged alternatively with murder or culpable homicide, and the jury found him guilty of the latter offence.[1] So also James Macghie was, on 17th January 1791, convicted of culpable homicide, by striking the deceased with a pair of heavy iron tongs, when lying on the ground. The provocation proved was, that the deceased had made a violent assault upon the pannel's father, in his presence, by throwing him on the ground, and severely beating him in that situation.[2] This would have made the homicide justifiable, if done with the fist or a stick, but the use of a lethal weapon, after the deceased had been thrown on the ground, and the plea of defence of his father was at an end, rendered it culpable in a high degree. Again, in the case of Lilburn and Buchanan, 12th February 1771, it appeared that the prisoners were passing the door of an inn, when they were attacked by a mastiff-dog, apparently set on them by the defunct, or his associates. One of them came up to the prisoners, when high words ensued, on which the deceased, with some others, left the inn, to assist their companion, when the prisoners, irritated by the continued attack of the dog, struck the deceased on the head with a spit, of which he died on the following day. This was considered as a case of culpable homicide, though no sentence followed, from an informality in the verdict of the jury.[3] Farther, in the case of Lieutenant George Story, 24th January 1785, it was proved that the deceased had, on a former night, in a frolic, thrown some *assafœtida* on the prisoner's clothes, on which the prisoner threat-

[1] Hume, i. 246.—[2] Ibid.—[3] Burnett, 14.

ened to break all the bottles in his shop; and that, accordingly, on the following night, he did come to the shop in a state of intoxication, and tossed about some bottles, and struck the deceased twice with them on the head, so as to occasion death. He was convicted of culpable homicide, and sentenced to eight months' imprisonment.[1] In like manner, in the case of Andrew Pyper, 4th January 1802, a quarrel arose between the prisoner and the deceased, who were fellow-servants, and, after some altercation, the deceased, who was the stronger man of the two, laid hold of the prisoner, and threw him violently on the ground, but without wounding him. On getting up, the prisoner immediately laid hold of a pair of iron tongs, and threatened to strike the deceased. This produced another altercation, in which, however, no blows were exchanged on either side. Shortly after, the deceased retired to a little distance, and, while standing with his back to the prisoner, the latter laid hold of the tongs a second time, and struck him such a blow on the head as produced death in two days after. The Court viewed this as a case of murder, seeing that the injury had taken place *ex intervallo*, and the motive for the fatal act appeared to have been not immediate resentment, but revenge; but the jury, moved by the consideration that the deceased was the original aggressor, found it culpable homicide only.[2] Again, in the case of Christian Paterson, December 22. 1828, it appeared that the pannel and the deceased had a quarrel in a house of ill-fame in Edinburgh, in which the deceased was partly to blame. All in the room were drunk and fighting together, and, in the course of it, the pannel struck the deceased on the head with a pair of tongs, and the wound, though not very severe, produced erysipelas, of which he died in the Infirmary. She was convicted of culpable homicide, and transported for seven years.

2. It is culpable homicide if death ensue in a quarrel, in consequence of an injury, not intended to produce death, and from which fatal consequences could not reasonably have been anticipated.

Numerous convictions have taken place of late years for culpable homicide, of this description; and, in general, it is the disposition of juries, where any extenuating or alleviating circumstances can be discovered, to save the offender's life by such a verdict. Thus in the case of William Stewart, Perth, September 1824, it appeared that the accused and his wife had for long lived on very bad terms, in consequence of a habit of drinking which she had acquired. He had beat her violently on many occasions, and her body, after death, exhibited livid marks from head to foot, but none of the blows were such, as *per se* seemed sufficient to account for death, excepting one on the head, which it was said might have proceeded from a fall. The Court considered the case as one of murder, but the jury brought it in culpable homicide, and the pannel was transported for life. The ground of the verdict was probably that the pannel's temper had been severely tried by his wife's intemperance, and that the blows were not of such a kind as necessarily proved a mortal or a reckless purpose. Further, in the case of Alexander Mackenzie, 14th March 1827, it was proved that the deceased was in the house of the pannel, which was a public house of ill-fame in Roxburgh Street, Edinburgh, when his purse, containing fifteen shillings, was stolen by a girl in the house. He immediately went and seized the purse, which she had in her hand, upon which she roared out that she was robbed of her money, and the pannel immediately came in, seized the deceased, threw him on the ground, and trampled on his groin, which brought on a lock-jaw, of which he died some days afterwards. The injuries inflicted were not serious, and would have been immaterial, but for the fatal occurrence of the lock-jaw. He was convicted of culpable homicide; and, as the death was occasioned when he was *versans in illicito*, both as defending a theft, and keeping a disorderly house, had sentence of transportation for fourteen years.[1] In like manner, in the case of Richard Hamilton, July 1807, the pannel had killed an infirm old woman, by several blows of the hand on the head; but it appeared in evidence, that, before doing so, he threw away a mell or hammer which he had in his hand, and the jury, in consequence, found him guilty of culpable homicide only, and he was transported for seven years.[2] Colin Telfer, on 27th February 1815, was convicted of culpable homicide, and transported seven years, for the death of Maclean, a joiner.

[1] Syme, 158; Hume, i. 236.—[2] Hume, i. 257.

He had taken offence at an offer which Maclean had made for some meat in his stall, and struck him on the head with the leg-bone of a cow, of which he died within a week; but, as the injury was not of such a kind as probably would have inferred death, he escaped the capital charge.[1]   Joseph Rae, on 22d July 1817, was convicted of culpable homicide, for the death of his apprentice John Fraser.   It there appeared that the boy stuck fast in a vent, which he had been sent up to sweep, and the pannel, with the assistance of Robert Reid, put ropes to his feet, and pulled him down with such violence that he died on the spot.   The case was one of the most savage cruelty, and which the Court viewed as murder; but the jury inclined to the lenient side, in consequence of the injury inflicted, however inhumane, not being one which obviously, or in reasonable probability, led to fatal consequences.   He was sentenced to fourteen, and Reid to seven years' transportation.[2] Judgment was long ago given, to the same effect, in the case of Gaspar Reysano, December 19. 1724, who had killed Robert Lamb, by throwing him down stairs backwards, whereby he received a wound on the head, of which he died.   The violence was culpable in the highest degree; but the act was not of such a kind as necessarily inferred a mortal or ruthless purpose, the pannel was only transported for life.[3]   So also, in the case of John Campbell and William Holm, 8th November 1827, it appeared that the pannels had, without the least provocation, assaulted Lawson, a poor Irish labourer, who had sought shelter, with his wife and children, in a hovel for the night.   They had dragged him out, naked as he was, and struck him some hard blows on the head with their fist, one of which knocked him to the ground, and he fell on some projecting stones, which fractured his skull.   The conduct of the men was cruel in the extreme; but the injury they inflicted could not have been anticipated to have produced fatal consequences, and would not have done so but for the accidental fall on the stones; and therefore they were convicted of culpable homicide only, and transported for seven years.[4]

. The distinction between these cases and others of a similar complexion formerly noticed, in which the crime was held to be murder in consequence of the injury being of a ruthless de-

---

[1] Hume, i. 257.—[2] Ibid. i. 258.—[3] Ibid. i. 236.—[4] Ibid i. 237.

scription, is thin, and may sometimes appear almost evanescent; but nevertheless it is founded in substantial justice. The great point to examine in this matter is, whether the whole evidence indicates that the pannel was utterly reckless of the consequences in the outrage which he committed; or was guilty merely of that inferior or measured degree of violence from which fatal consequences could not reasonably have been anticipated. In the first case, the crime is justly deemed murder; in the second, the more equitable as well as humane construction is for culpable homicide.

3. Culpable homicide is committed where death ensues in consequence even of the most inconsiderable violence, if the act producing it was illegal or improper.

The species of culpable homicide hitherto considered differ only by slight shades from murder. But some punishment is also due where death ensues in consequence of no intention either to kill or to inflict a serious injury, but merely to do some slight violence.[1] This usually takes place where the parties have been wrestling or boxing, and death ensues from some accidental occurrence, or latent weakness which could not have been foreseen, or was unknown. Thus, in the case of James Irving, 22d April 1815, it appeared that the pannel and the deceased had not quarrelled, but some wrestling and boxing had taken place; in the course of which Gow, though the stronger man, was, from an unlucky hit, thrown backwards, pitched on his head, and died from concussion of the brain. The pannel was convicted of culpable homicide, and sentenced to a month's imprisonment.[2] In like manner, in the case of William Mason, July 29. 1674, the parties had been wrestling, in the course of which the pannel threw the deceased down, and he fell with his temple on the corner of a chest, which occasioned a violent bleeding, and ultimately death. These facts were only found relevant to infer an arbitrary punishment; that is, to amount to culpable homicide.[3] So also in the case of Thomson and Aberdeen, January 23. 1769, the pannels had met the deceased on horseback, and they pulled him off his horse, in consequence of which he fell and fractured his skull on the pavement, and soon after died.[4]

[1] Hume, i. 234.—[2] Ibid.—[3] Ibid. i. 235.—[4] Ibid i. 237.

G

This was found only relevant to infer an arbitrary punishment. Again, in the case of Angus Cameron, 5th October 1811, it turned out that the deceased was an infirm and deformed lad, who died in consequence of a kick from the pannel; but that the injury would not have proved mortal, if he had not laboured under a rupture at the time, which was unknown to the accused. He had sentence of imprisonment for six months [1] Reference may also be made to the case of Corporal John Macfarlane, who was convicted of culpable homicide for the death of James Robison. The deceased, who was an idiot, had followed a military party through the country, and being suspected of having favoured the escape of a deserter, the pannel, in consequence, first shook him, and then discharged a musket so close to his ear that it produced his death. The jury, conceiving the fatal consequences had not been intended, but that the pannel only meant to frighten the deceased, found him guilty of culpable homicide; and he had sentence of imprisonment for nine months.[2] To the same purpose, on 12th July 1821, Thomas Wood was convicted of culpable homicide, done by striking William Steele a blow on the head with a rack-pin; and, on 14th July 1821, John Neil was convicted of the same offence for killing his mother with a blow from a hammer, which took effect on her instead of his brother, for whom it was intended. The blow was not serious, and would not in all probability have proved fatal but from her bad habit of body, from whence mortification ensued. He had sentence of imprisonment for six months.[3] John Tod, June 20. 1825, convicted of killing a man in a boxing-match, was sentenced to three months imprisonment; and James Gallaghar, September 28 1826, for killing his companion, by throwing him on the ground, where his head undesignedly struck a sharp stone, was sentenced to six weeks' imprisonment.

In the case of William Mailler, Perth, autumn 1824, the pannel was convicted of culpable homicide, and had sentence of imprisonment for four months. He was ploughing in a field near Dunning, and the deceased came up and used some irritating language, in consequence of which, in a fit of passion, he took up a stone and threw it at the deceased, and the blow taking effect on the head, concussion of the brain fol-

[1] Hume, i. 234.—[2] Ibid.—[3] Ibid. i. 235.

lowed, which proved fatal.[1] Again, in the case of John Macdonald, Glasgow, autumn 1826, the pannel was proved to have thrown a small stone at the deceased; but by a singular accident it struck the temple, and almost immediately occasioned death He was sentenced to three months imprisonment.[2]

To the same purpose, in the case of Henry Inglis and Andrew Colville, it appeared that the pannels had mixed snuff or some other hurtful stuff with some spiritous liquor, which they administered to a person with a design only to make him sick, but he died in consequence. The libel was sustained as relevant for culpable homicide, though the evidence proved defective, and they were acquitted.[3] In like manner, Adam Philip was convicted at Perth, on September 30. 1818, of culpable homicide, by having administered an excessive quantity of spirits, consisting of no less than *nine glasses*, to a boy of ten years of age, in consequence of which he died in a few hours: he was sentenced to twelve months' imprisonment.[4] Libel was found relevant against Alexander Forbes, Inverness, autumn 1828, for killing a man by causing him to drink three bottles of porter mixed with three mutchkins of whisky. The like would be the case of a woman who should desert and expose her infant child, in a situation where death was not *likely* to happen, as on the public highway in the day time.[5] If it were done in rigorous weather, and in a more solitary place, the crime would undoubtedly be murder, because such an act could proceed from nothing but a total disregard of the life of the infant. In like manner, if a preceptor or master were to kill his pupil or apprentice, in consequence not of such punishment as is cruel or excessive, or different *in kind* from that usually inflicted, but of an excess only in the usual and appropriate methods, he would be deemed guilty of culpable homicide. Thus, in the case of Robert Carmichael, January 19. 1700, the Court sustained an indictment for murder where a schoolmaster was charged with having killed a pupil by extraordinary and cruel methods of punishment, as by severely lashing him on the back and thighs, and beating him cruelly on the head and back, whereof he immediately died:[6] while, in the case of William Macewan, Perth, September 1830, the charge preferred against the pannel, who had killed an apprentice at a manufac-

---

[1] Unreported.—[2] Unreported.—[3] Hume, i. 237.—[4] Ibid.—[5] Ibid.—[6] Ibid. i. 238.

tory in Dundee by a blow on the shoulder with the fist, which dislocated the joint, was only culpable homicide. The indictment was sustained as relevant; but the pannel was acquitted in consequence of its appearing on the proof that the deceased had been of a very scrofulous and unhealthy habit of body, and that his death was owing rather to that, and the unskilful setting of the joint by an ignorant country practitioner, than to the blow itself, which would not have materially injured a person in ordinary health.[1] The case of Andrew Burk, Stirling, autumn 1804, has been already noticed, where a blacksmith was convicted of culpable homicide, and transported for fourteen years, in consequence of having killed his apprentice by a blow of an iron rod, an inch in diameter, on the head;[2] though the offence would have thus been more fitly visited by the pains of murder, which was the charge in the indictment, had the jury returned a proper verdict. Thus it appears that the only rule which can safely be adopted in such cases is, that it is culpable homicide where death results from an intention to inflict a small injury, but that the punishment inflicted will depend on the degree of recklessness or cruelty which the conduct of the pannel has evinced.

5. Culpable homicide is committed by an undue precipitance, or the unjustifiable use of lethal weapons, in defence of life or property, against a violent attack, even where the circumstances are not so aggravated as to make it amount to murder.

It has been already noticed, when treating of murder, that the use of lethal weapons is only *justifiable* where life is endangered by a violent assault, or property is injured from robbery, or the security of a house is on the point of being forced by housebreakers. But so jealous is our law of this recurrence to extreme measures, and so desirous of avoiding in all cases where it is possible the shedding of blood, that it looks narrowly into this alleged necessity, and holds the use of lethal weapons even in such circumstances unjustifiable, if a reasonable prospect of safety to life or property existed without their adoption.[3]

In the case even of an attempt upon life, it is not in every

---

[1] Unreported.—[2] Burnett, 34.—[3] Hume, i. 217

case a sufficient defence that the life of the pannel was endangered by an illegal attack : to have the benefit of an entire acquittal, it is necessary that he should farther prove that he has *fallen back as much as possible*, and only had recourse to lethal weapons when no other mode of escape existed.[1] It is true a homicide committed in this manner, upon apparent danger to life, will hardly ever amount to murder, but it generally will be considered as culpable homicide.[2] Although, therefore, in the event of a sudden attack on the highway, of which the consequences cannot be foreseen, it is undoubted law that the assailant may be instantly put to death ; yet if the danger is over, and he is seeking only to secure the culprit, or avenge his insult, and death ensue from the use of lethal weapons, it will amount to culpable homicide.[3]

The principle of the *moderamen inculpatæ tutelæ*, as it is termed by lawyers, is thoroughly established in our practice. Thus, in the case of Peter Maclean, March 1. 1710, it was found culpable homicide for a soldier to fire, though he had been abused with foul names, and an assault made on his person to wrest his piece from him.[4] He was not on duty at the time, or the homicide in defence of his arms would have been justifiable. Ensign Hardie was found guilty of culpable homicide, though he pleaded in defence that the deceased was the aggressor, that he stopped his horse by the bridle, struck him on the face with a rung to the effusion of his blood, and brought him to the ground from his horse. The Court, on June 9. 1701, expressly found these injuries only relevant to restrict the libel to an arbitrary punishment.[5] David Pretis pleaded against a charge of murder, on January 26. 1730, that the deceased had assaulted him in his own house, dragged him from thence, cut him in the head with a sharp instrument, and beat him to the ground. But the Court *only sustained* this plea in *exculpation*, viz. that the wounding of the defunct was in self-defence, when the pannel was put under the *imminent hazard of his life;* that is, they concluded the remainder, though proved, as still leaving him liable to an arbitrary punishment.[6]

Farther, the apprehension of the pannel must have been a reasonable apprehension, well founded in the circumstances of his situation. If therefore one kill a person who assaults

[1] Hume, i. 217.—[2] Ibid. i. 218.—[3] Ibid.—[4] Ibid. 223.—[5] Ibid.—[6] Ibid. i. 224.

him in sport with a foil, or mistakes the end of a whip for
a pistol, some punishment must undoubtedly follow; for the
law cannot entirely justify the extinction of life in consequence of such precipitate measures.[1]     Thus, in the case of
Captain John Price and others, November 24. 1690, it was
pleaded in defence, that being in a tavern, they were first
illtreated by the people of the house, and then assailed by
the multitude, who endeavoured to break in, and forced them
to barricade the doors, and that, when the guard arrived and
opened the doors, they fired, mistaking them for the assailants.     All this was found only relevant to restrict the libel
to an arbitrary punishment.[2]     So also in the case of Edward
Davies, December 6. 1712, the pannel, who was a soldier,
pleaded that the deceased and three more, all carrying staves,
attacked and beat him in the street; that he retired, and they
pressed on him, and cut him on the head, whereupon he called
for the assistance of the guard, and drew, and thrust with his
sword: but the reply was, that the danger, if it ever did exist,
*was over* when the fatal thrust was given; for that, on the
guard coming up, the mob retreated, and that this was in particular the case with the deceased, who received the thrust *in
his back.*     The defence was only found relevant to restrict the
libel to an arbitrary punishment.[3]     On the same principle, in
the case of Captain James Bruce and others, April 2. 1691,
who pleaded, when indicted for the murder of two soldiers of
the City Guard of Edinburgh, that they were violently assaulted by the guard while drinking the King's health.     But the
Court repelled this defence, " unless the pannels prove that,
before the killing, they were, by the guards aggressing them,
put *in present danger of their lives, and could not otherwise escape.*" [4]

  Farther, the crime will be deemed culpable homicide if any
undue excess appear in the mode or measure of resistance, or
by the use of lethal weapons, when not imperiously called for
by the circumstances of the pannel's situation.     He must have
done all that he could to extricate himself from the strife without shedding the assailant's blood; and if he have erred, or
exceeded in any of these particulars, some punishment must be
applied proportioned to the error.[5]     Thus, in the case of John

---

[1] Hume, i. 224.—[2] Ibid. i. 225.—[3] Ibid.—[4] Ibid. i. 226.—[5] Ibid. i. 227.

Govan, March 3. 1710, the Court " sustained the defences proponed for the pannel in these terms, viz. That the pannel was attacked by the defunct and his associate, and necessitate to fly to his own house; and that the defunct and his associate invaded him therein, and renewed the scuffle by beating of him ; and that the pannel, in dread of fear, laid hold of a sword for his defence, and that, during the continuance of the scuffle, the pannel gave the defunct the deadly wound, relevant to restrict the libel to an arbitrary punishment "[1] To the same purpose, in the case of John Macmillan, July 24. 1690, who was indicted for murder, the Court found " the defence that the pannel was assaulted and beaten by the defunct, with such a great rung as might have brained or killed him, and could not *get fled, nor save his life otherwise* than by drawing his sword, after he was so assaulted, relevant to restrict the libel to an arbitrary punishment."[2] In like manner, in the case of Urquhart and Webster, November 9. 1685, it was urged in behalf of Webster, that the deceased had bruised him with a large staff or baton, and trodden on him to the danger of his life. The prosecutor replied, that there was an *excessus moderaminis* on the part of the pannel, as he had brought the deceased to the ground by a stroke of his staff, and had afterwards so bruised him as to break his ribs, and occasion death. The Court sustained the defence as relevant to elide the charge of murder, and found the *reply of excess* relevant to take off the defence.[3]

At the same time, it must be observed as an equitable and necessary limitation of this principle, that, though the party assaulted is bound to retire from the assault, yet this is always under the provision that he can do so without materially augmenting his own danger, or putting himself in disadvantage with respect to his self-defence.[4] Thus, in the case of Captain William Barclay, November 12. 1668, the Court found " the qualification of self-defence relevant in this case, that the defunct or his accomplices were the first aggressors, and that he wounded the pannel's brother or servants, and thereafter pursued the pannel with a drawn sword or loaded pistol."[5] In like manner, though it is generally true that it is not legal to use a mortal weapon against one that is not mortal, yet if the swordsman is assailed by fearful odds, or is in danger of perish-

[1] Hume, i. 227.—[2] Ibid.—[3] Ibid. i. 228.—[4] Ibid. i. 229.—[5] Ibid. i. 230.

ing, without doubt he shall be entirely justified in the use of his lethal weapon.[1]

Nay, the law will make allowance, in very strong cases, for the perturbation consequent on an outrageous, rancorous, and dangerous assault, though the fatal stroke be not given for some little time *after* the danger has ceased. Thus, in the case of John Symons, 26th August 1810, it appeared that the deceased at midnight struck the pannel on the neck, in the street, several blows; that the pannel did not then draw his sword, but was again overtaken, 150 yards farther on, assaulted, and beaten by the deceased, who strove for his sword, knocked him down, and kicked him severely on the ground in the belly. The pannel then rose and pursued the deceased fifty yards, when he overtook him, and ran him through the body. The jury found the pannel *not guilty*—a decision which has the approval of Baron Hume; although, considering that the fatal thrust was given *ex intervallo*, when the danger was over, and the aggressor flying, it rather appears more agreeable to our law to have visited the pannel with a slight punishment.[2]

In like manner, in the case of housebreaking, it is quite fixed that the thief, making use of that violent mode of entry, or striving to effect it, may be killed on the spot. This is not only the common law of Scotland, but is expressly declared in the statute 1661, c. 22, already quoted. But while this is true on the one hand, it is not less material to observe on the other, that if the situation of the premises, or of the parties, be such that there is truly no danger of the violent entry being effected, then the law cannot sanction the use of lethal weapons; and, in the event of fatal consequences ensuing, will visit the party accused with a certain punishment proportioned to the degree of precipitance which his conduct has evinced. Thus if, instead of attempting to increase the security of the building, the owner shall purposely keep quiet for a time, and deliberately take aim at the thieves and kill them; or if he let them enter and then securely shoot them, his conduct seems deserving of some punishment.[3] The case would be very different, and the homicide clearly justifiable, if, in defiance of an express warning to keep off, the thieves should persist in their attempt to force open the building.[4]

These principles have been well illustrated by several cases

[1] Hume, i. 230.—[2] Ibid. i. 229; Burnett, 43.—[3] Hume, i. 220.—[4] Ibid. i. 221.

which have recently occurred in this country. Thus, in the case of William Williamson, Glasgow, September 7. 1801, it appeared that the accused was owner of a bleachfield, from which cloth had repeatedly been stolen, and he at length shot the thief in the night when in the act of entering the outhouse at a window, with intent to steal. The pannel had watched for successive nights with his gun, on purpose to destroy the thief if he should appear. The indictment was sustained by the Court; but the pannel had the good fortune to escape with a verdict of not guilty, a verdict hardly reconcileable with the principles of law, when it is considered that he gave no alarm to the thief, that the window broken was that of an outhouse only, and that there was no appearance of personal danger to himself.[1] Accordingly in the case of George Scott, Dumfries, September 1830, a verdict was pronounced under the direction of Lord Justice-Clerk Boyle and Lord Moncrieff, proceeding on sounder principles. The *species facti* there was that the pannel, who was butler in a country family, had been left in charge of the house, which contained some valuable plate, by his master, who was absent from home. The pannel, who was a young mason, had come in the night on a courting expedition, very common in that part of the country, to visit two of the maids. Not having been admitted by them as usual, he squeezed himself between two bars of the pantry window, and the noise which this occasioned wakened the butler, who immediately wakened two other men in the house, and proceeded to the pantry armed with a loaded gun. The deceased, hearing the noise of footsteps approaching, hastened to make his exit by the same window by which he had entered, but in the hurry he stuck in the bars, and was in the act of striving to force his shoulders through to get out when the pannel entered. He immediately called out to the deceased to tell his name, or he would fire; and having called out again without receiving any answer, he fired and killed the man. At this time, the two other men whom he had wakened were in the room, behind the pannel, and the deceased was unarmed. Lord Moncrieff laid it down that there was plainly here a precipitance in the use of lethal weapons: that the pannel being armed, and supported by two other men, was in no actual danger from a single individual,

[1] Hume, i 221.

situated as the deceased was: that the shot was fired when he was striving to escape, instead of forcing his way into the building; and that the more fact of not having answered did not in these circumstances warrant the use of lethal weapons. He was convicted, and had sentence of imprisonment for nine months.[1]  A similar decision was pronounced by the whole Court in the case of Lieutenant John Robertson, February 28. 1820.  The facts there were that a young man came to the neighbourhood of the pavilion near Melrose, at night, to visit a servant maid.  The pannel, who had previously been alarmed by report of housebreakers, hearing a noise, went down to the outer door and fired into the bushes, from whence the noise proceeded, and put out the eyes of the intruder, who had no felonious purpose in view, but was come on a courting expedition only.  He pleaded guilty under the advice of Mr Henry Cockburn, and received sentence of a month's imprisonment, having previously settled an annuity of £35 a-year on the sufferer; but the Court expressed a clear opinion that the use of fire-arms against *a real housebreaker* in such circumstances, of skulking and retreat, was unjustifiable.[2]  It is unnecessary, therefore, to add, that if a person at night should look over a window and see a thief trying to break into a lower window of the house, he certainly would not be authorized to shoot the aggressor without giving him any warning.  It would be otherwise if he saw the thief breaking into the room where he himself was; in such a case, as he had reason to apprehend the worst, he might legally use the most violent means of defence.

The following cases, which may be fitly quoted as authority in the Scotch courts, will show the limitation under which this doctrine must be received.  On 23d September 1816, William Tiffin was tried for the murder of William Reid, by shooting him with a pistol.  The pannel was a maker of crucibles, and in going his rounds at night as usual, with a lantern and loaded pistol, he observed a man lurking in the yard *within* the wall.  The pannel told him to be gone, or he would shoot him.  Instead of doing so, the man advanced towards the pannel, who told him the pistol was loaded, and again warned him to keep off; but the man still continued to press on, whereupon the pannel retired a few paces, and when the man

---

[1] Unreported.—[2] Unreported.

was two yards from him fired and killed him. The accused was *acquitted* by the jury, with the approbation of the Court, and there can be no doubt that in these circumstances the homicide was justifiable: for the pannel finding a person within his enclosed premises at the dead of night, and being alone, and finding the intruder *advancing upon him*, had good reason to dread the worst, if he did not destroy him before an assault was committed.[1] The case would have been otherwise, had the deceased fled or got over the railings when discovered; in such circumstances there can be no doubt it would have been culpable homicide.

In the case of a felonious and violent attack by robbers, or masterful depredators, or a lawless mob, upon a house, warehouse, or manufactory, there can be no doubt that homicide will be held to be justifiable, if the danger was urgent, and no other mode of deterring or keeping off the assailants appeared, and that equally, whether the violence is committed in the night or day time.[2] Thus, in the case of James Ripley and others, Old Bailey, 8th April 1815, it appeared that Mr Robinson's house had been attacked for successive days, and broken into by a mob. A guard of soldiers having been placed in the inside, and the attack renewed, they fired and killed a woman, who was a mere spectator. The Court were clearly of opinion that the homicide was justifiable, and that all within the house, soldiers, servants, and others, might lawfully kill in defence of the house against such an attack.[3] Whether the homicide will be justifiable or culpable in such cases, will depend upon the question, Whether there was a reasonable prospect of saving the property and keeping off the depredators, without having recourse to fatal extremities? Of course the peril will be esteemed greater, and the period, where killing may lawfully take place, be held to commence *earlier*, where there is a numerous convocation of assailants, than where the violence is threatened by one or two alone; for a few may be kept off by the mere strength of the building, or the dread of blows without death from those within; but a lawless mob must be intimidated by some severe example before they have made any considerable progress, or there is too much reason to fear that they will prove irresistible.

It has been already observed that the law of England, mak-

[1] Hume, i. 221.—[2] Ibid.—[3] Ibid. i. 222

ing greater allowance than the Scotch for the frailty of human passion, deems many cases manslaughter which we construe to be murder. Of course, all cases which we deem culpable homicide, they would consider as manslaughter; but many which they consider as the latter crime, with us amount to murder. Whenever death with them ensues from a sudden transport of passion, or heat of blood, upon a reasonable provocation, the offence is considered as manslaughter.[1] Thus even threatening words will be held as sufficient to reduce the crime to manslaughter, if the person provoked only strike with the fist, or a weapon not likely to kill; but if, on such provocation, he strike with a lethal weapon, it is murder.[2] And where an assault is made with circumstances of indignity, as by pulling the nose, and the person assaulted kills the aggressor immediately, it is deemed manslaughter.[3] Nay, they apply the same rule where the injury is much more inconsiderable, as jostling on the street, or whipping the manslayer's horse out of the track, if the killing take place on the first moment of irritation.[4] And in the case of trespasses upon, or injury to, property, if the trespasser be punished without circumstances of cruelty, as by merely flogging or ducking in a horse-pond, the case will be viewed in the same light, even though death ensue.[5] In like manner, if the pannel's son have fought with another boy, and being beaten return home bloody, and the father upon that take a cudgel and give a stroke not likely to destroy, it will be held manslaughter.[6] So also the consideration of the instrument used, if not likely to occasion death, is justly considered as materially extenuating the guilt of the prisoner. Thus where a man, upon being called by a woman the son of a whore, seized a broomstick and threw it at her from a distance and killed her, a pardon was advised of the capital sentence, upon the ground that the instrument used, and the distance, made death highly improbable.[7] In like manner, where a pannel had struck his boy with one of his clogs, and where a butcher took up a stake and threw it at a boy who had suffered some sheep to escape, and death ensued, in both cases it was considered manslaughter only.[8] But if the instrument

[1] Hale, i. 466; Hawkins, i. c. 30; Foster, 200.—[2] Foster, 291.—[3] Blackstone, iv. 191.—[4] Hale, i. 455.—[5] Foster, 291, Hawkins, i. c. 31, § 38.—[6] Foster, 294, 295.—[7] Hale, i. 455, 456, East. i. p. 236.—[8] Russell, i. 706; Leach, i. 378.

used be manifestly improper, and likely to endanger life, or if sufficient time have elapsed to have allowed the passions to cool, the opposite presumption will prevail, and the crime be considered as murder.[1]

The great peril of the use of lethal weapons has occasioned the passing of a special statute in England against stabbing. This is the 1st James I. c. 8, which enacts, " That every person that shall stab or thrust at any person that hath not then any weapon, or that hath not then first stricken the party which shall so stab or thrust, and if death ensue thereof within six months, shall be deemed guilty of felony, without benefit of clergy, even though it cannot be proved that the same was done of malice aforethought." There is an exemption of cases of self-defence, or misfortune, or in preserving the peace. But this statute has been considered by their greatest authorities as of doubtful expediency,[2] and rigorously construed in practice.[3] There seems little doubt that all cases falling under that act would be construed as murder by the common law of Scotland.

Cases of mutual combat are in England considered as manslaughter, if they fight even with mortal weapons on the spur of the moment, and before their passions have time to cool.[4] In such sudden combats, on equal terms, they consider it immaterial who struck the first blow.[5] And, if such a combat begin in equal terms, but in the course of it one of the parties use a lethal weapon, and death ensue, it will still be only manslaughter.[6] In all these particulars, their rules are entirely at variance with our practice.

6. If officers of the law, intrusted with the execution of legal diligence, make use of lethal weapons, and inflict death, without such a necessity as shews that their duty could not otherwise be discharged, they will be considered as guilty of culpable homicide, or murder, according to the circumstances of the case.

It has been already noticed, that the duty of officers of justice, intrusted with the execution of legal warrants, is to *advance* and discharge their commission, and that they will be

---

[1] Russell, i. 638, 639, 670, 707.—[2] Foster, 297, 300.—[3] Blackstone, iv. 193. —[4] Hale, i. 453.—[5] Ibid.—[6] East. i. 243

considered as justifiable if homicide be committed in defending *that advance*, on the same principles as a private individual would be considered as justified in defending his life.

It follows that culpable homicide may be committed by an officer of the law, or a soldier on duty, in consequence of undue precipitance in the use of lethal weapons, in the discharge of his duty. The circumstances in which recourse to such extremities is justifiable or blameable, cannot be distinguished by a more accurate rule than that already mentioned, contained in the 9th Geo. II. c. 35, which enacts, that " The officers, when resisted, in seizing or searching for goods, by persons passing with the same, armed with offensive weapons, may oppose force to force, and endeavour, by the *same methods* that are violently used against them, and by which their lives are endangered, to defend themselves, and execute the duty of their office." [1] " This statute," says Baron Hume, " is truly nothing more than declaratory of the powers which arise to the officer *vi juris*, from the command of the law to him, to *advance* and make the seizure. For, if the smuggler oppose him with mortal or offensive weapons, whereby the officer *shall come* to be in danger of his life, if, as in duty bound, he shall advance and persist to make his seizure, he must have a right to quell this rebellion by the necessary means, and cannot be answerable for any harm which ensues." [2] It is the precipitate and premature use of lethal weapons, which is likely to lead to questions of culpable homicide in such circumstances.

In the case of Patrick Anderson, 25th July 1799, it appeared that the pannel, in conjunction with two other officers of the revenue, set out to seize a cargo of smuggled spirits, the pannel being armed with a cutlass. On the road they met a party, consisting of a dozen of persons, carrying ankers of gin. Two of the men advanced with bludgeons, to give time to the remainder to fall back with the spirits, and one of them grappled with Anderson, who disabled him by a stroke of a cutlass on the arm. Another man grappled with the officer's assistant, and threw him down, getting above him  Anderson, upon this, gave the smuggler, who was grappling with his comrade, some strokes with his cutlass on the back, of which he soon died. The pannel was found not guilty, with the appro-

---

[1] 9th Geo. II. c. 35.—[2] Hume i. 215.

bation of the Bench.[1]  Again, in the case of Hugh Chalmers and others, 14th June 1813, the *species facti* was, that the pannels, with three persons more, eight in all, set out at night to interrupt a party of smugglers, coming from the Highlands to Glasgow, by the Garscube road.  The officers were all armed, some with cutlasses and others with pistols.  When dark the smugglers also arrived, eight in number, but armed with *bludgeons only.*  When they came up, the officers rushed upon them, and commanded the smugglers to surrender their goods.  In the dark a confused battle ensued, in the course of which three pistols were discharged, and two of the smugglers received wounds, which soon proved fatal.  In these circumstances the Court and jury were divided, but the majority were of opinion, that there was not such precipitancy in the use of lethal weapons as to constitute culpability in the officers; but the opinion of the minority seems deserving of much consideration, that, as the parties were here equally matched in point of numbers, and the officers all armed, while their antagonists had sticks only, there was an undue excess on their part, especially in not announcing their superiority in arms, which would probably have induced an immediate surrender.[2]  Lastly, in the case of John Jeffrey, 9th September 1817, it appeared that Jeffrey, who was mate of a revenue-cutter, had landed with a boat's crew of *eleven* in Arran, to seize some smuggled whisky, which had been put ashore.  They were opposed by a tumultuous band of two hundred, provided with sticks and stones.  Jeffrey ordered two shots to be fired over their heads, waved his cutlass in the air, and warned the people to keep off.  After a little the multitude gave three cheers, and advanced in a body: several of Jeffrey's men were thrown down, and he himself laid hold of, his cutlass and bayonet wrested from him, and his body brought to the ground.  In this extremity he fired his pistol, and ordered his men to do the like, upon which two persons were killed.  In these circumstances the pannel was clearly entitled to a verdict of not guilty, which he accordingly received from the Court.[3]

Most of the trials, of late years, for homicide by officers of the law, have terminated in the same result.  On July 29. 1776, George White was indicted for murder.  It appeared

[1] Hume, i. 215.—[2] Ibid. i. 216.—[3] Ibid.

that the pannel, who was an officer of excise, with an assistant, both armed with swords, were resisted by four smugglers, armed with staves, and that he was beaten and cut in the hand. The verdict was not proven.[1] In like manner, Peter France, on 22d September 1802, was indicted for the murder of a smuggler. It appeared that the smuggler had assaulted the officer who had just seized his goods, and presented a pistol at his breast. The verdict was, of course, and most justly, not guilty.[2] Peter Macintyre, Inverness, 3d April 1826, was acquitted of a charge of murder. He was one of a party from the Atalanta revenue-cutter, who had been sent to a moor above Beauly, to seize a still, and had there got into a struggle with one of the smugglers, who seized him by the privy parts, and wrestled hardly with him, in the course of which the pannel's pistol went off, and the smuggler was killed. Lord Pitmilly held, that whether this was by accident or design, the case was such that the pannel could not be convicted even of culpable homicide. Lastly, in the case of John Duncan, 14th October 1807, the pannel, who was an excise-officer, seized some smuggled salt in a cart. He was resisted, and a disorderly scuffle ensued, in the course of which the smuggler was killed. The verdict was not guilty, partly on the ground of self-defence, and partly because the fatal wound appeared to have been given accidentally with a dagger in the course of a personal struggle.[3]

By the law of England several nice, and what to us appear unsubstantial distinctions, are recognised in regard to homicide, by officers or private persons proceeding to arrest a criminal. An officer with them is justified in proceeding to the last extremity, whether for a civil or criminal arrest, if the party making resistance cannot otherwise be seized.[4] But they consider it manslaughter, and in some cases murder, to kill a person who is *flying* from arrest for a civil debt; while it is lawful to kill a *felon* flying from justice, if he cannot otherwise be apprehended.[5] In Scotland we are not disposed to adopt such a distinction, but follow one rule for all cases of resistance to a process, whether civil or criminal, that the officer must proceed with due circumspection, and not proceed to extremities, unless his duty cannot otherwise be discharged;

[1] Hume, 1. 214.—[2] Ibid.—[3] Ibid.—[4] Hale, 1. 494; Russell, i. 547.—[5] Russell, i. 547; Hale, 1. 489.

and the distinction between civil and criminal process appears chiefly, if not solely, in the greater dread which the officer is permitted to have, and the more violent measures he is allowed to adopt, against persons resisting warrants of the latter description.

7. A husband who finds a person in the act of adultery with his wife, is guilty of culpable homicide only, if he instantly put him to death ; but if he do so *ex intervallo,* it becomes murder.

The Scotch law, agreeing in this particular with that of England,[1] concedes so much to the just indignation of a husband, in such circumstances of extreme provocation, as to hold the taking away of life *on the moment* culpable homicide only.[2] Thus in the case of James Christie, it appeared that the pannel had stabbed the deceased with a sword, upon finding him in the act of adultery with his wife. This defence the Court found sufficient to restrict the libel to an arbitrary punishment.[3] But with us, equally as with them, if, instead of taking this summary redress of his wrongs, the husband shall confine him till next day, and then kill him, or castrate him, or force him to swallow a dose of laudanum, the case will be one of cold blooded revenge, which is always, whatever the provocation may have been, considered as murder.[4]

8. It is culpable homicide if death ensue in the performance even of an act not in itself criminal, if due care of others is not taken in the performance of it.

Cases of this description are the most numerous which occur under this branch of our law. They have of late years received a great increase from the common use of steam-vessels on friths of the sea and navigable rivers; and it is probable they will be still farther increased by the application of the power of steam to land-carriages. This branch of the law, therefore, is one of considerable importance.

The general principle is, that in acts, either of duty or amusement, all persons are bound to take due care that no injury is done to any of the lieges; and that if death ensue from the

[1] Russell, i. 488, Raym. 212.—[2] Hume, i. 215, 248, Burnett, 53.—[3] Ibid. i. 216.—[4] Hume, i. 252, Russell, i. 442.

want of such care, they must be answerable for the conse-quences.[1] Of course the *degree* of care which law requires, varies with the degree of peril which the lieges sustain from its want. It is greatest where the peril is most serious, and diminishes with the decrease in the danger incurred by negli-gence or inattention. Thus the masters of steam-boats, who are intrusted with the guidance of floating vessels of immense size, and moving with the greatest velocity, are bound to exer-cise the highest degree of vigilance · the drivers of stage coaches are answerable for the next degree of diligence, then drivers of ordinary carriages and riders on horseback. This arises from the different degrees of peril which the lieges sus-tain from such negligence, and the greater degree of skill ex-pected from those who are intrusted with the direction of the higher species of vehicles.

Thus, if one fire a gun, though loaded with powder only, in the streets of a crowded city, and a passenger is killed by its bursting, or by the wadding, or by a piece of metal or stone, which has, unknown to the person firing, been placed in the gun, he is guilty of culpable homicide; for to *fire at all*, in *such a situation*, was a reckless and dangerous act.[2] Accordingly, in the case of James Niven, December 21. 1795, who killed a passenger, by firing a small cannon in a lane of common re-sort, when several persons were passing at the time, the Court were unanimously of opinion, that, even on his own allegation, which was, that a bit of iron had, unknown to him, got into the wadding, the case was one of culpable homicide; but that if the case were proved, as laid in the indictment, which charged the iron with being knowingly put in, it would amount to murder, though no malice against any individual existed.[3] The same rule holds if one fire a gun so near a high road, as to endanger persons passing at the time, even though it is done in pursuit of game only. An indictment accordingly was sus-tained as relevant by Lord Meadowbank, at Ayr, in April 1827, which charged John Kilgour with having killed a child walking along a public road in Ayrshire, by discharging a gun loaded with small shot, at the distance of an easy gunshot from the road, in the direction of it, at a time when various of the lieges were likely to be passing. It appeared on the proof, that the distance was considerably greater, and that the shot went

[1] Hume, i. 192.—[2] Ibid.—[3] Ibid. and i. 23.

through the hedge, and pierced the eye of the child, and would not have injured it but for that unfortunate circumstance. The jury, in consequence, found the pannel not guilty.[1] Again, in the case of Peter Scott, Dumfries, April 1830, the pannel was charged with culpable homicide, in consequence of having culpably and recklessly discharged a gun in a house, loaded with small shot, which penetrated a hole in the partition of the room, and killed a woman passing in the passage on the outside. It appeared on the proof, that the pannel, who was a gamekeeper, had been present at a drinking party in the house, to which he had brought his gun; and, on getting up to go away, he had some altercation with one of the party, who pushed up his gun, which he was holding in a dangerous manner across his knee. He rose up soon after, and the gun went off, and the shot, passing through the hole, killed a woman in the passage on the outside. Some revengeful expressions were proved against him, which rendered it probable that the case approached to murder; but the jury, perplexed by contradictory evidence, brought in a verdict of not guilty.[2] Lord Gillies, however, laid it down as clear law, that the case was one *at least of culpable homicide*, as the pannel was a gamekeeper, acquainted with the use of fire-arms; and that, even though the gun was discharged by accident, he was blameable, for putting it in such a situation that it *could go off*, and injure the inmates of the house, while in his hands.

In like manner, if a man leave a fowling-piece loaded, and afterwards kill in trying the lock, or in discharging it in sport, some correction is due; for here has life been lost in consequence of an act of carelessness.[3] Accordingly at Glasgow, in April 1817, David Buchanan was convicted of culpable homicide, and sentenced to three weeks' imprisonment, for having shot his master's wife in handling a gun which he presented to her, not knowing that it was loaded.[4] So also if workmen, on the roof of a building, throw down slates or rubbish in a frequented street, without giving timely warning to the passengers.[5] To the same purpose, in the case of Henderson, Stirling 1789, an indictment was sustained as relevant, which charged a pannel with culpable homicide, in respect of having fired a pistol on the side of a highway to salute a marriage

---

[1] Unreported.—[2] Unreported.—[3] Hume, i. 192.—[4] Ibid.—[5] Ibid.

party who were passing, though the fatal consequences ensued from the wadding only.[1] A quack or ignorant practitioner also, who kills a patient by rashly administering powerful medicines unsuited to the complaint, or one dose instead of another, will be guilty of the same offence.[2] Such a case was that of the noted Edward St John Long, who was convicted at the Old Bailey in December 1830, before Mr Justice Park and Holroyd, of culpable homicide, and sentenced to pay a fine of £250. He had killed the deceased by rashly and ignorantly rubbing in powerful stimulants on the back to produce a counter-irritation, intended to ward off the danger of pulmonary complaints, which had not at the period of his treatment begun to manifest themselves. On the same principle, in the case of Matthew Graham, 27th April 1813, an indictment was sustained as relevant against a workman who had felled a tree on a roadside without due precaution, whereby a passenger was killed; but the jury acquitted the pannel. And on 25th April 1812, a charge of culpable homicide was found relevant by Lords Justice-Clerk Boyle and Hermand against James Cowan, for rashly discharging a gun, loaded with powder and wadding only, among a number of people assembled at a wedding.[3] Bernard Johnston and John Webster, Aberdeen, spring 1827, were convicted of culpable homicide, and sentenced to four months' imprisonment, for having culpably blasted rocks in a quarry on the road-side, near Aberdeen, and by the fall of one of the stones killed a person passing at the time.

9. In the management of carriages the driver is answerable for that degree of attention which persons of ordinary care and capacity exert in that employment, and for the due observance of all the rules of careful driving.

In driving along ordinary roads, and still more the streets of a city or village, where foot-passengers are frequent, a coachman or carter is bound to obey the following rules:—

1. To drive at a moderate pace, and never run races with another vehicle.

2. To have his horses well on hand, so as to be able to pull up if an accident should occur.

3. To keep a good look-out and not run against any persons

[1] Hume, i. 193.—[2] Ibid.—[3] Hume, i. 192.

or carriages who may be on the road, and, in an especial manner, not to get on the footpath.

4. To keep on the customary side on passing another carriage or horseman.

5. If he should have occasion to stop, not to leave his horses' head without some one to watch them, unless he is perfectly secure that they will not run off.

6. The proper place for a carter within the tolls of a town or village, or wherever there is a considerable concourse of passengers on the road, is at his horse's head.

If, in consequence of the neglect of any of these rules, which are so simple as to admit of being universally followed, any fatal accident should occur, the party in fault will be deemed guilty of culpable homicide. Numerous cases have occurred on this branch of the law, from which it will be sufficient to select the following :—

On 25th September 1804, Alexander Colquhoun was convicted of culpable homicide, and imprisoned a month, for having driven over an old man with a cart. The degree of culpability there was slight.[1] At Jedburgh, on 28th September 1805, Andrew and Adam Scott were convicted before the late Lord Meadowbank of killing an old man by furious driving with their carts. They were sentenced to six months' imprisonment.[2] Robert Jackson was convicted of culpable homicide on 14th September 1810, and imprisoned for a month, for leaving his cart and horse on the road while he went into an alehouse to drink, in consequence of which it went over an old woman, deaf, and nearly blind. The horses here had merely proceeded on the road without running off.[3] John Liddell, hackney-coachman, was, on 22d December 1818, convicted and sentenced to eighteen months' hard labour in Bridewell, for having driven rapidly in a state of intoxication along St Mary's Wynd, Edinburgh, and, in consequence, thrown down and driven over an old woman, of which she shortly afterwards died.[4] At Perth, on 22d April 1822, Thomas Crichton and Thomas Morrison were convicted of culpable homicide, for having run a race in their carts on the outskirts of Perth, and killed a woman. The one was sentenced to nine, the other to six months' imprisonment.[5] In like manner, in the case of

[1] Hume, i. 192.—[2] Ibid.—[3] Ibid.—[4] Ibid. i. 193.—[5] Ibid.

Robert Summers, 12th July 1823, the pannel had sentence of nine months' imprisonment for killing a man by recklessly driving over him at the Watergate, Edinburgh.[1]   On 4th July 1826, John Murdoch had sentence of imprisonment for twelve months in Bridewell for killing a man by reckless driving on Leith Walk.[2]   And on 14th July 1827, Robert Reid was imprisoned nine months for reckless driving on the road between Portobello and Edinburgh, whereby a man was run over on the footpath and killed.[3]   At Stirling, in April 1831, John Macmillan and others were convicted of culpable homicide, and sentenced to nine months' imprisonment, for having killed an old man by furious driving and racing in their carts on the road between Dollar and Alloa. The carts ran two and sometimes three abreast, and the poor man was thrown down on the footpath, so that the case was one of great culpability.[4] In like manner, at Perth, in April 1829, George Forfar was convicted of culpable homicide, and sentenced to three months' imprisonment. He had lashed his horses into a gallop on a road between Dollar and the North Queensferry, and driven in that state through a narrow pass in the road where there was barely room for two carts to pass abreast, whereby one woman was killed and another had her leg broke.[5]   At Ayr also, on September 11. 1827, Peter Brown was convicted of culpable homicide, and sentenced to four months' imprisonment. He had driven rapidly, and racing through a village in Ayrshire, and in consequence run over and killed a child.[6]

Numerous convictions have also taken place of late years, where the degree of culpability was much smaller than in these instances; adhering to the rule, that, in crowded situations, and where the danger to the public from the slightest deviation is considerable, proportional care is requisite from the driver.  Thus, at Glasgow, in April 1828, John Miller was convicted of culpably killing a child, though his only negligence consisted in driving along Duke Street, Glasgow, *seated in his cart*, without a sufficient command of his horse's head, and without looking at the persons in the street. The horse was going at a walk, and the child, who was only three years old, had wandered into the middle of the street of its own accord.[7] He received a month's imprisonment.  In like manner, in the

[1] Hume, i. 193.—[2] Ibid.—[3] Ibid.—[4] Unreported.—[5] Unreported.—[6] Unreported.—[7] Unreported

case of Daniel Macdonald, autumn 1826, the pannel was convicted of culpable homicide, and received a month's imprisonment. He had driven a horse and cart within the tolls of Glasgow, on the Dumbarton road, *seated in his cart*, and in consequence did not see, and rode over an old man who was crossing the road. His horse was only walking at the time; but Lord Justice-Clerk Boyle laid it down as clear law, that the proper place for a carter, within the tolls at least, is *at his horse's head*; and that, if any accident happens in such a situation, which might have been avoided had he been walking there with the halter in his hand, he is answerable for the consequences.[1] So also in the case of John Scott, Perth, April 1829, the pannel was convicted of culpable homicide before Lord Mackenzie, and received a month's imprisonment, though his neglect had been of the slightest kind. He was driving a horse from Ceres to Kirkcaldy, in Fife, and, after the manner of too many carters, fell a little behind his horse, talking with the other carters, whose vehicles were coming up in the rear. He *had not the reins in his hand*, and on turning a sharp corner near the town of Ceres, the horse, which was going at a walk, made a circuit, which brought it on, or close to, the footpath, which was there only eighteen inches broad, and on which a child of three years of age was then walking; the consequence was that the child lost its head, got among the horse's feet, and was killed. Lord Mackenzie laid it down that there was here a clear case of neglect, inasmuch as the carter should have been at his horse's head, and with the reins in his hands; whereas he was behind the cart, leaving the horse to take its own way; and that it was not sufficient that the horse was only walking at the time, for fatal results may ensue as probably from carts getting off the proper track when walking, as keeping on it when galloping.[2] And, on April 25. 1825, at Glasgow, an indictment was sustained as relevant against Robert Taylor, by Lord Justice-Clerk Boyle, where the principal ingredient in the charge was, that he was driving along the Trongate of Glasgow at a furious rate, which on the proof turned out to be at the *rate of nine miles an hour*. He was acquitted, from a discrepancy in the evidence as to the degree of the rapidity; but the Court expressed an opinion,

[1] Unreported.—[2] Unreported.

that, if that rapidity had been proved by satisfactory evidence, the case would have been deserving of some punishment, as it was clearly improper in that crowded thoroughfare.[1]  Richard Johnston, November 24. 1823, was convicted of culpable homicide, and sentenced to six months' imprisonment, chiefly on the ground that he had *loitered behind his carts*, and thereby allowed them to drive over and kill a child of three years of age.

It is to be observed, however, on the other hand, that there is an excessive and most culpable degree of negligence in the people in every part of Scotland, in going themselves, and still more in allowing their children to go, in the middle of the road, at the time that carriages and carts are passing.  It is impossible to travel in any part of the country without being sensible of this; and, therefore, if a person is killed in consequence of running before a cart, when the carter is walking at a moderate pace with the reins in his hand, certainly the carter is entitled to an acquittal.  And the like will hold with a coachman or charioteer if a similar accident occur, where he is trotting only, with his horses well on hand, and looking before him, and still more so if he has called to the person who sustains the injury; for every day's experience proves, that, from the excessive carelessness of the people, accidents will happen even with the most careful drivers.

Some punishment is also due where any of the lieges are *injured*, either in person or property, without being killed, by such acts of carelessness or neglect in the driving of carriages. Thus, in the case of J. Bartholomew and others, 21st November 1825, three carters were convicted of furious driving, and sentenced to twelve months' imprisonment.  They had driven their carts furiously three a-breast along the highway, and in consequence overturned a cart which they met, whereby a female had her leg broke, and several articles of furniture were much injured.[2]

No cases have yet occurred in the Supreme Court where culpable homicide was committed on persons *within* the carriage by furious driving on the part of the coachmen; but there seems no doubt that injury or damage done in that way is as much a relevant article of charge, as if it produced its effects on strangers on the road.  And, in the case of the Comet

[1] Unreported.—[2] Hume, i. 193.

Steam-boat, 22d December 1825, which was brought under the review of the Supreme Court from the Admiralty, on other grounds, no doubt seemed to be entertained that the charge was relevant, although all the lives lost were within the vessel, whose pilot and captain were placed at the bar.[1]

By the English law, if a person driving a cart or carriage happen to kill another, and it appears he might have seen the danger, but did not look before him, it will be considered as manslaughter for want of due circumspection.[2] And it is laid down in a work of great authority, " that the circumstance of the driver being in his cart, and going much faster than is usual for carriages of that construction, savours much of negligence and impropriety; for it is extremely difficult, if not impossible, to stop the course of the horses suddenly, in order to avoid any person who cannot get out of the way in time. And, indeed, such conduct in a driver of such heavy carriages might, under most circumstances, be thought to betoken a want of due care, if any, though but few, persons might probably pass by the same road. The greatest possible care is not to be expected; but whosoever seeks to excuse himself for having occasioned, by an act of his own, the death of another, ought at least to shew that he took that care to avoid it which persons in similar situations are accustomed to do.[3]

By the 1st Geo. IV. c. 4, it is enacted, " That if any person shall be maimed, or otherwise injured, by reason of the wanton and furious driving and racing, or by the wilful misconduct of any coachman or other person having the charge of any stagecoach or public carriage, such wanton and furious driving or racing, or wilful misconduct of such coachman or other person, shall be, and the same is hereby declared to be, a misdemeanour, and punishable as such by fine and imprisonment."[4] This act does not extend to hackney coaches drawn by two horses only. It extends to Scotland. And, by the 50th Geo. III. c. 48, § 15, a penalty, not exceeding £10, nor less than £5, is imposed upon a coachman, who, by furious driving, or by negligence or misconduct, shall overturn the carriage, or in any manner endanger the persons or property of the passengers, or of the owners of the carriage, unavoidable accidents being excepted.[5]

<hr>

[1] Hume, ı. 193 —[2] Foster, 263.—[3] East. ı. 263, 264.—[4] 1st Geo. IV. c. 4 —[5] Russell, ı. 627, last edition.

10. A rider on the highway, and still more in the streets of a town or village, is answerable for an ordinary degree of negligence in avoiding accidents; and will be held guilty of culpable homicide, if life be lost, from racing, furious riding, or evident negligence.

It is not in every man's power either to be a good rider, or to manage his horse dexterously on every occasion; but the law considers it incumbent on every person to know his own deficiencies, and take care that he does not proceed along the highway on a horse, which he is evidently incapable of managing; or to ride at so rapid a rate, whatever his skill in horsemanship may be, as to endanger the lives of the lieges who may be passing on the occasion. Thus, on May 14. 1830, James Grant was indicted for culpable homicide and furious riding, committed on the road between Stockbridge and Moray Place, Edinburgh. It appeared that he had galloped at a very rapid rate along the road, and, in passing some stone carts, at the distance of about one hundred yards beyond the toll-bar, his horse got upon the footpath, and knocked over two old women, one of whom was killed, and the other dangerously wounded. The libel was sustained as relevant; but the pannel was acquitted, owing to some evidence which he adduced tending to shew that the horse was a young one, apt to take fright, and set off at a gallop upon being alarmed; and that, on the occasion in question, the horse had run away with its rider, notwithstanding every exertion on his part, from some boys on the roadside clapping their hands.[1]

11. In the management of steam-boats, the master, pilot, and manager are bound to execute the highest degree of vigilance and attention, and will be held answerable for the effects of the most inconsiderable deviation from the established practice and regulations.

The principle has been already explained on which it is justly held that the master and pilot of a steam-boat are bound to exert the highest degree of vigilance in the management of their vessel, viz. that they are intrusted with the regulation of

---

[1] Unreported.

a moving power of such extreme force and rapidity, that the smallest inattention instantly produces fatal consequences; and, without the utmost vigilance on their part, vessels passing must be continually exposed to danger.

The same principle runs through all the analogous branches of the law. There is no fault in taking a lighted candle into an ordinary room; but it may be culpable, in the highest degree, to take it into a powder-magazine. There is scarcely any legal culpability in running along a crowded street; but there is so in galloping or driving in such a situation. To strike with a fist or cane may be a trifling misdemeanour; to cut with a sword, or stab with a dagger, is an offence of the gravest description. Universally the law measures the degree of care which it requires of those who are intrusted with instruments of power, by the degree of risk which attends their mismanagement.[1] On this principle, where one lays poison to kill rats, and another takes it and dies, this is misadventure; but this will only hold when it was laid in such a manner, as not easily to be mistaken for proper food, for otherwise it would betoken inadvertence, and might, in some cases, amount to manslaughter.[2]

In the navigation of steam-boats, the captain and pilot are bound to obey the following rules:

1. To have one or more persons constantly *on the look-out*, in such a situation as to have a clear view of the course which the vessel is taking. These persons are generally stationed at the bows, and certainly that is the appropriate station; but it is not unusual for the captain to take that duty on himself, standing on the paddle-box. It is not sufficient to intrust it to the man at the helm; for his vision is frequently obstructed by the passengers or luggage on deck; nor the sailors *generally*, for responsibility divided is gone, and what is everybody's business is nobody's business.

2. At night, or in hazy weather, to have *a light constantly burning* on a conspicuous part of the vessel; and, where the channel is very crowded, to take, where usually practised, the additional precaution of sounding a horn.

3. In passing a vessel in motion, to keep the ordinary rules, viz. In approaching each other each keeps to his own left; in

[1] Russell, 1. 540 —[2] Hale, i. 431.

passing one sailing in the same direction, the one proposing to pass steers to the right, the other to the left.

4. The vessel having the advantage of the wind and tide, makes way for the one beating up against them, and the vessel in motion is bound to avoid the one stationary or at anchor.

5. The man at the helm is bound to obey the orders of the captain; and the man on the look-out is exonered, if he gives the due notification to the former of these parties.

6. When a pilot is taken on board for a particular frith or piece of navigation, he is *pro tempore* responsible for the navigation of the vessel.

These principles have been illustrated in several cases.

In the case of William Blackwood and Alexander Macalpin, July 1. 1824, it appeared that the pannels, who were master and pilot of the steam-boat Hercules, were proceeding down the Clyde, at a place near Greenock, where it run foul of the Robert Burns Steam-boat, which it sank, and drowned several persons. The boats tried to avoid each other, but they, as sometimes happens with two persons meeting in the street, went to the same side, and so came into collision. The pannels had gone to the wrong side, but not very far, and they tried as rapidly as they could to get right; but, before the helm would come round, the vessels had struck. The jury, by a plurality, found the libel not proven.

Again, in the well known case of Duncan Macinnes and Peter Macbride, 22d December 1825, which related to the loss of the Comet, it appeared that the pannels, who were the captain and pilot of the Comet Steam-boat, had proceeded on their voyage from Fort-William up the River Clyde, during the night, without a conspicuous light in any part of the vessel, or keeping a proper look-out, both of which were contrary to the rules of good seamanship, the consequence of which was, that they ran foul of the Ayr Steam-boat, off Kempoch Point; the Comet was sunk to the bottom, and above fifty persons perished. No blame was attached to the master or pilot of the Ayr, in navigating his vessel, up to the moment of the collision, though he evinced great inhumanity in not stopping to relieve the sufferers after it occurred. Macinnes was convicted in the Admiralty, and sentenced to three months' imprisonment, chiefly on the ground of the want of a light; but the sentence was suspended in the Supreme Court, upon the ground of an informality in the way of making up the record in the Admiralty Court.[1]

In the case of Ezekiel Machaffie, November 26. 1827, it appeared that the pannel was master of the Dumbarton Castle Steam-boat, plying between Stranraer and Glasgow, and, in coming up the Clyde, off Kempoch Point, he ran down a fishing-boat riding at anchor, and drowned one of its crew. It clearly appeared in evidence, that the pannel had not put any person on deck specially intrusted with the duty of keeping a look-out, but intrusted that charge to all the seamen generally who might be on duty at the time. On passing Kempoch Point, he had gone below to collect the fares from the passengers, and the helmsman was not so placed as to be able to see distinctly ahead, and there was no person in the forepart of the vessel, to warn him of the appearance of any boats before them. The consequence was, that the steam-boat, advancing at the rate of ten miles an hour, came suddenly upon the small boat, and pursued its course right down upon it, so as in less than a minute to occasion a collision. The jury found the pannel guilty, upon the ground that he was bound to have attended to the first rule of seamanship, that of having a man constantly stationed on the look-out, and that no apology could be admitted for its neglect, in a river so frequently crossed by other vessels as the Clyde; and he received six months' imprisonment, besides being obliged to find caution not to navigate in a reckless manner again. A bill of suspension was unanimously refused in the Supreme Court.[2]

Again, in the case of David Smith, Norman Jamieson, John Macarthur, and Donald Macbride, January 11. 1828, the facts turned out to be that the two former were master and pilot on board the luggage steam-boat Favourite, and the latter master and seaman on board the steam-packet Fingal. The Favourite having the smack Carolina in tow, was proceeding up the river Clyde under the direction of the two first pannels, when they met the Fingal coming down the same river under the management of the two latter pannels. They approached each other, and came into collision near Roysperch, about half a mile above Dumbarton Castle, and at a place where there was ample room for several boats to pass abreast, when both were going at full speed, in consequence of which the Carolina, drawn in tow, was sunk, and five persons on board drowned. Both parties were to blame: the two first, for neglecting to keep to the left or larboard side, and slow the engine of the Favourite in sufficient time, and the latter for not steering the Fingal to their own left at all, but sailing straight down the middle of the river, which brought them right against the Carolina. As the persons in both vessels were to blame, the captain and pilot of both were put to the bar, and it appeared in evidence that the Fingal was most to blame, no alteration having been made in her course till she was within fifty yards of the other vessel, which, by working up against the stream with a smack in tow, was proceeding at a slower rate. The Admiralty Court considered the case clearly proved; but the jury, by a plurality, found the libel not proven.[1]

William Struthers, mate of the steam-packet Majestic, was, on November 27. 1826, tried for running down a boat near Kempoch Point, and drowning a person on board. The culpability consisted in this, that, though on the look-out on board the Majestic, he neglected his duty; and though he saw the small boat ahead, beating up against the wind in a rough sea, yet he gave no warning to the helmsman that any boat was in the ship's line, but began to coil up ropes, leaving the small vessel to get out of the way as it best could; the consequence of which was, that the small boat, impeded by the wind and tide, was unable to escape the collision of the large one, but was sailed straight over, and all its crew precipitated into the sea. The jury, in the face of that evidence, found the libel not proven; but it was laid down by the Court as fixed law, that the vessel, advancing with the wind and tide, was, by the common rules of navigation, bound to give way to that beating up against both, and that there was a culpable neglect of this rule in the case under consideration.[2]

### SECT. III.—JUSTIFIABLE HOMICIDE.

JUSTIFIABLE homicide is that which is committed with the intention to kill, or do a grievous bodily injury, but under circumstances which the law holds sufficient to exculpate the person who commits it.

[1] Unreported.—[2] Unreported.

1. A judge who, in pursuance of his duty, pronounces sentence of death, or the magistrates and inferior officers who carry it into execution, commit justifiable homicide.

It is evident that as the law prescribes the punishment of death for certain offences, it must protect those who are intrusted with its execution. A judge, therefore, who pronounces sentence of death in a legal manner on a regular indictment duly brought before him, and for a capital crime committed within his jurisdiction, is guilty of no offence; he is merely the organ of the law for the repression of offences destructive to the public weal.[1] But towards this complete protection, it is indispensable that the judge shall have cognizance of the crime which he has tried, and that he has proceeded in the usual manner, according to the settled practice of his Court. A sheriff, therefore, who should try for any of the pleas of the Crown, or a justice of the peace in a matter beyond his jurisdiction, or when his name was not in the commission, would, in strict law, be guilty of *murder*, from which his *bona fides* would be no legal protection, whatever claim it might afford for the mercy of the Crown.[2]

In like manner, the magistrate, sheriff, officers, and executioners, who carry the sentence into execution, are not less entitled to the protection of the law.[3] The magistrates and officers are bound only to look to the regularity of the warrant of execution, and are not answerable for any informalities which may have occurred in the previous stages of the proceeding, of which they have no sort of cognizance. Of course it is only the actual officers of the law who are thus privileged in carrying into execution a capital sentence; an outrageous mob who should break into a jail, seize a convict under sentence of death, and inflict punishment upon him, as in the case of the Porteous mob, with their own hands, would certainly not be the less the objects of punishment, that the days of the object of their vengeance had been numbered by a competent tribunal.[4]

No other magistrates can competently execute a sentence than those to whom it is addressed. If the magistrates of a burgh, therefore, should decline to execute the sentence put into their hands on a criminal in their custody, the lord lieutenant or sheriff

---

[1] Hume, i. 195.—[2] Ibid.—[3] Ibid. i. 196.—[4] Ibid.

of the county cannot interfere but at their own highest peril.[1] In conducting the execution, the magistrate must not vary in any material or essential particular from the terms of his warrant, as by beheading instead of hanging, or strangling in prison instead of publicly executing, or hanging at a different time or place from that prescribed in the death warrant.[2] If he does so, he acts without any authority, and will be answerable with his own life, for such wilful deviation from the terms of his warrant.[3] The like will hold if the magistrates proceed only on common report of a capital sentence having been pronounced without the death warrant, on which alone they can legally proceed, being put into their hands.[4]

But while this is true on the one hand, it is to be observed on the other, that any inconsiderable or trifling deviation from the terms of the warrant, though it may subject the offending party to fine or imprisonment, will not involve him in the serious penalties of murder. Thus, if the executioner disappear, or refuse to execute his duty, and no other means exist of carrying the sentence into execution, it is not to be supposed that the sheriff or other magistrate is not warranted in hiring another person to discharge the duty, or even in carrying it into effect with his own hands.[5] Or suppose that a mob arise and prevent the sentence being executed at the time and place specified in the warrant, it is not to be imagined that the magistrate commits a crime if he execute his duty on a tree or a signpost, or in any other way as near as possible to the time and place specified in the warrant.[6] In all such cases the rule obtains that the party intrusted with a particular duty, if prevented by violence or unavoidable misfortune, from specific implement, is liberated if he do his utmost to make the performance approach as nearly as possible to the prescribed terms.

2. Magistrates or other officers intrusted with the preservation of the public peace, are justified in committing homicide, or giving orders which lead to it, if the excesses of a riotous assembly cannot otherwise be repressed.

To maintain the King's peace, and punish rioters, is the duty of every magistrate within his bounds; and if this just and ne-

---

[1] Hume, i. 196.—[2] Ibid.—[3] Ibid.—[4] Ibid.—[5] Ibid. i. 197.—[6] Ibid.

cessary duty cannot be discharged without hazard to the life of the offenders, that those must answer for it who place him under the necessity of executing his duty in that perilous manner.[1] The only limitation to this rule is, that he must not proceed to these fatal extremities unnecessarily, or before the proper season.[2] The riot act makes no alteration on the common law in this particular; but merely, *in addition* to it, raises the *simple continuance* together for an hour after reading of the act to a capital offence, and authorizes the magistrate to employ force at the peril to life to enforce it.[3] It enacts, " That if any persons, to the number of *twelve or more*, being unlawfully, riotously, and tumultuously assembled together, to the disturbance of the public peace, and being required or commanded by any one or more justice or justices of the peace, or by the sheriff of the county, or his under sheriff, or by the mayor, bailiff or bailiffs, or other head officer, or justice of the peace of any city or town corporate, where such assembly shall be, by proclamation to be made in the King's name, in the form herein after directed, to disperse themselves and depart peaceably to their habitations, or to their lawful business, shall to the number of twelve or more, notwithstanding such proclamation made, unlawfully, riotously and tumultuously, remain or continue together, by the space of one hour, after such command or request made by proclamation, that then such continuing together to the number of twelve or more after such command or request made by proclamation, shall be adjudged felony without benefit of clergy."[4] The proclamation enjoined by the act is in these terms : " Our sovereign lord the King commandeth all persons being assembled immediately to disperse themselves, and depart to their habitations, or to their lawful business, upon the pains contained in the act made in the first year of King George for preventing tumults and riotous assemblies : God save the King." And in the event of the persons so unlawfully, riotously, and tumultuously assembled, continuing together to the number of twelve or more, for an hour after such proclamation made, it is declared lawful for the justice, magistrate, sheriff, or other officer, to seize and apprehend the offenders, and to summon to their aid all able bodied men ; " And if any persons so assembled shall happen to be killed,

[1] Hume, i. 197.—[2] Ibid.—[3] Ibid.—[4] 1st Geo. I. § 5, c. 5.

I

maimed or hurt, in the dispersing, seizing or apprehending them, or in the endeavour so to do, every such justice and constable, or other peace officer, shall be free, discharged and indemnified, concerning such killing, maiming or hurting." [1]   If proclamation be forcibly prevented from being made, those assembled are held not less bound to disperse than if it had actually been done, and the dispersers equally indemnified for the consequences.[2]   Prosecutions under the act are limited to twelve months after the date of the offence;[3] and sheriffs, justices of the peace, and magistrates in Scotland, are declared to have the same powers for putting the act in execution as justices, &c. have in England; and offenders against the act here are declared liable to the punishment of death and confiscation of moveables.[4].

Though these extraordinary powers are given to magistrates for the dispersion of riotous assemblies which have not as yet proceeded to any acts of violence, it is not on that account to be imagined that they are disabled from exerting the powers vested in them by the common law, before the period specified in the act has transpired, or before any attempts at reading it have been made.   On the contrary, it is intended for the case of riotous assemblages which have not yet proceeded to acts of open violence, and compels dispersion, after the hour, though none such have been perpetrated.   But if the mob have proceeded to such acts of violence, or are plainly preparing for them, either against persons, houses or property, unquestionably the magistrate is not only entitled but bound to exercise the powers of the common law for their instantaneous coercion or prevention.[5]   And if death ensue in the attempt to quell the riot or protect the persons or property of the lieges, it will be held justifiable if the violence was of such a kind, or the circumstances were such, that there was no reasonable probability of order being restored without proceeding to such extremities.[6]

A riot being so dangerous a thing, and tending rapidly to such fatal consequences, it is held that any private person may do what he can to appease such disturbances, by staying the persons assembled from proceeding to execute their purpose, or stopping others from joining them.[7]   Private persons also may arm themselves to suppress a riot, and in case of extreme ne-

---

[1] 1st Geo. I. § 3.—[2] § 5 —[3] § 8.—[4] § 9.; Russell, i. 257.—[5] Hume, i. 197.
[6] Ibid.—[7] Russell, i. 266

cessity use them;[1] and in all cases where a felony is about to be committed, as by breaking into a house, plundering a cart or vessel, or attempting the lives of the lieges, the bystanders are clearly entitled to interfere, and will be held justifiable if death ensue, provided the circumstances were such that there was no reasonable prospect of preventing the outrage in any other way.[2] It has frequently been subject of regret on the English bench, that the law was so much misunderstood on occasion of Lord George Gordon's riots in 1780, as that private persons deemed themselves not at liberty to use arms without the authority of a magistrate in those disgraceful tumults;—a proceeding which was clearly legal, and would probably have greatly checked the outrages which ensued.[3]

3. An officer of the law intrusted with the execution of a legal warrant, whether civil or criminal, will be justi-fied in committing homicide, if in the course of advancing to discharge his duty, he be brought into such peril that, without doing so, he cannot either save his own life or discharge the duty with which he is intrusted.

The law on this subject, and the cases illustrative of it, have already been amply illustrated.[4] It is sufficient, therefore, to observe, in general, that the situation of an officer intrusted with execution of a legal warrant, so far differs from that of an ordinary individual, that he is not only entitled, but bound, to *advance* against the object of his search; and that if, in the course of that advance, his life is brought into peril, he will be justified in killing, provided the circumstances were such that either his own life was evidently in peril, or his office and war-rant seriously endangered.[5] It must, however, be a reason-able and serious ground of danger, such as *cadit in constan-tem virum*, or was sufficient to intimidate a person of ordinary resolution. And the officer will be justified though he kill much earlier in the affray than a private individual; if at the time of killing the danger be in near and manifest preparation for him, so as to let him see that he shall come to be in peril of his life if he persevere in his duty.[6]

[1] Russell, i. 266; Hawkins, i. c. 65. § 11.—[2] Bos. & Pul. ii. 265; Russell, i. 266.—[3] Per Heath; Bos. & Pul. 266; Russell, i. 266.—[4] *Supra*, on Murder, p. 29, *et seq.*—[5] Hume, i. 204.—[6] Ibid.

The situation of an officer who bears an irregular or defective warrant, and the circumstances in which homicide will be justifiable in such a party, have also been considered.[1]

4. A soldier on duty will be justified in committing homicide, if he act in obedience to the commands of his officer, unless the command was to do something plainly illegal; or if he act on his own authority, provided the peril be so imminent that there appeared reasonable danger of his post being forced, or his arms taken from him, or his life endangered, unless he proceeded to that extremity.

An ample commentary on this important branch of the law will be found above[2]  The general result of all the decided cases on the subject will be found to be comprised in the above sentence.    .

5. A private individual will be justified in killing in defence of his life against imminent danger, of the lives of others connected with him from similar peril, or a woman or her friends in resisting an attempt at rape.

The act 1661, c. 22, has enumerated nearly all the cases in which an ordinary individual is justified in committing homicide.[3]  It enacts, " That the cases of homicide after mentioned, viz. Casual homicide, homicide in lawful defence, and homicide committed upon thieves or robbers breaking houses in the night; or in case of homicide the time of masterful depredation, or in the pursuit of denounced or declared rebels for capital crimes, or of such who assist and defend the rebels and masterful depredators by arms, &c., shall not be punished by death."[4]  The cases applicable to the present state of society which are here specified are, homicide in defence of life, in resistance against nocturnal housebreaking, and in defence against masterful depredators.  Hardly any others exist in which homicide can be relied on as absolutely justifiable at this day.

By the first principles of nature, homicide in defence of life is justifiable; but questions of the utmost nicety arise, as to whether the killing truly was in defence of life.[5]  Many illus-

[1] *Supra*, Murder, p 34, *et seq.*—[2] *Supra*, p. 39, *et seq.*—[3] Hume, i. 241.—[4] 1661, c 22.—[5] Hume, i. 218.

trations of the principles of the law on this subject have already been given in treating of murder; but the following instances embrace almost all the situations where it is clearly lawful to inflict death.

1. It is quite clear that if a person be on the highway, and is suddenly knocked down, or has a pistol fired or snapped at him, or a thrust made at him with a sword, he is entitled instantly to ward off the danger with which he is then threatened by destroying the assailant.[1] Nor is the right to kill in such circumstances confined to the person against whom the violence is directed, but extends also to any who may be in company with him, who are entitled to defend their companion equally as themselves against so unprovoked and threatening an assault.[2] And neither the one nor the other are bound to exercise the *moderamen tutelæ* which is required in other cases, it being a fair presumption that one who commences an attack in this way will instantly kill, " unless destroyed himself."[3] In such a case, the maxim of Cicero seems applicable : " *Gladius nobis ad occidendum, ab ipsis porrigitur legibus.*" [4]

But if the immediate peril be past, and the assailant has taken to flight, there seems to be no sufficient authority for holding that the injured party will be justified in pursuing and putting the offender to death in the course of the pursuit.[5] His powers on such an occasion are precisely the same as those of an officer of the law intrusted with a warrant for the apprehension of a felon : the assault of the criminal constitutes him an officer *pro hac vice*, and entitles him to exercise all the powers of such a situation.[6] But it is no part of the privilege of an officer, in our law, to inflict death upon a flying felon; nor even in case of resistance, unless the circumstances be such as to shew that his life may be endangered in the farther discharge of his duty, or that it cannot otherwise be performed. In general, therefore, the right of killing ceases when the prospect of danger is over; and the *dictum* of Burnett on this subject must not be received in the broad manner in which he has expressed it.[7]

A soldier on duty, with the strictest orders not to fire, will be justified in doing so, if he make out a clear case of instant

---

[1] Hume, i 218; Burnett, 39.—[2] Ibid.—[3] Burnett, 39; Hume, i. 218 —
[4] Pro Tito Annio Milone.—[5] Hume, i. 218.—[6] Ibid.—[7] Burnett, 403 ; Hume, i. 218; and Burnett, i. 43.

peril to his own life;[1] but he would not be justified if the peril
with such orders were to his post or arms only.   In all such
cases the right to kill may arise without any actual injury to
the person, if death be clearly threatened, as by firing though
the ball misses, or the piece flashes in the pan, or by thrusting with a sword though the wound do not take effect.[2]   And
cases may be figured where the pursuit is so much blended
with resistance to the assault as to justify the killing, though
the actual peril to life be past.   Of this kind, in the view of
the jury, was the case of Lieutenant Symonds, 30th August
1810,[3] already noticed; although, in the circumstances which
there occurred, it admits of doubt whether the interval was
not so great, and the circumstances such as to have rendered
the killing the result rather of revenge for injuries past than
of justifiable apprehension of danger to come.[4]

2. In case of an assault originating in a quarrel, or in circumstances where a murderous purpose in the aggressor could
not at first have been anticipated, homicide will be justified
when the party assaulted can show that he has *retired* as much
as he could from the danger, and only had recourse to extremities when matters had arrived at that pass, *morti proximum,*
where there was no reasonable prospect of escaping from the
assailant but by sacrificing his life.[5]   That homicide in such
circumstances is justifiable, no one can doubt; but the cases
mentioned under the head of murder demonstrate with how
much caution the doctrine is to be received in practice.[6]

Mackenzie lays it down, that the *moderamen tutelæ* may be
exceeded in *arms, time,* or manner of *resistance;* and that, if
the person assaulted exceed only in one of the three, the excess
is *culpa levissima,* and nowise punishable; if in two, it is somewhat punishable; but if in all the three, then it is *culpa lata,*
punishable by any pain short of death.[7]   There seems, however,
to be little practical use in such distinctions.   The general rule
is certain, that an assault with the fists, or a stick, will not
*justify* the use of a lethal weapon; nay, that in bad cases of
that description the killing will amount to murder.[8]   Of this
sort was the case of Lewis Marshall, 3d April 1644;[9] of Mitchell, May 1746;[10] and of Peter Scott, Aberdeen, spring 1823.[11]

---

[1] Burnett, 40.—[2] Ibid.—[3] Hume, i. 228.—[4] *Supra,* p. 103, and Burnett,
44, 45.—[5] Hume, i. 224.—[6] *Supra,* p. 12.—[7] Mackenzie, tit. Murder, p. 37.
—[8] Burnett, p. 46; Hume, i. 227.—[9] Burnett, 46.—[10] Ibid. 47, *nota.—*
[11] *Supra,* p. 15.

In the first of these cases, that of Lewis Marshall, it appeared that, previous to the scuffle, the deceased and pannel were on friendly terms: that the deceased gave the first provocation, by striking the pannel, and throwing his father on the ground: that he again struck the prisoner, and threw his father over a wall · that the deceased again returned and struck the prisoner, who drew his sword, and had his sword-arm held by a friend: that, while so held, he was attacked a third time by the deceased, who beat him with hands, feet, and knees; and that, on getting loose, he drew a knife from his pocket and mortally stabbed him. All this provocation, how violent soever, was found insufficient to save the accused from a capital sentence. In the second, the deceased, after the grossest verbal abuse, had collared the prisoner, driven him over a chest, dashed his head against the wall, and struck him on the head to the effusion of his blood, upon which the latter secretly drew a knife from his pocket and stabbed the aggressor in the belly. He was found guilty of murder, the Court having only sustained it relevant to exculpate, " that the defunct was killed by the pannel in the *just and lawful defence of his own life.*" [1] The circumstances of the third have been already given; [2] and they demonstrate both that these principles are *in viridi observantia*, and with how much caution the right of homicide in self-defence must be received in practice.

3. A woman may lawfully kill to defend herself from a rape, if her honour cannot otherwise be preserved; and the same privilege belongs to her parents, brother, or relatives, if they cannot otherwise save her from that calamity. [3] Nay, there seems no reason to doubt that an ordinary bystander, if he see a woman threatened with such an outrage, may aid her in resisting, even at the hazard of the assailant's life, on the same principle on which an attempted murder or highway robbery may be resisted by any person who witnesses it. [4]

By the English law, a man may lawfully kill in defence of his person, against any attempted felony. [5] In such cases he is not obliged to retreat, but may pursue his adversary till he finds himself out of danger; and if, in a conflict which then ensues, the assailant be killed, such killing is justifiable. [6] But the felonious intent should be apparent, and not left in uncertainty,

---

[1] Burnett, 47.—[2] *Supra*, p. 15.—[3] Hume, i. 218.—[4] Ibid.—[5] Russell, i. 549.
—[6] Foster, 273; Hale, i. 481, 445, 484; Hawkins, i. c. 28. § 21. 24.

so that, unless it plainly appear from the circumstances of the case, as the manner of the assault, the weapon, &c., that a felony was intended, the homicide will not be deemed justifiable.[1] And the rule applies to the case of an intended *felony* only; so that, if the offence evidently intended was an inferior injury, as an assault only, the killing will be deemed manslaughter.[2] But if the mode of assault be such as is calculated to excite great and immediate terror, the killing will be justifiable, though no felony was truly intended; as if several attack a person at once with deadly weapons, though they wait till he be on his guard, for so unequal a combat resembles more an attempt at assassination than a fair combat.[3]

6. Homicide is justifiable to prevent robbery, stouthrief, or housebreaking, in the night, provided those crimes be clearly attempted,

Depredation of any sort, when accompanied by violence, is considered so heinous an offence, that it is, by the laws of all civilized nations, considered lawful, in resisting it, to take the offender's life.[4] A forcible attempt at robbery on the highway, therefore, or a masterful intrusion into a house by a body of armed depredators, which constitutes the crime of stouthrief, or a violent entry, or attempt at entry into a house at night, with a view to commit housebreaking, unquestionably may be repelled at the hazard of the invader's life.[5] In like manner, if a lawless mob surround a house, shop, or manufactory, armed with fire-arms or bludgeons, and are proceeding, in spite of repeated warnings, to force the doors or windows, or to set fire to the premises, there is no doubt that those within may lawfully fire, though no actual entry has been effected.[6] Accordingly, in the case of James Ripley and others, Old Bailey, 8th April 1815, already mentioned, it was laid down as clear law by the English judges, that those intrusted with the defence of a house, whether servants, soldiers, or others, were as much entitled to kill in defence of the house, against such an attack, as the master himself would have been.[7]

The great difficulty in all such cases is to fix the degree of

---

[1] Hale, i. 484.—[2] Russell, i. 549; Hale, i. 484.—[3] Ford's case, East. i. 276.—[4] Hume, i. 210.—[5] Ibid.; Burnett, 40.—[6] Hume, i. 221.—[7] Hume, i. 221, 222.

violence which must have taken place before the homicide can lawfully be committed. Certainly it is not to be imagined that the moment a man sees a person in a threatening attitude on the road, or in suspicious circumstances near a house, or a mob hallooing in the street, he is entitled to assume that they are about to commit a robbery, housebreaking, or stouthrief, and instantly to fire among the supposed depredators. On the other hand, it is as little to be imagined that the person assailed is bound to wait till the pistol is at his breast, or the windows are actually broken open, or the mob have forced their way into the house, in the several cases which have now been supposed. Perhaps the nearest approach that can be made to a general rule is, that, in like manner, as life may not lawfully be taken till life has been put in imminent hazard, so lethal weapons may not be lawfully used in defence of property from violence, till that violence has proceeded to such a length as to show that, without imminent hazard, their use cannot longer be delayed.[1] If, therefore, the housebreaker be coming in at the window, or breaking open the door, or issuing from the chimney, he may without doubt be lawfully killed, if the circumstances were such as to leave no reasonable doubt that he had come there with a felonious design; but if he be lurking about the windows on the outside merely, or feeling the sash, without having actually raised it, or trying to pick the lock of the outer door, while as yet the strength of the building is unbroken, it would be deemed worthy of some censure in law, as unquestionably it would be in morals, if those within were, without any warning, to shoot the intruders.[2] But if warning has been given and disregarded, and the forcible entry still attempted, there can be no doubt that the intruders may lawfully be killed.[3] The cases which have been quoted under the head of Murder, show with how much caution this extreme right is to be exercised, and how slight are the shades of difference between justifiable and culpable homicide on such occasions. To fire when the person supposed to be bent on housebreaking is lurking under the windows of the drawing-room, among the laurel bushes, or when he is endeavouring to effect his escape, and is in such a situation that resistance on his part is impracticable, have been adjudged culpable in a serious degree.[4]

[1] Hume, i. 220.—[2] Ibid.—[3] Ibid.—[4] J. Scott's case, Dumfries, Sept. 1830, Lieutenant Robertson's case, Edinburgh; *Supra*, p. 105.

4

It has been already noticed that it is the use, or threatened use, of *violence*, which justifies the shedding of blood in any case of depredation; and therefore, that in any, even the most aggravated case of simple theft, though committed in a dwelling-house, it is unlawful to kill the thief. Nay, in some cases, the use of such extreme means against those committing such an offence may amount to murder.[1]

With respect to housebreaking *in the day*, there is an obvious distinction founded both in the nature of the thing and the enactment of the act 1661, c. 22. For while that statute enumerates the cases of inculpable homicide, it only mentions "killing robbers and thieves breaking houses in the *night*" among the number. And certainly a much stronger case of necessity must be made out for the use of lethal weapons against housebreakers in the daylight, when the trepidation consequent on an attack is so much less, and the means of procuring assistance are generally so much greater, than in the night time, when assistance is seldom to be had, and allowance must be made for the agitation consequent on so untimely an attack. But still this is not any general or unbending rule; for if the attack be made on a house in the day time in a remote situation, where no assistance is at hand, or in circumstances where it cannot be obtained; and more especially if there appear any disposition to persevere, notwithstanding warning of resistance, there can be no question that the violence may be repelled by force, and without regard to the consequences.[2]

By the English law the punishment of such cases is made the subject of special statute. The 24th Henry VIII. c. 5, enacts, "That if any person or persons be indicted or appealed of, for the death of any such evil disposed person or persons attempting to murder, rob, or burglarily to break mansion-houses as aforesaid, the person or persons so indicted or appealed of, and the same by verdict, so found and tried, shall be thereof, and for the same, fully acquitted and discharged." This statute is held to be declaratory only of the common law, and, though it mentions some cases, it does not exclude others where the principle and necessity is the same; so that the killing of one who attempts to burn a house is justifiable, without the aid of the statute.[3]

---

[1] *Supra*, p. 21.—[2] Hume, i. 222.—[3] Hale, i. 488; East. i. 272.

The cases of nicety which occur, are where doubt exists as to the intention of the person killed, and the circumstances which will vindicate the use of lethal weapons, where the felonious intent is not fully declared; for no assault, how violent soever, will justify the killing of the assailant under the plea of necessity, unless there be a plain manifestation of a felonious intent;[1] and a man cannot be justified in killing on the plea of necessity, unless he is wholly without fault in bringing that necessity upon himself.[2] In the case of Lovat, it appeared that, being in bed and asleep, his servant came to the door about twelve at night, conceiving that she heard thieves, and awakened her master. He immediately rose, and, with a drawn sword, proceeded down stairs. Meanwhile a young woman, who had been in the house to assist in washing, hearing the noise, ran into the pantry; upon which Lovat's wife exclaimed, There are the thieves, and he himself entering hastily, and not knowing who she was in the dark, stabbed her hastily, of which she instantly died. This was ruled to be misadventure;[3] but Judge Foster considers it should have been adjudged manslaughter, as due care and circumspection had not been used.[4] The better opinion, however, seems to be, that the homicide was justifiable, as proceeding not only on mistake, but on circumstances which rendered mistake nowise blameable. It differs from the case of Scott at Dumfries, September 1830, already noticed,[5] in this important particular, that the pannel had here reason to believe that a thief was in the house, and he was unsupported; whereas there, two men were in the room, and the man who had got into the house was in the act of forcing his body through the iron bars of the window to make his escape.

### SECTION IV.——CASUAL HOMICIDE.

1. It is Casual Homicide where a person kills unintentionally, when lawfully employed, and neither meaning harm to any one, nor having failed in the due degree of care and circumspection for preventing mischief to his neighbour.

[1] East. i. 277.——[2] Hale, i. 405, 440, 441, Russell, i. 551.——[3] Hale, i. 474.——[4] Foster, i. 299.——[5] *Supra* 104.

Under this class are comprehended all those cases, unfortunately too numerous, in which death ensues, not from any fault in any quarter, but from some misfortune or accident, and where, consequently, the person who is the innocent cause of another's death is more the subject of pity than punishment. Thus, if a person's gun burst in his hand, and kill his neighbour; or if the trigger be caught in going through a hedge, and the contents of the piece lodge in his breast; or a horse run away with its rider. in spite of all his efforts, and though he had no good reason to have believed he could not manage it, and kill a passenger on the road; or a cart go over a child in the street, though the driver was going moderately, and at his horse's head, and was so situated that he could not see it; or a coach drive over a person who foolishly attempted to cross before the horses heads, where they were going at the usual pace; or a steam-boat run down another vessel, owing to the darkness of the night or a thick mist, when every usual precaution to avoid a collision had been taken; in these, and the like cases, no blame is imputable to the party who occasioned the misfortune, and he is entitled to an honourable acquittal. The best definition which can be given of this kind of homicide is, that it obtains, when a person kills unintentionally, when lawfully employed, and neither meaning harm to any one, nor having failed in the due degree of care for preventing danger to his neighbour.[1]

2. It will be construed as casual homicide, though the fatal result might, by extreme care, or a totally different course, have been avoided, if, in the circumstances, the due degree of care has not been wanting on the part of the person who has inflicted the injury.

Cases of this sort usually occur, where the fatal event arises from some latent weakness and malady, unknown to the pannel, who has done nothing which could have injured a person in the health, which the appearance of the deceased gave reason to presume he possessed. Thus, in the case of William Bathgate, the defence was sustained that the death of the deceased, was solely owing to a fall, which happened in the

---

[1] Hume, l. 194.

course of a wrestling-bout for sport, and only proved injurious to the deceased, in consequence of his previous valetudinary condition.[1]  In like manner, in the case of William Murphie, 13th January 1810, it appeared that the deceased had engaged in a struggle with the pannel, in his (the pannel's) own house, where he had struck and abused him in a violent manner.  The pannel, in the struggle, had twisted his hand in the *outer* fold of the man's neckcloth, which drew the inner fold tight round his neck, and strangled him.  Now, here *resistance* to the assault was clearly justifiable, and there was no evidence that the consequence of the seizure of the outer fold was either known or could have been reasonably foreseen.[2]  Again, in the case of James Grant, May 14. 1830, the pannel was acquitted though he had rode over two women on the footpath, near Stockbridge, Edinburgh, and killed one, as it appeared in evidence that the horse, which was a young one, had run off with its rider, who could not manage it, in consequence of some boys clapping their hands.  So also in the case of William Buchan and Alexander Macintyre, December 14. 1829, the pannels were the captain and mate of a steam-boat, which occasioned the death of two individuals in the harbour of Greenock.  It appeared in evidence, that the deceased had set out in a small boat, with a cable from a sailing vessel lying about one hundred yards from the quay at Greenock, and which was warping in to the pier, to proceed to the shore, in order to make the vessel fast to the pier-head.  Before they had proceeded far, a steam-boat, under the guidance of the pannels, came up, and steered between the vessel and the shore, directly *across* the line of the boat's progress, moving at the rate of about nine miles an hour.  The cable which attached the boat to the vessel had sunk into the water, and of course could not be seen; and the steam-boat coming rapidly forward, came upon the small boat, sunk it, and drowned two of the boatmen.  There was a good look-out kept at the bow of the steam-boat, and the evidence shewed that the little boat was seen, but that no change of direction was deemed necessary, because if the boat had proceeded with the usual rapidity, it would have cleared the steam-boat.  In this way no alteration was made till it was too late to prevent a collision.

[1] Hume, 1 194.—[2] Ibid 1 195.

The anchor was raised on the sailing vessel; but it was not placed in such a situation as to insure its being seen from the steam-boat, and it was not known to those on board the steam-boat that the sailing vessel was warping in, though, by greater care, they might have seen it. The accident, therefore, was owing to the cable, which retarded the advance of the small boat, not being seen, and the Court, considering the homicide nowise blameable, directed an acquittal.[1]  The difficulty of the case consisted in this, that the motion of the steam-vessel had *not been retarded*, when so near the quay, and in a situation where the passage of other boats or vessels might so naturally have been expected, and that the steamer, contrary to usage, went *between* a vessel, which they might have seen, by a little attention, was warping in to shore, and the quay, instead of keeping on the outside, where there was plenty of water, and no risk whatever,—and, when these particulars are duly weighed, it will probably be thought that the pannels had good reason to congratulate themselves on the result of their trial.

In the case of Mr Campbell of Borland, Perth, autumn 1831, it appeared that the deceased had come to the house of the pannel at night, and asked to get in, as he had a letter to give to Mr Campbell.  Hearing the noise, the pannel rose, and took a double-barreled gun loaded with small-shot, with which he went out to the door, and asked the man what he wanted, desiring him, at the same time, to go off, or he would fire.  The deceased immediately retired, and soon after both barrels of the gun went off, and the man was killed at the distance of twenty yards.  The pannel alleged in defence, that he stumbled on the ground, which was proved to be rough and slippery, and that the gun went off by accident, and this was rendered probable by the shot slanting upwards in the body of the deceased. Lord Moncrieff laid it down that *intentional* firing, in these circumstances, while the deceased was retreating, would have *been clearly culpable;* but that there was not sufficient evidence to shew that the gun was fired intentionally, or disprove the pannel's defence of accident, and the jury accordingly acquitted him.

By the English law, Casual is termed Excusable Homicide by Misadventure, and is defined " where one doing a lawful

---

[1] Unreported.

act, without any intention of bodily harm, and using the proper precaution to prevent danger, unfortunately happen to kill another."[1] Thus, if people following their lawful occupations, use due care to prevent danger, and nevertheless a person is killed, this will be deemed misadventure ; or if workmen throw stones, rubbish, or other things, from a house in the ordinary course of their business, and a person is killed; this will be misadventure if it be done in a retired place, but manslaughter if in a place where there was any reasonable probability of persons passing.[2] In like manner, if a man go at a trot in an ordinary road, with a cart, and go over a person, it will be misadventure ; but if this be done in a place where people usually pass it will be manslaughter.[3] If a person be riding a horse, which springs out of the road, and kill a child, from a whip being cracked, or being lashed by another person, this is misadventure in the rider, but manslaughter in the person who lashed the animal.[4] When a farmer set himself, in the night time, to watch his corn, which had been much injured by deer, and set his servant in another corner of the field to watch, also armed with a gun, with orders to shoot whenever he heard a noise among the corn; and soon after, forgetting his own orders, rushed into the corn himself, and was shot by his servant, thinking the noise proceeded from a deer, this was adjudged misadventure ; but Hale held that if the master had not given such orders, it would have been manslaughter, because the servant fired before he saw the deer's mark.[5] In like manner it is misadventure only, if a commander, coming in the semblance of an enemy upon a sentry in the night, to try his vigilance, is taken for one, and shot as such.[6]

3. The caution which the law requires is not the *utmost* caution that can be used, but such reasonable precaution as is used in similar cases, and has been found by long experience, and in the ordinary course of things, to answer the end.[7]

Thus, in a case reported by Foster, a man went to his friend's house, carrying his gun with him; but before he went to dinner he discharged it. Returning home with his wife at night, he

[1] Russell, i. 539; East i. 221.—[2] Hale, i. 472; Foster, 262.—[3] East. i. 263.—[4] Hawk. i. c. 29. § 3.—[5] Hale, i. 476.—[6] Ibid. i. 42.—[7] Foster, 264.

took it up and touched the trigger, when it went off and killed her whom he dearly loved. It appeared in evidence that during his absence a person had loaded the gun, and replaced it where he found it, without the pannel's knowledge. "I did not inquire," says Foster, "whether the poor man had examined the gun before he carried it home; but being of opinion, upon the whole evidence, that he had reasonable ground for believing the gun was not loaded, I directed the jury to acquit, which was done accordingly." [1] "Accidents of this lamentable kind," says Foster, "may be the lot of the wisest and best of men, and commonly fall out among the nearest friends and relations, who love each other the best." [2]

A case decided on the same principles occurred at Ayr, spring 1827. John Kilgour, the pannel, was there charged with having fired a fowling-piece loaded with small shot, in a field within an easy shot of a highroad, where persons frequently passed, and in the direction of the road, and killed a girl passing at the time. The indictment was found relevant by Lord Meadowbank; but on the proof it appeared that the shot was really a long one, being above fifty yards, and that it proved fatal only by one of the leads having unfortunately penetrated the child's eye, while the other shot hardly penetrated the skin. The Court held the death accidental in these circumstances, and so the jury found.

If death ensue in consequence of such games as are entered into to give strength, skill, or activity in the use of arms, or for sport or recreation, as wrestling by consent, playing at cudgels, fencing, archery, &c. it is held in England misadventure.[3] The true principle which distinguishes such cases from those where death ensues in consequence of an intent to do a slight injury is, that here bodily harm is not the motive on either side.[4] Proper caution and perfect fair play should be used on both sides; for, if any improper advantage be taken, it will amount to manslaughter.[5] If a person be killed shooting at butts, game, or in any other lawful amusement, it will be misadventure; and though the person shooting at game be not qualified, that will not raise the case to manslaughter, if there be no culpability in the case.[6]

[1] Foster, 265.—[2] Ibid. 264.—[3] Russell, 1. 542.—[4] Foster, 260.—[5] East. i. 269.—[6] Hale, i. 475; Foster, 259.

# CHAPTER II.

### ON THE EVIDENCE NECESSARY TO SHEW THAT THE DECEASED DIED OF THE WOUND.

THE intention of the pannel is not the sole ingredient in the crime of homicide. It is moreover essential that the person injured has *died of the wound*. This constitutes the principal part of what lawyers termed the *corpus delicti*, and involves many nice and difficult questions as to the legal connexion between an injury received and supervening death.

1. It is essential to every species of homicide that a person have died of the injury received.

It is not sufficient, by the common law of Scotland, that a wound, however dangerous, have been inflicted, to forfeit the offender's life. It is moreover indispensable that the sufferer *has died* of the injury inflicted.[1] The crime of homicide, as the name imports, consists in the taking away of life by the act of another. Attempts to murder, however atrocious in themselves, are not by the common law, where standing *per se*, sufficient to infer the pain of death.[2] So it was expressly found in the case of Walter Buchanan of Boquhan, January 15. 1728.[3] The recent statute passed for the punishment of attempts at murder, by stabbing, cutting and poisoning, with death, will hereafter be considered.[4]

2. It is necessary, in every species of homicide, that the deceased died of the injury committed by the pannel, or with his accession, either directly, or by its usual and probable consequence.

It is under this branch of the law that the difficult and painful cases occur. An injury is inflicted, perhaps of a comparatively trivial kind; but, in consequence of some supervening

---

[1] Hume, i. 179.—[2] Ibid. i. 181.—[3] Ibid.—[4] *Infra*, on Statute against Stabbing.

K

malady, connected with the wound, but not its necessary and unvarying attendant, death ensues. Is the pannel answerable for the life of the deceased? A cut, for example, is inflicted on the arm or leg, in itself, and in ordinary cases, by no means dangerous: the sufferer is taken to an hospital, where he takes the erysipelas, or a contagious fever, or is obliged to suffer amputation, and in consequence dies. On the one hand, it may be urged that he would not have died if he had been let alone; that it was no act of his own which rendered removal to the hospital necessary; and that the consequences which there ensued may justly be visited on the person whose rash or criminal act has led to the chain of causes and effects which terminated in the fatal result. On the other, equity revolts at the serious pains of murder or culpable homicide being inflicted on one who has not done any thing which, in the ordinary course of events, would have occasioned death, but has done so in this particular case from a calamity which he certainly did not foresee, and could not, after his original wrong was committed, prevent.

1. One thing is perfectly clear, that if the death be owing not to the effects of the wound, but to a supervening accident or misfortune, though induced by the first violence, the pannel cannot be convicted of homicide. Thus if a person be wounded, no matter how severely, yet if he recover and engage in his ordinary avocations, and bear about with him no apparent seeds of his malady, the assailant cannot afterwards be involved in the consequences of his death, even though it was connected with the previous violence. So it was found in the case of Patrick Kinninmonth, November 22. 1697.[1] Or suppose that, in a combat between two persons, one is wounded, and the assailant flies, leaving him wounded on the field, and robbers come up and slay him in that defenceless state; certainly the pains of homicide cannot attach to the first assailant, though he was the original cause of the defenceless condition which led to the death of the deceased.[2] Or if a person be wounded, but recovers after a long confinement, which induces a consumption that ultimately proves fatal, still the death is here so remotely connected with the original violence, that human tribunals cannot consider the one as the cause of the other.[3] In short, to make out a charge of homicide, it is indispensable

that the death be connected with the violence, not merely by a concatenation of causes and effects, but by such direct influence as, without the intervention of any considerable change of circumstances, produced that effect.

2. It follows that, if the death be owing not to the natural and accustomed consequences of the injury, but to remote and improbable accidents which have since intervened, the pannel must be acquitted. Thus if a person receive a slight injury, in itself by no means dangerous, but which, by his obstinacy or intemperance, or by rash and hurtful applications, degenerates in the end into a mortal sore, he is himself answerable for the fatal result, and the first injury was only the occasion of his deed.[1] In the case of William Mason, July 18. 1674, it was pleaded in defence, that by the refusal of proper remedies, and persisting to keep abroad in the night in severe weather, the deceased had irritated a slight cut into a mortal complaint, and this was sustained as relevant to elide the libel by the Court; and, in the older case of Thomas Crombie, it was alleged that the deceased had *misgoverned* himself, as it was called, by hard drinking, keeping much company, and dancing at a bridal, contrary to the advice of his surgeon; and then the complainer in consequence abandoned the prosecution.[2] To the same purpose, in the case of Christian Paterson, 22d December 1823, it appeared in evidence that the deceased was struck on the head with a smoothing iron, which fractured her skull; some days afterwards she drank a quantity of whisky, and was ultimately carried to the Royal Infirmary, where erysipelas shortly appeared on the wound, of which she died. In these circumstances the charge of murder was departed from, and the accused found guilty only of the alternative charge of assault.[3]

In like manner, in the case of J. Campbell, Glasgow, April 1819, the pannel was gamekeeper to Lord Blantyre, and he had, in the course of a scuffle with a poacher, discharged his piece, which lodged its contents in his thigh. He was carried to the Infirmary at Glasgow, where erysipelas at the time was extremely prevalent; and having been unfortunately put into a bed formerly occupied by a patient with that disorder, he took it, and died in consequence. Till this supervened the wound bore no peculiarly dangerous symptoms. The

[1] Hume, l. 182 —[2] Ibid; Burnett, 550 —[3] Unreported

Public Prosecutor, Mr John Hope, afterwards Dean of Faculty, strongly contended, that, if the man had not been fired at, he never would have been exposed to the contagion of the erysipelas, and therefore that the death was by a circuitous but legitimate consequence owing to the wound; but this was deemed too remote a conclusion, and the pannel, under direction of Lords Justice-Clerk Boyle and Succoth, was acquitted.[1] In like manner, in the case of Hugh and Euphemia Macmillan, 17th December 1827, the pannels had thrown a quantity of sulphuric acid in the face of the deceased, and produced such inflammation in the eyes, that bleeding was deemed necessary. The orifice made to let the blood flow inflamed, and of this he died, but not from the injury in the face. The Court held this *second* injury, produced by a different hand, not so connected with the original violence as to support the charge of murder, which was accordingly departed from, and the pannel convicted of the assault only.

3. The same judgment must be passed on another set of cases, viz. that in which the injury inflicted by the pannel is only one circumstance among several which have all contributed to the fatal issue. Cases may often occur in which a glass of spiritous liquors, or even of cold water, improperly administered, may produce a fatal change in the state of the patient; but it would be going too far to hold that, in such cases, this adventitious circumstance, mixed up as it is with so many other elements, is to be taken as the cause of death. Thus, in the case of William Duff of Braco, November 10. 1707, a libel was dismissed as irrelevant which set forth that the pannel and others had broken into a house, and that the wife of the owner being in childbed at the time, was, " by the terror of the raging and roaring of the armed men about her, thrown into a fever of which she died."[2] And, in the case of Patrick Kinninmonth, August 11. 1607, it was one article of charge that he broke into a house, grievously alarmed the mistress, who was recently delivered, and so injured her health that her child soon after died. The injury to the mother was alone sustained as relevant; the death of the child being considered as a remote and uncertain result of that and probably other concurring causes.[3]

---

[1] Unreported.—[2] Hume, i. 183.—[3] Ibid.

3. If the death be owing to the usual and probable consequences of the injury, it is immaterial though a period of many months elapse between the one and the other, or in how feeble and declining a state the deceased may have been when he received the wound, or though, under more skilful treatment, he might have recovered.

In cases of this description, two different principles have been adopted in our law.

1. How feeble soever the condition of the sufferer may have been, and how short his tenure of life, it is equally murder as if the person killed had been in the prime of youth and vigour.[1] Accordingly, in the case of Robert Ramsay, March 24. 1713, it appeared that the deceased, who was a sick and infirm old man, was violently beat with a pair of tongs, of which in a few hours he died. These circumstances were found relevant to infer the crime of murder, though it was strongly urged that the death was rather owing to his previous infirm condition.[2] And an apt illustration of the same legal position may be found in the case which so often occurs of child-murder, where, if life be once proved to have existed, and been taken away, it is held altogether irrelevant to inquire whether the infant had ten minutes or eighty years to live.[3]

2. If the death be truly owing to the wound, it signifies not that, under more favourable circumstances, and with more skilful treatment, the fatal result might have been averted.[4] Thus if an assault be made which opens an artery, it will be no defence to plead that, by the assistance of a surgeon, the wound might have been staunched and life preserved.[5] Or, suppose a person receive a gunshot wound at a remote part of the country, where no skilful surgeons are to be had, and that he dies of the wound, notwithstanding the best care of the practitioners there, such as they are ; or that a person is robbed and severely beaten in the night in severe weather, and in a solitary place, so that lying there exposed to the cold till daylight he die upon the spot, or of the consequences shortly after; in all these and the like cases homicide is undoubted.[6] Thus, in the case of David Edgar, July 6. 1747, it appeared that the pannel was one of a party of smugglers who had fired at an

---

[1] Hume, i. 183.—[2] Ibid; Burnett, 550.—[3] Burnett, i. 550.—[4] Ibid. 551 ; Hume, i. 184.—[5] Hume, i 184.—[6] Ibid , Burnett, 551

officer of excise: the wounded man was carried to the nearest village, where he was attended by the surgeon of the country, who was not deficient in attention; but a great collection of matter having formed in the leg, and fever ensued, the patient died at the end of three weeks. The relevancy of this libel was strongly objected to, because it was said by skilful treatment the man might have recovered; but the Court found it relevant, leaving to the pannel to prove, if he could, that death arose *ex malo regimine*. The true distinction in all such cases is, that, if the death was evidently occasioned by grossly erroneous medical treatment, the original author of the violence will not be answerable; but if it arise from want merely of the higher skill which can only be commanded in great towns, he will, because he has wilfully exposed the deceased to a risk from which he had practically no means of escaping. Accordingly, in the case of William Macewan, Perth, September 1830, the pannel was indicted for the culpable homicide of a boy in a manufactory of which he was the overseer, by striking him on the shoulder, which dislocated the arm. On the proof it appeared that the boy's arm had been worked upon two days after the blow by an ignorant bonesetter, whose operations did more harm than good; and in consequence of the inflammation thus occasioned, acting upon a sickly and scrofulous habit of body, a white swelling ensued, which proved fatal. The jury accordingly, under the direction of Lord Meadowbank, acquitted the pannel. On the other hand, in the case of William Mackenzie, March 14. 1827, it appeared that the pannel seized the deceased by the throat, and bruised him severely in several parts of the body, in consequence of which lockjaw supervened, and he died. Skilful medical advice was not called in till near the end of the illness, when the lockjaw was already come on; and in the interval he had acted imprudently, and aggravated the symptoms. The medical evidence clearly proved that the lockjaw was owing to the injury, and was a frequent result of it. The Court was unanimous that the homicide was proved, and he was convicted, and transported for fourteen years.[1]

3. Though death do not ensue for weeks or months after the injury was received, yet if the wound be severe, and keep in a regular progression from bad to worse, so that the patient con-

---

[1] Syme, 158.

tinually languishes, and is consumed by it as by a disease, this in reason and law is quite the same as if he had died on the spot.[1]   Accordingly, in the case of Edward and James Scrymgeour, January 5. 1619, where the deceased was wounded in September, and died in the succeeding January, the defence founded on the lapse of time was repelled.[2]   Again, the like plea was repelled in the case of John Young, July 30. 1630, who was indicted for murder, by striking " with a whinger on the shackle bone" in June, of which the sufferer died in October.[3]   Nay, in the case of William Lowis, April 16. 1610, it appeared from the libel that the person wounded had survived the injury for *seventeen* months, notwithstanding which it was sent to an assize.[4]   In the case of Peter Leith, November 15. 1686, the deceased died at the end of three months; but the Court sustained the relevancy, the prosecutor undertaking to prove that, after receiving the wound, " he languished thereof constantly from evil to worse."   And, in the case of John Caldwall, July 1737, where the deceased, a postboy, was robbed, cut, and left on the ground all night, and death ensued at the end of two months, and it was proved by the medical evidence that the wound, with the cold which the deceased got by lying out all night, and the great loss of blood which followed on it, were the cause of death, the pannel was convicted of the murder as well as the robbery.[5]   So also in the case of William Somerville, December 1669, it appeared that the deceased received a wound in her forehead, not of its own nature mortal, with other fractures and contusions, and that the wounds, joined with the fractures, were incurable, and ultimately brought on a fever, which continued till the time of her death, which was *three months* after the injury.   A long and able argument was here maintained by Sir George Mackenzie for the pannel, in which it was offered to be proved that the wound was not in its nature mortal, and that the fever was acquired by contagion unconnected with the wound.   The libel, however, was found relevant, and the prisoner found guilty, though he obtained a pardon owing to an error on the part of the Court, in refusing to admit evidence that the death was owing to the fever acquired from another cause.[6]

By the law of England it is settled, that if a man give ano-

---

[1] Hume, i. 185 ;  Burnett, 552, *note.*—[2] Ibid.—[3] Ibid.—[4] Ibid.—[5] Ibid. —[6] Burnett, 551, 552 ; Hume, i. 186.

ther a stroke, not in itself so mortal, but that, with good care,
he might have recovered; yet if the party die of this wound
within year and day, it is murder, or other species of homicide as the case may be; though, if the wound appear not to
be mortal, and it clearly appear that the death was owing to
unskilful treatment, and not to the wound or its consequences,
then it is no species of homicide.[1]   But when a wound, not in
itself mortal, from want of proper application, or from neglect,
turns to a gangrene or fever, which is the immediate cause of
death, the party is deemed guilty of the homicide; for, though
the fever or gangrene be the immediate cause of death, yet the
wound being the cause of the gangrene or fever, is held the
cause of death *causa causati*.[2]   Thus it was resolved, that if
one inflict wounds on another, or neglect the cure of them, or
be disorderly, and do not keep the rule which a wounded person
should do; yet, if he die, it is murder or manslaughter, in the
original aggressor, according as the case may be, because, say
they, if the wounds had not been inflicted the man had not died,
and the neglect and disorder of the person who received the
wounds, shall furnish no excuse to him that gave them.[3]   How
sick soever the sufferer may be, before he receive the wound,
yet if the violence accelerate his death, it is homicide in the
person guilty thereof.[4]   But it is agreed that no person shall
be adjudged guilty of homicide, if the party injured does not
die within year and day after the stroke received, or cause of
death administered, in the computation of which the whole
day upon which the hurt was received is to be reckoned the
first.[5]

If a physician or surgeon give his patient a potion or plas-
ter, intending to do him good, but, contrary to expectation,
it kill him, this will, in the general case, be considered as
misadventure.[6]   But if the medicine were administered, or
the operation performed, by a person not a regular physician
or surgeon, the killing would be manslaughter.[7]   Nay, the
same will hold if the pretended remedy be obviously and notoriously perilous and unsuitable for the particular case where
it produced fatal consequences, an instance of which recently
occurred in the conviction of Mr St John Long for manslaughter, before the Old Bailey.

[1] Russell, L. 428. - [2] Hale, i. 428; Russell, i 428.—[3] Ibid.; Kel. 26; Russell, i. 429.—[4] Hale, i. 428.—[5] Hawkins, i c. 31. § 9, Erskine, i. 112, 343, 344.
—[6] Hale, i. 429; Russell, i. 428.—[7] Inst. 251; Russell, i. 428.

# CHAPTER III.

### OF CHILD-MURDER, AND CONCEALMENT OF PREGNANCY.

THE extreme facility of extinguishing the infant life, at the time, or shortly after birth, and the experienced difficulty of proving this unnatural crime, has led, both in the Scotch and English law, to the passing of statutes, calculated to facilitate the proof of the offence, and mitigate its punishment. This was formerly done by the Scotch act 1690, c. 21, which declared the crime punishable with death, and under which many inhuman convictions took place; but this statute being now happily repealed, the law stands on a comparative lenient footing, which presents no difficulty in the execution.

1. If a woman " shall conceal her being with child, during the whole period of her pregnancy, and shall not call for, or make use of, help or assistance in the birth, and if the child shall be found dead, or be amissing, she shall be imprisoned for a period not exceeding two years."[1]

By this statute it is not necessary to inquire whether the child has actually been killed or not; it is sufficient if the statutory presumptions are established, to subject the pannel to punishment. A concealment of pregnancy, and a failure to call for help or assistance in the birth, accompanied with the disappearance of the body, or its being found dead, are held to imply, *præsumptione juris et de jure*, that the infant died of the want of due and timeful assistance in the birth.[2]

In the interpretation of this statute it has been settled,

2. That it is incumbent on the prosecutor to establish that the woman *was pregnant* during such a period, as to have rendered the birth of a living child *possible*.[3] If

---

[1] 49th George III. c. 14.—[2] Hume, i. 293.—[3] Ibid.

the pregnancy, therefore, has only continued such a time as to occasion a miscarriage, or a premature and not living birth, at four or five months, it will be fatal to the case.[1]

Proof of the pregnancy during such a period as *might* have occasioned a living birth, is chiefly drawn from the appearance of the child or of the mother. Both are extremely delicate and difficult subjects. In the case of Smith, November 1761, the proof of the *corpus delicti* rested solely on the appearance of the woman's person. The symptoms proved were, that the pannel had milk in her breasts; that she had used means to put it away; and that she had, for some time previous to the birth, the appearance of a pregnant woman. The jury found the libel not proven.[2] Again, in the case of Ferguson, Glasgow, autumn 1809, the pannel's bulk had been observed for some time to have gradually increased, when all at once it diminished. Suspicion having arisen, the usual marks of a recent birth were discovered on her person, viz. the areola, or brown circle round the nipple, marks of tension round the belly, the parts of generation swelled, milk at the breasts, and some discharge going on from the vagina. These symptoms were proved by medical evidence never to *concur*, except in case of a birth, though they are often found taken separately, without that having taken place. On the other hand it was proved that, sixteen months before, she had had obstructions, which were removed, without any child having appeared. The jury found the pannel not *guilty*,[3] a conclusion hardly warranted by the doubtful state of the evidence.

3. It is not incumbent on the prosecutor to prove that the child was born *alive;* but, having established the mother's pregnancy for such a time as rendered a living birth *possible,* she is bound to shew that her issue was still-born, and certainly did not perish from neglect in the birth.

The presumption established by the statute, is by no means that the child *was killed* by its mother, after being born alive, for that would amount to child-murder; what it presumes,

---

[1] Hume, i. 293.—[2] Burnett, 574.—[3] Ibid.

from the concurrence of the requisites it enumerates, is, that the child perished either from neglect or inattention. The prosecutor, therefore, has done all that is incumbent on him, when he has established that the pannel was pregnant for such a time, as rendered a living birth possible; that she called for no assistance at the birth, and that the infant was found dead or was amissing. He need not go farther, and certainly it is not required to prove that the child was born alive, nor is it usual to do so, unless the charge of murder at common law, is intended to be insisted in.[1] But if the pannel bring forward credible evidence that her labour was brought on [    ]ident, and premature, and that the *fœtus* was previously destroyed in the womb, she is entitled to an acquittal.[2] Nay, it would rather appear that the same judgment must be given where the evidence goes to establish that the child was merely premature and still-born. Accordingly, in the case of Aurora Macleod, Inverness, September 1815, the pannel confessed that she had concealed her pregnancy, and did not call for assistance at the birth, and that the child was six weeks before its time, and *still-born* The case was certified for the opinion of the whole Bench, but no judgment was delivered, probably from an impression on the prosecutor's part that the case was untenable, and to this lenient construction Baron Hume has added the great authority of his opinion.[3]

4. The concealment must have continued during the whole course of the pregnancy, and down to the death or disappearance of the child, without disclosure to a single individual.

The prosecutor cannot be required to *prove* concealment · it is sufficient for him to allege it, and, like any other negatives, the proposition that she *did not reveal* her pregnancy, proves itself, unless disproved by contrary evidence, that she did.[4] But it will be a sufficient defence, if it appear that she revealed her condition to *any one individual*, if that disclosure be duly established. Accordingly, in the case of Isobel Taylor, March 4. 1709, the defence was sustained, that the pannel had revealed her pregnancy to one woman, who gave her lodging in

[1] Burnett, ι. 297.—[2] Ibid.—[3] Hume, l. 298, Burnett, 573.—[4] Hume, ι. 294

a barn the night before her delivery.[1]  In a former case this defence was overruled, when the disclosure to a single witness had occurred five weeks after conception; but if this proceeded on the circumstance of the disclosure being to one person, and not of the uncertainty of the communication at that early period of pregnancy, it is bad law.[2]

More difficulty occurs on the question, whether a disclosure *to the father* is sufficient to take the case from under the statute? In the case of Marion Burnet, March 5. 1709, the Court *sustained* " the defence proposed by the pannel, that she revealed being with child to the father during the time thereof, *and* that the child was not come to the full time when born.[3]"  In the case of Margaret Stewart, March 22. 1743, the father swore that the pannel had revealed her situation to him, but nevertheless she was convicted.  It does not appear, however, whether that was on the ground of the father being in that case unworthy of credit, or of a disclosure to him being no sufficient defence.[4]  Thus, on the whole, the weight of authority rather inclines to the humane construction ; and where to this is added, that the statute has made no distinction between a disclosure to the father, and any other individual, that the case, therefore, does not come within its letter if such a declaration has been made, that its spirit seems sufficiently evaded if the fact is made known to the person in the world who is under the strongest obligation to provide for the infant; and that penal clauses are not to be extended by implication beyond the law which they expressly include, it is thought that there can be little doubt what the decision of such a case will be, if it shall ever arise.

It makes no difference though the disclosure have not been voluntary, but unwillingly extorted by examination, or on a judicial declaration.  Still the pannel's defence is good, that even at the eleventh hour, and much against her will, she has taken her case out of the statute.[5]  Nay, it would rather appear that the same must hold, although the disclosure be in some degree doubtful, or expressed in ambiguous terms;[6] and, though it rest only on such an implied disclosure as may be gathered from openly, and before her family, providing childbed linens.[7]  Lastly, the concealment must continue down to

[1] Hume, i. 295.—[2] Ibid.—[3] Ibid.—[4] Ibid.—[5] Ibid. i. 296.—[6] Ibid.—[7] Burnett, 572.

the *death of the child*; even though the mother should not have divulged her situation prior to the birth, and called for no assistance on that occasion, still if she thus acknowledge and keep it, and it *afterwards* die, this acknowledgment, for how short a period soever, shall be held as atoning for her previous delinquency.[1]

5. To bring the case under the statute, the pannel must not have called for, and made use of, help or assistance in the birth.

However complete the former concealment may have been, if the pannel call for assistance in the birth, this, both on the reason of the thing and on the words of the statute, is a sufficient defence, for such a proceeding indicates the strongest intention not to deal unfairly by her offspring.[2]   On this point also the prosecutor is required to lead no proof; the negative that the pannel did not call for aid, proving itself, unless elided by positive proof that she did.   If the pains of childbirth come on unexpectedly, and the pannel send for assistance, but it arrives too late to save the life of the child, still having done what she could to repair her fault, she shall be held as liberated from the penalty of the statute.   Accordingly in the case of Stirling, November 1726, it was sustained as a sufficient defence " that the woman *called* for help in the birth." [3]

6. The statute applies indiscriminately to married and unmarried women.

Though the cases in which concealment are most likely to occur are those of unmarried women becoming pregnant, yet there are no words in the statute which restrict it to cases of that description, and it applies equally to both.   Accordingly in the case of Margaret Dickson, August 3. 1721, a libel, on the old act 1690, was found relevant against a married woman, and she was convicted and executed.[4]   Of course the same would hold with the more lenient statute, which has now come to supply its place.   In the case of Stewart, Aberdeen, spring 1786, a married woman was indicted under the old act, though

[1] Hume, i. 296 —[2] Hume, i. 297 —[3] Burnett, 573.—[4] Hume, i. 298.

the statutory charge was departed from for some reason not specified before the trial.[1] .

7. No person can be guilty of the statutory offence except as actor, the charge of art and part being inconsistent with the nature of the crime.

This follows evidently from the very nature of the charge; if any other person has been privy to the design, the statute is elided by that very circumstance, and therefore an indictment in such a case should never bear the charge of art and part.

In England it is provided by a special statute, that the trials of women charged with the murder of any issue of their bodies shall proceed by the same rules of evidence and presumption as are allowed to take place in respect to other trials for murder, " and that it shall and may be lawful for the jury, by whose verdict any prisoner charged with such murder as aforesaid shall be acquitted, to find, in case it shall so appear in evidence that the prisoner was delivered of issue of her body, male or female, which, if born alive, would have been bastard, and that she did, by secret burying or otherwise, endeavour to conceal the birth thereof; and thereupon it shall be lawful for the Court, before which such prisoner shall have been tried, to adjudge that such prisoner shall be committed to the common gaol or house of correction for any time not exceeding two years." [2] But this statute is so far defective and inferior to the Scotch act, that it makes no provision for a trial of the prisoner for concealment, independent of a charge of murder, which is accordingly incompetent by their law.[5] Under this statute it has been decided that a woman may be guilty of concealment, though from circumstances it appear probable that the child was still-born, and though the birth was probably known to an accomplice.

8. In cases of child-murder at common law, stronger evidence of *intentional* violence will be required than in other cases, it being established by experience that in cases of illegitimate birth, the mother, in the agonies of

---

[1] Burnett, 572.—[2] 43d Geo. III c. 58.—[3] Russell, i 476, *note*.

3

pain or despair, is sometimes the cause of the death of her offspring, without any intention of committing such a crime.

On occasion of a concealed or an illegitimate birth, the mother may be so overpowered by terror and despair, as to omit the care necessary to preserve the infant life; and the various accidents attending such a delivery may give the appearance of premeditated violence where none such had really been used.[1] Many pregnant women, under the influence of apprehension, become insane, and, from the state of mind they are in, would commit suicide, if they were not aware that such an action would lead to a detection of their shame. In this perplexity their distress of mind and body deprives them of all judgment, and they are delivered by themselves, sometimes dying in the agony of childbirth, and sometimes destroying their offspring without being conscious of what they are doing.[2] Accordingly it is a principle of law, that mere appearances of violence on the child's body are not *per se* sufficient, unless some circumstances of evidence exist to indicate that the violence was knowingly and intentionally committed; or they are of such a kind as themselves to indicate intentional murder. No stronger example of this can be figured than occurred in the case of Margaret Macintyre and Marjory Lennox, Glasgow, autumn 1829. These parties, mother and daughter, were indicted for the murder of the infant child of the latter, with an alternative charge against the daughter of concealment. It appeared in evidence that the only persons in the house at the time of the delivery were the two pannels, and the daughter of the former, who availed herself of her privilege of declining to give evidence against her parent. In these circumstances the case for the prosecution rested entirely on the appearances and disposal of the body, which were to the last degree suspicious. No assistance was called for in the birth; the pregnancy was concealed, and the body found some days after buried in the garden of the cottage where the parties dwelt. Considerable marks of violence were discovered on the neck, and in the inside of the throat and in the stomach were discovered several small pieces of straw, of the same kind as those which were in the bed where the birth took place. After the alarm was given, the mother absconded,

---

[1] Burnett, 571.—[2] Ibid

and was some weeks in concealment. The mother said in her declaration that the child died after birth; the daughter, that she heard it cry, and delivered it alive into her mother's hands. The medical evidence confirmed the statement that it had been born alive. In these circumstances there could be little doubt, morally speaking, that the child had been murdered; but on the ground that there was not distinct evidence which of the two pannels had been guilty of the act, that it did not necessarily imply a concert between them, but, on the contrary, might have been perpetrated by the one without the knowledge of the other; and that even the straw *might* have been forced into the throat and stomach during the agony of an unassisted birth, without the mother being aware of it, the Court recommended an acquittal of the charge of murder, and the daughter was convicted of the subordinate crime of concealment of pregnancy.[1]

Another case occurred at Aberdeen, in spring 1829, which also illustrates the difficulty of establishing the *corpus delicti,* without direct evidence of violence in cases of child-murder. This was the case of Catherine Butler or Anderson. It there appeared that the dead body of a child was thrown ashore by the river Deveron, a short way below Huntly. A few days before, the pannel was delivered of the child at Inverury, on the road to Aberdeen. Two days before it was discovered, she set out from Inverury to return to Huntly, with the child on her back, alive and well; and she was seen, with the child alive, proceeding on the road a few hours after, within nine miles of Huntly. Some persons who afterwards saw her on the road, observed that she had only a small bundle in her hand, much smaller than a child, and she arrived with such a bundle at her own house. A report having got up that she had made away with her child, the officers came to her house: she at first offered to produce it, and said they would find it in a cellar below the house; afterwards she said she could not tell where it was, and made light of what had happened, saying she had done no more than many married and unmarried had done before her. In her first declaration she said she was delivered near Aberdeen, and gave her child to a beggar-woman, and never saw it again; in her second, that it died of cold on

---

[1] Unreported.

the road from Inverury to Huntly, and that she threw it into the Deveron, and that the child there found was hers. It was proved to have been so by the witnesses who saw its dress at Inverury, and recognised the articles found on the child in the river. On the other hand, it appeared that the pannel had been kind to her child at Inverury, and that it was a cold day, with showers of sleet, when she was on the road, and that the infant might easily have perished of cold on its mother's back. In these circumstances there were the highest grounds of suspicion against the pannel; but on the principle that there was no decisive evidence that the death was not owing to natural causes, and that the subsequent concealment and false stories might have arisen from the desire to conceal an illegitimate birth, not to cover a murder, Lord Mackenzie directed an acquittal.[1]

One thing is very remarkable, and occurs in most cases of concealment and child-murder, viz. the strength and capability for exertion evinced by women in the inferior ranks shortly after childbirth—appearances so totally different from those exhibited in the higher orders, that, to persons acquainted only with cases among the latter, they would appear incredible In the case just mentioned, the mother, two or three days after her delivery, walked from Inverury to Huntly, a distance of twenty-eight miles, in a single day, with her child on her back. Similar occurrences daily are proved in cases of this description It is not unusual to find women engaged in reaping retire to a little distance, effect their delivery by themselves, return to their fellow-labourers, and go on with their work during the remainder of the day, without any other change of appearance but looking a little paler and thinner Such a fact occurred in the case of Jean Smith, Ayr, spring 1824.[2] Again, in the case of Ann Macdougal, Aberdeen, spring 1823, it appeared that the pannel, who was sleeping in bed with two other servants, rose, was delivered, and returned to bed, without any of them being conscious of what had occurred.[3] Instances have even occurred in which women have walked six and eight miles on the very day of their delivery, without any sensible inconvenience. Many respectable medical practitioners, judging from what they have observed among the higher ranks,

[1] Unreported.—[2] Unreported —[3] Unreported

L

would pronounce such facts impossible; but they occur so frequently among the labouring classes as to form a point worthy of knowledge in criminal jurisprudence; and to render perfectly credible what is said of the female American Indians, that they fall behind for a little, on their journeys through the forests, deliver themselves, and shortly make up to their husbands, and continue their journey with their offspring on their back.

The *exposure* of children, though not followed by fatal consequences, is of itself an offence cognizable in criminal courts.[1] If the child die, though by accident only, if it be an accident *connected* with the exposure, as by being trodden under foot by cattle, or rode over by a carriage, it will amount at the very least to culpable homicide;[2] if by such an one as was the *inevitable* consequence of the exposure, as by the rising of the tide above where the child was placed, to murder.[3] Thus, in the case of Isobel Kilgour, July 26. 1754, the libel was laid as for murder, on the charge that she had stuffed her infant, with its head foremost, into a hole, and gathered the sand about the mouth, although, owing to an error in the verdict, she escaped a capital sentence;[4] while in the case of Mary Graham, December 21. 1703, a libel was sustained as relevant for culpable homicide only, where the crime consisted in exposing a child naked in a field, where it was afterwards found dead.[5] More lately, in the case of David Buchanan, June 28. 1824, a charge of exposing a child simply in a whin-bush in a park in the parish of Strathmiglo, though death did not follow, was sustained as relevant, and the pannel was convicted and sentenced to six months' imprisonment.[6] Janet Craig and William Craig, Stirling, April 1827, were convicted of exposing a child in a yard, in cold weather, and sentenced to the same punishment.

The punishment for concealment is imprisonment: in most cases it is for a short period, from three to six months; but in aggravated cases, and especially where there is reason to believe that actual violence has been used, it is much longer,—from nine to eighteen months.

---

[1] Hume, i. 299.—[2] Ibid.—[3] Ibid.—[4] Ibid.—[5] Ibid.—[6] Unreported. A prior indictment against the same party was found irrelevant at Perth, April 1824, on an objection to the specification of the *locus*

# CHAPTER IV

## OF ATTEMPTS TO MURDER, AT COMMON LAW AND UNDER THE STATUTES

ATTEMPT at murder is an offence at common law, though to the effect only of inflicting an arbitrary pain.[1] It may be committed either by actual violence or by the secret administration of poison, and consequently gives rise to many nice and difficult questions as to the evidence requisite to convict of the murderous intent, and the length to which the attempt must have gone, to constitute the crime.

1. In judging of the intention of an accused who has committed an aggravated assault, the same rules are to be followed as in judging of the intent in actual murder, viz. that a ruthless intent, and an obvious indifference as to the sufferer, whether he live or die, is to be held as equivalent to an actual attempt to inflict death.

When a person stabs another in a vital part with a knife or sword, or when he discharges a loaded pistol at his head or body, it is impossible that he can be considered as actuated by any thing short of a mortal intent. It is nothing to the purpose that the sufferer has not actually died: if the act has been such as *might*, and frequently *does*, produce fatal effects, and, in consequence thereof, the person assaulted has run the hazard of his life, the intentions of the assailant must be judged of, as if his violence had produced its full consequences.[2] Accordingly, in all cases where an assault with lethal weapons, with intent to murder, has been proved, it has been visited by a very severe, generally the most severe punishment short of death. Thus in the cases of Alexander Syme, December 16. 1754, who

---

[1] Hume, 1 181, Burnett, 8.—[2] Hume, 1 328

L 2

was convicted of shooting at and wounding in the head; John Ogilvy, March 8. . 56, who was found guilty of stabbing in the belly; and Thomas Young, July 11. 1771, who was convicted of stabbing a person in the side as he lay asleep,—transportation for life was inflicted.[1]

A case of a very aggravated description occurred at Glasgow in April 1825, which was the immediate cause of the statutes to be immediately noticed being passed. This was the case of John Kean, who was convicted of discharging loaded fire-arms with intent to murder, at a weaver of the name of William Graham, whom he wounded in the most dreadful manner in the back, and maimed for life. The pannel belonged to a party of weavers who had struck work for an advance of wages, and he fired a pistol loaded with swan shot at the poor man on the public street, within a few yards of his body, because he had taken work at a lower rate of wages than the combination thought fit to prescribe. Several eye-witnesses having deponed to the commission of the crime, he was convicted and sentenced to be scourged, and transported for life, which was carried into execution, although his counsel Mr Cockburn strongly contended that the fact of the pistol having been loaded with swan shot, instead of ball, indicated an intention to maim rather than utterly destroy.[2] In like manner, in the case of William Macgarvie, Glasgow, September 1823, the pannel was convicted of stabbing another person on the side with a large butcher's knife, and sentenced to be publicly whipped and transported for fourteen years, which was carried into full execution His counsel strongly contended that stabbing in the body did not necessarily infer a murderous intent, but the presiding judge, Lord Hermand, holding the knife in his hand, asked the jury what intent he supposed the man would have who plunged that in his belly, and thereby put an end to such senseless distinctions. In the case of Archibald Knox, Glasgow, September 1828, the pannel was convicted of assault and stabbing, with intent to murder, and sentenced to seven years' transportation.[3] In the case of Mysie Brown, 13th March 1827, who was convicted of assault with intent to murder her husband, when lying asleep in bed, by hanging, eighteen months' hard labour in bridewell was only inflicted

[1] Hume, 1 328, 329 —[2] Unreported.—[3] Unreported

in consequence of a recommendation to lenity from the jury.[1] And in the case of Mary Ann Alcorn, 18th June 1827, on a conviction of " attempt to commit murder by the administering deleterious and poisonous drugs," was the crime charged; but the pannel being convicted only of the administering drugs, without the intent to murder, hard labour in bridewell for twelve months was inflicted.[2]

2. An attempt to commit homicide, however clearly established, does not necessarily infer an intent to murder, because the circumstances may be such as render it only culpable or justifiable; and the punishment must be proportioned to the magnitude of the offence.

If the situation of the parties during the scuffle has been such that the pannel, had the wounded man died, would have been guilty of culpable homicide only, he is entitled to the benefit of the same extenuating circumstances in diminishing the extent of his punishment, if of justifiable homicide, in altogether removing it. The same rules, therefore, must be followed in this department which have been the subject of so ample a commentary in the chapters relating to the more serious cases of homicide. It is sufficient to observe in general, therefore, that words will in no case justify blows, nor a blow with the fist or a stick, the use of lethal weapons, and that wounding with such instruments will then only be considered justifiable when matters have come to that pass, *morti proximum*, as to leave the person assaulted no reasonable prospect of escape but in their immediate use.

3. In attempts at murder, the crime is to be held as completed if the pannel has done all that in him lay to effect it, although, owing to accident or any other cause, the desired effect has been prevented from taking place.

If a person fire a pistol at his neighbour's head, but it miss fire, or the ball does not hit the object at which it was directed; or he strike with a dagger, but it light on a button and produce no injury, still the offender has done all that he could

[1] Syme, 152.—[2] Syme, 223

to effect his purpose, and he shall be judged guilty of attempt
to murder. Accordingly, in the case of Hume and Justice,
July 30. 1744, the libel was laid as for an attempt to murder,
in consequence of discharging a pistol which missed its aim.[1]

But farther, the crime is committed in cases where the attempt has not proceeded this length, *si deventum sit ad actum
maleficio proximum;* if the man have done that act, or part of
an act, by which he meant and expected to perpetrate his
crime. Thus, one who mingles poison with a draught or ba-
sin of liquid, and offers the contents to the victim, has done
his part in the crime as completely as when it is actually swallowed.[2] Accordingly in the case of Walter Buchan, January
1728, an attempt to commit poison, through the hand of an
ignorant person, was sustained as a relevant charge;[3] and in
the case of Roderick Dingwall, January 12. 1818, the charge
of "*attempting to prevail* upon John Gordon Robertson, surgeon
in Tain, to enter into a conspiracy to commit murder, by furnishing poison for that purpose," was found relevant to infer
an arbitrary punishment.[4] The pannel had there induced the
surgeon, who pretended to comply, to furnish him with doses
of arsenic to be administered to his wife, to act as medicines,
and also to visit the woman, and advise her to take the medicines which should be furnished by her husband. In the case
of Nicolson and Maxwell, January 1694, the act of *furnishing
poison* to destroy a certain woman, in conjunction with a deep
and complicated conspiracy to fix a charge on her of a conspiracy to murder her husband, were found relevant even to
infer the pain of death.[5] Lastly, in the case of Janet Ramage,
28th December 1825, it was sustained as a relevant charge,
" attempting to commit murder by means of poison," and
the administering any deleterious or injurious liquid or substance, with the wicked and felonious intent of doing a great
bodily injury. It was there stated in the minor, " that having found a tea-pot full of tea standing by the fire-place
in Margaret Macarthur's kitchen, and placed there for the
purpose of being drank by her at breakfast, she the pannel
put a quantity of oil of vitriol into the said tea-pot, and left
the said tea-pot there, in order that the same might be drank
by the said Margaret Macarthur on the said day." The trial
was prevented by an objection to the pannel's copy of the list

---

[1] Hume, 1 27.—[2] Ibid.—[3] Ibid.—[4] Ibid. 1, 28.—[5] Ibid. 1. 29

of assize; but this finding on the relevancy is decisive evidence of the rule of law on the subject. The attempt to poison, therefore, is held to be completed when the poison is mingled with the food which is *intended to be taken*, though it never actually enter the intended victim's lips.[1]

Whether the mere purchase of poison, or the mixing it up *with a view to mingling it* with the food that is intended to be taken, are to be taken as a complete commission of the crime, seems much more doubtful. In other departments of law the analogous cases are against such a construction. An incendiary letter written, but not sent or disclosed, a libel lying in the author's desk not published, a letter offering a bribe and inclosing the bank-notes, but still in the pocket of the writer, are no points of dittay:[2] nay, even a forged bank-note, though completed, is not the ground of punishment at common law, if not uttered.[3] Judging from these principles, there seems good ground to distinguish between those cases where the person meditating poison has merely purchased and mixed up the materials with that view, and those where he has actually *put them out of his hands*, and Providence or fortune only have prevented the effect. The one case is analogous to an incendiary letter written, but still in the pocket; the other, to such a letter put into the post-office, but intercepted on its route by some supervening accident.

By the common law of England, attempt at murder is considered as a misdemeanor of the highest kind.[1] But the great danger of such offences has rendered them the subject of a variety of penal statutes, which have been lately adopted with some slight variations into the Scotch law.

By the 6th Geo. IV. c. 126, intituled " an act for the more effectual punishment of attempts to murder in certain cases in Scotland," it is enacted, that if any person shall, within Scotland, wilfully, maliciously, and unlawfully present, point, or level any kind of loaded fire-arms at any of his Majesty's subjects, and attempt, by drawing a trigger, or in any other manner, to discharge the same at or against his or their person or persons; or shall wilfully, maliciously, and unlawfully stab or cut any of his Majesty's subjects with intent in so doing, or by means to murder or to maim, disfigure or disable such his Ma-

---

[1] Hume, i. 29.—[2] Ibid.—[3] Ibid.—[1] East. i 411, Russell, i 585.

jesty's subject or sub  ts, or with intent to do some other
grievous bodily harm to such his Majesty's subject or subjects;
or shall wilfully, maliciously and unlawfully administer to, or
cause to be administered to or taken by any of his Majesty's
subjects, any deadly poison or other noxious and destructive
substance or thing with intent thereby to murder or disable
such his Majesty's subject or subjects, or with intent to do
some grievous bodily harm to such of his Majesty's subject or
subjects; such person being lawfully convicted of any of the
aforesaid acts, shall be held guilty of a capital crime, and receive
sentence of death accordingly.    By section 2. it is enacted,
" That if any person in Scotland shall wilfully, maliciously
and unlawfully throw at or otherwise apply to any of his Majesty's subject or subjects any sulphuric acid, or other corrosive
substance, calculated by external application to injure the human frame, with intent in so doing, or by means thereof, to
murder or to maim, disfigure, or disable such his Majesty's
subject or subjects, or with intent to do some other grievous
bodily harm to such of his Majesty's subject or subjects, and
where, in consequence of such acid or other substance being so
wilfully, maliciously, and unlawfully thrown or applied with
intent as aforesaid, any of his Majesty's subjects shall be maimed, disfigured or disabled, or receive other grievous bodily
harm; such person being thereof lawfully convicted, shall be
held guilty of a capital crime, and shall receive sentence of
death accordingly: Provided always, that if it shall appear
upon the trial of any person accused of any of the aforesaid
offences, that, under the circumstances, if death had ensued,
the acts done would not have amounted to the crime of murder, such person shall not be held guilty of a capital crime, or
be subject to the punishment aforesaid; and provided farther,
that nothing contained in this or in any other statute shall be
held to affect the power of the prosecutor to restrict the pains
of law." [1]

No person has yet been executed under this statute, but
numerous prosecutions have taken place under it, and great
numbers of persons transported under its sanction.    On 17th
December 1827, Euphemia Macmillan was found guilty of
the statutory offence as libelled, and sentenced to death, but

[1] 6th Geo IV c 126

recommended to mercy. She had thrown a quantity of sulphuric acid in a man's face and eyes, and he died in consequence; but the charge of murder, which also was contained in the libel, was departed from in consequence of the death of the deceased being owing not to the natural consequences of the injury, but to erysipelas following *the bleeding*, which was deemed necessary. She was transported for life in pursuance of a pardon from the Crown.[1] On 28th November 1825, James Gowans was convicted under the statute, of cutting and wounding John Pryde with the blade of a razor upon the right shoulder or arm, and both wrists, with intent, as laid in the statute. He was transported seven years.[2]

A very atrocious case under this act occurred at Glasgow in autumn 1829. This was the case of James Maccumming and James Maccartney, who were indicted for ravishing a young woman in a close of Bridgeton, near Glasgow, and afterwards inflicting a severe wound in the interior of the vagina with the design of occasioning death, and concealing the commission of the original crime. The *corpus delicti* was clearly proved, and the girl swore positively to the commission of the crime by both the prisoners in a particular close, which she specified. She was seen on the night libelled going in that direction over the bridge leading towards the close, about ten minutes before the time she fixed on for the perpetration of the crime, and there were suspicious circumstances attending the situation and conduct of the pannels when apprehended the same night, which were strongly corroborative of their guilt. On the other hand, it was proved by a mass of overwhelming testimony, that no alarm or scuffle was heard in the close that night, and that vehement cries were heard at the time of the crime near the jail, on the opposite side of the water. It would appear, therefore, that the girl, from forgetfulness, confusion, or some other cause, had fixed on a wrong *locus*, and the jury, at a loss how to explain the matter, by a plurality of voices found the libel not proven.[3]

Several other convictions under the same statute have taken place, which it is unnecessary to notice more particularly, as it was only enacted for five years, and is now repealed by the 10th Geo IV. c 38, which forms the subsisting law on the subject, and is perpetual

---

[1] Hume, i 328.—[2] Ibid.—[3] Unreported

By this statute it is enacted, " That from and after the passing of this act, if any person shall, within Scotland, wilfully, maliciously, and unlawfully shoot at any of his Majesty's subjects, or shall wilfully, maliciously, and unlawfully present, point, or level any kind of loaded fire-arms at any of his Majesty's subjects, and attempt by drawing a trigger, or in any other manner, to discharge the same at or against his or their person or persons; or shall wilfully, maliciously, and unlawfully stab or cut any of his Majesty's subjects, with intent in so doing, or by means thereof, to murder or to maim, disfigure or disable such his Majesty's subject or subjects, or with intent to do some other grievous bodily harm to such his Majesty's subject or subjects; or shall wilfully, maliciously, and unlawfully administer, or cause to be administered to or taken by any of his Majesty's subjects, any deadly poison or other noxious and destructive subject or thing, with intent thereby, or by means thereof, to murder or disable such his Majesty's subject or subjects, or with intent to do some other grievous bodily harm to such his Majesty's subject or subjects; or shall wilfully, maliciously, and unlawfully attempt to suffocate, or to strangle, or to drown any of his Majesty's subjects, with the intent thereby, or by means thereof, to murder or disable such his Majesty's subject or subjects; or with intent to do some other grievous bodily harm to such his Majesty's subject or subjects; such person so offending, and being lawfully found guilty, actor, or art and part, of any of the several offences herein before enumerated, shall be held guilty of a capital crime, and receive sentence of death accordingly.

2. " That if any person in Scotland shall, from and after the passing of this act, wilfully, maliciously, and unlawfully throw at or otherwise apply to any of his Majesty's subjects any sulphuric acid, or other corrosive substance calculated to injure the human frame, with intent in so doing, or by means thereof, to murder or to maim, disfigure or disable such his Majesty's subject or subjects, or with intent to do some other grievous bodily harm to such his Majesty's subject or subjects, and where, in consequence of such acid or other substance being so wilfully, maliciously, and unlawfully thrown and applied with intent as aforesaid, any of his Majesty's subjects shall be maimed, disfigured, or disabled, or shall receive other grievous bodily harm, such person being thereof lawfully found

guilty actor, or art and part, shall be held guilty of a capital crime, and receive sentence of death accordingly.

" Provided always, that if it shall appear upon the trial of any person accused of any of the several offences herein before enumerated, that, under the circumstances of the case, if death had ensued, the act or acts done would not have amounted to the crime of murder, such person shall not be held guilty of a capital crime, or be subject to the punishment aforesaid; and provided also, that nothing contained in this or any other statute shall be held to affect or impair the power of the prosecutor to restrict the pains of law " [1]

The principal points to be noticed in thi  statute are—

1. That the clause declaring it capital  discharge, or attempt to discharge, by drawing the trigger, any loaded fire-arms at any of the lieges, *does not require* the intent to murder, or maim, disfigure, or disable. This intent is *inferred* in the statute from the  tempt to make such use of fire-arms, contrary to what is provi  d in regard to all the other offences which it enumerates.

2. That the clauses regarding the cutting, stabbing, and poisoning, *does require* this intent, and also that these attempts should have gone the length of actually reaching the person aimed at, as by actual cutting or stabbing, or the administration of poison. There seems nothing in the statute which warrants the opinion, that under it any person could be indicted for aiming a blow which did not take effect, or putting poison in the way which had not been swallowed. In this respect the clause regarding shooting is different from the others; for it declares it sufficient to bring the case within the statute, if the trigger of a loaded gun is drawn, though the piece does not go off.

3 That the clause regarding throwing sulphuric acid or corrosive acid requires, as a condition of its application, that, in addition to the acid being thrown with the intent specified, it shall have taken effect upon the person against whom it was directed, and shall have " maimed, disfigured, or disabled " him, or inflicted " some other grievous bodily harm." The mere throwing the acid, therefore, or its burning or destroying the dress, will not bring the case within the statute, some serious injury to *the person* is indispensable to its application.

4. That the clause regarding attempts to suffocate, strangle,

---

[1] 10th Geo. IV c 38.

or drown, requires only the application of personal violence, with the intent to murder, maim, or seriously injure, and does not also require serious injury to the person. It will be sufficient, therefore, if the accused have laid hold of another, and attempted to throw him into a draw-well, or deep river, or has strived to strangle or suffocate him, although no lasting injury at all has resulted from these nefarious attempts.

5. That the effects of such circumstances appearing on the trial as would have lowered the crime from the rank of murder, had death followed, is not to render the statute inapplicable, but merely to withdraw its capital sanction, leaving the statute in full vigour to the effect of authorising the infliction of an arbitrary punishment.

The 43d Geo. III. c. 58, commonly called Lord Ellenborough's act, provides, " That if any person or persons shall, either in England or Ireland, wilfully, maliciously, and unlawfully shoot at any of his Majesty's subjects; or shall wilfully, maliciously, or unlawfully present, point, or level any kind of loaded fire-arms at any of his Majesty's subjects, and attempt, by drawing a trigger, or in any other manner to discharge the same against their persons; or shall wilfully, maliciously, and unlawfully stab or cut any of his Majesty's subjects, with intent in so doing, or by means thereof, to murder or rob, or to maim, disfigure, or disable such his Majesty's subject or subjects, or with intent to do some other grievous bodily harm, or with intent to resist, obstruct, or prevent the lawful apprehension and detainer of the person or persons so stabbing or cutting; or shall wilfully, maliciously, and unlawfully administer, or cause to be administered, to or taken by any of his Majesty's subjects any deadly poison, or other noxious or destructive substance or thing, with intent that such his Majesty's subject or subjects thereby to murder, the person or persons so offending, their councillors, aiders, and abettors shall be and are hereby declared felons, and shall suffer death, as in cases of felony, without benefit of clergy." And then follows a clause that, " if such acts of stabbing or cutting were committed under such circumstances as that, if death had ensued therefrom, the same would not in law have amounted to murder, then the person so indicted shall be held to be not guilty of the felonies whereof they have been indicted, but shall be acquitted." [1]

[1] 43d Geo. III. c. 58.

From this quotation it appears that the English statute differs from the Scottish, framed upon its model, chiefly in the following particulars:

1. The English statute applies to assault with intent to *rob*, as well as murder or maim, while the Scotch applies to the latter of these only.

2. That the Scotch statute embraces attempts to murder by drowning, strangling, or throwing sulphuric acid, which is not the case with the English.

3. The English act applies to stabbing, or cutting with intent to resist the apprehension of the person having committed such an offence, which is not the case with the Scotch.

Under Lord Ellenborough's Act it has been held, that the loading must be of such a kind, as was capable, when discharged, of doing the mischief intended;[1] but that, if the loading be with paper and powder only, yet if it be fired so near, or in such a direction as to murder or maim, the statute applies.[2] But if the gun, though loaded, was not primed, it is not within the statute, for it is not capable of doing the mischief intended.[3] Striking on the face, with the sharp or claw end of a hammer, has been held sufficient to render the statute applicable,[4] but not with the blunt end, or with a square iron bar, or with the metal scabbard of a yeomanry sword, the sword being sheathed at the time, nor with the handle of a windlass.[5] But if cutting be inflicted, the case is within the statute, though the instrument used was not properly adapted for that purpose, or though the violence used was intended for a different object, as breaking the head, or lacerating, instead of effecting an actual incision.[6]

Cutting a child's private parts, so as to enlarge them for the time, is the infliction of a grievous bodily injury, though the wound be not dangerous, and though the ulterior object be the perpetration of a rape; yet, as the means employed are the infliction of a severe bodily injury, the case is within the statute.[7] If the intent laid be to disable, it must be a permanent disability, and not merely one which is temporary, or intended to prevent apprehension or pursuit,[8] but if the act done be in reality a grievous bodily injury, the fact of its having been in-

[1] Russell, 1 597.—[2] Rex v Kitchen, 1805, Russell, 1 596.—[3] Russell, 1 597.—[4] Ibid.—[5] Ibid—[6] Rex v. Hayward, Russell, 1. 598.—[7] Rex v. Cox, Russel, 1 598.—[8] Rex v. Boza, Russell, 1. 599

flicted to prevent apprehension, will not take the case out of the statute, though the intent laid be to inflict grievous bodily harm; for the twelve Judges have held that if both intents existed, it was immaterial which was the principal and which the subordinate one.[1]

Where the point is whether the shooting was designed or accidental, it has been held by all the Judges, that evidence may be given to shew that the prisoner, at another time, had shot intentionally at the same person, the two acts being within a quarter of an hour from each other, and part of one and the same transaction.[2] Where the intent charged is to do grievous bodily harm, it is immaterial whether such harm has actually been done or not, and general malice is sufficient under the statute, without any particular ill-will at the person injured, or though the wound was intended for another person.[3] If several persons are out for the purpose of committing a felony, and, upon the alarm being given, they all run different ways, and one maim a pursuer, to avoid being taken, the others are not to be considered as implicated in that act; but if the prisoners came with the same illegal purpose, and all prepared and determined to resist, the act of one will fix guilt upon all.[1] Where a party is present aiding and abetting, it is not necessary that his should be the hand by which the injury is inflicted, and, therefore, where several persons were present, knowing and abetting where one fired, the Twelve Judges were unanimously of opinion that they were all brought under the statute.[5]

[1] Rex v Gillon, Russel. &c.'    [2] Rex v. Voke, Russell, i 600.—[3] Rex v. Hunt, Russell, i. 600.—[4] Rex v. White and Richardson, 1806, Russell, i. 602. —[5] Rex v. Towle and Others, Russell, i 603.

# CHAPTER V.

### OF ASSAULT AND REAL INJURY.

ASSAULTS are of various degrees of atrocity, according to the intent of the guilty party, the degree of injury which he has inflicted, and the quality or situation of the person assailed. Assaults with intent to murder have been already considered, both at common law and under the statutes. But besides this highest of all aggravations, assault may be accompanied by other intents or qualities, which magnify its atrocity, and are justly considered as increasing the amount of punishment by which it is to be visited.

1. The crime of assault is held to be committed, if violence against the person has been attempted, though it has failed in producing actual injury.

The crime of assault does not require for its completion the application of any actual violence to the person; it is sufficient if such was intended, and the individual aimed at has incurred alarm and apprehension on that account.[1] Thus the shooting at, or thrusting at with a sword, constitute the crime, though the pistol miss its aim, or the sword do not reach the person.[2] Farther, the same will hold if blows be struck with the fist at the person, though they fall short and do not take effect;[3] or even if a gun be levelled, although it be not primed or the trigger drawn. This last point was unanimously determined in an indictment for assault by the Court of Justiciary, upon a bill of suspension from a judgment of the Sheriff of Edinburgh, who held that a verdict finding the pannel guilty of assault, by levelling a gun which was not primed, and without any attempt to draw the trigger, was a good conviction.[4] Certainly

---

[1] Hume, i. 329.—[2] Ibid.—[3] Procurator-Fiscal of Forfarshire v Stewart, 16th November 1829.—[4] Procurator-Fiscal of Edinburgh v Hog, February 6 1831, unreported.

2

this was carrying the principle as far as it could well go: and a greater length than, but for that decision, would seem consistent with the distinction between the perpetration of a crime and the separate offence of attempt to commit it.

The rule is the same in England. An *assault* with them is the attempt or offer with force and violence to do a corporal hurt to another, as by striking at him with a stick or other weapon, or without a weapon, though the party striking misses his aim. So drawing a sword or bayonet, holding up the fist in a menacing manner, presenting a gun at a person within gunshot, pointing a pitchfork at a person within reach, or any similar act as denote an intention, coupled with ability to use actual violence, will be held to amount to assault.[1] But no words, how provoking soever, will amount to assault.[2]

2. In judging of the defence of provocation, the same rule is to be followed as in cases of homicide; viz. that words will not justify blows, nor blows with the fist the use of a lethal weapon.

No words, how violent or contumelious soever, will justify a violent invasion or battery of the person; the first blow is the material point to which the law looks, which immediately excites the most indignant feelings, and prompts by an impulse often irresistible to immediate retaliation.[3] Innumerable cases, accordingly, have occurred in which this defence has been either repelled as irrelevant, or passed over as altogether unworthy of notice:[4] November 7. 1712, Joseph Skinner; George Douglass, January 1725; Andrew Macpherson, January 13. 1755.[5]

But though words will never *justify* blows, or relieve from every species of punishment for the assault which follows, yet it is not to be understood that they will not sometimes *alleviate* the offence. Certainly it is not to be denied that violent verbal abuse, as it extenuates the guilt, so it may diminish the pains of assault. So it was found in the case of Alexander Lockhart, June 23. 1746, where a proof of reproachful language was allowed to the effect of alleviating the charge.[6] In

---

[1] Hawkins, i. c. 62, § 1; Blackett, 120, Russell i. 604.—[2] Ibid; Hawkins; Ibid.—[3] Hume, i. 333.—[4] Ibid.—[5] Ibid.—[6] Maclaurin, No. 51, Hume, i 334.

like manner, in the case of Ensign Monro and others, 9th December 1700, the defence that the pannel had been called the son of a whore, without any provocation, was sustained to the effect of *alleviating* the punishment.[1] In modern practice, the extent of verbal abuse which precedes an assault is frequently the subject of consideration in alleviating punishment, although, from the whole circumstances of the case being at once laid before the jury, there is seldom to be found an interlocutor of relevancy precisely defining its legal effect.

3. In all cases of assault, it is of the utmost importance to ascertain who struck the first blow ; and the party who receives it will be excused for retaliating, if he do not exceed the just and fair measure of resentment.

Common sense, not less than legal principle, require that a person who is assailed by actual blows should be permitted to defend himself; and if the assailant be injured in the struggle, he alone is answerable for the consequence.[2] So it was found in a great variety of cases given by Baron Hume;[3] but it is unnecessary to quote authority on a subject daily practised in all criminal courts.

But, though fully justified in retaliating, the pannel must not carry his resentment such a length as to become the assailant in his turn, as by continuing to beat the aggressor after he has been disabled or has submitted, or by using a lethal or ponderous weapon. as a knife. poker. hatchet. or hammer. against a fist or cane, or, in general, by pushing his advantage in point of strength or weapons to the uttermost. In such cases the defence degenerates into an aggression, and the original assailant is entitled to demand punishment for the *new assault* committed on him after his original attack had been duly chastised.[4] Accordingly, in the noted case of Captain Charteris, August 4. 1707, a violent assault with a horsewhip and a sword was found sufficiently elided by a box on the ear, and a seizure of the sword, " except as to the wounding with the sword."[5] So also, in the case of Alexander Haliburton, it was not found sufficient to exculpate that the pannel had been knocked down and pushed out of the room, in respect that he

[1] Hume, l. 334.—[2] Ibid.—[3] Ibid.—[4] Ibid. l. 335.—[5] Ibid.—[6] Ibid.

had taken too severe revenge by striking on the head and thrusting in the mouth with a staff shod with iron.[1]

In modern practice, instances daily occur of the application of this rule. Thus, in the case of James Brown, Aberdeen, April 1829, it appeared that the parties had an altercation in the evening, in the course of which blows were exchanged; but the pannel having in the middle of it struck with a knife, he was convicted, and sentenced to six months' imprisonment.[2]

 4. Nothing is relevant as an alleviation of an assault but what occurred *de recenti* before the injury which is the subject of inquiry; it being rather an aggravation than an alleviation of assault that it is committed in pursuance of an old grudge, and on a principle of revenge.

If the law allow retaliation, it is with reluctance, and out of regard to the frailty of human nature, which is apt to be overborne by the heat of blood on a sudden injury to the person. In no case, therefore, will the law pardon an assault which is committed *ex intervallo*, after lapse of sufficient time for Reason to have resumed her seat. In cases of homicide, wherever the injury has been occasioned by cold-blooded revenge, the case is deemed murder; and in like manner, in assaults, the appearance of a cold-blooded determination to wreak resentment is an aggravation of the offence.[3]

It is not to be supposed, however, that the rule is to be followed so strictly as to exclude the consideration of every thing which has occurred prior to the assault. There is a certain latitude in the legal phrase *ex incontinenti*, which makes it admissible to alleviate, if, in the whole circumstances of the case, the pannel was in unavoidable heat of blood when he struck, even although the provocation was not received at that very hour. " Dictio *incontinenti*," says Carpsovius, " non præcise de momento temporis est intelligenda, sed cum aliquo spatio temporis est accipienda, quod neque maximum neque minimum sit, et quod magis intellectu percipi, quam elocutione exprimi possit."[4]

In judging of the time within which proof of provocation

---

[2] Hume, i. 335.—[2] Unreported.—[3] Hume, i. 366.—[4] Carpsovius, pars i. quæst. 31 No. 10.

can be admitted, our courts have never gone beyond *a day* preceding the injury. To extenuate the guilt of an assault in the evening, Mr Lockhart was allowed to prove provocation given in the same morning; but no plea of that kind can be carried farther than such a latitude.[1] In the case of Home and Justice, July 30. 1744, a train of provocation for a long time was offered to be proved; but the interlocutor limited the proof to what occurred on the *two days* preceding the assault. Such a latitude as was there permitted would not probably be now allowed. In the case of Alexander Paterson, March 1790, the pannel alleged a series of provocations, by personal rudeness to himself, and a woman under his protection by oppressive legal proceedings; but these allegations the Court found " not relevant either to exculpate or alleviate."[2] In the case of J. Lockhart, June 23. 1746, the Court found, " for alleviating the libel, it relevant to prove all facts and circumstances that happened *the day* the criminal facts libelled are charged to have been committed.[3]" In modern practice, it is the invariable course of the Court, on the one hand, to prevent the prosecutor from proving any indications or intentions of violence on the pannel's part for any considerable time before the commission of the assault; and, on the other, to exclude from proof any allegations of provocation which is not so recent as to have occasioned allowable resentment in the pannel's mind at the time of the assault. Thus, in the case of John Ross, Inverness, April 1823, it was offered to be proved on the pannel's part that he had sustained material injury from the person assaulted for some days before the crime was committed; but this was stopped by the Lord Justice-Clerk Boyle, as tending to establish the motive of revenge, and so injure rather than benefit his defence.[4]

5. Discharging loaded fire-arms is regarded as a peculiar and highly aggravated species of assault, necessarily involving, in almost every case, the intent to murder, or such recklessness as is equivalent to it; and generally, where the injury has been serious, punished with transportation.

---

[1] Hume, i. 336.—[2] Ibid i. 337.—[3] Maclaurin, No. 51.—[4] Unreported

To discharge loaded fire-arms is an act of such extreme
peril, and so universally known to draw after it fatal or highly
dangerous consequences, that it is uniformly regarded as one
of the worst species of assault, and deserving of the very highest pains short of death even at common law.  It is immaterial
though the injury may have happened to be inconsiderable;
what law looks to is the peril of such an outrage, and the ruinous consequences which would ensue, if the mere attempt to
commit so atrocious an injury were not universally understood
to be the fit subject of signal punishment.  These principles
have been always attended to in our practice.

In the case of Charles Lamond and John Smith, July 17.
1826, discharging loaded fire-arms with intent to murder, especially where committed on officers acting in execution of
their duty, was punished by fourteen years' transportation.[1]
Again, in the case of James Gordon and William Gordon, the
pannels, upon a conviction of the same offence committed
against officers of the law, " and especially when committed
by a number of persons assembled with intent to obstruct officers of the revenue in the discharge of their duty," were sentenced, on 16th July 1827, by the High Court, to transportation for life.[2]  In the case of James Carson, January 14. 1831,
transportation for fourteen years was inflicted for the same offence.[3]  John Kean was, at Glasgow, in April 1825, sentenced
to scourging and transportation for life, in pursuance of conviction of a very aggravated charge of discharging loaded fire-
arms, with intent to murder, attended with the most destructive
consequences to the health of the victim of his cruelty.[4]

Where the act of firing, however, has taken place in consequence of an erroneous opinion in point of law as to the right
to fire on intruders or suspected thieves, a more lenient course
has been adopted by the Court.  Thus, in the case of Lieutenant Robertson, February 28. 1829, who was convicted
on his own confession of discharging loaded fire-arms at a
young man at the pavilion near Melrose, whom he heard among
the shrubbery at night, and took for a housebreaker, though
in reality he was come to court one of the servant maids, one
month's imprisonment in the Castle of Jedburgh was the sentence, in consideration of his having settled £700 in the pur-

[1] Unreported.—[2] Syme, 245.—[3] Unreported.—[4] Unreported.

chase of an annuity on the suffering party.[1] And, in the case of James Corbet, 13th March 1828, who was convicted at common law of discharging a fowling-piece loaded with small-shot at a boy who was trespassing on the estate, apparently in search of game, nine months' imprisonment only was inflicted, in consideration of the crime having been committed under an erroneous impression of duty, and of the excellent character of the accused.[2]

6. It is a legal aggravation of assault, if it be committed with bludgeons or other offensive and lethal weapons, and still more so if to the effusion of blood and danger of life.

It has become usual, in modern practice, to charge assault in every case of personal violence where death or mutilation has not followed, and to state the serious parts of the charge as *aggravations* of the simple crime. In this way the facts which have really occurred are brought before the jury, while at the same time the inconvenience is avoided of the whole charge being endangered, if part of the aggravations are not established. And it has become another beneficial consequence of this system, that the ancient statutes imposing heavy punishments upon particular kinds of violence have gone out of practice; and assaults of serious kinds are stated with aggravations in such a manner that it is in the power of the jury, by finding part proven and part not proven, to accommodate their verdict to the real delinquency of the case.

The most ordinary aggravation of simple assault is, when it is committed with offensive and lethal weapons, as with bludgeons, knives, hammers, axes, bottles, pokers, tongs, large stones, or any heavy, cutting, or dangerous instrument. And the instances are numerous where, on a conviction for such an assault, if the injury to the pannel has been serious, or his life endangered, transportation has followed. Thus, in the case of Henry Niven, Stirling, September 1823, it appeared that the prisoner, along with an associate who was fugitated, had laid wait for a drunken tailor, who was returning from Carron to Falkirk near the railway in that vicinity, and beat him so severely with bludgeons that his nose was broken, and he was reduced to a state of insensibility: for this premeditated and

[1] Unreported.—[2] Syme, 339.

ferocious assault he was sentenced to seven years' transportation.[1]   Again, in the case of Hector Monro, Inverness, spring 1829, the facts were, that the prisoner, along with a great number of his associates, commenced a violent assault on several persons in the streets of Wick and Pultney Town, in consequence of which one of them was left on the ground for dead, dangerously wounded, while others were hurt in a lesser degree: for this offence he was sentenced by Lord Mackenzie to seven years' transportation.[2]   In like manner, in the case of Benjamin Ross, 11th May 1824, the pannel was sentenced to transportation for life by the High Court for an assault with a pair of iron tongs on his wife, by which her life was endangered.[3]   In the case of George Lugton, March 13. 1831, the prisoner was convicted of assaulting his wife during a drunken fit with a glass bottle on the head, which rendered her insensible, and throwing his child upon the fire and burning its arms: he was transported for seven years.[4]   At Stirling, September 1826, Neil Macpherson was transported seven years, for cutting a woman in several places with a knife.   On 12th July 1825, Alexander Mackay was convicted of assaulting and stabbing a man in the streets of Edinburgh with a knife, for which he was transported for seven years, and publicly whipped.[5] John Macdonald, Glasgow, May 2. 1825, was transported for seven years, for an assault with bludgeons within a house in Airdrie, to the danger of life, accompanied by much riot and other violence.[5]   And in the case of Neil Macilroy, November 21. 1825, the prisoner was transported seven years, for an assault on a woman in a state of pregnancy, to the danger of life, by kicking her in the belly, and striking her on the back.[6]   In the case of Mary Thomson, December 18. 1824, seven years' transportation was inflicted for stabbing a butcher in the back, with a large knife, to the danger of life.[7]   In the case of Robert Butter, December 7. 1829, High Court, the prisoner was sentenced to seven years' transportation, for a violent assault on a child, whom he seized by the neck, and twice threw down a stair, to the imminent danger of its life.[8]   Peter White, Perth, autumn 1827, for a similar offence, received the same punishment.   And, at Glasgow, autumn 1823, John Shaw was sentenced to fourteen years' transportation for a brutal assault on his wife, especially by kicking her on the belly, which

[1] Unreported.—[2] Ibid.—[3] Ibid.—[4] Ibid.—[5] Ibid.—[6] Ibid.—[7] Ibid.—[8] Ibid.

caused a severe internal hæmorrhage, and endangered her life.[1] In like manner, in the case of Robert and Alexander Duncan, April 23. 1831, seven years' transportation was inflicted on two brothers, for a violent assault on a woman, accompanied by stabbing in the belly.

The punishment in these cases will not be deemed too severe, when it is recollected how slight is the shade of difference, in point of moral guilt, between a person who is guilty of a furious assault, and one who commits murder; and that no lesser criminality on the part of the prisoner, but the intervention of Providence or accident in the direction of the blow, or the strength of a bone, has saved him from answering with his life for the death of a fellow creature.

In cases of inferior atrocity, the usual course of punishment is imprisonment for various periods, according to the magnitude of the offence, accompanied often by hard labour, and generally caution to keep the peace, when the prisoner's circumstances are such as to enable him to find such security. To this, by the late statute, it is now added as an indispensable requisite, that, in default of finding caution, the Court shall specify the additional period for which the confinement is to continue, on expiry of which the pannel is to be liberated, though such caution shall not have been found; so that in no event is the imprisonment to endure beyond a specified time.[2]

Thus in the case of Janet Thomson, July 23. 1826, eighteen months' confinement and hard labour in bridewell were inflicted for having struck a fellow servant repeatedly on the face and temple with an Italian iron, by which she was knocked down, rendered insensible, and put in danger of her life.[3] In the case of James Simpson, Inverness, spring 1826, the pannel was sentenced to twelve months' confinement in jail, for a most cruel and barbarous assault on a woman, whom he kicked so violently on the belly, that her intestines burst through the vagina, and fell down to her feet. There were peculiar circumstances in that case, arising from character and an infant family, which rendered transportation not advisable, or it most certainly would have been inflicted.[4] Again, in the case of Alexander Snadden and others, June 14. 1825, twelve months' imprisonment was inflicted for an atrocious assault committed on a collier, in pursuance of the purposes of a combination, by

---

[1] Unreported.—[2] 9th Geo. IV. c. 29.—[3] Unreported.—[4] Ibid.

which the unfortunate man was cruelly injured on the head, and for some time was in imminent danger of his life. They pleaded guilty, otherwise sentence of transportation would certainly have been awarded by the magnitude of the case becoming known.[1] In the case of Alexander MacCaughie and James Brown, Dumfries, April 1824, six months' imprisonment was the sentence for an assault with the fist only, but of a serious kind, one of the injured parties having been rendered insensible for six weeks, during which time his life was in danger from concussion of the brain.[2] Again, in the case of James Coghill and George Murray, Ayr, spring 1830, the prisoners were sentenced to eighteen months' confinement in bridewell, for an assault with a glass bottle upon a workman who was going to his labour in the morning, whereby he was knocked down and severely cut, both prisoners having been previously convicted of that offence.[3] At Inverness, spring 1829, William Munro and others received twelve months' imprisonment for an assault with large stones on the head and body, though not to the danger of life.

Cases of a more trifling description are visited with punishment of a slighter kind, as imprisonment from a month to six months, fine, or even a simple obligation to keep the peace. And, in general, it is the disposition of our courts to make the duration of the imprisonment as brief as is consistent with the infusion of a salutary terror into the public for a repetition of the offence; and always to take into account the amount of confinement which the pannel has endured before trial, in determining its duration after sentence.

7. Intent to ravish is a most serious aggravation of assault, and such as generally subjects the crime to a much higher punishment than the actual amount of violence perpetrated would otherwise require.

Assault with intent to ravish is no doubt a substantive offence, and may be charged as such in an indictment. But the risk of drawing it in that manner consists in this, that if the intent be not established, the whole charge falls to the ground, and, thus the prisoner escapes without any punishment, although his guilt to a certain extent may be clearly established.

<hr>

[1] Unreported.—[2] Ibid.—[3] Ibid.

To avoid this inconvenience, the more advisable course is to charge the simple assault as the substantive offence, and the intent to ravish as the aggravation; by which means the first may be found proven by the jury, without the intent, or the whole charge may be established according to the weight of the evidence.

In cases of this description, the material thing is the intent manifested; and, therefore, although actual violence, by striking, knocking down, or otherwise maltreating, is a material and most aggravating feature of the case; yet the crime is completed if such violence have been used, or is intended to effect, and might have accomplished, the object, but for the resistance offered. If, therefore, the man have seized the girl, and thrown her on the ground, or on a bed, and used indecent liberties with her person, the *assault* is clearly established; if, *in addition* to this, he have taken down his breeches, or made evident preparations for carnal connexion, the intent to ravish is proved. But, from the mere fact of indecent liberties having been taken, as kissing, putting on the knee, or even lifting the petticoats, &c. the intent to *ravish* is not, among the lower orders, as a matter of course to be inferred, though without doubt they are strong circumstances to make out that intent; for the slightest acquaintance with criminal cases must be sufficient to shew, that such romping or indecent behaviour is by no means unusual among that class of society, when no intent to *ravish* exists.

From the earliest times assault with intent to ravish, when clearly established, and more especially when accompanied by brutal violence, has been very severely punished. Thus for this crime, on June 22. 1732, Matthew Foulden was scourged and banished the town of Jedburgh;[1] James Wilson, on July 15. 1813, was ordered to be scourged, and transported for seven years; and Alexander Mackivor, September 17. 1813, at Ayr, subjected to the same punishment.[2] In these two last cases the assault had been of a most outrageous kind. On 22d December 1817, William Macward, in pursuance of an assault with intent to ravish, was transported fourteen years At Inverary, September 1825, John Jameson was convicted of this crime, and sentenced by the High Court to seven years' transportation, on a certification.[3] At Inverary, in September

---

[1] Hume, i. 309.—[2] Ibid.—[3] Ibid.

1826, John Heale was sentenced to seven years' transportation for the same offence. He had met the woman on the road in Argyleshire, and, after using the most improper freedoms, pursued her into a pond, whither she had run to avoid his attempts.[1] At Dumfries, in autumn 1825, George Scott was sentenced to be flogged, and transported seven years, for an assault with intent to ravish, on the road in Ewesdale, attended with very aggravated circumstances; and, at the same place, Alexander Crombie was sentenced to transportation for the same period, in autumn 1826, for the same offence, without so much brutality.[2] Lastly, in the case of James Macgowans, March 14. 1831, the prisoner was ordered to be scourged through the burgh of Haddington, and transported seven years, for the same crime.[3]

It has always, and most justly, been considered as a very great aggravation of this offence, if it be committed upon a girl of tender years, both on account of the greater danger to an infant from such an attempt, and of the depraved disposition which it indicates to feel passion at all towards a child below the age of puberty. The punishment, in such cases, accordingly, has generally been proportionally heavy. In the case of Gylor, February 1642, on a verdict, finding that a girl of ten years of age had her privy parts lacerated on an attempt to commit a rape, the pannel was whipped and transported.[4] On 14th July 1821, William Montgomery was sentenced to transportation for life, for an assault on a girl of ten years of age with intent to commit a rape.[5] At Inverness, in spring 1823, William Ingram was transported for fourteen years, for a similar assault on a girl of nine years of age.[6] Malcolm Maclean, May 11. 1829, was transported for seven years for an attempt to ravish a girl of eleven years of age.[7]

In cases of inferior atrocity, and more especially where the intent to ravish has been unaccompanied by striking, or any other violence, excepting that which goes to the gratification of desire, or where the levity or indiscretion of the woman has afforded any countenance to the attempt made on her chastity, the punishment has occasionally been much more lenient. Thus at Aberdeen, spring 1826, John Wylie escaped with twelve months' imprisonment in Bridewell, on a confession of an assault with this intent, unaccompanied by any circum-

[1] Unreported.—[2] Ibid.—[3] Ibid.—[4] Burnett, 102.—[5] Hume, l. 309.—[6] Unreported.—[7] Unreported.

stances of aggravation; and, in the High Court, Paul Fraser, on July 13. 1825, was sentenced to the same punishment for the same crime, with the same mitigated features.[1]

In judging of the punishment to be inflicted for this offence, and more especially in determining whether the additional penalty of flogging is to be imposed, the great matter to ascertain is, whether any brutal violence has been used, and whether the conduct of the accused indicated utter recklessness as to the victim of his passion. Such conduct is not only a very great aggravation of the offence, but it affords the strongest evidence that the assault was really and wholly against the girl's inclination; since, whatever may be said of little reluctance to indecent liberties, or even actual connexion, one thing is perfectly certain, that no woman will consent to blows or ill usage of that description. When such treatment, therefore, is proved, and more especially where the woman's person, or the medical evidence, proves the existence of such violence, the Court have not only proof of the aggravating circumstances, but evidence of the best kind to substantiate the want of consent, which, in all cases of this sort, is the most difficult article of proof.

In considering the evidence in trials of this kind, the same caution is to be observed as in cases of actual rape, viz. that the charge is easily made, hard to prove, but harder still to disprove, and therefore, that the most conclusive evidence is requisite to establish that the attempted connexion was against the woman's consent. The mere fact of her having been found struggling, or crying out, when discovered by the witnesses, is not conclusive evidence of the whole having been contrary to her inclination; for it often happens, especially with young women employed in manufactories, that they retire to the country for the purpose of illicit connexion, and, when accidentally discovered, cry out and make a show of resistance in order to save their character. The great points to be looked to, therefore, are, 1st, Whether they made resistance and cried out *before* they were discovered, and, 2d, Whether they had received *blows and actual injury;* it being quite certain that at least that violence was inflicted against the will. The circumstance of early giving information is also material, but its ab-

---

[1] Unreported.

sence is by no means decisive; for many women, who have really suffered violence of this sort, decline to give information from a dread of exposure, which, to sensitive minds, is worse than death itself.

All difficulty, with respect to *consent*, is avoided in the case of an assault with intent to ravish a child below the years of puberty. It is held *præsumptione juris et de jure* that they cannot consent, and, consequently, an attempt to ravish such an infant requires no evidence of want of consent on its part.[1]

8. Assault, with intent to rob, is also a most serious aggravation of the offence, and such as generally leads to the punishment of transportation.

As the crime of robbery is one of a very heinous kind, and which generally is punished with the highest corporal pains, and never with less than transportation, so assault, with intent to commit that crime, is justly considered as one of the worst kinds of that offence.[2]

The intent to rob is to be established by such violence as clearly indicates a design to deprive the person assailed of his property, as putting the hand in the pocket, tearing at or snatching the watch, pulling at a bundle on his back, &c. But juries should be cautious in finding this serious aggravation proven, from the mere fact of such violence being proved during the scuffle, because it may often occur in the confusion of an assault, that such acts may take place without any serious intention to carry off property. But where such acts are proved during an assault, and any *previous* intention to commit depredation is established, they afford the best indication of the intent with which the violence was committed, and justly authorise a conviction of the assault with the aggravation.

9. Assault is aggravated when committed in pursuance of an intent to compel a rise of wages, or deter from working at a certain rate, or of a combination entered into for these illegal purposes.

Simple combination to procure a rise of wages is no longer a relevant article of dittay. By the 6th Geo. IV. c. 129, a

_____
[1] Hume, i. 303.—[2] Ibid. i. 329.

great variety of statutes against combinations among workmen for a rise of wages are repealed, and, after the specific repeal, the statute in general repeals " all enactments in any other statutes or acts, which, immediately before the passing of the 5th Geo. IV. c. 95, were in force throughout any part of the United Kingdom of Great Britain and Ireland, relative to combination to obtain an advance of wages, or lessen or alter the hours or duration of the time of working, or to decrease the quantity of work, or to regulate or control the mode of carrying on any manufacture, trade, or business, or the management thereof, or relative to combinations to lower the rate of wages, or to increase or alter the hours or duration of the time of working, or to increase the quantity of work, or to regulate or control the mode of carrying on any trade, manufacture, or business, or the management thereof, or relative to fixing the amount of the wages of labour, or relative to the obliging workmen not hired to enter into work, and every enactment extending or enforcing the said several enactments, shall be, and the same are hereby, repealed." [1]   By the same statute it is declared that meetings for settling the rate of wages to be received, or the hours of work to be employed, by the persons meeting, are legal; and that " persons so meeting for the purposes aforesaid, or entering into any such agreement as aforesaid, shall not be liable to any prosecution or penalty for so doing, any *law* or statute to the contrary notwithstanding." By the force of this clause the common, as well as the statute, law on this subject is repealed.

By the same statute provision is made for the punishment of those assaults by workmen, which too often form the disgraceful accompaniments of such associations.   Section 3. enacts, " That if any person shall, by violence to the person or property, or by threats or intimidation, or by molesting or in any way obstructing another, force, or endeavour to force, any journeyman, manufacturer, workman, or other person hired or employed in any manufacture, trade, or business, to depart from his hiring, employment or work, or to return his work before the same shall be finished, or prevent, or endeavour to prevent, any journeyman, manufacturer, workman, or other person not being hired or employed, from hiring himself to, or

---

[1] 6th Geo. IV. c. 129, § 2.

accepting work or employment from, any person or persons;
or if any person shall use or employ violence to the person or
property of another, or threats or intimidation, or shall molest
or in any ways obstruct another, for the purpose of forcing or
inducing such person to belong to any club or association; or
to contribute to any common fund, or to pay any fine or penalty, or on account of not belonging to any club or association,
or not having contributed, or refused to contribute, to any common fund, or to pay any fine or penalty; or, on account of his
not having complied, or refused to comply, with any rules, orders, or regulations made to obtain an advance or reduce the
rate of wages, or to lessen or alter the hours of working, or to
decrease or alter the quantity of work, or regulate the mode of
carrying on any manufacture, trade, or business, or the management thereof; or if any person shall, by violence to the
person or property of another, or by threats or intimidation,
or by molesting or in any way obstructing another, force, or
endeavour to force, any manufacturer or person carrying on
any trade or business, to make any alteration in his mode of
carrying on or conducting such manufacture, trade, or business; or to limit the number of his apprentices, or the number
or description of his journeymen, workmen, or servants; every
one so offending, or aiding, abetting, or assisting therein, being
convicted thereof in manner herein after mentioned, shall be
imprisoned only, or imprisoned and kept to hard labour for any
period not exceeding three calendar months." [1]    And the mode
of prosecution to warrant the infliction of this punishment
pointed out in the act, is by complaint on oath emitted within
six months of the commission of the crime, before one or more
Justices of the Peace, who is thereupon empowered to issue
his warrant for calling upon the person so charged to appear
before " any *two* such justices at a certain time and place specified," or at once to issue warrant for apprehending the person
so charged: and, upon his appearance, they are empowered
" to make inquiry touching the matters complained of, and to
examine into the same by the oath or oaths of *one or more* credible persons as shall be requisite, and to hear and determine
the matter of every such complaint " [2]

By these enactments a speedy and summary mode of prose-

---

[1] 6th Geo. IV. c. 129, § 3.—[2] § 7

1

cution was provided for offences of this frequent and dangerous
description, without the intervention of a jury, or of the delays
incident to the ordinary mode of trial.   But they did by no
means take away the ordinary cognizance which the common
law takes of such offences, or hinder them from being stated
as aggravations of an ordinary assault.   The cases have been
numerous, accordingly, both before and after the statute, in
which the intent of interfering with the free employment of
labour has been sustained as a most serious aggravation of
assault.

In the case of William Ewing, John Gourlay, and others,
Glasgow, April 1821, the crime charged was " assault, especially when committed by persons who have struck work in a
body, or in great numbers at one or nearly one and the same
time, on account of a reduction of their wages, or the prices of
their work, upon any other workmen or artificers willing to
work at reduced wages, with the intent of intimidating them
from so working."   The case was certified from the Circuit
Court to the High Court, and, on 19th November 1821, the
charge was found relevant.[1]

In the case of Alexander Mackay, Peter Macconochie, and
others, Glasgow, September 1823, the crime charged was " assault, and pouring vitriolic acid on the person and clothes of
the lieges, especially when done with the illegal, wicked, and
felonious intent of deterring any workman or workmen from
entering into the employment of any master, manufacturer, or
employer of operative workmen, or of compelling any workman or workmen to leave the employment of such master,
manufacturer, or employer, contrary to the inclination of such
person, or of controlling, thwarting, or counteracting any master, manufacturer, or employer of operative workmen, in the
choice of his workmen, or the wages he is to give, or the terms
on which he is to employ them, or of controlling, thwarting,
or counteracting any operative workman or workmen in the
choice of the master, manufacturer, or employer they are to
serve, or the wages they are to receive, or the terms on which
they are to be employed ; and more especially still, when done
by several persons acting in concert, and with the same illegal
and felonious intent of concussing, intimidating, or controlling

[1] Hume, i 329; Shaw's Cases.—[2] Unreported.

any master, manufacturer, or employer of operative workman
or workmen as aforesaid." This indictment was sustained as
relevant by the Lord Justice-Clerk and Lord Hermand, and,
after a long trial, the whole prisoners, six in number, were
convicted and sentenced to fourteen years' transportation. The
*species facti*, as it appeared on the proof, was, that the prisoners, who had an ill-will at a young man on account of his
working at a lower rate of wages than they had fixed on, enticed him into a public-house, where, after some conversation,
the candle was put out, and a vial of oil of vitriol was poured
on his back, which completely destroyed his coat and other
parts of his dress, but fortunately did not injure his skin: he
was at the same time struck with the fist on the eye, and beaten
about, but not materially injured. The Court, at pronouncing
sentence, declared, that if the destructive acid had burnt his
skin, they would, in addition to transportation, have inflicted
corporal punishment.[1]

In the case of John Kean and Daniel Lafferty, April 26.
1825, the crime charged was assault, especially when committed by discharging loaded fire-arms, and with intent to murder, to the effusion of blood and imminent danger of life, and
more especially when committed with the intent of deterring
any workman, &c. as in Alexander Mackay's case, already
given. Kean was convicted and sentenced to be flogged and
transported for life, and Lafferty, who had not fired the pistol,
but only concurred in the assault, was sentenced to eighteen
months' hard labour in bridewell.[2]

In the case of James Steel, Glasgow, April 1826, the pannel
was charged with assaulting, striking, and jumping on the body,
to the effusion of blood and serious injury to the person, especially when committed " with the wicked and felonious intent
of deterring the said Alexander Davidson and all others from
entering into the employment of the said James Lindsay Ewing, or of compelling him to leave the said employment, or of
controlling, thwarting, or counteracting the said James Lindsay
Ewing in the choice of the workmen he was to employ, or the
wages he was to give, or the terms on which he was to engage
them." He was convicted, and, on a certification to the High
Court, sentenced to twelve months' imprisonment.[3] This case

---

[1] Unreported.—[2] Ibid.—[3] Hume, i. 320.

was *subsequent* to the statute, declaring simple combinations not punishable, already quoted.

In the case of John Robertson, William Armstrong, Samuel Williamson, and others, Glasgow, April 1824, the crime charged was illegal combination or conspiracy to raise the wages of labour; or for the purpose of assaulting, maltreating, or employing others to assault or maltreat, masters or employers, workmen or artificers, for the purposes of such illegal combination or conspiracy; " as also illegal combination or conspiracy to shoot and put to death any of the lieges; as also the wickedly and maliciously writing and transmitting to any of the lieges letters containing threats of personal violence; as also the invading the houses of any of the lieges, and discharging loaded fire-arms into the same, or threatening violence and injury to the persons within the same." [1]   There can be no doubt that these crimes, with the exception of the more illegal combination or conspiracy to raise the wages of labour, are still undoubted articles of dittay; for the statute declaring simple combination not punishable, has not only made no alteration whatever either on the common or statute law, against acts of violence to forward the purposes of such combination or combinations, to carry into effect such violence, but has made new and important regulations for their summary conviction, when that method of prosecution is preferred.   In like manner, in the case of James Frew, James Pettegrew, and Thomas Allan, Glasgow, 23d April 1828, the pannels were convicted of " assault, especially when committed with iron tongs, paling, stobs, or knives, to the effusion of blood and serious injury of the person, and more especially when committed by invading and breaking into the houses of the lieges, with the wicked and felonious purpose of compelling any master manufacturer to dismiss certain persons from his employment, or of compelling any workman to leave the employment of their masters," and were sentenced to seven years' transportation each. [2]

10. Assault is aggravated by being committed on a magistrate, either when in the execution of his duty, or in contemplation of, or in revenge for, its discharge.

As law has imposed upon magistrates of every description

[1] Unreported.—[2] Ibid.

N

the important and often perilous duty of deciding the differences of the lieges, and maintaining the public peace, it is indispensable that it should protect their persons and property by high and peculiar pains. An assault upon a magistrate, therefore, for any matter connected with the discharge of his official duty, is justly regarded as a very serious offence, and, though not attended with severe corporal injury, is severely punished. Accordingly, in the case of Robert Laughlan, who was convicted of such an assault, committed against William Cunningham of Lainshaw, a magistrate of Ayrshire, at Ayr, September 1821, the pannel was sentenced to twelve months' imprisonment, and to find caution to keep the peace for five years [1] And, in the case of Robert Duncan, 3d December 1827, who was found guilty of an assault, by a blow with the fist, aggravated by being committed on a magistrate, on account of a judgment he had given, and more especially still by his having conceived previous malice and ill-will on that account, the pannel, on a confession of the assault, aggravated as libelled, but without the previous ill-will, was sentenced to six months' imprisonment.[2]

11. Assault is aggravated by being committed upon officers of the law in the discharge of their duty, or with a view to deter them from such discharge, or in revenge for their having performed it.

Cases under this head are among the most numerous which come under the cognizance of courts of justice. It is an acknowledged principle of the law, that, as soon as any statute has prescribed any regulation of trade, or granted any revenue to His Majesty, the common law extends its protection in a peculiar manner to the officers who are charged with the enforcement of it, and views as a higher offence any assault made with a view to obstruct him in the execution of his duty, or in revenge for his having done so.[3] The assaults upon excise and sheriff officers, on account of the invidious duty which they are called upon to discharge, occupy a large portion of the time even of our Supreme Courts; and it is of importance, therefore, to attend to the practice which has taken place in regard to them.

In the case of David Barnet and John Brown, 16th January

---

[1] Hume, i. 329.—[2] Syme, 280.—[3] Hume, i. 329.

1820, the pannels, upon conviction of an assault, which charged them with violently assaulting, beating, and wounding, to the effusion of blood, especially when committed upon an officer of the revenue, when employed in the execution of his duty," were sentenced to eighteen months' imprisonment.[1] A similar case, that of James Clark, Perth, September 1827, was visited with imprisonment for the same duration. For a much slighter assault committed to the effusion of blood " against an officer of the revenue, employed in the execution of his duty, or against any person assisting him therein," John Fraser was sentenced to three months' imprisonment at Inverness, April 1823.[2] In the case of Joseph Watson, John Gordon, and William Bain, Aberdeen, April 12. 1823, the pannels, for an assault on excise-officers attempting to seize illicit whisky, on a road near the Dee, were sentenced to six months' imprisonment each.[3] In the case of Alexander Gordon and Donald Macpherson, April 21. 1826, Perth, the prisoners, upon a conviction of assaulting revenue officers, employed in the execution of their duty, especially when committed with bludgeons, and to the effusion of blood and serious injury of the person, were sentenced to twelve months' imprisonment, besides security to keep the peace.[4] George Young, convicted of assaulting officers of excise in the execution of their duty, was sentenced at Perth, in September 1824, to six months' imprisonment.[5]

It has been already observed, that where the assault, committed on officers of the law, has been aggravated by discharging of loaded fire-arms, it is uniformly visited by a very heavy punishment. For this offence, so dangerous to society, and indicating so ruthless a disposition on the part of the assailant, transportation for life was inflicted in the case of James and William Gordon, 16th June 1827;[6] and for fourteen years, in the cases of Charles Lamond and John Smith, July 17. 1826; and of James Carson, January 14. 1831.[7]

12. If assault has been carried the length of mutilation of limbs, or real and irreparable injury of the person, it is considered as so serious an aggravation as generally to lead to transportation.

---

[1] Hume, i. 329.—[2] Unreported.—[3] Ibid.—[4] Ibid.—[5] Ibid.—[6] Syme, 245.—
[7] Both unreported. *Supra*, p. 180.

Mutilation, as it is an irreparable injury, is unquestionably one of the worst kinds of assault. It may be charged either as an aggravation of the simple crime, or as a separate offence, under the name of Stellionate and Real Injury, and is generally visited with a severe punishment. Indeed, in former times, the only doubt appears to have been, whether it was not in itself a capital offence; but this was settled in the negative, in the noted case of the Bishop of Orkney, January 1678, which was laid for mutilation as well as other crimes, and concluded for the pains of death, but the Court, after full deliberation, found it only relevant to infer an arbitrary punishment.[1]

Banishment and scourging have been the usual punishment for this offence. Thus, in the case of James Campbell, January 22. 1722, for a most cruel act of stellionate and real injury, by putting hot coals on the privy parts of a man, confined in the same cell with the pannel in jail, this punishment was inflicted. So also in the case of Archibald Mathie and Robert Falconer, September 3. 1791, for an atrocious case of beating and real injury; and of John Macallister, December 27. 1791, scourging and banishment from Scotland were inflicted.[2] In the case of John Gaul, Aberdeen, April 1823, transportation for seven years was the sentence for a conviction for real injury, by throwing a destructive acid in the face, whereby the sight of one eye was totally destroyed, and the other seriously injured.[3] So also in the case of Charles Macewan, 13th July 1824, who was tried on an indictment, which charged him with " assaulting, maiming, and mutilating the lieges," flogging and imprisonment for twelve months, and labour at the tread-mill, were inflicted. He was convicted of having sprung upon a man, who was lying on the ground in a state of intoxication, and bit off a considerable part of his nose.[4] The sentence was transportation for seven years on William Gibson and George Gibson, Glasgow, spring 1824, who were convicted of two acts of throwing sulphuric acid, whereby the persons and clothes of two different persons were injured, though not severely.[5]

13. Assault is aggravated by being committed by a child on its parent, by a husband on his wife, or by any person upon another within his own house.

[1] Hume, i. 331.—[2] Ibid.—[3] Unreported.—[4] Hume, i. 331.—[5] Unreported

Assaults by a husband on his wife, or by a child on its parent, are so obviously contrary to natural feeling, that they are clearly an aggravated species of the ordinary offence. They are daily considered as such, accordingly, in practice. Witness, among many other examples that might be given, the case of Benjamin Ross, 11th May 1824, who was transported for life, and that of John Shaw, Glasgow, autumn 1823, who was transported fourteen years, for brutal and ferocious assaults on their wives, accompanied by imminent danger to their lives. [1]

The crime of hamesucken to be immediately considered, consists in entering a person's house, with the design of assaulting him, and inflicting violence in pursuance of that intent. But, besides this offence, an assault may be committed in a person's own house, or in his shop, counting-house, or place of business, by a person who entered it without any design of committing violence, but who takes up the intention in consequence of some grudge conceived, or provocation offered, at the moment. This is not hamesucken, because the entry was not made with the design to assault; but it is an aggravated species of assault, because it implies a greater recklessness and violence of disposition to commit such violence upon a man in his own house or place of business, than in a casual rencontre on the road or elsewhere. [2] It is usual, accordingly, in all cases of hamesucken, to libel an alternative charge of assault, especially when committed on a man in his own house, of which the pannel may be convicted, if the evidence do not support an entry with the design of using violence. Accordingly, in the case of James Macredie, April 30. 1825, Glasgow, six months' confinement in Bridewell was inflicted on the pannel, in pursuance of a conviction of assault, committed on a woman in her own house, by which the bone of her nose was injured. [3] Again, in the case of Alexander Macdonald and John Fraser, 18th September 1818, the libel was laid for hamesucken, alternatively with assault, " especially when committed on a person in his own house." The jury found the pannels guilty of the assault, as aggravated, but without the hamesucken, and they were sentenced to six months' imprisonment. [4]

14. Assault, like any other crime, may be aggravated

---

[1] Unreported.—[2] Hume, i. 313,—[3] Unreported.—[4] Hume, i. 318.

by a previous conviction for the same offence; and, if such be proved, the punishment is proportionally heavier.

In the case of William Bell, Dumfries, April 1824, upon a conviction of assault, with sticks, to the effusion of blood, especially when committed by a person who had been previously convicted of that offence, six months' imprisonment, and heavy security to keep the peace, was inflicted.[1]  And, in the case of James Coghill and George Murray, Ayr, spring 1830, the pannels, upon a conviction of assault with a glass bottle, to the effusion of blood, aggravated by two previous convictions against both pannels, hard labour in Bridewell for eighteen months was the sentence.[2]

15. In prosecutions at the instance of the Lord Advocate for the public interest, no remission by the private party injured can have any effect; and, even in prosecutions at the instance of that party himself, an abandonment of the right to prosecute is not to be inferred, except from express or written agreement.

When assault or real injury are prosecuted at the instance of the public prosecutor, it is evident that no settlement of the disputes between the parties can take away his high and paramount right to bring the offenders to punishment for the breach of the public peace, of which he has been guilty.[3]  But even when the prosecution is at the instance of the private party, with concourse of the public prosecutor, no remission is to be inferred from any thing but the most express declaration of an intention not to prosecute.  No casual meeting of parties at table, therefore, nor familiar conversation, is to be construed as producing this effect.  The whole defences accordingly founded on these and similar fallacious appearances, were repelled in the cases of James Campbell, January 8. 1722; Douglas of Broughton, January 7. 1825; and Baillie of Torrance, March 8. 1726.[4]  It is unnecessary to enter more minutely into this matter, which, from the change of practice, and disuse of private prosecutions, is more matter of curiosity than practical use.

---

[1] Unreported.—[2] Ibid.—[3] Hume, i. 338.—[4] Ibid.

# CHAPTER VI.

## HAMESUCKEN.

THE crime of hamesucken consists in "the felonious seeking and invasion of a person in his dwelling-house."[1] The mere breaking into the house, without the personal violence, does not constitute the offence; nor does the personal violence without an entry with intent to commit an assault. It is the combination of both which completes the crime.[2]

1. It is necessary that the invasion of the house should have proceeded from forethought malice; but it is sufficient if, from any illegal motive, the violence has been meditated, although it have not proceeded from the desire of wreaking personal revenge properly so called.

1. It is an undoubted requisite of the crime of hamesucken, that the entry of the house have been effected with a view to the perpetration of personal violence; for it is in the premeditated seeking of the person at his home to assault him, that the aggravated and distinctive character of the crime lies.[3] No outrage, therefore, how violent soever, which a person suffers in his own house, is to be regarded as hamesucken, if it happen in consequence of a quarrel taken up at the moment, or of an altercation with the invaders, who came there peaceably and lawfully at first.[4] Accordingly, in the case of William Den, Aberdeen, April 1827, Lord Mackenzie found an indictment for hamesucken relevant which did not specify that the entry to the house was with a view to an assault. Nay, the same will hold if the invasion of the house has taken place in consequence of a scuffle in the street, or on the outside, and the assailant has merely followed the person assaulted into his own

---

[1] Hume, L 312; Burnett, 86.—[2] Burnett, 86.—[3] Hume, L 319.—[4] Ibid.

house, whither he had fled to avoid the violence; for, though
the entry has here taken place during the heat of passion, it
is not that deliberate and premeditated intention of violence,
which constitutes the essence of the crime.[1]   In the case of
Thomson and Inglis, November 1719, accordingly, which was
a case of one person pursuing another into his house and assaulting him, after a scuffle in the street, the prosecution, after
a full argument, was restricted, and the charge of hamesucken
departed from.[2]

But though this is well established on the one hand, it is
equally fixed on the other, that, if the house has been entered
with the design of committing violence, the crime of hamesucken is committed, though the ulterior, and possibly the
principal, object was not violence, but depredation, rape, abduction, or any other offence.[3]   It is sufficient, in the estimation of
the law, if, in the prosecution of this felonious design, the assailants have resolved to commit violence to the persons of the
inmates of the house; the existence of other motives will not
take away the legal effects of a resolution to commit violence.
Accordingly, in the case of Campbell, July 1. 1678, and Car-
negy and others, June 20. 1681, the crimes charged were abduction, rape, and hamesucken; the object in both cases being the carrying off of young women, although no trial took
place in either instance[4]   Farther, in the case of the Macgregors, July 1752, and January 1753, the object was a forcible
marriage, but nevertheless hamesucken was charged, and sustained as relevant by the Court, though objected to in the
prisoner's information, on the ground that injury to the person
was not charged as the primary object of the violence.[5]   In
like manner, in the case of Potts, Glasgow, spring 1792, the
indictment bore a charge of hamesucken, and stated that the assault was made in the dwelling-house with intent to commit a
robbery; and this was sustained as relevant.[6]   To the same
purpose, in the case of Gray, Glasgow, April 1800, the indictment charged hamesucken among other crimes, and the minor
set forth that the prisoners entered the house armed with
bludgeons, " with a wicked and forethought intent to assault
and injure the persons of the said Ludovick Colquhoun and his
servants, and by *that means commit a theft or robbery in the said
house.*"   The relevancy of this charge was objected to on the

---

[1] Hume, i 319; Burnett, 86.—[2] Ibid.—[3] Burnett, 87.—[4] Ibid. 88.—[5] Ibid.
[6] Burnett, 90, 91

ground that the usual incentive of *personal enmity* was here awanting, and that entry done *animo lucri* could not support a charge of hamesucken; but to this it was sustained as a sufficient answer, that personal violence was considered as a means necessary to attain the end, and that *malitia* in the eye of law means any wicked and felonious purpose. The prisoner accordingly was convicted and executed.[1] Hamesucken was found to be a relevant charge where the intent libelled was " to assault and commit a rape," at Glasgow, winter 1828, in the case of Richard Beats.

It will not, however, be sufficient to support a charge of hamesucken, if the entry have taken place with an intent to commit not a crime of *violence*, but a crime of *stealth*, as theft, fire-raising, &c., and the violence has ensued in consequence of the offender being detected, and in the course of the efforts made to apprehend or secure him.[2] The mere felonious intent will not be sufficient, if it be not a felonious intent in which violence is contemplated as a principal ingredient. Farther, if the house have been entered under some mistaken idea of right, or in prosecution of some irregular act, as under an irregular warrant, or by mistake for some other person, and in consequence violence ensues; certainly this is a point of dittay, but cannot be considered as hamesucken.[3] Much less would it be construed to amount to that crime, if the error lay in excessive and undue execution of a warrant in itself correct and lawful.[4]

2. The place where the assault was committed must have been the proper dwelling-house of the party injured, and not a place of business, visit, or occasional residence.

The principal circumstance which renders hamesucken so serious an offence is, the violation of the security of a man's proper home. It cannot, therefore, be committed on a tradesman in his booth, shop, or warehouse, as was found in the case of John Kirkwood, March 12. 1678;[5] nor on a comedian in his theatre or place of business, as was determined in the case of Mungo Murray, June 4. 1669;[6] nor on a miller in his mill, a cobbler in his stall, a banker in his counting-house, or the like.[7] As little is it hamesucken if the assault have taken

[1] Burnett, 90, 91.—[2] Hume, i. 319.—[3] Ibid.—[4] Ibid.—[5] Ibid. i. 313.—[6] Ibid.—[7] Ibid.

place, not in the party's proper home, but under the roof of a stranger, or in an inn, hotel, or place of temporary residence.[1] So it was found with respect to a lodger in an inn, in the case of Peter Leith, November 15. 1686; and with respect to troopers in a tavern, in the case of the Master of Tarbat and others, August 18. 1691.[2]

But this high protection is not confined to the *proprietor* of the house; the privilege applies also to the tenant or possessor, even though the invasion have been committed by his own landlord.[3]  So it was found in the case of Keith of Linbush, January 11. 1692, where the interlocutor of relevancy express- ly required that not the property only, but the possession, should have been in the pannel at the time.[4]  And it applies not to the master of the family only, but his wife, children, and servants, and, in general, all the members of his house- hold who are there at bed and board permanently at the time.[5] Accordingly, in the case of Campbell and Mackinnon, June 1725, the pannels were executed on a charge of hamesucken, for having violently broken into the house of Fraser of To- pachy, and beat and wounded his servants.[6]  The like judg- ment was given in the case of George Johnston, 1754, where the assault was on a lodger with the family, who had dwelt there for some months, and had no other home;[7] and in the case of Peter Gray, Glasgow, April 1800, where the Court were clearly of opinion that the crime of hamesucken was com- mitted on servants.[8]  In the case of Richard Hamilton, 21st July 1807, the assault was committed on an old woman, who occupied a single apartment immediately over the pannel's dwelling-place, and a part of the same tenement or building, though entering by a separate stair from without, and not from any part of Hamilton's house  This was considered as hamesucken by the Court, and Mr Hume adds that the same principle holds in the case of *lands* or floors, which are certain- ly separate houses.[9]  This derives some support from the prin- ciple of the English law, which, in cases of burglary, holds apartments let to several lodgers, and of which they keep the keys, as their respective dwelling-places, though the entrance to them is by a common passage, if the owner of the premises do not occupy any part of the house.[10]

[1] Hume, i. 313.—[2] Ibid.; Burnett, 92.—[3] Hume, i. 314; Burnett, 92.— [4] Hume, i. 314.—[5] Burnett, 92; Hume, i. 314.—[6] Hume, i. 314.—[7] Mac- laurin, No. 65.—[8] Burnet, 92.—[9] Hume, i. 314.—[10] Leach, i. 50, 118, 140, 198.

In the case of an innkeeper there is room for a distinction. It is not hamesucken to invade a publican, *being already in his house*, as was the opinion of the Court in Muir's case, 8th November 1675, but only an aggravated assault.[1] The like was found in the case of John Torrance and William Baillie, March 15. 1726.[2] But if the entry be made not after the usual fashion of coming into an inn, but violently and unlawfully, as by forcing his window in the night, the same protection applies to him as to any other individual.[3] Accordingly, in just such a case, the petition of Bernard Clunes for bail was refused;[4] and the Court found, after full argument, in the case of Johnston and Mason, 9th December 1754, held that it was hamesucken to enter a brothel with intent to assault a female lodger, and there perpetrate the violence.[5]

Hamesucken is not committed any where but *within* the dwelling-house. An assault, therefore, within the precincts, or in the court-yard or offices, is not this serious crime, but only a common assault.[6] So it was found in the case of David Home, October 1729, where an assault committed in the close or court-yard of Seaton was found only relevant to infer an arbitrary punishment.[7]

But, on the other hand, the crime is hamesucken, if the injury be inflicted within the house, in pursuance of a seeking to commit violence there, although the assailants have neither crossed the threshhold, nor in any way entered the house, as by firing at the inmate from without, or thrusting at him through an opening.[8] Nay, it seems to be no lesser offence if the seeking be from without, and the safety of the house be violated, although the principal offence be committed on the outside; as if a band of ruffians go to the door, knock, and when the master opens, rush upon him, and drag him out into the highway or street, where the beating takes place. Here the assault *begins* within the premises, and is only *continued* on the outside. Accordingly, in the case of Robert Macgregor, January 1753, the pannel was convicted and executed for hamesucken, committed by the forcible abduction of Jean Key from the house, done without any beating or other violence, though in opposition to her struggles.[9] The same will hold if

---

[1] Burnett, 93, 94, Hume, i. 315.—[2] Ibid.—[3] Hume, i. 35.—[4] Ibid.—[5] Burnett, 94.—[6] Hume, i. 315, 316.—[7] Ibid. i. 316.—[8] Ibid.—[9] Maclaurin, 62; Hume, i. 317.

a band of ruffians beset and break into a house, and the master
leap from a window to escape from the violence, and they follow, overtake, and wound him.[1]    But notwithstanding the authority of Mackenzie to the contrary,[2] it is not hamesucken if
the invader by artifice entice his victim to quit his house, and
there assaults him when he has come forth ; any more than it
is theft to abstract an article of which, on false pretences,
possession has been obtained.    Accordingly, in the case of
Arbuthnot and Falconer, February 2. 1728, which was just
such a case, the interlocutor restricts the libel to an arbitrary
punishment.[3]

It seems not to be a settled point whether hamesucken can
be committed on a shipmaster or sailor in their *ship*.    On the
one hand, this is undoubtedly the proper domicile and resting
place of these persons, though in harbour, while engaged in
actual service ; on the other, the security of the dwelling-house
seems to have been the principal object of the law.    In the
case of John Haldane and others, February 1719, the question
was, whether a ship was, in the sense of law, a *dwelling-house ;*
the pannels having entered a ship lying in the harbour of Prestonpans, assaulted the master, forced him to leave the ship,
and broken open the hatches.    The indictment was laid for assault and robbery, and the Judge-Admiral seems to have evaded
the difficulty by pronouncing a special interlocutor, finding the
acts of violence libelled relevant to infer an arbitrary punishment[4]    A similar finding took place before the same judge in
the case of Watson and others, 25th November 1740.[5]    In
these circumstances, it cannot be affirmed that such a crime is
any thing more than an aggravated assault ; and it would be
prudent to lay it as such in all charges for such offences.

3. Hamesucken is committed equally in the day as the
night, and not only by effraction of the building by actual force, but by an entry obtained by fraud, with the intention of inflicting personal violence, followed by its perpetration.

Though this crime is usually committed in the night, it
may be perpetrated equally in the day.[6]    And it is sufficient if

---

[1] Hume, i. 317.—[2] Mackenzie, tit. Hamesucken.—[3] Hume, i. 317.—[4] Burnett, 93.—[5] Ibid.—[6] Hume, i. 318.

there have been an entry against the King's peace, with the felonious purpose of invading and grossly injuring some of the inhabitants, though not made by some actual effraction of the building.[1] Hamesucken, therefore, equally as housebreaking, may be committed by terrifying the inmates of the house to open the door, or by enticing them to open under some false pretence.[2] Accordingly, in the case of Johnston, in 1754, the entry was effected by threats, until the door was opened;[3] and in the case of Macgregor, in 1752, the discovery of where the young woman carried off lay concealed, was obtained by threats.[4] In like manner, in the case of Alexander Macdonald and John Fraser, 18th September 1818, the *species facti* set forth in the libel was, that the pannels went to the door and *demanded admittance*, and the door having been opened by Lewis Bain, the master of the house, they set upon him, and beat him violently, " at and near the door of the house, and he having run into the house, they followed him in there, and beat him to the danger of his life. This was objected to as not hamesucken; but Lord Pitmilly repelled the objection. The jury, however, found the pannels guilty of the assault upon Lewis Bain, at his own house only, upon which he was imprisoned six months.[5]

4. It is not hamesucken unless the injury to the person be of a grievous and material injury, though all the other requisites to the crime have occurred ; but if this be the case, it is immaterial whether the violence be done *lucri causa*, or from personal spite.

The most violent effraction of the external strength of a house is not hamesucken, unless accompanied by violence to the persons of the inmates of the house.[6] Not only so, but the personal violence must be of a serious and grievous kind, and not merely such a slight injury as savours more of contumely than actual injury. Accordingly, in the case of John Haldane, August 5. 1718, where the libel charged that the master of a house was caught by the throat, had a cane shaken over his head, and was raised from his bed in the night-time by a party of armed men, who forced him into the street, the Court

[1] Hume, i. 318.—[2] Ibid.—[3] Maclaurin, No. 65, p 168.—[4] Ibid. No. 60, p. 137.—[5] Hume, i. 318.—[6] Ibid. i. 320.

found, " that the facts, as libelled, were not of so *atrocious a nature* as to infer the crime of hamesucken.[1]"

But though this is well established on the one hand, it is equally settled on the other, that if the injury be of the due rank and degree, it signifies nothing of what *kind* it be, or with what weapon, or in what manner inflicted. Thus it is equally hamesucken to beat a person violently with the fist, as to thrash with a stick or cudgel, or fire at and wound with a pistol, or cut or stab with a sharp instrument.[2] Accordingly, in the case of William Ritchie, 8th January 1819, a charge of hamesucken was sustained, and the pannel transported seven years, for a horsewhipping deliberately inflicted upon a medical examinator, by one of the young men whom he had been instrumental in rejecting.[3] Farther, it is hamesucken to enter a house in order to commit a rape on the owner there, and there commit, or attempt to commit, that violence, or violently to carry her away from thence, whether with a view to a rape or a forcible marriage, though without any farther violence than is necessary to the abduction; as was found, after full argument, in the case of Robert Macgregor, in 1752,[4] who suffered death for that species of the offence. Nay, the same will hold even though no actual violence be done to the person, if a serious personal injury be attempted, as if a pistol be discharged though it do not hit, or a thrust be made with a sword, though it be averted or fall short [5]

But it is immaterial whether the injury be committed *lucri causa*, or from personal spite. Accordingly, in the case of Peter Gray, Glasgow, April 1800, the *species facti* was, that the pannels entered the house of Colonel Colquhoun, knocked down a maid-servant, whom they met in the passage; rushed into the parlour, and attacked the Colonel and his two friends there with sticks, threatening to fire with pistols, if resisted. They were vigorously resisted, however, the clergyman fighting desperately with a poker, and the other gentlemen escaping in different directions. They then attacked the man-servant, and broke open cupboards, but in the end retired, without getting any thing. This was charged hamesucken, and assault with intent to rob; and it was sustained as such, though the objection was stated that the violence was clearly *lucri*

[1] Hume, i 320.—[2] Ibid.—[3] Ibid.—[4] Maclaurin, No. 62, p. 60.—[5] Hume, i. 320.

*causa,* and the entry had not been made with intent to do personal wrong.[1]

Of late years hamesucken has generally been charged in those cases of stouthrief, or attempt to rob within the dwelling-house, which call for the severest punishment. Thus, in the case of James Whiteford, 14th July 1819, the pannel was indicted for hamesucken and robbery, and the charge bore, that he knocked at the door of a toll-house, in order to commit violence on the inmates of the house, and by that means perpetrate a robbery in the said toll-house; and that the door having been opened, he knocked the woman, who opened it, on the head, and rushed into the house, where they completed the robbery.[2] Upon this charge he was convicted and executed. A similar outrage was more correctly libelled as stouthrief and hamesucken, in the case of Brine Judd and Thomas Clapperton, 28th November 1819. The libel there stated that the pannels went to James Brydon's house, with intent to assault him and his wife, and perpetrate a robbery in the house: that they forced open the door, assaulted and knocked down the man and his wife, and, in a masterful manner, carried off above £41, and various other articles. The jury found them guilty of the " crimes libelled," and they were condemned and executed.[3] In a still later case, that of John Stuart, July 14. 1827, a libel for hamesucken was found relevant, which charged the pannel with having gone to the house of John Kerr, with intent to assault him, and that, having got access, he presented and drew the trigger of a loaded pistol at him, which flashed in the pan; and that a struggle having ensued, in the course of which Mr Kerr had five teeth knocked down his throat. It was here objected, that there is no instance of a conviction for hamesucken without the intent to assault, and a serious injury to the person; but it was unanimously held by the Court, that the intent to concuss into submission to demands, and failing that, to use violence, was quite sufficient to support a charge of hamesucken; and that the case of Gray in 1800, when the intent to rob was the motive of the entry, and subsequent violence, and a blow on the arm was all the injury which the owner of the house received, was decisive on the point. Notwithstanding a powerful charge from Lord Gillies, and in the face of the clearest evidence, the jury found the libel not proven.[4]

---

[1] Burnett, 90; Hume, i. 322.—[2] Hume, i. 322.—[3] Ibid.—[4] Syme, 236.

5. The punishment of hamesucken, in aggravated cases of injury, is death : in cases of inferior atrocity an arbitrary punishment.

Hamesucken has been, by our old lawyers, classed with robbery and rape as a capital crime.[1]  In the case of Campbell and Mackinnon in 1725, and the Macgregors in 1752, and of Gray in 1800, the law was carried into full execution ; but in the case of Richard Hamilton, July 1807, the Court were of opinion that the series of precedents were not so uniform as to compel them to apply, in every instance, the highest pains, and, accordingly, they sentenced the pannel only to transportation for life only, though the case was in some respects very aggravated. But it justly weighed in his favour that he had struck with the hand only, and thrown away a mell or hammer which he had in his hand ; that the assault was occasioned by sudden resentment, from water spilling through from the upper floor, where the old woman lived, and not by any previous ill-will, and that ten years had elapsed between the perpetration of the crime and the trial.[2]

In the case of James Coghill and David Gemmel, Ayr, September 30. 1828, fourteen years' transportation was inflicted on Coghill, who was convicted of hamesucken, by breaking open the door of the house of Morris Girvan, and stabbing him with a pitchfork in the eye  He had been previously convicted of assault ; and his companion, who did not actually thrust with the grape, and had not been convicted, was sentenced to nine months' imprisonment[3]

Formerly it would appear that this course was liable to a prescription of unusual shortness.[4]  But this is so far departed from in later times, that, in the case of Hamilton just mentioned, the libel was sustained, and the pannel convicted, at the distance of ten years from the assault[5]  The only effect, therefore, of such a delay in prosecution, is to expose the prosecution to difficulty in the mode of proof ; an effect common to this with every other crime.

[1] Burnett, 24.—[2] Hume, i. 312; Burnett, 96, 98.—[3] Unreported.—[4] Reg. Maj iv. c 10.—[5] Burnett, 98.

# CHAPTER VII.

## OF RAPE.

THE crime of rape has always been considered, and still is, a capital crime in our practice. It consists in the forcible carnal knowledge of a woman's person against her will.[1]

1. Rape is completed by penetration of the privy parts and entry of the body, without any proof of actual emission.

It has long been disputed among lawyers, both in this and other countries, whether rape is completed by penetration, or emission is farther requisite. Mr Hume declines giving any opinion of his own on the subject;[2] but Burnett expresses a clear conviction, that penetration alone is not sufficient, and refers to the usual practice of the Courts, where the question asked of the woman is whether the prisoner had " carnal dealings with her," or " had his will of her," or had such " carnal knowledge as a man has with a woman." [3] But these words are ambiguous, and may mean complete penetration without emission. The ordinary and established style of indictments throws no light on this question, as it merely states that the prisoner " had carnal knowledge of her person, forcibly, and against her will, notwithstanding the utmost resistance in her power." But it may be inferred from this style, that emission is not indispensable; it being an established principle of law, that every essential quality of a crime must be expressly alleged in the indictment. Mr Hume quotes a great variety of cases from the older records,[4] as illustrating this question, but they are by no means decisive of the point; because they are all cases of rape or attempted rape on young girls under the years of puberty, and therefore the physical difficulty to which the verdicts allude, as preventing the completion of the crime,

---

[1] Hume, 1. 301 ; Burnett, 101.—[2] Hume, 1. 301.—[3] Burnett, 101.—[4] Hume, 1. 302.

o

may have been, and probably was, that which arises from the
smallness of the female parts in the person injured, which
prevented complete penetration, and not the want of actual
emission. But this point was settled in the case of William
Montgomerie, July 18. 1821, where Lord Gillies laid it down,
with the concurrence of the Court, that rape may be perpetrated by complete penetration, without emission; and that when
the injured party is below the years of puberty, it is enough if
her body had been entered, though not to the degree which
takes place with a full grown woman.

In the law of England the greatest doubt has been entertained on this important question, on which the life of prisoners has often in their practice come to depend. That there
must be actual penetration, or *res in re*, is acknowledged in
all their authorities,[1] though a slight penetration, and such as
does not break the hymen, is considered sufficient, that being
a membrane sometimes an inch and a half within the orifice
of the vagina.[2] But whether there must be emission, as well
as penetration, was long the subject of dispute. In the case
of the King v. Sheridan, Judge Bathurst directed the jury,
that if the man had penetration, and did not withdraw till he
chose to do so, the crime was complete without proof of actual
emission;[3] and in this opinion Judge Ashhurst concurred in
another case.[4] But in a later case, which was reserved for the
opinion of all the Judges, and penetration was positively sworn
to, but there was no direct proof of emission, it was held by a
great majority of the Judges that both were necessary.[5] This
doctrine was applied in a case of sodomy, which is governed by
the same rules, and where, upon proof of complete penetration
and emission, but the latter being out of the body of the sufferer
by the violence, the Judges held *injectio seminis* indispensable,
and that the conviction was wrong.[6] At length, therefore,
though with great difficulty, and after many vacillations of
opinion,[7] the doctrine was settled that penetration and emission
must both be proved.

But all this notwithstanding, they held that penetration is
*prima facie* evidence of emission, unless the contrary appear

[1] Hale, i. 628; Hawkins, c. 48, § 3; Russell, i. 558.—[2] East. i. 438, 439;
Russell, i. 558.—[3] Russell, i. 559.—[4] Rex v. Russell, East. i. 438, 439; Rus-
sell, i. 559.—[5] Rex v. Hill, 1781; East. i. 439; Russell, i. 559.—[6] Rex v.
Parker; Russell, i. 560.—[7] Foster, 274; East. i. 436.

probable from the circumstances of the case; and that, whether it has occurred or not, is a question for the jury.[1] Accordingly, where the woman swore that the prisoner had his will of her, and remained in her body as long as he pleased, Judge Buller held that sufficient evidence of a rape to be left to the jury, though she could not speak to the actual emission;[2] and even where the woman was dead, it was left to the jury to gather from the circumstances of the case, and the deposition she had emitted before the magistrate, whether emission had taken place.[3]

But all these doubts are now removed in England by the statute 9th Geo. IV. c. 31, § 18, which has enacted, that the crimes of rape, sodomy, and carnal abuse of girls under twelve years of age, are complete " upon proof of penetration only." This statute punishes with death the unlawful and carnal knowledge and abuse of a girl under ten years of age; if above ten and below twelve, the offender is punished with imprisonment and hard labour only.[4] It does not very well appear why the period from ten to twelve is the only one in a woman's life during which her person may be violated without peril to the offender's life. This statute does not extend to Scotland; but the reasons on which it is founded will, doubtless, if the case should arise, have great weight with our Courts.

Certain it is, that, in practice, the difficulty as to emission is almost always evaded in our Courts by the question being asked in general terms, whether the pannel had his will of her, or whether he had carnal knowledge of her person; an answer to which in the affirmative is always held to be sufficient proof of the completion of the crime. So it was held in particular in the case of James Burtnay, 18th November 1822, where the pannel had sentence of death for a rape on a child of eight years of age, who could not distinctly depone to the emission, from the tenderness of its years.[5]

2. The knowledge of the woman's person must be against her will; but it is immaterial whether her consent be forced by actual violence or by threats, or the administration of stupifying drugs.

[1] East. i. 440; Russell, i. 560.—[2] Rex v. Harmwood, 1787; East. i. 440.—[3] Leach, ii. 854.—[4] 9th Geo. IV. c. 31, § 18.—[5] Unreported; on this point see the case in Hume, i. 303.

As robbery and stouthrief is committed by the use of such threats as compel a party to part with his property against his will, so rape is complete if the woman's person be known under the terror of such threats as have deprived her of the unbiassed exercise of her will. Thus it is equally rape to have connexion with a woman with a pistol at her head, or a dagger at her breast, as if she is held till the nefarious purpose is completed.[1] In the case, accordingly, of William and Alexander Fraser, November 14. 1744, a libel was found relevant, which set forth that the woman was carried into Stratherrik, " where she was detained in captivity for several days and nights, and carried from place to place, and thereby, and *by the terror of her life*, compelled to submit to the said William Fraser, his unlawful purposes.[2] The like judgment must be given if the woman faint in the struggle, through terror and fatigue, or if from natural infirmity she is incapable of opposing any effectual resistance. So it was found in the case of James Mackie, February 20. 1660, who was condemned to die for a rape on a poor cripple woman, who was lying bedfast in her father's house alone, and incapable of making any resistance.[3] Indeed, in most cases, it is not so much by the subduing the woman's *bodily* strength as by overcoming her *resolution* by the threat of death, that the crime is completed. In the case, accordingly, of John Murray, Aberdeen, April 1826, an indictment for rape was sustained as relevant, where the principal ingredient of the violence was the drawing of a knife by the pannel, and threatening to stab the girl if she made any resistance.[4] He made a narrow escape, by an objection to the principal witness. In the case of James Thomson and John Dobbie, July 19. 1830, the pannels were convicted and justly suffered death, for a most atrocious case of rape and murder committed on a woman, in a state of semi-stupefaction from blows and ill-treatment, on the high road near Gilmerton in Midlothian. They first ravished her and then thrust sharp stones up the vagina, which entered the intestines and produced death, accompanied by excessive torture. They were convicted of the assault and murder only, the death of the woman having rendered complete proof of the rape impossible.

Mr Hume seems to incline to the opinion that the like judgment should be given in the case of a woman who is stupified

[1] Hume, i. 302.—[2] Ibid.; Burnett, 103.—[3] Hume, i. 303.—[4] Unreported

by drugs,[1] and Burnett adopts the opposite view.[2]   The true
solution of such a case is to be found in the previous conduct
of the parties; if the woman had previously given any indications of consent, the essential character of rape is wanting, and
the administration of the drug cannot be considered as decisive
evidence of a violent proceeding; if the reverse have occurred,
it is as much a rape as if the pannel had struck her on the
head, and, during the insensibility then produced, accomplished
his nefarious purpose.   Accordingly, in the noted case of Luke
Dillon, April 1830, the prisoner, a young man of family and
fashion at Dublin, was convicted, and sentenced to death for a
rape on a young lady to whom he had given a stupifying drug
in a hotel there, and during her stupefaction carried to his bed.
Her conduct had been rather questionable in going with him
alone to a hotel in a town where her parents were living, but,
nevertheless, the Court and the jury held the case proved.   He
was afterwards transported for life, at the earnest intercession
of the girl and her relations.

3. In charges of rape, the quality of violence is only required in females above the age of twelve years; below
that age it is held that consent cannot be given, and that
the connexion must have been involuntary.

In the case of females below the age of puberty, there is only
a constructive force, or force in the estimation of law; a girl
of those tender years being held to be incapable either of the
desire or discretion, which must combine, to have a will in the
matter; so that the deed may justly be said to be without her
will, even when she makes no resistance.[3]   On this account,
and on account of the greater depravity implied in such an attempt on an innocent and helpless infant, the pains of law have
always been more rigorously applied in such cases than in ordinary rape.   Accordingly, on March 8. 1693, William Currie
was capitally convicted for a rape on a child of nine years of
age; and on September 11. 1671, William Riply, for a rape on
a child of six years old, was sentenced to death.   This sentence
was pronounced after a certification to the whole Court, who
found " that the crime of which the said William Riply stands
convicted is capital, and adjudged him to be executed accord-

---

[1] Hume, l. 303.—[2] Burnett, 103.—[3] Hume, l. 303.

ingly."[1]   And on 18th November 1822, James Burtnay had
sentence of death, and was executed, for a rape on a girl of
eight years of age.   The infant had been examined on declaration only, and her declaration was received, notwithstanding
an objection that she was of weak intellects, the proof of that
last objection having failed.[2]

4. A rape may be committed on any female, whether
maid, wife, or widow, and even on a common prostitute,
provided clear and decisive evidence of the act having been
perpetrated by violence is laid before the jury.

The character of unchastity is, without doubt, the strongest
possible presumption against a charge of rape; because it is
natural to suppose, that a woman who has once yielded, and
still more one who has made prostitution a profession, will not
seriously resist on another occasion.   But this is only a *præ-
sumptio hominis*, though, without doubt, one of the strongest
kind, and as such may be elided by distinct and unequivocal
evidence of actual violence on the occasion libelled.[3]   Thus, if
a woman be knocked down on the highway and ravished by
one who is an entire stranger to her, it is no defence against
the charge of rape that she is a woman of loose character, or
even who has made a traffic of her person.[4]   The lesser amount
of the injury she has sustained seems rather the subject for the
Royal clemency, than for the Court or the jury.   Accordingly,
in the case of J. Cummings and James Maccartney, Glasgow,
spring 1828, a charge of rape was sent by the Lord Justice-
Clerk to the jury, along with a most brutal charge of stabbing,
in the private parts, the woman ravished, though several witnesses for both sides spoke lightly of the woman's character;
there being contradictory evidence on that point, and a *presumption* of violence in the connexion from the unquestionable
violence with which it was followed.[5]   Certainly, however, in
the general case, a charge of rape is entirely dependent upon
the fairness of the woman's character; and nothing can be
more difficult than to substantiate the case, if it be impeached
on probable grounds.

It is a more doubtful question, and not yet decided in our
books, whether a rape can be committed on a woman who is

[1] Hume, i. 303.—[2] Ibid.—[3] Ibid. i. 304, 305.—[4] Ibid.—[5] Unreported.

actually in a course of prostitution at the time, and perhaps in the very haunts where she carries on her infamous calling. On the one hand, it may be urged that the injury done in such a case is truly elusory; that the resistance, if it really existed, must have been from mere perversity; and that the facility of trumping up false stories of resistance in such circumstances is a most serious consideration. On the other hand, even the lowest classes of society are entitled to protection;—robbery may be committed on a beggar as well as a prince, and because a woman makes a traffic of her person, that is no reason why she should be forcibly subjected to a man with whom she does not choose to have connexion, against her will. Burnett's opinion is against the competency of a charge of rape in these circumstances;[1] and certainly it is difficult to imagine a situation in which it would be more difficult to make out a case of legal evidence.

In the law of England, rape may be committed on a common strumpet, or even on the concubine of the ravisher;[2] these circumstances being only held as clogs on the prosecution. A husband cannot commit a rape on his own wife, but he may aid and abet a rape committed on her by another; for, though she has surrendered her person to him, he has not thereby acquired the right to prostitute her to others.[5]

5. In cases of rape, the previous character of the woman may competently be made the subject of investigation.

A remarkable change has been introduced into the Scotch law of evidence, in consequence of the decision in Burke's case, 24th December 1828, to be hereafter mentioned, touching the competence of asking questions tending to discredit a witness. But before this alteration had taken place, the extreme injustice of giving the same credit in cases of rape to a woman of loose as to one of unsullied character, had led to a relaxation of the rule in that particular case. Accordingly, in the case of James Wilson, 15th July 1813, evidence was admitted on the prisoner's part to impeach the chastity of the woman, by imputing to her acts of criminality *subsequent* to the events libelled, the prosecutor having previously called witnesses to support her character. Lord Meadowbank senior was adverse to this judg-

[1] Burnett, 104.—[2] Blackstone, iv. 214; Hawkins, l. c. 41. § 7.—[3] Hale, i. 620.

ment, and Baron Hume expresses his opinion rather against
it;[1] but, notwithstanding these great authorities, it seems impossible to hold, that, *in some way or other*, such evidence is
not to be let in, and that a witness, possibly of the most abandoned character, is to be presented to the jury as equally worthy of credit with one of the most unsullied reputation, in a
case where life is at stake.   More particularly was such evidence competent in Wilson's case, as the prosecutor had previously led evidence to support the woman's character; for if
such testimony is to be excluded, it ought, in fairness, to be so
on both sides.

It is indispensable, however, to the admissibility of such evidence, that the pannel shall duly have lodged defences before
giving warning of his intention to impeach the woman's testimony by discrediting her character.   In the case of Alexander
Mackeiver, accordingly, Ayr, 17th September 1813, Lord Pitmilly rejected such offer of proof, in respect no warning had
been given of such an intention on the prisoner's part.[2]

By the decision in Burke's case, it was found competent to
*ask* a witness, on cross examination, whether he had ever been
implicated in another crime of the same kind as the one under
investigation; and, in the subsequent case of George Ferguson,
James Lindsay, and others, the Cupar rioters, June 28. 1829,
it was unanimously held by the High Court, upon a bill of suspension and liberation from a judgment of the Sheriff of Perth-
shire, that it was competent to discredit a man adduced as a
witness on a charge of rioting, by asking him whether he had
ever been engaged *in the lifting of bodies;* it being always explained to the witness, before answering, that he was at liberty
to decline answering the question.[3]

Under these authorities, therefore, it seems to be settled that
it is competent to test the credibility of the woman's story in
cases of rape, not only by cross examining her as to previous
irregularities, but adducing evidence to prove previous improper proceedings on her part.

In judging of the length, however, to which this privilege is
to be carried, it is important to keep in view the restrictions
under which the doctrine is received by the English law.   " On
the trial of an indictment for rape, evidence," says Phillips, " is
admissible on the part of the prisoner that the woman bore a

---

[1] Hume, i. 304.—[2] Ibid.—[3] Unreported.

notoriously bad character, for want of chastity and common decency, or that she had before been criminally connected with the prisoner; but it cannot be shown that she had a criminal connexion with other persons. And on an indictment for assault, with intent to ravish, general evidence of the woman's bad character previous to the supposed offence is clearly admissible; but evidence of particular facts to impeach her chastity cannot be received in this case more than the last, not even for the purpose of contradicting her answers in cross examination."[1] It is worthy of observation, that, in the case of Wilson, above mentioned, the Court here went so far *beyond* the rule thus guarded in the law of England, as to admit evidence of *specific* acts of impropriety with *others subsequent* to the events libelled, a latitude which unquestionably would not have been permitted in the English practice. This matter is deserving of special consideration, when the points shall again come under consideration.[2]

6. The account which the principal witness has given of the transaction, *de recenti* after the injury, to others, is competent to be given in evidence on the prisoner's part.

Whatever doubt may exist as to the competency of admitting evidence of the account which the woman has given of her injury recently after its reception to others in the general case, there can be none as to its admissibility in cases of rape. The obvious importance of such an inquiry in a case where so much depends on her testimony, has long fixed the principle, that evidence of this account is admissible in this particular case. Accordingly, in the case of James Burtnay, 18th November 1822, such an account was received in evidence by the High Court, though given by a child only eight years of age.[3] In the case of J. Cumming and James Maccartney, Glasgow, April 1828, such an account was admitted by the Lord Justice-Clerk; and in the case of Thomas Mackenzie, 18th February 1828, evidence was admitted by the Supreme Court of the story told by the principal witness to different persons the day after the injury.[4]

[1] Phillips, i. 175, 5th edition; Russell, i. 563, opinion of Twelve Judges in Rex v. Hodgson, Russell and R. 211.—[2] Hume, i. 304.—[3] Unreported on this point.—[4] Syme, 330.

7. It is equally rape if the woman's person be violated against her will, whether it be done for the sake of lust, or of ambition, or any malignant passion.

As lust is indispensable to the completion of the crime, so it is immaterial what is the ultimate object of that lust, whether the gratification of the offender's passion or any other unlawful or wicked motive. Accordingly, in the case of Simon Fraser of Beaufort, February 17. 1701, who, partly on account of ambition, partly of revenge, and partly to possess himself of a large jointure, committed an abduction, forcible marriage, and rape, the prisoner was outlawed on a charge of rape.[1]

8. A prisoner may be convicted as art and part of a rape, though the crime can be committed only by a single person.

Several pannels may be convicted of the crime of rape, though the actual perpetrator, of course, is only one person.[2] Accordingly, in the case of Turnbull, Edgar, and Potts, Aberdeen, April 1794, Turnbull was " found guilty of the crime libelled, and that J. Edgar and J. Potts were aiding and abetting him in the commission of these crimes." [3] And in the case of J. Cumming and J. Maccartney, Glasgow, spring 1828, the indictment charged each prisoner with perpetrating a rape on one girl, while his companion was art and part in the crime, and again lending his assistance to his companion when similarly engaged. The charge was sustained as relevant by Lord Justice-Clerk Boyle, and the prisoners made a most narrow escape.[4] Nay, a husband may be convicted as art and part of a rape committed by another on his own wife, both by the Scotch[5] and English law.[6]

9. If a woman who has been carried off and ravished shall acquiesce in the wrong, and cohabit with the offender, and declare when unbiassed, however falsely, that she went off of her own accord, the offender shall not be condemned to death, but only suffer fine, imprisonment, or confiscation of moveables.

[1] Hume, L 305.—[2] Ibid. L 306; Burnett, 106.—[3] Burnett, 107.—[4] Unreported.—[5] Hume, L 306.—[6] Hale, L 629.

By the statute 1612, c. 4, it is enacted, that " if any, being art or part of ravishing of women, be pursued for that offence, and defend themselves be the subsequent consent of the woman ravished, or be her declaration that she went with him of her own free will or consent (albeit in that case the woman's declaration of consent may excuse them from capital punishment) that if the woman's parents or nearest of kinsfolk, or his Majesty's advocate, be able to verify, be determination of the assize, that the fact was at first violably and forcibly done against the parties' will and without their consent, the subsequent declaration of the party shall not exume the offenders from his Majesty's arbitral punishment of warding their persons, confiscation of their goods, and imposing upon them pecunial penalties at his Majesty's pleasure." [1]   In the construction of this statute, which, from the change of manners, has now become a matter of curiosity rather than use, it has been settled that the man's life will be spared if the woman declare, however falsely, that she went off with the ravisher willingly.[2] But this declaration, though it need not be on oath, must have been emitted soberly and deliberately in a situation where she was entirely free from restraint, and subject to no improper influence, experience having proved that no reliance could be placed on declarations, how solemn soever to appearance, if impetrated under the influence of the ravisher.[3]

If the woman subsequently intermarry with the ravisher, this is held to be such conclusive evidence of her previous consent as will bring the case within the protection of the statutes.[4]

Besides the party injured, and the Lord Advocate, her kinsmen and near relatives are entitled to prosecute.[5]  Accordingly, in the case of Carnegie, June 20. 1681, a father-in-law pursued in name of the woman; and in the case of Colonel Charteris, November 12. 1723, a husband for a rape on his wife; and in the case of James Cheyne, July 6. 1602, a parent for a rape committed on a child; and in the case of Wedderburn, 1602, a mother for a rape on her daughter.[6]  There is no limitation in our present practice of the time within which the prosecution may be brought in this more than in any other crime.[7]

10. In cases of rape, perhaps more than any other

---

[1] 1612, c. 4.—[2] Hume, i. 306.—[3] Ibid. i. 307; Burnett, 106.—[4] Burnett, 106.—[5] Hume, i. 307.—[6] Ibid.; Burnett, 107.—[7] Hume, i. 308.

crime, it is indispensable to look minutely into the accounts told by the woman, and the support which they receive from the other circumstances of the case, it being an
easy matter to prefer such a charge where there has been
no violence perpetrated, and exceedingly difficult to disprove it.

The circumstance which renders a minute consideration of
the evidence in cases of rape or assault, with intent to ravish,
more necessary than in any other offence, is, that the facts attending it bear so close an affinity to voluntary connexion, and
that it is so easy a matter for a woman, who has fallen into an
illicit connexion, for the preservation of her character, in revenge, or to extort money, to get up a story which, in every
other particular but the violence said to have been used, may
be not only strictly true, but completely supported by the other
parts of the evidence.  It is not sufficient, therefore, by the
Scotch law, to bring forward the woman and support her evidence by proof, that the parties had been seen together about
the time in the most suspicious circumstances, for all that may
be true, and yet the connexion may have been voluntary on her
part, and the subsequent story got up for the most nefarious
purposes.  The principal point to attend to is, whether her
statement, in regard to the *violence* used, is duly corroborated;
and this is done in the most unexceptionable way by such physical appearances as afford real evidence of the truth of her
story, and after that by the evidence in regard to her subsequent disclosure of the crime to her relations, or the public
authorities, and her previous character for modesty and correct
demeanour.

" It is true," says Lord Hale, " that rape is a most detestable crime, and therefore ought severely and impartially to be
punished with death ; but it ought to be recollected, that it is
an accusation easily made, hard to be proved, but harder still
to be disproved, though the party accused be never so innocent.
We should be more cautious upon trials of this nature, wherein
the Court and jury may with so much ease be imposed upon
without great care and vigilance, the heinousness of the offence
transporting the judge and jury with so much indignation, that
they are over hastily carried to the conviction of the person
accused thereof by the confident testimony sometimes of mali-

5

cious and false witnesses."[1] If the woman presently discovered the offence, and made search for the offender; if she showed circumstances and signs of the injury, whereof many are of that nature, that women only are proper examiners; if the place where the fact was done were remote from inhabitants or passengers; if the party accused fled from it,—these and the like are concurring circumstances which give greater probability to her evidence. But if, on the other hand, the witness be of evil fame, and stand unsupported by others; if, without being under control, or the influence of fear, she concealed the injury for any considerable time after she had an opportunity of complaining; if the place where the fact is alleged to have been committed was near to persons by whom she might probably have been heard, and yet she made no outcry; if she has given wrong description of the place, or varied in the account to different persons of the violence committed upon her,—these and the like circumstances afford a strong, though not conclusive, ground for suspecting that her testimony is feigned.[2]

The usual physical appearances consequent on rape, however, are by no means decisive of the charge, because they are produced equally by voluntary and involuntary connexion. Thus the rupture of the hymen, swelling and inflammation of the orifice of the vagina, staining of the clothes with blood, &c. are as usual after the one species of connexion, where it occurs for the first time, as the other. They are important evidence, if the question be whether connexion has taken place, but of little weight in the consideration whether or not it was involuntary. More important evidence is to be found in appearances of violence on the other parts of the woman's person, as marks of blows, symptoms of having been thrown violently down, marks of grasping by the throat, &c., for, whatever may be said of the other, it is certain that *these* appearances have not been produced with her concurrence.

The *place* where the crime is alleged to have been committed is one of the most important indexes in the inquiry, as to the want of consent on the woman's part. If the assault took place on the roadside, or in a situation not such as is usually selected for illicit intercourse, it affords a presumption that her story is well-founded, and that she was the victim of a passion

[1] Hale, i. 635, 636.—[2] Blackstone, iv. 213; East. i. 445.

suddenly conceived by a reckless impetuous man, totally re-
gardless of the consequences.   On the other hand, if there be
any appearance of the parties having retired to a more seques-
tered situation, as by going off the road into a field, or a wood,
or a shed, or of her having gone out of her way with him previous to the alleged offence, or the like, it affords such an obstacle in the way of a conviction, as, in the general case, will
prove insurmountable.   In considering the evidence on this
point, it is a material consideration that passion is much more
rapid and impetuous in the male than the female sex, and,
consequently, that the presumption of violence having been
used, is much strengthened by the place being such as a woman would not have selected for any improper purposes.

Undue weight is frequently attached to the fact of *cries* having been heard.   Their importance depends' on a distinction.
If the woman was aware that she had been discovered, or
caught in the act, her screams cannot be relied on, because
they may have been, and frequently are, uttered to give a colour of violence to a voluntary proceeding: if they took place
*before* any discovery to her knowledge had been made, and
alarmed persons at a distance, they are the strongest evidence
of resistance.   For want of this species of evidence, an acquittal took place in the following circumstances, where the whole
other requisites of rape concurred.   Thomas Mackenzie was indicted for rape on 18th February 1828.   He was a spirit-
dealer at Newhaven, near Leith, and lived alone.   The girl,
who was a servant in a family in the neighbourhood, came to
his house late at night for some tea, where, according to her
story, she was detained by him, and forced into a bed in a
room behind, where she lay all night, and was twice violated.
Her character was unimpeachable : she told the story next day,
and repeatedly afterwards, to her relations: she was seen by
the neighbours going into the shop at night, and her person
bore physical evidence of recent connexion committed under
more than usual violence.   The pannel denied in his declaration that any girl had been in his house that night at all, or
that he had had any connexion with any woman.   On the
other hand, it was proved by the watchman, who went his
rounds repeatedly close to the house, that he heard no cries
during the night, and that the neighbours who were also in the
near vicinity were no ways alarmed.   The jury, by a plurality

of voices found the libel not proven; a result which, notwithstanding the strong presumption against the pannel, seems consonant to strict justice.[1]

In general, the falsehood of the woman's story may be elicited by a well conducted cross-examination, directed to such
minute circumstances as were not likely to have been considered by her previous to the trial. A remarkable instance of
this occurred in the trial of J. Stewart, June 18. 1830. The
pannel, who was a police-officer in Edinburgh, was there
charged with a rape, committed on a young girl in one of the
cells of the police-office, when sent to lock her up for the night.
She swore positively to the rape, committed, as she alleged,
when the door of the cell was a-jar, and when a prisoner was
in an adjoining cell; and asserted that his hand was placed
over her mouth, which prevented cries. She adhered with
tolerable steadiness to this story on a cross examination; but
when asked to go into her subsequent conduct, she gave such
an absurd and contradictory statement, as at once proved fatal
to the prosecution.[2]

In our ancient law, it was held indispensable that the woman should not delay making her complaint *ultra unam noctem.*
If she did so, her complaint was no longer to be listened to,
and she was to be punished as a calumnious accuser.[3] This
strictness is no longer preserved as a legal bar to the charge;
and, accordingly, in the case of Matthew Foulden, February
1732, there had been a delay of three days on the woman's
part in communicating the fact.[4] But unquestionably any
undue delay in communicating the outrage, at least to the most
confidential relations, still does, and always must, form a serious objection to her testimony.[5] And unless some extraordinary circumstances are established to justify the delay, the
omission to communicate the disaster, even for twenty-four
hours, will in general form an important feature in the case.

But while this is perfectly true on the one hand, it is not
less material to observe on the other, that women, especially
of tender years, have a strong, frequently an insurmountable,
aversion to communicating such an outrage even to their nearest and dearest friends; and, therefore, it is not in every case
to be taken as *per se* decisive against the sufferer, that she has

[1] Syme, 323.—[2] Unreported.—[3] Hume, i. 308; Burnett, 553.—[4] Hume, i.
308.—[5] Burnett, 554.

endeavoured even permanently to conceal her disgrace. In
endeavouring to distinguish this species of concealment from
that culpable kind which arises from the desire to get up a false
story, the character, appearance, and manner of the witness,
are to be taken into consideration; and it is chiefly in the
power of making such a discrimination that the value of jury
trial consists.

11. The injured woman is a competent witness to
prove the injury done to her person; but her credibility
may be tested by cross-examination, or proof as to her
having given different accounts of the transaction to other
persons on previous occasions.

If the prosecution be at the instance of the Lord Advocate,
or of her relations, she is of course a competent, and indeed
the principal, witness to give an account of the injury.[1] But if
she be herself the prosecutor, she cannot be allowed to depone
in her own case; a difficulty which should always prevent the
adoption of that mode of prosecution.[2] If the crime has been
perpetrated on a child of tender years, she is permitted to give
her declaration, and, in confirmation of her account, the statement given by her to her relations and friends *de recenti* is admissible.[3] Accordingly, in the case of James Burtnay, 18th
November 1822, the declaration of the injured girl, an infant
of eight years of age, was admitted, and proved the principal
evidence against the accused, who was convicted and executed.[4]
A still more remarkable example of the admissibility of testimony, occurred in the case of Alexander Martin, June 13.
1823, where a woman deaf and dumb, upon whom a rape was
alleged to have been committed, was allowed to give evidence,
the Court having previously ascertained, by the evidence of sworn
interpreters, who understood her peculiar mode of expressing
herself by signs, that she was of sufficient capacity to understand an oath.[5]

But as a woman is thus permitted to give an account of the
injury she has received, and to support that testimony by the
accounts she has previously given to others *de recenti* after the
outrage, it follows that she may be discredited by proof of ha-

[1] Hume, i. 308; Burnett, 554.—[2] Burnett, 554.—[3] Hume, i. 308; Burnett,
554.—[4] Hume, i. 303.—[5] Shaw, 101.

ving given a different account of the transaction on such occasions, and varied in the versions she has given to different persons.[1]  Accordingly, in the case of James Young, Ayr, September 1823, for assault with intent to ravish, Lord Succoth allowed the question to be put to William Kenneth, an exculpatory witness, " Whether the woman assaulted had at any time in April told him that she had not been very ill used by James Young in the field ?"[2]  But, in all such cases, the question should not be allowed from *others*, unless a foundation has previously been laid in the cross-examination of the principal witness; and indeed Mr Hume hesitates as to the admissibility of such evidence, even where the way has been so previously prepared.[3]  But, in the case of William Hardie, January 24. 1831, it was solemnly decided by the High Court that it is competent to question a witness *himself* as to previous and contradictory accounts which he has given of the story to others; but that it is not competent to contradict his story by the evidence of others adduced on the prisoner's part.[4]  After this decision, there can be no question of the competency of such a course of examination from the principal witness in cases of rape; and considering the vast importance of her testimony in considering the evidence of such a crime, there seems no sufficient reason for refusing to admit evidence of contradictory statements by her made *de recenti*, if such a foundation has been laid in her cross-examination.  In England, the rule is well established, that the credit of a witness may be impeached by proof that he has made statements out of court on the same subject, contrary to what he swore at the trial.[5]

11. Indecent practices with female children, under the years of puberty, are punishable with an arbitrary pain.

Besides the serious and capital charge of rape, and the subordinate offence of assault with intent to ravish, the law of Scotland punishes with exemplary severity those corrupt and unnatural practices with female pupils which are not less fatal to the virtue of their sex.  The relevancy of this charge was first fixed in the case of James Forbes, the master of a charity school, on 24th July 1758, who had sentence to be scourged

---

[1] Hume, 1 309 —[2] Ibid —[3] Ibid.—[4] Unreported.—[5] Ersk. ii. 489, Philip, 1. 301, 4th edit.

and transported for life.[1]   In the case of John Bell, December 2. 1777, a schoolmaster, for a conviction of an offence of this description, was sentenced to be scourged and banished Scotland for life.[2]   On July 20. 1819, George Smythe, on a conviction following a confession of indecent practices, by exposing his person before young girls, and putting his hands up their petticoats, was sentenced to seven years' transportation.[3]   The like judgment was given in the case of A. Purves, Jedburgh, September 1819.[4]

12. Forcible abduction and marriage constitute a crime punishable with the highest arbitrary pains.

It was formerly doubted whether forcible abduction and marriage did not amount to a capital crime.   But, in the case of Thomas Gray and others, July 1751, it was settled, after full consideration, that the crime warranted only an arbitrary punishment.[5]   In the case of the Macgregors, July 1752, forcible abduction and marriage were charged along with other offences of a capital nature; and the Court found the libel relevant to infer the pains of law, and inflicted transportation for fourteen years;[6] but as the other charges were capital, the sentence of death which followed was no impeachment of this judgment.[7]

By the statute 9th George IV. c. 31, § 20, it is declared, " That if any person shall unlawfully take, or cause to be taken, any unmarried girl, being under the age of sixteen years, out of the possession, and against the will of her father or mother, or of any other person having the lawful care or charge of her," he shall be punished with fine, imprisonment, or both. And, by § 19. of the same statute, it is declared punishable with transportation for life, or any term not less than seven years, or imprisonment for any term not exceeding four years, to take away, or detain against her will, *from motives of lucre,* any woman who has any interest, legal or equitable, present or future, absolute, conditional or contingent, in any real or personal estate, or who is an heiress presumptive or next in kin to any one having such an interest, if this done " with intent to marry or defile her, or to cause her to be married or defiled

[1] Hume, i. 310.—[2] Ibid.—[3] Ibid.—[4] Unreported.—[5] Hume, i. 310; Burnett, 108.—[6] Maclaurin, 59.—[7] Ibid. 62; Hume, i. 310.

by any other person."[1]   This is an English statute; but the
common law of Scotland has power sufficient to inflict the same
chastisement on the offence.[2]  In the case of Sir Patrick Churn-
side, 8th November 1616, an indictment was preferred against
the pannel for carrying off a boy of fourteen years of age, with
a view to concuss him into a marriage with his daughter, which
was at length accomplished.   No doubt seems to have been entertained of the relevancy of the charge, although the prosecution came to nothing from the boy's declaring that he did not
concur in the process.[3]

The offence of abduction, if committed without any intention of marriage or rape, belongs to another class of crimes,
and will be considered under the head of *Plagium* and Theft.

# CHAPTER VII.

## OF ROBBERY AND STOUTHRIEF.

ROBBERY consists in the violent and forcible taking away
the property of another.   As such it might be supposed that it
should be considered rather as an aggravation of theft than as
a separate offence;  but it is settled in our practice that they
are separate crimes, and that, under an indictment charging
robbery, it is not competent for the jury to return a verdict of
simple theft[4]  This distinction, how unfounded soever in reason, being fully established in law, should be always attended
to in practice, by drawing the charge, where there is any
doubt as to the violence, alternatively for theft or robbery.

Stouthrieff was formerly the expression used for every species of theft, accomplished by violence to the person; and as
such it is used both by Hume and Burnett as synonymous
with robbery.[5]  But of late years this has become the *vox sig-
nata* for forcible and masterful depredation within or near the
dwelling-house; while robbery has been more peculiarly ap-

---

[1] 9th Geo. IV. c. 31, § 19. & 20.—[2] Burnett, 108.—[3] Ibid.—[4] Shaw, 30;
Peter Wallace and Others, May 21. 1821.—[5] Hume, i. 104 , Burnett, 145.

plied to violent depredation on the highway, or unaccompanied by housebreaking. But, though this has been the ordinary use, the practice has not become so inveterate as to found any legal objection to the indiscriminate use of either term to depredation accomplished by personal violence.

It does not appear, however, to be settled by any fixed rule that stouthrief is a separate crime from theft; and consequently there is no reason for departing from the dictates of common sense on that subject. On the contrary, in the case of James Graham and others, April 16. 1824, Dumfries, who were tried for stouthrief, the Lord Justice-Clerk Boyle expressed a clear opinion that stouthrief is only forcible theft, and that it would be proper to add to the words usually employed in that charge, " violently seize, and in a lawless and masterful manner carry away," the words, " in a lawless, masterful, *and theftuous* manner."[1] And, in the case of James Donaldson and William Buchanan, Aberdeen, April 1823,[2] Lord Pitmilly threw out a suggestion, that the aggravation of being habite and repute a thief should added to the charge of *stouthrief;* an aggravation which could not be made to a charge of *robbery,* and could proceed only on the principle that the crimes of stouthrief and theft are substantially the same, the former being only an aggravated species of the latter. In this view they are evidently considered by Mr Hume;[3] and it is difficult to perceive any sufficient reason for holding depredation committed by breaking into houses an aggravated species of theft, and yet that the crime is totally changed if, after invading the house, personal violence is resorted to.

1. It is essential to the crimes either of robbery or stouthrief that property should be seized and carried off by violence; but it is immaterial whether this violence is applied to the person or the will of the suffering party.

Violence, in the sense of law, is not confined to an actual assault of the person, by beating, knocking down, or forcibly wresting from. On the contrary, whatever goes to intimidate and overawe, by the apprehension of personal violence, or by the fear of life, with a view to compel delivery of property,

---

[1] Unreported —[2] Ibid —[3] Hume, i. 104

equally falls within its limits.[1] The mere display of force, and preparation of mischief, whether shewn by the display of weapons, or the words, gestures, or carriage of the whole party, if in the circumstances of the situation they may reasonably intimidate and overawe, are therefore a proper description of violence to found a charge of robbery.[2] Accordingly, in the case of Samuel Riccards, June 20. 1710, it was found a sufficient specification to support a charge of murder, that the prisoner had, " in a rude and violent manner, with a mortal weapon in his hand, attacked Eliza Bruce upon the highway and robbed her of money and goods."[3] So also in the case of Stuart, Bannatyne and Paul, June 20. 1791, the pannels had sentence of death for an act of robbery, though the assault was not accompanied by any shew of arms, or bodily harm to the person robbed, farther than by laying hold of him and pulling him to the ground.[4]

In estimating the degree of violence which shall be held sufficient to support a charge of robbery, regard is also to be had to the age, sex, and situation of the person assaulted; it being justly deemed that a much smaller degree of threats or violence will be sufficient to effect the spoliation from a woman, or an infirm person, in a remote situation, than from a young or robust man, in a frequented spot[5] Thus if a woman be rudely accosted on the highway, and a demand made for her money, though no direct violence is used to her person, she will be held to have been robbed, if she deliver up her money, under the influence of that intimidation, such as it was.[6] Accordingly in the case of Barclay, July 31. 1758, a capital sentence was pronounced, although an objection was stated that no arms or offensive weapon had been shewn on the occasion.[7] In like manner, in the case of Hugh Lundie, March 25. 1754, the charge bore, that he jumped over a wall to a highway, where two women were passing, and called out, " Damn you, stand," and immediately gripped one of them, and put his hand into her pockets, and took but eightpence halfpenny Sterling. In another charge in the same libel, the charge was merely, that he came up to a woman, asked her if she had any money, and thereupon gripped her pocket, and took out two shillings.

[1] Burnett, 146, Hume, i. 107.—[2] Hume, i. 107 —[3] Ibid.—[4] Ibid.—[5] Burnett, 146 —[6] Ibid.—[7] Hume, i. 107.

He had sentence of death. Again, in the case of James Campbell, 13th December 1824, the libel charged him with robbing an old gentleman, Mr John Horner, in Nicolson Street, Edinburgh, and striking him in the face. He pleaded guilty to the robbery, but not the assault, and had sentence of death.[1] In short, any reasonable fear of danger, arising from a constructive violence, which is gathered from the mode and circumstances of the demand, being such as are attended with awe and alarm, and may naturally induce a man to surrender his property for the safety of his person, is sufficient to constitute a taking against the will of the sufferer, which is the essence both of robbery and stouthrief.

The putting one in fear of his life is not essential to robbery, any more than an actual wounding of the person.[2] It is sufficient if the property be taken away under the dread of immediate personal danger of any sort, provided it be of a serious and alarming description. In the case of Patison and others, Stirling, May 1775, it was objected to an indictment for robbery, that " it did not libel a putting in fear of life, or any thing that could infer it, nor personal violence." The libel, nevertheless, was found relevant, and the pannels transported for life.

2. It is not necessary that the thing be taken from the *person*; it is sufficient if, in consequence of force applied to the person, or threats to the will, goods are taken from the custody of the sufferer.

In cases of stouthrief it generally happens that goods are not taken from the persons of the sufferers, but from their custody or control. The course of proceeding usually is, that the assailants break into the house, knock down, bind, or intimidate the inmates, and openly, in their presence, unlock the drawers, and rifle the house of its most valuable contents. In all such cases the crime of stouthrief is as plainly committed as if the depredation had taken place on their own persons.[3] It is the same thing if, by force or menaces, delivery of a key is compelled, or the inmates are obliged to shew where their property is secreted, as if it is violently wrested from their cus-

---

[1] Hume, i 107 —[2] Burnett, 146.—[3] Ibid. 148.

tody.[1] Accordingly, in the case of Macdonald, Inverness, September 1772, it was objected to an indictment for robbery, that the ordering one to give up a key was not robbery; but the answer was sustained, that the doing so by threats, as charged, and then opening the chest with the key, is robbery.[2] In the case of William Macmillan and Spence Gordon, 23d November 1829, High Court, the only violence alleged or proved was, that the prisoners broke into the house of an old woman near Tranent, and shook a stick over her head till she unlocked her drawers, and shewed where her property was placed, which they carried off, and on this they had sentence of death.[3] In like manner, in the case of David Little and others, Glasgow, Christmas 1830, the indictment set forth, that they broke into the house of Mrs Hill, and bound the hands of two servant-maids, and then proceeded up stairs, and compelled Mrs Hill and her daughter, by threats of instant death, to unbolt the door of their room, and having then got in, they compelled them to deliver up the keys, and shew where their valuable property was kept, which they carried away in considerable quantity. Upon this charge Matthias Little, who alone was apprehended, was condemned and executed.[3]

3. The violence requisite to constitute robbery or stouthrief must be present, and either personal or threatened to be applied to the person, and not threats of future evil, or of some other and different kinds of oppression.

The will may be coerced not only by threats of present violence, but by intimidation of a different kind, as by threatening to set the house on fire, or to carry the sufferer to jail, or to bring an infamous charge against him; and the question occurs, whether the extorting of money or other property by such menaces, constitutes the crime of stouthrief or robbery. This matter may be resolved by a distinction. If the threat be of instant or near and personal danger, as if matches be exhibited, by which it is proposed immediately to set fire to the house, or cords be produced for binding the person, preparatory to dragging him on a false charge to jail, there seems no difference between such a case and the extortion of money by the me-

naces of immediate death.[1]  But if the threat be of a future
or contingent danger, and such as, by the interposition of law,
or by other means, may be averted, the crime is not to be considered as robbery, but as oppression, which is a crime *sui generis* of a very serious, though not a capital kind;[2] more especially if, in consequence of such threats, the money be delivered
not immediately, but *ex intervallo*, as by sending it by letter,
placing it under a stone designed by the criminal, or the like.
In such cases the crime is not considered robbery any more than
if it had been obtained under the terror of an incendiary letter.[3]

The law of England has attained much greater precision on
this subject than has yet been reached in our practice.  If violence be made use of to obtain the property, it is not the less
robbery, on account of the depredator having had recourse to
some specious pretext to effect his purpose.  Thus where a
bailiff handcuffed a woman, under pretence of carrying her
with greater safety to prison, and by violence extorted money
from her while so handcuffed, it was held robbery.[4]  In like
manner, if the violence be originally used with a different intent, as to commit a rape, and the woman, to avoid such an
outrage, offer money, which is taken, it is also robbery;[5] or if
violence have preceded, and alms are then begged and given,
under such circumstances as may fairly be held to have been
yielded under the fear of a repetition of the attack, the crime
remains the same.[6]  Nay, it is not the less robbery, if the assailants, finding little money about the man whom they have
attacked, make him swear, by menaces of death, to bring a
larger sum, and he do so, if the fear of that menace was upon
him at the time of making the delivery.[7]

The fear requisite to constitute robbery with them, may not
only be fear for the person of the sufferer, but for his child or
estate.  Thus money delivered under a threat, that otherwise
the child of the person threatened would be destroyed, has been
more than once held to be an act of robbery.[8]  Threats by a
mob to tear in pieces a stack of corn, and level the house of
the prosecutor, have been held to amount to the violence required in this offence.[9]  Nay, money obtained by a threat, that

---

[1] Burnett, 147, Hume, i 108.—[2] Burnett, 147.—[3] Hume, i. 108.—[4] Leach,
i. 280; Russell, ii. 70.—[5] East. ii. 711; Russell, ii. 71.—[6] Blackstone, i. 241;
Russell, ii. 71 –[7] Hale, i. 532, East. ii. 711, Russell, ii. 71 —[8] East. ii. 718,
735; Russell, ii. 72.—[9] East. ii. 731

the house of the person threatened should be pulled down at a *future time*, has been held to be robbed money.[1]

But the fear of being sent to prison has been held by the Twelve Judges to be not of itself a sufficient ground of terror to constitute robbery,[2] for that is an evil from which law will give redress. And parting with money, under the threat of accusing of an unnatural offence, if done not under the feeling of intimidation, but with the design of afterwards prosecuting the offender, does not constitute robbery.[3]

In one particular class of cases, threats have always been sustained in England as sufficient to constitute a charge of robbery, and that is where a charge of sodomy is either express or implied. In Jones' case in 1776, the prosecutor swore that he delivered money, under a threat which he understood meant that a charge of sodomy would be preferred; and, upon a reserved case, the Judges gave their opinion that it amounted to robbery, and the prisoner had sentence of death.[4] So also, in Donally's case, a direct threat to accuse of an unnatural crime, if money was not instantly paid, was held by all the Judges to amount to robbery. On this occasion it was laid down by Judge Willis, who delivered the result of their deliberation, " that the circumstance of actual fear need not be proved upon the trial, for if the fact be done violently, and against the will, the law *in odium spoliatoris* will presume fear; that there need not be actual violence, a reasonable fear of danger caused by constructive violence being sufficient; and that when such terror is impressed upon the mind, as does not leave the party a free agent, and he deliver money in order to get rid of that terror, he may clearly be said to part with it against his will, so as to constitute robbery."[5]

4. To constitute robbery or stouthrief there must be a taking of property at the time, in consequence of the violence used or threatened; but it is immaterial of how trifling a value that property may be.

Robbery or stouthrief are not committed unless some article is carried off; but if this is done, it is of no importance whe-

---

[1] Astley's Case, East. ii. 720; Russell, ii. 75.—[2] Knewland's Case, Leach, ii. 721; Russell, ii. 76.—[3] Fuller's Case, Russell, ii. 87.—[4] Jones' Case, Leach, i. 139; Russell, ii. 78.—[5] Donally's Case, East. ii. 715; Russell, ii. 79, 80

ther it is an article of the smallest or greatest value.[1]   Of this
no stronger proof can be imagined than occurred in the case of
William Higgins and Thomas Harold, Glasgow, September
1814, who were convicted and had sentence of death, on a charge
of robbing two persons, from one of whom they took a memo-
randum-book, and from the other a thread purse, containing a
sixpence.[2]   In like manner, on 20th January 1817, John Larg
and James Mitchell had sentence of death, on a libel which
charged that they had taken from the master of the house two
forged notes, which were of no sort of value.   An objection,
grounded on this circumstance, was repelled by the Court.[3]
And, in the case of Thomas Donaldson, William Buchanan,
and William Forbes Duncan, Aberdeen, spring 1823, a charge
of stouthrief was found relevant, and terminated fatally for the
two former of these parties, where the only articles carried off
were a pair of old boots not worth one shilling.[4]

But it is indispensable that something should have been
*taken.*   Though an assault be made with intent to commit depredation, yet if the intention has not been carried into effect,
it is neither stouthrief nor robbery, but assault with intent to
commit those crimes.[5]   In all cases where there is any doubt
as to the completion of the crime, the libel should be drawn alternatively for robbery, and assault with intent to rob.

In the construction of what shall be deemed a *taking,* law
attends chiefly to the fact as to whether the invader has once
got possession of the thing by means of violence.   A person
shall therefore be held to have been taken, though the owner,
being intimidated, have, with his own hand, delivered it on
demand, or though it have fallen to the ground in the struggle
between them, and he have picked it up, or though the owner
cast it aside, and the robber espy it and pick it up.[6]   Accordingly, in the case of Anderson, Paul, and Bannatyne, June 20.
1791, one of the articles robbed was the hat, which had fallen
from the head of the person assaulted, and then was laid hold of
by one of the party.   This the Court held to be as much robbery
as taking money from his pocket.[7]   In like manner, if a snatch
be made at a watch-chain, but the article is firmly fastened,
and a struggle ensues, in which the owner is collared, and his
hand held till at last the watch, with a portion of cloth at-

[1] Burnett, 149.—[2] Hume, 1 105.—[3] Ibid.—[4] Unreported.—[5] Hume, 1.
104.—[6] Ibid. p. 105, Burnett, 149.—[7] Ibid.

tached, is torn from the fob, this is a completed act of robbery.[1]

5. The crime is completed as soon as the article has
fairly passed into the custody of the assailant, though he
do not succeed in carrying it off, but not till then.

As soon as the article has fully passed from the possession
of the person assaulted into that of the assailant, the crime is
completed though he be apprehended on the spot, nay though
from fear, or not deeming it worth keeping, he has thrown it
away.[2]  Accordingly, James Cranstoun, on September 11.
1723, had sentence of death, for taking one article only, with
which he was apprehended on the spot, and in presence of the
person assaulted.[3]  In like manner, in the case of James Holland, 12th December 1808, a libel was sustained as relevant
for robbery, which merely set forth, " that he struck John
Hay, and immediately thereafter seized and took from his person a seal and chain of a watch, and did rob him thereof, and
some person having come up to assist the said James Holland,
the prisoner was immediately taken into custody." [4]  From defect of evidence of the *amotio*, the jury found the prisoner
guilty of assault with intent to rob only; but the Court expressed a clear opinion, that if the watch, chain, and seals were
forcibly torn away by the prisoner, though they had dropt in
the scuffle, and had not, strictly speaking, been at any time in
his possession, there was a sufficient taking to complete the
act of robbery.[5]

In like manner, if goods are removed from their proper place
of keeping, in presence of the owner, who is either forcibly
prevented or overawed from interfering, the robbery or stouthrief is completed, though they never pass out of the room,
shed, or cart, in which they were placed.[6]  If a carrier is stopt
by a person on the highway, and any article is forcibly taken
out of the waggon, though the taker is seized before he has
made off with it, it is clearly robbery; for it has passed from
its place of deposit into the custody of the assailant, and it is
of no consequence for how short a period that custody has continued.[7]

[1] Hume, 1. 105, Burnett, 149 —[2] Ibid —[3] Ibid —[4] Hume, 1. 106 —[5] Burnett, 149.—[6] Ibid.—[7] Ibid

But if the removal of the goods was only attempted, and *in course* of being effected, but not actually completed, the crime amounts to an attempt only. Thus in the English case of Edward Farrell, Old Bailey, December 1787, it was found by the Twelve Judges, that when the prisoner stopt the prosecutor, as he was carrying a feather-bed on his shoulders, and threatened to shoot him if he did not lay it down, upon which the man *laid it down,* but before the prisoner could *pick it up* he was seized : this was not robbery but only attempt.[1] " So also," says Hale, " where A had his purse tied to his girdle, and B attempting to rob him, in the struggle the girdle broke, and the purse fell to the ground, B not having previously taken hold of it, nor picking it up afterwards, it was ruled to be no taking "[2]

But it is immaterial with them, though the possession was for an instant only. Thus where a robber took a purse from a gentleman, and returned it to him immediately, saying, " If you value your purse, you will please to take it back, and give me the contents," and was apprehended before the contents were given, this was held to be a completed robbery.[3] In like manner, where a lady was stepping into her carriage, and the prisoner snatched at her ear-ring, and separated it from her ear, by tearing the flesh entirely through, but there was no evidence that it ever was in his hand, and it was found at night in a curl in the lady's hair, the Twelve Judges were of opinion, that there was a sufficient taking to constitute robbery, though the possession had only been retained for an instant.[4]

6. It is not, however, robbery, but theft, if an article is taken away by a sudden snatch, although it be violently wrested from the possession, if no attempts have been made to subdue the strength or overawe the will.

If a man make a sudden snatch at a lady, for example, who is carrying a reticule, or a man's watch-seals, and they are carried off, this is not robbery, but theft. Accordingly, in the case of Peter Wallace and others, Perth, April 1821, who were indicted for robbery only, it turned out that the pannels had snatched a man's hat and watch from him by surprise, without

---

[1] Leach, i. 222.—[2] Hale, 1 533.—[3] Peat's Case.—[4] Lapier's Case, Leach, i. 320 ; Russell, n. 63.

any demand or griping of his person: the jury accordingly convicted them of *theft* only, the consequence of which was, that the pannels escaped altogether without punishment.[1]  In like manner, in the case of Arthur Highlands, Glasgow, autumn 1829, which was one of sudden snatching of a pocket from the person, Lord Justice-Clerk Boyle held that the crime was rightly charged as theft.[2]  So also in the case of Alexander Smith, Glasgow, spring 1828, the pannel had taken a reticule from a lady, in a stair in Glasgow, by grasping her round the waist, and snatching it out of her hand.  No farther violence was used, and the whole was over in a moment.  The case was charged alternatively as theft and robbery; but the Lords Justice-Clerk Boyle and Moncrieff were of opinion that it was theft, of which he was convicted accordingly.[3]  The like was found in such a case of sudden snatching, in the case of William Duggin and John Kitchin, December 1. 1828, where a watch was seized much in the same manner.  In England, in like manner, it is fully established, though after some diversity of opinion, that a sudden snatching or taking of property will not constitute robbery, unless some injury be done to the person, or there be some previous struggle for the possession of the property, or some force be used to obtain it.[4]

7. The violence must have been used with the intent of lucre; but it is immaterial whether the felonious intent have been taken up, before or after the assault, provided it existed at the time of the taking.

Robbery or stouthrief can only be committed for the sake of gain; if the violence has been perpetrated with a different design it is assault or hamesucken only.  This holds although, in the course of the struggle, some article of property has been carried off; if, in the whole circumstances of the case, it is evident that this was done in frolic, or from malice or accident, and not *animo retinendi lucri causa*.[5]  Accordingly, in the case of Edgar Wright, December 15. 1788, which was one of a drunken squabble and mutual violence between the parties, in the course of which a pistol was carried off; the verdict was not guilty of the robbery, but of the assault only.[6]  It fre-

---

[1] Hume, i 106.—[2] Unreported.—[3] Unreported.—[4] Leach, i. 287, 291; East ii. 703; Russell, ii 64.—[5] Burnett, 150; Hume, i. 108.—[6] Hume, i. 108.

quently happens in practice, that, after a quarrel of this description, in the course of which some article has been carried off, perhaps in triumph or from inadvertence, or has been lost, by the person who was worsted in the affray, a charge of robbery is preferred against the victorious party, though nothing was farther from his intention than to commit such a crime. It behoves prosecutors to be rigidly on their guard against such perversions of the real transaction which has occurred, and to endeavour to restrict charges of this serious description to cases of real felonious depredation.   In the case of James Graham, James Wilson, and John Wright, Dumfries, April 16. 1824, the *species facti* was, that the pannels broke into the house of one of the water-bailies of the river Annan, and forcibly carried off a fishing-net, which he had the day before seized on the shore of that river, in terms of an act of Parliament.   The case was laid alternatively for stouthrief, and for a minor offence.   The housebreaking and violence were clearly proved; but as the *animus lucri* was awanting, the Lord Justice-Clerk held that the charge of stouthrief was out of the question; and, as there was an error in the commission of the water-bailie, which proved fatal to the subordinate charge, the pannels escaped altogether without punishment.[1]   In like manner, in the case of David Bruce and James Macalpine, Glasgow, autumn 1829, it turned out, on the examination of the principal witness, that a scuffle took place on the high road between Glasgow and Airdrie, in the course of which the witness was deprived of a ruling-measure, a hat, and a variety of other articles out of his pockets, which were afterwards found on the road-side; but, as it turned out that he was tipsy at the time, and the article might have been lost in the scuffle, without an intention of felonious appropriation on the pannel's part, the Lord Justice-Clerk Boyle directed an acquittal.[2]

But it may happen that an assault is commenced from some other motive, and, in the course of it, a depredation, evidently done *lucri causa*, is committed, suggested perhaps by the unforeseen exposure of some valuable property, or the defenceless condition to which the owner is reduced in the course of the affray.   In such a case it is not the less robbery, that the intention to appropriate arose after the assault.[5]   Accordingly,

<hr>

[1] Unreported —[2] Unreported.—[3] Burnett, 150.

5

in the case of Young, autumn 1801, Glasgow, the fact turned
out on evidence, that, from a purpose of malice, the pannel
had lain in wait to assault the object of his malice; a scuffle
ensued, and, during the struggle, the person assailed lost a
bundle, which was never afterwards recovered. The Court
laid it down, that, if the intention of depredation existed at the
moment of the taking, the case was robbery, though the assault
commenced from a different motive; but the jury, doubting
the evidence, acquitted of the robbery, and convicted only of
the assault.[1] If one, in a frolic, goes to the highway, presents
a pistol to a traveller, obtains his money, and then gives it
back, this is not robbery, as the thing was not taken with a felonious intent, but it is a high outrage, and severely punishable.[2] To assault another, with a view to the recovery of the
assailant's *own property*, conceived to be illegally detained, is
not robbery: it is rather a spulzie, for the defence of *res sua*
is good against robbery.[3] This, however, must be understood
with the due limitation; for if the assailant has, for a valuable
consideration, vested the right of *possession* in another, though
upon a defeasible title, as by pledge, loan, or location; the articles so transferred are in the *lawful possession* of the party
who has acquired them, and it is not less robbery to carry off
articles in the lawful possession of another than his actual property. And it is certainly not, in the general case, a defence
against robbery, that the violence was committed with a view
to recover the property of the depredators, conceived to have
been illegally seized or detained, if there was not a reasonable
ground for such an opinion.[4] To assault an excise-officer, and
take from him by force or menaces the goods which he had
regularly seized, is unquestionably robbery at common law, independent of the 19th George II. c. 34, specially enacted for
that particular case.[5]

To concuss another, by force or threats, into subscribing a
bill, or delivering up papers of value, subscribed by the assailant, is not so properly robbery as a separate offence, which
should be libelled by a general description of its character in
the major proposition, or at least such a general description
should always be charged alternatively with that crime. A
libel, in such a case, was sustained as relevant by Lord Hailes,

[1] Burnett, 150.—[2] Ibid —[3] Ibid.—[4] Ibid. 151 —[5] Ibid.

drawn in that way in the case of George Adam, Aberdeen, spring, 1791.[1] In the case of John Milne, Aberdeen, April 1805, the libel was laid not for robbery in such a case, but the " wickedly and feloniously enveigling any person into a remote place, and there assaulting, intimidating, concussing, and compelling him, by threats, to deliver up any writing contrary to his will," which was sustained as relevant by the Court.[2]

8. Stouthrief is the general appellation in every species of masterful depredation, but where the crimes are complicated, the same acts may be charged under different denominations.

In our earlier practice, it seems not   usual to libel in cases of complicated depredation and violence, robbery and theft, by housebreaking and stouthrief. Such a course was adopted in the case of Robert Calder, against whom the libel set forth, that he entered a lady's bedchamber in the night, by opening the casement of her window, to which he mounted by a ladder, and that, on her wakening and being alarmed, he, by threats and violence, compelled her to deliver up certain jewels which were in the room at the time.[3] In like manner, the libel was laid for stouthrief and robbery in the case of John Larg and James Mitchell, 20th January 1817, where the thieves had obtained entry to a house in the night by means of violent threats to pull it down, and when admitted they presented a pistol at the master of the house, and compelled him and his wife to deliver up their money.[4] They were convicted and hanged. On 5th September 1817,     rd and Hugh Macilvogue and Patrick Macchristal were tried on a libel which charged stouthrief, robbery, rape, and assault, and had sentence of death on a conviction of the crimes libelled;[5] and on 7th February 1820, William Macghur and Charles Britton had sentence of death on a libel which charged stouthrief and robbery.[6]

It may frequently be necessary to charge theft by housebreaking as well as stouthrief in such cases, because part of the depredation may have been committed before the personal violence began, and at such a distance from it, in respect of time and place, as to be incapable of being considered as part of the

Burnett, 152 —[2] Ibid 151 —[3] Hume, i 109.—[4] Ibid.—[5] Ibid.—[6] Ibid.

3

violent depredation; but though certainly not irrelevant, it is difficult to see what is the use of charging robbery as well as stouthrief, the latter of these expressions being the generic term for every species of violent depredation. The libel, accordingly, in later cases, has always been laid for theft and stouthrief, or stouthrief alone, without any mention of robbery. This was done in particular in the cases of Donaldson, Buchanan, and Forbes, Aberdeen, spring 1823; Maxwell, Muir, and Hamilton, 11th December 1820; Alexander Martin, 14th July 1829; of John Craig and James Brown, Glasgow, autumn 1820; and Matthew Little, Glasgow, Christmas 1830; all of which terminated in sentence of death being pronounced on the pannels.[1]

9. Legal evidence, in cases of stouthrief or robbery, consists in the evidence of two witnesses, or of one witness supported by circumstantial evidence before or after the violence, or of such a train of circumstances as, without any direct evidence, leaves no reasonable doubt of the guilt of the accused.

There is no class of cases in which the difficulty of evidence is more severely felt than in robbery, or in which it is more frequently pressed on juries, that they are bound to acquit, although there is no doubt, morally speaking, of the guilt of the prisoner committed to their charge. It is of importance, therefore, to investigate the principles of evidence as applicable to this subject, and to examine what amount of evidence has been deemed sufficient in time past to convict prisoners of the offence.

When it is said that the law requires the evidence of more than one witness, it is only meant that it will not do for a prosecutor to call one witness and conclude his case. Unquestionably, how clearly soever that witness may identify the pannel, and swear to the robbery by him, if he be totally unsupported, the verdict must be not proven.

But while this is perfectly clear on the one hand, it is material to observe on the other, that the testimony of one witness speaking directly to the fact, accompanied by other evidence which, though not confirming the actual assault, connects the

---

[1] All unreported.

pannel with the person robbed before or after the crime, is sufficient for conviction.   Nay, a train of circumstances alone,
without any direct evidence, is sufficient, provided only it be
pregnant and conclusive to a reasonable mind.[1]

The evidence usually adduced in cases of robbery consists in
the direct evidence of the person assaulted, coupled with that
of persons who saw him near the scene of violence, or in company with the principal witness shortly before the robbery, or
trace part of the robbed goods into his possession.   If these circumstances be proved by credible witnesses, they in general are
amply sufficient, with rational juries, to convict the prisoner.

Thus, in the case of William Doig, Perth, May 1755, the
jury returned the following special verdict : " Find it proved
that part of the goods found in the pannel's possession, when
apprehended, were the property of the deceased : that the body
of the deceased was found in a ditch in Mosswoodend, and,
from the marks of violence thereon, find it proved that he was
murdered : find that the pannel and the deceased met on the
road betwixt Perth and Methven, and travelled westward, with
many others, till they came to the Mill-town of Carsehead,
when the deceased and the pannel parted from the rest, and
went together, as they gave out, toward the moss-side of Ma-
therly : that the pannel arrived there alone, and that the deceased was not seen afterwards till his body was discovered."
Upon this verdict the prisoner had sentence of death, nor was
any objection moved to the evidence as insufficient, though he
was defended by Mr Wedderburn, afterwards Lord Chancellor
Loughborough, and Mr Rae, afterwards Lord Justice-Clerk.[2]

In like manner, in the case of John Douglas, December 24.
1823, it was proved by several witnesses that the pannel, who
was totally unacquainted with the person robbed, had, on various pretexts, attached himself to him in Edinburgh, and was
seen in different public-houses with him there ; that he learned
he was going to Portobello, and set out on the road with him ;
that they were seen together half way between that place and
Edinburgh ; and that, after he returned, he had the silver
watch which belonged to the man robbed, which was produced
at the trial.   The man robbed added that he went with the
prisoner to Portobello, and was knocked down and robbed by

---

[1] Burnett, 518.—[2] Ibid. 522.

him of his watch in a lane off the main street of that village; and his appearance when he came to the nearest house clearly proved that he had been thrown on his back on the road. On this evidence the accused was convicted, and had sentence of death.[1]

Again, in the case of James Stevenson, April 29. 1825, it was proved by the person robbed that he was assaulted on a road near Glasgow, by two men, and robbed of his watch, but, from the violence of the blows received, and the darkness of the night, he was unable to identify the prisoner as one of them. But a few days afterwards he presented the watch robbed to a pawnbroker in Glasgow, and an associate of the prisoner turned King's evidence, and identified him as the man who struck the blows previous to the robbery. His testimony was corroborated in every particular by the man robbed, except as to the identification of the pannel. He was convicted and executed.[2]

In the case of William Thomson, James Thomson, and John Fram, January 22. 1827, it appeared that Mr Dickson, a farmer near Dalkeith, was attacked and robbed at seven o'clock in the afternoon on the high road between that place and Edinburgh by four men, one of whom he identified as the prisoner William Thomson, but he could not identify the others. The prisoners were proved to have left the neighbourhood of Musselburgh about three o'clock that afternoon, and were traced by successive witnesses to the vicinity of the place where the robbery was committed; and a *socius criminis*, who came with them to the scene of action, gave a full account of the transaction, and pointed out a place in a field, on the road back towards Musselburgh, where part of the stolen property had been deposited, where, shortly after, a number of papers belonging to Mr Dickson were discovered. They were condemned, and William Thomson, the principal culprit, executed,—the sentence of the others having been commuted to transportation.[3]

Andrew Stewart, George Buckley, and James Dick, were brought to trial at Glasgow on September 25. 1826, for the robbery of an Italian on the streets of that city. It appeared that the Italian was assailed on the Gallowgate by a number of blackguards, about seven at night, and knocked down

[1] Unreported.—[2] Unreported.—[3] Unreported

by one of them and robbed of a gold watch of considerable value. He thought Stewart resembled the man who struck him, but could not identify him. A girl of the town saw the prisoners, with a large party of lads, following the Italian; another saw Stewart knock him down, while Buckley was close behind, and the third prisoner was on his right hand; and a third saw him knocked down, but thought it was done by Buckley. Two *socii criminis*, who were in the party, deponed to the robbery, and gave an account of a meeting for the division of the spoil in the Green of Glasgow, and one of them swore to Stewart feeling the pockets of one of the lesser lads, to whom the watch had been given. Stewart acknowledged knocking down the man, but denied any intention of robbery, alleging that he had a quarrel with the foreigner, and only intended to assault him. Stewart was condemned and executed; James Dick was sentenced to fourteen years' transportation; and Buckley, from the error of the woman, who conceived he was the actual assailant, was fortunate enough to escape with a verdict of not proven.[1]

J Macfarlane, at the same circuit, was brought to trial for the robbery of a carter near Camlachie. It appeared in evidence that he was drinking with the prisoner at a public-house on the roadside, where he had an opportunity of seeing his watch. They were seen by the landlord setting out together at eleven at night, for Tollcross, which was about a mile distant. The carter deponed that, after they had gone a short distance along the road, the prisoner grasped him firmly round the waist, while his companion came up and pulled his watch out of his fob, with which they both got clear off. On arriving at Tollcross at twelve, he gave an account of the transaction to a man whom he roused there from his bed, and he wanted his watch. Here, therefore, though there was but one witness to the fact, it was confirmed both by the persons who saw him in company with the prisoner immediately before, and spoke to his condition immediately after, the robbery. Macfarlane was convicted and transported for fourteen years.[2]

In the case of William Adams, December 8. 1829, High Court, the person robbed deponed that the prisoner, whom he had never seen before, made up to him in the Pleasance,

---

[1] Unreported —[2] Unreported.

under pretence of purchasing his coat, and they went together into a public-house there: that he then led him, under the same pretence of taking him to the purchaser, to the Cowgate, and up a stair leading from a close there to the West Bow: that, when in the stair, which was quite dark, he was suddenly knocked down and robbed of the whole money in his pocket, consisting of a one pound note and seven shillings and sixpence in silver. Two women who came up, alarmed by the noise, found the man just rising, and heard the footsteps of a person running up the stair. The landlord of the public-house in the Pleasance identified the prisoner as the man who was along with the man robbed in his house before the robbery; and two different shopkeepers proved that the prisoner came running into their shop about an hour after, without his hat, wishing change for a pound note, which they could not give him. At Melrose's shop, South Bridge, the prisoner at last got it changed; and the note was put by the shop-boy into a drawer along with a great many other notes; and in that drawer, on the following day, the person robbed picked out his note, which he identified, by having observed two manuscript letters on the back. On this evidence the prisoner was convicted and executed.[1]

H. Macleod was brought to trial at Inverness in autumn 1831, for the murder and robbery of a pedlar of the name of Grant, in a desolate part of Assynt, in the summer of 1830 It appeared in evidence that Grant set out from Lochbroom in Sutherland, about a month before his death, having about £40 worth of goods in his pack. He came in the beginning of June into the neighbourhood of Loch Tor-na-Eign, in Assynt, where he slept in the house of one Graham, and in the room with his sons, one of whom was an intimate friend and neighbour of the prisoner, and had an opportunity of seeing his money, which was kept in a leathern bag, and consisted of £36 in silver and notes, the produce of the sales of almost all the pack. On a Friday morning, June 19., the prisoner was in a cottage along with Grant, and they left the village together, taking the road towards the place where the body was afterwards found. The prisoner was, at two o'clock on that day, seen by a girl at the distance of about five miles from that village, and within 200 yards of the spot where the body of

---

[1] Unreported.

Grant was afterwards discovered; and he told her not to mention that she had seen him there. The deceased himself, about the same hour, set out from a cottage about a mile off, after having asked the road to a place, in going to which he behoved to pass near that spot. The prisoner was not again seen, but it was proved that he was not at school, as he should have been, that day ⟨⟩ ⟨⟩ soon afterwards he began to shew a considerable comm      of money, having changed a £5 note with a grocer in the      ghbourhood, bought a gun for thirty shillings, and squandered various small sums to the amount of two or three pounds more. Previous to that day, he was in such needy circumstances that the neighbours would not have trusted him for five shillings, and his relations were all as poor as himself. The body of the deceased, who was never again seen in life, was found about six weeks afterwards floating in Loch Tor-na-Eign, at the distance of about 200 yards from the place where the prisoner had been seen by the girl. A place was discovered close to the shore, where the body had lain for some time previous to its immersion in the lake, covered with heath. The body bore several ghastly marks of wounds, such as could not have been inflicted by suicide or accident; and the prisoner, when the crowd were examining the body, stood aloof on a hill, without approaching the bloody object. Shortly after he set out in company with his friend Graham, in whose house the deceased had slept the night before, to a minister about five miles off, requesting an order to bury the body at the public expense, representing the death as evidently one of suicide. A few days before the death of the deceased he had purchased some stockings from an old woman in the neighbourhood, and one of these pairs was afterwards identified by her, having been left by the prisoner some time afterwards, at a house where he took them off his feet on occasion of being wet. Two other pairs of the same kind, and having the same number of bars of blue and white as those sold to the deceased, were found on the prisoner, or in his house, after his apprehension. When in prison he exhibited two bank-notes, one of which he got changed at far less than its value by a fellow prisoner, to whom he tendered it through the window of his cell. This evidence left no doubt in the mind of any reasonable man of the prisoner's guilt, and he was convicted and executed.[1]

[1] Unreported.

From these authorities, it is evident that, although it is undoubtedly still part of our law that a conviction for robbery, any more than any other offence, cannot take place without more than the evidence of one witness, yet a very slender support is now deemed sufficient, if that witness is of unexceptionable character. It makes up the measure of legal evidence if such corroboration be afforded as the circumstances of the case will admit. Law does not forget that highway robbers generally select for their victims the most unattended and defenceless of the people; and for the places of their outrage the most lonely and unfrequented spots. To require the evidence of two witnesses for the conviction of such offenders, would be equivalent to a proclamation of impunity for their crimes. All that is required, therefore, is, that the person injured should himself be worthy of credit, that he should identify the pannel as the author of the violence, and that his narrative before and after the violence should be supported by such persons as had an opportunity of witnessing his previous and subsequent condition. If, instead of this identification, any part of the robbed property be traced *de recenti* to the pannel, it will amount to as complete evidence as if the person robbed had sworn to his person.

In cases of stouthrief the same rules are observed. Thus, in the case of Thomas Donaldson, William Buchanan, and William Forbes Duncan, Aberdeen, spring 1829, it appeared that the farm-house of a poor man of the name of Cooper, in Aberdeenshire, was broken open by four ruffians, who seized hold of Cooper, dragged him to the front of the door, and there beat him in the most barbarous manner. They were identified by him, and by an old sister who lived in family with her brother; and a pair of old boots which they had carried off were traced to the possession of Donaldson. Forbes Duncan pleaded guilty; the two others were convicted and executed.[1]

In the case of John Craig and James Brown, Glasgow, autumn 1829, it appeared that the house of an old man, who lived with an old maiden sister at Foxbar, in the county of Renfrew, was broken open in the night by two men, who entered the house, while a third remained at the door to keep guard. The old man was severely beaten with a stick, and bound with ropes, and his sister thrown on the ground, where

[1] Unreported.

she soon after fainted. He thought Brown was one of the men, but-could not identify the others. A large quantity of articles were carried off, comprising among others a number of spoons, and a divider and some toddy-ladles. Craig was proved to have shortly after offered some of the spoons at a shop in Glasgow; and Brown pledged the divider and the toddy-ladles with a pawnbroker in Belfast, about a week after the robbery. A passenger in the steamboat to Belfast proved that he offered some of these articles for sale there, and a *socius criminis* detailed the circumstances of a meeting in a field near Foxbar, where the spoil was exhibited, and divided between the two pannels and their third associate. They were both convicted and executed.[1]

In the case of William Mackinlay and A. Spence Gordon, High Court, the house of an old woman, called the Witch's House, near Tranent, was broken open, ransacked, and goods to a large amount carried off. The only violence offered to her consisted in shaking their sticks over her head till the keys of her drawers were produced. They had blacking on their faces, and were so disguised that she could not identify the prisoners. But they were proved to have set out from Aberlady, about eight miles distant, about five o'clock in the afternoon, in company with a fourth person, who was examined as a *socius criminis*, and were traced by successive witnesses to Prestonpans, about three quarters of a mile from the scene of the robbery. They were traced also back the following morning by a different route to Aberlady, where they were all apprehended in one room about eleven o'clock of the same day. In the recesses of that house were found, some weeks afterwards, a considerable number of small articles, which were identified by the old woman as her property; and in a field at a short distance from the road by which they returned, were found by several reapers, some weeks after, a large quantity of the robbed property. The *socius criminis*, though with great reluctance, and many attempts to screen the prisoners, detailed nearly the whole circumstances which occurred from their leaving Prestonpans, on the road to Tranent, till the booty was deposited in the field. They were all convicted and sentenced to death, but, in consideration of their having used no personal violence, the punishment was commuted into transportation for life.[2]

[1] Unreported.—[2] Unreported

In the case of Alexander Martin, 14th July 1824, it appeared that the cottage of an old man, ninety years of age, had been broken into, in a solitary part of Aberdeenshire, and robbed of a number of articles. He himself, with an elderly daughter who lived with him, appeared and gave evidence, and distinctly identified the prisoner. He had remained in the house a considerable time, and forced them to light a candle and shew him where their valuable property was concealed. He was traced to the neighbourhood of the house, chiefly by a red waistcoat which he wore at the time of the violence, and also returning from it on the following day. He was con and executed.[1]

In the case of Matthias Little, Glasgow, Christmas 1830, the house of Mrs Hill, near Glasgow, was proved to have been broken into by a party of men, with crape on their faces. The man-servant forced his way through the stauncheons of the window of his room, and roused the servants from the farm-offices, who alarmed the depredators, and struck one of them who was running away such a violent blow on the face as was thought at the time to have effectually disabled him, although, by creeping into the bushes, he contrived to elude pursuit and escape. The prisoner was proved to have told two persons with whom he lodged in Glasgow, that he had been engaged in the house-breaking, and detailed it in a way in every respect consonant to the testimony given by the suffering person; and a *socius criminis* identified him as the person who had watched on the outside, while the others entered the house. One of the most convincing, and, in truth, an irresistible article of evidence, was elicited by the man who struck the blow, who, being desired to point out the part of the face where he struck the man, went down to the prisoner and pointed out the scar still remaining above his eyebrow.[2]

Thus it appears that the direct evidence of the person robbed, coupled with very slender adminicles, is sufficient to convict of stouthrief; and that, if it be wanting from inability to identify, the defect may be supplied by recent possession of the robbed articles, supported by a train of circumstances; or by the testimony of a *socius* similarly supported, provided it appears in itself credible, and cohere well with the other circumstances of the case.

[1] Unreported.—[2] Unreported.

# CHAPTER VIII.

### OF THEFT AND ITS AGGRAVATIONS.

THE fundamental requisites in the crime of theft consist in the felonious taking or appropriation of the property of another. But this occurs also in swindling; and, therefore, it is material to distinguish between the offences which fall under the one denomination, and those that are embraced by the other.

1. Theft consists in the secret and felonious abstraction of the property of another for the sake of lucre, without his consent: Swindling is the fraudulent impetration of that consent on false pretences.

The above definition includes the essential requisites of these two crimes. Though nearly allied, they are nevertheless distinct from each other. The theftuous abstraction implies that the thing is *ab initio, clam et fraudulenter*, taken out of the custody of its possessor. " A furto omnimodo excusatur," says our old law, " qui *initium suæ detentionis* habuit per dominum."[1] On this principle, the following points are fixed in regard to the distinction of the two offences.

2. It is not the less theft that the owner has intrusted the property to the thief, provided that was done for a temporary and transient purpose, and not with the intention of transferring the real rights, or subjecting the depositary to a mere action for account.

It happens continually in the business of life, that the possession of property is, for temporary purposes, entrusted to others, without any intention either of transferring the right of custody, or of calling the custodier to account merely by an

---

[1] Reg. Mag. 3, 9, 4 & 5.

action of account. Thus plate is intrusted to the butler, linen
to the chambermaid, horses to the groom, stores to the house-
keeper, clothes to the footman, sheep to the shepherd, tools to
the gardener, and the like. In all such cases there is no intention of transferring the property: the custody is still retained
*animo* by the proprietor, and he is still held to be possessing
by the hand of his servants, according to the rule, *Qui facit
per alium facit per se.* In all of them, accordingly, the abstraction of the articles by the person intrusted is theft.[1]
This point was settled so long ago as August 10. 1608, in the
case of Margaret Heartside, an attendant on the Queen, who
was indicted for the theft of sundry jewels, her Majesty's property, of which she had the custody. She pleaded in defence
that the crime was not theft, but breach of trust; but this plea
was overruled by the Court.[2] It is matter of every day's practice, accordingly, to libel such cases as theft; and the rule that
abstraction in such circumstances by the custodier is no minor
offence constantly referred to as fixed law on the Bench.

Farther, the same rule applies in circumstances a shade more
favourable to the pannel, and where the person intrusted is a
higher species of servant. An apprentice or shop-servant is
guilty of theft if he abstract any part of the goods contained
in the shop, though he is intrusted with the power of selling
them for a *bona fide* price.[3] Accordingly, on 27th December
1803, Agnes Gray was indicted for stealing the shop goods under her charge as shop-servant, and was sentenced to six months'
imprisonment;[4] and, on July 27. 1789, fourteen years' transportation were inflicted on Peter Mathieson, an apprentice, for
theft of his master's tools.[4] So also George Chalmers, March
13. 1828, was convicted of theft, and sentenced to twelve
months' imprisonment, for the abstraction of various articles
from his master's shop, on a libel which set forth theft by a
shop-servant of his master's goods, as an aggravated species of
theft;[5] and, in the case of Daniel Alexander Murray and John
Tait, November 18. 1829, an indictment was sustained as relevant, which charged the latter of these parties with theft of
haberdashery articles and gloves, from the shop in which he
was shop-boy at the time.

The law of England proceeds upon the same principles.

[1] Burnett, 112; Hume, i. 63.—[2] Hume, i. 65.—[3] Ibid.; Burnett, 112.—
[4] Ibid.; Hume, i. 68.—[5] Unreported.

The clear maxim of the common law, established by a variety of cases, is, that where a party has the bare custody or charge of the goods of another, the legal possession remains in the owner, and the party may be guilty of trespass or larceny, in fraudulently converting the same to his own use.[1] And this rule holds *universally* in the case of servants, whose possession of their masters' goods, by their delivery or permission, is the possession of the master himself.[2] Thus, in Paradise's case, 1766, the prisoner was indicted for stealing a bill for £100, the property of a mercer at Devizes, to whom he was foreman and book-keeper, receiving a yearly salary, but not living in the house, and who had delivered him that bill, among others, to inclose in cover, and send by post. This was held theft by all the Judges.[3] In like manner, a porter in the employment of the prosecutor, who had embezzled £80 worth of gauze belonging to his master, and which had been delivered to him with a view to delivery to customers;[4] and a servant, who abstracted five quarters of oats from corn-factors in the River Thames, were found by all the Judges to have been guilty of larceny.[5] So also, a servant going off with money, which his master had given him to carry to another, and applying it to his own use;[6] and a servant, who had obtained ten guineas from her mistress, on pretence that she knew where she would get them changed, and immediately ran off with them, were found by all the Judges to have committed theft.[7]

3. If goods are delivered to a stranger or carrier for a special and particular purpose, independent of any transfer of property, as to be conveyed to a particular place, or subjected to a particular operation, the abstraction of them by the person intrusted is theft.

Where the custody is for a special and particular purpose only, as by delivery to a porter to carry to a specified place, or a letter-carrier to deliver at a particular door, or a tradesman's servant, who is sent with an article to be delivered to a customer, or a hackney-coachman, who gets an article along with a person who hires his vehicle, the right of custody is

---

[1] East. ii. P. c. 564, Russell, ii. 197.—[2] Ibid.—[3] East. ii. 565, Russell, ii. 198.—[4] Russell, i. 198.—[5] Leach, ii. 824, Russell, ii. 200.—[6] Russell, ii. 201. —[7] Leach, i. 302; Russell, ii. 201.

temporary only, and the case is clearly held to be theft.[1]   For a very long period, accordingly, such cases have been considered in this light.

Thus in the case of James Shand, December 11. 1764, a tailor's workman was found guilty of theft, for running off from his master's house with a suit of clothes, which he had been employed to make.[2]   In the case of Daniel Mackay, assistant-porter at the Post-Office, July 6. 1781, and of Adam Johnston, postmaster, 25. 1780, the crime of abstracting money from letters was found to be theft, at common law, as well as under the statute; although, in the latter case, it was strenuously contended to be breach of trust only.[3]   And, in the case of Andrew Laurie, 8th January 1802, a libel was found relevant at common law, which charged a letter-carrier with the theft of money contained in a letter put into his hands for delivery.[4]   So also, in the case of Archibald Drummond, 14th March 1815, a porter at the Post-Office, was convicted of stealing £200 from a sealed parcel given him at the office, to deliver according to the address.[5]

The same principle has been applied to analogous cases of every other description. Thus, in the case of Alexander Mackay, 27th December 1826, it was held to be a clear case of theft, that he had carried off and concealed a portmanteau, and its contents, for which the owner had sent him, as a porter, to bring from a shop in Aberdeen to his lodgings, about a quarter of a mile off.[6]   The like judgment was given in the case of Edgerton Wylie, July 1829, where an indictment for theft was sustained as relevant, which charged the prisoner with stealing a box of goods, placed on his back as a porter, at the Register-Office, Edinburgh, as he was following the person to whom it belonged along the South Bridge.[7]   On 23d March 1815, Archibald Paterson and Alexander Marr were indicted for stealing a woollen web from a carrier's warehouse, where they were regularly employed to load and unload the carts, and sentenced to seven years' transportation.[8]   In the case of William Glen, May 18. 1827, an indictment was objected to, which charged the pannel with stealing the contents of a parcel wrapped up in a silk handkerchief, which was committed to his charge as an occasional carrier between Lin-

---

[1] Hume, i. 64, 65, Burnett, 112, 113.—[2] Hume, i. 67.—[3] Ibid.—[4] Ibid.—[5] Ibid.—[6] Ibid. i. 64, Syme, 53.—[7] Unreported.—[8] Hume, i. 65.

lithgow and Falkirk, on the ground that the offence was not theft, but breach of trust. The case was certified by Lord Gillies from Stirling, and, after being fully argued before the High Court, it was unanimously found that the crime was theft.[1] A judgment proceeding on the same principles was pronounced in the case of Brown, Gilchrist and others, July 14. 1831. Gilchrist was one of the *part owners* of a coach running between Glasgow and Edinburgh, and he was charged with having broken open the locked boot, and stolen a parcel of bank-notes containing £5400. This was held clearly theft, though he was one of the owners of the coach, and he was condemned to death and executed.

The same principle rules the case of money committed to the custody of clerks, or others, connected with mercantile or banking-houses in the course of business. At Glasgow, on October 5. 1799, William Dick was indicted for theft, committed by stealing a large sum of money, the contents of a sealed parcel which he had been hired to carry. The objection stated, " that as the libel stated that as the parcel was *given* to the pannel, the fact charged was breach of trust." Answered for the prosecutor, " That the parcel was given to the pannel for a special purpose, to be carried by him to a particular place, and the breaking it up was an act of theft." The Court repelled the objection.[2] This decision was confirmed by another recently pronounced, after great consideration, by the whole Court, in the case of Daniel Alexander Murray and J. Tait, November 18. 1829. The *species facti* here was, that the former of these parties was a clerk in a mercantile house in Glasgow, and in that character was in the habit of being intrusted with the payment of large sums into the cash-account of his employers. Having fallen into difficulties, he formed the design of abstracting one of these sums, and emigrating with it to America. The indictment set forth, that, on the day libelled, he was intrusted by his employers with a large sum, to be instantly paid into their cash-account to their credit; but that, instead of fulfilling his instructions, he did, with the assistance of the pannel Tait, abstract the whole, and appropriate it to their own purposes. The indictment was objected to at the Glasgow Circuit, on two grounds, 1*st*, That the crime charged amounted to breach of trust only; and, 2*d*, That the accession of Tait to the crime was not duly set forth in the charge. The

[1] Unreported.—[2] Hume, i. 66

Judges there (Lords Justice-Clerk Boyle and Moncrieff), expressed a clear opinion that the case was one of theft, but they certified both points, with a view to obtain an authoritative judgment from the Supreme Court; and, after hearing a full argument, their Lordships unanimously expressed a clear opinion, that the crime was rightly charged as theft; and the charge of theft against Tait having been waved, and the reset only insisted in *quoad* him, the libel was found relevant to infer the pains of law. The conviction of both offenders was afterwards prevented by the circumstance of their being taken as witnesses to detail conversations which they had with Emonds in Edinburgh Jail, relative to the Haddington murders with which he was charged.[1]

The same rules are adopted in the English law. Thus, where a person hired a servant, for the special purpose of driving sheep to a fair, and the man, on the road, converted part of them to his own use, it was held by all the Judges, on a reserved case, that it was theft.[2] In like manner, where a clerk had the management of the cash concerns of the prosecutors, and had authority to get their bills discounted as occasion might require, and absconded with the proceeds of one of the bills which he had got discounted, this was held by Justice Heath to be clearly theft.[3] In Hammon's case, it appeared that a banker's clerk had falsely informed a customer of the house, where he had paid in money to his credit, and thereby induced the customer to give him a check for the amount, and received the money which he appropriated, and then, to prevent discovery, made fictitious entries in the books. This was held by all the Judges to be larceny Justice Grove, in delivering their opinion, declared, " The true meaning of larceny is the felonious taking of the property of another without his consent: the fact of this can answer every part of this definition: the taking of the property is clear: the taking with a felonious intent, against the will of the owner, is equally clear, from the circumstance of the prisoner's having made false entries, to conceal the means he had artfully made use of to obtain it." [4]

It has been decided that it is felony at common law, and in-

<hr/>

[1] Unreported.—[2] Stocks' Case, Russell, ii. 201.—[3] Chipchage's Case, Leach, ii. 699; Russell, ii. 202.—[4] Hammon's Case, May 1812, Leach, 1083; Russell, ii. 203.

dependent of the statutes, for a clerk, letter-carrier, or other person in the Post-Office, to abstract money from a letter. So it was held in the case of Thomas Hassell, a letter-sorter, 16th October 1730;[1] and, in the case of Timothy Skutt, Old Bailey, July 1774, the pannel was convicted, at common law, of theft, for stealing money from letters which had come into his hands as a letter-sorter.[2]

But the English were embarrassed on this matter with a difficulty which is not experienced in our practice, viz. the principle thoroughly established in their law, that property is not to be considered as ever delivered into the owner's possession, if it has been merely delivered to a servant for his use. On this ground they held that if the servant have done no act to determine the original possession which he has acquired, as by depositing the goods in his master's house, warehouse, or the like, if he appropriated the goods to his own use, he was not guilty of larceny, but of breach of trust.[3]  Upon this principle it was held, that where the prisoner had received East India bonds for behoof of the Bank of England, of which he was a cashier; but, instead of depositing them in the place of deposit of the Bank, had put them in his private desk, of which he had the key, and there purloined and sold them for his own behoof, he was guilty not of theft but breach of trust.[4]  And this was confirmed in a subsequent case, where it was ruled that a banker's clerk, who was intrusted to receive bank-notes and cash at the counter, and give a discharge for the same, instead of putting a £ 100 note into one of the drawers, where it should have been placed, secreted it about his person, and converted it to his own use, this was not theft, but breach of trust.[5]

In consequence of this decision, the statute 39th Geo. III. c. 85, was passed, which made provision for the embezzlement by clerks or servants which had not yet reached their masters' possession.  But that statute is now repealed, and, in lieu thereof, the 7th and 8th Geo. IV. c. 29, provides for the punishment of such offenders.  This statute enacts, " that if any clerk or servant, or any person employed for the purpose, or in the capacity of a clerk or servant, shall, by virtue of such employment,

<hr/>

[1] Leach's Cases, No 1 —[2] Ibid  No 63.—[3] Russell, ii. 204.—[4] Waite's Case, Leach, i 28, Russell, ii. 404.—[5] Bazeley's Case, 1799, Leach, ii. 835, Russell, ii 205.

receive or take into his possession any chattel, money, or valuable security for, or in the name or on account of, his master, and shall fraudulently embezzle the same or any part thereof; every such offender shall be deemed to have feloniously stolen the same from his master, although such chattel, money, or security was not received into the possession of such master otherwise than by the actual possession of his clerk, servant, or other person so employed; and every such offender being convicted therefor, shall be liable, at the discretion of the Court, to any of the punishments which the Court may award, as herein before mentioned." [1] Any punishment not exceeding fourteen years' transportation may be inflicted under this act.

It was decided in England in the case of Benjamin Walsh, July 1812, that it is not theft where the prosecutor delivers a bank-check to a broker for the purpose of the proceeds being applied to a particular purpose, and he appropriates the proceeds to his own use, although at the time of receiving the check he had formed that intention.[2] In consequence of this decision, the 52d Geo. III. c. 63, was passed, which declared such an offence punishable with transportation. This act is now repealed, but in its stead it is enacted by Mr Peel's act, 7th and 8th Geo. IV. c. 29, " that if any money, or security for the payment of money, shall be intrusted to any banker, merchant, broker, attorney, or other agent, with any direction in writing to apply such money or any part thereof, or the proceeds of any part of the proceeds of such security for any purpose specified in such direction, and he shall, in violation of good faith, and contrary to the purpose so specified in such direction, in anywise convert to his own use or benefit such money, security, or proceeds, or any part thereof respectively, every such offender shall be guilty of a misdemeanour, and shall be liable to be transported at the discretion of the Court for any period not exceeding fourteen nor less than seven years, or to suffer such other punishment by fine or imprisonment, or by both, as the Court shall award; and if any chattel or valuable security, or any power of attorney, for the sale or transfer of any share or interest in any public stock or fund, whether of this kingdom or of Great Britain, or of Ireland, or of any foreign state, or in any fund of any body corporate, company

---

[1] 7th and 8th Geo IV. c 29 § 47 —[2] Walsh's Case, Russell, ii 114

or society, shall be    trusted to any banker, merchant, broker, attorney, or other ag  _t, for safe custody, or for any special purpose, without any authority to sell, negociate, transfer, or pledge; and he shall, in violation of good faith, and contrary to the object or purpose for which such chattel, security, or power of attorney, shall have been intrusted to him, sell, negociate, transfer, pledge, or in any manner convert to his own use or benefit such chattel or security, or the proceeds of the same, or any part thereof, or the share or interest in the stock or fund to which such power shall relate, or any part thereof; every such offender shall be guilty of a misdemeanour, and being convicted thereof, shall be liable, at the discretion of the Court, to any of the punishments which the Court may award, as herein last before mentioned." [1]

. These enactments unquestionably relate to England only; and there seems no necessity for their extension to this country, because the common law of Scotland is amply sufficient for the punishment of all such offences under the name of breach of trust.   And wherever there is any doubt as to the completion of delivery to the person from whom the depredation has been committed, the indictment should be laid alternately f r theft or breach of trust; under either of which alternatives as severe a punishment may be inflicted as is authorised by the English statute, as will be amply shewn in the chapter on breach of trust.

It is hardly necessary to observe, that the pannel has no sort of defence against a charge of theft in those less favourable situations where the particular thing has not at all been committed to him, but his station has merely afforded him a convenient opportunity to steal.   As if a servant open his master's repositories with the keys which he has found mislaid, or taken out of his pocket; or if, being sent with a key to fetch an article from some locked place, he take the opportunity to secrete some other article; or if he take his pocket-book out of his pocket when brushing the clothes, or if the groom carry off the plate from the butler's pantry, or the butler take a horse from the stable.   In all these and similar cases, there is no sort of custody or trust reposed in the servant, and his felonious appropriation is unquestionably theft, and daily treated as such in our practice.[2]

[1] 7th and 8th Geo IV. c. 29. § 49.—[2] Hume, 1 68.

4. It is theft, although the article stolen be obtained on some false pretence, or by a trick, from the true owner, provided there was no consent obtained by false representations to the actual transfer of the property of the article in question.

It will afterwards be shewn, that when possession is obtained by such false representations as induce the owner to sell or part with *the property*, the crime is swindling  But a variety of cases frequently occur in which the possession is obtained, not on any contract or agreement adequate to pass the *property*, but on some inferior title, intended only to give the pannel the right of *interim custody*.  Thus, a man hires a horse professedly to go a particular journey, but instead of doing so he instantly rides the horse as hard as it can go in a different direction, and there sells it for the best price he can get; or a person gets linen on the false pretence of being a bleacher, and immediately upon obtaining it, packs it up and flies, or sells it and pockets the price: in all such cases the crime is nothing less than theft.[1]  The distinction between such cases and those in which the property is obtained on a false pretence lies here,—that, in the one case, the proprietor has agreed to transfer the property, therefore he has only been *imposed upon* in the transfer; in the other, he has never agreed to part with his property, and therefore the subsequent appropriation is theft.[2]

Accordingly,   the case of John Marshall, Dumfries, April 1792, it appeared that the pannel had hired a horse at Sanquhar to ride to Leadhills, a distance of ten miles, instead of which he rode directly to Edinburgh as fast as he could, and there sold the horse for his own behoof.  This was held by Lord Hailes to be theft, and the prisoner, having confessed, was transported for seven years.[3]  So also in the case of Walter Tyrie, Perth, autumn 1827, the *species facti* set forth in the indictment was, that the prisoner hired a horse at Cupar in Fife professedly to ride a short distance near that place; but, having got on his back, he crossed the Dundee ferry and rode to Stonehaven, where he sold him for his own behoof.  It was strenuously argued against the libel, which was laid alternatively for theft and fraud, that the offence only amounted to the latter

---

[1] Hume, i. 68, 69; Burnett, 113.—[2] Hume, i. 69.—[3] Ibid , Burnett, 114.

of these crimes; but Lords Pitmilly and Alloway, after a full and able argument from Mr Menzies, repelled the objection, and sustained the libel as relevant which charged the offence as theft. The pannel then pleaded guilty to the fraud, which the prosecutor agreed to, as the point of law was determined, and was sentenced to twelve months' imprisonment.[1] This has been more recently confirmed by the opinion of the whole Court in the case of John Smith, January 8. 1829, High Court. The *species facti* here was that the pannel went to a stable-yard in Rose Street, where he hired a horse to ride about Edinburgh for two days, but instead of doing so he directly rode off to Glasgow, where he sold him for his own behoof. The libel charged theft alternatively with fraud, but the Court expressed a clear conviction that the case was one of theft, and that the proper *locus* of the theft, in such a case, is the place where the horse was first obtained by the pannel, with the design of abstracting it, and, to avoid a capital conviction, the libel was restricted to the charge of swindling, and the pannel was sentenced to seven years' transportation.[2]

The law of England seems to be settled on the same principles, it being fixed that if the owner has not parted with the *property* in consequence of the false representation, but only with the *possession*, the subsequent felonious appropriation is theft.[3] Thus, where a hosier, by desire of the prisoner, took a variety of silk stockings to his lodgings, where the prisoner pretended to purchase them, and then sent for some more and decamped with the articles, this was held to be larceny, on the ground that the whole of the prisoner's conduct manifested an original and tortuous design to get possession of the goods.[4] So also where the owner of goods sent them by his servants to be delivered to a real purchaser, and the prisoner procured them to be delivered to himself, by fraudulently pretending that he was that servant, this was held by all the Judges to be theft.[5] In like manner, to obtain fraudulently a chest of tea from the India House, by means of a request-note and permit, was adjudged by the same high authority to be larceny.[6] In another case, the prisoner offered to accommodate the prosecutor by giving him gold for bank-notes, upon which the prosecutor put

---

[1] Unreported —[2] Unreported —[3] Russell, ii. 118 —[4] Sharpless's Case, Leach, i. 93; Russell, ii. 119.—[5] Wilkins's Case, Leach, i 520, Russell, ii. Hercules's 120 —[6] Case, Russell, ii. 120

down a number of notes, which the prisoner immediately took up and carried off; this was adjudged theft, if the jury believed that the prisoner intended to run away with the notes, and not return with the gold.[1]  Again, where the prisoner induced the prosecutor to deliver twenty guineas and four doubloons, by way of pledge for a counterfeit jewel, pretended to have been found, with intent to steal the money, it was adjudged theft by the Court of King's Bench;[2] and this was afterwards confirmed by all the Judges in another case precisely similar.[3]  Where the prisoner induced a person to deliver bank-notes to him on the pretence of ring-dropping, upon the usual agreement, that the notes should be returned, and the value of the found jewel divided, this was held by all the Judges to be larceny.[4]  So also where the prisoner hired a horse on the pretence of taking a journey, and almost immediately afterwards sold it; this was held by all the Judges to be theft, after great consideration.[5]  This was soon after confirmed in another case, where the horse hired was sold on the same day on which it had been received by the prisoner.[6]  And in Major Semple's case, where the prisoner obtained a post-chaise by hiring, with the design of converting it to his own use, and he afterwards sold it for his own behoof; this was adjudged to be theft, and the prisoner was transported for seven years.  In this case the Court said, " If the owner only intended to give the prisoner a qualified use of the chaise, and he had no intention to make use of that qualified possession, but to convert it to his own use, he did not take it upon the contract, and therefore did not obtain the lawful possession of it." [7]  Goods also obtained by the fraudulent use of legal process, or by fraudulent ejectment, are held to be stolen or robbed, according as the case occurred without or with violence.[8]

The principle on which these cases proceed is the more worthy of consideration by our Court, because it is settled in the English law equally with our practice, that if the *property* in the goods taken has been *parted with* by the owner in consequence of false representations, the crime is not theft, but swindling.[9]  Thus, where the prisoner bought a horse at a fair,

[1] Oliver's Case, Leach, ii. 1072,  Russell, ii. 122.—[2] Moore's Case, Leach, i. 314; Russell, ii. 125.—[3] Marsh's Case, Leach, i 345,  Russell, ii. 125, *note* —[4] Watson's Case, Leach, ii. 640 ; Russell, ii 126 —[5] Pear's Case, Leach, i 212; Russell, ii. 127 —[6] Charlewood's Case, Old Bailey, 1786, Russell, ii. 128. —[7] Semple's Case, Leach, i 420,  Russell, ii 130.—[8] Hale, i. 507; Chadwick's Case, East. ii. 660,  Russell, ii. 130, 131.—[9] Russell, ii. 118

and rode away with it, ..ter it was delivered, without paying the purchase-money, this was held not to be theft, on the ground that there was a complete contract of sale and delivery, and that the *property*, as well as the possession, had been completely parted with.[1] So also where the prisoner, with a fraudulent intent to obtain goods, ordered a tradesman to send him some, to be paid for on delivery, and gave the servant who brought them fabricated bills which were of no value, this was ruled not to be larceny, upon the ground that the servant had parted with the property by accepting such payment as had been offered.[2]

5. If goods be delivered to a carrier, whether by land or water, it is theft by the English law if he, or any one under his orders, open out the packages and steal the articles.

A carrier has no sort of property in the goods intrusted to his care for transport; his contract is to deliver them at the specified place; he is *pro hac vice* servant of his employer, and therefore would seem as much guilty of theft if he appropriate them to his own use, as the butler if he steal the plate, or the shepherd the sheep. Mr Hume, however, delivers the contrary doctrine[3] in the case of a regular and established carrier. But however that matter may be ultimately settled, it is advisable in the mean time to draw all libels for such offences by carriers, or others intrusted with goods, alternately for theft and breach of trust.[4]

In the English law it seems upon the whole settled, though with some apparently unsubstantial distinctions, that such an appropriation on the carrier's part is theft. Thus it is settled, that if a carrier open a pack and take out part of the goods, or a weaver take part of the silk which he has received to work, or a miller take part of the corn which has been delivered to him to grind, such takings, if done with a felonious intent, will amount to theft.[5] So also, where a warehouseman took out the wheat out of certain bags which had been delivered to him for safe custody, this was unanimously held by all the Judges to be larceny.[6] But they have sanctioned a distinction on the

---

[1] Harvey's Case, Leach, i. 467, Russell, ii. 109.—[2] Parker's Case, East. ii. 671; Russell, ii 110.—[3] Hume, i. 58.—[4] *Ante*, p. 253, 254.—[5] Hale, i. 505; Hawkins, i. c 33 § 4; Russell, ii. 134.—[6] Brasier's Case, Russell, ii. 134.

subject, which need not be held up for our imitation, viz. that though it is theft, if the carrier *open* and abstract part of the package, yet it is not theft if he take away the *whole* without opening.[1] No hesitation need be felt in condemning this distinction, so obviously contrary to reason, since the English lawyers themselves stigmatise it as " savouring a little of contradiction, and standing more upon positive law than sound reasoning." [2] Wherever the delivery of the goods is for a special and specific purpose, the possession is held to reside with the proprietor, and if the possessor abstract, he commits theft. Thus it is theft to abstract plate set before a person in a tavern, or if a watchmaker appropriate a watch delivered to him to clean, or a washerwoman carry off clothes delivered to her to wash, or any one plunder goods delivered to him for custody in a locked chest with the key.[3]

6. It is not the less theft that the owner has put the article stolen in the prisoner's way, or given it into his custody for a short period, if there was no contract for the transfer of the property.

Cases of this sort are of daily occurrence. Thus, a man delivers a portmanteau to a porter to be carried to a particular place, and he instantly runs off with it; or a shopkeeper produces goods to one who inquires for them, and he runs off with them as soon as they are put into his hands; or a person gallops off with a horse which he has mounted to try his paces; or, under pretence of giving change to one who asks for it in the market, some villain gets the note into his hand and immediately runs off; in all these and the like cases the crime is theft.[4] Accordingly, in the case of William Renwick, Jedburgh, September 1818, a libel was found relevant for theft, which stated that the prisoner having sold a pony to a purchaser, and immediately afterwards asked him to allow him to ride a bay-mare belonging to the purchaser to Melrose, which he was allowed to do, in company with the purchaser's boy, and that, when on the road, he started off and galloped away with the mare.[5] In like manner, in the case of Richard Mac-

---

[1] Hale, i. 505, Russell, ii. 134.—[2] Kelly, 83; East ii 695, Russell, ii. 134.—[3] Hawkins, i c. 33. § 10; Russell, ii. 107.—[4] Hume, i 64; Burnett, 114.—[5] Hume, i. 64

kinney, Perth, April 1821, it was held to be a relevant charge
of theft, that he had snatched and run off with a watch from
the hand of a person who pulled it out to shew him the hour
on his asking it.[1]

It has been already stated, that any article abstracted by
a *snatch* or sudden pull, even though a momentary exertion of
force have been exerted to get the command of it, is held to be
*stolen*, not robbed, upon the principle that robbery is the violence which is directly applied to overcome the physical
strength, or indirectly to control the will.[2]  Upon this principle, if a man's hat be snatched from his head, or his watch
from his fob, or a lady's reticule from her hand, or her purse
from her bosom, it is theft, and not robbery.[3]  So it was found
at Glasgow in the case of Alexander Smith, autumn 1829,
where the prisoner snatched a reticule from a lady in a common stair and ran off with it; this was held to be theft:[4] and
at Edinburgh, in the case of W. Duggin and J. Kitchen, December 1. 1828, where the snatching of a watch from a fob,
while the owner was only jostled, was also adjudged to be that
crime.[5]

The rule of the English law is the same.  Thus, where a
boy was carrying a bundle along the street in his hand, and
the prisoner ran past him and suddenly snatched it, the Judges
held that it was not done with the force and violence requisite
to constitute robbery.[6]  In like manner, where two little boys
were carrying a parcel of cloth to one of the inns at Bath, and
the prisoner came up suddenly and snatched it from the one of
them, this was held to be theft.[7]  The same doctrine was held
in two other cases, in one of which the hat and wig of a gentleman were snatched from his head in the street; and, in another, an umbrella was snatched out of the hand of a woman as
she was walking the street.[8]  But the distinction between such
cases and those where the crime is robbery, is very thin; for,
if any injury be done to the person, or there be any struggle
on the part of the owner to keep possession of his goods, it will
be robbery.[9]  Thus, where the prisoner made a snatch at a
sword hanging by a gentleman's side, and he caught hold of

[1] Hume, 1. 64.—[2] *Ante*, p 253.—[3] Hume, 1. 64; Burnett, 115.—[4] Unreported.—[5] Unreported.—[6] Macauley's Case, Leach, i. 287, Russell, ii. 67.—
[7] Robin's Case, Leach, 1. 290, Russell, ii 67.—[8] Steward's Case, East ii. 702,
Russell, ii. 68, Horne's Case, East. ii. 703; Russell, ii. 68.—[9] Russell, ii 68.

the scabbard, and a struggle ensued, the result of which was that the scabbard remained in his hand, and the prisoner made off with the sword, this was adjudged robbery;[1] and the like judgment was given by all the Judges in another case, where it appeared that the prosecutor's watch was fastened by a guard-chain round his neck, the seal and chain hanging from his fob, and the prisoner pulled the watch from the fob, but the chain held it, and by two jerks he broke the chain.[2]

The mere possession for the moment will not render the crime less than theft, if this possession was obtained *animo furandi.* Thus where the prisoner agreed with the prosecutor to discount a bill of exchange, and the bill accordingly was delivered into the prisoner's hands, upon a promise to give the prosecutor cash when he came to his lodgings, the prosecutor sent his clerk with him to receive the money; but the prisoner having got out of the clerk's sight on the road, and escaped with the bill; this was held by all the Judges to be larceny.[3] The same rule obtains where the owner has exposed his property to be stolen, by affording the suspected thief some facility towards the accomplishment of his purpose, as by allowing his watchman to give a seeming assent to a proposal made to him by the prisoner to rob the house, and to facilitate their purpose by opening a certain door.[4] In like manner, where a house was hired under a certain lease for twenty-one years, with a view to steal the lead and other fixtures, this was clearly theft; and so it was held by all the Judges.[5]

7. It is essential in theft that there be not only a taking, but a carrying away; but it is sufficient to complete the crime if the thing be removed for the shortest time, and for a small distance from its proper place and state of keeping.

How clearly soever the intention to steal may have been manifested, to abstract property with a felonious intent the crime of theft is not committed without an actual *asportatio,* or removal of the thing from its place of keeping.[6] Thus, if a boy has his hand in my pocket, and has got hold of my purse,

[1] Davie's Case, Leach, L 299, Russell, ii 68.—[2] Mason's Case, Russell, ii 68.—[3] Ackle's Case, Leach, i 294; Russell, ii. 122—[4] Eggington's Case, Leach, ii. 913, Russell, ii. 105—[5] Munday's Case, Leach, No 312.—[6] Hume, i. 70; Burnett, 121.

but there I seize his hand, and the purse is never withdrawn; or if a vagabond in passing make a snatch at linen upon a hedge, but it sticks to the thorns and is not removed; or having got into a waggon to steal, he raise a package on its end, but do not remove it from its place; in none of these cases is the crime theft, it is only attempt to steal, a different and well established point of dittay.[1]

But, while this is fixed on the one hand, it is not the less material to observe on the other, that the crime will be held as completed though there has been no complete removal of the article from the premises, or place of keeping where it was, provided it has once got into the hands of the thief, and been by him shifted from its former place of deposit. Though the thief is seen in the very act of taking, and is instantly pursued, and throws it down, the offence is nevertheless theft.[2] Thus, in the case of Smith and Forrester, December 15. 1686, it was held a relevant article of dittay, under a charge of theft, that they had laid hold of poultry in a close or court-yard, but, being discovered, they threw down the poultry and fled.[3] So also, in the case of Samuel Riccards, June 27. 1710, it was found to be a good charge of robbery, which is governed on this point by the same principles as theft, that he had run off with a woman's plaid, and threw it from him in the field near the spot of the robbery.[4]

Farther, it is theft in every instance where the thing is taken out of its proper place of keeping, under such circumstances as clearly indicates the intention of the taker.[5] On this principle, the crime is completed as soon as the horse is carried out of the stable, or the cattle out of the enclosure in which they were kept.[6] Accordingly, Thomas Gordowan, February 5. 1782, had sentence of death for sheepstealing, on evidence that he had lifted two sheep over the wall of the field where they had been at pasture, and was there caught with the carcasses on the spot. Again, in the case of Anderson and Lindsay, 15th June 1818, two butchers were convicted on a libel for theft, who had stolen an ox from the door of a booth to which it was tied in a common shambles, and had moved it to another booth a few doors off and there slaughtered it.[7] Nay, there seems no reason to doubt that the crime is completed, though the animal

[1] Hume, i. 70, Burnett, 121.—[2] Hume, i. 70; Burnett, 122.—[3] Ibid.—[4] Ibid.—[5] Burnett, 121, Hume, i. 71.—[6] Hume, i. 71.—[7] Ibid.

be not removed from the enclosure where it had pastured at will, provided it have been seized and brought clearly into the possession of the thief; as, if a sheep be seized in a large field, and the thief is caught with the animal on his back in the act of carrying it across the park; or the horse has been caught, and is in the act of being led along its field, when the theft is discovered.[1]

Farther, still the same shall hold where the *amotio* has been much more inconsiderable, provided the article has been clearly removed *animo furandi* from its proper place of keeping or deposit. Thus it is quite fixed with respect to any article which has a peculiar and safe place of keeping within a house, that it is theft to remove it from that situation.[2] A servant is unquestionably guilty of theft who forces the lock of any repository in his master's house, and takes out the contents; or a stranger who has entered a house, and broken up a chest, cupboard, or the like, and removed the contents to the floor with a view to their being afterwards packed up and carried away.[3] Accordingly, on December 19. 1698, Alexander Snaile had sentence of death on a proof which established that he had entered a house by means of a false key, on a Sunday, and that, having opened a chest by means of the key, which was standing in the lock, he had abstracted an article of small value, with which he was taken in the room.[4] On this principle, if a housebreaker be caught with a hat on his head which he has taken out of a hat-box, or books have been lifted down from their shelves and put in a bag, or goods have been taken down from the shelves of a shop and laid on the floor packed up, the *amotio* is complete.[5] So also if a purse be taken from the pocket, a watch from the fob, or an ear-ring from the ear, the crime has been completed.[6] And, in general, if the state of fixture in which the thing naturally is be altered, or the particular provisions, how slender soever made, for its safe custody overcome, this, joined with the least removal in respect of place, consummates the guilt.[7] Thus a charge of theft is good if wool be picked from a sheep, or fruit from a tree, or if a strong chest fastened to the floor be unscrewed and removed how little soever from its place; or if a piece of cloth in a bleachfield be unpinned, rolled up, and removed to a small dis-

---

[1] Hume, i. 73.—[2] Burnett, 121; Hume, i. 71.—[3] Ibid. i. 72; Burnett, 122.—[4] Hume, i. 72.—[5] Ibid. i. 73.—[6] Ibid.—[7] Ibid.

tance; or if a thief cut a web out of a loom and fold it, or take
a person's breeches with money in it from under his pillow as
he sleeps, and be hastening with it out of the room, when he is
seized.[1]

Accordingly, in the case of John Welsh, November 1808, it
appeared that the thief had broke into a shop in the night, and
laid hold of a jar full of vinegar, and which he had moved into a back area of the building   He had also taken a quantity
of sugar out of a paper parcel, which he had put into a canvass
bag, with a view to carry it off, which he had put on the top
of a chest in the shop.   When he had proceeded thus far he
was scared, and made off, leaving the articles in these situations.   The *amotio* was held complete as to *both* articles, and
the pannel was transported.[2]   So also in the case of Macqueen
and Baillie, 15th January 1810, the thieves were caught in the
shop, with some of the shop goods displaced from the shelves
and lying on the floor.   The Court were clearly of opinion
that, had the evidence clearly shewn that the goods had been
removed there by the act of the thieves, the crime was complete; but it appeared doubtful on the evidence whether the
removal had not taken place during a scuffle which took place
with the police officers.[3]   Again, in the case of John Perry,
Hugh Robertson, and John Birrell, Glasgow, April 1819, it
was held to be a sufficient removal that the pannels had cut
the straps which fastened a trunk behind a carriage travelling
on the road, so that the trunk fell to the ground, though they
were detected in the fact and ran off without lifting it from
the ground.[4]   In like manner, in the case of Robert Thomson and J. Brown, May 1823, it was held to be a clear case
of removal that the pannels had taken some blankets and other
bedclothes off a bed in Merchiston Castle, into which they had
feloniously obtained entry, and rolled them up in the same
room in which they had been placed, without any farther removal[5]   This was confirmed in the case of John Paterson and
Alexander Glasgow, 15th March 1827, where it was unanimously held by the High Court, to make a sufficient case of
theft,  that the pannels had entered into an unoccupied house,
and removed certain blankets and counterpanes from the beds
and apartments in which they were placed, and having bundled

---

[1] Hume, 1. 73.—[2] Ibid. 1. 72.—[3] Burnett, 122, Hume, 1 73 —[4] Ibid 1 72
—[5] Unreported.

them up, had placed the bundle in a passage near the back door in the sunk floor, whither the men returned the following night to carry it off.[1] The like judgment was given by Lords Justice-Clerk Boyle and Pitmilly, in the case of J. Macdonald, Aberdeen, spring 1823, where it was held that goods were sufficiently removed to constitute theft which had been taken out of various open places of deposit in a cottage, and placed on the thief's handkerchief in the middle of the floor, preparatory to removal, but without the handkerchief having been tied, or any farther removal effected [2] On the other hand, it was held by the Lord Justice-Clerk Boyle, at Glasgow, autumn 1826, in the case of John Boyle, that the removal was not complete, where the thief had rolled the bedclothes to the bottom of the bed, evidently with a view to removal, but was scared before he had proceeded farther.[3] And, in the case of Irvine Macewan, Glasgow, autumn 1826, that the *asportatio* was not complete, where a shirt was rolled up but not taken out of the drawers where it had been placed, but that it would have been otherwise if the article had been taken out of the drawers, though it was thrown instantly down on the floor.

The law of England is fixed upon the same principles. It is settled with them that the felony lies in the very first act of removing the property, and, therefore, that the very least removal of the thing from where it was before, with intent to steal, is sufficient to asportation [4] Thus, when a guest in an inn had taken the sheets from his bed, with the design to steal them, and carried them into the hall, but was apprehended before he could get out of the house, it was held that he was guilty of larceny.[5] The like judgment was given where a person had taken a horse in a close, but was apprehended before he could get it out; and where a person intending to steal plate, took it out of a trunk where it had been deposited, and laid it on the floor, but was surprised before he could carry it away.[6] In a later case it was held by all the Judges to be theft to remove a parcel from the head to the tail of a waggon, with intent to steal;[7] but the reverse was found where the parcel was only altered in *its position* in the waggon, or being put on its end,

[1] Syme, 174.—[2] Unreported.—[3] Unreported —[4] Blackstone, iv. 231, East ii. 555.—[5] Hale, i 507, 508.—[6] Simson's Case, Kil 31, Russell, ii 95.— [7] Coslet's Case, Leach, i 236, Russell, ii 95

instead of being laid lengthwise, without being removed from
its place. The Judges held that some removal of the goods
from the place where they were is necessary, and that the pannel must, for the instant at least, have had the entire and absolute possession of them.[1]  But if every part of the thing has
been removed from the place which that part occupied, though
the whole thing is not removed from the place which it occupied, this will render the asportation complete.[2]  Thus the
lifting of a bag from the bottom to the top of the boot of a
coach, though the prisoner had not got it out of the boot,
was held to be a completed theft by all the Judges:[4] and the
same would hold of a sword partly drawn out of a scabbard.[4]

On the other hand, it has been held not to be theft where
goods tied by a string to the counter, and lifted up and carried
by the thief as far as they would go, because here there was no
severance;[5] and where the thief took from the pockets of the
owner a purse, and was apprehended with the purse in his
hand, but still hanging by the string, it was ruled not to be
larceny.[6]

8. It is indispensable to theft that the taking shall
have been for a felonious purpose, and *lucri causa*; any
appropriation done from a different motive, or on a mistaken idea of right, being a different species of crime; but
if it be taken away for this motive, subsequent restitution
will form no defence.

The taking and carrying away must be with a felonious
purpose by one who knows that the thing belongs to another,
and who means notwithstanding to deprive him of his property.  It is not therefore theft, though known to be the property of another, if the taker's intention was irregular and improper only, and not *lucri causa*, for the sake of appropriation.[7]
Thus if a servant ride his master's horse in the night on his
own errand; or, if finding his neighbour's plough lying in the
field, a farmer uses it in tilling his own ground; or, if he drive
his neighbour's cattle into his own enclosure, in the night, to
poind them there, under pretence of a trespass, this is not

<hr>

[1] Cheny's Case, East. ii. 556, Russell, ii. 96.—[2] Russell, ii. 96.—[3] Walsh's
Case, Russell, ii. 96.—[4] Russell, ii. 96.—[5] East. ii. 566, Russell, ii. 96.—
[6] Hale, i. 502; Russell, ii. 90.—[7] Hume, i. 73; Burnett, 121, 115.

theft.[1] We do not admit the *furtum usus* or *possessionis* of the Roman law.[2] Accordingly, in the case of Dewar, Glasgow, October 1777, it appeared that the prisoner was an apprentice to a printfield company, the proprietors of which were possessed of a secret for mixing and preparing colours, the receipt of which was kept in a pocket belonging to one of the partners, kept in a lockfast room. The prisoner, being desirous to get possession of the receipt, broke open the room and carried it off; copied it, and afterwards replaced it where he had found it. The Court, upon an argument on the relevancy, did not consider this as a case of proper theft, the paper having been fraudulently abstracted, with a view merely to copy and return it; but they held it an irregular and punishable act, and inflicted imprisonment and banishment from the county.[3]

As little does it amount to theft, though the taker mean to dispose of the thing as his own, if he take it in the belief, however erroneous, if serious, and founded on probable grounds, that the thing is his own. Accordingly, in the case of Ker and Stables, Aberdeen, September 1792, the pannels were indicted for theft, as principal and accessary. The *species facti* appeared to be, that Ker, a younger brother, conceiving that he had a right to a certain share of his father's moveable effects, made a demand upon his elder brother for a share of them, which was refused. Upon this Ker, instigated by Stables, came in the night-time, and clandestinely carried off cattle and other effects, which formerly belonged to their father. The jury found the facts proved as now stated; but " that the conduct of the pannels in this respect, though highly culpable, does not amount to the crime of theft, there being no sufficient evidence that the articles he carried away were the property of John Ker" (his elder brother). This verdict had the approbation of the Court.[4] In like manner, if John carry off James's goods, by poinding, how irregular soever the diligence may be, or oppressive the proceedings, still the taking in this form, even in its worst form, can never infer theft or stouthrief, but only spuilzie or oppression, punishable with an arbitrary pain.[5] Many cases of this sort formerly occurred, some which are collected by Mr Hume;[6] but the change of manners

---

[1] Hume, l. 73.—[2] Burnett, 115.—[3] Ibid. 115.—[4] Ibid. 118; Hume, l. 74.
[5] Hume, l. 74.—[6] Ibid.

has rendered them now rather matter of curiosity than use, and, if prosecuted now, would certainly be under the name of spuilzie or oppression.

But to make way for this favourable construction, the person accused must have a colourable ground for believing that the thing taken was his own.[1] That sort of belief which is directly in the face of the law, and is grounded only on the violent passions, or singular ideas of the man, can establish no sort of defence. A smuggler, therefore, who breaks into a custom-house, and takes away goods which have been seized and condemned, is as much guilty of theft by housebreaking, as if he broke into the house and abstracted the goods of his neighbour.[2] Accordingly, in the case of Alexander Williamson and others, January 12. 1767, who had broken into an excise warehouse, and seized some casks of brandy, which had been seized and deposited there, the Court disregarded the plea that this was neither theft nor robbery, the goods not having been condemned, and, upon the libels being restricted, inflicted transportation for life.[3] A case somewhat similar occurred at Dumfries, September 1800, on the trial of John Lockhart. The goods had here been seized, but not condemned, and, in that intermediate state, they were stolen back again by the original owner. He pleaded, that it is the act of *condemnation* alone which transfers the goods to the Crown, and that till that is done, it is uncertain whether the seizure was lawful, or the state of ownership changed. To this it was answered, that the seizure must *prima facie* be presumed to be regular, till the contrary be shewn; that, till condemnation, they were *in manibus curiæ*, and a *quasi* property vested in the Crown, independent of special statute, and that the condemnation afterwards pronounced drew back to the original seizure. The Court had some doubts on the case, but they were relieved by the jury finding a verdict of not proven.[4] In all cases of this description, where the state of ownership is doubtful, the libel should be drawn alternatively for theft, and the insubordinate offence, described in general terms, by the complexion of what has actually occurred. This accordingly was the course adopted in the case of Macdonald and Chisholm, Inverness, 2d May 1814, who had broken into the King's warehouse at Inverness,

[1] Burnett, 118, Hume, i. 74.—[2] Hume, i. 75; Burnett, 119.—[3] Burnett, 118, 119.—[4] Burnett, 119; Hume, i. 77.

and carried off three ankers, one belonging to Macdonald, the others to some other person, but not condemned. They were convicted of the alternative charge, and transported seven years.

If the taker believed on rational grounds, that the owner would not object to his taking the goods, the crime will not be theft. This presumed consent may be inferred from the near relationship of the parties, or their intimate connexion, in the way of friendship, partnership, or business; and these, where sufficiently pregnant, will do away the *prima facie* evidence of a felonious intent from the way in which the thing was taken.[1] But if the owner have exposed his goods, in a situation where they were likely to be stolen, as with a view to detect and punish the thief, this is not such a consent as will serve as a defence against the charge of theft; on the contrary, it is the strongest indication of a contrary inclination, and a wish to discover and punish the offender.[2]

No one can commit theft of his own goods;[3] but he may of another, though the party, from whose custody they were taken, be not the true owner, but a custodier only for the most temporary cause. Thus goods deposited or lent to a third party, watches in the hands of a watchmaker, clothes in the hands of a washerwoman, &c. may be, and every day are, held as stolen from the persons in whose custody they are.[4] This is matter of daily practice, and, accordingly, every indictment for theft bears, that the goods specified were stolen and theftuously taken away, "being all the property, or *in the lawful possession* of the said A B." Under these words it is sufficient to prove that the goods libelled as stolen were taken from the lawful custody of A B, without specifying who the real proprietor was.

But it is farther indispensable to be for the sake of lucre and profit.[5] This, however, only means, that the thing shall have been taken away " with intent to *detain it from the owner,*" or possessor; or that a charge of theft will not lie where the thing is destroyed out of malice, without being removed, as when a man's cattle are slaughtered and left dead on the field, or a mob enter a house, and break and deface his effects, without carrying any article away.[6] But if the thing has once been feloniously removed the crime is complete, although the ob-

---

[1] Burnett, 120.—[2] Ibid.—[3] Ibid.—[4] Ibid. 121.—[5] Hume, i. 75.—[6] Ibid.

ject of that removal was to destroy it, for that was the *lucre*
which he proposed to himself in the depredation.[1] If, therefore, a herd of cattle be driven from the grounds, and slaughtered at a distance, the charge of theft is good, for the gratification of a malignant passion is the advantage which the depredator has proposed to himself by the removal.[2] Accordingly, in the case of John Mathieson, October 1758, who had
maliciously destroyed another person's mare, the indictment
charged him not with theft, but with "maliciously killing or
destroying a mare, the property of the private pursuer, without his knowledge or consent;" and the like course was adopted
in the case of J. Anderson, Perth, autumn 1809, who, for stabbing and killing an ox, was sentenced to seven years' transportation.[3] Malicious mischief is the proper designation of such
a crime, and, as such, the stabbing of a mare was prosecuted
in the case of William and James Wilson, Ayr, spring 1827.[4]

But, on the other hand, if the *amotio* has been completed,
though evidently with a malicious intent, and not the design
of gain, the proper designation of the crime is theft, and as
such as it has always been treated. Thus in the case of Gilchrist, 6th March 1741, who was one of a mob that had broken
into Bell's Mills, near Edinburgh, and carried off a quantity
of grain, the defence pleaded against an indictment for theft,
was, " that the act was done *animo injuriandi*, and *non lucri
faciendi causa*, and therefore that it was not robbery; the rule
being " *Non factum quæritur, sed causa faciendi;*" but the answer
was sustained, that " the libel charged that the meal was carried away, and not that it was destroyed or consumed, and,
therefore, that its being done from a malicious or mischievous
intent, did not make it less a robbery." The pannel was transported for seven years.[5] The same form of charge, and the
like result, took place in the case of Allan, 18th June 1716,
and June 13. 1727, in both of which such a felonious depredation was charged as theft, and punished as such.[6]

Generally speaking, therefore, the *animus lucri* is to be presumed from the act itself of taking away the thing. Every object is lucre in the estimation of law, which tempts a person to
covet the *keeping and possession* of that which belongs to another. Thus if a criminal purloin from the Sheriff the written

[1] Hume, i. 75, Burnett, 116.—[2] Ibid.—[3] Burnett, 116.—[4] Unreported.—
[5] Burnett, 116.—[6] Ibid.

documents which constitute the evidence of his guilt, or if an antiquary steal gems or books for the pleasure of admiring them, or any one steal a child from love to the child, or spite to its relations, in all these cases the crime is theft.[1] It need hardly be added that theft is committed of any article, however trifling, and though it be of no value whatever to any one but the owner. This is matter of daily practice, and was exemplified in the case of Larg and Mitchell, January 20. 1817, who were executed for stouthrief, though the articles taken consisted only of two forged notes;[2] and the case of William Wilson, July 14. 1827, where the pannel, who was habite and repute a thief, was transported fourteen years for the theft of an old cotton bag, certainly not worth one halfpenny.[3]

The law of England is in the main the same. In the case of Henry Clarke, a conviction was sustained by all the Judges for stealing a number of promissory notes for one pound each, which had been paid and extinguished by the bankers, and, consequently, were of no value to them, except in so far as they could be re-issued by them;[4] and, in the case of Thomas Ranson, a servant of the Post-Office was convicted of larceny, who had secreted a letter containing a number of notes, in the same situation, and *in cursu* of being conveyed to the bankers, for the purpose of being re-issued.[5]

Where the *animus furandi* is not clear, the prisoner is found guilty of a trespass only.[6] Thus, if a man leave a plough or harrow in a field, and another having land in the same field uses them;[7] or where a man, having cattle on a common which he cannot readily find, takes his neighbour's horse which is pasturing on the common, and rides it about to find his cattle; these are trespasses only.[8] Accordingly, where the two prisoners took two horses from a stable, rode them to a considerable distance, and there left them, proceeding on their journey on foot, and the jury found that the horses were taken by the prisoners only to ride them, and afterwards leave them; this was held by all the Judges to be a trespass only.[9] In like manner, property taken by mistake, as a stranger's sheep mixed with the prisoner's own flock, will not constitute felony;[10] and

---

[1] Hume, i. 76.—[2] Ibid. i. 77.—[3] Syme.—[4] Leach, No. 346.—[5] Ibid. 350.—
[6] Russell, ii. 97.—[7] Hale, i. 500.—[8] Hale, i. 509.—[9] Phillips and Strange's
Case, East. ii. 662; Russell, ii. 98.—[10] Hale, i. 503.

the circumstance of the goods being taken on a claim of right, if colourable, may also negative the theftuous intent.[1]

Where goods are *found*, it will not amount in the general case to felony to take them, even though it be done *animo furandi*.[2] Accordingly, if A find the purse of B on the highway, and carry it off, it is not felony.[3] But this doctrine must be received with great limitations; for if goods be found in a place of ordinary, or usual deposit, to abstract them is theft.[4] And if the circumstances were such as should have led to the knowledge of who the proprietor was, the taking will be viewed in the same light.[5] Where a gentleman left a trunk in a hackney coach, and the coachman took and converted it to his own use, this was held to be felony.[6] And this was confirmed by all the Judges in a late case, where a box was left in a hackney coach, which had been uncorded and left at a Jew's by the coachman.[7] And it has been held that, where a parcel of bank-notes is found by a party who knows the owner of it, or there be any mark upon it by which the owner may be ascertained, and the party, instead of restoring the property, converts it to his own use; this is felony.[8] In a case in Chancery it appeared that a large sum of money was found in a bureau, which had been delivered to a carpenter for the purpose of being repaired, Lord Chancellor Eldon said, " There cannot be a doubt that this is felony. There is no doubt that this bureau, being delivered for the purpose of being repaired, if the carpenter broke open any part not necessary for the repair, with intent to appropriate what he could get, that is felony. If a pocket-book containing money be left in a hackney coach, and there were ten people in it in the course of the day, and the coachman did not know to which it belonged, he acquires it by finding, certainly; but not being intrusted with it for the purpose of opening it, that is felony according to the modern cases."[9]

It has been delivered as law by all the Judges, that the true meaning of larceny is " the felonious taking the property of another without his consent, and against his will, with intent

---

[1] Hal., i. 513.—[2] Hawkins, i. c. 33, § 2, Russell, ii. 100.—[3] Hale, i 506; Russell, ii. 100.—[4] Hale, i. 506.—[5] Ibid i. 507 —[6] Lamb's Case, East. ii. 664; Russell, ii. 101 —[7] Wynne's Case, Leach, i. 413, Russell, ii. 664.—[8] Russell, ii. 102—[9] Cartwright v. Greaves, Leach, ii. 952; Vez ii 405

to convert it to the use of the taker." [1] But the *lucre* essential to the crime is not confined to pecuniary advantage; a taking with intent to destroy, if for the supposed advantage of the person committing the offence, or a third party, is sufficient.[2] And it has been held, that a servant's abstracting corn to give his master's horses is theft, especially if his own labour be thereby diminished.

9. It is indispensable to theft that the thing taken be the property of another, but if it be so, it is immaterial whether it is the property of an individual, an incorporation, or a number of persons.

Although a person cannot steal his own property, yet it is no objection to a charge of theft that the goods are the property of a person deceased, or are in a waif or stray condition, or are *in transitu*, or lodged with another on commission, or for the performance of some manufacturing operation, or impledged for the security of a debt.[3] A certain latitude in this respect is indispensable in the manifold operations of life. Accordingly, as already noticed, every libel for theft bears an alternative of the goods being the property, *or in the lawful possession*, of the person stolen from. Nay, this holds good, though the actual owner be uncertain or unknown, if the articles have been taken from the custody of some known person; and accordingly, in the case of Macdonald and Jamieson, August 9. 1770, a libel was sustained as relevant for breaking into the shop of Alexander Macdougall and stealing goods from therein, " being the property of the said Alexander MacDougall, or of some other person to the prosecutor unknown." [4] This is now matter of daily practice.

Theft may be committed, whoever is the owner of the thing stolen, whether a private person, the King, an incorporation, a private society, a parish, or though the case be such that it is impossible to describe correctly the true owner. Thus, in Smith and Brodie's case, August 27. 1788, the money stolen was part of the Royal revenue; and on 6th December 1556, Adam Sinclair and Henry Elderlons had sentence of death for breaking into the church of Forres, and stealing money, chalices, and

---

[1] Hammond's Case, Leach, ii. 1089.—[2] Russell, ii. 94.—[3] Hume, i. 77.—
[4] Ibid. i. 78.

church ornaments.[1]   In the case of William Norval, 21st May 1602, the pannel was banished for stealing money from the poor's box in the session-house at Aberdeen,[2] and William Martin, spring 1750, for stealing £11 of poor's money, had sentence of death.   In the case of J. Cochrane and others, December 11. 1829, the pannels were convicted of theft for breaking into and carrying off free-masons' robes and other insignia belonging to the Canongate Lodge, from a house of one of the office-bearers in Leith.[3]   We are not in this matter embarrassed with the difficulties, and what to us appear the technical distinctions, of the English law, but are content with such a description of the thing as makes the title of possession or management clear, and excludes all pretence of right in the pannel to take it away.[4]

10. Theft may be committed of every inanimate thing, which is either moveable or capable of being severed from that which is naturally or artificially attached to it.

In Scotland no distinction is admitted in regard to the objects on which theft may be committed.   Every thing that can be carried off, without the knowledge or consent of the owner, may be the subject of theft.[5]   Thus, in the case of James Inglis, November 1. 1720, an indictment for theft was sustained as relevant, which charged the tearing of wool from a sheep's back and carrying it away.[6]   So also in the case of James Miln, March 13. 1758, the pannel was transported for stealing shorn corn, shearing and carrying away grass, and pulling up and carrying away growing peas.[7]   In like manner, Andrew Young was transported seven years on 26th December 1800, on a libel which charged the theft of sundry large quantities of potatoes growing upon different fields within the parish of Duddingston.[8]   So also in the case of James Watson and John O'Brien, Glasgow, 22d April 1828, the pannels were convicted of breaking into an unfinished but locked house, and carrying off the lower sash of one of the window-frames which was fastened to the window frame.[9]   The stealing of lead from the roof of houses is daily made the subject of indictment and punishment under the name of theft; and the same seems to hold in the abstrac-

¹ Hume, i 78.—² Ibid.—³ Unreported.—⁴ Hume, i. 78.—⁵ Ibid. i. 79; Burnett, 124.—⁶ Hume, i. 79.—⁷ Ibid.—⁸ Ibid. i. 80.—⁹ Unreported.

tion of coal from a coal-pit, stones from a quarry, or fuel from a moss, if done in the felonious and clandestine manner which form the characteristics of that crime.[1]

With respect to *writings*, the law has been settled in the same way by a great variety of precedents, which are quoted by Baron Hume.[2] To carry off a bond, bill, or promissory note, or writing of any description, is as much theft as to steal a horse or a bag of money.[3] To give a few out of innumerable instances, William Mitchell was convicted on 23d August 1811, of stealing a bill for £48; and William Swan and Duncan Hunter, 20th March 1815, were put on their trial for stealing a bill from a letter put into a private letter-box.[4]

It is also theft at common law, independent of the statutes, to steal from the mail. Such an offence, accordingly, was visited with death in the case of John Seton, 3d July 1691, whose offence was committed before the act 1690, c. 3, anent stealing for the packet, although the relevancy of the indictment was objected to on that very ground.[5] Almost all the indictments in late years for stealing from the mail have been laid upon *the common law* as well as the statutes, and they have all been sustained as relevant. Thus, in the case of Charles and James Jamieson, December 18. 1786, an objection to the charge of stealing from the mail, at common law, was repelled.[6] In the cases of James Clark and Alexander Brown, 10th November 1802, and of George Warden, 12th March 1819, libels in post-office cases for theft were found relevant at common law as well as under the statutes; and in the case of William Oliver, 31st October 1809, there was an express finding of relevancy on the common law charge alone.[7]

11. Theft may be committed on such living creatures as are *sub dominio* and constitute property, and on an infant child from the custody of its parents or guardians.

With regard to the abstraction of animate things, our practice acknowledges a distinction. Such animals as are truly *feræ bestiæ*, as deer, hares, foxes; or such birds as are altogether wild, as partridges, grouse, ptarmigan, wildgeese, plover, &c.

---

[1] Burnett, 124; Hume, i. 80.—[2] Ibid.—[3] Ibid.—[4] Hume, i. 80.—[5] Ibid. i. 81.—[6] Ibid.—[7] Ibid.

are incapable of being stolen; for this plain reason, that they do not belong to, nor are they in the lawful keeping of, any individual.[1] In the only prosecution for an offence of this sort not laid on the game acts, accordingly, which appears on record, that of Ronald Macdonald and others, December 24. 1711, the libel is laid not for theft but for a trespass.

On the other hand, all domestic creatures, such as sheep, horses, poultry, and the like, are the proper subjects of theft; and this holds, in like manner, with animals of a wild kind, if so kept and confined that they cannot escape, as deer in a pen, or limited enclosure, rabbits in a house, or *young* pigeons in a dovecot.[2] And even with regard to wild animals more at large, as deer in a park, rabbits in a warren, doves in a dovecot, fish in a pond, it has been declared by the acts 1474, c. 60; 1535, c. 13; 1587, c. 59, and 1579, c. 84, that the committers of these offences shall be held guilty of theft. The acts 1535, c. 13, and 1555, c. 58, extend the same pains to the stealers of bee-hives; but there seems no doubt that the theft of bees *in a hive* is theft at common law.[3] and so it is uniformly treated in modern practice, where prosecutions for such thefts have been very numerous, though chiefly before the Sheriff Courts.

But by far the most atrocious theft of this description is that of a human being, more especially of an infant child, the *crimen plagii* of the Roman law. This is obviously a crime of the very greatest atrocity, from the unequalled agony and distress which it necessarily inflicts on the unfortunate parents who are in this cruel manner bereaved of their offspring. " Nihil tamen tristius concepi potest," says Voet, " quam lugere vivos, dolere raptos, dura, aspera nefanda nonnunquam experturos, qui sinui parentum molliter fuissent fovendi; ut proinde mirandum non fuerit, si leges posteriores severissimi in tam horrendi luctuosique criminis reos animadverti voluerint."[4] From the earliest times, accordingly, this atrocious offence has been punished with death by the Scotch law.[5] Nor is it any defence that the child is taken away for affection to itself, or from any other motive, and not for the sake of lucre, taken in its ordinary sense, for the detainer has at least that advantage and benefit which he coveted in taking away the

_____

[1] Hume, 1 81.—[2] Ibid. i. 82.—[3] Ibid.—[4] Voet ad tit. de Lege Fabia de Plagariis.—[5] Hume, i. 84.

child; and this is sufficient to constitute theft in the estimation of law.[1]

The first instance of a trial for this offence was that of Torrence and Waldie, February 2. 1752, who were charged with stealing a child of nine years of age, in order to sell its body to surgeons for dissection; and the indictment bore not only murder but " the stealing or away-taking of a living child." The Court pronounced a general interlocutor of relevancy, and the pannels were convicted " of stealing the child, and soon thereafter selling and delivering its body, then dead, to some surgeons." Upon this they had sentence of death.[2] Again, in the case of Margaret Irvine, Aberdeen, September 1784, a libel for *plagium* or man-stealing was found relevant after a full debate on the relevancy of the charge,[3] and the prisoner, upon conviction, sentenced to death. Farther, in the case of Rachel Wright, 23d November 1808, and 25th January 1809, it was proved that the pannel had stole Flora Amos, a child of three years of age, from her father's house, in Ayrshire; and the case having been certified to the High Court for consideration of the punishment, the sentence of death was unanimously inflicted.[4] The sentence was afterwards commuted into transportation for life; but with such an expression of opinion from the Secretary of State, as proved that in that quarter no doubts were entertained of the legality of the sentence.[5] On 8th September 1817, Janet Douglas had sentence of death for the same crime, which was also commuted into transportation for life[6] The latest cases on the subject are Elizabeth Mill, 20th September 1826, Perth, who was transported fourteen years on a similar conviction; and Janet MacCallum, September 1828, who was convicted of stealing a child at Stirling, on her own confession, but the diet was continued on account of her apparent insanity; and it afterwards appeared that she had recently before made her escape from a lunatic asylum at Greenock. In these circumstances no sentence was moved for by the public prosecutor.[7]

The offence of raising a dead body from the grave is a separate crime, distinct from theft, known under the name of *crimen violati sepulchri*, which will be hereafter treated of. But it is

<hr>

[1] Hume, i. 84.—[2] Maclaurin, 152; Burnett, 133.—[3] Burnett, 133.—[4] Hume, i. 84, Burnett, 134.—[5] Hume, i. 84.—[6] Ibid. i. 85.—[7] Unreported.

theft to steal a dead body, *before* it is interred, from the custody of the relations or executors of the deceased. Thus, in the case of Mackenzie, Inverness, May 1733, a libel was sustained as relevant, which charged the theft of a dead body out of a house, but the prisoner was acquitted.[1]

12. The aggravation of housebreaking is incurred whenever the security of the building has been overcome, and an article carried off or removed from its place in the interior of the dwelling.

The most ordinary, and at the same time the most important, aggravation of theft is housebreaking. This is in every instance considered as a capital crime;[2] and, therefore, it is of great importance to attend to the circumstances which mark its completion.

The evident danger and alarming nature of this offence, which violates the security of private dwellings, and is always attended with terror and peril to innocent persons, has led to a rigid construction of the rules as to its perpetration. Thus it is held that the security of the building has been overcome, and the crime of housebreaking committed, although no actual effraction has taken place, if the entry has been effected by what is not the usual or intended mode of entrance. Thus to come down the chimney, or force an entry up a sewer, is not less housebreaking than to break open a door or force a window.[3] So it was found in the case of Randall Courtney, August 6. 1743, who entered a house by means of coming down the chimney.[4] This was confirmed in a later case, that of George Scott Middleton, Aberdeen, autumn 1824, where the Lord Justice-Clerk Boyle held it clear law that housebreaking is committed by coming down the chimney; and the pannel was convicted of housebreaking in that way accordingly.[5] And, in the case of John Hunter, 17th March 1801, it was sustained as a relevant charge of housebreaking into a mill, to state that the pannel entered into the mill " by means of the water-wheel." The pannel was convicted and transported seven years.[6]

But what shall be said of an entry effected, not by any of

---

[1] Burnett, 124; Hume, i. 85 —[2] Hume, i 98.—[3] Ibid. i. 99 , Burnett, 137 —[4] Ibid.—[5] Unreported.—[6] Hume, i. 99

these extraordinary and unusual methods, but in a way more likely to invite the thief; as by a skylight in the roof unclosed, or by a window which has been accidently left open? On this point there seems room for a distinction. If the window is so near the ground that one can step in from the outside without climbing, the proprietor has himself to blame for having left his house in such an unguarded condition; and an entry by such an opening, albeit not the proper way of getting into the house, will not amount to housebreaking.[1] This is matter of daily practice. On the other hand, if the window was at such a distance from the ground as to render it impossible to effect an entry without external application or aid, as by mounting on a man's shoulders, getting on a barrel, ascending by a ladder, the proprietor was entitled to rely on *that difficulty* as constituting the defence of the building; and, therefore, to enter by this unceremonious fashion, is housebreaking. Accordingly, in the case of Gadesby, 21st December 1790, where the indictment had charged housebreaking, " by forcing open a window or entering in at the same," and the jury pronounced a general verdict, the Court overruled the objection that, as the *breaking* was not found proven, the entering by an open window was not housebreaking.[2]

To raise a sash of a window, though not kept down by any means whatever, is certainly housebreaking. This was decided in the case of John Watson, February 6. 1773, who had sentence of death for two acts of theft committed in this way; and the same was found in the subsequent case of William Mills and Archibald Stewart, July 18. 1785; in which last case there was no mention of any force having been applied to raise the sash.[3] This is now matter of daily practice; and universally it is held that, if the sash has been raised, the *effractio* was complete, though no force was required to raise it, nor any bolt or nail affixed in the inside to keep it down.

Nay the same rule holds if a window be left raised only a few inches, and the thief pushes it further up, and so obtains an entrance. For, in this case, equally as the preceding, the security of the building has been overcome, and the intruder, by an act of his own, and not by the mere negligence of the proprietor, has effected his entrance. So the law was laid down at Glasgow by Lord Justice-Clerk Boyle, in the case of

Hume, i. 98.—[2] Burnett, 137, Hume, i. 98.—[3] Hume, i. 100, Burnett, 137.

John Dick and John Jeffrey, Glasgow, autumn 1829.[1]  The law has been repeatedly laid down in the same manner from the Bench, though only in illustration of other questions on this subject.

13. It is equally housebreaking to break through the wall, cut through the floor from a tenement above or below, make a hole in the roof, force open the door or any of the windows, or enter by means of false keys, or by the true key which had been previously stolen, or by means of the true key taken out of a place of concealment in the neighbourhood, or by unlocking the outer door by means of the true key left in the lock on the outside with the door locked.

No authority is required to shew, that if an entry be effected by breaking a hole in a wall, by cutting a hole in the floor, by making an aperture in the roof, the housebreaking is complete.  Nor does it make any difference although the floor cut through is the ceiling of an inferior, or the floor of a superior tenement; for, in either case, the intermediate storey, if it form a separate house or warehouse, is forcibly entered.  In the case of James Prior and others, accordingly, Aberdeen, September 1830, the housebreaking was charged in the indictment as having been effected by cutting a hole in the floor of the warehouse broken into, which was the second storey of a tenement in Aberdeen, from a shop below, belonging to different parties, into which the thieves had obtained entrance without violence.[2]

It is equally housebreaking to enter a house by means of false keys, or picklocks, as by putting aside the bolt, or bursting open the lock.[3]  Nay, the same holds if the entry be effected by means of the true key, which has been previously stolen, or fraudulently obtained, either immediately before the entry, or at a more remote period.[4]  In all the recent cases, accordingly, of housebreaking by picking of locks, the style is to charge the entry as effected " by means of false keys, or by means of the true key which you had previously stolen."  Thus, in the case of Colin Fraser and Daniel Gunn, 2d July 1827,

[1] Unreported.—[2] Unreported.—[3] Burnett, 136; Hume, i. 98.—[4] Burnett, 138, Hume, i. 99.

the entry was charged as having been effected " by opening the door of the said house with a key, which had been used for the lock of the said door, and which you had stolen when it was in the lock of the said door." This indictment was found relevant, and the pannels transported for fourteen years.[1] So also, in the case of Thomson, Burke and Hunter, 4th June 1827, a libel was found relevant which charged a housebreaking by opening the outer door of the house libelled by means of the key which the thief had stolen from a house, where it had been placed as a temporary place of deposit.[2]

Farther, it is equally housebreaking if the entry has been effected by taking the key out of a hole or hiding place where it had been secreted, as is very frequently the case with the labouring classes, when they leave the house to go to their work. Accordingly, in the case of Alexander Macdonald, Perth, April 20. 1826, an indictment was sustained as relevant by Lords Pitmilly and Alloway, which charged the pannel with " unlocking the outer door of the said house by means of the key thereof, which you found concealed in a hole, or under a stone near the said door." He was convicted, and transported seven years.[3]

But if the key have been left in the door, locked on the outside, decisions have varied. In the case of Charles Brown and Mary Stewart, Perth, April 1826, where the pannels were charged with " unlocking the door of the said house, which had been left locked with the key in the lock on the outside, with intent to steal;" this was objected to as not housebreaking, and the objection was sustained by Lords Pitmilly and Alloway.[4] On the other hand, in the case of Alexander Vallance, December 29. 1825, the indictment charged the pannel " with unlocking the door of the said shop by means of the key thereof, which you had previously stolen, or otherwise to the prosecutor unknown." The proof established that the key was *left in the door* on the outside, after it had been locked. It was laid down by the Lord Justice-Clerk Boyle, with concurrence of Lords Pitmilly and Meadowbank, that this was clearly housebreaking, and that the *modus operandi* was sufficiently included under the words " otherwise to the prosecutor unknown." [5] In this state of the decided cases, it is difficult to pronounce with confidence how the law lies; but, *in dubio*, the

[1] Hume, L 98.—[2] Ibid.—[3] Unreported.—[4] Unreported—[5] Unreported.

3

decision of the High Court is certainly superior to the authority of any Judges, however eminent, on the Circuit; and certainly, on principle, it is as much housebreaking to unlock a door in which the key has been accidentally left, as to lift the sash of a window; and the authority both of Hume and Burnett seem clear upon the point. The former observes, " It is equally housebreaking to enter a house by means of false keys or picklocks, *or by anyhow putting aside the bolt*, as by bursting open the lock;[1] and Burnett says, " One who opens a chest, bureau, *dwelling-house, or shop*, with a false key or picklock, or by putting aside the bolt which secures them, *or turning the key left there by the owner*, and steals, is guilty of a violent theft."[2] The weight of authority, therefore, concurs with principle in including this in the class of housebreakings.

It is hardly necessary to observe, that it is clearly not housebreaking if the door be merely closed, or standing shut by the latch, if by merely turning the handle on the outside it can be opened. But if the door have no means of opening from the outside, and the latch is burst open by pressure from without, this is housebreaking; for the security of the dwelling has there been clearly overcome by violence.[3]

By the law of England, burglary or housebreaking may be committed by making a hole in the wall, forcing open the door, putting back, picking or opening the lock by means of false keys, breaking the window, cutting out a pane of glass, or by pushing back the leaf by drawing or lifting the latch, if the door be not otherwise fastened, turning the key where the door is locked in the inside, or unloosing any fastening by which the door is hindered from opening.[4] It is housebreaking to push open a window which is fastened by a wedge, to open it by raising or lowering the sash, or to creep down the chimney.[5] The breaking may be of the *inner* as well as the exterior door, if the burglar has found the outer door open;[6] and it is burglary if a servant, who already is in a house, open the chamber door of his master or mistress, whether latched, or otherwise fastened, with intent to commit a felony;[7] or if persons in an eating-house slip up stairs, pick the lock of a chamber-door, and steal plate.[8] But it is settled that breaking an

---

[1] Hume, i. 98.—[2] Burnett, 136.—[3] Hume, i. 98, Burnett, 136.—[4] Hale, i. 552; East. ii. 487; Russell, ii. 3.—[5] Russell, ii. 3.—[6] Hale, i. 553; Russell, ii. 3.—[7] Hale, i. 553; Russell, ii. 0.—[8] Hale, i 524.

area-door to a town-house is not burglary, that being no part of the security of the dwelling properly so called.

14. Housebreaking may be committed not only by actual breaking of the premises, but by entering through concert with a servant who gives the thieves access from within, or violently forcing an entry after the door has been opened by the owner.

It is evident that the security of a dwelling may be effectually broken not only by an actual effraction of the building, but by concert or connivance with a servant or other person, who has the means of giving admission. In such a case the crime is housebreaking in all concerned.[1] The same holds if a thief knock at a door in the night, on pretence of asking the way, or of a wish to see some one within, and the moment it is opened rushes in; or if a party surround a house at night, and the owner opens the door to drive them off, and they overpower him and force an entrance.[2] In the case of Patrick Macgregor, July 17. 1665, and John Brown and James Wilson, June 28. 1773, which were just such cases, and the doors were opened on such pretences, the pannels were convicted of robbery and house pillaging.[3] Stouthrief seems the more appropriate designation for all such offences.

It is also clearly housebreaking, if one who is lodged in a barn or other outhouse shall leave it, and enter the mansion-house, or any of the other outhouses, by forcing open the door or window;[4] but if the thief be already lawfully lodged in a house, as being the occupier of a hired room, or a guest in an inn, it is not housebreaking, but theft, by opening lockfast places, to force open the door of another locked chamber in the inn or house, and steal the property therein placed.[5]

The violence may be committed not only at the time of the entry, but before it, if done with the design of subsequently taking advantage of the effraction thus made, and committing depredation.[6] Thus one who, being lawfully within a house, takes the opportunity of throwing up the sash of a window, or removing any of the fastenings or bars, and subsequently returns and obtains entrance, by means of the change thus effected, is clearly guilty of housebreaking.[7]

[1] Hume, i. 101 —[2] Ibid. , Burnett, 138.—[3] Ibid.—[4] Ibid.—[5] Ibid.—[6] Ibid.
[7] Ibid

If the thief obtain entry to the house by stealth without violence, there conceals himself, commits theft, and then breaks *out* of the house, he is not guilty of housebreaking, but only of an aggravated kind of theft. In the cases, accordingly, of James Mackenzie, January 27 1774, and William Wright, 10th August 1774, which were just cases of that description, the libel was laid for theft only.[1] And in the case of Edward Kennedy, Dumfries, 11th April 1831, Lord Mackenzie decided, that where the entry is voluntarily given by the inmates of the house, and the violence is committed by the thief breaking out with goods stolen within the premises, this is not housebreaking. In the law of England special provision is made for such a case by the 7th and 8th Geo. IV. c. 29. § 11, which enacts, " That if any person shall enter the dwelling-house of another, with intent to commit a felony, or being in such dwelling-house shall commit any felony, and shall, in either case, break out of the said dwelling-house, in the night-time, such person shall be deemed guilty of burglary."

In England, also, if in consequence of violence commenced or threatened, in order to obtain entrance to a house, the owner, either from apprehension of violence, or in order to repel it, open the door, and the thief enters, such entry will amount to a breaking in law.[2] So also, if entry be obtained to a house by fraud, as by pretending to have a search-warrant, or by raising a hue and cry, and bringing a constable to the door, and rushing in when the door is opened, this also, if done in the day, is housebreaking, in the night burglary.[3] In like manner, if admission be obtained on a fraudulent pretence,[4] or by deluding the person left in charge of it; this also is the same offence:[5] and the obtaining entry to a dwelling-house, by a conspiracy with a servant or lodger within, who admits the thieves by a door or window, is viewed in the same light.[6]

15. The entry is held to have been completed, if the thief has succeeded in seizing and removing something placed within, and under the safeguard of the dwelling.

It is not necessary to complete the crime, that the thief should have been actually within the premises. it is sufficient if so much of his body has been within it, as enables him to commit his de-

---

[1] Burnett, i. 130.—[2] Hale, i 553; Russell, ii 8 —[3] Leach, i. 284, Hale, i 552, 553.—[4] Russell, ii. 9.—[5] East i. 485.—[6] Hale, ii 354, 355 , Russell, ii. 10.

predation.[1] Thus, if he lift the sash, or force open the casement of a window, and reach in his arm, snatch up an article, and carry it off, this is as much housebreaking as if he had leapt in to commit the depredation. So it was found, after deliberate argument, in just such a case as that of William Gadesby, December 21. 1790, who had sentence of death for such an offence.[2] In England it is held that the crime of burglary is committed by any, even the least entry, with the whole or any part of the body; as with a hand or foot, or an instrument introduced for the purpose of committing a felony.[3] Accordingly it has been ruled, that where a prisoner cut a hole in the window shutters, and put his hand through the hole, and stole some watches within reach, this was burglary.[4] And the same decision has been given where the thief broke the window of a house in the night-time, with intent to steal, and put in a hook to seize goods, though neither his hand, nor any part of his body, was within the window.[5]

The law is settled in the same way in Scotland, where depredations, by raising the sashes of windows, and reaching in, and carrying off goods, are daily the subject of trial and punishment, under the denomination of Theft by Housebreaking.

16. Theft by housebreaking may be committed not only by those who actually enter the building, but by those who are art and part in that offence, by aiding and abetting those principally engaged.

Like every other crime, theft is capable of being committed not only by those actually engaged in the offence, but by those who are accessary to its commission,—in the language of law, by those who are *art and part*. Thus, Donaldson broke into and entered a shop,—Calder watched without, procured a light, and received the goods which Donaldson threw out to him; for this accession Calder had sentence of death along with Donaldson. April 6. 1780, Calder and Donaldson.[6] In like manner, in the case of Wilson, Hall, and Robertson, March 1786, the office of Robertson, as charged in the libel, was to watch at the door of the inn while his associates above stairs were employed in breaking the door of the chamber.[7] If a gang of

[1] Hume, i. 102.—[2] Ibid.—[3] Blackstone, iv. 227; Russell, ii. 10.—[4] Fost. 107, 108.—[5] Hale, i. 555.—[6] Hume, i. 102.—[7] Ibid.

housebreakers execute their purpose by stationing one to keep watch to prevent surprize, another to receive the goods, and a third to forward their escape, all these, though at some distance from the scene of action, are, *constructione juris*, present at the time, and participate in the deed.[1]

Nothing is more usual than this species of accession. A gang of thieves enter into a combination or joint adventure of plunder: they set out to a particular place, lodge all in the same house, and concert their plans so that each undertakes a separate part of the adventure, meet occasionally in the course of the day, assemble together at night, divide their booty, and lodge all in one apartment. Though not actually present at each theft, they are all art and part in all the depredations which are committed by any members of the gang. Such a case occurred at Aberdeen, and the law was laid down in this manner in the case of Wright and others, April 1803. The Court were clearly of opinion that they were all art and part in each particular theft, and must be held as virtually present at each, from the circumstances of the previous concert, intermediate meetings near the scene of action, and subsequent division of the whole spoil.[2] Judgment was given to the same effect by Lord Mackenzie in the case of James Prior and J. Maclachlan, Aberdeen, September 1830. It there appeared that a pawnbroker's establishment in Aberdeen was broken open between Saturday night and Monday morning, and goods to an immense amount carried off. Prior's coat and clothes were found in the premises which were broken open, which demonstrated that he had been present at the depredation, but none of Maclachlan's; and the only circumstance to connect him with the housebreaking was the subsequent possession of some of the stolen property. In truth, there was some reason to believe that Maclachlan had carried on the depredation many hours *after* Prior had broken the shop open, and on that account it was contended that he was not implicated in the *housebreaking*, but only in the *theft*. But as there was evidence of previous meetings between the prisoners, and the possession by Maclachlan of the stolen goods demonstrated that he had got a part of the spoil, Lord Mackenzie delivered it as clear law that both prisoners were implicated in the housebreaking as well as

[1] Burnett, 274 —[2] Ibid 276.

the theft.[1]  The same opinion was expressed by the High Court in the case of Wilson and Macdonald, June 15. 1818.  It there appeared that a party of young men had gone to the neighbourhood of Eyemouth, in Berwickshire, when part of them went out at night to commit depredations, and others remained at the inn where they resided, receiving the stolen goods, and making arrangements for the farther prosecution of the felonies. The Court were clear that all were accessary to all the thefts which were committed.[2]  The law was laid down in precisely the same way in the cases of William Boyd, Henry Wilson, and Henry Marshall, Glasgow, September 1823; and George Laidlaw and George Spittal, Glasgow, September 1823, in both of which it appeared in evidence that one only of the thieves had actually entered the house, the two others having remained at a little distance; but the one was stationed as a watch, and the other assisted in carrying away the stolen property to the resetters, where it was disposed of by all three.  All were convicted of the housebreaking as well as the theft, and the former sentenced to fourteen years' transportation, the latter to be executed, which was carried into execution against Laidlaw.[3]

17. Not only dwelling-houses, but shops, warehouses, manufactories, stables, byres, cellars, and locked outhouses, whether connected with a dwelling or not, fall under the description of buildings protected by the law of housebreaking.

There is a remarkable difference between the law of Scotland and that of England in regard to the buildings, by entering which the crime of housebreaking may be committed.  In Scotland it is not essential that a house, strictly so called, should be entered; any shop, wareroom, or office, whether adjoining to, or disconnected with, a dwelling-house, is deemed a house in the eye of law, and considered entitled to the protection of such.[4]  The construction applies to every edifice, to what use soever destined, whether it be a counting-room, public office, place of work, store, or business; so as it be a shut or fast building, and not a mere open shed, booth, or temporary place for lumber.[5]  Charles Cunningham, accordingly, received sen-

[1] Unreported.—[2] Hume, i. 116.—[3] Unreported.—[4] Burnett, 138; Hume, i. 103.—[5] Hume, i. 103.

tence of death on 12th March 1783, for breaking into a wash-house and brush-maker's workhouse: Alexander Mowat, on 8th April 1783, for breaking into a counting-room: Smith and Brodie, on 27th August 1788, for breaking into the excise-office.[1]   On 14th July 1791, David Mitchell was convicted of theft by housebreaking, for breaking into a seed-loft and stable: Christopher Beattie and Margaret Thomson, on 11th July 1791, for breaking into a waste-house containing lumber: Alexander Leitch and James Wilmer, on 17th December 1785, for break-ing into a coach-house.[2]   The same principles are matter of daily practice in modern times.   Thus, to give a few examples of those cases which might appear at first sight to be more doubtful.   On 26th April 1826, Charles Macdonald was con-victed at Aberdeen of theft by housebreaking, for forcing his way into a stable-loft through the window: on 21st April 1824, James Donelly and William Wood, for breaking into a wash-ing-house: on 24th April 1824, William Galbraith and others, for breaking into a stable; Andrew Menzies and George Spicer, on 13th November 1824, for breaking into a dairy and wash-ing-house; Robert Clenachan, Dumfries, April 1824, for break-ing into a coach-house; Robert Finlay and James Pearson, at Glasgow, on October 2. 1826, for breaking into a cellar used by a shopkeeper as a place of deposit, at a distance from his place of business; James Fairlie, September 30. 1826, for breaking into the bonded cellar of a merchant on the west quay of Greenock; James Innes, on March 16. 1826, for breaking into a school-room; and Robert Macgregor and Martin Mac-gregor, at Glasgow, on 27th September 1825, for breaking into a church.[3]

By the English law, on the other hand, the crime of bur-glary can only be committed by breaking into a *dwelling-house,* and that, too, in the night season, with intent to commit a fe-lony.[4]   The intended felony with them may not only be theft, but rape, murder, or any other felony.[5]   This limitation of the crime to a peculiar species of housebreaking, has introduced a variety of distinctions as to breaking into an edifice within or without the *curtilage,* as it is called, or enclosure which sur-rounds the dwelling-house;[6] with all of which, under the

[1] Hume, i. 103.—[2] Ibid.—[3] All unreported.—[4] Hale, i. 549; Russell, ii. 2. —[5] Ibid. ii. 33.—[6] Ibid. ii. 12. 15.

generic description of the crime in Scotch law, we are happily unacquainted.

18. Where a house is occupied in distinct floors by separate tenants or proprietors, each floor is a separate house; and where a floor is subdivided among different poor persons, who inhabit one or two rooms each, each room is a separate house, and entitled to the protection of such.

It frequently happens among the tenements tenanted by the poorer classes, that one building contains a great number of different families, many of whom frequently reside on one floor, sometimes several in one room. In such a case, each of the separate rooms or "*houses*," as they are called, is to be regarded as a separate dwelling; and any breaking into *that* room, though from the passage which is common to the whole tenants, will be esteemed housebreaking. So the law was laid down by Lords Justice-Clerk Boyle and Pitmilly in the case of Alexander Cowie, Aberdeen, September 1824. The *species facti* there was, that the house which was broken into entered from a common passage or entry, the door of which stood open; but the prisoner broke open the *inner door* forming the outer door of a family living in the land, several of which entered from the same passage. This the Court held to be clearly housebreaking, though the external door, or safeguard of the whole tenement, was not broken.[1] And, indeed, as the common stair or passage in such tenements necessarily must always be left open for the entry of the numerous persons who thereby obtain access to their dwellings, it is evident that, if any other rule were followed, the houses of the poor, which of all others stand most in need of this high protection, would be altogether deprived of it

In England the question of the ownership, which with them is very material in cases of housebreaking, depends on the points whether the owner sleeps under the same roof with the tenants or lodgers, and whether there is but one outer door. It is settled law, that if the owner, who lets apartments in his house for other persons to sleep under the same roof, which has but one outer door where he and they indiscriminately enter, all

---

[1] Unreported.

the apartments of such lodgers are to be considered as parcels of the one dwelling of the owner; but if either the owner do not dwell in the same house, or if he and his lodgers enter by separate outer doors, the apartments so let are to be held as the mansion for the time being of each lodger respectively.[1] So upon an indictment for robbery in a dwelling-house, where it appeared that the *whole* house was let out to three families, with one outer door, which was common to all the inmates, it was decided by all the Judges that the charge was well laid as having been committed in the dwelling-house of the particular inmate.[2] And in a subsequent case, the same decision was given by the Twelve Judges, where the owner did not occupy any part of the premises himself.[3] In Scotland the obvious mode of avoiding the difficulty, is to lay the house broken alternatively as the property of the landlord and the lodger, and where there is any doubt as to its being a house, properly speaking, which was invaded, it is advisable to put an alternative clause of theft, by opening lockfast places. And if the owner of the property be himself the housebreaker of one of his tenants, and live in the same tenement, this seems the appropriate form of charging the offence.[4]

19. Theft by housebreaking, of course, cannot be committed unless some article be abstracted; but housebreaking, with intent to steal, is a separate and indictable offence, though nothing has been taken.

How extraordinary soever it may appear, it is certain that the crime of housebreaking, with intent to steal, was not recognised as a separate and indictable offence till the year 1810. It was then made the subject of a deliberate judgment from the Court in the case of Charles Macqueen and Alexander Baillie, 25th January 1810, and finally settled, that the violent breaking into a house or shop, with intent to steal, is a cognizable charge, and relevant to infer an arbitrary punishment. In that case the pannels received sentence of fourteen years' transportation each.[5] The whole law already explained, with reference to theft by housebreaking, is here applicable, with this dif-

---

[1] Blackstone, iv. 225; Russell, ii. 29 —[2] Trapshaw's Case, Leach, i. 427, Russell, ii. 29.—[3] Rogers' Case, Leach, i. 89, Russell, ii. 30.—[4] Russell, ii. 31. —[5] Burnett, 142; Hume, i 102

ference only, that the intention of depredation has not been carried into effect, and no article removed.

The punishment of this offence varies of course with the magnitude of the violence which has been used, and the audacious nature of the attempt made; but in no case has a severer sentence than transportation for fourteen years been inflicted, while, generally, the punishment has been only seven years, and of late years not unfrequently modified to nine, twelve, or eighteen months' imprisonment. Thus, in the case of George Buckley, Glasgow, spring 1819, transportation for seven years was inflicted for this offence;[1] and the same punishment was awarded in the cases of John Campbell, 10th November 1824, John Ferguson, 21st February 1825, and John Sutherland, 21st February 1825.[2] On the other hand, the more lenient course was followed in the cases of J. H. Brown and D. Kelly, 11th June 1827, who received nine months' imprisonment on a conviction of breaking open the door and window of a warehouse, with intent to steal;[3] of Andrew Smith, Glasgow, autumn 1829, where imprisonment in Bridewell for twelve months was the sentence awarded;[4] of Adam Hilson and James Craig, 13th March 1827, where it was eighteen months' hard labour in Bridewell.[5]

20. Theft may also be aggravated by being committed by opening lockfast places, which makes a species of theft almost always punished with transportation, though seldom in modern practice with death.

Theft may be committed not only by housebreaking, but by breaking open lockfast places; a species of violence generally necessary to obtain access to the more valuable articles which are deposited in places of security.[6] It matters not what is the value of the article carried away in pursuance of this violence; what the law chiefly looks to is the audacity of the thief, who thus violates the most secure asylums of property, and the danger to the lieges in having their secured repositories thus ransacked by a lawless depredator.[7] In the estimation of law, it is immaterial whether the security of the lockfast place is overcome by actual violence, as by

[1] Shaw, 73.—[2] Hume, i. 102.—[3] Syme, 209.—[4] Unreported.—[5] Syme, 150. —[6] Burnett, 136.—[7] Ibid.

forcing open the lock, staving in the door or lid, or the like; or by picking the lock, or stealing the key, or using false keys. In the case, accordingly, of James Gray, Dumfries, April 1824, the prisoner was transported seven years for breaking open a chest in a stable-loft, by staving in the lid. In the case of Samuel Inglis, Dumfries, April 10. 1824, twelve months' imprisonment was inflicted for a theft from a locked drawer, "by means of the key of the said drawer, of which the prisoner had unlawfully obtained possession." And, in the case of George Beath and John Beath, Perth, September 13. 1827, seven years' transportation was the punishment for opening a locked chest of drawers by means of false keys, or by means of the true key, of which the thief had unlawfully obtained possession.[1] If the key has been left in the lock on the outside, it is said by an authority to be theft by lockfast places to open the lock and steal the goods therein contained.[2] But it is to be observed, that the analogy of housebreaking, in this particular, will not hold; for it is unquestionably housebreaking to raise a sash of a window and enter a house; but it is not theft by lockfast places to open a closed drawer which is not locked; and the better opinion would rather appear to be, that one who is so negligent as to leave his key in such a tempting situation, has lost the protection of the law in this particular But, if the key has been concealed, or taken out of its place, and laid down on a table, shelf or chair, the full crime is committed, if it be taken from that situation and the lock so opened. So the law has been repeatedly laid down from the Bench.

The punishment of theft by opening lockfast places has of late years been in general seven years' transportation; mitigated, in favourable cases, occasionally to twelve or nine months' imprisonment. Very frequently it occurs in combination with housebreaking, and then it is held so serious an aggravation as almost in every instance to lead, upon conviction, to transportation for fourteen years.

21. Theft, like every other crime, may be aggravated by previous conviction for the same offence; but the aggravation of being committed by one who is habite and repute a thief, peculiar to this crime, raises it in every instance to a capital crime.

[f] All unreported.—[1] Burnett, 136.

Every offence whatever is held to be legally aggravated by being committed by a person previously convicted of that crime; but, in addition to this, the crime of theft is susceptible of aggravation by the *previous character* of the accused, if it has become so bad as to amount to habite and repute a thief. As this is an aggravation, now become, from the increasing depravity of the lower orders, unhappily too frequent, and as it forms an exception to the ordinary rule in regard to character, it requires particular attention.

From the earliest time this charge of being habite and repute a thief was allowed to be proved in Scotland against a person accused of a specific act of theft.[1] Not only so, but, upon proof of this character *alone*, independent of any specific charge, the prisoner was liable to the highest punishment, according to the rule, *Latro defamatus et latro probatus æquiparantur*.[2] This severity, however, is now most properly departed from, and the general character cannot legally be proved till a specific act of theft has been established.[3]

It is not sufficient to establish this character, that the accused is a person of a suspicious or doubtful character. He must have been marked as a *known thief* by the common bruit and report of the neighbourhood, and have had a character affixed to him as a brother of the trade.[4] As little is it sufficient that he is considered as a bad character by the neighbourhood, or has been guilty of repeated immoral or atrocious acts; nothing can fix this character upon him, but the specific *mala fama* of being *a thief*.[5] Even the character of being a robber or a resetter, how nearly soever akin to that of a thief, will not support this peculiar and specific aggravation.[6]

The ordinary and best method of establishing this aggravation in great cities is by the evidence of police-officers, supported as it frequently is by the record of previous convictions for theft; and this, accordingly, is the mode of proof adopted in nineteen out of twenty of the cases which daily occur before the courts. The observation of Mr Burnett,[7] that the evidence of police-officers is not, on this point, so worthy of credit as that of the neighbours of the pannel, only proves how rapid has been the progress of vice in this kingdom since the composition of

---

[1] Hume, i. 93; Burnett, 127.—[2] Burnett, 127; Hume, i 92.—[3] Hume, i. 92; Burnett, 128.—[4] Hume, i. 93, Burnett, 130.—[5] Ibid.—[6] Hume, i. 94.—[7] Burnett, 130.

his work; for the depraved habits, irregular life, and constant changes of domicile of the professional thieves of the present day, are such as to render it equally impossible to say who are their neighbours, or to find persons among their associates upon whose testimony any reliance can be placed. In truth, the only persons, excepting those of their own gang, who keep their eye upon them, and can speak from personal knowledge of their profession and avocations, are the police-officers, into whose hands they frequently come on charges of theft, and whose business leads them to be in a peculiar manner conversant with persons of their habits. While nothing is more common, therefore, than to hear this authority quoted against the evidence of police-officers, it is uniformly overruled by the Bench, and rejected by all persons practically acquainted with these matters.       .

In country places, however, or small towns, the neighbours of a man may still be considered as the best evidence as to whether he is habite and repute a thief; because, unless they entertained such an opinion of him, he cannot be said to bear such a character, whatever his demerits in this particular may actually be [1]  It is rarely, however, that such persons are called to speak to this point, from the great difficulty of getting country people to understand what is really meant by the expression, or to give any distinct account of the matter, even where the charge is in reality best founded.

Though previous convictions are sometimes tendered in support of the charge of habite and repute, along with parole evidence, yet it is by no means to be understood that they constitute either the best or the only proof of this aggravation.[2] Such a plea is frequently urged, but as uniformly overruled by the Court. This was done, in particular, by Lords Justice-Clerk Boyle and Alloway, in the case of James Brown, Glasgow, spring 1828, where the objection that the charge of habite and repute was proved only by parole evidence, without any conviction, was expressly overruled.[3] In truth, the aggravation of habite and repute, referring as it does to *character*, may exist without any conviction; for a man may both be a thief, and bear the character of such, without having ever been brought under the lash of the law; while, on the other hand,

---

[1] Hume, i. 94.—[2] Ibid.; Burnett, 130.—[3] Unreported.

he may have been convicted once or twice, at considerable intervals from each other, without having either become a professional thief, or been known as such to the officers of justice.

. Habite and repute can be laid only as an aggravation of a specific act of theft; and, therefore, the general charge cannot competently be made the subject of proof until the specific charge is established by legal evidence.[1] It follows from this, that, if the special charge is not established, the jury cannot find the prisoner guilty of being habite and repute a thief alone, or, if they do, no sentence can follow on the verdict. So it was determined by the Court in the case of Allan Henderson, Glasgow, 15th September 1802; John Fleming, Stirling, April 1817; and David Beatson and John Macpherson, 17th July 1820: in all of which the Court determined that, upon a verdict finding the principal charge not proven, but the aggravation of being habite and repute a thief established, no sentence could follow.[2]

.This aggravation may be proved either by the testimony of two witnesses, or by the testimony even of one witness, coupled with several convictions for theft.[3] The first is the ordinary and unexceptionable mode of establishing the charge; but instances are not awanting of its being made out by the other and complex mode of proof. Thus, in the case of John Johnstone, June 19. 1786, three convictions were *per se* sustained as sufficient evidence of this aggravation; and, in the case of Rachel Ferguson, 13th March 1801, one conviction only was founded on in the libel with the testimony of a single witness.[4] It is not safe, however, to trust the proof of this character to a single witness, unless he is supported by a series of convictions for theft extending over a course of years.

Contrary to the opinion of Burnett,[5] it is now fixed, that, if the pannel be acquitted on a specific charge of theft, aggravated by being habite and repute a thief, he may be tried again next day, on another charge, aggravated by the same character. So the Court found, upon such an objection being stated in the case of John Reed, 1st August 1774, who was tried in that year on a charge of theft, aggravated by being habite and repute, although he pleaded that he had been tried on such a charge and acquitted eight years before.[6] In truth, there is

[1] Hume, i. 94.—[2] Ibid. i. 94, 95.—[3] Hume, i. 94; Burnett, 130.—[4] Hume, i. 94.—[5] Burnett, 131.—[6] Hume, i. 95; Burnett, 131.

no foundation on principle for the objection, not only because the pannel may have *acquired* the character of a thief, though he had it not before, in the interval between the two trials, but because the character being laid only as an aggravation, necessarily shared the fate of the principal charge to which it was annexed, and the jury were compelled to acquit him of the whole, if the proof of that specific charge failed, how clearly soever it may have been established in evidence before them.[1].

It was held by the Court, in the case of Peter Davidson, Aberdeen, September 1824, that it was not sufficient to stamp a pannel with the character of being an habitual thief that the police-officers swore he had borne that character for *six weeks* prior to the specific act charged against him.[2] On the other hand, it is matter of every day's practice to find the aggravation proven by this character, having been fixed upon a prisoner at the police-offices for eight or ten months. In judging of this matter, it is material to inquire, whether the prisoner has abandoned his lawful calling, if he ever had any, and has had for some time no visible means of subsistence, except depredation : for, if he has done so, there seems no ground either in law or justice, on which the aggravation of character, if it has endured for this period, can be found not proven. Perhaps six months may be stated as the shortest period which has yet been held sufficient to stamp this character upon a prisoner.

The police-officers frequently say that the prisoner was once well known to them as a common thief, but that of late years they have lost sight of him ; or that he works occasionally, and at other times relapses into his habits of stealing. In such cases, it is a proper jury question, whether or not the particular crime charged was committed under this aggravation ;— keeping in view, on the one hand, that, though a man may once have been an habitual thief, the stain may be washed out by subsequent and steady good conduct ; and, on the other, that a man may be not the less a thief because he occasionally works in the intervals of his depredations.

If the charge of habite and repute be once established by concurring witnesses, it is no sufficient answer to it to prove, by the

---

[1] Hume, i. 95.—[2] Unreported.

testimony of one or more persons, who speak merely to particular dealings they may have had with him, or which may
have fallen under their observation, for such a proof meets not
the charge of habite and repute; and it is inconclusive in itself,
because it does not follow that even a common thief will, in
every instance, be dishonest.[1] A signal instance of this occurred at Aberdeen, September 1830, in the case of Margaret
Cathie and Ann Ross, who were proved by the most conclusive
evidence to be habite and repute, and previously convicted; although several of their neighbours declared they always found
them quite correct in their dealings, and knew nothing against
their characters.[2] This affords an illustration of the observation formerly made, that the police-officers, in large towns, are
much better judges of the character of such persons even than
those who have long dwelt in their neighbourhood; because
their irregular habits have brought them under the observation
of the one and not of the other.

22. The charge of habite and repute is peculiar to theft,
and cannot be stated as an aggravation either of housebreaking with intent to steal, or robbery, or reset of theft.

The obvious expedience of getting quit of habitual thieves,
by transportation, when detected in the analogous practices of
housebreaking with intent to steal, robbery, and reset of theft,
has led to frequent attempts to state the aggravation of habite
and repute, as applicable to these charges; but all such attempts have been resisted by the Court. In the case of George
Buckley, 12th July 1822, the Court found the aggravation of
being habite and repute not relevant, in connexion with housebreaking with intent to steal.[3] Again, in the case of Mary
Bentley and Houston Cathie, 9th January 1822, it was found
that it is not relevant to charge either the aggravation of being
habite and repute a thief, or habite and repute a resetter, or
previously convicted of theft, as connected with the charge of
reset of theft.[4] And, although it has not yet been *in terminis*
decided, that the aggravation of habite and repute cannot be
charged in connexion with the crime of robbery; yet as it has
been thought that the crimes are so much distinct, that, on an

[1] Burnett, 130.—[2] Unreported.—[3] Shaw's Cases, 73, Hume, i. 94.—[4] Ibid.

indictment for robbery, it is not competent for the jury to return a verdict of guilty of theft,[1] it may be anticipated that no
such attempt would be successful, until a variation in the law
in this particular has taken place.

But with regard to *stouthrief*, it deserves consideration whether there is any incompetency in charging this aggravation as
applicable to that crime. In the case of Donaldson, Buchanan,
and Forbes Duncan, Aberdeen, April 1823,[2] it was stated by
Lord Pitmilly, that there was no legal incompetency in stating
the aggravation to a charge of stouthrief; and, in the case of
James Graham and others, Dumfries, April 1824, it was
strongly stated by Lord Justice-Clerk Boyle, that stouthrief
was forcible theft.[3] This also is the opinion of Baron Hume;[4]
and, in the case of James Milne, Perth, September 1824, Lord
Justice-Clerk Boyle laid it down, that there could be no objection to the aggravation of habite and repute being connected
with a charge of stouthrief.[5] In these circumstances, there
seems no incompetency in point of law, as there assuredly is
no impropriety in point of reason, in charging habite and repute as an aggravation of the violent theft implied in stouthrief, as well as of the clandestine abstraction recognised in the
simple crime.

23. In considering the evidence against an accused
party, it is not legal to lay any stress on the character of
habite and repute, however clearly established, unless a
specific act of theft has been once established.

No legal proposition is so frequently stated from the Bench,
in criminal courts, as that proof of habite and repute cannot be
legally taken into view as a make-weight of evidence against
an accused party. The jury must be satisfied that the accused
is guilty of an act of theft, before they approach the question
whether he committed the crime under the aggravation of
being an habitual thief. Thus far the law is clear; but it is
to be wished that this rule was as well founded in reason and
justice as it is in authority. Certainly it requires repeated ad-
monitions from the highest legal quarter to convince a jury,
that the same evidence is necessary to establish the guilt of an

---

[1] Shaw's Cases, 30, Peter Wallace, May 21. 1811.—[2] Unreported.—[3] Unreported.—[4] Hume, i. 110.—[5] Unreported.

upright and virtuous man, who has never been known to commit a fault, as of a person who has for ten years lived by thieving; or that there is much equity in the rule which allows the prisoner, in doubtful cases, to cast the balance in his own favour, by adducing evidence of *good* character, and debars the prosecutor from rebutting that inference, by proof of the most systematic and long continued depravity, by one who has for years lived by the trade of thieving.

24. The punishment of an habitual thief, originally death, is now generally transportation ; but in fixing the sentence, the Court proceed almost entirely on the character of the pannel, without regard to the amount in value of the special article abstracted.

In judging of the punishment to be inflicted on a person convicted of theft, aggravated by being habite and repute a thief, the Court most properly considers chiefly the character established against the pannel.   Originally it was the uniform practice to follow such convictions with a sentence of death;[1] but the more humane and enlightened practice of modern times has commuted this punishment, wherever the theft is unaccompanied with violence, to transportation.   In awarding this sentence, however, the practice is rather to consider the length of time that the prisoner has borne the character of an habitual thief, than the specific value of the particular theft of which he has been convicted ; and never to visit a person convicted under this character with a smaller punishment than transportation.   In the case, accordingly, of William Wilson, July 14. 1827, the Court awarded fourteen years' transportation, where the article abstracted was only a cotton bag, not worth a penny, in consideration of a long previous character of a thief proved against him.[2]   Whatever the value of the article may have been, if the character of habite and repute for a course of years is established, transportation for fourteen years, or for life, is the usual punishment.[3]

25. Previous conviction forms a legal aggravation of theft, as well as of every other offence, provided the conviction be of the same crime with that now charged, that

---

[1] Hume, i. 93.—[2] Unreported.—[3] Syme's Cases, *passim*

it have proceeded before a competent court, and that the proceedings *ex facie* of the record produced appear to have been fair and regular.

Common sense demonstrates, that a man who, in defiance of repeated previous punishment, persists in a life of depredation, is a more hardened character, and deserves a severer chastisement, than one who is put on his trial for a first offence. It is settled law, accordingly, that a previous conviction for the same offence, with that which is again charged against a prisoner, is in every instance a relevant aggravation of the specific charge. So it was found by the Court, in the case of Alexander Campbell, June 3. 1822,[1] on a certification of the point from the north circuit. Since that period it has been the invariable practice to charge previous convictions for theft as aggravations of any new charge for the same crime, where the requisite evidence of the former conviction could be obtained.

But it is only when the previous conviction is for the *same offence*, as the new one charged against the prisoner, that this aggravation can be competently stated. Thus it is legal to charge a previous conviction for theft, as an aggravation of any subsequent charge for the same crime; or a previous conviction for reset as an aggravation of a new charge of that description; but it will not do to charge previous convictions for reset as an aggravation of a charge of theft, or previous convictions for theft as an aggravation of a charge of reset. The reason is, that a pannel's whole character is not to be made the subject of investigation, but only such parts of it as have an immediate and direct connexion with the special charge under consideration; and that law visits with a severer punishment not a repetition of offences in general, but of that particular crime, which has formerly been, without the hoped-for success, visited with chastisement.

The previous conviction also must have taken place before a competent court. If it appear *ex facie* of the record produced, that the Court was incompetent to try for the offence, it amounts to a mere nullity, to which no legal weight whatever can be attached. Thus if, on a trial for robbery, a previous conviction for that crime by any inferior court were to be pro-

[1] Shaw's Cases, 66.

2

duced, no attention whatever could be paid to so irregular a production. In like manner, a conviction for theft was rejected by Lord Alloway at Aberdeen, in the case of John Hardie, autumn 1827, in respect that it bore to be before a *single Justice* of the Peace, whereas the Acts of Parliament require every such conviction to be before " *two or more* of his Majesty's Justices of the Peace." [1]

The description of the conviction must be such as truly applies to the extract produced. Thus if a conviction be described as having been obtained before the Magistrates of Edinburgh, but it appears from the extract itself that it was obtained before the Magistrate presiding in the *Police Court*, the conviction cannot be proved; because the court referred to in the libel is not the court specified in the extract, even though the same judge may preside in both. Such was found in the case of George Gowans, 25th June 1827. [2]

Farther, the conviction cannot be established, if the extract produced bears evidence of any considerable irregularity in the mode of conducting the previous trial, as, for example, by convicting the pannel on the declarations of witnesses not emitted on oath. Thus the police convictions for Edinburgh, by their usual form, bore that the witnesses were " sworn and examined;" but some convictions of that police court having been produced, which bore that they were " examined" only, the Court held that they must be withdrawn; as the record itself demonstrated that a fatal irregularity had taken place in the previous proceeding. So it was found by the Court, in the case of Allan Grant and others, 5th March 1827, [3] and Ann Dykes and Helen Goodall, 9th November 1827. [4]

But if the extracts of the convictions produced be themselves formal and regular, no allegation can be admitted of their having been improperly or irregularly obtained. It is to the record alone that the Court can competently look; and no allegation of irregularity, how gross soever in the previous steps of the trial, can be attended to, in this matter of receiving the conviction, if not established on the face of the conviction produced. So the Court found in the case of Gunn and Macgregor, 2d March 1829 [5] Least of all, can any allegation offered to be established by parole evidence, be admitted to control, explain, or contradict a regular record;

---

[1] Unreported.—[2] Syme, 223.—[3] Ibid 144.—[4] Ibid. 263.—[5] Unreported.

and, therefore, where it was even offered to be proved that the defender was not allowed to adduce witnesses in excul. pation, the Court, with many expressions of regret at not being able to get at the truth in such a case, felt themselves obliged to preclude the proposed investigation.[1]   Indeed, it is evident that the faith of the records imperatively requires that they should bear faith in judgment till regularly set aside; and, therefore, that no exceptions should be admitted against them, but such as appear and are established on the face of the extract produced.

The punishment of theft, when committed by one often previously convicted, was formerly death,[2] but it is now almost invariably restricted to a lighter chastisement.   This aggravation is not in general considered by the Court in so serious a light, as that of being habite and repute a thief, upon the ground that the depravity of character is not generally so great in one who occasionally steals, and has been punished, as in one who has entirely devoted himself to the trade, and actually lives by thieving.   Where the theft itself is trifling, and the previous convictions few, imprisonment for nine or twelve months is generally the sentence; but if either the theft be more serious in itself, so as to approach to a *furtum grave*, or the previous convictions are numerous, transportation is invariably awarded. Of course, wherever previous convictions co-exist with habite and repute, which is very often the case, or where any of them have been by the Sheriff and a jury, or by the Court of Justiciary, transportation is the appropriate sentence.

Theft also may be committed by one who, although not previously convicted, is charged in the same libel with many different acts of depredation.   In such cases, the rule formerly was, that *three* charges of theft, how trifling soever, were sufficient to warrant a capital sentence;[3] and, though this rule is now happily annulled by the humanity of modern practice, unless the theft be extremely serious, or accompanied with some other aggravation, in so far as the actual infliction of death is concerned, yet it still occupies an important and useful place in regulating applications for bail.   A magistrate, therefore, will be justified still in refusing bail, where a prisoner is either charged with three acts of theft, or with a single

[1] Gunn and Macgregor, 2d March 1829, unreported.—[2] Hume, i. 95, 96. —[3] Ibid 96.

act, aggravated by two previous convictions.[1]  In the case of James Kelly, 8th January 1810, the pannel had sentence of death for three acts of theft, committed by picking drawers, although the articles abstracted were of no great value in any one instance.[2]

27. Theft may be aggravated, independently of the character of the thief, or the violence attending its commission, by the value of the article stolen, which, if that amount to a *furtum grave*, raises the offence to a capital crime.

According to our ancient and undoubted law, the punishment of a *furtum grave* was death; but what value in the article stolen raises it to this serious denomination, no precise rule has yet been precisely fixed in our practice.[3]  In the case of Alexander Thomson, Jedburgh, May 1714, the Court found " the pannel's stealing William Douglas's pack, and goods therein, the same being of *considerable value*, relevant to infer the pains of death." [4]  What the " considerable value" is which shall produce this serious consequence, has not yet been precisely fixed; but in the case of James Loss, April 1821, where the pannel was accused of breaking open a house, forced a lockfast press, and stealing therefrom £112, the aggravation of housebreaking was passed from, and the question remained whether the verdict of the jury, which found the pannel " guilty of the *theft as libelled*," warranted a capital sentence The point having been certified, the Court found that " the crime, of which the pannel, by the verdict of assize, was found guilty, is relevant to infer a capital punishment;" [5] but this judgment cannot be held as decisively settling the point, because the " theft libelled" was still a theft by opening lockfast places ; and although this was not set forth as a separate aggravation in the major proposition, the Court expressed a clear opinion that, in considering the punishment, they were entitled to take into consideration the *modus operandi* specified in the indictment, and found proven by the jury; and, therefore, the verdict of guilty of the " theft libelled," was in effect a verdict of guilty by opening lockfast places.[6]  Upon the whole, there-

---

[1] Hume, i. 96.—[2] Ibid.—[3] Burnett, 131 ; Hume, i 90, 91.—[4] Hume, i. 90 —[5] Ibid.—[6] Hume, ii. 170 , Shaw, 29.

fore, it still remains an open point, what amount of value raises the crime to a *furtum grave;* but if a magistrate were to refuse bail, in any case where the value of the article stolen exceeds £100, there does not seem to be any ground for holding he would be acting illegally. In considering the more delicate and important point of pronouncing sentence, the Court is now almost uniformly relieved of all anxiety by the practice now almost grown into a custom, of restricting the libel, in almost all cases of simple theft, how great soever the value of the article stolen, to an arbitrary punishment. Of this no stronger proof can be given than occurred at Aberdeen, September 1830, in the case of Matthew Prior and James Maclachlan, where, upon a verdict finding the former of these parties guilty of theft of jewellery, to the amount of £2000, by housebreaking, the sentence was fourteen years' transportation; upon the latter, who was convicted of the simple theft, seven years.[1] In like manner, in the case of Catharine Brown, Grace Mackenzie, and Margaret Bowie, who were convicted of stealing £90 from a country man, in a house of ill-fame in Edinburgh, the sentence was fourteen years' transportation on the principal, and seven years on the two minor offenders[2] And in the case of Jean Strachan, September 14. 1827, Perth, the pannel being convicted of picking a man's pocket of £100, in a house of ill-fame in Dundee, was sentenced to seven years' transportation only.[3] Upon the whole, the disposition of our practice is to consider not the value of the article stolen so much as the character of the thief, the daring nature of the offence, and the skilful way in which it has been committed.[4] This is in an essential manner the case in pocket-picking, where the prisoner is in general utterly ignorant of the value of the prize at which he snatches, and may stumble, without any additional depravity, on a pocket containing £500, as on one containing £5 Accordingly, in the case of Grace Sharp, 22d March 1826, the Court, while they found that a simple theft of £14 from the person was too serious a case to admit of trial by the Sheriff without a jury, held that, in many cases of dexterous audacious thefts of that description, fourteen years' transportation would not be too severe a punishment, without any aggravation whatsoever, while, in others, seven years would

---

[1] Unreported.—[2] Unreported.—[3] Unreported.—[4] Hume, i 91.

be sufficient for a theft of £100.[1]  And this principle was put in force by Lord Justice-Clerk Boyle, at Inverary, autumn 1826, in the case of Charles Macdonald, Mary Campbell, and John Macmillan, the former of whom being convicted of a dexterous theft of twelve shillings from the person of a country man at a fair at Tarbert in Argyleshire, along with a theft of some goods in a pack in a house, to the value of £10 or £12, was sentenced to fourteen years, and his two companions, who were only accessary to the theft of the pack, to seven years' transportation.[2]

There is one theft of a peculiar nature, which, on account of the excessive depravity of heart which it evinces, it has always been the disposition of our practice to punish with great severity.  This is the theft of children's apparel, by wretches who decoy them into remote or secluded situations, and there strip them and leave them.  Thus, on 12th July 1827, Janet Irvine had sentence of transportation for life, for stealing a tartan frock from the person of a chimney-sweeper's child, three years old, whom she had decoyed into a common stair, in one of the Edinburgh closes, stript, and there left.  She was also habite and repute a thief.[3]  In like manner, Janet Macbeath was, on 7th July 1828, sentenced to fourteen years' transportation, for a theft of a tartan frock from a child, whom she had decoyed into the King's Park, near Edinburgh, aggravated by the like aggravation.[4]  And in the case of Ann Dunlop, Glasgow, 15th April 1828, transportation for life was inflicted on a woman, habite and repute, and previously convicted, who was found guilty of stealing their clothes from two different poor children, whom she had decoyed into unfrequented places in the town of Paisley.[5]

28. Theft of a single sheep is not capital; but theft of more than one sheep, or of a single horse or ox, is punishable with death.

The theft of horses and cattle of every description is, from the exposed situation in which they are placed, and the necessity of protecting property of this description with peculiar care, a species of depredation which has always been punished

---

[1] Unreported on this point.—[2] Unreported.—[3] Syme, 231.—[4] Hume, i. 91.
[5] Unreported.

with great severity. The theft of *one* sheep, indeed, has been found relevant only to infer an arbitrary punishment. This was done in the case of William Crichton, May 1. 1714, Jedburgh;[1] but the theft of *more* than one sheep has always been deemed a capital offence. Thus, in the case of George Edgar and John Young, 3d February 1829, the pannels had sentence of transportation for fourteen years, for stealing four sheep in one night, from two adjoining fields; and Lord Gillies, in proposing sentence, declared that if the libel had not been restricted, a capital sentence must have been pronounced.[2] In like manner, in the case of James Forgie, 5th December 1825, the prisoner, upon a conviction of stealing four wedders, escaped a capital sentence, solely in consequence of a restriction of the libel by the Lord Advocate, after the verdict was pronounced, on their recommendation to mercy.[3] Lastly, in the case of Peter Oliver, 9th July 1827, who was convicted of stealing thirteen sheep at one time, the pannel had sentence of death, after a debate as to whether the offence, of which he stood convicted, warranted a capital punishment.[4] The sentence for stealing one sheep is generally transportation for seven years, as was done in the cases of Andrew Craig, Aberdeen, April 1815,[5] and John Calder, December 8. 1829.[6] But if either such a single act of depredation has been repeated, or more than one have been taken at the same time, the punishment is almost always transportation for a longer period. Thus David Muir, at Ayr, April 1817, was transported fourteen years for stealing three sheep, two at one time and one at another.[7] On February 3. 1829, George Edgar and John Young were transported fourteen years for stealing four sheep, three from one place and one from another.[8] In the case of Donald Macphie, Donald Campbell, and Lachlan Cameron, Inverary, April 1828, fourteen years was the punishment on all the pannels, for stealing one sheep on one occasion, and three sheep on another.[9] And, in the case of William Mackenzie, Aberdeen, September 1830, Lord Mackenzie sentenced a pannel to fourteen years' transportation for two acts of sheep-stealing, embracing in all five sheep.[10]

---

[1] Hume, i. 91,—[2] Unreported.—[3] Hume, i. 90.—[4] Ibid i. 89.—[5] Ibid —[6] Unreported —[7] Hume, i 89.—[8] Unreported.—[9] Unreported.—[10] Unreported.

With regard, again, to cattle-stealing or horse-stealing, it admits of no doubt that, in strict law, a single act is a capital offence.[1] Thus in the case of Thomas Nelson, September 10. 1661, the prisoner was hanged for stealing a single horse, without any aggravation.[2] James Grant, on May 4. 1791, was sentenced to be hanged for stealing one horse, though the jury, in consideration of there being only that single charge, recommended him to mercy.[3] And in the case of Andrew Aitken, 26th June 1798, the Court expressed a clear opinion, that stealing a single horse from a stable is a capital crime.[4] It admits of still less doubt, that, where several acts of horse or cattle stealing have been committed, or more than one animal has been abstracted, the crime is capital, and numbers have suffered death for such offences. Thus Alexander Wilson was sentenced to be hanged for stealing two horses on one occasion, at Inverness, May 2. 1791;[5] George Walker, on 21st July 1801, for stealing two horses at once; and Smith and Thomson, on 8th December 1806, for stealing three horses in one night, from two different stables.[6] Lastly, at Ayr, in May 1811, George Watson had sentence of death for two acts of horse-stealing, committed from different stables, after an argument at the bar as to the extent of pains which such a conviction warranted.[7]

In the case of John and Donald Roy, Inverness, May 1. 1712, the like judgment was pronounced by Lords Minto and Roystoun, finding the theft of cattle capital.[8] And in the case of David Murdoch, August 1661, who had confessed the theft of seven cows, the Court referred the punishment to the Privy Council, who, as an extraordinary stretch, in consideration of various alleviating circumstances, gave sentence of banishment instead of death.[9]

But though such is the undoubted law, still *in viridi observantia* in the matter of bail, it has been the disposition of modern practice to punish this crime with transportation only. This is of course done by means of a restriction of the libel. Thus, in the case of Lindsay and Anderson, transportation for seven years was inflicted on two butchers for the theft of an ox.[10] In the case of John Gall, Aberdeen, September 1827, transportation for fourteen years was inflicted for two separate

<hr/>

[1] Hume, i. 89 —[2] Ibid. i. 88.—[3] Ibid. i. 89 —[4] Ibid.—[5] Ibid.—[6] Ibid.—
[7] Ibid.—[8] Ibid.—[9] Ibid. i. 91.—[10] Ibid. i. 89.

acts of theft at the same time, one of two stots, and another of three cows, from a field in the vicinity; and in the case of Andrew Howie, same circuit, seven years' transportation was the punishment for the theft of two stots at the same time, from one proprietor, the libel having been restricted in both cases.[1] And in the case of Alexander Macmath, Dumfries, April 1824, fourteen years' transportation was inflicted for the theft of two stots on two different occasions.[2] The like sentence was pronounced in just such a case, Aberdeen, September 1830, James Morrison, by Lord Mackenzie.[3]

Even in the case of horse-stealing, the lenity of modern practice almost always interposes to save the offender's life. In the case of Robert Waugh, Jedburgh, September 12. 1825, fourteen years' transportation was inflicted for the theft of a mare.[4] In the case of John Tweddal, Glasgow, winter 1828, the pannel, being convicted of four acts of horse-stealing, was sentenced to be hanged, but his punishment commuted into transportation for life.[5] In the case of Christopher Edgar, autumn 1824, fourteen years' transportation was the punishment for the theft of a single horse; and in that of George Bannerman, Aberdeen, autumn 1830, the same sentence was pronounced for the same offence.[6]

29. Legal evidence in theft consists either of the direct evidence of the persons who witnessed the crime, or of such a train of circumstances as leaves no reasonable doubt of the prisoner's guilt.

As in other crimes, so in theft, the most important branch of criminal jurisprudence is that concerning which the least information is to be found in the books, viz. what is the *amount of evidence* requisite to convict a prisoner of the offence. This evidence may be either direct or circumstantial.

It rarely happens that the direct evidence is altogether decisive in cases of theft, in consequence of the caution with which it is usually committed, and the unguarded moments which are selected for the depredation. It is chiefly in cases of pocket-picking or shop-lifting that the proof by eye-witnesses forms a material part of the evidence, and where it is clear and explicit,

---

[1], Both unreported.—[2] Unreported.—[3] Unreported.—[4] Unreported.—[5] Unreported.—[6] Both unreported.

without doubt it is the most satisfactory of any. It consists, for the most part, either of the evidence of the person himself who saw or was conscious of the depredation, or of that of some of the bystanders, who had an opportunity of perceiving what was going forward. In all such cases, if either two witnesses saw the theft, or one witness saw it, and he is corroborated by circumstances, as by the sudden flight of the thief from the spot; his being seen to throw away the stolen article; its being found near the line of his flight; his being caught with it in his possession, or near his feet; his being seen to hand it to an associate in his flight, or the like, the measure of evidence is held to be complete. In addition to this, which, however, seems of itself to be abundantly sufficient, some corroborating evidence is generally deduced from the prisoner's declaration; where either some falsehood occurs, or the story told is so utterly incredible and absurd as to demonstrate that some delinquence required to be concealed.

But by far the most usual cases are those where there is no direct evidence at all, but the fact of the depredation is satisfactorily established, and the prisoner's guilt is left to be inferred from a variety of circumstances which are in any reasonable view inconsistent with his innocence. Such indirect evidence usually is of this description. A shop is broken open during the night: early in the morning the prisoner is seen moving along one of the streets in the neighbourhood with a bundle on his back, which proves to be part of the stolen property. No doubt can exist in such a case of his guilt, unless he can satisfactorily shew that he got it from some other person, under such circumstances as either exclude his guilt altogether, or reduce it to that of a resetter merely. A curious case of this description occurred at Aberdeen, autumn 1824, in the trial of John Downie and Alexander Milne. The *species facti* here was, that a carpenter's workshop was broken open on a particular night at Aberdeen, and some workman's tools carried off. On the same night the counting-house of Messrs Davidson at Footdee, and of Messrs Catto and Co. on the Links at Aberdeen, were both broken, and goods and money to a considerable extent stolen. The prisoners were met at seven in the following morning in one of the streets of Aberdeen, at a distance from either of the places of depredation by two of the police. Upon seeing the officers, conscience-struck, they began to run; and being pursued and taken, there was found in the possession of each a considerable quantity of the articles taken from Catto and Co.; but none of the things taken either from the carpenter's shop or Davidson's. But in Catto and Co.'s warehouse were found a brown coat and other articles got from Davidson's, and which had not been there the evening preceding, when the shop was locked up; and in Davidson's were found the tools which had been abstracted from the carpenter's. Thus, the recent possession of the articles stolen from Catto and Co.'s proved that the pannels were the depredators in that warehouse; while the fact of the articles taken from Davidson's having been left there, connected them with that prior housebreaking; while, again, the chisels belonging to the carpenter's shop, found in Davidson's, identified the persons who broke into that last house with those who committed the original theft at the carpenter's. The result was, that the pannels were both convicted of all the thefts, upon evidence which left no doubt in the mind of any reasonable man.[1]

Another case very similar, but still more extensive in its delinquency, occurred at Aberdeen in April 1826, in the trial of Charles Bowman. This man was accused of no fewer than nine different acts of theft by housebreaking, committed in and around Aberdeen at various times during the summer of 1825 and winter 1825–6. No suspicion had been awakened against the pannel, who was a carter, living an industrious and apparently regular life, until one occasion, when some of the stolen articles having been detected in a broker's shop, and traced to his custody, a search was made, and some articles from all the houses broken open found amongst an immense mass of other goods evidently stolen, in a large chest, and concealed about various parts of the prisoner's house. Their number, variety, and the place where they were found, were quite sufficient to convict him of reset; but, as they were discovered at the distance of many months from the times when the various thefts had been committed, the difficulty was how to connect him with the actual theft.

The charges selected for trial were five in number, and as nearly connected with each other in point of time as could be obtained. In none of them was the prisoner identified as the

---

[1] Unreported.

person who had broken into the houses, although the thief was seen, and more than once fired at; but in all the first four houses which had been broken into were discovered some of the articles taken from the others, and in the pannel's custody were found some articles taken from them all, which sufficiently proved that all the depredations had been committed by one person, and the mark of an iron-instrument was found on three of the windows broken, which coincided exactly with a chisel left in the last house. Two days after the housebreaking of that last house, an old watch, belonging to the owner Mr Bruce, was shewn by the pannel to a shopkeeper in Old Meldrum, to whom it was soon afterwards sold, and delivered up to the officers. Upon this evidence the prisoner was convicted of all the charges of housebreaking, with the approbation of the Court (Lords Pitmilly and Alloway), and received sentence of death, which was afterwards commuted into transportation for life, a remarkable instance of the increased humanity of modern practice.[1]

In the case of James Prior and James Maclachlan, Aberdeen, September 1830, it appeared that a broker's shop in Aberdeen was broken open, and watches, jewellery, silver, money, and other articles, to the amount of £2000, taken away. The thieves had got access by breaking into a workshop immediately below the broker's, and cutting a hole in the floor. The shop was shut, safe, and secure on Saturday night, and on Sunday about six in the evening, one of the shopmen returning scared the thieves, who were then in the shop, and who instantly took to flight, leaving the great bulk of the stolen property packed up in the workshop below the broker's. Two men were seen at this time by several witnesses running rapidly in a direction from the broker's, through several adjoining streets, and one of them, who was running on his stocking-soles, was identified as the prisoner Maclachlan. In the bolster of his bed, when he was apprehended that night, was found a watch-key, which was identified as part of the stolen property, and £4, 16s. in silver, of which he declared in his declaration he knew nothing. None of the stolen property was found upon Prior, but a fur cap, jacket and waistcoat, proved to belong to him, were found in the broker's lying on the floor; and it was

[1] Unreported

in evidence that he came home much heated and agitated in the course of the evening, and uttered several suspicious expressions to his landlady, at the same time jingling silver in his pocket. It was proved that, for several evenings before, the two prisoners had been frequently out together, and that they were absent together from ten to twelve on the preceding night. No doubt could remain of the prisoners' guilt, and they were both convicted and transported [1]

In the case of George Laidlaw and George Spittal, Glasgow, September 1823, the *species facti* was, that the shop of Moses Solomon, in Glasgow, was broken open, and watches and jewellery to the amount of £600 carried off. Laidlaw had been frequently about the shop, and he was proved to have purchased, a few days before the shopbreaking, a key, which opened the door. Three days after the crime was committed, a considerable quantity of the stolen goods was traced to his possession, especially in a steam-boat going down the Clyde, where he gave them away in the most prodigal manner to newly formed acquaintances Spittal pleaded guilty. They were both convicted, and Laidlaw was sentenced to be executed, while Spittal was transported for life.[2]

In the case of William Boyd, Henry Wilson, and Henry Marshall, Glasgow, autumn 1823, it appeared that a house situated in Stirling road, near Glasgow, was broken open, and some shirts and other articles of dress carried off. These goods were the same night discovered in the house of a notorious resetter of the name of Buchanan, in the Gallowgate, who was also at the bar charged with the crime of reset. Two *socii criminis* deponed to the circumstances of the theft and housebreaking, in which all the prisoners had some concern; and the prisoners were apprehended that very night in the resetter's house, with part of the stolen goods lying near them. They were all convicted and transported.[3]

One of the most curious chains of circumstantial evidence which ever occurred was brought to light in the trial of James Murray, February 16. 1825. This man, who was a notorious English thief, who had made his escape from New South Wales, was charged with the theft of a parcel of bank-notes, amounting to £8000, from the mail-coach, at or near the village of

[1] Unreported.—[2] Unreported.—[3] Unreported.

Kirkliston, on the road from Stirling to Edinburgh. It appeared on the proof that the bank-notes were safely lodged in the mail-coach, in the box under the guard's seat, at Stirling, and left that town at three o'clock for Edinburgh. The guard had occasion to put his hand into the boot at Winchburgh, a few miles to the westward of Kirkliston, and there he was sensible the money parcels were all right: he left his seat and attended to harnessing the horses for a few minutes at Kirkliston, but did not again examine the boot till he got to Edinburgh, when it was discovered that they were all gone. A woman at Kirkliston saw a stranger leap from the guard's seat during his temporary absence at that place, and make off hastily towards a field in a northerly direction. Two country men met two men running in great haste a little farther on in the same direction, in the lane leading from Kirkliston to the South Ferry. The prisoner was proved to have come down to Edinburgh and lived a retired quiet life, driving out frequently in a gig, for six weeks previous to the theft. On the day libelled he hired a horse and gig from a livery-stable in Edinburgh, with which he drove out to the Queensferry, and about five in the evening drove off in the direction of Kirkliston. The horse and gig were found overturned in a ditch about 200 yards from the place where the theft was committed, and directly in the line which the two men who were met running were taking. A handkerchief proved to belong to the pannel was found near the gig, and farther on towards Kirkliston. In about two hours the pannel returned alone to the inn which he had left at Queensferry; ordered a chaise, drove to Stockbridge, got out of it a few yards on the outside of the toll, and walked to his lodgings On the following day he took a place in a feigned name for York in the mail, walked out of Edinburgh, and was taken up by the coach a little way on the western side of Portobello He was apprehended at Newcastle, and four ten pound notes of the Bank of Scotland, and a five pound note of Ramsay, Bonar and Company, were found in his possession; which corresponded to the description of notes lost in the stolen parcel in particular a five pound Ramsay and Bonar note was there proved to have been abstracted. To the officer who apprehended him he made various statements highly suspicious, if not implying his guilt; as that " he was done now," &c. In his declaration he gave

an absurd and incredible account of his motives for hiring the
gig, leaving it and the horse in such a plight so near the scene
of theft, and setting off with such expedition on the following
day for England. The Court, after the evidence was concluded, recommended to the prosecutor not to demand a conviction, with which he complied: but it is to be regretted that
the matter was not pressed to the judgment of the jury, for it
has since been ascertained that they had no doubt whatever of
the prisoner's guilt; and the prisoner, who was one of a most
daring and skilful set of bank robbers in England, afterwards
offered, if he was liberated from the charge of returning from
transportation, to restore the whole stolen property; a proposal
which was of course rejected, and the law allowed to take its
course for that minor offence.[1]

The case of William Heath and Elizabeth Crowder, Glasgow, September 1831, was attended with a different result.
They were charged with breaking into the Glasgow Bank, situated in Virginia Street, Glasgow, and stealing £6000 from
the repositories of that establishment. It appeared in evidence
that the bank was safely locked up on the 24th December, and
that it was found to have been broken into when the clerks
returned on the morning of the 26th, the intervening day having been a holiday. The iron-safes had all been forced open.
The pannel Heath had been seen in Virginia Street more than
once, about three weeks before the robbery. On Christmas
day, a woman extremely like Elizabeth Crowder rang at the
bank door, and repeatedly looked past the servant who opened
the door up the stair. The prisoners came to Glasgow about
six weeks before the theft, living together, and left their first
lodgings about a fortnight before Christmas for another, in
which they lived till Christmas-day, when they finally left it.
They frequently went out carrying a box, which they always
brought back; and when at home they were frequently engaged,
with the windows closed, in a noisy work like breaking of iron
with hammers. On the day of the theft they were seen in
Virginia Street by two witnesses lounging about during the
time of divine service. Heath had repeatedly called at an
ironmonger's in Glasgow, for some weeks previous, to get blank
keys, and to get them bored and altered, and that ironmonger

---

[1] Unreported.

5

identified a fragment of a key found in the lock of the safe of the bank as what he had made for Heath; and on the dresser of the lodgings they occupied in Glasgow were found circles such as would have been produced by making keys similar to one of which a fragment was found in the safe of the bank which was robbed, and the catches of a vice found in Crowder's house in London coincided with the markings on a board in Heath's lodgings in Glasgow. On the day after the theft the prisoner Heath set off in the coach to Edinburgh, under a feigned name, and was traced in the mail by Edinburgh to London. On the 31st December he was found at a jeweller's shop in Dover exchanging two Scotch notes for French gold; and to the mate of the steam-boat between Dover and Calais a person resembling the prisoner Heath tendered a twenty pound Scotch note. In their declaration, both prisoners refused to answer any questions. Upon this evidence Heath was convicted and executed, and Crowder escaped by a verdict finding that she was in the previous knowledge of the theft, but had no actual participation in it; a verdict which the Court justly considered as equivalent to not proven.[1]

A similar case, which came to the same result, was that of James M'Coul or Moffat, June 12. 1820. This man was accused of breaking into the Paisley Union Bank, in Paisley, by means of false keys, and stealing notes and money to the amount of £20,000. The evidence was partly direct and partly circumstantial. It appeared that the pannel had come down to Paisley, where he had lived for several weeks, and again returned to London, with a great variety of impressions of the wards of locks in wax, where they were formed into skeleton keys by one Scoltock, the blacksmith of the gang. He then returned to Paisley, and was seen by one witness sitting on a wall near the bank early on the morning succeeding the night when the theft was committed. On that day he was traced travelling in post-chaises to Edinburgh, the last of which was dismissed in Maitland Street. He again went on the same evening to London, and was taken up in Greenside Street by a coach which conveyed him to York. He was traced travelling post to an inn at Barnett, where he was identified by the waiter as having been seen sitting in a room with two other

[1] Unreported.

men, with a great number of large Scotch notes before them, spread all over the table, which they were apparently in the act of dividing. The prisoner had changed some large Scotch notes on the road, but none which were identified as part of the stolen property. He was convicted, and sentenced to be executed, but died in jail, after receiving a transportation pardon.[1]

Possession of the stolen property recently after the theft is the circumstance of all others which most strongly militates against a pannel; and, unless explained by him in some way consistent with his innocence, almost always leads with sensible juries to a conviction.[2] What is the precise period within which the possession of the stolen goods is held to have this decisive effect against the pannel, has not been fixed by any unbending rule; nor indeed is it possible that it can be so, because the weight to be attached to that circumstance mainly depends on the other circumstances which are connected with it. If the prisoner has confessed, when brought before a magistrate, or in his declaration, or to the persons who apprehended him; if he was seen hastily making off from the place of the theft, or loitering about it without any visible reason before; if picklocks or instruments for breaking doors and windows are found upon him, and the crime was perpetrated by the aid of such instruments; if he had purchased recently before, or was in possession of, a key which opens the lock, and the theft was committed by means of false keys; if any part of his dress, or any articles belonging to him, are found in or near the place from which the goods were taken, or within the house broken open; if the marks of his shoes coincide with the marks left by the thieves; if he offer to deliver up part of the goods, or bribe to be let off; if he deny that he has the goods, and they are found with the marks effaced secreted in his possession, or about his person, or within or near his house, or place of usual haunt; if he have sold part of the goods at inferior prices, or to known resetters of stolen property; if he tell in his declaration an absurd or incredible story as to the way in which he got the articles, as by finding them on the road, receiving them from a stranger whom he does not know, and cannot produce, &c.; certainly any of these articles of pre-

---

[1] Unreported.—[2] Hume, i. 111, Burnett, 555

sumptive evidence, coupled with recent possession of the stolen goods, unexplained on any rational grounds, is a sufficient ground for a legal conviction. Hundreds of prisoners are justly convicted every year upon such evidence.[1] When it was the fashion of the Court to pronounce special interlocutors, the recent and unexplained possession of stolen goods was frequently of itself sustained as a sufficient ground of conviction.[2] This was done, in particular, in the case of the Roys, Inverness, 1st May 1712; Alexander M'Coull, Inverness, May 2. 1731; James Inglis, 1st November 1820; and John Scott, February 11. 1734.[3]

In modern practice, though recent possession is almost always, in circumstantial cases, a most important article of evidence, yet it is usually accompanied with some other circumstance, generally slight indeed, but confirmatory of the inference deducible from that leading fact. This is more especially the case where an interval of days has elapsed between the commission of the theft and the goods being found in the pannel's possession. Thus, in the case of Smith and Stevenson, 8th December 1806, two men, horse-dealers, having been seen the evening before the horses were stolen near the place where the theft was committed, and in the course of a few days found with them at Newcastle, were found guilty, and had sentence of death[4] In like manner, in the case of Walker, July 1801, the prisoner was proved to have been in possession of the stolen horse three days after the theft; but he pleaded reset, and specified the person from whom he had bought the animal· as it turned out, however, upon the exculpatory proof, that the prisoner had been seen with the person thus set forth as the thief the day preceding the theft, and that something had passed between them like an agreement to meet on the following day, this destroyed the defence, by establishing previous concert, and the prisoner was convicted of the theft.[5] In the case of John Gall, Aberdeen, September 1827, the cattle were stolen from some fields in the neighbourhood of Banchory, on the Dee, in Aberdeenshire. The prisoner was traced along the road from Aberdeen, on the preceding day, to within two miles of the place of the theft, and on the following morning found in the possession of cattle answering the description a few miles

---

[1] Hume, i. 111; Burnett, 556, 557.—[2] Burnett, 557.—[3] Ibid.; Hume, i. 557.—[4] Hume, i. 112.—[5] Burnett, 555.

to the southward, on the road leading across the Grampians to Fettercairn; and he was traced with these animals under his charge to Brechin, where they were found in a field in which he had placed them, and identified by the owner, who had joined in the pursuit: upon this evidence the prisoner was convicted.[1]  In the case of John Wales, Glasgow, spring 1828, the *species facti* was, that a shop in Glasgow was broken open between a Saturday night and a Monday morning, and about £30 in silver carried off; and suspicions fell on the prisoner. There was found in his lodgings, when he was apprehended on the Monday, about eleven o'clock in the forenoon, a good deal of silver, comprising an old dollar, corresponding with an old coin of the same description which had been carried off, but which of course could not be identified.  To compensate, however, this defect, there was found in the ashes of the grate in the prisoner's room, the iron-heel of a shoe, which corresponded in size, form, and the number of holes, to the iron of a shoe which was left in the shop broken into  The morning of the Monday was wet, and the stocking-soles were wet and dirty, though the pannel was in bed, and said he had not been out that morning: the prisoner was convicted on the most convincing evidence, and transported for life.[2]  Lastly, in the case of D. Lantwheler and others, 11th December 1826, the prisoners were convicted upon proof that the theft and housebreaking was committed, and that, two days afterwards, they were found wearing part of the stolen property, of the acquisition of which they could give no satisfactory account; though they had been never seen near the plundered premises[3]

It frequently happens that the identification is not complete, but nearly so; and, in such circumstances, it is a matter of much nicety to determine whether the evidence arising from recent possession is sufficient.  Of course, more evidence is required to support such *semiplena* identification, than where it is unequivocal; but still, where the other circumstances are pregnant with suspicion, it will fill up the measure of legal evidence.  Thus, in the case of John M'Kechnie and Alexander Tolmie, Glasgow, spring 1828, it appeared that the soapboiling premises of William Johnston and Company, near Glasgow, were broken into, by breaking open a hole in the wall, and 120 pounds of yellow soap abstracted.  This took place on a Satur-

[1] Unreported.—[2] Unreported —[3] Syme, i. 33.

day night; on the same night, at eleven o'clock, the prisoners were met by the watchmen near the centre of the city, one of them having 40 pounds of brown soap on his back, and the other his clothes all greased over with the same substance. The prisoners, on seeing the watchmen, attempted to escape, but were seized. The owner declared that the soap was exactly of the same kind, size and shape, with that abstracted from his manufactory; but, as it had no private mark, it could not be identified more distinctly. One of the prisoners had formerly been a servant about the premises; and both in their declarations declared they got the soap in a public house from a man whom they did not know. On this evidence, though not amounting to complete identification, they were convicted, and transported seven years.[1] A similar case occurred at Glasgow in the same circuit, attended with the same result. This was that of William Young. A workshop was there broken into on an evening about six o'clock, and £10 in silver stolen from a locked drawer. The effraction had been accomplished in a very peculiar way, and evidently by a person well acquainted with the premises. A fierce watch-dog left in charge of the premises had not been heard to make any noise by the neighbours, although he would in all probability have seized and torn a stranger. The prisoner, who had formerly been a servant in the shop, and was well acquainted with the premises, and familiar with the dog, was seen by a watchman in a neighbouring street at five o'clock; and there was found in his chest £9, 18s. in silver, including a crooked sixpence, which the owner thought was one which she had long possessed, or at least it exactly resembled it. He was convicted and transported.[2]

In cases of theft, the same question frequently arises which has been noticed in relation to other offences; viz. What weight is due to the testimony of a single witness, and what amount of proof is required to support each step in a chain of evidence? Upon this point, it seems to be fixed, on the one hand, that the testimony of a single witness, without any corroborating circumstance, is not sufficient for the whole case; and, on the other, that more than one witness is certainly not required to each link, however material, in a chain of evidence. It wont

---

[1] Unreported — [2] Unreported

do for the prosecutor to examine one witness, and conclude his case; but, on the other hand, if the *corpus delicti* is established by one witness, and he is corroborated in that essential fact by any circumstance, it is sufficient to establish that a crime was committed. Nay, it is enough if this corroborating fact be one of the *indiciæ* tending to fix guilt on the prisoner. For example, if one swear to the theft, a second see the pannel in the vicinity, and the third apprehend him *de recenti* with the stolen goods in his possession, without all doubt the proof is here complete in all its parts. True there is only one direct witness to the fundamental fact of a theft having been committed; but his testimony is supported by the circumstance of finding the goods in the possession of the pannel, which is spoken to by a third party. So the law was laid down, after a full argument, at Perth, spring 1829, by Lord Mackenzie, in the case of Mary Mason; and it is matter of every day's practice to convict prisoners upon this species of evidence. It is sufficient, therefore, to prove the *corpus delicti* by one witness; and the circumstances attaching to the pannel each by another. Nay, in cases of direct and positive circumstances inferring guilt *de recenti* after the crime was committed, it is often sufficient to establish the guilt of the pannel by one witness, if the *corpus* have been previously established by another. For example, if a man feel a hand in his pocket, and discover instantly that his pocket-book is stolen, but without being able to identify the thief, and another apprehend the thief at a little distance running off with it in his hand, there can be no doubt that the proof is complete, though there is only one witness to the *corpus*, and another to the prisoner's guilt; for this reason, that each of these witnesses corroborates the other; the witness to the *corpus* being supported by the discovery of the stolen property in the pannel's possession, and the witness to that fact by the person who identifies it as the goods which had just been taken from him. Such a proof was accordingly sustained as sufficient at Glasgow, spring 1825, in the case of Hugh Laird, and of Thomas Brown and James Adams, Glasgow, spring 1828.[2] In like manner, if the owner of a house swear that he closed his windows at night, that in the morning he found them broken open, and part of his plate stolen, and a

---

[1] Unreported.—[2] Unreported.

watchman depone that he apprehended the prisoner running along the street in a direction from the house early in the morning, with a bundle on his back, which on his apprehension proves to be the identical plate abstracted from the house, and as such is immediately identified by the proprietor, there is no reasonable jury who could hesitate as to convicting the prisoner; because, though there is only one witness to each fact, yet they mutually support each other, which is all that the law requires. Such a proof, accordingly, was sustained as sufficient by Lord Moncrieff, at Glasgow, spring 1828, in the case of Buchanan Wilson and John Cunningham.[1] Here one witness proved the locking up of a hen-house at night: and another, who was a watchman, swore to meeting the prisoners about fifty yards from the hen-house, coming as if from it, at five o'clock in the morning, one of whom had a bundle in his hand, which he immediately dropped, and they both ran, but were afterwards seized. The bundle proved to be cocks and hens, which, being taken to the owner, were immediately identified, and the premises found to be broken open; while in the pocket of the one who had not the fowls was found a knife, stained with recent blood, two of the fowls having had their throats cut. In these circumstances, they were both convicted; and, being habite and repute thieves, transported fourteen years. The reason why more than one witness is generally brought forward, both to substantiate the *corpus delicti*, and to bring home guilt to the prisoner, is not that more than one is legally required, on each point, if sufficiently explicit, but that it is so difficult to find one who can himself and singly speak to the requisite facts.

It is not sufficient, however, though the *corpus delicti* be ever so clearly established, to convict a prisoner, that he has simply confessed in his declaration. Without doubt that is a most material, and, with a slight addition, if the *corpus* be previously established, decisive circumstance against him; but of itself, and unsupported, it is not sufficient So it was held by the whole Court, in the case of John Dunlop, James Armour, and others, December 8. 1823, where the *corpus* was proved, and the prisoner confessed, but, for want of any other article of evidence, an acquittal was directed.[2]

---

[1] Unreported.—[2] Unreported.

In cases of this description, the evidence of associates is frequently of decisive importance, and, therefore, it is important to attend to the principles on which the consideration of their testimony is regulated. It is evident that a man does not become disqualified for giving testimony, by the mere fact that he admits that he has been accessary to a depredation, because the interests of society, *ne crimina maneant impunita*, imperiously require that this species of evidence, which is often the only one that can be obtained, should not be rejected. On the other hand, it is to be recollected, that this evidence is that of worthless characters, who admit that they have been implicated in grave offences, and, by their habits of life, are not likely to be materially influenced by the reverence for an oath. The only mode (and it almost always proves effectual) of sifting such evidence, is by minutely examining the *socii* as to the circumstances of the alleged crime; and if this testimony coincide in all the minute particulars with the account of the appearances of the premises after the depredation was discovered, by unexceptionable evidence, it affords a presumption almost irresistible, that the story was true; for here, as every where else, the maxim will be found applicable, that " Truth is one, but errors are many, and every man has a different one." In the cases, accordingly, of John Gilchrist, Glasgow, autumn 1826, and J. Devine and others, Glasgow, autumn 1823, the case for the prosecution rested mainly, in each case, on the evidence of an associate; but his evidence was so strikingly corroborative, in the minutest particulars, of the account of the marks and effects of the theft, by housebreaking, which was given by the owners of the premises, that not a doubt could remain of their guilt, and they were accordingly convicted.[1]

Where, as very frequently occurs, witnesses of this stamp speak imperfectly out, or strive to screen a particular favourite associate, it is very unreasonable to hold that they must, on that account, be entirely rejected. On the contrary, what is squeezed, by the force of minute and long continued examination, out of a witness of this description, is frequently of more weight with an intelligent jury than if it had been at once and voluntarily emitted by him. The reason is obvious, that he is speaking *against* an evident desire to conceal the truth; and, therefore, the motive for concealment being all against the pro-

[1] Unreported

secutor, what he does admit against his associate is entitled to the more consideration. On the other hand, where there appears an undue anxiety to fix the crime, in an especial manner, upon one, in preference to the others, the testimony of such a character is to be taken with the more caution ; and absolutely rejected, if it either vary from the real and unsupported evidence of the case, or if there be any grounds for supposing that he is influenced by a vindictive or malevolent motive.

In cases of theft, much important evidence is frequently derived from the prisoner's declaration. Guilty persons are usually extremely at a loss how to account for their possession of stolen articles. They generally say that they found them on the road ; that they got them from a person whom they never saw before, and would not know if they saw again ; that they received them from one who put them into their hands, and desired them to carry them for a short distance, and then absconded, and so on. It is unnecessary to observe, that all such absurd stories, unless supported by evidence, are totally undeserving of weight. If the account which the pannel gives of the way in which he got the article be supported by credible testimony, it is as material a circumstance for, as, if totally unsupported by evidence, it is against his defence. Even though unsupported by evidence, the story as to the *modus acquirendi* is often of weight in favour of the pannel, if it be in itself rational, told voluntarily, and with candour and consistence ; but if it be either incredible or absurd in itself, or varied at different times, or inconsistent with the other evidence in the case, it not only is of no weight in his favour, but a material circumstance against him.

It is also a legitimate ground of inference against a pannel, if he admit, in his declaration, that he was in company or connexion with one who has confessed his guilt, at or about the time of the commission of the crime. In admitting such a circumstance to weigh against him, we are not allowing the declaration of one prisoner to militate against another, contrary to a received and acknowledged principle of jurisprudence ; we are only admitting the weight which must necessarily belong to the admitted fact, that the prisoner was in connexion with an acknowledged thief about the time the crime was committed. And, on the same principle, though the declaration of one pannel is not evidence against another; yet the fact, that the testimony of a *socius* is confirmed by the declaration of one of the pannels, must be received as a support to that testimony, even in considering the case against the other pannel. So the law was laid down by Lord Justice-Clerk Boyle, with the concurrence of the whole Court, in the case of George Edgar and John Young, February 3. 1828,[1] and on various other occasions.

# CHAPTER X.

### OF RESET OF THEFT.

Reset of Theft is the receiving and keeping of stolen goods, knowing them to be stolen, with the design of feloniously retaining them from the real owner.[2] Unless both requisites concur, the crime is not completed; for, unless the goods are known to be stolen, there is no crime in their reception, and, unless they are feloniously detained, every clerk of Court who is intrusted with the custody of stolen goods, would be guilty of this offence.[3]

1. It is indispensable to this crime, that the goods are received into the prisoner's keeping; but if this be once done, it is immaterial on what terms they were received, or into whose hands they are afterwards passed, if it be not those of the real owner.

It is the fundamental circumstance in the description of this crime, that the stolen goods are received into the offender's possession. The mere harbouring of the thief, therefore, will not constitute this offence; but, on the other hand, the reset will not be the less committed, though the thief be harboured, if the stolen goods have passed into the custody or keeping of the prisoner.[4] In the case of John Tennant and others, Au-

[1] Unreported.—[2] Hume, i. 113 ; Burnett, 155.—[3] Burnett, 155.—[4] Hume, i. 113.

gust 11. 1714, accordingly, the prisoner Tennant was convicted of reset, although the thieves were taken in his house,
he having part of the stolen goods in his pocket, and part concealed in his house.[1]   To the same purpose was the verdict in
the case of William Boyd, Henry Marshall, and others, Glasgow, autumn 1823, where the resetters, William Buchanan
and his wife, were convicted of reset, although the thieves
were apprehended in their house, and the stolen goods were
found in a bundle lying on the floor, two associates in the
theft having deponed to the goods having been looked at by
the resetters, when the thieves came into the house, and to
some communing having taken place about their purchase,
which, however, was not finally concluded.[2]

But if the pannel once receive the goods into his keeping, it
is immaterial on what footing this is done; whether by purchase, pledge, barter, or as a mere depositary for the thief.[3]
Nay, though he buy them for full value, the crime is the same;
because he knowingly detains them from the true owner; but
the fact of a fair price having been paid is an important circumstance to outweigh the presumption of the guilty knowledge.[4]

2. It is not indispensable to the crime of reset, that the
goods shall have been received directly from the thief;
the guilt is the same, though they have passed through
several intermediate hands, provided the pannel was
aware that they were stolen.

When the prosecutor has proved that the goods were stolen,
and that they were found in the prisoner's possession, under
circumstances implying a knowledge that they were stolen, he
has made out his case.   He is not bound to go farther, and
trace all the hands through which the goods have gone in their
progress from the real owner to the prisoner.[5]   The crime is
equally committed, although the goods may have passed through
twenty intermediate hands, if it is evident that he knew in
what way they passed from the hands of the true owner.[6]

But it is indispensable that the knowledge of the goods being
stolen should be brought home to the pannel.   Unless this be

Hume. i. 113.—[2] Unreported.—[3] Burnett, 155, Hume, i. 113.—[4] Hume,
i. 113.—[5] Ibid. i. 114.—[6] Ibid , Burnett, 156.

done, the prosecutor has no case; if it is done, the prisoner has none. But it is necessary that the guilty *knowledge* should be brought home to the prisoner. Suspicion merely that they are not honestly come by will not suffice; and, accordingly, in the case of James Johnnie, 23d May 1775, where the jury found merely that " the pannel bought the goods, *suspecting* them to be stolen," he was assoilzied and dismissed from the bar [1]

This rule, however, must be understood in a reasonable sense. Certainly it is not requisite that the prisoner should have been informed by direct evidence that the goods were stolen : it is sufficient if they were received under circumstances which could have left no doubt, in any reasonable mind, that they had been thus acquired. Owing to the jealousy and caution so natural in this sort of traffic, it often happens that no express disclosure is made, and yet the theftuous acquisition of the articles in question, is as well understood as if the resetter had actually witnessed the depredation.[2] In this, as in other cases, therefore, it is sufficient, if circumstances are proved, which, to persons of an ordinary understanding, and situated as the pannel was, must have led to the conclusion that they were theftuously acquired.[3] Thus, if it be proved that the pannel received watches, jewellery, large quantities of money, bundles of clothes of various kinds, or moveables of any sort, to a considerable value, from boys, or other persons destitute of property, and without any lawful means of acquiring them; and, more especially, if it be proved that they were brought, at untimely hours, and under circumstances of evident concealment, it is impossible to arrive at any other conclusion, but that they were received in the full understanding of the guilty mode of their acquisition. This will be still farther confirmed, if it appear that they were purchased at considerably less than their real value; concealed in places not usually employed for keeping such articles, as under beds, in coal-cellars, in mattresses, up chimneys, if their marks were effaced, or false and inconsistent stories told as to the mode of their acquisition [4] And it is a still farther ingredient towards inferring guilty knowledge, if they have been received from a notorious thief, or one from whom stolen goods have, on previous occasions, been received.[5] Nor is it necessary that all these circumstances

---

[1] Hume, u. 115; Burnett, 153.—[2] Hume, i 114.—[3] Ibid , Burnett, 156 —[4] Hume, i 114, 115 , Burnett, 158.—[5] Burnett, 157; Hume, i. 115.

should concur in any one case; it is sufficient if the goods stolen
be found in the prisoner's custody, without any evidence of
honest acquisition, and he either prevaricates as to the way
in which they were got, or has concealed them, or effaced
their marks, or received them from such persons, or in such a
way, as could not have been deemed consistent with their
having legally come into his author's possession.[1]

3. Reset is the act of one unconnected with the original depredation; and, therefore, if there be evidence of a
previous agreement or concert, as well as subsequent participation in the stolen property, the pannel is not a resetter, but art and part in the original theft.

The crime of reset being so nearly akin to theft, it often becomes a matter of nicety to distinguish between the circumstances which infer the one crime, and those which warrant a
conviction of the other. The only rule which can be laid down
in these cases is, that if the pannel were previously aware of the
theft, and took any steps to promote its accomplishment, his
subsequent possession of part of the stolen property will amount
to evidence warranting a conviction, not of reset but of theft;
but that if he were not implicated in the original crime either
by counsel, knowledge, or co-operation, his subsequent guilty
possession is evidence of reset only. The rule itself is clear,
but its application to particular cases is often extremely difficult.
If two pickpockets are plying their trade in different parts
of the same market-place, and one of them runs off with a
purse, which, in the course of his flight, he hands to his associate, the latter is not a resetter, but art and part in the theft.[2]
In like manner, if a person having stolen a pack of goods from
a waggon in the street *straightway* repair with it to the house
of a known thief, who instantly secretes the property, and receives a share of the spoil, it may be a very doubtful question
whether, by such instantaneous co-operation, though subsequent
to the event, the assister may not become accessary to the original theft.[3] But whatever may be thought of such cases, one
thing is quite clear, that where immediate subsequent co-ope-

ration is combined with any sort of previous knowledge of the
particular deed, or any sort of assistance but towards the perpetration, the crime amounts to actual theft.[1]   Accordingly in
the case of Anderson and Marshall, December 4. 1728, the
*species facti* was, 'hat Anderson was a gipsy, and Marshall
kept a house of resort for vagabonds, and both were charged as
art and part of a robbery committed on Bailie Rule.   It appeared that the gipsies were lodged in Marshall's barn on the
night of the robbery ; that Marshall knew of Rule's intention to
pass that way at night, which he communicated to the gipsies.
Anderson rose in the night alone and robbed Rule, and, on returning, was heard to desire Marshall to take care of his money,
who answered " that it was as safe as his shirt."   In these circumstances Marshall was justly convicted, not of reset, but of robbery, and had sentence of death accordingly.[2]   To the same
purpose was the judgment of the Court in the case of Macdonald
and Wilson, 15th June 1818.   It there appeared that Macdonald
went on a predatory expedition to Berwickshire with two
younger lads, and they took their quarters together at Eyemouth.   Macdonald sent out the lads to steal, with instructions
not to bring the booty to their lodgings, but to lodge it in the
fields.   They did so accordingly, and on the following day they
set out together for Edinburgh, and in the course of the journey the lads brought the goods to Macdonald, and they were
divided among them, he receiving a share of the plunder.   In
these circumstances he was justly convicted as art and part of
the *theft* libelled, though he had neither been present when the
goods were stolen, nor pointed out, nor given any information
regarding the particular places where they were to be committed.[3]   And the law was laid down in the same way by Lords
Justice-Clerk Boyle and Pitmilly in the case of William Boyd,
Henry Marshall, and others, Glasgow, autumn 1823, where
one of the persons convicted as accessary to the theft was a
person who was not present at the housebreaking, but belonged
to the gang, and received part of the goods to carry away at a
considerable distance from the place of the original crime.[4]

But unless the prisoner can be connected with the original
depredation by previous knowledge, concert, or co-operation,
or by presence, or acting as art and part on the occasion itself,

---

[1] Hume, i. 116.—[2] Ibid.—[3] Ibid.—[4] Unreported.

or *immediate* subsequent assistance, his crime is not theft but reset. And in all cases where a charge of art and part guilty of theft is founded upon mere recent possession of the stolen goods, without any evidence of previous concert or knowledge, the subsequent assistance must have been *immediate*, and such as to infer, by reasonable inference, previous knowledge or preparation, as we do not acknowledge the accession after the fact of the English law.

It is hardly necessary to observe, that these observations relate exclusively to the case where the pannel has sufficiently fixed the theft on another, and the only question is, whether he was art and part with him, or a resetter only; because, if no other thief be pointed out, the recent possession is of itself an almost conclusive article of evidence to warrant a conviction of theft [1]

4. If the goods be once received into the resetter's possession, the crime is completed, though they be retained for the shortest time, or though the object be not permanent possession, but temporary concealment.

The crime of reset consists in the guilty *receipt* of stolen goods, and is nowise dependent upon the period of their detention. In the same way, therefore, as theft is complete the moment the goods are abstracted, though it be but for an instant, so reset is committed the moment the goods are feloniously received, though no intention of ultimate detention existed.[2] In truth, it is in this criminal *concealment* of stolen goods, whether for behoof of the thief or the resetter, that one of the most dangerous qualities of this crime consists. Although, therefore, it would be hard to fix on a prisoner a charge of reset, merely because goods are thrown in at his window, or thrust in at his door, before he is well aware what is going forward; yet, if he once acquiesce in the placing of the goods there under circumstances inferring his guilty knowledge, and still more if he lend any aid towards their concealment, even though it be only to screen the thief from detection, or extricate him from pursuit, his guilt is incurred. So it was laid down by Lord Justice-Clerk Boyle in the case of Robert Finlay, James Pearson, Jean

---

[1] Hume, i. 117.—[2] Ibid. i. 113

Macgregor, and others, Glasgow, autumn 1826. It there appeared that the thieves came running up the stair where the prisoners charged with reset lodged, and hastily threw the stolen goods upon a bed, where they were covered by Jean Macgregor, a lodger in the house, who instantly leapt from the window, and in the fall broke her leg and was taken. Her counsel contended that there was not here the requisite detention or appropriation of the stolen goods; but this was overruled by the Court, and she was convicted and sentenced to eighteen months' imprisonment in Bridewell.[1] And in that case it was also determined that reset may be committed by concealing in a house, not only by the owner, but any lodger or temporary occupant; the essence of the crime consisting in the concealment of the stolen goods from the true owner, which may be done as well by a visitor or temporary lodger as the proper householder.

5. Legal evidence in reset consists in proof of the theft followed by reception of the goods by the pannel, with the design of concealing and detaining them from the proprietor under such circumstances as infer knowledge that they had been theftuously acquired.

The proof in cases of reset usually consists in the discovery of the stolen goods in the possession of the pannel, secreted or altered in such a way as evidently demonstrates that he was aware how they had been acquired. For example, if jewellery, watches, laces, or other valuable articles are discovered stuffed into a mattress, thrust into a hole in the chimney, concealed under a bundle of old clothes, with the marks picked out, or the like, it is impossible to draw any other conclusions but that they were secreted in such situation, or altered in that manner, to avoid detection, and from a knowledge that they had been stolen. Such evidence, accompanied by the inability of the prisoner to give any rational account of how he got them, is accordingly every day sustained as sufficient proof of the guilty knowledge, and as inferring the design of felonious concealment, which is essential to the crime. Witness, for example, the case of Dunlop, Hunter, and Armour, December 8. 1823,

---

[1] Unreported.

where the latter of these parties was convicted of reset to a
great extent, and transported fourteen years, upon evidence
that they were partly stowed away in concealed places in his
house, partly sent off by the first conveyance to Belfast.[1]

It is not sufficient, however, to prove that goods were found
in the prisoner's possession, under such circumstances as clearly indicated a knowledge that they were stolen : the prosecutor
must go a step farther, and prove from whom they were taken,
and the time, place, and mode in which the theft was committed; if, therefore, either any of these circumstances have not
been set forth in the libel, or any of them fail in the proof, the
prisoner must be acquitted.[2]   In the case, accordingly, of Robert Byers, July 16. 1824, where the prosecutor had neglected
to libel on the mode of the previous theft, or the person to
whom the stolen goods belonged, the charge of reset was found
to be irrelevantly laid.[3]   And so completely is the crime of reset held to be dependent on the establishment of the previous
crime of theft, that any failure in the proof of the first offence
will prove fatal to the second,[4] even though the fact of the
goods having been stolen *somehow* be ever so clearly established.   The prosecutor is bound to establish not merely that the
goods were received after having been stolen, but after having
been stolen at the precise time and place specified in the indictment.[5]   If, therefore, the libel assert that the goods were
stolen from the house of John Cooper, and it turn out that they
were stolen from the house of James Cooper; or that they were
stolen from a house in George Street, and it appear that they
were stolen from a house in Prince's Street, the subsidiary
charge of reset must fall to the ground.

It is not, however, indispensable that the prosecutor should
establish *the person* by whom the theft was committed, for this
he very often has no means of ascertaining; it is quite sufficient
if he libel and prove the person from whom the depredation
was committed, and the time and mode of its accomplishment.
This he always has it in his power to ascertain, if the theft
have been detected by unexceptionable evidence; the other depends upon the discovery of a criminal who is frequently beyond his reach.   In the case of Robert Byers, accordingly, already mentioned, where the amended libel set forth the mode

[1] Unreported.—[2] Hume, i. 114.—[3] Unreported.—[4] Hume, i. 114.—[5] Ibid.

of the theft, and the owner of the stolen goods, though without
the name of the thieves, the prisoner was convicted of reset,
and transported for seven years.[1]

It is quite competent to adduce some, or even all, the thieves
as witnesses against the resetters, and this is frequently done
with the very best effect, especially where the latter are old
and hardened offenders, who have made use of juvenile depredators to ply the trade from which they derive the principal
emolument.  Of course the evidence of the thieves who are
adduced as *socii criminis* must be received with the due degree
of caution; but if it be credible in itself, given with the appearance of candour, and supported, in so far as it could be by the
other evidence in the case, it forms an unexceptionable ground
of conviction.  In the case of William Whyte, John Paisley,
and others, accordingly, Glasgow, autumn 1823, where Mr Urquhart's (the perfumer) shop had been broken open in that city,
and jewellery to a large amount abstracted, the proof against
the resetter, who kept a notorious house of prostitutes and
thieves in the Old Wynd there, consisted in the evidence of two
of the boys employed in the theft, who proved the bringing of the
stolen articles to their house, coupled with the finding of some
vinagrettes and other small articles in their possession, and the
absurd story told as to the mode of their acquisition by the
prisoners in their declaration.[2]  In the case of Betty Sheills
and Janet Kilgour, 2d March 1818, which was a suspension of
a sentence of the Sheriff Court of Fife, the objection stated
against the sentence was, that the thief could not be adduced
as a witness against the resetter, but, if known, must be tried
in the first instance, and that the principal thief in that case
was not only known but adduced as a witness against the prisoner.  But this objection was unanimously repelled.[3]  In
England also, it is competent to adduce the thief as a witness
against the resetter.[4]

In considering the evidence against persons charged with
this crime, much weight is justly laid upon the declaration of
the pannel, because, being an offence, whereof the criminality
consists in guilty knowledge, the account which he himself
gives of the mode in which, and the persons from whom, he
acquired them, must of course form a most important element

[1] Unreported.—[2] Unreported.—[3] Hume, i 120.—[4] Leach, i. case 194.

for consideration. If the account given by the prisoner, when apprehended, to the officers or others concerned in his seizure, is different from that afterwards told in his declaration; or if his declarations or statements be at variance with each other; or if the account he gives be contradicted by the evidence, or totally unsupported by testimony on his side; or if it be in itself incredible, unlikely, or absurd; or if he claim the goods proved to have been stolen as his own property, or that of any of the members of his family, certainly any of these circumstances, if coupled with the discovery of the goods in his possession, in suspicious circumstances, or places of concealment, or with the marks of former ownership effaced, form a sufficient ground of conviction, and upon which juries every day proceed in trials for this offence.

6. It is competent to try the resetter on the same libel and at the same diet with the principal thief, or before the thief has been discovered or apprehended, or though he be in custody and has not been brought to trial, or though he be employed as a witness against him.

It was formerly doubted whether the resetter could be tried before the principal thief, if he were known and in custody.[1] But these doubts have long ago been at an end; and it has long been the settled practice to try the thief and the resetter at one and the same time, and in one and the same libel. Such a charge was accordingly sustained in the noted case of Murdieson and Miller in 1773, and in that of Macdonald and Jamieson, August 9. 1770, where the objection, that the thief must be previously discussed, was overruled. Since that time it has been matter of daily practice to try the thieves and resetters at once, on the same libel.[2] And in the case of Campbell, Ker, and Welsh, 22d April 1822, where these three men were put to the bar on a libel which at the same time charged three women, Miller, Young, and Anderson, with reset of the stolen goods, an objection stated to the accumulation of persons and charges was repelled.[3]

Farther, it shall not alter the case though the thief have not

---

[1] Mackenzie's Theft-Boot, No. 4, Hume, i 120.—[2] Hume, i 120.—[3] Ibid.

been discovered, or though it be ascertained by the list of witnesses served on the resetter, that he is known, and, instead of
being tried, is meant to be adduced as a witness against him.[1]
Thus, in the case of Morgammoch, Inverness, September 1766,
it was objected " that the libel did not condescend upon the
persons who stole the goods alleged to have been resetted, and
that the reset of theft could not go to proof till the original
theft was established, or the principal thief convicted. But this
objection was repelled." [2]　And this authority has since been
always followed as law, and the trial of the resetter before the
thief, and where the latter is taken as a witness against him, is
now matter of daily practice. Witness the case of William Boyd,
Henry Marshall, and others, Glasgow, autumn 1823, where,
on the evidence of the thieves, the resetters were convicted and
transported fourteen years ; and that of Duncan Macdonald
and Ann Farrel, Glasgow, April 27. 1825, where the female
prisoner being convicted of reset chiefly by the evidence of one
of the thieves, and it being proved that she had been previously
eight times convicted in the Police Court of the same offence,
transportation for fourteen years was the punishment.[3]

7. A wife cannot be charged with reset for receiving
or concealing the stolen goods brought in by her husband,
unless she make a trade of the crime, and has taken a part
in disposing of the stolen goods.

A wife may, doubtless, be accessary to a theft committed by
her husband, and as such may be tried on the same libel with
him; and she may also be tried on the same libel with him for
reset, in which they are *both* implicated; but she cannot be
charged with resetting the goods which he has stolen and
brought to their common house,[4] unless it appear that she was
not merely concealing the evidence of his guilt, but commencing a new course of guilt for herself, in which she took a principal share, as by selling the stolen articles, or carrying on long
the infamous traffic. If she have done either of these things,
her privilege ceases ; and, accordingly, in many cases of *that*
description, the wife has been convicted of resetting her hus-

---

[1] Hume, l. 121 ; Burnett, 289, 290.—[2] Burnett, 289.—[3] Unreported.—[4] Mackenzie, tit. Reset.

band's stolen goods, in particular that of Boyd Maccormick and Mary Maccormick, his wife, Aberdeen, September 1827. The reason of the rule in the general case is, that the wife is considered as bound, by the humanity of the law, to cherish and protect her husband, and, so far from informing against him, to conceal his delinquencies, and protect him from punishment. The concealment of stolen goods, therefore, which forms the essence of the crime, is in her only the discharge of a domestic duty. In the case, accordingly, of Thomas Malloch and Margaret Rennie, Glasgow, spring 1828, where the husband was charged as thief, and his wife as resetter of the stolen goods, the public prosecutor, with the approbation of the Lord Justice-Clerk Boyle and Lord Moncrieff, departed from the charge against the wife, and the husband alone was convicted and transported.[1] This being matter of evidence, however, must be pleaded to the jury, and cannot be stated as an objection to the relevancy of a charge of reset against a wife. There is no authority, however, for a similar rule in regard to the husband, who receives the stolen goods of his wife, because she is presumed to have done wrong *ex reverentia mariti;* but no similar excuse can be pleaded for such criminal acts on his part.

.8. The punishment of reset is arbitrary, varying from a few months' imprisonment to transportation; but it is generally made severe where either the property resetted is of great value, repeated previous convictions are proved, or the keeping of an infamous receptacle of thieves and prostitutes is brought to light.

Reset of theft is justly considered as a very serious and most dangerous offence, it being certain that, if there were no resetters, there would be hardly any thieves, and that the greatest encouragement to delinquency of every sort, and especially juvenile depravity in both sexes, arises from the facilities afforded for the disposal of stolen property. At no period, however, was reset punished capitally in our practice;[2] and, in the case of Murdison and Miller, January 1773, the Court expressed an opinion that even repeated reset is only punishable with an ar-

---

[1] Unreported —[2] Hume, i 119

bitrary pain[1]  But that the highest arbitrary pains may be
legally inflicted, is not the subject of dispute.[2]

In judging what punishment should follow a conviction for
reset, the Court look chiefly to the value of the articles received,
the description of house which it is proved to have been, and
the previous character of the pannel.   On the first ground, in
the case of Alexander Robertson and others, 2d March 1819,
er  goods to the value of £232 were stolen from a house in
Glasgow, and the thieves were sentenced to be executed, the resetters were sentenced to fourteen years' transportation[3]  In
like manner, in the case of David Wylie, William Johnston,
and Mrs Dunsmure, Glasgow, autumn 1823, where a house in
Glasgow had been broken into, and gutted of almost all its contents, during the absence of the owners in the country, transportation for fourteen years was inflicted on the female resetter,
who was a person in a superior rank of life to most criminals of
that description.[4]  Upon the second principle, viz. the infamous
character proved against the house where the reset was committed, the Court, in the case of William White, Maria Sinclair, and
others, Glasgow, autumn 1823, sentenced the resetters to fourteen years' transportation.   They were proved to have kept an
infamous house in the Old Wynd, where thieves and prostitutes
were constantly harboured, and the double temptation of spirits and women were held out as incitements to youthful depravity; and, on this account, though the articles proved to
have been resetted were merely some trifling articles of jew'-
lery, they were sentenced to this severe punishment.[5]  Upon
the same principle, in the case of Campbell and Ross, Aberdeen, autumn 1827, transportation for fourteen years was inflicted on resetters, proved to have kept a house of bad fame
for juvenile delinquents.[6]  Lastly, on account of repeated acts
of reset, either charged and proved at the trial, or substantiated
by previous convictions, Robert Stewart and Catherine Stewart,
his wife, were, on 8th June 1818, transported for life; and
Ann Farrel, Glasgow, April 27. 1825, against whom eight previous convictions were proved, was transported for fourteen
years.[7]

Unless in cases of such aggravation, however, the usual pun-

[1] Maclaurin, No 89.—[2] Hume, 1 118, 119.—[3] Hume, 1 118.—[4] Unreported.—[5] Unreported.—[6] Unreported.—[7] Unreported

ishment for reset is imprisonment, varying for different periods, from one to eighteen months, according to the magnitude of the offence.

Habit and repute a resetter, though once sustained as a relevant charge a century ago,[1] is not a legal aggravation in modern practice. So the Court held, after full argument, in the case of Houston Cathie, 27th January 1823,[2] which has always been held to have finally settled the point.

By the English common law, reset of theft was only a misdemeanour; but by several statutes, now consolidated by the 7th and 8th Geo. IV. c. 29, receivers of stolen goods were declared accessaries after the fact, and may be either prosecuted as such, or for a substantive felony.[3] The cases chiefly valuable decided under the old statutes, are those which distinguish between the cases of an accessary to the theft and a resetter. Thus, where some seamen employed in conveying barilla in a boat stowed part of it under some ropes, and the prisoner assisted in conveying the barilla thus separated from the rest, after it had been detached, into another boat, for the purpose of carrying it off; and it was objected that this was accession after the fact, or reset only, the Court held that the prisoner was art and part in the original offence.[4] But where the goods have been so completely taken away from the premises, or actual possession of the owner, that their farther removal could not be deemed a continuation of the original taking, the party concerned in such farther removal was held by the Twelve Judges to be a resetter only.[5] But where a man committed a larceny in the room of a house, and threw a bundle containing the stolen goods out of a window to an accomplice, who was waiting below, it was held by the same authority that the accomplice was a principal, and should have been convicted as such.[6]

It was unanimously held by all the Judges, that an indictment for reset was good, though it did not state who was the principal thief;[7] but where the thief was known, it was thought he should have been named in the indictment.[8] The principal felon, though not convicted or pardoned, is a competent wit-

[1] John and Elizabeth Bell, June 1736, Hume, i. 118.—[2] Hume, i. 118.—[3] Russell, ii 253.—[4] East. ii. 767, Russell, ii. 255.—[5] King's Case, Russell, ii. 256.—[6] Owen's Case, Russell, ii. 257.—[7] Thomas's Case, East. ii. 761, Russell, ii. 257.—[8] Russell, ii. 258

ness against the receiver[1], but it is competent for the receiver to controvert the guilt of the principal, and even to open up a conviction of him for theft, though it be presumptive evidence that all was right by shewing that the offence in him, of which he was convicted, did not amount to felony, or the peculiar felony with which he was charged.[2]

# CHAPTER XI.

### OF POST-OFFICE OFFENCES

THE peculiar importance of preserving letters sent by the public Post-Office from being either detained, mislaid, or opened, and, still more, from having their contents abstracted, has led to the formation of a separate code for all persons in this department, and also to the passing of a number of statutes, imposing penalties of extraordinary severity upon all persons whatever guilty of robbing the mail, or in any way interfering with the safe transmission of letters. The consideration of these statutes, and of the cases adjudged therein, forms an important part of modern criminal jurisprudence.

The embezzlement and stealing of letters, or their contents, by persons employed in the public Post-office, is the subject of the 5th Geo. III. c. 25, 7th Geo. III. c. 50, and 42d Geo. III. c. 81. § 1; but it is unnecessary to refer particularly to these statutes, because they are all now consolidated into the 52d Geo. III. c. 143, which forms the ruling statute on the subject.

1. It is a capital crime for any persons employed in the public post-office, to secrete, embezzle, or destroy any letter containing money, or any voucher or security for money, or to steal such contents, or any part of them, from such letter.

By 52d Geo. III. c. 143, § 2, it is enacted, " That if any deputy, clerk, agent, letter-carrier, post-boy or rider, or any

---

[1] Harlam's Case, Leach, i. 418 , Russell, ii 259.—[2] Foster, 365 ; Smith's Case, Leach, 288.

other officer or person whatsoever, employed by, or under the Post-Office of Great Britain, in receiving, stamping, sorting, charging, carrying, conveying, or delivering letters or packets, or in any other business relating to the said office, shall secrete, embezzle, or destroy any letter or packet, or bag or mail of letters, with which he or she shall have been intrusted, in consequence of such employment, or which shall in any other manner have come to his or her hands or possession, while so employed, containing the whole, or any part or parts of any banknote, bank post-bill, bill of exchange, exchequer bill, South Sea and East India bond, dividend warrant either 'e bank, South Sea, or East India bond, or any other comp. society, or corporation, navy, or victualling, or transport bill, ordnance debenture, seaman's ticket, state-lottery ticket or certificate, bank receipt for payment on any loan, note of assignment of stock in the funds, letter of attorney for receiving dividends or annuities, or for selling stock in the funds, or belonging to any company, society, or corporation, American provincial bill of credit, goldsmith's or banker's letter of credit, or note for or relating to the payment of money, or other bond or warrant, draft, bill, or promissory note whatsoever, for the payment of money; or shall steal and take out of any letter or packet with which he or she shall have been so intrusted, or which shall have so come to his or her hands or possession; the whole or any part or parts of any such bank-note, bank post-bill, bill of exchange, exchequer-bill, South Sea or East India bond, dividend warrant either of the bank, South Sea, East India, or any other company, society, or corporation, navy, or victualling, or transport bill, ordnance debenture, seaman's ticket, state-lottery ticket or certificate, bank-receipt for payment of any loan, note of assignment of stock in the funds, letter of attorney for receiving annuities or dividends, or for selling stock in the funds, or belonging to any company, society, or corporation, American provincial bill of credit, goldsmith's or banker's letter of credit, or note for or relating to the payment of money, or other bond or warrant, draft, bill, or promissory note whatsoever for the payment of money: every person so offending, being thereof lawfully convicted, shall be adjudged guilty of felony, and suffer death as a felon, without benefit of clergy." [1]

The fourth section of the statute, regarding accession to any

[1] § 2.

of these offences, enacts, " That if any person shall counsel, command, hire, persuade, procure, aid, or abet, any such deputy, clerk, agent, letter-carrier, post-boy or rider, or any officer or person whatsoever employed by or under the said office, in receiving, stamping, sorting, charging, carrying, conveying or delivering letters or packets, or in any other business relating to the said office, to commit any of the offences herein before mentioned; or shall, with a fraudulent intention, buy or receive the whole, or any part or parts of any such security or instruments, as herein before described, which shall have been contained in, and which, at the time of buying or receiving thereof, he shall know to have been contained in any such letter or packet so secreted, embezzled, stolen, or taken by any deputy, clerk, agent, letter-carrier, post boy or rider, or any other officer or person so employed as aforesaid; or which such person so buying or receiving as aforesaid, shall, at the time of buying or receiving thereof, know to have been contained in, stolen and taken out of, any letter or packet stolen or taken out from or out of any mail or bag of letters, sent and conveyed by such post, or from or out of any post-office, or house or place for the receipt or delivery of letters or packets, or bags or mails of letters sent or to be sent by such post: every person so offending, and being thereof convicted, shall be adjudged guilty of felony, as well before as after the trial or conviction of the principal felon; and whether the principal felon shall have been apprehended or amenable to justice or not." [1]

All other offences against the post-office, capital by former statutes, are declared in this act " to be felony with benefit of clergy, and punishable only as such, unless the same shall also be declared to be felony without benefit of clergy, by this act." [2]

Under a previous statute, 7th Geo. III. c. 50, which had enacted, that no person shall be capable of exercising any employment relating to the post-office, unless he shall have first taken the oath therein mentioned, it was objected to an indictment charging the prisoner, as a servant of the post-office, with embezzling a letter, containing a bill of exchange, that he had not taken the oath, and so could not be considered as a servant of the post-office; but the objection being submitted to the con-

[1] § 4.—[2] § 1.

sideration of the Twelve Judges, was overruled.[1] It has been held that a bill of exchange may be laid in the indictment as a warrant for the payment of money.[2] Where an indictment charged the prisoner as a person employed in sorting letters in the post-office, with secreting a letter containing a draft, purporting to be drawn in London, but which appeared from the evidence to have been drawn at Maidstone, but without any stamp upon it, contrary to the 31st Geo. III. c. 25, § 4, it was held that this is not a draft for the payment of money within the statute.[3] In the course of the argument on this case, Lord Chancellor Eldon observed, that the legislature had not made it felony to secrete any letter; but to secrete any letter containing any of the securities specified in the statute. A servant of the post-office, employed as a facer of letters, who secreted a letter containing the *paid* notes of a country bank, in course of conveyance from the London bankers who had paid, to the country bankers who would re-issue them, was held to have committed an offence under the statute;[4] and where an indictment charged the prisoner, as a person employed in the business of the post-office, with secreting certain bills of exchange sent by post, it was held sufficient to allege in part description of the bills, that they were subscribed by A and B, without saying that they were made by them.[5]

Convictions have been numerous, under the post-office acts, of persons stealing from letters in this country. The libels against Adam Johnston, September 25. 1780, and Daniel Mackay, July 6. 1781, were laid on the acts then in force, as well as on the common law, and an indiscriminate relevancy sustained in both, and the pannels had sentence of death.[6] Andrew Lawrie, on 8th January 1802, was capitally convicted for stealing money from letters delivered to the pannel as a letter-carrier;[7] and William Oliver, on 31st October 1809, was transported fourteen years for a like offence, upon a restriction of the libel.[8] On 12th March 1819, George Warden, clerk-assistant in the Post-office, Aberdeen, was convicted and had sentence of death at common law, and on the 42d Geo. III. c. 81, for stealing sundry letters and bank-notes, con-

[1] Clay's Case, East. ii. 580; Russell, ii. 230.—[2] Willoughby's Case, East. ii 581; Russell, ii. 231.—[3] Pooley's Case, Leach, ii. 887; Russell, ii. 233.— [4] Ranson's Case, Leach, ii. 1090; Russell, ii. 233.—[5] Dawson's Case, East. ii. 603, Russell, ii 234.—[6] Hume, i. 67, 68.—[7] Ibid.—[8] Ibid

taining orders and drafts.[1] And, in the case of Peter Henderson, June 9. 1828, sentence of death was passed upon the prisoner, upon a confession of five different acts of secreting, detaining, or opening letters, containing money or bills; but he subsequently received a transportation pardon, in consequence of its having appeared that he had been insane both previous and subsequent to the commission of the act.[2]

Questions of nicety have arisen as to what truly amounts to an employment by the Post-office, so as to bring the accused under the capital sanction in the statute. It has been already stated, that the taking of the oath has been found by the Twelve Judges to be not necessary to constitute such employment;[3] but the difficulty is where the pannel has not been appointed by the Post-office, but by individuals, to facilitate the transmission of letters in remote parts of the country, from the Post-office to their houses, but still has become possessed, by such employment, of the post letters. In the case of John Macnab, Stirling, September 17. 1826, who was charged with altering and advancing the postage of letters, and destroying post-paid letters, it was stated in the indictment, that the pannel had been appointed letter-carrier or runner between the Post-office at Falkirk, and the Penny Post-office at Larbert; but it was not said either that he had been regularly appointed by or under the Post-office of Great Britain, at Falkirk, or taken the oaths; and it was objected at the trial that he was only a casual assistant, without any regular appointment, and had never taken the oaths, and that this was manifest on the face of the indictment; but this was overruled by the Lord Justice-Clerk Boyle, who observed both that a formal minute of appointment was not necessary, and that, in the prisoner's declaration, he had confessed having been sworn. He was convicted on his own confession of one charge, and transported seven years.[4] In the case of Donald Ross, Inverness, spring 1830, the *species facti* was, that the pannel had been appointed by the Post-office, in a remote district in Cromarty, to carry the mail-bags to the separate houses of the gentlemen in the county, and on the road he had abstracted money from a letter, but which had not come regularly into his hands as a post-runner, but been privately delivered to him to be delivered,

[1] Hume, i. 81.—[2] Unreported.—[3] Clay's Case, Russell, ii. 230.—[4] Unreported.

without entering the mail-bags; and the doubt was whether he
came under the capital sanction of the statute, as one employed ' by or under" the Post-office.   The indictment was
laid at common law, and on the 52d Geo. III.; and, though
the point was not expressly decided, in consequence of his
having pleaded guilty at common law only, Lord Moncrieff is
understood to have rather inclined to the opinion, that he came
under the statute, in consequence of the broad and comprehensive words, " by or *under* the post-office," and " or which
shall, in any *other manner*, have come to his or her hands or
possession, while so employed."   A similar case occurred at
Inverness, spring 1831, Peter Mow.., where the prisoner
pleaded to the theft at common law, as well as the statute, and
was transported seven years.   But whatever decision may ultimately be given on this point, the indictment against persons
in such an ambiguous situation should always be laid at common law, as well as on the statute.

2. Independent of the statutes, it is an offence at common law, punishable by an arbitrary pain, for any person
employed in the Post-office, whether by Government
or not, to secrete, detain, destroy, or fail to deliver any
letter, in course of transmission by the public post, and
whether containing money or not, or to open any mail-
bags with intent to steal, or to advance the postage of any
letter beyond the authorised amount.

The interests of the Post-office being so paramount to all
the lieges, the conduct of all persons employed in it fall under the cognizance of the common law, as well of the statutes.   It has, accordingly, been repeatedly sustained as a relevant charge at common law, to accuse a person employed in
the Post-office of secreting, detaining, destroying, or failing to
deliver any letters intrusted to his keeping for any purpose
connected with the conveyance or delivery of letters.   In the
case of Donald Smith, 12th July 1827, it was found relevant
at common law, as an " act of wilful neglect of duty of his
office as a letter-carrier in the said Post-office, that he being a
servant of the Post-office, and intrusted with the delivery of a
certain letter, opened the seal, and detained it for fifteen days,
and having resealed it, did at the end of that time deliver it,

and that he also detained and failed to deliver a certain other letter for several days.[1]   In that case none of the letters in question were money letters, nor was there any charge of the letters having been opened with intent to steal ; and the relevancy was sustained after a full argument.  In the case of James Macintosh, July 17. 1826, the pannel pleaded guilty to a charge of " wickedly and feloniously opening any sealed mail-bags, containing letters transmitted by the public post, without legal authority, especially when committed with intent to steal or abstract money, bills, or other valuable documents contained in the letters lying in the said sealed bags," and was transported seven years [2]   In that case it was also sustained a relevant charge at common law, " the wickedly and feloniously breaking open any sealed letters transmitted by the public post, especially when committed with intent to steal, and more especially when committed by a clerk in the Post-office ;" but the pannel was not convicted of this charge in the indictment.  In the case of Peter Henderson, June 9. 1828, not only was the charge of stealing money from letters sustained at common law, but also of " secreting, embezzling, or destroying any letters in the course of transmission by the public post, containing bank-notes or bills, especially when committed with intent to steal, and more especially still when committed by a clerk in the public Post-office :" he had sentence of death on the statutory charge [3] In the case of John Macnab, Stirling, September 1826, it was found relevant to charge the pannel with having advanced and altered the postage charged upon letters sent by the public post, and received the advanced sum from the persons to whom they were addressed, without accounting for it to the proper party, he being a servant in the post-office ; as also with having destroyed, secreted, or detained post-paid letters, and appropriated the money paid with the same, in violation of his duty as a letter-carrier or runner in the employment; and, upon a confession of the first charge, the pannel was transported seven years, though the act of embezzlement confessed amounted only to one shilling.   In this case, however, a statutory charge, grounded on the same facts, founded on the 5th George III. c. 25, and 7th George III. c. 50, was added ; but both were sustained as relevant.[4]  Lastly, in the case of John Graham, March

---

[1] Syme, p 185, 233.—[2] Unreported.—[3] Unreported.—[4] Unreported.

1. 1830, 1828, an indictment was sustained as relevant which charged the prisoner, being a person in the employment of the Post-office, with having feloniously, and in breach of his duty as a letter-carrier, detained and secreted various letters which came into his hands in the course of his employment as such, though without opening them, or doing any thing farther than retaining them in his possession undelivered, and though none of them contained money or money securities of any sort. He pleaded guilty to nine different acts, and, in consideration of various alleviating circumstances in his case, received only twelve months' imprisonment;[1] and the similar case of William Morgan, Aberdeen, April 1831, was visited with six months' imprisonment. A similar case, tried before the Sheriff of Edinburgh and a jury, had a similar result: William Cunningham, June 4. 1830.[2]

3. It is also felony by statute for any person in the employment of the Post-office to secrete or destroy letters which so come into his hands, though not containing money or bills, or embezzle, or advance, or fail to account for the postage received for them.

By 5th George III. c. 25, § 19, it is enacted, " That if any deputy, clerk, agent, letter-carrier, or other servant, appointed, authorized, and intrusted to take in letters or packets, and receive the postage thereof, shall embezzle or apply to his, her, or their own use, any money or moneys by him her, or them, received with such letters or packets, for the postage thereof; or shall burn or otherwise destroy any letter or letters, packet or packets, by him, her or them, so taken in or received; or who, by virtue of their respective offices, shall advance the rates upon letters or packets sent by the post, and shall not duly account for the money by him, her or them, received for such advanced postage, every such offender or offenders being thereof convicted as aforesaid, shall be deemed guilty of felony." And by 7th George III. c. 50, § 3, it is enacted, " That if any deputy, clerk, agent, letter-carrier, officer, or other person whatsoever, employed, or hereafter to be employed, in any business relating to the Post-office, shall take and receive into his, her, or their hands or possession, any letter or letters, packet or

---

[1] Unreported —[2] Unreported

I

packets, to be forwarded by the post, and receive any sum or sums of money therewith for the postage thereof, shall burn or otherwise destroy any letter or letters, packet or packets, by him, her or them, so taken in and received; or if any such deputy, clerk, agent, letter-carrier, officer, or other person whatsoever so employed, or hereafter to be employed, shall advance the rate or rates of postage, upon any letter or letters, packet or packets, sent by the post, and shall secrete and not duly account for the money by him or them received for such advanced postage; every such offender or offenders being thereof convicted as aforesaid shall be deemed guilty of felony." It was under these statutes, as well as at common law, that John Macnab, at Stirling, in September 1826, who was a post-runner between Larbert and Falkirk, was convicted of advancing the postage of a letter, and transported seven years.[1]  In the case of Sloper in 1772, the jury found that the prisoner was an officer employed in the business of the Post-office in stamping and facing letters; that he secreted the letter in question, without opening it, or knowing that it contained a ten pound note, and that he secreted it for the purpose of defrauding the King of the postage which had been paid. The case was certified for the opinion of all the Judges, because, as the letter was not *destroyed*, the case did not fall under the 5th George III.; but the determination of the Judges was never known, though it was probably unfavourable to the prisoner, as he remained in jail till July 1777.[2]

4. It is also a misdemeanour, punishable by fine and imprisonment, for persons in the Post-office to abstract newspapers or proceedings in Parliament from the Post-office.

By the 5th George IV c. 20, § 10, it is enacted, " That if any deputy, clerk, agent, letter-carrier, letter-sorter, postboy, or rider, or other officer or person whatsoever, employed, or hereafter to be employed, in receiving, stamping, sorting, charging, conveying, or delivering letters or packets, or in any other business relating to the Post-office in Great Britain, shall wilfully purloin, embezzle, secrete, or destroy, or shall wilfully permit or suffer any other person or persons to purloin, em-

---

[1] Unreported —[2] Leach, i 81, Russell, ii. 235.

bezzle, secrete or destroy, any printed votes or proceedings in Parliament, or printed newspapers, or any other printed paper whatsoever sent, or to be sent, by the post without covers, or in covers open at the sides, each and every person or persons so offending shall be deemed and taken to be guilty of a misdemeanour, and shall be punished by fine and imprisonment;" and such offences shall and may be inquired, or tried and determined, either in the county where the offence was committed, or where the party shall be apprehended.

5. Stealing or robbing letters from the Post-office by persons not connected with it is a capital crime, both at common law and under the statute.

It has already been stated, that stealing letters from the Post-office is a capital crime at common law;[1] but for a long time past the statutory has superseded the common law on this subject.

By 7th George III. c. 50, § 2, it is enacted, " That if any person or persons whatsoever shall rob any mail or mails in which letters are sent or conveyed by post of any letter or letters, packet or packets, bag and mail of letters, or shall steal and take from or out of any such mail or mails, or from or out of any bag or bags of letters, sent or conveyed by post, or from or out of any post-office, or house or place for the receipt or delivery of letters or packets sent or to be sent by the post, any letter or letters, packet or packets, although such robbery, stealing or taking, shall not appear or be proved to be a taking from the person, or upon the King's highway, or to be a robbery committed in any dwelling-house or coach-house, stable, barn, or out-house belonging to a dwelling-house, and though it should not appear that any person or persons were put in bodily fear by such robbery, stealing or taking; yet such offender or offenders being convicted thereof as aforesaid, shall nevertheless respectively be deemed guilty of felony, and shall suffer death as a felon without benefit of clergy."

Farther, by 52d George III. c. 143, it is enacted, " That if any person shall steal and take from any carriage, or from the possession of any person employed to convey letters sent by the post of Great Britain, or from or out of any Post-office, or house or place for the receipt or delivery of letters or packets,

[1] *Supra,* p. 345

or bags or mails of letters sent or to be sent by such post, any letter or pa  ct, or bag or mail of letters sent or to be sent by such post, o1  all steal and take any letter or packet out of any such bag or mail; every person so offending, and being thereof lawfully convicted, shall suffer death as a felon, without benefit of clergy; and such offences shall and may be inquired of, tried and determined, either in the county where the offence shall be committed, or where the party shall or may be apprehended."

Where the prisoner, by the artifice of pretending that he was guard, obtained the mail-bags by the delivery of a person in the Post-office to him while on the outside, it was held to be a stealing out of the Post-office, under the statute.[1]   In a case where the prisoner was employed by the Post-office to deliver letters but not to sort them, but he did sort them, when regularly he ought not to have done so, and while sorting stole a letter, the indictment charged him as a sorter with secreting, and as a common person under the 52d George III. with stealing; but as it appeared that the sorting was out of his department, he was acquitted of the secreting, but convicted of the stealing.   Upon this, it was objected that he could not be convicted under the third section of the 52d George III., because he was employed by the Post-office, and that cla se related only to strangers; but this was overruled by all ne Judges, who held that a man who stole was not less a person stealing because he had some employment in the office, and that an opposite construction would lead to the absurdity, that, if a person in the office stole, but not in the course of his employment, he would be altogether unpunishable.[2]   It has been held that a letter-carrier taking letters out of the office intending to deliver them to the owners, and only embezzle the postage, but who was detected with them in his pocket in the neighbourhood of the clerk's office, cannot be indicted as for theft, and that a conviction of the prisoner for that offence could not be supported.[3]   And it is evident that, as the *animus furandi* was wanting, the judgment was right, and that the prisoner should have been indicted for destroying or secreting letters, and embezzling the postage.

6. It is also a misdemeanour for any person to secrete,

[1] Pearce's Case, East ii 603; Russell, ii 237.—[2] Brown's Case, Russell, ii 238.—[3] Howatt's Case, Russell, ii 239

keep or detain, any mail-bags or letters in course of conveyance by post, and dropped or found on the highway or
elsewhere.

By 42d Geo. III. c. 81, § 4, it is enacted, " That if any person or persons shall wilfully secrete, keep, or detain, or being required to deliver up by any deputy, clerk, agent, letter-carrier,
postboy, rider, driver, or guard of any mail coach, or any other
officer or person whatsoever employed or to be employed in
any business relating to the Post-office, shall refuse, or wilfully
neglect to deliver up any mail or bag of letters sent or conveyed, or made up in order to be sent or conveyed by the post,
or any letter or letters, packet or packets, sent or conveyed by
the post, or put for that purpose into any post-office, or house
or place for the receipt or delivery of letters or packets sent or
to be sent by the post, and which letter or letters, packet or
packets, bag or mail of letters, shall have been found or picked
up by the same, or any other person or persons, or shall by or
through accident or mistake have been left with or at the house
of the same, or any other person or persons, each and every
person or persons so offending shall be deemed and taken to be
guilty of a misdemeanour, to be punished by fine and imprisonment."

Under these statutes, numerous convictions have taken place
in Scotland of persons for robbing or stealing from the mail.
Thus, in the case of William Oliver, 31st October 1809, the
Court sustained an indictment for robbing the mail laid both
at common law on the act 1693, c. 3, and the 7th George III.
c. 5; and the prisoner, being convicted, only escaped with
transportation for fourteen years by a restriction of the libel.[1]
William Ross, at Inverness, spring 1822, was convicted at common law, and under the 52d Geo III., of stealing a letter containing a five pound and a one pound note, and transported.[2]
William Shearer, Aberdeen, spring 1809, was indicted on the
7th Geo III. c. 50, and at common law, for stealing a money
letter containing a twenty shilling note, and transported seven
years[3] George Blyth and George Walker, both in the employment of the Post-office, indicted for stealing letters without money, and secreting and embezzling letters, at common
law only, were convicted, and imprisoned nine months[4]

[1] Hume, i. 67.—[2] Unreported.—[3] Unreported.—[4] Unreported.

# CHAPTER XII.

## OF BREACH OF TRUST

THE distinction between theft and breach of trust is to be found chiefly in the terms or way in which the thing taken originally came into the criminal's possession;[1] and the rule seems to be, that wherever the article is obtained upon a fair contract, not for a mere temporary purpose, or by one who is in the employment of the deliverer, then the subsequent appropriation is to be considered as an act of breach of trust.[2] But, in the application of this rule, many nice cases require to be distinguished.

1. If the article be delivered with the design of transferring the real right, or of subjecting the receiver to a mere action for account, and not for a mere temporary purpose, or to a servant of the deliverer, the subsequent conversion to the receiver's use is breach of trust.

The subsequent appropriation of goods that have been delivered on credit, or impledged; of goods given in loan, or for hire for a long period; or of goods where the trust is of such a kind as implies a power of management or disposal, is not theft, but breach of trust.[3] If a watch, therefore, has been given in loan for a length of time (for it would be otherwise if the period was a few minutes or hours only), or goods delivered on credit without the price having been paid, or a debtor has impledged any moveable article with his creditor, the subsequent appropriation is the same crime.[4] In like manner, if a furnished house be taken for a term, and the heir afterwards disposes of some of them for his own use, he is guilty of

---

[1] Burnett, 111.—[2] Hume, i. 58, Burnett, 111.—[3] Ibid.—[4] Burnett, 111; Hume, i. 58, 59.

breach of trust only.[1] Nay, though it is quite fixed that a butler who abstracts the plate, or a shepherd the sheep, is guilty of theft, yet a livery-servant who sells his clothes furnished by his master is guilty of breach of trust; though, if he abstract his master's clothes, put into his hands to brush, he commits theft.[2] The reason of the difference is, that the interest which the servant has in his own livery-clothes is of a much higher kind, and his right of possession much longer, than those of his master merely put into his hands for a special and temporary purpose. This point was settled in the case of Alexander Steele, August 13. 1669. The pannel there pleaded, " That he did actually *wear and make use of* the said clothes and goods during the year of his service;" and the Court, "anent the articles of dittay as to the stealing of the clothes and arms, found the same not relevant (as theft), unless it be alleged that he stole these goods such a day by breaking of his master's doors, chests or trunks." [3]

Under the same rule falls the case of a factor who runs off with his employer's rents, or an overseer or steward who fraudulently disposes of the grain which has come into his possession in the course of his management, for his own behoof: for the wrong here does not lie in the original acquisition of the thing, but in the concealment of receipt and breach of trust in regard to subjects wherewith he was not only entitled but bound to intromit.[4] So the Court found in the case of Archibald Tait, February 17. 1776. This was a suspension of a judgment of the Justices of the Peace for West Lothian, against the pannel, for fraud and embezzlement, upon the ground that the *species facti* set forth in the minor amounted to theft, and could not be tried without a jury; but the Court found, " that the libel did not contain a charge of theft, but of fraudulent concealment of his master's goods, and by false contrivances endeavouring to prevent those proceeds coming to his master's knowledge, and as such could be tried without a jury." [5] William Dickson, factor to Robert Dundas, Esq. of Arniston, who was charged with embezzling property to the amount of above £1000, belonging to his employer, was brought to trial in March 1828, on an indictment for falsehood, fraud and embezzlement, and the indictment found relevant, though the

---

[1] Hume, i. 59; Palmer's Case, Leach, ii. 680.—[2] Hume, i. 60; Burnett, 111.—[3] Hume, i. 60.—[4] Ibid.; Burnett, 111.—[5] Ibid.

case was not ⸱ecuted to an issue from the difficulty of proving such complicated transactions.

2. Wherever the prisoner was possessed of the money or goods embezzled, not as a *corpus* to be redelivered in specie, but as a trust to be accounted for, the fraudulent intromission is breach of trust.

This principle applies to all who are in a responsible state as officers, and are intrusted not with the custody only, but the possession and administration of money; as cashiers and tellers of banks, collectors of taxes or parochial rates, treasurers of bodies corporate, judicial factors, and the like.[1] It is implied in the nature of such appointments, that the officer has the management less or more of the cash in his hands, which is intrusted to him in the mean time, under the obligation of accounting; and this obligation is not specific to return the identical pieces of money or notes delivered, but generally to account for their amount. " Si quis pecuniam ita deposuerit, ut neque clausam, neque obsignatam, sed numeratam tradiderit; quo casu nihil aliud eum debere (accipiendum est) apud quem deposita est, nisi tantundem pecuniæ solvere." Accordingly, on March 2. 1705, Robert Pringle, teller of a bank, who had embezzled the money intrusted to his care, was convicted of breach of trust.[2]

Numerous cases have occurred of late years, accordingly, where fraudulent embezzlement by persons intrusted with money or goods in this manner, has been prosecuted, and always under the name of breach of trust. Thus, in the case of William Stewart, clerk to the deputy-postmaster at Perth, 7th August 1809, the libel charged short accounting, and appropriating to his own use part of the money which had come into his hands in that capacity, under the name of breach of trust.[3] In like manner, on 20th November 1820, John Douglass, clerk to a banking company, who was convicted of embezzling part of his employer's money, to the amount of £1300, was convicted of breach of trust, and transported seven years.[4] And, on 28th March 1825, John Corner pleaded guilty to a charge of breach of trust and embezzlement, and was impri-

[1] Hume, i. 61.—[2] Ibid.—[3] Ibid.—[4] Shaw's Cases, No 16.

soned for twelve months, he having been employed by James
Mackenzie, writer to the Signet, in a public office, and embezzled part of the money which thus came into his hands in
that character.[1]   The like judgment was given at the Old
Bailey, February 1743, in the case of John Waite, cashier to
the Bank of England, who had abstracted and sold six East
India bonds, the property of the bank, intrusted to his keeping.[2]
And this precedent was followed by all the Judges in the case
of Joseph Bazely, a banker's clerk, who was tried for appropriating a bank-note for £100, which had been paid to him by
a customer of the house in the course of business, on the principle that, as the note never was in the possession of the
banker, the intromission with it could not amount to theft.[3]

Robert Galbraith was indicted for falsehood, fraud, breach
of trust, and embezzlement, at Edinburgh, 12th June 1826,
and imprisoned nine months.   He had been employed by
Messrs Mudie and Son, manufacturers in Glasgow, as their
foreman and clerk, and had in that character embezzled large
sums belonging to his employers, and concealed the fraud by
means of false entries.[4]   George Mills and Charles Mackenzie,
both clerks in the General Post-office at Edinburgh, who had
embezzled postages received by them from persons to whom
letters or parcels had been transmitted by the mail, were, in
like manner, in May 1822, indicted for falsehood, fraud,
and breach of trust.[5]   Ebenezer Anderson, cashier of the Fife
Banking Company, charged with most extensive fraud, breach
of trust, and embezzlement, in his situation as cashier, was outlawed for not appearing, at Perth, spring 1828; as was Robert
Cochrane, agent for the Bank of Scotland at Kirkcudbright, at
Dumfries, spring 1824.[6]   Thomas Gray, clerk to Inglis and
Company, bankers in Edinburgh, was convicted of three acts of
fraud, breach of trust, and embezzlement upon his employers,
supported by false entries in the books, and transported seven
years; [7] and David Langlands, convicted of embezzling the
funds of a Benefit Society, of which he was treasurer, to the
amount of £227, and concealing the fraud by means of false
entries, was, on December 8. 1828, sentenced to the same punishment.[8]   George Knox, treasurer to the Lessudden Savings
Bank, who pleaded guilty to embezzling the funds of the bank

---

[1] Hume, i. 61.—[2] Leach, No. 14.—[3] Ibid. i. 849.—[4] Unreported.—[5] Unreported.—[6] Both unreported.—[7] Syme, 254.—[9] Unreported.

to the amount of £430 was, in consideration of an uncommonly good previous character, sentenced to twelve months' imprisonment only.[1]  And Charles M'Culloch, excise-officer, charged with wilful neglect of duty and breach of trust as an excise-officer, and making false entries to conceal his frauds, was, on November 10. 1828, sentenced to nine months' imprisonment.[2]

3. A shopkeeper's clerk, bookkeeper, guard of a mail-coach, or carrier who is intrusted with money, not sealed up but open, for behoof of his employers, or to be delivered at a distance to particular people, is guilty of breach of trust, if he appropriate part of the money which thus comes into his hands to his own purposes.

In cases where a shopboy takes money out of his employer's till or repositories, he unquestionably commits theft; but the case is different on principle where a clerk or bookkeeper receives payment of an account, or is intrusted with funds for behoof of his master, and he fraudulently intromits with it; or when a carrier embezzles goods put into his hands to be delivered to a particular person.[3]  In such a case, the money has never been properly in his master's possession; and, besides this, free permission to touch and meddle with the money implies a special reliance on the individual as worthy of trust.  Accordingly, in the case of William Paterson, 30th December 1817, who was accused of six trespasses of this sort, laid alternatively for breach of trust or theft, the Solicitor-General, at calling, restricted the charge to the breach of trust libelled.[4]  So also in the case of Andrew Welser, Aberdeen, May 1783, Lords Hailes and Henderland sustained as relevant a libel which charged a carrier with embezzlement and breach of trust for abstracting a parcel committed to his charge, and for which he had given a receipt[5]  In like manner, in the case of William Todd, Glasgow, April 1825, the pannel, who was guard of a stage-coach, was indicted for embezzling £76 delivered to him, in order that it might be delivered to several different individuals, under the name of fraud and breach of trust, and outlawed for not appearing.[6]  To the same purpose George Leslie,

---

[1] Unreported.—[2] Unreported.—[3] Hume, i. 58.—[4] Ibid. i. 62.—[5] Burnett, 113.—[6] Unreported

to whom £150 had been delivered near Banff, in order that it
might be delivered to a banking house and other places in
Aberdeen, and who appropriated £51 to himself, was indicted
for breach of trust, and sentenced to twelve months' imprisonment.[1]   And, on 25th April 1826, Charles Learmonth, a
flesher, who had received £52 from an occasional employer,
in order to pay the price of a quantity of sheep which he had
purchased at the distance of thirty miles, and who embezzled
the money on the road, was convicted of fraud and breach of
trust, and sentenced to six months' imprisonment.[2]   The like
course was adopted in the indictment of Donald Cameron, a
postrunner, Perth, autumn 1827, who had embezzled £41 put
into his hands, not through the post-office, but as an ordinary
carrier, to be delivered at various places on his route, and
who was sentenced to nine months' imprisonment for having
appropriated it to his own use.[3]   Such cases, where a carrier is
intrusted with the disposal of open money, seems different
from that of a carrier intrusted with a sealed parcel; the appropriation of which appears to be theft.

4. If goods are put into a tradesman's hands for the
purpose of being repaired, and the operation is of such a
kind as necessarily requires considerable time for the operation, the subsequent felonious appropriation is breach of
trust.

It has been already noticed when treating of theft, that if
goods are carried off which have been put into any person's
hands for a temporary purpose, as a porter's, to be conveyed
to a particular place, or a clerk's, to be conveyed to a bank, or
the like, the felonious abstraction is theft.[4]   But the case is
different, both on principle and authority, where goods are put
into a person's hands not for such a specific and transient purpose, but to undergo some lengthened operation, as linens to
be bleached at a bleachfield, books to be bound at a bookbind-
er's, watches to be repaired at a watchmaker's, or the like.
In all these cases the depositary stands in a different situation
from a mere clerk or porter sent on a particular errand; his
profession, and the purposes of his receiving the goods, imply

---

[1] Unreported.—[2] Unreported.—[3] Unreported.—[4] *Supra*, p. 302

a much higher power of intromission, alteration, and manage-ment, and therefore his felonious abstraction or embezzlement falls under the description of breach of trust.  In the case of William Burton, accordingly, Jedburgh, autumn 1824, a watch-maker who had embezzled a watch put into his hands for the purpose of being mended, was prosecuted for breach of trust and embezzlement, and sentenced to six months' imprisonment.[1] The like course was adopted with another watchmaker, who had embezzled and carried off watches to a very great extent, Daniel Johnston Ross, Inverness, autumn 1827, who was sen-tenced to seven years' transportation.[2]   On the same principle Archibald Mackain, convicted 12th March 1830, of having em-bezzled, and sold for his own behoof, forty-two head of cattle, put into his hands to graze for two months on his farm, was sentenced to seven years' transportation.

5. If the wrong consist only in a failure to deliver the article lent by the time agreed on, the case is breach of trust only.

We do not recognise the *furtum usus* of the Roman law, and therefore, if the criminal or other improper act, consist only in a failure to redeliver the article at the time appointed, the case, in the most unfavourable view, can be only breach of trust, and, generally, will not even amount to that[3]  Thus, if a thing be lent me to be returned by a particular day, and I keep it longer, or a horse be hired for a certain place, and I ride it far-ther in the same direction, or a carrier keep a bale of goods, neither broken open nor concealed after his arrival at the place of their destination, the crime is destitute of the felonious in-tention, to appropriate which is essential to theft, and of the intention to *embezzle*, which is the worst ingredient in breach of trust and embezzlement.  This offence, therefore, if it be so serious as really to amount to a point of dittay, is only wilful neglect of duty and breach of trust *quoad* delivery, and, as such, merits only a slight castigation.[4]

6. It is not theft, but breach of trust, if a person appro-priate goods which he has found in a situation which does not necessarily infer a knowledge of the real owner.

---

[1] Unreported.—[2] Unreported.—[3] Hume, i. 59.—[4] Ibid

If a person find any article under circumstances which necessarily imply a knowledge of the real owner, as if he see a handkerchief just dropped from another's pocket, or a hackney coachman see a passenger take a bundle into his coach, and he get out, leaving the bundle there, so that there can be no doubt as to the owner, there seems no doubt that the case is one of theft, and it is treated as such in the English law;[1] but, in cases of a more doubtful import, the offence is breach of trust. Thus, if a landholder find a stray animal in his field, or a treasure in his ground, or have wrecked goods thrown upon his shore, or a person find a book upon the road, and he may discover to whom it belongs, it is not theft if the finder appropriate the thing to himself. The wrong does not lie in the first occupation, for *res nullius cedit occupanti*; but in the failure to redeliver where the owner might have been discovered, or in the neglect of the due notices to discover the true proprietor, either of which is breach of trust only.[2] Mr Hume[3] considers the same ru applicable to the case of one who pilfers goods in the course of their removal from a house on fire, even though he be acting in presence only, and without the orders or request of the proprietor; but there is no authority for such an opinion, and, on principle, it seems unquestionably to amount to theft.

It has been already stated, that, in consequence of the decision of all the Judges in Bazely's case, the 39th Geo. II. c. 85, was passed for the more effectual punishment of bankers' clerks and others embezzling the moneys or securities put into their hands, and which had not come into the actual possession of their employer.[4] It has been decided in England, that this act extends to clerks and servants of all persons whatsoever,[5] and that it will embrace the case of a servant who embezzled money received from a customer, to whom his master had given it to try his honesty.[6]

---

[1] Wynne's Case, Leach, i. 415; *Supra*, p. 308.—[2] Hume, i 62.—[3] Ibid.—
[4] *Ante*, p. 304.—[5] Russell, ii. 208.—[6] Whittingham's Case, Russell, ii. 212;
Leach, ｜ Headge's Case, Leach, ii. 912.

# CHAPTER XIII.

### OF FRAUD AND SWINDLING.

ALL those falsehoods and frauds by which another is deprived of his property under fraudulent and false pretences, especially by the assumption of a false character, or substituting one thing for another, or by using a false or vitiated document as the instrument of deception, may be prosecuted as crimes, and subject the offender to the highest arbitrary punishment.[1] Under this head fall the numerous set of cases known in common, and sometimes also in legal, language, under the name of swindling, as well as those more complicated frauds, by the vitiation or substitution of documents which involve the crime of forgery. Our common law takes cognizance of all such offences without requiring, as the English common law, the shewing of any false token to support the charge.

1. The fundamental requisite in a charge of swindling is the assur o  of a false character, or a false representation of some  , which occasions the giving credit, the most extensive fraud committed by merely ordering goods on credit, and not paying for them, without any such false representation, not falling under this species of crime.

Falsehood, fraud, and wilful imposition, is the *nomen juris* by which the crime of swindling is designated in our law, and from the earliest times it has formed an article of dittay by the common law. Without going farther back than 1789, in the case of Thomas Hall, July 21. 1789, an indictment was sustained as relevant, which charged the pannel with falsely assuming the character of a trader, hiring a shop, filling it with

----

[1] Burnett, 165

fictitious bales, and thereby inducing persons to furnish goods on credit.[1] " The case," says Mr Hume, " was thus distinguished from the bare civil wrong of failure to pay for goods obtained on credit, inasmuch as there was throughout the assumption of a false character and intention of business:[2] he was transported seven years. Again, on 14th June 1791, George Smith was indicted for fraud and wilful imposition, by commissioning, under a feigned name and character, large quantities of goods and the proceeds, and banished Scotland for life.[3] So also in the case of Thomas Kirby, 27th March 1799, the pannel was charged " with fraudulent and wilful imposition and falsehood, more especially when practised in order to obtain, by false and untrue pretences, the money or goods of others." He had obtained a considerable sum of money from a banker in Leith, upon the false allegation that he had a large balance in the hands of his banker in London, and by drawing a bill on a house there, which owed him nothing, which of course returned protested:[4] he was transported for five years It was here strongly objected to the relevancy of the indictment, " that no fraud can be stated as a crime, unless it be supported by the using of a false document, or the assumption of a false name ;" but to this it was sustained as a sufficient answer, " that though no false name was assumed, or false document urged, yet false pretences were used, and a false character assumed, inasmuch as money was obtained on the false allegation of the pannel's having funds in the banker's hand in London." The Court sustained the relevancy of the indictment, observing that a man might no doubt often obtain credit without funds, from the hope of their being realized before the period of payment arrived, but that such a measure as drawing a bill on a banker with whom he had no dealings, was a clear false and fraudulent representation.[5] At Dumfries, September 1768, Edward Warren was indicted for extorting money, by fortune-telling. The relevancy was sustained at common law, and he was sentenced to a year's imprisonment.[6] And at Aberdeen, September 1802, Alexander Reid was convicted of fraud, by assuming the character of an excise-officer, and extorting money under pretence of compounding for smuggled goods, and sentenced to six months' imprisonment.[7]

[1] Hume, 1 173, Burnett, 106.—[2] Hume, 1 173.—[3] Burnett, 166.—[4] Burnett, 167, Hume, i. 174.—[5] Burnett, 170 —[6] Ibid. 173.—[7] Ibid.

In like manner, in the case of Adam Fraser, Inverness, spring 1801, the pannel had advertised extensively in Ross-shire that he was about to purchase cattle, and a great number having, in consequence, been brought to him, he, instead of paying cash, shewed the people a letter, purpo ing to be from a man of the name of Watson, authorizing him to purchase cattle on his account, and stating that they would be paid by application at the Tain Bank. On the strength of this he got 200 cattle, and no person of the name of Watson ever had been heard of at the Tain Bank. He was sentenced to the pillory, and to be banished Scotland for seven years.[1] Again, in the case of James Munro and John Macfarlane, 20th March 1809, two apprentices had enlisted and sworn before a Justice of the Peace that they were not apprentices, whereby they obtained payment of eleven guineas each. The libel was found relevant, but the case remitted for trial to the Sheriff.[2] Alexander Kinnaird had sentence of imprisonment for six months, having been discharged from the army on account of a rupture, and afterwards enlisted in a regiment of militia, received a bounty of £45, and sworn before a magistrate on that occasion that he was free from rupture, or any other complaint.[3] Andrew Harvey, on 23d August 1811, had sentence of transportation for seven years, on a libel charging fraud and wilful imposition, George Scott having lodged two bales of goods in the cellar of Robert Ferguson, publican in Leith, to lie there till called for, and the pannel having obtained delivery of them from Ferguson on the false pretence of having been employed by Scott.

In like manner Bethia Hamilton, 27th June 1817, was transported seven years, on a charge of having obtained, in three instances, money and goods from shopkeepers under the false and assumed character of housekeepers to certain ladies, and supported this by producing false notes as if from those ladies.[4] Neil Douglas, 12th July 1816, was imprisoned six months for having obtained money from various persons on the false pretence of having influence to obtain employment for them from Lord Melville at the Admiralty.[5] Mary Hutchison, 22d June 1818, for having cheated a poor girl out of various sums, amounting in all to £27, 14s., under pretence of telling fortunes, by means of incantations and enchantments, was sen-

<hr/>

[1] Burnett, 171.—[2] Burnett, 172; Hume, I. 174.—[3] Hume, I. 174.—[4] Ibid. —[5] Ibid.

tenced to six months' imprisonment.[1] Joanna Rickerby, 21st June 1824, on a confession of two acts of obtaining wearing apparel of some value, by assuming a false name and designation, and pretending to have lost her own clothes by shipwreck, was sent to Bridewell for nine months.[2] Isobel Provan, on a confession of seven acts of fraud and wilful imposition, was sentenced at Glasgow, April 26. 1825, to seven years' transportation; and Jane Watt, for three acts of the same crime, and one charge of theft, was visited with fourteen years.[3] For five acts of swindling, John Ballantyne, at Jedburgh, April 30. 1827, was transported seven years; and Elizabeth Hall, for stealing a deposit-receipt for £625, and thereafter procuring a woman she met in the street to take the receipt, endorsed, to the bank and draw the money, under the false representation that she was authorised to receive it, was transported fourteen years.[4] George Scott, convicted of having obtained delivery of 2000 stones of hay from a farmer in West Lothian, upon the false and fraudulent pretence that he was a contractor's clerk, taking up stores for the use of the cavalry at Piershill Barracks, was, on June 18. 1828, sentenced to eighteen months' confinement in Bridewell.[5]

2. Like every other offence, swindling may be aggravated by previous convictions for the same crime, and, when proved, generally leads to transportation.

The competence of aggravating a charge of falsehood, fraud, and wilful imposition, by a previous conviction for the same offence, was fixed on a certification from the Circuit Court at Inverness, in the case of John Campbell, 3d June 1822. He was convicted accordingly under that aggravation, of having, in seven different instances, and under various names, falsely assumed the character of a person appointed by the Society for the Propagation of Christian Knowledge, and thereby obtained, besides board and lodging, loans of money, clothes, and a horse, and sentenced to fourteen years' transportation.[6] For three acts of the same crime, committed by getting goods under a feigned name from tradesmen, aggravated by previous conviction, John Law was, on 13th July 1824, sentenced to

[1] Hume, ı. 174.—[2] Ibid. ı. 175.—[3] Both unreported.—[4] Unreported.—
[5] Unreported.—[6] Hume, i. 175

seven years' transportation;[1] and Henry Hill, Glasgow, spring 1880, convicted of four acts of swindling, aggravated by a previous conviction at Dumfries Circuit for the same offence, was sentenced to the same punishment.

3. It is also an aggravated species of the offence, and such as is almost always visited with transportation, when the acts of swindling or fraud are supported or accompanied by the exhibition of false or fabricated documents.

In the assumption of a false character it frequently happens, that a party is induced or driven to exhibit some fictitious or fabricated document to support his pretensions, or even to forge the signatures of real or pretended persons; and wherever the crime appears in conjunction with such an addition, it is visited with a very severe punishment. Thus, on 20th March 1820, Patrick Branaw, William Brown, Isaac Eccles, and others, were convicted on a charge of falsehood, fraud, and wilful imposition, of presenting false passes or certificates, in imitation of those by which the wives and children of soldiers embarked for foreign service were entitled to certain allowances, and thus obtaining from a kirk-treasurer certain payments of money. Fisher was transported for seven, Brown for five years, and the others imprisoned for various periods.[2] In like manner John Macleod Gillies was, on 30th June 1828, brought to trial and transported fourteen years, for fraud, and false personation of a person entitled to Greenwich Hospital allowances, and thereby drawing £6:7:11 of prize-money due to that individual. This was a very laborious and complicated operation, for he had first to ascertain the name, services, and ships, on board which the person to be personated had served; next to write letters to the proper officers at Greenwich Hospital; then counterfeit the signature of the supposed applicant, justice of the peace, three ministers, and four elders, to the several certificates and documents required to enable him to draw the prize-money; and, lastly, to draw the money from the collector of excise at Aberdeen, on a false receipt, under a mark bearing to be that of the applicant. The indictment was laid at common law, for falsehood, fraud, and wilful imposition, and forgery of genuine and fictitious names, as well as on

---

[1] Hume, i. 175.—[2] Ibid.

the 59th Geo. III. c. 56, and 5th Geo. IV. c. 56, which punish frauds of this description on Greenwich Hospital with transportation; and, after a long and complicated trial, the prisoner was convicted, and transported fourteen years.[1] Again, in the case of Peter Hill, Aberdeen, April 25. 1826, the pannel was convicted of six acts of swindling, one of which was supported by the delivery of a forged document, though without any signature, and sentenced to seven years' transportation.[2]

4. Personating, or causing another to personate, a person to whom a parcel or letter is addressed by a carrier or post, and thereby obtaining possession of such letter or parcel, is a point of dittay at common law.

If by personating another, or on a false pretence of authority received, one prevail with a carrier, whether by land or water, to deliver to one a bale or parcel addressed to another, this may be charged and punished as a fraud at common law.[3] It is an offence of the same description if one, by the like false pretence, prevail on a person in the employment of the Post-office, to deliver him a letter addressed to another, and he detain and open such letter, and make use of the contents for his own purpose, though no money was abstracted, nor any pecuniary fraud intended. Such a charge was accordingly found relevant by the High Court, in the case of Alexander Borland, 5th June 1826. This person had applied personally, and through an agent at the Post-office in Paisley, to obtain letters addressed by one John Caldwell to his wife there, on the false allegation that he was employed by the wife to obtain delivery of the letters for her, and which he was to forward to their destination; and, having thus obtained delivery of the letters, he opened them and read their contents, which were of importance to him in business. The offence was charged in the major " as the wickedly, unlawfully, and feloniously obtaining, by means of cozenage and false pretences, and intercepting, opening, or detaining, or causing or procuring to be intercepted, opened, or detained as aforesaid, letters transmitted through the public Post-office." The relevancy was strenuously resisted by the Dean of Faculty Moncrieff; but the objections

---

[1] Hume, 1. 175.—[2] Unreported.—[3] Hume, 1. 175.

were unanimously repelled by the Court, and the pannel was convicted by the jury; and, in consideration of his good character, and the recommendation of the jury, sentenced only to six weeks' imprisonment.[1]  Of course it is a more serious offence, and should be stated as an aggravation of such a charge, if it is done for the purpose of getting possession of a money-letter, and embezzling the contents.  Such an offence was the subject of trial before the Sheriff of Fife (A. Clephane, Esq.), in the case of Isabella Morrison, 2d May 1827, who was indicted for falsehood, fraud, and wilful imposition, especially when committed by applying at the Post-office for letters addressed to another, and so obtaining delivery of them, and opening and embezzling their contents.  The prisoner, who had in this way got possession of a letter containing a one pound note, which she embezzled, was convicted, and sentenced to six weeks' imprisonment, and, though acting under able legal advice, she did not bring the judgment under review by suspension.[2]

5. It is an indictable offence for any person to make use of false, forged, or fabricated letters of recommendation, or certificates of character or distress, as a means of obtaining charity.

It is a common practice for persons who make a trade of begging to support their claims by fabricated certificates, or letters of recommendation, or by actual forgeries of the signatures of known charitable persons to such documents.  Such means of imposing on the public expose the committer to punishment.  In the case, accordingly, of John Brown, Stirling, 15th September 1821, the prisoner received three months' imprisonment for raising money by means of exhibiting a forged minister's certificate of recommendation of him as an object of charity, and his subscription of 5s. at the paper.[3]  In like manner, in the case of William Ross, Glasgow, spring 1819, the prisoner was convicted, and sentenced to six months' imprisonment, for having forged the name of several persons to a letter of recommendation of the prisoner as an object of charity, and levied money from the public by that fraudulent device.[4]

[1] Hume, i. 175.—[2] Unreported.—[3] Hume, i. 175.—[4] Unreported

# CHAPTER XIV.

## OF FALSE CONSPIRACY

Conspiracy to fix a false charge upon an individual, and expose him not only to the disgrace and patrimonial injury, but the risk of trial and punishment consequent upon its commission, is one of the most diabolical species of offences, and has long been visited with condign punishment by our common law.

1. It is an indictable offence at common law, to conspire to fix an unjust imputation of a crime on any of the lieges.

One of the earliest recorded cases on this subject is the noted one of Nicol Muschet and James Campbell, March 31. 1721. The *species facti* here was, that Campbell, having agreed for a sum of money to obtain false affidavits or testimony to the adultery of his wife, so as to enable him to procure a divorce, by the foulest contrivances, got the woman's person into his possession, and there stupified her and laid her in bed, where he put a man into bed with her, and introduced witnesses into the room, for the purpose of seeing him in the act of having connexion with her. These witnesses were not privy to the fraud, and deponed only to what they actually saw; but under the name of false conspiracy and machination, the offence was prosecuted at common law, and Campbell was found guilty, and transported for life. The libel in that case bore, as its major proposition, " The contriving or executing of wicked projects, deceitful and false machinations, for loading of innocent persons with heinous crimes, in order to subject them to the severest punishments." [1]

Another case of the same complexion was that of Elliot, Nicolson, and Campbell, January 1. 1694. It here appeared that

[1] Hume, i. 170.

A a

Daniel Nicolson, a writer in Edinburgh, was engaged in an adulterous intercourse with Marion Maxwell; and, in order to carry it on more fully, they resolved to get quit of Jean Sands, Nicolson's wife. For this purpose, having failed in a design to dispatch her by poison, they resolved to fix on Mrs Nicolson, and her sister Margaret Sands, the atrocious crime of attempting to poison Nicolson. For this purpose Nicolson waited on the Lord Advocate, and laid an account of what he pretended he had discovered before him, and Elliot, a druggist, having been sent for, confirmed the story. The Lord Advocate ordered Elliot to furnish the poison, and take a receipt for it if it could be obtained; and they soon after called on him with such a receipt, which was in truth forged. Warrant was immediately issued for the apprehension of Mrs Nicolson and her sister, but, after they had been apprehended, one thing came out after another, chiefly in consequence of the previous bad character and notorious intercourse of Nicolson and Maxwell, and the result was, that they were themselves apprehended along with Elliot, on a charge of conspiracy, forging and using the receipt, and Nicolson and Maxwell with notour adultery. Elliot was found guilty of forging the receipt, and of conspiracy, and Nicolson and Maxwell of uttering the forged document, conspiracy and notour adultery, and all three were executed. The conspiracy to fix the intent to poison on Jean Sands, jointly with furnishing it, was found relevant to infer death, independent of the forgery or uttering; but this is not a precedent to be now relied on for that extreme pain, however good for the highest arbitrary punishment.[1]

In the case of J. Watson, Aberdeen, autumn 1819, an offence of this description was the subject of conviction and punishment in modern times. This person, along with another associate, had entered into a conspiracy for the purpose of fixing a charge of housebreaking upon an innocent party. Their design had very nearly succeeded, as they got the articles, intended to be charged as stolen, brought into the house of their victim, and placed there in the most suspicious circumstances, which led to her apprehension on a charge of having committed the crime; but one of the party having turned King's evidence, the conspiracy was discovered, and they were brought to trial, convicted, and sentenced to seven years' transportation.[2]

[1] Hume, i. 171.—[2] Unreported.

# CHAPTER XV.

## OF FORGERY, AND UTTERING FORGED INSTRUMENTS.

THE crime of Forgery and Uttering Forged Instruments, as it is one of the most dangerous crimes which can be committed, so it is one whose frequency is continually on the increase with the progress of wealth, and the increase of commercial transactions. Its prosecution and punishment, therefore, constitute an important part in every system of criminal jurisprudence.

Forgery is the fabrication of false and obligatory writs, to the prejudice of another, with intent to defraud; and it is completed by uttering or putting it in circulation. The first point to be considered is the species of writing which constitutes the crime; the second the act necessary to its being put in circulation.

1. It is not essential to the crime of forgery that the writing of the person forged on should be correctly imitated, or his name properly spelt, or his Christian name correctly given: it is sufficient if a signed writing is used which has been forged, which was intended to pass for his signature, and might by ordinary persons be mistaken for a genuine instrument.

The most ordinary species of capital falsification is the felonious making and publishing of a writing, as the *signed* instrument of the person who has not signed it. In such cases the usual course of proceeding is to imitate the handwriting of the person whose name is forged; and, in such a case, it is no defence to the pannel that he has proceeded in the most awkward or clumsy manner, or misspelt the name, or omitted part of the person's subscription.[1] A blunder of this kind occurred

---

[1] Hume, i. 141; Burnett, 180.

in the case of Mary Nisbet, 1726, who, in forging a name of the Duchess of Gordon, who was not a Peeress in her own right, had omitted the Christian name; so that the subscription forged was not that which the Duchess used; notwithstanding which the charge of forgery was sustained, as it was obviously intended for her.[1] The same objection was repelled in the case of Davidson, 21st September 1791, by Lord Hailes, when the accepter's name to a bill was misspelt; and this matter was fully argued in the case of Richard Myndham, 17th July 1800. It 'ere appeared that the notes charged as forged were not a correct imitation of the real notes; the real notes being those of *Surtees, Burdon* and Co., while the forgery was that of *Sentees, Bendon* and Co.; so that both the names in the firm of the forged notes were different from those of the firm on which the forgery was set forth as having been committed. The Court repelled the objection, upon the ground that wherever an imitation is *meant*, and a false subscription made with that view, it is a forgery, though the name be wrong spelt, or a wrong christian name be added; and that it is a question for the jury whether the party really intended to be forged on is the one set forth in the indictment.[2] The same objection was repeated at Glasgow in the case of Scott and Adamson, April 1805, and in like manner repelled.[3] More lately, in the noted case of Malcolm Gillespie, Aberdeen, September 1827, the indictment contained several charges, in which a wrong Christian name was inserted for the persons forged on: in particular, " *William* Leith, Moss-side, Auchlea," instead of the true name " *James* Leith, Moss-side, Auchlea," and " *Alexander* Johnston, farmer and miller, Milltown Harrow," instead of " *John* Johnston, farmer and miller there;" and, in order to bring out the question, it was set forth in the indictment that these words were used by mistake for the true names which were mentioned; but Lords Alloway and Pitmilly, without hesitation, found the libel relevant, and the pannel was convicted and executed.[4]

The principle of the English law on this point, and which appears in itself reasonable, is, that the false instrument should carry on its face the *semblance* of that for which it is counterfeited; but that it is not necessary that the resemblance to the

---

[1] Hume, i 141. Burnett, 180.—[2] Burnett, 181.—[3] Ibid.—[4] Unreported on this point.

known instrument should be exact: it is sufficient if the instruments be so far alike, that persons, in general, using their ordinary observation upon the subject, may be imposed upon by the deception, though it would not impose upon a person particularly acquainted with them.[1]   Thus where a prisoner was indicted for the forgery of bank-notes, and a Bank of England clerk said he could not have been deceived by the forgery, it was held that as the forgery was such as would impose upon ordinary persons, it was complete.[2]   Again, a conviction for the forgery of a bank-note was held to be good, although, in the forged note, the word " pounds" was omitted, and there was no water-mark in the paper.[3]   On the same principle it was held, that engraving a counterfeit stamp like part of a real stamp, but unlike in others, and then cutting out the unlike parts, and concealing the part cut out, is forgery.[4]  Justice Grose there laid it down, " An exact resemblance, or *fac simile*, is not required to constitute the crime of forgery; for if there be a sufficient resemblance to shew that a false making was intended, and that the false stamp was made so as to have an aptitude to deceive, that is sufficient."   A mere literal mistake will make no difference, as Desimockex for Desormeaux.[5]   Nay, a forgery may be committed of a will, though it is wrong in the *Christian* name of the person, whose will it purports to be; as where a will was forged, bearing the signature " *John* Perry, his mark," though it began with the words, " I *Peter* Perry," and Peter was the man's real name.[6]   But, where the forged instrument has no resemblance to the true one, or is illegal in its very frame, the case is not considered as forgery.[7]   Thus where a bill of exchange was directed to John *Ring*, and the acceptance was by John *King*; and the indictment set forth, that the prisoner had forged the acceptance in the name of John King, judgment was arrested, because Ring could not purport to be King.[8]

2. It is not indispensable to forgery, that the writing forged be an imitation of the handwriting of another; the crime is complete if a signed instrument is put in cir-

[1] East. ii. 858; Russell, ii. 342.—[2] Hoost's Case, East. ii. 950.—[3] Elliot's Case, Russell, ii. 342.—[4] Collicot's Case, Russell, ii. 343, Leach, ii. 1048.— [5] Clinch's Case, Leach, i. 540, Russell, ii. 344.—[6] Fitzgerald's Case, Leach, ii. 344.—[7] Russell, ii. 345.—[8] Reading's Case, Russell, ii. 346.

culation, whereby the estate of another is lesed, though it be the signature of one who could not write which is forged, or of an entirely fictitious person.

Imitation of a subscription and of handwriting, is the most ordinary and dangerous, but not the only kind of forgery. Every writing is false which narrates a falsehood, and is used as a document to the hurt and prejudice of another.[1] In many such cases there is no forgery of a handwriting at all. Thus, suppose money is obtained by the false acceptance of a bill, in the name of one to whom it is specially addressed by name and description, but who could not write, this, nevertheless, is as much forgery as the imitation of a genuine signature.[2] In the case of John-Robertson, accordingly, 9th December 1709, no objection was moved to the indictment, on the ground that two of the receipts said to be forged, was of persons who could not write.[3] And in Gillespie's case, Aberdeen, autumn 1827, many of the subscriptions forged proved to be those of persons who could not write, notwithstanding which he was convicted of all the charges.[4] Numerous cases have occurred in later practice, where the signatures forged proved to be those of persons who could not write, notwithstanding which convictions have uniformly followed where the evidence was complete.

On the same principle, it is now completely settled in our practice, that the crime of forgery is complete, though the signature forged is not that of a *real*, but a *fictitious* person, provided that, by the use of that fictitious name, the patrimonial interests of a third party have been prejudiced. Mr Hume states this point as undecided;[5] but it has since been settled, in the case of Alexander Anderson, May 20. 1822, where the High Court were clear, that a charge of forgery was good, though the name forged was that of an entirely fictitious person.[6] Again, in the case of Patrick Miller Maclatchie, Dumfries, April 16. 1824, the pannel was charged with uttering a bill for £20, in which the signature of the drawer was that of a fictitious character, or of an unknown person, and that of the accepter of a real person. Lord Justice-Clerk Boyle had no doubts of the relevancy of the whole charge, and he was transported for life.[7] More lately

[1] Burnett, 177.—[2] Hume, i 141, Burnett, 179.—[3] Hume, i. 141.—[4] Unreported.—[5] Hume, i. 142.—[6] Unreported.—[7] Unreported.

still, this point came again under the consideration of the whole Court, in the case of Andrew Ovens, November 24. 1828. The indictment against this person set forth, that he had entered into a fraudulent design of raising money and purchasing goods, by means of forging the subscriptions of fictitious firms, or persons, to the bills granted for payment of these goods, and charged three different acts of purchasing and obtaining goods, by uttering notes on which were the signatures of fictitious persons and mercantile houses. The indictment charged both forgery and uttering, and also falsehood, fraud, and wilful imposition. especially when committed by uttering promissory notes, " having such false, fraudulent, and fictitious subscriptions thereon, of any person or persons, or company firms, as drawers, indorsers, or accepters thereof." The Court had no doubt that the charge of forgery was relevantly laid, though the whole subscriptions were charged as being fictitious; but the prosecutor, being desirous to avoid a capital conviction, departed from the charge of forgery, and the pannel having been convicted of the fraud aggravated by uttering the fictitious bills, was transported for fourteen years.[1] In the case, also, of Malcolm Gillespie, Aberdeen, September 1827, several of the charges were laid alternatively as the forgeries of a person specified, or of " some person to the prosecutor unknown," and the indictment was found relevant, and a capital execution followed.[2] An indictment was found relevant by Lord Pitmilly, against James Whyte, September 13. 1827, at Perth, which charged the forging and uttering of bills, having some real and some fictitious signatures, and the pannel was transported seven years.[3]

The law of England is founded on the same principle. Thus it is established that the use of a mere fictitious name is of itself sufficient to constitute a forgery.[4] A bill of exchange drawn in fictitious names, where there was no such persons existing as the bill imports, is a forged bill within the 2d George II. c. 25.[5] An order on a banker in a fictitious name, or in the name of one who had no authority to draw, is within the 7th George II. c. 22, and amounts to forgery.[6] It is clearly forgery to indorse a bill with a fictitious name, though the money

---

[1] Unreported.—[2] Unreported.—[3] Unreported.—[4] Bolland's Case, Leach, i. 83; Russell, ii. 328.—[5] Wilk's Case, Russell, ii. 328.—[6] Lockett's Case, Leach, i. 94; Russell, ii. 320.

might have been as well obtained by indorsing it in the real
name of the person who uttered it, and no additional credit
has been used by adhibiting the false name.[1]  It is the same
crime to give to the drawer of a bill of exchange a receipt in
a false name, as for the prisoner's own name, for the contents
of the bill indorsed in blank, to avoid detection, though no additional credit has thereby been gained to the prisoner.[2]  And
it was held forgery to draw a draft upon a banker in a fictitious
name, assumed by the party at first for the purpose of fraud,
though the credit was given not on the assumed name but the
personal appearance of the prisoner.[3]

3. It is also forgery if one put his own name on a ne-
gotiable instrument, instead of one of the same name,
but of a different designation, for whom it was intended;
and by this substitution of his own name for that of another prejudice a third party.

The most extensive and dangerous forgeries may be committed in this way.  Thus, suppose that one has, by accident or
fraud, got possession of a bill which stands indorsed to another
person of the same name and surname, but who is of better
credit, and is fully described in the indorsement, and that he
transfers and indorses this with his own name, and gets the
value from some one who mistakes him for the person described
in the indorsation; though he sign his own name and surname,
and do not counterfeit the hand of the real indorsee, still he
signs for him and assumes his person and character, and therefore he is guilty of nothing less than forgery.[4]  In England,
accordingly, it is settled that such an act is forgery.  Thus it
was held, that if a bill of exchange payable to A B on order
get into the hands of another person of the same name as the
payee, and such person, knowing that he is not the real payee,
in whose favour it was drawn, indorse it for the purpose of
fraudulently possessing himself of the money, it is forgery.[5]
But if the prisoner have merely assumed the character of being
the real indorser of a bill, but written nothing upon it, and uttered it as such, it is a fraud, not a forgery.[6]

[1] Taft's Case, Russell, ii. 329; Leach i. 172.—[2] Taylor's Case, Leach, i.
172; Russell, ii. 330.—[3] Shepherd's Case, Russell, ii. 332; Leach, i. 226.—
[4] Hume, i. 142.—[5] Mead v. Young, 4th Term. Rep. 28; Russell, 321.—[6] He-
vey's Case, Russell, ii. 324.

4. Forgery is also committed if the name of a person really existing be assumed, and an obligatory writ be uttered in his name to the fraud of another.

If a note be uttered in the name of another person, who is either really existing or represented so to be, it is a forgery. Thus in Hadfield's case, the prisoner assumed the name and character of brother to the Earl of Hopetoun, and in that character drew a bill upon a gentleman in the neighbourhood, who would have paid it had the imposture not been discovered. He was convicted and executed.[1]

5. Where the name of the person signed is one who never existed, but to whom at the time a certain character and description is attributed to increase its circulation, or where authority to sign for a real person is falsely asserted, and signature for him is adhibited, it amounts to forgery.

A charge of this complex description has been more than once the subject of trial in the Scotch Courts. Thus, in the case of William Hunter, February 5. 1708, it appeared that he had obtained a confirmation of *Margaret Grieve, spouse of John Hodge, as executor to her deceased brother Robert Grieve*, who was creditor to the African Company. In truth, there was no such person as Margaret Grieve; John Hodge was dead, and the name of his widow was not Margaret Grieve, but Agnes Crauford. Hunter proceeded to forge an indorsement in his own favour of this certificate of the debt to the African Company, in the name of John Hodge and Margaret Grieve, and he was condemned to die without any exception as to the forging the name of Margaret Grieve.[2] Here, however, the forgery of the name of a real person, John Hodge, rendered it perhaps not worth while to plead the objection. But in the case of Mungo Strachan and William Hunter, February 5. 1708, the point occurred without any such addition. The requisite number of persons had there conspired to frame a false deed, signed by two notaries and four witnesses; and this was done of course without the imitation of any handwriting, but by the

[1] Russell, ii. 327.—[2] Hume, i. 143.

mere false assertion of a mandate, authorizing the signature of
the notaries. It was held as forgery in all concerned, and they
were condemned to die, though the only falsehood consisted in
the false narrative of the authority to the notaries.[1] Every
obligatory writ signed as for another, without his knowledge
or authority, is as much forgery as if his handwriting be imitated.[2] Thus, if one personate another who cannot write, and
then impose on notaries and give them a mandate to sign for
the assumed and absent person, this is undoubtedly forgery.
So the Court held in the case of David Donaldson, December
12. 1611, and of John Watson, July 16. 1623.[3] In England
the rule is the same. In the case of Elizabeth Dunn, September 1765, who had made a note in an assumed name and character, by desiring another person to sign for her, as she could
not write, and by this instrument got some money as a seaman's
executrix, it was held to be forgery.[4] Indeed, since the decisions that have since that time been pronounced, finding the
affixing a fictitious signature forgery, there can be no doubt
that the assumption of a false name and character amounts to
that offence.

6. It is forgery in England to counterfeit the mark or
initials of another, and hold out that mark or initials as
his valid subscription.

The question whether the imitation of a mark or initials
amounts to forgery depends on this, whether, by such irregular instruments, the law permits a man's estate to be bound; for
if it do, there is no reason why such false affixing of a binding
signature should not amount to forgery as well as the imitation
of his name. Now, a bill signed by initials,[5] or by a mark,[6]
without the subscription of witnesses, is insufficient to authorise summary diligence, but may be received as an adminicle
of evidence in an action for constituting the debt.[7] The point
therefore is, whether this secondary and more loose species of
obligation created in this irregular fashion will raise the imitation of the mark up to the rank of forgery. There is no decided case yet on the subject, but from that very absence it may

---

[1] Hume, i. 143; Burnett, 177.—[2] Burnett, 177.—[3] Hume, i. 144.—[4] Russell, ii. 326.—[5] Monro v. Monro, Nov. 14. 1820.—[6] Stewart v. Russell, July
11. 1815; Bell, i. 30.—[7] Cockburn v. Gibson, Dec. 8. 1815; Fac. Coll.

fairly be inferred that the point has been considered by our lawyers as doubtful. Mr Burnett is of opinion that such an act is forgery,[1] and Mr Hume rather seems to incline to the opinion that it is not.[2] But if the forger write the name of the person whose mark is signed round the mark, which is the ordinary course, it seems difficult to distinguish such a case from the forgery of a person's name who cannot write at all, which is clearly held with us to be forgery, because, in both cases, there is the forgery of a signature of one who *could not* write, with the addition in the former of the imitation of a mark which he *could* adhibit. In the English law it has been settled by the opinion of all the Judges, that the forgery of a signature by mark falls under their capital statutes.[3]

7. Forgery is committed by separating a genuine subscription from another deed, and affixing it to a forged instrument, or drawing a forged instrument over a subscription of another deed, or intended for a different purpose.

The transference of a genuine signature from the deed to which it stood affixed to a forged instrument, or the making out a forged instrument above such a genuine signature, is forgery.[4] Though the subscription be genuine, its application is a false act of the offender. Accordingly, in the case of Halliday, Laurie, and others, February 8. 1597, it was found to be a capital charge, that the pannels having got a blank paper from Captain William Nisbet, intended to be filled up with a decree-arbitral, they falsely filled up this paper with the discharge of a bond for 1200 merks.[5] In like manner, in the case of William Forbes, 6th November 1820, the pannel pleaded guilty to a charge of having drawn over the subscription of John Thomson, agent at Glasgow for the Royal Bank of Scotland, a draft, or letter of credit, for £6000, in favour of John Ross, a fictitious person, and employed him to personate John Ross, and present the draft for payment. He was transported seven years.[6] If, however, a person have obtained a blank stamp signed, either for a bill or receipt from a party, that is

[1] Burnett, 179.—[2] Hume, i. 145.—[3] Dewar's Case, Russell, ii 326; Fitzgerald's Case, Russell, ii. 344.—[4] Burnett, 178, 179; Hume, i. 145.—[5] Hume, i. 145.—[6] Ibid.

a mandate to fill up the paper with either of these writings to
the extent authorised by the stamp,[1] and therefore, if there be
nothing more done than merely filling up the stamp with a receipt or bill for such a sum as the stamp will cover, the charge
of forgery will not lie; but the case comes under fraud, if any
misrepresentation or deceit were practised in obtaining the
blank signature.

By the English law the rule is, that the fraudulent application of a true signature to a false instrument, or *vice versa*, will
be forgery.[2]   So, if a man find a signature at the bottom of a
letter at a considerable distance from the other writing, and he
cut off the letter, execute a release above the name, and affix
the seal taken from the letter to the signature, it is forgery.[3]
So also it is forgery to insert in a will legacies not authorised
by the testator.[4]   The fraudulent alteration of the material part
of a deed is forgery; as altering the manor of *dale* into the
manor of *sale*, or making a bond for £500 one for £5000.[5]
Altering the date of a bill of exchange, after acceptance, and
thereby accelerating the term of payment, falls under the same
rule.[6]   So also the alteration of a bill of exchange from £10
to £50, both in the words and the figures, was held to be the
same offence.[7]   Altering a banker's note, by substituting the
word ten for the word one, or discharging one indorsement on
a bill and inserting another, is forgery.[8]

The expunging, by means of lemon juice, an indorsement on
a bank-note, was held to be a *razing* of the indorsement, which
amounts to an alteration.[9]   Where the prisoner had procured
a deed to be forged, and, after the death of one of the supposed
granters, had procured the forged deed to be altered by enlarg-
ing the granter's estate to a fee, this was adjudged forgery by
all the Judges.[10]   But a man cannot be guilty of forgery by bare
*non passance*, as by omitting to insert a legacy which he was
directed to insert, unless by so doing he materially alter the
limitation of a bequest to another.[11]

## 8. A fabricated solemn instrument falsely relating acts,

[1] Collis *v.* Ennoch, Hen. Bla. i. 313; Russell *v.* Langstaffe, Douglas, 496.
—[2] East. ii. 855.—[3] Hawk. i. c. 70, § 2, Russell, ii. 318.—[4] Russell, ii. 318 —
[5] Hawk. i. c 70, § 2, 3, Russell, ii. 317.—[6] East ii. 853.—[7] Teague's Case, East.
ii. 979.—[8] Russell, ii. 320.—[9] Ibid.—[10] Kender's Case, East. ii. 855; Russell,
ii. 320.—[11] Russell, ii. 320

or imposing obligations, which had no existence, is one of the worst kinds of forgery, though the signature of no real person have been counterfeited.

Forgeries even of the worst kinds may be completed without any counterfeiting of a real signature. A notary may draw an instrument falsely relating a seisin of lands which he never gave, and to this instrument he may affix his own genuine signature and the signatures of imaginary witnesses; or a bankrupt, wishing to favour some of his creditors on the eve of insolvency, may antedate a deed to elude the law concerning preferences, and forge the names of fictitious persons as witnesses to its execution; there can be no doubt that such acts are forgery[1] And the rule would rather seem to be the same, if the signature of a witness to a deed be forged, although the deed itself be genuine and authentic; for, although the subject matter be true, the mode of authentication is false.[2] No doubt whatever can be entertained that it is a complete forgery, if, beside the attestation of the witnesses being fabricated, the deed itself be false or fraudulent, or intended to carry through or cover a fraudulent transaction. In the case of J. Macleod Gillies, accordingly, already mentioned (June 16. 1828), a charge of forgery was sustained for counterfeiting the signatures of various persons as Justices of the Peace, ministers, or elders, to the affidavits or certificates necessary for drawing certain allowances at Greenwich Hospital: and in the case of James Dow and William Dick, July 14. 1829, who were charged with a most extensive fraud upon the Excise, committed by embezzling the money charged against the Crown as paid to particular individuals on the public account, a charge of forgery was sustained, not only of the names of the persons who were entitled to have drawn the allowances, but of the official persons whose signatures were intended to check or vouch the transaction.[3]

9. It is equally forgery to imitate the subscription of persons to the most irregular as the most solemn instruments, provided the writing be of such a kind as was intended to create an obligation against the party whose

[1] Hume, i. 146, Burnett, 177.—[2] Hume, i. 145.—[3] Unreported.

subscription is counterfeited, or seriously to affect his patrimonial interest.

Our law holds it a capital offence to forge an obligatory document, whether it be in the shape of a solemn and regularly attested deed, or of a holograph writing, or a naked subscription *in re mercatoria*, as to a bill or promissory note.[1] Accordingly, in the case of Raybould, January 19. 1768, the defence was at once overruled, that forgery could not be committed by the imitation of an unauthenticated subscription;[2] and no such plea has since been maintained. The same objection had previously been overruled in the case of Baillie, February 1765, who was convicted before the Court of Session of counterfeiting notes of the British Linen Company.

Farther, if the forgery be of an obligatory document, and intended to lese the party whose subscription was imitated, it signifies nothing though it be executed in so clumsy or imperfect a manner as to render it highly probable that the attempt would prove unsuccessful, or drawn out in such terms as rendered it incapable of achieving the object for which it was intended.[3] Thus the offender shall answer for it as a forgery, though he have used ordinary instead of stamped paper for a bill or receipt; or one sort of a stamp instead of the correct one; or the word legate and bequeath instead of dispone, in a conveyance of heritage; or have omitted the testing clause, or to add witnesses to a deed where by law they are requisite.[4] Accordingly, in the case of John Anderson and James Barry, Inverness, September 19. 1827, the objection to a charge of forging a bill, that it was attested before it was fully completed by the signature of the drawer, was repelled, in respect a bill incomplete in the drawer's name constitutes a good claim against the accepter's estate.[5]

In the English law the rule is the same. Thus they hold that forgery of a bill is complete though executed on unstamped paper;[6] or of a promissory note though on the same paper, in opposition to the directions of statute;[7] or though the writ forged be the will of a person living, though of course it could not take effect till his death.[8] Judge Buller observed that the very definition of forgery excluded the doubt; for that it was

---

[1] Hume, i. 146; Burnett, 182.—[2] Hume, i 146.—[3] Ibid.—[4] Ibid.—[5] Bell, i. 396.—[6] Hawkwood's Case, Russell, ii. 340.—[7] Morton's Case, East ii 955.—[8] Sterling's Case, Leach, i 99

the making a false instrument with intent to deceive; and that, as such, the intention to deceive was manifest, and the falsehood of the instrument was proved.[1]

Forgery may be committed of all writings intended to be obligatory; whether public, as a notorial instrument, a revenue certificate, an extract of a decree, or sentence of a court of justice; or private, as a bill, bond, bank-note, letter of credit, power of attorney, or the like.[2] Nay, the same holds of the forgery of writings intended to answer any purpose of personal security or revenge, or any other gratification or advantage in itself of a graver or serious nature.[3] Thus Robert Binning, July 3. 1662, was convicted of forgery, in counterfeiting letters of suspension; Mungo Strachan, Feb. 5. 1708, for forging two deeds of factory; Dr Elliot, January 15. 1694, for fabricating an acknowledgment of the receipt of poison from an apothecary, with intent to fix a charge of poison on an innocent person; Margaret Nisbet, January 15. 1694, for fabricating a declaration tending to fix a charge of forgery on an innocent person; Andrew Adam, February 20. 1710, for forging a bond of caution in a suspension; Patrick Gordon, November 20. 1706, for forging a bond of caution in law-burrows; Joshua Noble, March 1. 1805, after a full debate as to whether it was a capital charge, for forging a bond of caution in a suspension; William Mitchell, August 23. 1811, for forging a letter ordering a bill to be discounted, which the forger had recently before stolen;[4] Lindsay Craufurd, and Bradley, February 4. 1812, for forging, altering, and vitiating a number of writs, entries, and doquets, in order to establish Lindsay's propinquity to the family of Lindsay Craufurd.[5] Peter Steven, March 12. 1824, for stealing six retired drafts for payment of money, altering their dates, and drawing money for them; Francis Adam, July 1822, for forging a number of letters, acknowledgments, and receipts, intended to defraud Sir Robert Abercrombie of a large sum of money;[6] William Macgilvray, Inverness, May 1824, for forging a letter of guarantee and a bill;[7] John Macleod Gillies, June 23. 1829, for forging various certificates, attestations, depositions, and signed writings, intended to enable the forger to commit a fraud by drawing money from Greenwich Hospital, in the name of sailors entitled to prize-money;[8] James Park, Glas-

[1] Cogan's Case, Leach, i. 449, Russell, ii. 339.—[2] Hume, i. 147.—[3] Ibid. —[4] Ibid. i 148.—[5] Ibid. i. 160.—[6] Unreported.—[7] Unreported.—[8] Unreported.

gow, September 1828, for forging letters of recommendation, for the purpose of enabling the forger, or those in league with him, to obtain the goods of others, by presenting the letter of recommendation;[1] John Tweddal, Glasgow, winter 1828, and John Williamson, Glasgow, winter 1828, for severally forging letters of guarantee, and transported each for seven years.

10. The fraudulent vitiation or alteration of any obligatory writ, is, by the common law of Scotland, forgery, though not warranting the infliction of capital pains.

The vitiation or alteration of a deed, bill, or bond, is a species of forgery as dangerous as any other; but, as it is not so daring an offence as the creation of an entirely new forged document, it is only punished by the common law of Scotland with an arbitrary pain.[2] And this holds good as to all the different modes of vitiation, whether by antedating an instrument, erazing words, interpolating others, falsely signing as a witness, or the like. Thus William Dunbar, February 26. 1762, was transported for life, for erazing and vitiating an interlocutor; and James Leatch, for vitiating a bill, had sentence of pillory and infamy.[3] Belsher and others were imprisoned and suspended for antedating the registration of a bond in July 19. 1788; and Daniel Aitken, June 2. 1750, for altering material words in a letter, was imprisoned and declared incapable of trust.[4] At Glasgow, on October 7. 1812, Alexander Falconer was sentenced to a year's imprisonment for altering a receipt of property-tax for £ 6, 4s., so as to make it answer a different year;[5] and Alexander Nimmo Stirling, October 1812, was sentenced to the pillory and six months' imprisonment for altering a writing, having forged the words *in gremio*, intended to pass for a missive of tack of a piece of land.[6]

In the case of Thomas Mathie, March 10. 1727, a remarkable case of this description occurred. This man had been factor to the York Buildings Company; and he was charged with having, after the recal of his factory, uplifted or taken bills for certain rents and sums of money owing to the company, and had given receipts on these occasions, which, as well as the bills, he had antedated to conceal the fraud; and that,

[1] Unreported.—[2] Hume, I. 160.—[3] Ibid. I. 161.—[4] Ibid. I. 160.—[5] Ibid. I. 161.—[6] Ibid

in one instance, he had cancelled a bill payable to the company, and taken a new one with a false date, in his own name, for the sum. The libel was laid as for forgery as well as fraud, and he was convicted of one article of charge.[1]   John Lindsay Craufurd and J. Bradley's case, 4th February 1812, was still more curious.   These persons were charged with a long series of falsehoods and forgeries, the object of which was to establish Lindsay's propinquity as heir of the first Viscount Garnock, and support his claim of a general service before the Sheriff of Edinburgh.   For this purpose they had, by a chemical process, discharged parts of the writing in sundry old letters, and inserted new passages in lieu of them; had forged two complete letters, erased the subscriptions of the witnesses to certain old tacks, had substituted other subscriptions for them, altering at the same time the testing clause of the deeds, and forged various signed entries in a book of accounts.   These forged or vitiated writings were all produced in support of the claim of service.   They were convicted, and sentenced to fourteen years' transportation; the presiding Judge, Lord Meadowbank, observing at the same time, that if the indictment, instead of charging that the forgeries were uttered to establish right to a certain character by a general service, had charged, as it might have done, a combination and conspiracy to carry off a large estate from the true heir, it would have warranted a capital punishment.[2]

11. By special statute, the altering any bill, note, order, or warrant for payment of money, is capital.

By 45th George III. c. 89, which extends to every part of Great Britain, it is enacted, " That if any person or persons shall falsely make, forge, counterfeit or alter, or cause or procure to be falsely made, forged, counterfeited or altered, or wilfully act or assist in the false making, forging, counterfeiting, or altering any deed, will, testament, bond, writing, obligatory bill of exchange, promissory note for payment of money, indorsement or assignment of any bill of exchange or promissory note for the payment of money, acceptance of any bill of exchange, or any acquittance or receipt either for money or goods, or any accountable receipt for any note, bill, or

[1] Hume, i. 100.—[2] Ibid.

other security for payment of money or delivery of goods, or
any warrant or order for payment of money or delivery of
goods, with intention to defraud any person or persons, body
or bodies politic or corporate whatsoever; or shall offer, dispose of, or put away, any false, forged, counterfeited, or altered deed, will, testament, bond, writing, obligatory bill of exchange, promissory note for payment of money, indorsement
or assignment of any bill of exchange or promissory note for
payment of money, acceptance of any bill of exchange, acquittance or receipt, either for money or goods, accountable receipt
for any note, bill, or other security for payment of money, warrant or order for payment of money and delivery of goods,
with intent to defraud any person or persons, body or bodies
politic or corporate, knowing the same to be false, forged,
counterfeited or altered; every such person so offending shall
be deemed guilty of felony, without benefit of clergy."[1]   It
has been already noticed that this act extends to Scotland;
and Peter Steven, having pleaded guilty to six charges of altering retired drafts and presenting them for payment, under this
act as well as the common law, was, on a restriction of the libel,
sentenced to fourteen years' transportation.[2]

Under this act, or the prior act 2d George II. c. 25, which
was of the same tenor, but applied only to England, it has been
decided, that a power of attorney is a *deed* within the words of
the statute;[3] and that a power of attorney to transfer Government stock, signed, sealed, and delivered, was a deed within
the second of these acts.[4]  A bill drawn upon the Commissioners of the Navy is a bill of exchange in the sense of the statutes;[5] and a promissory note,[6] or a note payable to the prisoner's own order, and uttered without indorsement, is also
within their purview.[7]   A forged receipt for bank-notes is not
a receipt for money or goods within the statute; but an entry
of the receipt of money or notes made by a cashier of the Bank
of England in the bank-book of a creditor, is an accountable
receipt within the 7th George II.;[8] a distinction which appears
to us singularly thin and unsubstantial.   Forging a receipt,
in order to found a claim of payment thereon against a third

[1] 45th George III. c. 89, § 1.—[2] Hume, i. 160.—[3] Lyon's Case, Russell,
ii. 456.—[4] Fauntleroy's Case, Russell, ii. 456.—[5] Chisholm's Case, Russell, ii.
457.—[6] Box's Case, Russell, ii. 460.—[7] Bicket's Case, Russell, ii. 461.—[8] Har-
rison's Case, Leach, i. 180.

person, is as much within the statute as forging it to defeat a claim by the person whose name is forged.[1]

In the construction of the words, " warrants or orders for the payment of money or delivery of goods," it has been ultimately settled, though after some conflicting decisions, that the statute is not confined to commercial transactions, and that a bill of exchange may be stated as an order for the payment of money:[2] but, in order to constitute an order for the payment of money, there must bo some payee; and, therefore, a bill drawn upon the Treasurer of the Navy, payable to blank or order, was held not to fall within the statute;[3] nor a forged note to a tradesman requesting him to let the bearer have certain goods, in respect the person whose name was forged was not the owner of the goods intended to be delivered.[4]  The order must be directed to the holder, or person interested in, or having possession of, the goods;[5] but if the order *purport to be* one which the party had a right to make, though, in point of fact, he had no such right, and although no such person as the order purports to be made by exists in fact, it falls within the penalty of the statute.[6]  On this principle, a forged order on a banker is held to be within the statute, though made in a fictitious name, as it purported to be made by a person who kept cash with a banker;[7] and it is not necessary that the particular goods should be specified in the order, if it is conceived in terms intelligible to the parties themselves to whom the order is addressed;[8] and the statute applies though the order proved in the end not available, by reason of some collateral objection which the prisoner had not foreseen.[9]

12. By special statute it is felony to engrave or forge any plate of the Bank of England notes, or to have any such in one's possession.

The great importance of the securities issued by the Bank of England has given rise to a variety of statutes, punishing with great severity any attempt even at forging any of its notes.

[1] Thomas's Case, Russell, ii. 468; Leach, ii. 882.—[2] Shepherd's Case, Leach, i. 226; Russell, ii. 468.—[3] Richard's Case, Russell, ii 470.—[4] William's Case, Russell, ii. 470; Leach, i. 114.—[5] Clinck's Case, Russell, ii. 474.—[6] East. ii. 940; Russell, ii. 474.—[7] Locket's Case, Leach, i. 94; Russell, ii. 475.—[8] Jone's Case, Russell, ii. 475.—[9] Macintosh's Case, East. ii. 942; Russell, ii. 475.

By 45th George III. c 89, § 2, it is enacted, " That if any person or persons shall forge, counterfeit or alter, any bank-note, bank bill of exchange, dividend warrant, or any bond or obligation under the common seal of the Governor and Company of the Bank of England, or any indorsement thereon, or shall offer, or dispose of, or put away, any such forged, counterfeited or altered note, bill, dividend warrant, bond or obligation, or the indorsement thereon, or demand any money therein contained, or pretended to be due thereon, or any part thereof, of the said company, or any of their officers or servants, knowing such note, bill, dividend warrant, bond or obligation, or the indorsement thereon, to be forged, counterfeited or altered, with intent to defraud the said Governor and Company, or their successors, or any other person or persons, body or bodies politic or corporate whatsoever; every person or persons so offending, and being thereof convicted in due form of law, shall be deemed guilty of felony, and suffer death without benefit of clergy."

By the 3d section of the same act it is enacted, that any persons, other than officers of the bank duly authorized, making or using, or having in their possession, any frame or instrument for making paper of a certain description, or manufacturing, or having in their possession any such paper, or causing the sum or amount of any bank-note, bank bill of exchange, bank post-bill, blank bank-note, blank bill of exchange, or blank bank post-bill, to appear in the substance of the paper, are declared guilty of felony, and subject to transportation for fourteen years.[1] Section 4th provides, that the act is not to prevent persons from issuing any bills of exchange or promissory notes having the sum in guineas, or in a *numerical figure in pounds*, visible in the substance of the paper; and section 5th provides, that act shall not prevent any persons from making or publishing any paper having waving or bar lines, &c. provided the same do not imitate the paper used by the Bank of England. And by section 7th it is enacted, " That if any person or persons shall engrave, cut, etch, scrape, or by any other means or device make, or shall cause or procure to be engraved, cut, etched, scraped, or by any other means or device made, or shall knowingly aid or assist in the en-

---

[1] 45th George III. c. 89, § 3.

graving, cutting, etching, scraping, or by any other means or device making, in or upon any plate of copper, brass, steel, pewter, or of any other metal or mixture of metals, or upon any wood or other materials, or any plate whatsoever, any bank-note, bank bill of exchange, bank post-bill, or blank bank-note, blank bank-bill of exchange, blank bank post-bill, or part of any bank-note, bank bill of exchange, or bank post-bill, purporting to be the note or bill of exchange, or bank post-bill, or blank bank-note, or blank bill of exchange, or blank bank-post bill, or part of the note or bill of exchange, or bank post-bill of the Governor and Company of the Bank of England, without an authority in writing for that purpose from the said Governor and Company of the Bank of England, or shall use any such plate so engraved, cut, etched, scraped, or by any other means or device made, or shall use any other instrument or device for the making or printing any such bank-note, bank bill of exchange, or bank post-bill, or blank bank-note, blank bank bill of exchange, or blank bank post-bill, or part of a bank-note, bank bill of exchange, or bank post-bill, without such authority in writing as aforesaid; or if any person or persons shall, without such authority as aforesaid, have in his, her, or their custody, any such plate, instrument or device, or shall without such authority as aforesaid, knowingly and wilfully utter, publish, dispose of, or put away, bank-note, bank post-bill, bank bill of exchange, or blank bank-note, blank bank post-bill, blank bill of exchange; every person so offending, and being convicted thereof, shall be adjudged a felon, and transported fourteen years."

These offences are not very likely to be committed in this country; but that contemplated in the following clause has occurred, and is very likely to recur, and come under the consideration of our courts: " That if any person or persons shall purchase or receive from any other person or persons, any forged or counterfeited bank-note, bank post-bill, bank bill of exchange, or blank bank-note, blank bank post-bill, blank bill of exchange, knowing the same to be forged or counterfeited, or shall or willingly have in his, her, or their dwelling-house, out-house, lodgings or apartments, any forged or counterfeited bank-note, bank post bill, bank-bill of exchange, or blank bank-note, blank post bill, or blank bank-bill of exchange, without lawful excuse, the proof whereof shall lie upon the person accused, every person or persons so offending, and being thereof convicted according to law, shall be adjudged a felon, and shall be transported for fourteen years." On 27th June 1814, Thomas Gray was brought to trial, under the statute, for having in his possession two forged notes of the Bank of England, and *two forged notes of the Bank of Scotland.* The statute expressly extends to Scotland; but the point of difficulty and importance was, whether it embraced the possession within Scotland of any other forged notes than those of the Bank of England. The point was fully debated, and the Court found, " that the act of Parliament libelled on extends to notes issued *by the Bank of Scotland,* as well as to the notes of the Bank of England." [1] But this judgment, which was passed by the narrowest majority, is now considered to be bad law; and though the point has not been expressly brought under their notice, it is understood that the Court is now unanimously of opinion that the act applies only to Bank of England notes. Indeed an attentive consideration of the intention of the statute, framed in all its parts for the protection of the Bank of England, and of its phraseology, which is every where applicable solely to its paper or securities, or their manufacture, must, it is conceived, lead to that conclusion; and the frequency of the offence of bringing over large quantities of forged notes, especially from Ireland, loudly calls for an enactment extending the provisions of this statute to the guilty possession of forged bank-notes of every description. Indeed cases have frequently occurred of late years in which persons apprehended with four or five hundred forged notes of Scotch banks in their possession, recently imported from Ireland, have been liberated without trial, in consequence of the want of any statutory enactment which reached their case.

13. By special statute, it is declared a crime, punishable with imprisonment or transportation, to engrave, use, or possess the plates of any private banks, or to make or use the paper used in their formation.

By 41st Geo. III. c. 57, which extends to Scotland, passed for the protection of private bankers, and all banking corpora-

[1] Hume, i. 149.

4

tions, it is enacted, " that any person who shall make or use any mould for making paper, with the name or firm of any persons or body corporate appearing in the body of the paper, without a written authority for that purpose; or shall make or vend such paper, or cause such name or firm to appear in the substance of the paper, whereon the same shall be written or printed, shall be imprisoned, for the first offence, not less than six months, nor more than two years, and for the second offence, be transported seven years." And by § 2, " if any person shall engrave or make any bill or note of any person or banking company, or use any plate so engraved, or any device for making or printing such bill or note, or shall, knowingly, have in his custody such plate or device, or shall utter such bill or note without such a written authority for the purpose, he shall be punished in the same manner." And the third section enacts, " that if any person shall engrave or make on any plate any subscriptions subjoined to any bill or note of any person or banking company, payable to bearer on demand, or have in his possession any such plate, he shall, for the first offence, be imprisoned not exceeding three years nor less than twelve months, and for the second offence be transported seven years.[1]

The 43d Geo. III. c. 139, § 2, enacts, " that persons engraving plates for any foreign bill of exchange, promissory note, or undertaking or order for the payment of money, or printing them without authority, shall be deemed guilty of a misdemeanour, and for the first offence may be imprisoned for any term not exceeding six months, and for the second offence be transported fourteen years." [2]

These statutes, both relating to the forgery of the Bank of England and of private banks, have no dependence on the uttering of the forged instrument. The crime is complete, though the forged note intended to be made have never been uttered, nay, though it be only in the course of preparation. It is the secret preparation and commencement of the process of forging which it is the object of the statutes to prevent and to punish.

A variety of other statutes, much too long for enumeration here, have been passed for the protection of the Excise and

---

[1] 41st George III. c. 57.—[2] 43d George III. c. 139.

Customs against forgeries on their several departments of the revenue, and also against forgeries of stamps. An abstract of them would of itself fill a volume, and they are of the less importance in Scotland, as the crimes to which they relate, generally speaking, are sufficiently embraced by our common law.

14. It is forgery at common law to forge any Excise stamp, or other security, for the collection of the revenue, and the crime is punishable with an arbitrary pain, to which, by special statutes, the pain of death is, in many cases, superadded.

The forging of *revenue stamps*, the subject of such anxious provision in the British statute law, is also a point of dittay by the common law of Scotland. This matter was fully discussed in the case of Brown and Macnab, 18th March 1798, who were charged at common law, and also under the 26th Geo. III. c. 51, with forging the stamps on starch. The indictment was objected to, in so far as laid on the common law, on the ground that the Scotch law, independent of statutes, recognises no such forgery as that which is now set forth; but the Court, after a full argument, sustained the charge at common law, to the effect of warranting an arbitrary pain.[1] Since that decision, it has never been contested that the counterfeiting any stamp, certificate, or other security, for the collection of the revenue, is an indictable offence, and several cases have been laid and found relevant both at common law and on the statutes; in particular, that of Ferguson, 10th October 1809, for counterfeiting stamps on paper, who was prosecuted both at common law and on the statutes, and of Heughan, 12th July and 14th August 1810, for counterfeiting Excise debentures.[2]

By the statutory law of the realm, the forging or transposing of stamps, is in general declared to be punishable with death.[3] But by the leading statute on the subject, 52d Geo. III. c. 143, it is enacted, " That in all cases where any act to be done or committed in *breach of, or in resistance to*, any part of the laws for collecting his Majesty's revenue in Great Britain, would, by the laws now in force, subject the offender to suffer

---

[1] Burnett, 196.—[2] Ibid. 197, Hume, i. 169.—[3] Russell, ii. 410

death, such act to be done or committed shall be deemed and taken to be felony, with benefit of clergy, and punishable as such, unless the same shall also be declared to be felony, without benefit of clergy, by this act." To discover the forgeries of public stamps punishable with death, we have only to examine the cases described as felony without benefit of clergy, in this act. It is impossible to give an abstract, even within the limits of this work, of the different enactments it contains, nor is it of much consequence, as the humane practice of restricting the libel renders it immaterial in most cases what forgeries are capitally punishable. The statutes on this subject will be found well digested in Russell's Crown Law, ii. 410: They are, 52d Geo. III. c. 143; 55th Geo. III. c. 184; 55th Geo. III. c. 185; 56th Geo. III. c. 56, § 37; 13th Geo. III. c. 59, relative to forging the assay marks on gold and silver plate; 24th Geo. III. sess. 2, c. 53, on the same subject. The 55th Geo. III. c. 184, declares the fraudulent cutting or getting off any stamp from any paper, with intent to use the same upon any other paper chargeable with the duties, a capital offence. The 12th Geo. III. c. 48, contains some provisions on the same subject, which, on account of their importance, should be generally known. It enacts, " That if any person or persons shall write or engross, or cause or procure to be written or engrossed, either the whole or any part of any writ, mandate, bond, affidavit, or other writing, matter or thing whatsoever, in respect whereof any duty is or shall be payable by any act or acts made in that behalf on the whole or any piece of vellum, parchment or paper, whereon there shall have been before written any other writ, bond, mandate, affidavit, or other matter or thing, in respect whereof any duty was or shall be made payable as aforesaid, before such vellum, parchment or paper shall have been again marked or stamped according to the said acts; or shall fraudulently erase or scrape out, or cause to be erased or scraped out, the name or names of any person or persons, or any sum, date, or other thing written in such writ, mandate, affidavit, bond, or other writing, matter or thing as aforesaid, or fraudulently cut, tear, or get off any mark or stamp, in respect whereof or whereby any duties are or shall be payable, or denoted to be paid or payable as aforesaid, from any piece of vellum, parchment, paper, playing-cards, outside paper of any parcel or pack of playing-cards, or any part thereof, with intent to use such stamp or mark for any other writing, matter, or thing, in respect whereof any such duty is or shall be payable: every person so offending, and every person aiding and abetting him in such offence, shall be liable to transportation for seven years."

Though the aid of the British statutes is requisite to punish offences of this description with the pain of death, yet it is not to be supposed that they do not fall as high misdemeanours, warranting the infliction of the highest arbitrary pain, under the common law of Scotland. As soon as any stamp-act passes, this article is thenceforward the lawful property of his Majesty and his successors, and enjoys, as much as any other property, the protection of the common law of Scotland, which will defend it from all manner of fraudulent devices, and especially from all that are executed by means of falsehood and forgery; which crimes are not in the least more excusable because directed against the public revenue, and not that of an individual.

15. It is indispensable to the crime of forgery that the making or uttering be felonious, or with intent to injure; but it is sufficient if any sort of gain or advantage is to be obtained from another by the falsehood, though it should not amount to cheating him out of the whole sum contained in the forged writing.

It is not forgery if one, to accommodate another who cannot, or is unwilling to write, and at his desire, signs a draft or receipt in the name of that other, not even though he make no mention of his own name, but simply adhibit that of his author; for there is here no fraudulent intention, nor intent to injure.[1] This practice is very common among the lower orders, and an example of it occurred in the case of Jackson v. Williamson, 18th December 1824, in the Civil Court.[2] But, on the other hand, it is not less forgery, though the advantage to be gained be not the full sum contained in the bill or note, if it amount to a real and sensible advantage to the offending party; as, for example, if a discharge be forged for an account really paid, but of which the voucher has been mislaid.[3] In such a case, however, of mitigated delinquency, or, possibly, of innocent intention, the extenuating circumstances would unquestionably

[1] Hume, i. 154.—[2] Shaw and Dunlop, Dec. 16. 1824.—[3] Hume, i. 155.

be fully considered by the Court in pronouncing sentence.[1] Accordingly, in the case of Moir, Aberdeen, spring 1786, the defence that the person who had forged a receipt had truly paid the money, and that he had no intention to defraud, was overruled.[2]

16. A person may be guilty of forgery not only by actually writing the forged instrument, but by such assistance or aid towards its perpetration, as, on the ordinary principle of accession, renders him art and part in the offence.

Like every other offence, which is capable of being performed by more persons than one, forgery is susceptible of accession, and pannels may be convicted of it under the charge of art and part.[3] But the importance of the subject renders a more detailed statement necessary.

There can be no question that one becomes art and part in forgery, by immediate assistance lent in the fabrication of the deed itself. Thus, if one person furnish the scroll of a false deed, another dictate the deed from that scroll, a third write it, and a fourth affix a false subscription in presence of the others; without doubt, all are implicated in the offence. Thus, in the case of Halliday and others, February 8. 1597, it appeared that Marjoribanks the notary, dictated a scroll of the false discharge to Halliday, after consultation between them on the matter: Halliday sent it to Lowrie, who filled it up in the blank signed paper, with the assistance of John Lowrie and Winzet, and Winzet signed as a false witness. All these persons had sentence of death.[4] In like manner, in the case of James Tarbet and Finlay Ferne, February 15. 1600, Tarbet copying a scroll delivered to him by Finlay Ferne, wrote a part, and employed John Kennedy to write the remainder, of a charter, to which he had previously seen Ferne affix his father's name.[5] They were both convicted. In regard to those who sign as witnesses on such occasions, though they do nothing but sign their own names, and after their ordinary fashion, yet they are not the less art and part in the charge, as they attest a falsehood, and so become impli-

[1] Hume, i. 155, Burnett, 192.—[2] Burnett, 192.—[3] Burnett, 197; Hume, i 155.—[4] Hume, i. 155.—[5] Ibid.

cated in the principal forgery.[1]    Much of the same description
was the case of Malcolm Gillespie and James Edwards, Aberdeen, autumn 1827.   The *species facti* there was, that Gillespie,
who was an excise-officer in Aberdeenshire, got involved in difficulties, and, to raise money, engaged in a most extensive plan
of forging bills, signed by small farmers in his vicinity, which
he intercepted by payment before the period of their becoming
due, and thus the fraud was for a long time not discovered.
The bills were executed for the most part by Edwards, who
generally forged the names by tracing them on the window
over the genuine signature of the parties, which he got on various pretences, and the body of all the bills was in his handwriting; but this was done with the knowledge of Gillespie,
in his house, and for his benefit, and Gillespie himself uttered
all the bills and received the proceeds.   In these circumstances
it was laid down as clear law by the Bench, that Gillespie, as
the utterer, was art and part in the forgery, and Edwards, as
the forger, was art and part in the uttering, which took place,
with his connivance, through the hand of Gillespie.   Gillespie
was convicted and executed, and though Edwards escaped from
that charge owing to an informality in the mode in which the
verdict was worded by the jury, yet he afterwards pleaded
guilty to the same indictment in the High Court, on November
18. 1827, and was transported for life.[2]   A similar case of accession occurred in the case of Andrew Ovens, November 24.
1828.   In that case the prisoner, along with several other persons, had engaged in a most extensive scheme of fabricating
bills drawn on fictitious persons, and raising money by means
of discounting them, or delivering them in payment of goods
furnished.   The   .gery was accomplished by many persons in
a public-house in a close in the High Street of Edinburgh;
one furnished the engraving and paper on which the forged instruments, which were admirable imitations of Hamburgh bills
of exchange, were drawn; one the ink of different shades and
colour, employed in fabricating the names of the different parties to the bills; another signed the subscriptions of some of
the fictitious parties; and a fourth, with red ink, affixed the
markings in imitation of the notings put on by the different
banks or mercantile houses through which they passed.   Only

---

[1] Hume, ᴵ. 155 —[2] Unreported on this matter.

one of the prisoners was put to the bar, the others being absent or adduced as witnesses; but the Court expressed a clear opinion that all were art and part in the offence.[1]

17. The user or vender of a false writing, though not himself connected with the forging, becomes an accessary to the offence, if it be uttered knowing that it was forged.

The person who utters a false instrument, though nowise connected with the actual fabricator, is nevertheless as guilty as he: nay, it is as presumptively art and part in the vending, that the fabricator himself is punished, unless in the cases embraced in special statutes.[2] The obvious reason is, that though the vender has not been from the first an associate in the adventure, which, however, is generally the case, he partakes in, and associates himself with its guilt, which, by his industry or accession, he brings to its destined accomplishment[3]; to which it may be added that the utterer must be presumed to be the forger, unless by evidence he can throw that guilt upon another.[4] Numerous cases, accordingly, have occurred, and are of daily practice, in which the utterers of forged instruments have been punished as the actual forgers. Indeed the act 1540, c. 80, confirmed by the act 1551, c. 22, expressly declares, that the " users of false writs wittingly shall be punishable as falsifiers." Among other instances of capital sentence for uttering only, may be mentioned that of John Macaffee, November 26. 1782,[5] and that of Malcolm Gillespie, Aberdeen, September 1827; in which last instance, although the libel charged both forging and uttering against the pannel, the evidence only brought home the uttering to him, and he was convicted of " forging and uttering," in consequence of the principle of law laid down by the Bench, that the utterer, if the act have been done in the guilty knowledge that the deed was forged, is necessarily art and part of the original falsification.[6] This principle is so well established, that it is unnecessary to refer to that important class of cases, unhappily now too numerous, in which uttering merely is made the matter of substantive charge, altogether independent of any connexion with the actual fabricator.

[1] Unreported.—[2] Hume, i. 155.—[3] Ibid.—[4] Ibid.; Burnett, 185.—[5] Hume, i. 156.—[6] Ibid. i. 149.

3

Thus, in the case of Roderick Macinthie, 13th October 1797, the pannel was found guilty of " fraudulently using and uttering the notes libelled, knowing them to be forged," and sentenced to death.[1]  Samuel Bell, 23d July 1800, on a similar verdict had a similar sentence; as had John Macneil and Michael O'Neil, 20th March 1801, on a libel restricted before it went to the assize, to the charge of uttering only.[2]  Peter Hughan, 17th December 1810, was found " guilty of uttering the forged debenture libelled on, knowing it to be forged," and transported seven years; James Wood, 1st February 1813, on a confession of the uttering, without the forgery, was transported for life; and James Macgall, 4th July 1814, on a verdict finding the pannel guilty of the uttering, and the forging not proven, had sentence of death.[3]  Lastly, at Glasgow, April 1817, James Macneil and William Mackay were tried on an indictment which charged the forging of bank-notes at Belfast, in Ireland, and uttering them in Scotland.  This brought out the question, whether the forging being done *extra territorium*, could be tried in Scotland; but the Court, after hearing the objection pleaded at great length, repelled the objection, and Mackay had sentence of death.[4]

18. It is competent to charge the wickedly and feloniously uttering forged instruments, knowing them to be forged, without any allusion to the actual forger.

As capital convictions had frequently taken place, in pursuance of a conviction for uttering only, the practice at length was adopted of drawing the libel, with a charge of uttering only.  After this practice had gone on unchallenged for a course of years, it was made the subject of objection and debate, in the case of Ebenezer Knox, 9th June 1817.  It was pleaded for him that the libel bore no charge of actual forging, and that it did not state when or where that preliminary offence had been committed.  The public prosecutor answered, that the uttering a false writ is in itself a cognizable offence, and that it is proper to omit the charge of forgery, where there is no reason to believe that the utterer is himself guilty of that offence.  The Lords sustained the indictment;[5] and, since that

[1] Hume, i. 156; Burnett, 195.—[2] Ibid.—[3] Hume, i. 156.—[4] Ibid.—[5] Ibid.

time, it has been the invariable practice, in cases of uttering forged notes, to omit the clause of actual forging altogether.

Where this is done it is indispensable that both the major and minor propositions should set forth the terms " wickedly and feloniously," and " knowing the same to be forged." [1]  It is not the mere act of uttering, but the uttering in the guilty knowledge of the forgery, which constitutes the offence; and, therefore, unless these words, which necessarily imply the guilty knowledge, are stated in the indictment, no offence is charged against the prisoner.

Cases of uttering forged notes have been extremely common of late years; and the punishment, which was at first too often capital, is now for the most part, owing to a restriction of the libel, limited to transportation.  Uttering a single forged note is now in general punished with seven years' transportation; but, when two or more charges are brought home to the prisoner, it is commonly augmented to fourteen years, or life. In estimating the amount of the punishment, the principal point the Court usually look to, is whether the prisoner is merely a hand put forward by more guilty persons, in which case he is frequently more an object of commiseration than any thing else; or himself engaged in the wholesale traffic or disposal of forged notes.  In the former case the punishment is generally made as light as possible, and has been occasionally limited to imprisonment only; in the latter it is invariably transportation for a very long period.  The evidence on which this rests is generally the number of notes issued by the prisoner, or the quantity found in his possession, both of which are competent objects of inquiry, if the preliminary and indispensable matter of issuing one forged note has been established.

Cases were formerly very frequent of a capital conviction passing, and even being carried into execution, for uttering forged notes.  Thus at Glasgow, 19th September 1821, Ann Wilson or Moore was sentenced to death for uttering one forged note.[2]  At Dumfries, April 1823, John Mackana, Joseph Richardson, and William Richardson had sentence of death for three charges of uttering forged notes for one guinea each.  This was a very aggravated case, for there were found

[1] Burnett, 186.—[2] Hume, i. 157.

on the pannels no less than 235 forged notes, so that there could be no doubt of their being wholesale dealers.[1] William Macteague and Margaret Macteague, on a charge of uttering five forged notes, had sentence, the first of death, the second of transportation for life.[2]  At Ayr, April 1827, John Hobson had sentence of death on a conviction for uttering two forged notes, but the lenity of the Crown prevented the execution of the sentence.[5]

On the other hand, the examples are much more numerous of a restriction of the libel, and the infliction of transportation, in such cases.   Indeed, of late years, this has become so usual, as almost, except in cases of very great delinquency, to amount to a settled practice.   Thus, at Inverary, September 1823, John Boyle, for uttering a forged five pound note of the Bank of Scotland, was sentenced to fourteen years' transportation. In that case eight forged five pound notes were found in his possession.[4]   On March 12. 1823, James Curley, on a confession of uttering three one pound notes, was transported for life.[5]   Walter Graham and James Cameron, convicted of three acts of uttering one pound notes, were transported fourteen years each.[6]   William Innes, Perth, April 1823, on a confession of issuing three similar notes, was sentenced to the same punishment.[7]   Ellen Hughes, Aberdeen, September 1825, on a conviction of uttering two forged one pound notes, was sentenced to fourteen years' transportation.[8]   John Wallace, Aberdeen, September 1826, convicted of uttering two forged one pound notes, and proved to have had fourteen more in his possession, received the same sentence.[9]   The like punishment was inflicted on Margaret Thine, Glasgow, September 1826, on a confession of uttering two forged guinea notes.[10]   Peter Lannigan, Glasgow, September 1826, on a confession of uttering a one pound forged note, was transported seven years.[11] John Wilson, 7th November 1826, High Court, on a confession of uttering a forged one pound note, was punished in the same manner.[12]  Michael Logan, on a confession of uttering two forged notes, was, on 3d December 1826, transported fourteen years.[13] Peter Macmahon, on a conviction of uttering three forged notes, was, by the High Court, February 20. 1826, sentenced to trans-

---

[1] Unreported.—[2] Unreported.—[3] Unreported.—[4] Unreported.—[5] Unreported.—[6] Unreported.—[7] Unreported.—[8] Unreported.—[9] Unreported.—[10] Unreported.—[11] Unreported.—[12] Syme, 11.—[13] Ibid. 29.

portation for life.[1] Edward Roney, Glasgow, September 1826, on a conviction of uttering one forged note, was transported seven years.[2] James Devlin, Glasgow, spring 1828, convicted, on two indictments, of uttering three forged notes, and proved to have had a thick bundle of others in his possession, was transported for life.[3]

Of the still more lenient course of punishment, which, in cases where the pannel is obviously an instrument in the hands of others, seems perfectly consonant with justice, instances occurred in the case of Mary Cameron, Aberdeen, autumn 1824, who was sentenced to eighteen months' imprisonment, on a conviction of uttering one forged note;[4] and in that of Mary Smith, or Selkridge, Perth, September 1827, who, on a similar conviction, received only six months' imprisonment.[5] In this last case there were very extenuating circumstances. Lastly, in the case of Helen O'Neil, Ayr, spring 1830, the prisoner, an old woman, on a similar conviction of uttering one forged note, under alleviating circumstances, was sentenced to nine months' imprisonment.[6]

19. The crime of forgery is not completed, unless the forged instrument be uttered; but if this has been done, it is of no consequence though it was immediately rejected, or no patrimonial loss has arisen from the crime.

No point of law is better established than that, how artfully or completely soever the forgery may have been executed, it cannot be made the subject of trial or punishment, unless it it is also uttered or put to use[7] How clear soever the evidence may be of an intent forthwith to put to use, if this has not been actually done, the crime is not cognizable by any human tribunal.[8] Accordingly, in the case of Alexander Ramsay, 16th July 1716, where the libel did not state that the forged instrument had been put to use, the Lords found the libel not relevant.[9] In like manner, in the case of Charles Anderson, Perth, autumn 1827, where the jury " found the pannel guilty of the forgery, but found the uttering not proven," the public prosecutor declined to move for sentence.[10] In the

---

[1] Unreported.—[2] Unreported.—[3] Unreported.—[4] Unreported.—[5] Unreported.—[6] Unreported —[7] Hume, i. 148, Burnett, 184.—[8] Hume, ibid.—[9] Hume, i. 148.—[10] Unreported

case of James Devlin, Glasgow, spring 1828, the proof on one of the charges did not come completely up to the strict definition of uttering; the forged note in question having not been handed over the counter, but only taken out of the prisoner's pocket, and put into his hand, from whence it fell to the ground, and before it could be taken up the prisoner was apprehended. In these circumstances Lord Justice-Clerk Boyle stopped the proof on that charge, though the prisoner was convicted on others.[1] Lastly, in the case of Malcolm Gillespie and George Skene Edwards, Aberdeen, autumn 1827, the jury found the prisoner Edwards " guilty of the *forgery* libelled," but without saying any thing of the uttering, while they found Gillespie guilty of the forgery and uttering. In these circumstances the prosecutor, with the approbation of the Court, declined to move for sentence.[2]

But, while this is quite clear on the one hand, it is not the less material to observe on the other, that the great danger, in a commercial country, of this crime, has established a rigorous construction, in the matter of the uttering, against the prisoner. It is sufficient, therefore, to complete the crime, if the forged instrument have been uttered, that is presented in payment, or made the foundation of a claim, though no advantage whatever was gained from the act, nay, though it was challenged immediately as a forgery, and returned to the prisoner.[3] So completely is this established in practice, that, by the ordinary style of the indictments for issuing forged notes, it is set forth as having been used and uttered " in payment, or *as a tender of payment, for* a gill of whisky there purchased, or proposed to be purchased by you, the said A B "

The same principle holds in the forgery of other instruments. A libel is good, therefore, for forgery and uttering, if the false bond has been made the ground of action or diligence, or has been produced and pleaded on in the way of claim or defence, though not abiden by upon challenge."[4] Accordingly, in the case of William and Thomas Mackie, February 2. 1636, the pannels were convicted of forgery and uttering, who had pleaded on a false discharge of a bond.[5] In like manner, in the case of Andrew Adam, February 15. 1710, the uttering was held to have been completed by the tendering of the bond

[1] Unreported.—[2] Hume, i. 149.—[3] Ibid. i. 150.—[4] Ibid. i. 152.—[5] Ibid.

of caution, in a suspension to the proper officer.[1]  So also, if a forged disposition has been followed by resignation or infeftment, or has been put into the hands of a notary for that purpose, or if the note or bill has been presented for payment, though challenged the moment it was seen by the clerk who took it.[2]  Indeed, the Legislature have declared, by the act 1621, c. 22, that it shall not protect from the pains of falsehood, to pass from the writing on challenge, or engage not to make use of it in future.[3]  On the same principle it is a clear uttering if a deed is registered for diligence, or in obedience to the injunction of law, in order to render it effectual as a groundwork of a claim, as in the case of seisins, hornings, abbreviates of adjudication, resignations *ad remanentiam*, petitions for sequestration, or the like.[4]  But it seems extremely doubtful whether the mere registration *custodiæ causa*, is a proper uttering; for the deed is put there for preservation only, and may or may not be afterwards made use of for the patrimonial advantage of the guilty party.[5]

The recent practice of the Court has been entirely in conformity with these principles.  Thus, in the case of William Mitchell, 29d August 1811, the pannel had sentence of death on a conviction for theft and forgery, he having stolen a bill, and presented it for payment, though no money had been received on it.[6]  At Ayr, spring 1818, Charles Affleck was transported fourteen years for forging and uttering a bill for £20, although it was stopped at the bank as soon as uttered; and the like course was followed in the case of James Sloan, Ayr, April 1818, who had sentence of death for forging and uttering three bills, one of which only was paid, the other two having been stopped on the offer to discount.[7]  In like manner, in the case of Robert Hughes, Ayr, spring 1830, the pannel was convicted and transported fourteen years for the theft of a deposit-receipt of the Ayr bank, and uttering it with a forged indorsation at the office of the bank, though the clerk who received it challenged it as a forgery the moment that he saw it.[8]

Sometimes it is matter of considerable nicety to fix the place or period when the uttering, in the sense of law, has taken place.  The principle is, that the uttering, if made through the medium of an agent, is completed the moment that it is

[1] Hume, i. 152.—[2] Ibid.—[3] 1621, c 22.—[4] Hume, i. 154.—[5] Ibid.—[6] Ibid.
—[7] Ibid.—[8] Unreported.

lodged with the agent with instructions, or in the view that
it should be produced in a process, or made the foundation of
a claim, or in any way tendered for the benefit of the pannel,
provided that such production, tendering, or claim, is afterwards made by the agent.    Thus, in the case of Francis Adams,
Inverness, 1st September 1820, who was indicted for forging a
series of obligations, letters, receipts, &c., against Sir George
Abercrombie, and also for uttering them knowing them to have
been forged, the indictment stated, that he had caused these
writings to be delivered to Richard Graham, writer in Annan,
for the purpose of being by him used and employed as true and
genuine, for the purpose of obtaining for the said Francis
Adams' behoof a large sum of money from the said Sir Robert
Abercrombie.    The like charge was made as to the transmission of these writings to William Johnston, writer to the Signet,
and John Patison junior, writer to the Signet, his agent or
agents for the time; and then it charged that his agents executed
a summons against Sir Robert, and produced the writings in
the clerk's hands before Lord Pitmilly.    It was objected to the
two first charges that they did not amount to an uttering;
though it was admitted that they might be referred to in modum
probationis of the third charge, which it was contended was
the true uttering.[1]    The Lords repelled the objection, which,
indeed, was clearly ill founded; the true period of the uttering
by the pannel being the time when he first parted with the documents to a third party, and put them in that train which ultimately led to their being made the foundation of a claim
against the person on whom the forgery was committed; and
the subsequent tracing of the documents being only necessary
to shew, that this uttering received its intended accomplishment by being made the foundation of a claim in a court of law.
On the same principle, in the case of Alexander Baillie, 14th
March 1825, indicted for falsehood and forgery, the indictment
in the 12th charge stated, that the prisoner did " use and utter
the whole of the said false and forged documents above libelled,
by placing them in the hands of the said James Todd, your
agent, with directions to him to found thereon judicial proceedings against the trustees of the said William Scott junior," &c.
It was objected to this charge, 1. " That the uttering in Glas-

[1] Hume, l. 153.

gow was stated as having been made to the pannel's own agent
Mr Todd, and the documents were not charged as having been
uttered as genuine    2. That it is not stated when or how Mr
Todd put forth the documents, or whether he put them forth
as genuine.    3. That it is not said who lodged them in the Bill-
Chamber, nor whether they were there lodged as genuine."
The Court held the uttering rightly charged as having been
made through Mr Todd, the prisoner's agent; but that the libel
should have set forth the deed as having been delivered to him
for the purpose of being uttered *as genuine*, and this followed
up by a distinct narrative of when and how, by Mr Todd's
agency, the forged deeds were lodged as genuine in process.[1]    Lastly, in the case of John Scott, Aberdeen, autumn
1830, a libel was sustained as relevant, which charged the
pannel with having uttered a forged bill, by delivering it to his
agent to be by him uttered as genuine, and followed this up by
a statement of when and where the forged instrument thus put
in circulation was tendered against the party forged on.[2]    On
the same principle, if a forged instrument be uttered through
the Post-office, the time and place to be charged for the uttering is that when the writing was put into the post-office, which
should be followed up by a narrative of its having been conveyed in course of post to the place of its destination.

Cases frequently have occurred of late years, in which the
utterers of forged notes did not tender the notes themselves,
but gave them to others, who were put forward as the cat's-
paw on this perilous mission.    In such cases, the instrument
should be charged as delivered for the purpose of being tendered as genuine, at the time and place where it was delivered to
the hand who uttered it; and this followed up by a narrative
of the time, place, and mode of presentment which this hand
adopted in uttering it as genuine to a third party.    Such a
mode of charging the uttering has been repeatedly sustained as
relevant, and followed by conviction and exemplary punishment; and in all such cases, the hands put forward are competent witnesses against the pannel.    So the Court held in the
case of James Devlin and Alexander Leith, Glasgow, spring
1828, who issued forged notes through the medium of girls, who
were sent forward to the shops for that purpose.    The deliver-

---

[1] Unreported.—[2] Unreported.

ing was charged as having been made to these girls at the place where the notes were delivered to them by the pannels, for the purpose of being passed as genuine; and this followed up by a narrative of when and where these girls fulfilled their instructions, and passed them as genuine on the public.[1] The same style was adopted and sustained in the case of Patrick Hendrie, Glasgow, spring 1828, who was transported fourteen years. In the case of Bell and Mortimer, 22d July 1800, the competence of proceeding in this manner was fully recognised by the Court. The libel there charged that Bell had delivered one of the forged notes, particularly described, to his associate Young, in order that he might vend it, and that Young accordingly did so. The jury found Bell "guilty of fraudulently and feloniously using, uttering and vending the note libelled on," without any mention of the uttering having taken place through Young. An objection having been stated to the sufficiency of this verdict, and its application to the libel, the Court held that Young was to be considered as a hand through which Bell uttered the note, so that Bell was substantially art and part of the vending by Young; and, in consequence, Bell had sentence of death.[2]

20. It is a crime punishable by the highest arbitrary pain, to utter or vend forged notes, knowing them to be forged, to an associate, at less than their nominal value, for the purpose of their being passed as genuine upon the public.

In the cases hitherto discussed, the uttering of the forged instrument has been always, either directly by the pannel, or circuitously through a third party by his contrivance, to the public as genuine. But there is another case of not unfrequent occurrence, viz. where a pannel has uttered forged notes to an associate in the trade, in the full knowledge that they are forged, for less than their nominal value; as where a parcel of forged notes have been uttered for five shillings each. This important question first occurred for discussion in the case of Richard Myndham, 31st July 1800. This man was charged with uttering, using and vending false notes, by delivering them to

---

[1] Unreported.—[2] Hume, i. 150; Burnett, 188.

others *at an under value.* It was objected to the indictment, that delivery to a *socius* is not an uttering in the sense of the law, inasmuch as forgery consists in the deception practised by uttering a forged writing as genuine, which is awanting where it is vended in the knowledge of the forgery at an under value. But the Court expressed a clear opinion, that the giving notes to a *socius* at an under value for the purpose of being circulated, was an uttering or using in the sense of law.[1]   A similar question occurred on 16th July 1810, in the case of John Macfarlane, who was charged with using, uttering, and vending, counterfeited coin to an accomplice, for the purpose of their being circulated.   The Court sustained the objection that the libel was *illogically* drawn, inasmuch as the major proposition charged the passing the false money *as genuine,* and the minor related sundry acts of vending false pieces to an associate *as false;* so that the major and minor did not correspond.[2]   But at length this question received a deliberate judgment of the whole Court in the case of John Horne, July 15. 1814, who was charged *inter alia* with " feloniously delivering, vending, or disposing, of any such forged or counterfeited notes or obligations, *as forged or counterfeited, for a valuable consideration, less than the nominal value thereof;* and for the fraudulent and felonious purpose of their being used, uttered, or vended, as genuine."   And the minor stated, that he had disposed of four one-pound notes *for five shillings each,* and for the fraudulent and felonious purpose of their being uttered as genuine.   The Court, after a full argument, unanimously held that, though this does not amount to the capital crime of forgery, it is a criminal act or point of dittay, relevant to infer the highest arbitrary pains.[3]

Since that time, this offence of vending forged notes at an under value, has been frequently made the subject of trial and punishment at common law.   In particular, such a charge was sustained, and followed by conviction and transportation for fourteen years, at Glasgow, spring 1828, in the case of Patrick Hendrie junior;[4] and again at Glasgow, autumn 1831, Henry Macmillan was convicted and transported fourteen years for vending five forged one-pound notes at an under value, with the intent that they should be passed off as genuine on the public.

[1] Burnett, 190.—[2] Hume, i. 150.—[3] Ibid. 151.—[4] Unreported.

21. It is by special statute a capital crime, to dispose
or put away any forged Bank of England notes, whether
for their nominal or an under value, with intent to defraud
the Bank or any other person.

By the 15th Geo II. c. 13. § 11, the forging and uttering
Bank of England notes was made punishable with death.   The
provisions of that act are now in a great measure superseded
by the recent act 45th Geo. III. c. 89, which enacts in sect. 2,
. ' That if any person or persons shall forge, counterfeit or alter, any bank-note, bank bill of exchange, dividend warrant,
or any bond or obligation under the common seal of the Governor and Company of the Bank of England, or any indorsement
thereon, or shall offer or dispose of, or put away any such
forged, counterfeited or altered note, bill, dividend warrant,
bond or obligation, or the indorsement thereon, or any part
thereof, of the said company, or any of their officers or servants,
knowing such note, bill, dividend warrant, bond, or obligation,
or the indorsement thereon, to be forged, counterfeited or altered, with intent to defraud the said Governor and Company,
or their successors, or any other person or persons, body or
bodies politic or corporate whatsoever, every person or persons
so offending, and being thereof convicted in due form of law,
shall be deemed guilty of felony, and suffer death as a felon
without benefit of clergy."   This act extends to Scotland.

Under the act of Geo. II. it has been held, that where one of
the prisoners knowingly delivered a forged bank-note to the
other prisoner for the purpose of its being knowingly uttered
by her, and she uttered it accordingly, the prisoner who delivered such note might be convicted of having " disposed of
and put away" the forged note.[1]   And it was decided by all
the Judges, that, in an indictment under the last of these statutes for disposing of and putting away forged bank-notes, the
offence may be held as completed, though it appear that the
notes were furnished by the prisoners to agents employed by
the bank to procure them from the prisoners, and that the notes
were delivered to such agents as forged notes, for the purpose
of being disposed of by them.[2]   And it was held that, where the
bank have indicted a prisoner for the capital offence of having

---

[1] Palmer and Hodgson's case, Leach, u. 978, Russell, u. 406.—[2] Holden's
case, Russell, ii. 406.

uttered forged notes, and also for the minor one of having such forged notes in his possession, an acquittal on the minor charge should not be directed, though the facts proved amounted to the major; and also that it is not necessary that the signing clerk at the bank should be produced at the trial, if witnesses acquainted with his handwriting swear that the signature of the note is his handwriting.[1]

22. When extant and accessible, the false writing must be produced at the trial; but its absence, if it be proved not to exist, is no bar to the trial proceeding, more especially if it has been destroyed by the prisoner himself, to prevent its being adduced in evidence against him.

In any prosecution for forgery, it is a sufficient objection in bar of trial that the forged document exists, and is not libelled on as a production;[2] for the general rule in the law of evidence is, that the best evidence which can be procured must be laid before the jury, and witnesses; and, of course, the best evidence as to the forgery of a writing is to be drawn from inspection of it by the witnesses in presence of the assize.[3]  But what if the forged writing has perished; is it competent in such a case to adduce parole testimony as to the forgery by the witnesses who saw it when in existence?  The principle of the rule there fails, because the best *existing* evidence is still produced; but it is evident that the want of such an important production must be in most cases an insurmountable difficulty in the way of obtaining a conviction.[4]  In such a case, accordingly, the objection that the forged document is not produced is justly repelled as a bar to trial.[5]  So it was found in two cases in the Court of Session, William Chatto, 6th February 1753, and John Cameron, 9th August 1754;[6] and, in a recent instance, the same rule was adopted in the Court of Justiciary.  In the case of Robert Hay, Aberdeen, 27th September 1819, it was stated in the indictment, that, on the committal of the prisoner, he asked to see the forged bill founded on, and instantly put in his mouth and chewed it till it was totally illegible.  The want of the forged document was here founded on in bar of trial, and also

[1] Russ. and Ry, 378; Russell, ii. 407.—[2] Hume, i. 164; Burnett, 200.—[3] Burnett, 200.—[4] Hume, i. 164.—[5] Ibid.; Burnett, 200.—[6] Fac. Coll. i. No. 60 and 113

the incompetency of taking parole evidence respecting the contents of a writing not libelled on, as a production at the trial; but both these objections were repelled by Lords Hermand and Succoth, and the prisoner was transported seven years.[1] More lately still, the same rule was followed by Lords Justice-Clerk Boyle and Pitmilly, in the case of Alexander Alston, Glasgow, September 1826; the indictment there stated, that, while under examination, the pannel got hold of the note, and tore off and swallowed the parts containing the forged signatures; but the Court were clearly of opinion, that this was no bar to the trial proceeding in the circumstances here set forth, and the pannel pleaded guilty and was transported seven years.[2]

It has not yet been decided whether it is competent to proceed with a trial for forgery, where the forged instrument is not produced, without any fault on the prisoner's part It may be anticipated, that, in all such cases, the *casus amissionis* must be clearly established, and the best secondary evidence produced: but, if this be done, there seems to be no bar to the trial proceeding, whatever difficulty there may be, in such circumstances, in obtaining a conviction.[3] It need hardly be observed, that the rule would unquestionably be the reverse, if the destruction or disappearance of the forged instrument could be in anywise traced to the prosecutor, or those acting for him: for, on the same principle in which secondary evidence as to the contents of a forged writing is competent where the writing has perished by the prisoner's act, it would be rejected where the prosecutor was in any degree implicated in the proceeding.

23. In trials for forgery, the person forged on is a competent, and in general necessary, witness for the prosecution; but his testimony is liable to the observation of the evident interest which affects his situation.

It being a fixed rule in the law of evidence, that the best proof of which the case will admit must be laid before the jury, it follows, as a necessary consequence, that the person forged on should, if still alive, be adduced at the trial, because it is to be presumed that no person is so well acquainted with his sig-

----

[1] Shaw's Cases, No. 29.—[2] Unreported.—[3] Hume, i. 164; Burnett, 200.

nature as he himself is. Nor is it any objection to the competence of such testimony that he is under an evident interest, inasmuch as, if he succeed in establishing the forgery, he will get quit of all responsibility for the debt; for our law, differing in that respect from the English, in no case holds an injured party disqualified from giving testimony by the interest which may eventually arise to him from the conviction of the offender. This point was first made the subject of serious objection and argument, in the case of Thomas Wilson, January 25. 1790, who was indicted for forging the indorsement or acceptance of Dr Lindsay, Thomas Brown, and others, to certain bills. The Court repelled the objection to their admissibility, reserving their credibility to the jury; and this has been the rule invariably followed ever since that time.[1]

The common law of England is founded on different principles: the objection of interest against the person forged on, is there sustained, unless obviated by a release.[2] This, however, has been always regarded as an anomaly by the English lawyers. " Upon what principle," says Lord Ellenborough, " this anomalous rule has been so settled, I cannot pretend to say; but, having been so settled, it cannot now be remedied but by the Legislature."[3]. Such a remedy has now been applied. By 4th Geo. IV. c. 32, it is enacted, that the party whose name has been forged shall be a competent witness in all prosecutions for forgery.[4]

The person whose name is forged is a necessary witness in the general case, in all cases in which he is alive. But to this rule there are, in the case of the signature of bank-officers, two important exceptions. Where the signature of the social firm is in use of being adhibited by different persons, it is not necessary to bring any of those persons; but it is sufficient if a bank-officer is brought who can swear that the signature forged is that of one or other of them. So it was held by Lords Pitmilly and Alloway, at Perth, autumn 1827, in the case of Mary Smith or Selkridge. It was there objected to the proof of forgery of the signature " Forbes, Hunter & Co." of Sir W. Forbes's Bank, that no one authorized to sign the social firm was adduced as a witness, but only Mr Young, who was not a partner, but only a clerk acquainted with their signatures. But to

this it was sustained, as a sufficient answer, that many different partners are authorized to adhibit the signature of the
social firm, and that if one partner were a necessary witness,
they would require to be all summoned in every case; because,
although each was the best evidence as to his own signature, he
was not the best as to that of his copartner, and that the clerk
who knew the signatures of them all, was equally good, as to
the signature of the others, as one of the partners themselves.[1]
Secondly, It has been determined that, where a bank-officer, in
use to sign notes, has been disabled from attendance by necessary absence, or ill health, the other signing officer may speak
to his signature, and a conviction take place, though he is alive
and has not been examined. So it was held by the High Court,
in the case of Christian Kennedy, November 9. 1829.[2] It has
been already noticed, that the rule is the same in England, and
that it is sufficient to prove the signature to the Bank of England notes, by the clerks who are well acquainted with them,
though the actual signer has not been adduced.[3] Of course, if
the person whose name has been forged is actually dead, proof
by others is at all times competent as to whether the signature
founded on as a forgery is genuine or not.

24. The best evidence in cases of forgery is the oath of
the person forged on, that it is not his handwriting; the
next that of persons acquainted with his writing, and who
have seen him write; next, that of persons who have corresponded with him, though without having seen him
write; next, a *comparatio literarum* with his genuine
writings; and, lastly, that of professional persons accustomed to compare the similitude of handwriting, on their
productions.

No authority is required for the position, that the best evidence in cases of forgery is the testimony of the person himself, who declares that the signature produced, purporting to
be his, is not his handwriting. Next to that is the evidence of
a witness who swears that he has seen the pannel write, and
the more frequently the better, and has in this way gained a
knowledge of his handwriting.[5] Next in degree to this, and

---

[1] Unreported.—[2] Unreported.—[3] Russ. and Ry, 378; Russell, ii. 407.—See
Hume, ii. 395.—[5] Hume ii. 395, Phillips, i. 485, &c

certainly admissible, is the testimony of one who has received, or has had occasion to see, letters or writings from the pannel, and has either heard him acknowledge they were his, or speak of them as his own writing, or has reason to believe, from their being in answer to letters of his own, addressed to the writer, that they were genuine, or had acquired this information from the statements of others, or in any other way.[1] Next comes the evidence *comparatione literarum*, from an actual comparison, by the jury, or witnesses in their presence, of the writing said to be forged, with the admitted or proved writings of the party forged on; and, lastly, the testimony of engravers, and other skilled persons, upon the conclusions which their sagacity, sharpened by experience in these matters, has drawn from such a comparison.[2]

These principles have, from a very early period, been recognised in our practice. " *Comparatio literarum*," says Lord Royston, " may be used in a circumstantial proof, though not sufficient *per se*; as if one witness saw the prisoner write the paper, then *comparatio* may be proved in support of it."[3] In the case of Campbell, 29th June 1721, the hardship of a proof *comparatione* was urged, but the Court found the pannel guilty. In the case of Clerk and Brown, 9th November 1802, the Court allowed a letter to be produced, which was only *comparatione literarum*, and, by comparison with another letter, proved to be the pannel's.[4] In the case of Melville *v.* Crichton, March 1821, the competency of such proof *comparatione* was argued in the Jury Court, and they held that it was admissible *valeat quantum*, and this was confirmed after a hearing in presence by the First Division.[5] Lastly, in the case of John Macleod Gillies, June 20. 1828, tried for falsehood, fraud, and forgery; two engravers were examined who had compared the false certificates with the writings proved to be the pannel's, and the prisoner was convicted; but evidence, both direct and circumstantial, was there previously laid before the jury, tending to implicate him in the forgeries founded on.[6]

25. In cases of uttering a forged writing, it is indispensably necessary that the writing libelled on as forged

---

[1] Hume, i. 395; Phillips, i. 492.—[2] Hume, ii. 395; Phillips, i. 492, fifth edition; Burnett, 502.—[3] Burnett, 503.—[4] Hume, ii 396.—[5] Murray's Reports, ii. 237.—[6] Hume, ii 396.

be dist᾽ ictly proved to have been uttered by the prisoner, or that he was art and part in that offence.

In cases of uttering any forged writing, and more especially forged notes, it is indispensable that the writing libelled on be distinctly brought home to the prisoner; and no other evidence can be relied on in this particular, but either a marking by the person who received it at the moment of its being uttered, or before it went out of his possession, or distinct evidence by every person who got the note afterwards, as to how he disposed of it, until it was finally marked by some one who can swear to his signature. This it is very material to attend to, for it frequently happens that a forged note is distinctly recognised by the person who received it, when examined in precognition shortly after the event, who yet is unable to swear to it without some marking of his own, when exhibited to him at the trial some months after. The only way of obviating this inconvenience is either to get the person who received the note to mark it with his initials before he parts with it, or if it have got unmarked into the hands of others, to examine every person, without exception, into whose hands it got before it was marked, as to the note which he received being the same which he passed on to others. Cases, doubtless, do sometimes occur where the chain of identification is complete without such detailed evidence, but nothing else should be relied on as likely in every case to prove satisfactory.

In like manner, if the forged note have been put into a pocket, drawer, or box, with others, the proof of identification will almost certainly fail, unless some means have been taken to enable the person so doing to recognise it from the others with which it has thus become blended. This may sometimes be done by its being the only note of a certain bank, which was in that parcel or pocket; but as that is a point concerning which the memory is extremely apt, especially after the lapse of months, to prove fallacious, it is not to be relied on, unless the witness be extremely clear on the subject, or can give some satisfactory *causa scientiæ* which enables him to distinguish that note from the others with which it may so easily have become confused. It often happens that the witness says that the forged note was the only note of *any kind* put into the till, pocket, or drawer; and if he be quite distinct on that point,

the chain of identification will of course, in that one link, be
complete.   But, in general, the sooner that a note suspected to
be forged is marked with initials the better, and, before this is
done, the safest course is to examine every person into whose
possession it got, both as to how he disposed of it and his *causa
scientiæ*, that no confusion of it with another note took place
while in his custody.

This minuteness is less necessary where the forged instrument is a bill, bond, or other writing, because the chances of
mistake are so much less, and the means of identification so
much greater in that case, than where the forged instrument
is a bank-note.   But still a clear chain of identification is indispensable in that as well as in other cases; and if the note
or writing have been put into any place where it ran the chance
of being mistaken for another instrument, a clear *causa scientiæ*
as to its identity, or some marking or circumstance which leads
to its being satisfactorily distinguished, will justly be required
for the conviction of the jury.

26. In cases of forgery it is competent to adduce the
forger against the utterer, or *vice versa*.

The general rule as to the competence of adducing a *socius
criminis* against a pannel, admits of no exception in cases of
forgery.   It is competent, accordingly, to adduce the forger
against the utterer, or the utterer against the forger, though
their evidence of course be subject to the observation of the
stain with which, on their own shewing, it is affected.   In the
case of Mrs Nisbett, already mentioned, February 1727, the
evidence of the person she had suborned to forge the writing
was admitted without objection.[1]   In like manner, in the case
of Malcolm Gillespie, Aberdeen, autumn 1827, the evidence of
two of the *socii criminis* were admitted without objection as to
their competency, though with many animadversions as to their
credibility to the jury.   So also in the case of James Devlin
and Alexander Leith, Glasgow, spring 1828, the evidence of
the hands whom they had put forward to utter the forged notes
was admitted without objection, though, in regard to one of
them, the Porteous Roll for the same circuit contained an indictment for being herself engaged in issuing forged notes.[2]

[1] Burnett, 198.—[2] Unreported.

27. It is competent, in cases of forgery, to adduce evidence of previous unsuccessful attempts to utter instruments suspected to be forged by the prisoner; not as substantive articles of charge, but *in modum probationis* of the charges in which the crime was actually completed.

It frequently happens that a prisoner who is proved to have uttered a forged instrument had made previous and unsuccessful attempts to utter either that or some other similar note. And it is competent to prove such previous unsuccessful attempts to utter, as articles of evidence tending to fasten the completed acts on the prisoner. This rule is part of the general principle, that general behaviour about the time is admissible to fasten a particular charge on a prisoner; as having picklocks, skeleton keys, or dark lanterns, is admissible in cases of housebreaking.[1] This evidence was admitted in the case of Nathaniel Blair, 1814, who had uttered a two pound note, which after his apprehension he had got back and destroyed, though these facts were not specially libelled on.[2] But, in the case of Ebenezer Knox, 9th June 1817, various attempts to utter were set forth in the libel; and it was objected " that it is not relevant to prove that at one time or place a pannel attempted to commit any particular act, either of receiving or uttering forged notes, or of any other crime which may consist in repeated acts, such as assault or the like, in order to infer from thence that he actually succeeded in committing a different act of the same crime, completed at a different time or place." But to this it was sustained as a sufficient answer, " that the attempts to utter objected to are not stated as separate charges, but *in modum probationis* of the specific charges set forth; and that it is of no consequence whether the persons to whom the notes were uttered received them as genuine, if they were tendered as such."[3] Since that time, it has been frequently the practice to libel on attempts to utter, *in modum probationis* of the completed acts set forth. This was done, in particular, in the case of William Hay, Glasgow, winter 1829, where, *in modum probationis* of a charge of having uttered a forged five pound note, a previous unsuccessful attempt to issue a one pound forged note was set

---

[1] Phillips, i. p 432.—[2] Hume, i. 157 —[3] Ibid.

3

forth in the libel, and admitted to proof by the Court; and the pannel was convicted, and transported fourteen years. But on all these occasions it is indispensable that the previous attempts to utter be set forth in the indictment, and the time and place specified with as much accuracy as the completed acts on which the indictment is founded;[1] and the prosecutor must establish that the notes attempted to be uttered were forged, by the same means, and with the same accuracy, as the notes libelled on in the principal charges. It does not seem to be indispensable, however, that on every one of the occasions on which an attempt to utter took place, he should prove that it was made with the guilty knowledge: for that is the *sine qua non* of the principal charges libelled on; and it is the precise object of proving these attempts to infer from their number or circumstances, that the particular notes libelled on in the specific charges must have been issued in the knowledge that they were forged instruments.

28. Legal evidence, in cases of uttering forged writings, consists in proof that the instrument libelled on is forged; that it was uttered by the prisoner, or with his accession; and that it was uttered by him knowing it to be forged.

In cases of uttering forged instruments, the three points which the prosecutor has to establish are, 1. That the deed is a forgery; 2. That it was uttered by the prisoner, or that he was art and part in that offence; 3. That it was uttered by him in the guilty knowledge of the forgery.

The preliminary point that the deed is forged, requires little illustration. Of course, unless this fundamental point is established, there is no offence to form the subject of investigation. The usual evidence adduced on this head consists of the oath of the person whose signature has been imitated, who must be produced to the jury, if he be alive; unless in the cases already mentioned, where, in cases of sickness or absence, one bank-officer is allowed to swear to another's signature, and a clerk is allowed to swear to the signature of the social firm by one of the partners, though none of the persons entitled to adhibit that signature has been adduced.[2] It is sufficient, in strict

---

[1] Hume, i 157 —[2] *Supra,* p 411.

law, if the person forged on proves that his signature is forged; and, accordingly, in the case of Malcolm Gillespie, Aberdeen, autumn 1827, several of the forged signatures were proved to be forgeries only by the persons themselves forged on; and the same occurred with several of the forged signatures in the case of J. Macleod Gillies, June 28. 1818, High Court.[1] In truth, this is but a branch of the general rule of law, that the *corpus delicti* in all crimes may be proved by one witness, provided he be sufficiently explicit and worthy of credit, if in the circumstances of the case it appear that more could not be got. But as no reliance can be placed on the principal witness being sufficiently clear and explicit, it is advisable, in all cases where it can be got, to be provided with another witness, to corroborate the principal one, in the event of there being any deficiency in his testimony. Or it will equally fill up the measure of legal evidence, if the genuine signature of the party, adhibited before witnesses who can prove the fact, be laid before the jury, to be by them compared with the writing libelled on as forged in the indictment. This was done in a great many instances in Gillespie's case; the parties, when examined in precognition, having been desired by the procurator-fiscal to sign in their usual way on a slip of paper, which was annexed to the forged writing, and made a production to the jury along with it, and proved by the party who wrote it, and the procurator-fiscal or one of the clerks in whose presence it was adhibited. In the selection of such supplementary evidence, attention should be paid to the rules already laid down, of the superiority of the evidence of those who have seen the party write over those who are only acquainted with his handwriting, and of both over that of engravers and other professional men, who speak only from acquired skill and a comparison of hands.

The prosecutor must next establish that the writing was uttered, that is, either paid or tendered in payment, or to obtain payment, by the prisoner, or by another person with his connivance or accession. It is immaterial, in considering this question, whether the pannel has *himself* uttered the forged writing, or done so by means of a hand whom he has sent forward on the occasion; in either case he is accessary to the of-

---

[1] Unreported on this point.

fence, and must answer for his own or his associate's acts.[1] It has been already noticed, that, at Glasgow, in spring 1828, Patrick Hendrie, James Develin, and Alexander Leslie, were convicted of uttering forged notes, by means of girls to whom they had delivered them, and whom they sent forward into the shops for that purpose; and, in the case of Elizabeth Hall, December 26. 1826, High Court, the prisoner was convicted of uttering a bill for £ 646, which she had stole, by means of a woman whom she sent forward into the bank for that purpose.[2]

It is indispensable that the writing charged as forged, and produced on the table, should be traced clearly back by an unbroken chain of evidence into the prisoner's hands. There must be no hesitation or doubt as to that being the identical instrument which came from his possession; for this is not a point on which a certain latitude can be allowed to the witnesses, while they substantially prove the prisoner's guilt; if there is the least hesitation here in any one link, not adequately supplied by other evidence, the case against the prisoner is at an end. In the case, accordingly, of J. Hobson, Ayr, spring 1827, Lord Meadowbank stopped the proof of two of the charges, though the prisoner was convicted on the others, upon the ground that, in each charge, a witness swore that he gave the note to another witness, and got it back, and that other witness was not adduced to establish that the note which he returned was the same which he had received. The note here had not been marked, or this would have been of no consequence.[3]

The most difficult, and not the least indispensable point to be established, in all cases of uttering, is, that it was done in the guilty knowledge that the instrument was forged. This is in general to be made out by circumstantial evidence; because, unless the utterer be the actual forger, or received the instrument, with such information, or in such circumstances, as could have left no doubt of its being forged, his guilty knowledge can be inferred only from his own conduct, or the articles found in his possession.

The most important circumstance, and which generally is *per se* decisive as to the guilty knowledge, is, if other forged

---

[1] *Supra*, p. 405.—[2] Unreported.—[3] Unreported.

notes are found on the pannel. If four or five forged notes, and especially forgeries on the same bank with that uttered, are found on the prisoner, it is hardly possible to form any other conclusion than that he is a dealer in these dangerous instruments, caught in the very act of disposing of them. This will amount to moral certainty, if the other forged notes are found concealed in his possession, as in his hat, in a concealed pocket, sewed between his coat and the lining, or the like. On the other hand, the weight of this circumstance, always great, must be held as diminished, if the notes found on him were nowise concealed, and were exhibited by him without any suspicious circumstances, or appearance of conscious guilt. In innumerable cases this has been found the chief, if not the sole circumstance, from which the guilty knowledge was inferred.

Another circumstance, always of great, often of decisive importance, in the consideration of the guilty knowledge, is the conduct of the prisoner in regard to the suspected instrument. If he has sent forward another to present it, while he himself is at hand, and could equally well have done so in person; if, when challenged, he has exhibited evident symptoms of conscious guilt; if he has taken to flight, as soon as he could, or snatched at the note, or tried to destroy it, these, or similar proceedings, are the natural indications of a guilty conscience, and the best evidence of that knowledge of the forgery, which law considers indispensable to the criminality of uttering. In almost all cases of uttering, some indications of this conscious guilt appear. One of the most conclusive circumstances of this description, where forged bills have been passed at a bank, is the intercepting the bank notices of the bill being due to the persons whose names have been forged. This circumstance was the principal ingredient in the indirect evidence which brought home the guilty knowledge to Malcolm Gillespie, convicted of forgery and uttering at Aberdeen, autumn 1827.[1] It is, however, to be remarked, on the other hand, that the mere circumstance of having exhibited symptoms of terror or agitation, when the note was challenged, and still more when the police-officers were sent for, is not *per se* conclusive evidence of conscious guilt; for many innocent persons are seized with

[1] Unreported.

5

alarm at the thoughts of having passed, however unconsciously, a forged instrument, and the prospect of a jail is sufficient to intimidate many, especially of the lower orders, how innocent soever they may be of any offence. The great thing, therefore, to be attended to in the inquiry, is, what was the conduct of the prisoner *before* the instrument was challenged as a forgery? for whatever may be said of innocence feeling alarm after that event, certainly nothing can be said for its taking precautions for concealment or security before it.

A third circumstance of much importance in such cases, is the nature of the excuse which the prisoner can make for having presented the instrument. If, therefore, he had no such excuse, it must militate as much against, as, if it had, it must weigh for him. For example, if a person is detected passing a variety of notes, and accumulating silver about his person, without being able to give any rational account of his reason for so doing, and one or more of these notes turn out to be a forgery, it is impossible to avoid feeling an unfavourable impression against him; for, if his only object was to pay for a trifling article, why change another note when he already had plenty of silver in his possession. It is always, therefore, a material circumstance against the prisoner, if he has passed a forged note for payment of a trifling account, as a gill of whisky, a bottle of porter, &c. when he had a much larger quantity of change in his possession; and this of course becomes the stronger, in proportion as the store of change was the greater. As this is a presumption only arising from the nature of the transaction, it may be elided by evidence of the reason for which the additional change was sought; but this it lies upon the prisoner to establish, and thus rebut the inference which his own conduct affords against him.

Similar to this, and of still more weight in the scale of evidence, is the circumstance of a number of forged notes having been uttered, or attempted to have been uttered, about the same time by the prisoner. This it lies upon him to explain; both by shewing how he came to be changing so many notes of *any* kind, about that time, and how it happened that several of these notes were forgeries. If, therefore, a note have been challenged as bad, when first uttered, and he nevertheless persists in attempting to pass it in different shops; or if different acts of uttering distinct notes, which turn out to be forgeries, are proved against him about the same time and place, he is placed in an awkward predicament, from which he can hardly escape, but by shewing the peculiar circumstances which innocently brought so many forged instruments into his possession, and innocently compelled him to pass them.

The last circumstance of weight in this inquiry, is the account which the prisoner has given, when the note is presented, where it is challenged, or at any time afterwards, of the way in which it came into his possession. The accounts which the prisoner gave at any time of the way in which he acquired the forged instrument, is competent matter of proof, both by the parole evidence of those who heard what he said, and by production of his written declaration taken before a magistrate; and, by comparing these accounts together, important conclu· sions may generally be arrived at in regard to his guilt or innocence. If these accounts are in themselves rational and probable; if they are consistent with each other, and still more if they are in any part supported by evidence, they form a material circumstance on which the prisoner may rely in vindicating the innocence of his intentions before the jury. On the other hand, if the account given of the acquisition of the forged instrument is in itself incredible or absurd; if it has varied at different times, and is supported by no sort of evidence, it is impossible to arrive at any other conclusion, but that there was something to conceal, which made these different fabrications necessary. The stories usually told by utterers of forged notes, is similar to that so commonly resorted to by thieves, to account for the possession of stolen goods, viz. that they found them on the street or in a stair; that they got them from a man whom they never saw before, and would not know if they saw again; that they received them in exchange for a watch, which they sold in the street, or in a public-house, which they could not point out, &c. &c. It is quite evident that all such stories are utterly inadmissible, unless supported by some sort of evidence; and if, in addition to the absence of such evidence, they have varied at different times, and to different persons, they afford the most legitimate ground on which a jury can proceed in inferring the guilty knowledge.

29. The trial of forgery is competent either before the Court of Session or the Justiciary Court; but if the latter

be the Court selected, the proceedings against the accused in any previous civil court are not *probatio probata* against him, and the evidence previously led must *de novo* be taken and considered before the jury.

The prosecution of forgery has, from the earliest times, been attended with this peculiarity, that it may be brought either in the Justiciary Court or the Court of Session; and that, though commencing in the civil, it frequently terminates in the criminal court.[1] The frequency of this crime coming to light in the course of proceedings in the civil court, has given rise to the custom of trying it before that judicatory; to which was added, in former times, the difficulty of concluding the proof in intricate cases of this description within the limits required in proceedings before an assize.[2] Indeed, so frequent was the use of this judicatory in these cases in former times, that Mackenzie goes the length of affirming, that the Court of Session are exclusive of the Court of Justiciary in the first instance.[3] But this opinion, which has no countenance from the statutes, was overruled in the cases of Nicolson and Elliot, January 1694, John Howison, November 1705, and William Baillie and others, September 6. 1715[4] Indeed, in later times, and for the last half century, the trial of almost all cases of forgery, whether the proof was direct or circumstantial, has taken place before the Court of Justiciary; and the mode of proceeding before the Court of Session has become rather a matter of curiosity than practical use.

The form of process before the Court of Session may either be by process of reduction or improbation, raised by the private party, with concourse of the Lord Advocate; in the course of which, the defender, if in custody and appearing, may be found guilty of the forgery, and punished or remitted to the criminal court, if the writing challenged be produced and proved to be a forgery; or by summary complaint, either at the instance of the Lord Advocate, or the private party with his concurrence.[5] But unless the writings are produced, nothing but decree of certification can pass; nor any punishment be inflicted on the accused,[6] unless the writing has perished from the prisoner's

---

[1] Hume, i. 162.—[2] Ibid.—[3] Mackenzie, Tit. Falsehood, No. 4.—[4] Hume, i. 163; Burnett, 108.—[5] Hume, i. 163-4; Burnett, 198.—[6] Ibid.

fault, or by his act.[1]  The course of proceeding in such cases is
by hearing parties on the libel and defences, after which an interlocutor of relevancy is pronounced, and evidence taken on
both sides in presence of the Court.[2]  Under the new regulations and the Judicature Act, the prosecutor would doubtless
be compelled to lodge and abide by a revised condescendence,
in which all the circumstances alleged would require to be stated
with the same precision as in a criminal indictment.  Upon the
evidence, when then adduced, the Court may themselves punish
with any arbitrary pain short of death; but if the case requires the forfeit of the offender's life, all they can do is to
remit the pannel to the Court of Justiciary, there to undergo a
new trial and condemnation.[3]

The proceedings there are by indictment and list of witnesses, as in ordinary cases of crime.  But what is to be made of
the proof formerly taken in the Court of Session in such a case,
and is it to be taken as *probatio probata* against the accused, or
at all admitted in evidence against him?  The rule on this subject, however singular, is settled by immemorial custom to be
this,—that the prosecutor is only obliged to prove that the pannel is the same person who was convicted in the Court of Session; and the productions are merely the extracted decree of
the Court of Session, which proves itself, and the forged writings authenticated by the subscription of the President of that
Court, sworn to by that judge and a clerk of Court.  No farther proof is competent on the part of the prosecutor;[4] and it
was decided in the case of David Reid, August 12. 1780, that
no farther proof can be admitted on the pannel's side.[5]

In former times, it was even strenuously maintained by our
lawyers,[6] that the decree of the Session was to be taken as *probatio probata* of the pannel's guilt; but this rigorous doctrine
was gradually relaxed, and it is now completely established
that the assize are entitled to look into the evidence contained
in the extracted decree of the Court of Session, and exercise
their own judgment on that evidence in convicting or acquitting the pannel.[7]  But if the decree of the Court of Session has

[1] William Chatto, 6th February 1753; John Cameron, 9th August 1754;
Fac. Coll., Acts of Sederunt, 5th February 1754; Hume, 1. 164; Burnett,
199.—[2] Hume, 1 164.—[3] Ibid. 165; Burnett, 200.—[4] Hume, 1. 165.—[5] Burnett, 201, Hume, 1. 165.—[6] Ersk. Tit. Crimes, No. 72; Mackenzie, Tit. Falsehood, No. 7; Jurisdict. of Session, No. 3.—[7] Hume, 1. 167; Burnett, 200,
Raybouldican, January 18. 1768, Maclaurin

been an *absolvitor* to the pannel, the prosecutor is not at liberty to prosecute him anew before the criminal court, but must abide by the issue of the prosecution before that Court which he has selected.[1]

It was also maintained in former times, that a remit from the Court of Session constrained the Justiciary to pronounce a capital sentence.[2]   But this opinion also gave way in the progress of humanity, and after various instances in which, on a remit from the civil court, it had been followed only by an arbitrary pain,[3] it was at length unanimously agreed by the Court, in the case of Mrs Nisbet, January 23. 1727, that they had the power of judging of the punishment to be inflicted in this as well as in other cases of forgery.[4]

It does not seem to be as yet a settled point, whether inferior, and especially the Sheriff Courts, can competently try for this offence.   Mr Hume lays it down, that all process of reduction and improbation, and all original and separate process for punishment of forgery, are reserved as matters of difficulty for the peculiar cognizance of the Supreme Court.[5]   But there does not seem to be any decision which has yet established that *the Sheriff*, whose jurisdiction is general over all offences, unless excluded by statute or usage, is not competent to try for this offence; and the opinion of Mr Hume, as to the difficulty of proof, savours more of the practice of ancient than the ideas of modern times, where the most intricate cases of forgery are daily submitted to the decision of juries, and the increasing practice of the Sheriff Courts has habituated their judges to handling the most intricate evidence.   Of late years, accordingly, numerous instances have occurred in which trials for uttering forged notes have taken place before the larger Sheriff-Courts of Lanark, Fife, Forfar, Mid-Lothian, Perth, and Ayr, and an objection to the jurisdiction more than once repelled by their learned judges.   Nor are instances awanting in which, upon remits from the Justiciary Court, trials in inconsiderable cases of actual forgery and uttering have taken place before the Sheriff-Courts.   This took place in particular in the case of George Robertson and John Robertson, Perth, autumn 1827, charged with forging a certificate of banns, which was remitted

---

[1] Hume, i. 168.—[2] Mackenzie, Tit. Falsehood, No. 7; Royston, Tit. Falsehood, No 25.—[3] Craig's case, March 15. 1605; Forsyth's case, 1038.—[4] Hume, i. 168.—[5] Ibid.

from the Circuit Court at Perth, where Lords Pitmilly and Alloway presided, to the Sheriff of Perth, and the pannels afterwards convicted by that learned and able judge, and sentenced to two months' imprisonment.[1]

30. The punishment of forgery is capital in all cases where the forgery consists in the making or publishing of a forged instrument, as the signed and obligatory writing of another; but it only warrants an arbitrary punishment where the writing forged has no direct patrimonial consequences.

The question of the punishment of forgery was formerly of more moment than it has now for a considerable period become, in consequence of the increased humanity of modern practice, which almost invariably interposes by a restriction to save the offender's life, except in those flagrant cases where, beyond all dispute, the punishment of death may be awarded. But still the question of what cases of forgery are by law capital, is of importance in defining the legal rights of the prosecutor and pannel, and fixing the cases in which bail may legally be demanded.

1. The most undoubted mode of capital falsification is the felonious making and publishing of a writing to the prejudice of another, as the *signed instrument* of the person who has not made it.[2] If such a forgery has been completed and published, it is of no moment how small the sum is which the instrument contains; of which no other proof need be adduced than the frequency of the cases in which, for merely uttering a forged one-pound note, a capital sentence has been pronounced and executed.[3]

2. Though the counterfeiting a man's hand is the principal, it is not the only species of capital forgery. If money is obtained by the false acceptance of a bill in the name of one to whom it is specially addressed by name and description, and by assuming the person and signing the name of the true party, it is just as much a capital falsification as if the signature had been forged;[4] nor will it alter the case, though the name and surname thus adopted be the real name of the forger, but in-

---

[1] Unreported.—[2] Hume, I. 140.—[3] Ibid. 141.—[4] Ibid.

tended to apply to a different person of that name;[1] or though
the signature forged is entirely fictitious, if money has been
raised upon it from a third party.[2]

3. It is immaterial whether the signature has been adhibited
by writing, or engraving, or any other method. Such an objection was repelled in the case of Scott and Adamson, Glasgow, 1st May 1805.[3]

4. A capital forgery is also committed without the imitation
of any signature, by the false and fraudulent machination of
signing by means of two notaries and four witnesses; that being
a falsification of a mode of adhibiting a subscription recognised
by the law of Scotland.[4]

5. The affixing a genuine subscription to a false obligatory
deed to which it was not intended to be attached, or drawing
an obligation over a genuine signature without the knowledge
or consent of the party, is a capital forgery;[5] as also the forging
the     es of witnesses to a false and fraudulent deed.[6]

6 . · writings tending to patrimonial profit or loss may be
the .   ject of capital forgery, as bills, bonds, bank-notes, holograph writings, missive letters, discharges, whether of money
or obligations, charters, dispositions, testaments, assignations,
resignations, and that however small the sum contained in the
obligation.[7]

7. A false attestation or execution of a doquet, seisin, or
other deed, to which he alone is competent, by a notary-public,
is, on account of the importance and solemnity of such instruments, a capital offence;[8] as also the false execution of such a
writing by one falsely assuming to himself that character.

On the other hand, other and inferior falsification of writs,
are liable at common law to be punished only with an arbitrary
pain. This class of cases, which embraces all *alterations* of a deed
to the profit of the forger, as by altering the sum in a bill or bond,
secretly inserting a clause in one's own favour in a testament
or other deed, is not capital at common law: but they are made
so in regard to all warrants for payment of money, receipts for
money or goods, or the like, by the 45th Geo. III. c. 89.[9] The
forging of writs not directly inferring patrimonial consequences,
however serious in their ultimate effects, as certificates of mar-

---

[1] Hume, i. 142.—[2] *Ante*, p. 374.—[3] Burnett, 181 ; Hume, i. 141.—[4] Hume,
i. 143 ; Burnett, 178.—[5] Hume, i. 145 ; Burnett, 179.—[6] Hume, i. 146 ; Burnet, 179.—[7] Hume, i. 147-8.—[8] Ibid. 158, Burnett, 177.—[9] Hume, i. 160.

riage, proclamation of banns, baptisms, deaths or burials, or
writs intended to substantiate a claim to a certain legal character, or certificates of good character, or for the purpose of obtaining charity or relief, belong to the inferior class, to which
at common law the capital sanction does not reach.[1]

The course of punishment in cases of forgery has become so
much more lenient of late years than it formerly was, that precedents showing the present course of practice in this respect
can be drawn only from a very recent period. Malcolm Gillespie, hanged at Aberdeen, September 1827, was the last instance of a capital sentence for forgery being carried into execution; but that was a very peculiar case, not only because the
forgeries were very numerous, above twenty different acts
standing in three different indictments against him, on one of
which, embracing five charges, he was convicted, but because
they were committed in connection with another charge of fire-
raising, for committing which, at Gillespie's instigation and for
his behoof, two other prisoners were convicted at the same circuit. The usual course of punishment is transportation for life
or fourteen years in extensive forgeries or aggravated cases, and
for seven years in instances of inferior guilt, smaller sums, and
evident contrition. Of the course of practice of late years, the
following instances will give an idea. Walter Ewing Taylor,
convicted of forging and uttering two bills, one for £50 and one
for £47, was, on March 14. 1826, transported for life.[2] James
Barry, convicted of forging two bills, one for £140 and one for
£75. was, at Inverness, September 1827, transported for fourteen years[3] Alexander Alston, September 26. 1826, Glasgow,
was transported seven years, on a confession of having forged
a bill for £104. James Whyte, Sept. 13. 1827, on a confession of having forged two bills, one for £53 and one for £54,
was transported for the same period.[4]

---

[1] Hume, i. 161-2.—[2] Unreported.—[3] Unreported.—[4] Both unreported.

# CHAPTER XVI.

## OF WILFUL FIRE-RAISING, AND ATTEMPT TO COMMIT THAT CRIME.

By the laws of all countries, wilful fire-raising is considered as a crime of the most atrocious nature, both from the malignant spirit from which it proceeds, and the disastrous consequences with which it is attended. It is in Scotland numbered among the pleas of the Crown, which, on account of their importance and difficulty, can be tried only in the Court of Justiciary.

1. It is essential to the crime of fire-raising, that some part of the tenement set on fire should have been actually ignited; but, if this has been done, it is immaterial how small a portion that may be, or for how short a time the flames may have continued.

Whatever opinion may be formed of the guilt of the offender, it is fixed law, that the complete and capital crime of wilful fire-raising is not committed, unless some part of the subject set on fire has actually been consumed. If, therefore, the matches only have been kindled, and tossed among the corn, or in at the window, or into the stack-yard, or upon the roof of the house; still, if the purpose has failed, and no actual burning has taken place, it is not wilful fire-raising, but attempt at wilful fire-raising, which has been committed.[1]   Accordingly, in the case of Barbara Phinnick, July 8. 1670, who, being left alone in her master's house, had torn the bed-quilt, and placed it under the bed, with a lighted candle stuck into its middle, and then left the house, and locked the door, evidently with intent to destroy the house; but, owing to the bed-tick being of leather, the quilt was not quite consumed, and the floor was

---

[1] Hume, i. 127; Burnett, 220

only beginning to be touched, no sentence followed on the verdict establishing these facts.[1]   She was clearly guilty of the *attempt*; but that was not the crime laid in the indictment. To constitute, however, the capital offence, it is necessary that the thing ignited be some part *of the house*, or of the fixtures which properly form part of it, as shelves, thatch, floors, joists, doors, windows, or the like; for the burning any of the *effects within it*, is an inferior offence, punishable only with an arbitrary pain.[2]

But, while this is clear on the one hand, it is equally well settled on the other, that the offence is completed if the subject set on fire has once *begun to burn*, for how short a period, or in how small a degree soever.[3]   The fire-raiser shall be involved in the capital pains, though no stack in the farm-yard be consumed, or no chamber in the tenement be destroyed, if the fire has once laid hold of, or been raised in the premises, so as to occasion alarm for their safety, and put them in danger of being consumed.[4]   Accordingly, in the case of the Frasers, 7th November 1720, the Court found " their having wilfully set fire to the barn, or corns in the barn-yard libelled, whereby the said corns, *or any part thereof*, were burnt or consumed, relevant to infer the pain of death."[5]   So also in the case of Robert Allan, Glasgow, April 1756, the libel was found relevant to infer the pain of death, though the libel set forth that the fire was extinguished before it had proceeded far.[6]   On 28th July 1819, a libel was found relevant against Aaron Bramwell, which charged wilful fire-raising, in respect he had wilfully put a candle in a small closet, which was afterwards locked up, and that " the said fire took effect, and communicated to the said counting-house, and consumed great part of the *wood work of the said closet*, or safe, and part of the *floor of the said counting-room.*  Lastly, in the case of William Sutherland, 15th March 1825, a libel was raised against the pannel, charging him with having set fire to the shop by putting in combustibles whereby the " said fire did consume the floor of the said shop, *or parts thereof.*"   An objection to the citation prevented the case being tried; but the opinion of the Court was expressed on a former libel in the same case, 14th February 1825, that if the fire had once fastened on the floor of

---

[1] Hume, i. 127.—[2] Burnett, 220.—[3] Burnett, 220; Hume, i. 127.—[4] Hume, i. 127.—[5] Ibid.—[6] Burnett, 220.—[7] Hume, i. 127.

the house, and consumed any part, though small, of the wood, the capital crime was committed.[1] Indeed, in the case of Margaret Nicolson, August 16. 1711, who was charged with setting fire to a thatched roof of her master's, the pannel's life was only saved by a restriction of the libel, though the fire was almost immediately discovered and extinguished.[2]

If any articles of furniture within a house are set on fire, but it has not spread to any of the *fixtures* of the building, the crime of *attempt at fire-raising* only has been committed. Accordingly, in the case of William Douglas, 28th May 1827, the indictment charged the crime of attempt at wilful fire-raising, and supported that charge in the minor, by a statement that the pannel had set fire to a chest of drawers and bureau, with intent to consume the house; that the drawers and bureau were in great part consumed, and the flames *beginning* to communicate to the wood-work of the house, when they were discovered and extinguished. This libel was found relevant, thereby proving the sense of the Court that this *species facti* amounted to the minor offence of attempt to commit the capital crime. The pannel was convicted; but, being proved insane at the time, he was ordered to be confined for life.[3]

2. The rule in regard to the tenements which may be the subject of wilful fire-raising, is the same with that in regard to those on which housebreaking may be committed, and embraces every subject, whether dwelling-house, shop, barn, or out-house, communicating with, or forming part of, the premises.

The fire may not be communicated to a house or shop, strictly speaking, but to some outhouse or building connected with them; and an important question for the pannel may arise as to the buildings by the ignition of which the capital crime is committed. Now, on this subject, the rule seems to be, that wilful fire-raising is committed if a building is set on fire which communicates with, and forms part of, the premises of either a shop or dwelling-house, though forming no part of such a tenement itself. According to this rule, it is as much capital to set on fire a barn, shed, stable, byre, cart-house, or coach-house, as

---

[1] Unreported.—[2] Hume, i. 128.—[3] Ibid.

a dwelling-house or shop, provided the inferior species of building thus put in flames communicates with, or is so situated as seriously to endanger either a house, shop, or stack of corns.[1] Thus on 31st July 1806, Janet Hamilton and James Campbell had sentence of death for wilful fire-raising, on a libel which related that they had set on fire a cart-house adjoining a dwelling-house, whereby the cart-house, stable, byre, and dwelling-house were consumed. At Ayr, September 1817, Margaret Crossan had sentence of death for setting on fire a barn, whereby a stable, byre, and barn-yard were partly destroyed.[2] In the case of Alexander Perth, April 1801, a boy was convicted of wilful fire-raising, for setting fire to a *lint-shade;* and, in the case of Margaret Macinnon, Inverness, September 1787, the like crime was held to have been committed by setting fire to a small storeroom belonging to a ship-carpenter.[3]

The law of England is the same. Arson with them is the wilful burning of the house of another; but, under the word *house,* they include all outhouses which are *parcel thereof,* as they say, though not adjoining thereto, or under the same roof.[4] And, at common law (for the rule was altered as to burglary, by 7th and 8th Geo IV. c. 29, § 13), they hold all buildings to be parcel of a house which form part of its premises, though not, strictly speaking, connected, as outhouses, warehouses, barns, stable, cow-houses, and dairies.[5]

But there seems to be no authority, at least in the Scotch law, for holding that it is wilful fire-raising to set on fire an outhouse or byre at a distance from, and nowise endangering, any shop or dwelling-house; as, for example, a milk-house in the corner of a field, a dovecot in an orchard, or the like. That such an offence is punishable with high arbitrary pains cannot admit of a doubt; but there seems good reason to distinguish it from the terrible offence of burning buildings, whereby the persons and most valuable property of the lieges may be placed in imminent danger.[5]

3. The fire must have been kindled wilfully, and not by negligence, how gross soever; but, if this be the case, it matters not how circuitous may have been the mode of operation selected, or though the injury intended to have

---

[1] Hume, i. 132 —[2] Ibid i. 129.—[3] Burnett, 221.—[4] Blackst iv. 221, Hale, i 570; Russell, ii. 489.—[5] Hale, i 550, Russell, ii 14.

been done was not the actual burning of a house, but some inferior mischief.

If fire be kindled recklessly, or from misgovernment, as it is called in our old statute, 1426, c. 75, the crime is not wilful fire-raising, but an inferior delinquence, punishable by fine or imprisonment.[1] But, if the fire has been intentionally applied, and applied in such a way, or to such a place, as to spread to a house, or such a building as law considers as equivalent to a house, the crime is committed, though the flame originally was kindled at a distance.[2] To set fire to any thing contiguous to a house, with the design of the flames communicating to it, and it is thereby burnt, is wilful fire-raising. Thus if one discharge a gun at the thatched roof of a dwelling-house, with intent to consume the building, and the flames take effect, it is fire-raising[3] Whether the fire be raised by one person, or, as was determined in the case of William Spencer, December 13 1784, by a mob, whether he apply the torch by his own hands or by those of another, whom he has counselled or equipped for the deed; whether he apply it directly to the tenement meant to be destroyed, or to something contained in or nearly connected with it, so that the one being on fire the other is likely to kindle, the law is the same.[4] Accordingly, in the case of James Campbell and Janet Hamilton, 31st July 1806, the pannels were convicted of wilful fire-raising for setting fire to a cart-house adjoining a dwelling, whereby both were consumed.[5] In like manner, if one kindle a stack of fuel contiguous to a farm-yard, and the flames spread to the corn-stacks, which are consumed, without doubt the capital crime is committed. Or, if the flames be applied to an article of furniture in a house, with the design of consuming the building, and the flames spreading from the furniture fasten on the wood-work of the dwelling, the rule is the same. So it was found in the case of James Douglas, August 10. 1682, who, having broken into a writer's chamber, and stolen some articles, to conceal the depredation, wilfully placed a lighted candle among the papers in a writing-desk, whereby the house was set on fire and burned;[7] and, in the case of Margaret Tallasdale or Anderson, 22d May 1826, who was charged with ha-

[1] Hume, 1 128.—[2] Ibid. 1. 129.—[3] Burnett, 220.—[4] Hume, 1. 129.—[5] Ibid
[6] Ibid. i. 130.—[7] Ibid.

E e

ving set fire to the furniture in her house with intent to burn
and destroy the premises, the flames of which, with her knowledge and consent, spread to the wood-work of the building,
and consumed great part of it.[1]

In the construction of the wilful intent or malice essential to
the crime, the rule seems to be the same as is followed in cases
of homicide, viz. that gross and utter neglect of his neighbour's
property, committed in pursuance of a wilful design to injure,
is held equivalent to the actual intent to destroy. Thus, one
who is actuated by malicious purpose against his neighbour,
and, in pursuance of that spirit, does him an essential injury,
which ultimately leads to fire-raising, is as much guilty of the
capital offence, as if he applied the torch at once to his roof.
If, therefore, he set fire to his furze or heath, with the design
merely of injuring him, and the flames spread and consume his
corns or houses, he shall be punished in the same manner as
if he had applied the flames directly to these articles.[2] Or if
a mob break into a man's house, and pull his effects to pieces
and pile up the fragments in front of his house and set fire to
them, and the flames spread to and destroy the house itself,
without doubt this is the capital crime.

4. If fire-raising have been wilfully committed on a
house or corns, it is of no consequence, although malice,
strictly speaking, were not the offender's motive, but some
other impulse actuated him, whether lucre to the criminal,
or the concealment of a depredation, or any public and
violent passion.

Malice to an individual is the usual, but by no means the
only or the necessary, motive in wilful fire-raising[3] The
crime is the same if the fire be wilfully kindled in pursuance
of any other illegal or criminal act. Thus, if thieves set fire
to a house, either with intent to plunder it during the conflagration, or to conceal a depredation already committed, it is as
much wilful fire-raising as if they did it from spite at the proprietor. So it was found in the case of James Douglas, August
10. 1682, who set fire to a desk and consumed part of a house,
to conceal a theft;[4] and the opinion of the Court was ex-

[1] Hume, i. 130.—[2] Ibid.—[3] Burnett, 220; Hume, i. 130.—[4] Burnett, 220.

pressed in the same way in the case of John Farquhar and
James Thomson, February 24 1825, who were convicted of
having broken into and plundered a house in the Crosscause-
way, in the course of which it appeared on the proof, that they
had wilfully set fire to the house, though the flames were
speedily extinguished.   The Court expressed an unanimous
opinion, that this might have been charged as wilful fire-raising.[1]   In like manner, if a mob assault a jail to rescue prisoners, and, to obtain an entrance, they set fire to the doors or
windows, it is fire-raising.   So it was found in the case of Maclachlan, tried as an accessary to the outrages of the Porteous
mob.[2]   So also in the case of James Ford, Jedburgh, September 1792, a charge of wilful fire-raising was sustained for burning a toll-bar and toll-house, in a fit of irritation at the imposition of the toll, but the prosecutor restricted the libel.[3]

The most usual cases which occur on this subject are where
a prisoner has set fire to the house let to him by his landlord,
with a design to defraud the insurers with whom he has insured
the furniture, and, in consequence, his landlord's property is
consumed.   There seems no reason to doubt that this is wilful
fire-raising, although the motive to the commission of the crime
was not malice to another, but lucre to himself; because, for
that object, he was still willing to destroy his neighbour's property, just as a robber who commits homicide in the course of
his violent depredation is justly considered as actuated by the
*dolus malus* requisite for murder.[4]   Nor does it alter the case,
that the tenant has a right of possession in the subject, for still
he has wilfully consumed what was another's property.   Many
cases, accordingly, have occurred where such an act on the
tenant's part has been charged and sustained as wilful fire-
raising.   Thus, in the case of Margaret Drysdale, May 22.
1826, a charge of wilful fire-raising was sustained against a
woman for burning a house, of which she was tenant, and in
possession.[5]   And in the case of John Martin, July 17. 1822,
it was sustained as wilful fire-raising, and followed by transportation for life, on a restriction where a tenant had set fire to
his shop with a view to defraud the insurers.[6]   So also in the
case of Malcolm Gillespie, George Brownie, and Alexandrina
Campbell, Aberdeen, autumn 1827, the indictment charged

[1] Unreported.—[2] Maclaurin, No. 93.—[3] Burnett, 220.—[4] Hume, i. 132.—
[5] Unreported.—[6] Unreported.

these parties with wilful fire-raising, in respect of their having set fire to the house which Gillespie occupied in Aberdeenshire, called Crombie Cottage, and which was the property of Mr Crombie of Phesdo. There was a nicety in the case, from this circumstance, that the house had been built by Gillespie himself on Mr Crombie's ground, which he held on a nineteen years' lease, and the fire was kindled with a view to defraud insurers, so that there was some doubt whether the crime committed was burning one's own house in order to defraud insurers, or burning another's with that design, and so wilful fire-raising. The indictment charged the crime alternatively under the description of wilful fire-raising, and the fraudulent burning of the pannel's own house to defraud insurers, to meet either view of the house being considered as the property of the landlord or the tenant; but Lords Pitmilly and Alloway were clearly of opinion, upon the principle, *quod solo inedificatum domino soli cedit*, that the house was the landlord's property, and, consequently, that the crime was wilful fire-raising. Gillespie himself had been previously capitally convicted under a charge of forgery; and, as he was the chief delinquent, the libel was restricted as to the others, and they were convicted and sentenced to seven years' transportation.[1] In like manner, in the case of William Sutherland, 15th March 1825, the pannel was charged with wilful fire-raising, for having set fire to a shop, of which he was tenant, to defraud the insurers of the shop goods, which had been insured far above their value. The case was prevented being brought to a decision, from a critical objection to the citation, which was sustained by the Court; but no doubt was entertained by the Court that, in these circumstances, the crime was wilful fire-raising.[2] It may therefore be considered as fixed, that, if the offender's interest in the subject burned is any thing less than the complete right of property; as, for example, if it be that of a tenant, usufructuary, or liferenter, his wilfully setting fire to the subject will be held as amounting to the capital offence [3]

The law is different in England, it being held with them that a tenant in possession, under an agreement for years, is not guilty of arson if he burn the subject.[4] This, however, is against the opinion of Foster;[5] and Lord Mansfield has ex-

[1] Unreported.—[2] Unreported.—[3] Hume, i. 132; Burnett, 216.—[4] Holme's Case, Russell, ii. 487 —[5] Foster, 113, 115.

pressed great regret at the law being so settled.[1] But they hold that, if the tenant wilfully sets fire to the house inhabited by himself in order to burn the adjoining house, and the adjoining house is in consequence burned, this is undoubtedly arson.[2]

5. It is wilful fire-raising if the proprietor of a house wilfully burn his own house in the possession of a liferenter or tenant.

The converse of the case just considered may occur; that of a person who burns his own house in the possession of a liferenter or tenant, either from malice at these parties, or from a design to defraud insurers with whom he had insured the subject. In such a case the crime is wilful fire-raising.[3] So it was found by the Court in the case of John Buchanan, January 15. 1728, who had set fire to his own house in the possession of a liferentrix; this was held to be wilful fire-raising.[4] But if the tenant or liferenter have not actually obtained possession, but only had a title to enter, there seems no authority for holding that the landlord or fiar, by burning the house in that intermediate state, is guilty of the capital offence; nor do the same reasons of justice and expedience occur in this case as the other, there being none of the imminent peril to life or property which must occur if fire be set to a building inhabited by others.[5] For the same reason there is no authority for extending the capital sanction to the case of a landlord who burns a subject over which another has a lien or security, not followed by actual possession, in the case of an adjudger or holder of an heritable bond.[6]

In England, if a landlord or reversioner set fire to his own house, of which another is in possession under a lease from himself or from those from whom he derived his estate, it is arson; for, during the lease, they consider the house as the property of the tenant.[7] And it has been held by the Twelve Judges that it is not arson for a man to burn his own house, though surrendered to the use of a mortgagee, but remaining in his own possession.[8]

[1] Leach, 1. 242.—[2] Ibid.—[3] Hume, 1. 133, Burnett, 216.—[4] Ibid.—[5] Hume, 1. 133.—[6] Burnett, 217.—[7] Foster, 115, Blackstone, iv. 221.—[8] Spalding's Case, Leach, 1. 108

6. Wilful burning one's own house with a view to defraud insurers, is an offence punishable with the highest
arbitrary pain, but not wilful fire-raising, unless the house
were so situated as to endanger other houses, and they in
consequence are burnt, from a fire thus maliciously or
fraudulently kindled, in which case the capital crime is
completed.

Towards the completion of the crime of wilful fire-raising,
it is indispensable that the subject burned shall be the property
of *another*.[1] If, therefore, a man burn his *own house*, whether
out of whim, caprice, or from a design to defraud insurers, it
is not wilful fire-raising, but an inferior offence.[2] Indeed, if
the house burned be at a distance from any other, so that there
is no danger of the flames spreading to any adjoining buildings,
and the fire be kindled without any fraudulent design, it is evidently not a point of dittay at all.[3]

But if one burn his own house adjoining that of a neighbour,
out of spite to that neighbour, and from the design of consuming his house, and the flames accordingly spread and accomplish the object, this is wilful fire-raising.[4] Nay, if the burning the pannel's own house be attended with obvious risk to
adjoining tenements, and one of them be actually burned in
consequence, the guilty party, as for *culpable and reckless fire-
raising*, is amenable to a severe punishment.[5]

In the case, of too frequent occurrence of late years, of the
pannel's having burned his own house, which he had insured
at a high rate of insurance, the criminal act, as a fraud of the
worst kind, is punishable with the very highest arbitrary pains,
but it is not capital.[6] This holds equally whether the fraud
have taken effect or not, by recovery of the money from the
underwriters, and though only the pannel's own house have
been destroyed.[7] The first case in which this point occurred
was that of Thomas Muir and James Cant, December 6. 1773,
who were charged with " wilful fire-raising, especially when
committed to defraud insurers," and there the libel set forth
that the house burned was the property of the pannels. It was

[1] Burnett, 215.—[2] Hume, i. 134; Burnett, 215.—[3] Ibid.—[4] Ibid.—[5] Burnett, 215.—[6] Hume, i. 134; Burnett, 217.—[7] Hume, i. 134.

objected to the libel, that this is not wilful fire-raising, but fraud, and informations were ordered to be given in; before advising which, the pannels gave in a petition praying to be transported for life, which was accordingly done.[1]   Again, in the case of John Ker, 19th December 1791, it appeared that the pannel was proprietor of a tenement of houses near Dunbar, possessed partly by himself and partly by his tenants, which he had insured much above their value in the Sun Fire Office of London.  The libel charged wilful fire-raising, especially when committed with intent to defraud insurers, and then set forth that the houses burned were partly possessed by tenants and partly by the pannel.  Informations were ordered, and the Public Prosecutor restricted the libel, which was found relevant.[2]  The point cannot be said, therefore, to have received an express determination; but, from the course adopted by the Prosecutor in these two cases, it may fairly be concluded that he had no great chance of obtaining in either case a capital conviction; and indeed the principles of law, as well as the authority of our criminal writers, are clearly in favour of the milder construction.[3]

One point, however, seems perfectly settled.  If, in consequence of the flames thus kindled by a proprietor from a fraudulent design in his own house, his neighbour's house is burned, this is wilful fire-raising.[4]  The case is analogous to homicide committed in pursuance of an intent to commit a felony, which is unquestionably murder.

In England, it is fixed, that if one set fire to his own house maliciously and unlawfully, in order to defraud an insurance office, and from the flames thus raised a neighbour's house is consumed, this is arson; but, if his own house only is consumed, it is at common law only misdemeanour.[5]  And the burning a man's own house in a town, and near other houses, so as to endanger other houses, though the case does not fall within the definition of arson, yet at common law it is a great misdemeanour, deserving of the most exemplary punishment.[6]  In an indictment for arson, they justly hold it indispensable that the ownership of the house should be correctly stated, so as to shew it to be the house of another;[7] and, therefore, an in-

---

[1] Burnett, 217.—[2] Ibid. 219; Hume, i. 134.—[3] Ibid.—[4] Ibid.—[5] Isaac's Case, East. ii. 1031   Russell, ii. 487.—[6] Probert's Case, East. ii. 1031; Russell, ii. 489.—[7] Menton's Case, East. ii. 1033; Russell, ii. 494.

dictment is bad which merely states that the prisoner set fire to a house in a certain parish, without specifying to whom it belongs.[1]  With regard to the nature of the possession, they hold that a house, in part of which a man lives, and other parts of which he lets to lodgers, may be described as his house.  It appeared that Fearne occupied part of the house, and let out the rest to lodgers: the room set fire to belonged to the prisoner: five months before the fire Fearne was discharged as an insolvent debtor, and had previously executed an assignment, including this house, to Davie, who never took possession.  In these circumstances, the Twelve Judges held that the *whole house* was in the possession of Fearne; the possession by his tenants being his possession: and they were also of opinion that the prisoner's own room might be deemed his house.[2]

By Mr Peel's act, 7th and 8th Geo. IV. c. 30, it is made capital " unlawfully and maliciously to set fire to any church or chapel, or any house, stable, coach-house, out-house, warehouse, office, shop, mill, malt-house, hop-work, barn or granary, or any building or erection used in carrying on any trade or manufacture, or any branch thereof, whether in the possession of the offender or any other person, with intent to injure or defraud any person."  This statute, intended to prevent fraudulent fire-raising to defraud insurers, does not extend to Scotland.

7. By special statute it is capital to burn, or otherwise wilfully destroy, any insured vessel, with intent to prejudice the underwriters or others concerned.

A British statute, 29th Geo. III. c. 46, enacts, " That if any person shall maliciously and unlawfully set fire to, or in anywise destroy, any ship or vessel, whether the same be complete or in an unfinished state, or shall maliciously and unlawfully set fire to, cast away, or in anywise destroy any ship or vessel, with intent thereby to prejudice any owner or part owner of such ship or vessel, or of any goods on board the same, or any person that hath underwritten, or shall underwrite any policy of insurance upon such ship or vessel, or on the freight thereof, or upon any goods on board the same; every such offender shall suffer death as a felon "  This statute

[1] Rickman's Case, East. ii. 1034 — [2] Ball's Case, 1824, Russell, ii. 495

extends to Scotland,[1] although the statute in which it is re-
enacted, Mr Peel's act, 7th and 8th Geo. IV. c. 30, is only applicable to England.

8. Not only the wilful burning of houses, but of corns,
coal-heughs, and woods, is by the common and statute
law of Scotland a capital offence.

By the statute 1526, c. 10, the crime of wilful fire-raising
is raised to the rank of treason. " The auld lawis," it says,
shall be keepit, with this additioune, that quha cummis and
byrnis fock in their housis, and all byrnings of *housis and cornis*
and wilful fire-raising, be treason."[2]    The pains of treason
were afterwards applied by 1592, c. 148, to the burn-rs of
coal-heughs; and, by 7th Anne, c. 21, fire-raising, in all cases
where it had been raised to the rank of treason, is again lowered to a capital crime.    By 1st Geo. I. c. 48, § 4, it is enacted :
" That if any person shall maliciously set on fire or burn, or
cause to be burnt, any wood, underwood, or coppice, or any
part thereof, such malicious setting on fire, burning, or causing
to be burned, shall be, and is hereby declared and made felony, and the offender and *offenders* shall suffer and be liable
to all the penalties and forfeitures, as other felons by the law
now are ; and, where such offences are committed in that part
of Great Britain called Scotland, such offender and offenders
shall suffer and be liable, as wilful fire-raisers, according to an
act passed in the 7th of Queen Anne, entitled, ' An Act for
Improving the Union of the Two Kingdoms.' "

The species of fire-raising, therefore, which are by the Scotch
law capital, are the wilful burning of houses, corns, woods,
coal-heughs, and ships, with intent to defraud.    In the case of
Andrew Ross, Inverness, 27th September 1822, the indictment
charged the prisoner with wilful fire-raising, in respect that he
had set fire to a heath in a muir contiguous to a wood, with intent to consume the wood ; that a large tract of the heath was
consumed, and that the fire spread to within a few yards of
the wood, and that it was with great difficulty extinguished.
It is evident that this was not the capital crime, but an attempt only to its commission ; for although, if the fire had
spread from the heath to the wood, it would have been the

[1] Hume, 1. 134.—[2] Thomson's Acts, ii. 316.

same thing as if the flames had been applied to the wood itself; yet as the flames did not reach the wood, it was only an attempt to commit the capital, and an actual commission of the minor, offence of burning heath. The objection to the indictment was accordingly sustained.[1]

Corn is equally protected by the capital pains, whether it is in the field growing, or cut down in the stack-yard or barn.[2] In the cases of William and Alexander Fraser, November 4. 1720, and David Young, July 24. 1728, capital convictions took place for burning corns, in both of which cases they were in the barn-yard.[3]

9. Wilful burning of heath, furze, mosses, stacks of fuel or hay, or any sort of moveables, though not by law capital, is an indictable offence, punishable according to the magnitude and peril of the offence with severe arbitrary pains.

The wilful combustion of heath, hay, whins, furniture, carriages, wooden articles, clothes, books, or moveables of any sort, is an offence punishable with the highest arbitrary pains; but it is not wilful fire-raising, or at least it is not the capital branch of that crime, and should not, correctly speaking, be indicted under that name.[4] It constitutes an offence which may be called, " the wilfully and feloniously burning any heath, muir," &c. according to the article to which the flames have been communicated. In the cases of Peter Lamont and James Gray, Aberdeen, autumn 1826, the setting fire to heath was indicted under the name of " malicious mischief, particularly the maliciously setting fire to any heath, moss, or pasture, belonging to or in the occupation of others;" but the flight of the pannels prevented the case being tried.[5]

10. Attempts at wilful fire-raising, or instigations to commit, or threats of perpetrating it, are cognizable offences, and punishable with arbitrary pains.

As in other cases of atrocious and dangerous offences, attempt at wilful fire-raising is a crime cognizable by the criminal courts, and justly warranting the infliction of severe arbitrary pains.[6] In judging of the degree of progress which the

[1] Hume. i. 121.—[2] Ibid. i. 131.—[3] Ibid. i. 132.—[4] Ibid. i. 131.—[5] Unreported.—[6] Hume, i. 135 , Burnett, 222.

offender's design must have made, the same rule is adopted as in other cases, viz. that *si devenit ad actum proximum* : if the combustible has *nearly* produced the desired effect of burning the house or corns, the attempt is held to have been committed.[1]   If, therefore, the furniture has been set on fire, and in part consumed, though no part of the tenement itself has been in flames; or if the lighted torch has been applied to the roof or joists, or the ignited peat put under the stack, though neither the wood nor the corns have begun to burn, the attempt has been completed.   Accordingly, in the case of Walter Buchanan, January 15. 1728, the casting a kindled peat into a house with the design to burn the tenement was found relevant to infer an arbitrary punishment, though the fire had not taken effect.[2]   In the case of Robina Spence, also, February 24. 1824, a libel for attempt at wilful fire-raising was sustained, where the mischief set forth in the indictment was, that the pannel had set fire to a mattress in her room, with design to burn the house, which was her landlord's property, but the flames were extinguished before they had spread farther than the mattress itself   After the libel was found relevant, it was remitted to the Sheriff for trial of the *attempt*; and the pannel was convicted, and sentenced to two years' imprisonment.[3]

Farther, the soliciting or instigating others to commit fire-raising is itself a point of dittay by our practice, even although they refuse compliance, and nothing beyond the mere *conatus* has taken place.   In the case, accordingly, of William and Alexander Fraser, November 14. 1720, the Court found the inviting or soliciting others to set fire to a barn, or corns in the barn-yard, relevant to infer an arbitrary punishment.   The libel stated, that the persons tampered with had refused the solicitation ; notwithstanding which the prisoners were transported for life.[4]

Nay, so far does our practice carry its jealousy of this offence, that the mere uttering of threats of fire-raising, though unaccompanied either with any solicitation of others, or attempt at individual performance, is relevant to infer an inferior punishment.   Accordingly, in the cases of Grizel Somerville, April 5. 1686, and Ludovick Grant, June 7. 1712, such threats were sustained as sufficient to infer an arbitrary punishment, though no damage had ensued in either case.[5]   The

[1] Hume, i 135.—[2] Ibid.—[3] Unreported.—[4] Hume, i. 136.—[5] Ibid. i 135.

same course was adopted in the case of Patrick Hepburn, March 12. 1714, where fire had been raised in the premises soon after the threats, but without any evidence of its having been done in connection with them.[1]

11. Wilful fire-raising is one of the pleas of the Crown, and can only be tried in the Justiciary Court; but attempts, instigations, or threats to commit the crime, can be competently tried in inferior tribunals.

From its peculiar danger and atrocity, the wilful fire-raising has for long been ranked as one of the pleas of the Crown, and as such can only be tried in the Justiciary Court. But the inferior delinquencies of attempts, instigations, or threats to commit it, can be competently made the subject of trial and punishment in inferior tribunals. In the case, accordingly, already mentioned of Robina Spence, February 24. 1824, the alternative charge of attempt at fire-raising was remitted from the Justiciary Court to the Sheriff of Edinburgh; and though the sentence pronounced was diminished by the Court of Justiciary, on account of its severity, on a bill of suspension, no doubt was expressed of his competence to try the offence [2]

12. Legal evidence in cases of wilful fire-raising consists, in proof, that the fire was intentionally raised, accompanied by such direct or circumstantial evidence as leaves no reasonable doubt that the pannel was implicated in that offence.

There is, perhaps, no crime in which evidence is so difficult as in this, both on account of the secrecy and privacy with which it is usually committed, and the devouring nature of the element raised, which destroys all the usual traces and *indiciæ* by which in other instances guilt is detailed. The spectacle of a wilful and an accidental fire is the same; and the more complete the success of the enterprize, the more thoroughly are all the means of detecting it destroyed. Nevertheless, it is not to be imagined that, on account of this difficulty, the prosecutor is to be considered as relieved from any part of his obligation to make out his case; but only that, in default of direct testi-

[1] Hume, i. 135.—[2] Unreported

mony, which is very seldom to be obtained, a conviction may be legally and safely obtained on circumstantial evidence, if it be only sufficiently weighty.[1] To require direct evidence of the wilful completion of the crime would be in most, and generally the worst cases, to secure absolute impunity to the criminal.[2]

Unlike other crimes, the proof of the *corpus delicti* in wilful fire-raising is generally mixed up with that which goes to fix guilt upon the prisoner; nor, indeed, in cases where direct evidence cannot be obtained can it well be otherwise, as the first effect of the flames taking effect is to consume the combustibles which raised it. The *indiciæ* which go to substantiate at once the *corpus delicti* and the guilt of the prisoner, are chiefly the facts that the fire broke out suddenly in an uninhabited house, or in different parts of the same building; that combustibles have been found strewed about, or dropped at intervals, or placed in convenient situations to excite a combustion, as under beds, under thatch, under a stack, &c.; that the prisoner had a cause of ill-will at the sufferer, or had been heard to threaten him, or had been seen purchasing combustibles, or carrying them in the direction of the premises, or lounging about them at suspicious hours. To this is to be added, where the fire was raised to defraud insurers, the important facts of the premises or its furniture having been insured at a high value, or in different offices at the same time, and of a claim having been made, or attempted to be made, at both offices.

In almost all the convictions for wilful fire-raising which have been obtained, the evidence has been of a circumstantial kind. In the noted case of Meldrum, August 1663, who was convicted of burning the Tower of Frendraught, under circumstances of great atrocity, the whole proof, both as to the *corpus* and the prisoner's accession, was circumstantial, but there seems some doubt whether the *indiciæ* rested on were sufficient to warrant the prisoner's conviction.[3] In the case of Phennick, June 1670, the chief circumstances founded on were the declaration of the prisoner, her being seen near to, or at the house, at the time, denying there was fire in it, refusing the keys when asked for, and exhibiting evident marks of confusion.[4] These circumstances certainly inferred suspicion, but

[1] Burnett, 566; Hume, i 128.—[2] Burnett, 507.—[3] Hume, i 129.—[4] Burnett, 568

they do not amount to legal evidence. In Cunningham's case, 30th July 1677, stronger presumptions were accumulated: he was a servant at Glammis, and had been dismissed his master's service the day before; he had been seen preparing combustibles, was found near the house immediately after the fire, could give no account of himself, pretended he had not seen the flames, and when seized endeavoured to make his escape. He was convicted.[1] In Young's case, June 1738, the *induciæ* chiefly insisted on were threats and malice on account of a lawsuit, being seen lurking about the house a few nights before the fire, and on the night of the fire being seen taking a burning peat from his house, putting it in an earthen pitcher, going away with it, not returning till next morning, and when apprehended trying to escape. The jury found the libel not proven; and something certainly was awanting to fill up the measure.[2] In the case of Burnett, Aberdeen, autumn 1784, a conviction was obtained on the following grounds; that the pannel was seen a short time before the fire, near the house, which he pretended he had used to light a tobacco-pipe, but which he had never used in that way, accompanied by evidence, though slight, of previous enmity.[3] Much stronger evidence was procured, but deemed insufficient by the majority of the jury, in the case of Margaret Fallardale or Drysdale, May 26. 1826. It there appeared, that the prisoner, who kept a house of bad fame in the West Bow, at Edinburgh, of which she was tenant, had insured her furniture in two different offices, at the same time, for much more than their probable value; that on the night of the fire she was sitting in her room with a witness, and made no attempt to put it out, nor expressed any astonishment or alarm at its occurrence; that she made out a list of furniture she had lost, which was much larger than that contained in another list which her landlord had made out on a petition for sequestration; and that she made an affidavit with a view to claiming the value of this larger list from one of the insurance offices No reasonable doubt in these circumstances could exist of the prisoner's participation in the crime, and the Court held it clearly proved but the jury thought fit by a majority to acquit.[4] In the case of William Douglas, May 28. 1827, it was proved that the prisoner was seen coming down the stair

---

[1] Burnett, 558.—[2] Ibid 869.—[3] Ibid.—[4] Unreported

from the room in which he lodged in his master's house, and that a smoke and smell of fire was immediately perceived; and when the inmates of the house went up they found a candle placed under a chest of drawers containing clothes, so as inevitably to set it on fire, and the clothes and other articles in the room burning. The prisoner was convicted, but being proved to have been insane at the time, was ordered to be confined for life.[1]

Direct evidence, however, has been obtained in some cases Thus, in the case of Isobel Nicolson, August 1711, the prisoner had been actually seen with her hand at the thatch of the house, where the fire broke out immediately after: some burnt flax was found in the roof, which was found to be of the same kind with that in the prisoner's master's house She confessed her guilt extrajudicially before the Justices of the Peace. She was seen shortly before near the place, and she had previously threatened the owner of the burnt dwelling. In these circumstances, a conviction was of course obtained.[2] In the case of John Hood, Dumfries, April 11. 1824, the case rested almost entirely on the judicial confession of the prisoner in one of his declarations. He pleaded guilty, and was transported for life.[3] Lastly, in the case of James Brownie and Alexandrina Campbell, Aberdeen, autumn 1827, the evidence consisted almost entirely of the depositions of two *socii criminis*, who turned King's evidence, and detailed the whole circumstances of the wilful conflagration, with proof of the insuring the house and furniture by Gillespie, the principal party in the plot, in two insurance offices at more than their values, taking both together, and the taking of steps by him to claim the sums insured from both offices. They were convicted and transported; Gillespie himself having been previously sentenced to be executed for forgery.[4]

[1] Unreported.—[2] Burnett, 569.—[3] Unreported —[4] Unreported.

# CHAPTER XVII.

## OF MALICIOUS MISCHIEF

THE expression *Malicious Mischief*, is indiscriminately applied, in legal language, to the wanton or reckless destruction of property, and the wilful perpetration of injury to the person The more appropriate appellation, however, of the latter offence is Real Injury, and under that head it has already been considered in the chapter relating to Personal Assaults. In this chapter, therefore, that division of Real Injury is alone to be considered which relates to mischief wantonly and maliciously inflicted on property, whether animate or inanimate.

1. At common law, every act of serious and wilful damage done to the property of another, whether from malice or gross misapprehension of legal right, is an indictable offence.

Besides wilful fire-raising, which is the most serious of any, many other kinds of injury to property may be committed, both by individuals and numbers of persons assembled together. Thus to enter a neighbour's lands, with a convocation of servants, and cast down the houses, or corn stacks, or dikes, or to root up or lay waste the woods, or cut away or destroy the crops, or set fire to the peats or coals, or deface inclosures, or break down sluices, aqueducts, or mill-dams, or to destroy or burn boats or nets, or the like, is an undoubted article of dittay at common law.[1] So it was found in regard to casting down houses, in the case of Donald and Charles Robertson, March 9. 1671, and William Leitch and others, November 17 1764;[2] in regard to forcibly intruding into lands, beating and hounding off cattle, breaking down dikes, and the like, in the case of

---

[1] Hume, 1 122.—[2] Ibid.

2

William Leitch, November 17. 1674;[1] in regard to pulling
down a dam-dike, and stopping a mill thereby, in the case of
Glass of Sauchie, December 19. 1718;[2] in regard to entering
nursery grounds, treading down and destroying plants, destroying turf, and the like, in the case of Rigg of Morton, December 6. 1714; in regard to poisoning poultry, by mixing arsenic
with their food, in the case of Thomas Billie, November 5.
1600.[3]  In regard to such cases, the general rule seems to be
this; that if serious or extensive mischief is inflicted on property, as by cutting or mangling cattle, sheep, or dogs, the act
in every case forms the fit subject of criminal prosecution, how
covertly soever perpetrated by the offender; but that if the
mischief is of a more inconsiderable kind, or such as may reasonably be supposed to have arisen from a mistaken apprehension of right, or from the excusable desire to vindicate what is
supposed to be one's own property, the acts will not be sustained as a relevant article of *criminal* dittay, unless they are
accompanied with such circumstances of violence or outrage,
as shew an evident disregard of the authority of the magistrate,
in which case the most inconsiderable acts become the fit subject of trial and punishment.[4]

2. By special statute certain acts of malicious mischief
committed against animals at stated times, highly injurious to the public, are punishable with death.

In certain cases of wilful mischief, peculiarly alarming on
account of their danger, or the ease with which they may be
committed, the powers of the common law have been strengthened by special statute.  Thus, by 1581, c. 110, and 1587, c.
83, the breaking or destroying of ploughs or plough-gear, in
time of tilth; the killing, goring, or houghing of oxen, horses,
or other cattle, at seed-time or harvest; and the breaking or
destroying of mills, are declared to be punishable as theft, and
with death.  This, however, is to be understood only where
the damage is done out of malice to the owner, and not from
any sudden anger at the animal itself.[5]  In the case of George
Walter and Ingram Scott, February 20. 1616, the pannels
were condemned to die, under these statutes, for the slaughter-

---

[1] Hume, 1 122.—[2] Ibid.—[3] Ibid 1 124.—[4] Ibid.—[5] Ibid 1 125

F f

ing of sheep; an act of severity which would certainly not be repeated in modern times.

3. The wanton or malicious perpetration of mischief to cattle, animals, or property of any sort, is, in modern practice, visited with an arbitrary punishment, varying according to the magnitude of the offence.

Although the killing of oxen or cattle would certainly not be punished in these days with death; yet, as a most dangerous and diabolical crime, it is visited with the most exemplary arbitrary pains. Thus, in the case of William Wilson junior, Ayr, April 20. 1827, the slaughtering a horse belonging to another was sustained as malicious mischief, and, though the jury thought fit to acquit, the Judge intimated that he considered the offence as deserving of a very serious punishment.[1]  In the case of Peter Clark, Inverary, September 1826, the affixing a stob, armed with iron nails, to the tail of a pony, by which the animal was wounded in the hind legs, was punished, on a confession, with two months' imprisonment.[2]  In the case of Nicolson Muir, Ayr, spring 1825, it was held relevant as malicious mischief, to charge a collier with knocking away the props of a colliery, whereby the roof fell in; but the flight of the party prevented the case being tried.[3]  At Jedburgh, spring 1823, Nicol Burton, convicted of cutting the throats of four sheep, was sentenced to twelve months' imprisonment.[4]  Burning and injuring a chariot, by means of sulphuric acid, was sustained as a relevant article of charge, at Inverary, autumn 1823, in the case of Colin Campbell, though the jury, in the face of the clearest evidence, acquitted the prisoner.[5]  Wilful breaking open a window, by throwing against it a large stone, which shattered and destroyed the frame, was sustained as malicious mischief by Lord Justice-Clerk Boyle, at Glasgow, in September 1829; but the evidence being contradictory, a verdict of not proven was returned.[6]  Cornelius Vaudenburgh, convicted of destroying a large part of the glass-work of a hothouse, at Woodhall, Lanarkshire, was, at Glasgow, spring 1828, sentenced to nine months' imprisonment in Bridewell.[7] J. Ingram, convicted of slaughtering a cow, and stealing the

[1] Unreported.—[2] Unreported.—[3] Unreported.—[4] Unreported.—[5] Unreported.—[6] Unreported.—[7] Unreported.

hide, at Glasgow, spring 1828, was sentenced to fourteen years' transportation.[1] George Monro, July 17. 1831, convicted of maliciously letting some oil-casks run off, whereby oil to the value of £300 was lost, was sentenced to eighteen months confinement in Bridewell; the Court, at the same time, expressing very great doubts whether transportation should not have been the punishment, and none that it was competent.[2]

# CHAPTER XVIII.

### OF COINING, AND UTTERING FALSE COIN.

By the old law of Scotland offences against the coin were, for the most part, raised to the rank of treason; but, without embarrassing the present practice with such matters, which now are more objects of curiosity than use, it is sufficient to explain the law as now practically enforced on the subject of Coining and Issuing False Coin.

1. The uttering false or base coin, knowing it to be false, is an offence at common law, punishable, in ordinary cases, with imprisonment, and in aggravated circumstances, or after previous conviction, with transportation.

Uttering false coin, knowing it to be false, is a very common offence in modern times, and its trial and punishment a material object of inquiry. The rules formerly explained in regard to the uttering of forged notes, are here precisely applicable, so far as the test of what shall amount to a legal uttering, the necessity of proving the guilty knowledge, the relevancy of the charge without any connexion with the actual coiner, and the means by which the guilty knowledge is to be established are concerned. Without doubt, therefore, the mere uttering the base money is a completion of the crime, although it be not accepted, or has been immediately refused, or although no loss whatever has accrued to any party from the act. The prosecutor is bound to prove that the coin passed is bad; that

[1] Unreported.—[2] Unreported.

it was uttered by the prisoner, and that it was uttered by him in the guilty knowledge of its being base; but having done this, he has done all that law deems necessary for a conviction of the offender.

The offence of knowingly uttering false British coin, is, by 15th Geo. II. c. 28, punishable with six months' imprisonment for the first offence; and, in the case of a *common utterer*, with twelve months' imprisonment; and, in the case of a third offence, or of an act of uttering by one previously convicted as a common utterer, with death.[1] There is much doubt whether this statute extends to Scotland;[2] and it seems unnecessary to embarrass ourselves with the inquiry as to whether it does, because the common law of the country possesses powers amply sufficient for the cognizance of the offence. In the case of Weir, Hallywell, and others, July 6. 1699, the vending of false coin, jointly with the procuring materials subservient to the coining, was found relevant only to infer an arbitrary punishment.[3] Ever since this decision, the crime of knowingly uttering or vending false coin has been held a cognizable offence by the common law of Scotland, and its punishment has varied from a few months' imprisonment to transportation.

Thus, in the case of Catherine Macarthur, Perth, April 1822, the prisoner, convicted of four acts of uttering false shillings, was sentenced to six months' imprisonment.[4] Again, in the case of Elizabeth King, or Marshall, September 27 1825, twelve months of Bridewell was inflicted on a confession of one act of uttering a false half-crown, accompanied by three previous convictions in the inferior court for that offence.[5] In the case of Susan Robertson, Perth, spring 1824, the prisoner, on a conviction of six acts of uttering shilling and half-crown pieces, was sentenced to twelve months' imprisonment.[6]

But, though imprisonment is the usual, it is by no means the only, punishment that is in use. In the case of Robert Henderson *alias* Peter Stalker, Aberdeen, September 1827, seven years' transportation was inflicted on the prisoner, on the conviction of uttering a single bad shilling, aggravated by a previous conviction for that offence, and by 180 bad shillings having been found in his possession.[7] In like manner, in the case of William and John Braidwood, 15th March 1830, the High Court

[1] 15th Geo. II c 28.—[2] Hume, 1 565.—[3] Ibid 1 566.—[4] Unreported.—[5] Unreported.—[6] Unreported.—[7] Unreported

inflicted the same punishment on the prisoners, who pleaded guilty to three charges of uttering bad shillings and sixpences, and upon whom a considerable quantity of bad shillings, and some powder and other apparatus for colouring base shillings, had been found.[1]   So also, in the cases of Christian Tweedie, June 22. 1829, and Helen Goodall, February 4. 1830, transportation for seven years was inflicted on the prisoners, who were severally convicted of two acts of uttering false shillings, only aggravated in each case by seven or eight convictions in the Police-court for the same offence.[2]

It is to be observed, too, that although imprisonment is the punishment inflicted, in ordinary cases, of vending false coin, yet this is to be understood only of cases where half-crowns, shillings, and sixpences have been tendered; for the uttering of *gold* coin, whether guineas, half-guineas, sovereigns, or half-sovereigns, has been always put on the same footing with uttering forged notes, and punished, even in the case of a single act, without any aggravation, by transportation.   Thus in the case of John Miller and John Macmillan, Glasgow, April 1828, the pannels, who pleaded guilty to a charge of uttering a forged £1 note, a bad sovereign, and a bad half-sovereign, were sentenced, by Lords Justice-Clerk Boyle and Alloway, to fourteen years' transportation; the Court stating, at the same time, that one half of the punishment was inflicted for the sovereigns, and half for the forged note.[3]   To the same purpose, in various other cases, the pannels have been transported for uttering bad sovereigns, without any other aggravation.[4]

2. In the proof of the coin being bad, it is not necessary to adduce officers of the Mint; the evidence of goldsmiths, or any persons of skill, is sufficient.

All the lieges are presumed to be more or less familiar with the distinction between good and bad coin, and, therefore, in trials for uttering such base pieces of metal, it is not necessary to adduce the officers of the Mint, or any persons engaged in the actual process of coining, but it is sufficient to prove the fact by the opinion of persons, qualified by their habits to form an opinion on such subjects.[5]   In the case, accordingly, of Hugh

[1] Unreported.—[2] Unreported.—[3] Unreported.—[4] Unreported.—[5] Hume, ii. 395

Johnston, Aberdeen, April 1805, the objection was repelled to
the proof of the coin being bad, that it was proved, not by the
officers of the Mint, but by dealers in silver goods.[1]   The like
judgment was given by the whole Court, in the case of John
Glass, June 12. 1826, where no proof was led by the prosecutor that the coin was bad by officers of the Mint, but the Court
held that proof by goldsmiths and other persons skilled in such
matters was perfectly sufficient.[2]   But *some proof* by persons
of skill is necessary; and, accordingly, in that case their Lordships directed an acquittal, because no goldsmiths were adduced.

3. In cases of uttering base coin, it is indispensable
that the coin laid on the table, and proved to be bad,
should be shewn to be the identical one issued by the prisoner; and no evidence can be relied on as sufficient for
this purpose, but the oath of every person into whose
hands it got after being issued, till it was finally marked,
so as to be always distinguishable.

In the uttering of false coin, even more than in the uttering
of forged notes, the most minute and scrupulous chain of evidence is justly required to shew that the piece of metal uttered
by the prisoner is the same as that exhibited to the jury; and
for this sufficient reason, that it is even more difficult to distinguish one coin than one note from another; and, therefore,
the risk is the more imminent of convicting the prisoner,
though he has uttered a different coin from that proved to be
bad.   The only evidence that can with certainty be relied on
as sufficient to make out this vital branch of the case, is the
oath of every person, without exception, who got the coin into
his hand, that the coin he delivered up, or gave to another, is
the same as he received; and this must be continued without
interruption, from the time it left the prisoner's hand, till it is
marked in such a way as to be always distinguishable.   It is
very material to attend to this; because witnesses often say in
precognition, that the coin exhibited to them is the same as
that they saw uttered, where they will hesitate to say so at the
distance of months, in a court of justice, and when, in truth,
they can specify no sufficient *causa scientiæ*, to enable them to

[1] Hume, ii. 395.—[2] Unreported.

distinguish that particular coin from others of a similar denomination. The question which should always be asked from
them, in such circumstances, is, whether they are quite sure
that the coin they put out of their hands is the same as they
got into it; and what grounds they have for their belief that
it is so.

4. The guilty knowledge in uttering base coin must be
established in the same manner, and from the same *indiciæ,* as in cases of uttering forged notes.

As the guilty knowledge is the *inter essentialia* of this offence, the prosecutor must be prepared with such circumstances as shall establish it to the satisfaction of a reasonable
jury. These are the same, for the most part, as in uttering
forged notes, and consist in the discovery of other base coin
about his person, or in his possession, which, if found in concealed situations, or in large quantities, will generally be of itself decisive of his guilt; in the possession by him of powders,
pans, moulds, uncoloured stamped copper, or other articles evidently used for forging money, which is also decisive against
him; in his conduct after issuing the coin; the quantity of
other change which he had about him when he tendered the
piece in question; the account he gives of the way he got the
coin, and the like. Here, too, as in uttering forged notes, the
number of charges brought home to him about the same time
is a most suspicious, and, if not explained, decisive circumstance; for, although it is possible that an innocent man may
have had a quantity of bad coin given him in change, yet it is
highly improbable that this should be accompanied by the necessity, about the same time, of changing them in different
places, and for different purposes. In such a case, therefore,
it lies upon the prisoner to give a rational account of the way
in which he got the coin, and support the statement, if in his
power, by some sort of evidence, and also to give an explanation of the circumstances which led him about the same time
to pass such a quantity of change; and, if he cannot do this,
the only conclusion is, that he is guilty of the offence with
which he is charged.

Here, too, as in uttering forged notes, it is competent to lead
evidence of unsuccessful attempts to utter, not as substantive

charg.     ..it as articles of evidence, tending to fix the guilty
knowlec..e in the completed charges libelled against the prisoner; but equally here as there, where this is intended, a fair
and intelligible narrative should be given in the libel of these
unsuccessful attempts by time, place, and circumstances, and
where this is not done, the proof of them should be stopped [1]
The same observation also here applies which was there made,
viz. that, in drawing inferences from the conduct of the prisoner, it is his conduct *before* the coin is challenged as bad, or
he is apprehended, which is chiefly to be relied on, and not after that event; because, on the one hand, no innocent man
would take precautions, or send forward others in issuing
coin, which he was not aware was bad; and, on the other,
many persons, though innocent, may strive to escape from the
officers of justice, or, when threatened with a jail, evince symptoms of alarm, hardly if at all distinguishable from those of actual guilt.

5. Issuing base coin, at an under value, to others, for
the purpose of being uttered to the world, is an indictable
offence, punishable with an arbitrary pain.

On the same principles on which it is justly held that the
act of vending forged notes, at an under value, for the purpose
of their being circulated among the lieges by the vender, as
genuine, is an offence cognizable by the common law, and punishable with an arbitrary pain, it must follow that the vending
of base coin at an under value, for the same fraudulent purpose, is a similar crime. No pros.~utions for this offence have
yet taken place; but, from the s.a'   .y of law in other particulars, there can be no doubt that.  ~   .. they shall occur, they
will be sustained as relevant, without the aid of any new enactment.

6. In cases of actual coinage, the crime is completed by
the bare act of counterfeiting or throwing off the coin,
though not accompanied with any act of uttering.

The essence of the crime of false coining does not consist in
the mere act of striking off a piece of metal with a die, or even

---

[1] *Supra,* p 416

tendering it in payment, but in imitating some of the current
coin of the realm. In this there is a double offence, if the coin
be an imitation of gold or silver coin, by a coloured or coated
baser metal, in the usurpation of the royal prerogative, which
alone extends to the coining of money of that precious kind,
and in the fraud thus commenced or intended upon the public.[1]
And, even although the coin contain no mixture of alloy, but
be really worth the sum which it bears, still it is a very high
offence to interfere with the royal prerogative in this particular, or usurp the exercise of those acts, which, for wise and sufficient purposes, the legislature has, in every country, confined
to the sovereign authority.[2] But, on the other hand, it is only
the coinage of some of the current coin of the realm which
falls under this rule; and, therefore, the mere striking a piece
of metal with a die, and even offering it in payment as a medium of exchange, is nowise an illegal act, if it be not formed
after the similitude, or intended to pass for some known national coin.[3]

The offence of false coining is committed by the bare act of
counterfeiting or throwing off the coin, in imitation of the current coin of the realm, and does not require, as forgery, for its
completion, any act of uttering or tendering either to an associate for an under value, or to the public as genuine, because
the offence of usurping the royal prerogative has been already
completed by the very act of the coinage[4] The rule also, that
the coining, to be a subject of prosecution, must be in imitation
of some of the current coin of the realm, must be understood
in a reasonable sense; for certainly the law will not permit the
royal prerogative to be usurped, and the punishment of the
offence evaded, by the mere device of making the coin differ,
in some minute and hardly perceptible particulars, from the
current national coin.[5] The principle here is the same as in
the forgery of bank-notes, viz. that the offence is complete if
the article manufactured bears such a resemblance to the genuine one, as would deceive persons of ordinary understanding,
in the inconsiderate intercourse of daily life.

This principle is fully recognised in the English law.[6] Thus
in the case of John and Patrick Welsh, in 1785, the Twelve
Judges were of opinion that a counterfeit shilling, though quite

---

[1] Hume, i. 565.—[2] Ibid.—[3] Ibid.—[4] Ibid.; Hale, i. 215, Russell, i. 61.—
[5] Hume, i 565.—[6] Russell, i. 59, Hale, i. 178, East i. 164

smooth, and without impression of any sort, was sufficient to support an indictment for coining, having a reasonable likeness and similitude to the genuine coin, which time has so defaced, and which yet passes in circulation.[1] The same decision was given in the case of J. Wilson, in 1783.[2] It has been held too, that, where the false coining is effected by means of melting down a small quantity of silver among a large quantity of baser metal, and then putting the piece of metal into aquafortis, which brings all the silver to the surface, the offence was completed as soon as the blanks had been dipped in the aquafortis, for that brought out the silver, and only required rubbing to make them pass.[3] But, on the other hand, where the false coin is so imperfect as not to be passable, the offence of counterfeiting will not be held to be completed, as where the prisoner had forged the impression of a half guinea on a piece of gold, which was hammered but not rounded, the Judges held the offence not completed, as the thing could not pass for any current coin.[4]

7. The coining of copper or brass money, is, by statutes deemed applicable to Scotland, punishable with an arbitrary pain.

The old Scotch law punished the offence of coining copper or brass money with death.[5] But, in the case of William Deans, November 11. 1729, it was found that, on a conviction for having coined and vended brass and copper money, the pillory and transportation only could be inflicted. This decision renders the difficult question of little importance, whether the English statutes on this subject, 15th Geo. II. c. 28, and 11th Geo. III. c. 40, apply to this country.[6] In truth, the decision seems to imply that they do; for else the pains of law, for which the libel concluded in the case of Deans, must have been death; the undoubted penalty attached by the Scottish statutes to the coiner of copper money[7] At all events, there can be no doubt that, according to the practice of modern times, a restriction of the libel would be interposed to save the offender from this extreme and unsuitable penalty for the crime. In libelling for offences of this sort, it seems proper to

[1] Leach, i. 364; Russell, i. 59.—[2] Leach, i. 285; Russell, 59.—[3] Case's case, Leach, i. 154; Russell, i. 31.—[4] Varley's Case, Leach, i. 76; Russell, i. 60.—[5] Hume, i. 554.—[6] Ibid.—[7] 1469, c. 40; 1696, c. 42.

[illegible] both on the common and statute law of Scotland, and the English statutes.

8. By the Act of the Union, the treason law of England is communicated to Scotland; and, by that law, the coining of gold or silver money of the realm is high treason.

The Act of the Union having transferred the English law of high treason *per aversionem* to this country, and all the more serious offences against the coin having been raised by the statutes of that country to high treason, it becomes necessary to give a summary of their enactments on the subject.

The " king's money " is the only proper subject of high treason by the English law; and it is held that any money once legally made and issued by the king's authority from the Mint, continues to be the king's money till recalled, notwithstanding any change in the authority from which it emanated.[1] The statute 25th Edward III. st. 5. c. 5, declares it to be high treason " if a man counterfeit the king's money;" and, as there are no accessaries in high treason, it follows that all who, by furnishing the necessary tools, or other means, aid or assist in the coining, are as much guilty as he whose hand is employed in the operation.[2] But, by the expression " king's money," is understood gold or silver only, with a certain alloy, constituting what is called *sterling* coin, and issued by the king's authority.[5]

Besides counterfeiting the gold or silver current coin of the realm, the offence of high treason may be committed by marking on the edges of any of the current or diminished coin of the kingdom, or counterfeit coin made to resemble it, with letters or grainings, or other marks or figures, like those on the edges of money coined in the Royal Mint. By 8th and 9th William III. c. 26, § 3, made perpetual by 7th Anne, c. 25, it is enacted, " that if any person other than the person employed in his Majesty's Mint shall mark on the edges any of the current coin of this kingdom; or if any person whatsoever shall mark on the edges any of the diminished coin of this kingdom, or any counterfeit coin, resembling the coin of this kingdom,

[1] East. i. 140; Russell, i. 54.—[2] Russell, i. 53.—[3] East. i. 147; Hale, i c. 17, Russell, i 53.

with letters or grainings, or other marks or figures, like unto those on the edges of money coined on his Majesty's Mint, every such offence shall be adjudged high treason."

It is further provided by 15th Geo II. c. 28, § 1, " That if any person shall wash, gild, or colour any of the lawful silver coin called a shilling or a sixpence, or add to or alter the impression, or any part of the impression of either side of such lawful or counterfeit shilling or sixpence, with intent to make such shilling resemble, or look like or pass for a piece of lawful gold, called a half guinea; or shall file, or anywise alter, wash, or colour any of the brass money called halfpennies or farthings or add to or alter the impression of either side of a halfpenney or farthing, with intent to make a halfpenny resemble, or look like or pass for a lawful shilling, or a farthing resemble or look like or pass for a lawful sixpence, such offenders, their aiders, counsellors, abettors, and procurers shall be guilty of high treason."

By the 8th and 9th William III. c. 26, it is provided, " that if any person shall gild or case over with gold or silver, or with any wash or materials producing the colour of gold or silver, any coin resembling any of the current coin of the kingdom, or any round blanks of base metal, or of coarse gold or coarse silver, of a fit size and figure to be coined into counterfeit milled money, resembling any of the gold or silver coin of this kingdom; or if any person shall gild over any silver blanks of a fit size and figure, to be coined into pieces resembling the current gold coin of this kingdom, all such offenders, their counsellors and procurers, aiders and abettors, shall be guilty of high treason."

The statute 56th Geo. III. c. 68, § 17, enacts that all and every act and acts in force immediately before the passing of that act, respecting the coin of this realm, or the clipping, diminishing, or counterfeiting the same, or respecting any other matters relating thereto, shall be applied and put in execution with respect to the silver coin to be coined in pursuance of the directions of that act, as fully and effectually as if the same were repeated and re-enacted in that act.[1]

The crime of counterfeiting foreign coin, either gold, silver, or copper, is made highly penal by several statutes. By 1st Mary, st. 2, c. 6, and 14th Elizabeth, c. 3, such offences are

---

[1] Russell, i. 56.

declared treason and misprision of treason respectively, according as they relate to foreign coin, current or not current, in this realm.[1] Additional provisions are made on this subject, by the 37th Geo. III. c 126. and the 43d Geo. III. c. 139, &c of which an abstract will be found in Russell's Crown Law.[2]

# CHAPTER XIX.

### OF VIOLATING THE SEPULCHRES OF THE DEAD.

The crime of violating the sepulchres of the dead, is naturally regarded with strong feelings of horror in all civilized states. Nor is this feeling in the least diminished by the acknowledged necessity of procuring subjects for medical instruction, because experience has demonstrated that such subjects can be procured in sufficient quantities by proper police regulations, from vagrants, hospitals, and workhouses, without injuring the feelings of any human being. It has accordingly been always regarded as a point of dittay in the Scotch criminal law.

1. To raise a dead body from the grave is an offence at common law, punishable, in ordinary cases, with imprisonment; but, in cases of great aggravation, or previous conviction, by transportation.

The *crimen violati sepulchri* is not considered as a branch of theft; for our practice acknowledges no property in the remains of deceased relations after they have been committed to the grave; but, as a crime *sui generis*, punishable with an arbitrary pain. Before interment, however, an indictment for theft may be raised for an abstraction of a corpse So it was found in the case of J Mackenzie, Inverness, May 1733.[3] The crime of raising a dead body from the grave was found to be a point of dittay in the case of John Samuel, July 5. 1742; and, since that time,

---

[1] Russell, i. 56.—[2] Ibid. i 57.—[3] Burnett, 124.

the number of cases on the subject have been very numerous.[1] On 14th January 1809, Archibald Begg was banished Scotland for fourteen years, on his own petition, for this offence.[2]   On 15th February 1819, Archibald Wilson was convicted, on his own confession, of raising two dead bodies from their graves, in the Church-yard of Abbotshall, and had sentence of imprisonment for nine months.[3]   On 17th March 1821, George Lawrie, on a confession of one act of raising a dead body, was sentenced to six months' imprisonment.[4]   Thomas Hodge and Andrew Miller, 19th March 1821, convicted of raising two dead bodies from the grave in the Church-yard of Lanark, was imprisoned for six months.[5]   At Glasgow, spring 1828, Henry Gillies was sentenced to nine months' confinement in Bridewell, on a conviction of raising two dead bodies from a church-yard near that city.[6]

But in cases of aggravation, especially such as arise from a previous conviction for the offence, it is competent to inflict the punishment of transportation.   Thus, in the case of Thomas Stevenson *alias* Thomas Hodge, 2d June 1823, the prisoner, on a conviction of raising a dead body from the grave, aggravated by a previous conviction for the same offence, was sentenced to seven years' transportation.[7]   He afterwards received a pardon from the Crown, not from any doubt as to the magnitude of the punishment, but from doubt thrown by medical authorities as to the sufficiency of the evidence as to the identity of the body.

2. In cases where the crime has been committed by students or others, for the sake of study or science, the punishment is usually made as lenient as possible.

In the cases hitherto mentioned, the pannels brought to the bar were professional body-lifters, or at least persons who sold the bodies to others, and engaged in the traffic from motives of gain; but cases of a different and far more melancholy description frequently occur: those of young men of ardent and enthusiastic minds, who undertake such perilous enterprizes from a desire of scientific instruction, and a laudable wish for improvement.   Whenever such cases occur, the Court are care-

[1] Hume, i. 85.—[2] Ibid.—[3] Ibid.—[4] Ibid.—[5] Ibid.—[6] Unreported.—[7] Hume, i. 86.

ful, while they sustain of course the relevancy of the charge, equally, as in other instances, to apportion the punishment to the diminished delinquency of the case. Thus, in the case of John Campbell, Aberdeen, 29th April 1815, the pannel, a student of medicine in that place, who had raised a dead body from the grave for his own study, was ordered to be imprisoned only fourteen days, and to pay a fine of £100 to the Infirmary of Aberdeen.[1] On the same principle, in the case of Alexander Crombie Matthew, Aberdeen, autumn 1826, the prisoner, also a student of medicine, who had, from the same motive, lifted a body in the Garioch, was sentenced to one months' imprisonment, and to pay a fine of £20.

3. The act of attempting to raise a dead body from the grave, is a point of dittay at common law, as well as the completed act.

Sometimes it happens that the prisoners, in the act of carrying into execution their design, are interrupted. In such case the attempt to commit the crime is a relevant point of dittay, punishable with an arbitrary pain. So it was found in the case of George Campbell, John Ker, and George Maclean, 21st June 1819, who was indicted alternatively for " violating or attempting to violate the sepulchres of the dead." An indiscriminate relevancy was found on both charges; and it appeared on the proof that they were interrupted and taken, after they had raised the turf from a grave and dug up a portion of the mould. They were found guilty of attempting to violate the sepulchres of the dead, as libelled, and sentenced to be imprisoned twelve months, as the thing was done under circumstances of considerable aggravation.[2] In like manner, John M'Quilkan, 11th February 1828, was convicted of opening a grave in the church-yard of Libberton, with intent to carry away a corpse.[3] He had opened the grave and affixed the instrument in the head, but without having actually lifted the body. The Court held, that if the body had been raised out of the shroud, though ever so little, the crime would have been completed. He was sentenced to six months' hard labour in Bridewell.

---

[1] Hume, i. 85.—[2] Ibid.—[3] Syme, 321.

4. It is indispensable that the prisoner should be convicted of raising the identical body from the grave, set forth in the indictment, and if it turn out to be another body, he is entitled to an acquittal.

An indictment for this offence to be relevant must not set forth in general that the prisoner has lifted dead bodies from the grave, but that he has lifted an identical body or bodies, described by name and former place of residence. The description of the body must be correct by name, trade, parish, and county; and a variation in any of these particulars, between the evidence on the trial and the statements in the libel, will be fatal to the charge. In the case, accordingly, of Henry Gillies, Glasgow, spring 1828, it was set forth in one of the charges that the prisoner had raised the body of " *Robina* Macneil, daughter of Archibald Macneil, cotton-spinner." It appeared on the proof that the girl's name was not *Robina*, but *Archibin*, a contraction for *Archibina*, and that she had been christened by that name. An acquittal was immediately directed by the Court on that charge.[1] But it is not necessary that the name or abode of the person interred should in every instance be set forth in the libel, or proved at the trial; for if the person were a pauper, vagrant, or one whose name or residence was not known, it is sufficient to describe her as such without any farther designation. So it was found in regard to one of the charges in the case of Henry Gillies, Glasgow, spring 1828, already mentioned.

It is indispensable of course in all trials for this offence, that the interment of the body libelled shall be first proved, and then that the body raised was that body. It is very necessary to be cautious in the consideration of the proof of the identity of the body raised with that interred; for, *a priori*, it could not be imagined how like one body, after it has been some time in the earth, is to another. Of this a curious instance occurred in the case of Thomas Stevenson or Hodge, 2d June 1823, already mentioned. The witnesses there swore positively that the body found in the prisoner's possession was the body of a young woman who had been interred in the parish of Larbert about three weeks before, and their testimony was so positive

[1] Unreported.

that it outweighed with the jury the evidence of several medical gentlemen adduced for the prisoner, who declared that, from the state in which the body was when discovered, it *could not* have been that of a person interred so long before. After conviction, however, the prisoner demonstrated that the body taken was *not* that of the young woman which it was supposed to be, but of another woman buried a few days before the crime was committed with which he was charged, and that he had himself raised the body of the other some weeks before, and sold her to a medical man in Edinburgh. It was on this being substantiated that he received the royal pardon, already mentioned.

# CHAPTER XX.

## OF PERJURY.

PERJURY, or the judicial affirmation of falsehood upon oath, is justly regarded as a transgression of a most heinous nature, both as implying a wilful disregard of the sanction of an oath, and as tending directly to undermine the security on which all judicial proceedings and the most important contracts of life are founded. But as the penalties attached to it are severe, so it is justly held necessary that its perpetration should be committed in a clear and unequivocal manner.

1. It is essential to the crime of perjury that a direct and unequivocal falsehood has been affirmed.

If either the true state of the fact, or the true sense of the pannel's words, be at all doubtful; or if they can in any reasonable way be reconciled with the truth, or with an innocent intention, a charge of perjury will not lie. Towards the relevancy of such a charge, it is indispensable that a direct and absolute falsehood has been affirmed; one, concerning which there is no possibility of doubt, uncertainty, mistaken recollection, or eventual. Accordingly, in the case of Archibald Mackillop, November 8th 1784, it appeared that this man had been a witness with others in the trial of certain revenue-officers, and had sworn favorrably to the pannels. Among other things he had sworn that they addressed the revenue-officers in a moderate and inoffensive manner, " desiring them to walk soberly, and make no disturbance." For this he was indicted for perjury, inasmuch as it was offered to be proved, that the men in question went up violently to the officers and demanded their arms, and threatened to blow them up if they resisted. It was objected by the pannels that these circumstances were not conclusive, inasmuch as the two statements might relate to different periods of the affray; and the Court, accordingly, in their interlocutor of relevancy, made an exception of this article of the charge.[2] To the same purpose, in the case of Robert Orrock, December 24 1711, the pannel had sworn as arrestee in a process of forthcoming, that he owed to Craig, the common debtor, such a sum by bond, and so much more as the residue of the price of malt. In truth he owed him a still greater sum by bill; but the bill might have been omitted from inadvertency, since no question was put about it; and having deponed that he owed a larger sum than that contained in the letters of arrestment, the pannel might naturally have conceived that the subject of the reference was exhausted, and that he was not bound to detail any thing farther in regard to his private affairs. In these circumstances the libel was justly found not relevant.[3] Indeed, from the proceedings in the case of Martin Gray, 6th July 1718, it may be inferred, that it is not possible to make a relevant charge in a case of this description upon a mere omission, unless the circumstance omitted was specially put as an interrogatory, and the prisoner distinctly swore to its non existence.[4]

Such being the just strictness of the law in this particular, it is indispensable that every libel for this offence should set forth specifically and distinctly in what particular, and for what reason the affirmation on oath is charged as having been false. In the case, accordingly, of Lawson of Westerton, June 27. 1795, who was charged with perjury for taking the trust oath, though he well knew " that his pretended title thereto

[2] Hume, i. 366; Burnett, 393.—[3] Hume, i. 367.—[4] Ibid.—[4] Ibid.; Burnett, 394.

was nominal and fictitious," the Court found the libel irrelevant, in respect the particulars were not specified from which it was inferred that the title was fictitious.[1]

2. The falsehood, to amount to perjury, must have been affirmed absolutely; under the limitation, however, that an affirmation of *non memini* or *nihil novi*, if made in circumstances where the recollection must have been fresh, will not elude the punishment.

The falsehood must have been directly affirmed; that is to say, a person shall not be liable to a prosecution for perjury if he has sworn doubtfully, or according to the best of his recollection, and with reference to such things about which, from their distant date or otherwise, he might naturally be uncertain.[2] For this limitation must, in all such cases, be distinctly understood, that if the matter concerning which the oath was taken was recent, and such as must have been fresh in the recollection of the swearer, he shall not escape the pains of perjury by pretending imperfect recollection on such a subject.[3] Accordingly, in the case of George Montgomery, January 19. 1716, the defence of want of distinct recollection was repelled, in regard to a consent given to the preference of certain creditors, though it was alleged to have been made upwards of two years before.[4] It is always to be recollected, in such cases, that a witness is bound to tell the truth, and the *whole truth*, by the oath he takes; and that, therefore, the concealment of truth, by suppressing what is recollected, or pretending indistinctness of recollection in what must be well known, is as much a violation of the oath as a direct allegation of what is known to be false.[5]

3. The falsehood must be wilfully affirmed, as to a matter of fact or undoubted notoriety, by one who knows the truth, and out of malice, partiality, or some corrupt motive, resolves to suppress or alter it.

The wilful nature of the false affirmation is as necessary to a charge of perjury, as the knowledge of goods being stolen to one

---

[1] Hume, i. 368.—[2] Ibid.; Burnett, 203.—[3] Ibid.—[4] Hume, i 368.—[5] Ibid.

of respect of theft.[1] In the case, accordingly, of Gabriel Halliday, February 1797, a libel for perjury was found not relevant, in respect it was not alleged that the falsehood had been wilfully affirmed.[2]

It results from this, that, in the ordinary case, the oath must be to a matter of fact, and not to one of opinion, inference, or apprehension.[3] If, therefore, the matter sworn to be one of opinion merely, as a medical opinion, an oath of calumny, or in lawburrows, it cannot in the general case be made the foundation of a prosecution for perjury.[4] But this is true only in the general case, for if the oath in lawburrows be emitted in circumstances which clearly and indisputably imply a falsehood, it may still be the subject of criminal prosecution.[5] In like manner, though an oath of calumny, or on a *meditatio fugæ*, cannot in the general case be made the ground-work of criminal proceedings, in so far as relates to the opinion which a party entertains of his own case, concerning which the frequency of mental delusion is well known. Yet if it occurs in circumstances where misconception was impossible, as if a party pursues on a bond or bill of which he is proved to have received payment recently before, or knowingly to have the discharge in his possession, or if it assert *a fact* which is false in addition to involving an absurd opinion, certainly in such a case the general rule must suffer an exception.[6] In like manner, though a medical or scientific *opinion* cannot in general be challenged as a perjury, because the uncertainty and division of opinion in the medical profession is proverbial; yet if it assert a fact, or draw an inference evidently false, as, for example, if a medical attendant swear that a person is unfit to travel who is in perfect health, or an architect shall declare a tenement to be ruinous which is in good condition, certainly the gross falsehood of such an assertion, shall in neither case be protected by the plea that it related to a matter of professional investigation, concerning which a diversity of opinion might exist.[7] It is unnecessary to observe that, in narrating *a fact*, a medical or scientific witness of any kind is such *in pari casu* with any other person; and that, if there be any evidence of his having been bribed, or

---

[1] Hume, i. 368.—[2] Maclaurin, No. 75.—[3] Burnett, 204; Hume, i. 369.—
[4] Ibid.—[5] Smith c. Baird, January 26 1799, Fac. Coll.; Burnett, 205.—
[6] Burnett, 205; Hume, i. 375.—[7] Ibid.

keted from corrupt or malicious motives, his protection is at an end.[1]

4. The falsehood must be in a matter pertinent to the issue, and competent to be asked of the witness; but if this be the case, it matters not in how trivial a matter the falsehood may consist, or how far from the original relevant matter the witness may have been led before he makes the false affirmation.

It is laid down by Mr Hume, that the oath which is the foundation of a charge of perjury must be material to the point at issue;[2] while it is maintained by Burnett,[3] that it is not essential in every case that the falsehood challenged be material to the matter at issue, or to the point which is in controversy. The truth seems to be, that it is only essential to perjury that the subject matter of the oath should have *commenced* with a relevant and competent subject of investigation; because it often happens that the most important contradictions or falsehoods are elicited from witnesses in the course of an examination, in which they have been purposely led from the matters in which they had prepared a false story, to others in which, from want of such previous preparation, this falsehood is at once apparent. It is impossible, too, to say, that any thing is irrelevant to the question at issue, which goes to convict the witness of concealment or falsehood; because the maxim immediately applies, *falsum in uno, falsum in omnibus,* and the witness' whole testimony is set aside in consequence of his perjury, even in an inconsiderable particular. Mr Hume's doctrine accordingly has not been followed in later times, since the principles of evidence, from the great increase of criminal practice, have come to be better understood. Thus, in the case of Elizabeth Muir, Glasgow, spring 1830, the pannel was convicted, and sentenced to seven years' transportation, for perjury, the preceding Circuit at Glasgow. She had been adduced as a witness in exculpation, and had sworn that the police-officers who apprehended the prisoner then at the bar had got drunk, and conducted themselves in the most improper manner during and subsequent to her apprehension; a fact nowise mate-

---

[1] Burnett, 205.—[2] Hume, i. 369.—[3] Burnett, 206.

rial to the prisoner's case in itself, farther than that her falsehood in it went to destroy her credibility in other matters which she deponed to, and which really were essential to the first prisoner's defence.[1]  In like manner, it is unquestionable that perjury may be committed by a false oath upon an examination *in initialibus*, as on the most material fact *in causa*; for what can be more material to the issue of a cause, than the conviction of a witness of perjury in the questions relating to the purity of the evidence which he is to give.[2]

There is one exception, however, to this rule, where the matter on which the perjury was alleged to have been committed was such, as it was not competent to examine the witness upon, however material to the issue; for law cannot lend the terrors of its punishment to protect a party in pursuing an incompetent and illegal train of investigation.  On this ground it was that the decision went in the case of Patrick M'Curly, 4th August 1777, who had been precognosced with a view to a criminal trial, and afterwards, as often happens, had given a different account of the matter on the trial itself.  Towards the close of his deposition, he was asked whether he had ever given a different account of the matter, and he swore he had not.  Upon this last falsehood he was indicted for perjury; and after a debate on the relevancy, the prosecutor abandoned the charge; nor, in truth, does it seem possible to maintain an indictment for perjury in such a case, where the question put was clearly incompetent, and the witness would have been entitled to decline answering it.[3]


5. The oath must have been before a judge or commissioner legally entitled to put it, and in relation to a matter involved in some judicial process or investigation.


How great soever may be the guilt, morally speaking, of one who calls God to witness the statements of a falsehood, even of the most inconsiderable kind, and of his own accord, it is not to such instances of depravity that the law of perjury relates. What it principally looks to in this matter is the interfering with the course of justice, and corrupting the sources of judicial investigation.[4]  The oath, therefore, must have been emitted

---

[1] Unreported.—[2] Burnett, 206, Hume, i. 369.—[3] Hume, i. 370, Burnett, 206.—[4] Burnett, 205.

before some magistrate, judge, or other person who has authority or commission to receive or exact it;[1] and it must relate either to a depending process, or some matter of legal or judicial investigation.[2] The most solemn asseveration, accompanied by oaths before a private person, or any voluntary affidavits, even to the most important facts before a magistrate, are not the fit subjects of prosecutions for perjury[3]

No indictment for perjury can be maintained on account of what is sworn in a church court; for an oath in ecclesiastical proceedings is not properly a *judicial* oath, the Court having no cognizance as to its civil effects; and though it may be afterwards founded on as an article of evidence in a civil court, its not being taken *coram judici* is an objection to its being made the foundation of an indictment for perjury. In the case of Barclay, 25th April 1601, this prisoner, who had falsely sworn before the Presbytery of Edinburgh, was only sentenced on the ground of his having come in the King's will, in other words, waived all objections to the competency of the proceeding; and in the later case of J. and W. Wilson, Aberdeen, autumn 1803, where the pannels were charged with perjury in consequence of a false oath before a kirk-session, regarding a bastard child, the diet was deserted in consequence of the court entertaining serious doubts as to the relevancy of the charge.[4]

It is not essential, however, to a charge of perjury, that the matter concerning which the oath is emitted be properly speaking a depending *process*. It is the same thing if the oath took place in the course of a judicial investigation or proceeding, in which, for certain civil effects, the law requires an oath to be taken. Thus prosecutions have repeatedly been sustained for perjury in the statutory oaths emitted by bankrupts before the Sheriff, which are declared indeed by the Sequestration act to be under the sanction of perjury; as, for example, in the case of J. Baillie, 19th May 1823,[5] and of John Carter, July 20. 1831,[6] both of whom were transported seven years. So also, on 16th July 1824, William Hay was indicted at common law for perjury, committed by falsely taking the oath prescribed in the Sequestration act, and being convicted, was transported seven years.[7] In like manner, in the case of Matthew Steele, 10th February 1623, who was indicted for perjury at common law, and under

[1] Hume, l. 370.—[2] Burnett, 205.—[3] Hume, l 370; Burnett, 205.—[4] Ibid. 206; Hume, l. 371.—[5] Ibid. l. 371.—[6] Unreported.—[7] Hume, l 371

the Sequestration act, for having falsely emitted an affidavit to
a claim of debt before a magistrate, the indictment was found
relevant at common law, but not under the statute, because it
did not set forth that Steele was a creditor on the bankrupt
estate.[1] On the same principle, the oath of bribery and of trust
and possession at elections, a debtor's oath to obtain the benefit of the act of grace, a *cessio bonorum*, or a discharge of debts
under the Sequestration act, a suspender's oath at passing his
bill on juratory caution, are all oaths which are emitted under
the sanction of perjury.[2] For in all these cases the swearer has
taken the oath by the appointment of the law, and in a matter
of judicial proceeding in which others besides himself are interested.[3] On the same principle, a prosecution for perjury
may be founded on falsehood contained in any of the numerous
oaths required in revenue matters, or in giving up a false in-
ventory of moveable or heritable property in the Commissary
or Sheriff Courts or the like.[4] In all cases, in short, where an
oath is required and imposed by law, either as a safeguard to
the revenue, or for the protection of the interest of a number
of other persons, or as a necessary step towards making effectual a legal right, and the oath has been emitted before the person authorised and appointed to receive it, falsehood wilfully
committed is considered as the fit subject of the pains of perjury.[5] In the case accordingly of Andrew Paterson, March 16.
1825, a prosecution for perjury was founded on a false oath
emitted by a soldier before a Justice of Peace, in order to obtain prize-money for enlisting in a new regiment, in which he
falsely declared that he was not already in the service; and although the prosecutor, in consideration of a confession, with-
drew the charge of forgery, and limited the case to the fraud
libelled, the Court had no doubts as to the relevancy of the former charge.[6] In like manner, in the case of William Taylor,
Perth, September 1826, an indictment for perjury was sustained, grounded on falsehood, deponed to in the course of an oath
emitted before a magistrate of Dundee, with a view to obtain
the benefit of the act of grace.[7] And at Perth, September
1824, Andrew Hay was outlawed on a charge of fraud and perjury, committed by emitting false affidavits to fraudulent claims
of debt, with a view to their being used in a sequestration; a

---

[1] Hume, i. 374.—[2] Ibid.; Burnett, 207.—[3] Hume, i. 375.—[4] Ibid.; Burnett, 207.—[5] Ibid.—[6] Unreported.—[7] Unreported.

proceeding which, independently of being clearly perjury at common law, is expressly declared to be such by the Sequestration act, 54th Geo. III. c. 137.

6. Perjury may be committed on a reference to oath, or in an oath put *ex officio judicis* to elicit the truth, equally as in one administered in the ordinary course of legal procedure.

It is *triti juris* that a reference to oath is the termination of strife; but if the referee has sworn falsely, he is liable to a prosecution for perjury.[1]    Accordingly, in the case of Montgomery, November 1715, an indictment for perjury was sustained for what was deponed to on a reference to oath; and the like in the case of Kilpatrick, Dumfries, April 1755, where the objection that an indictment for perjury could not be maintained, for what was deponed to *parte referente* was repelled.[2] The same holds with false oaths, emitted in pursuance of interrogations put *ex officio judicis,* for the discovery of truth.[3] But an oath *in litem* cannot be made the foundation of a prosecution for perjury, unless the falsehood was so gross as to place the matter beyond a doubt; because such an oath is to a certain degree on a subject on which allowance must be made for difference of opinion.[4]    Accordingly, in the case of Robertson, 19th September 1709, where an act of perjury was founded on an oath *in litem,* contrasted with a prior oath, the Court found the libel, as libelled on the instructions produced, not relevant; in other words, that the contradiction or falsehood founded on was not so gross as to warrant such a prosecution.[5] In the case of Thomas Somerville, 16th February 1813, the pannel had, in a suspension, swore on a reference that he had given full value for a bill, and, in consequence, the letters were found orderly proceeded.    But the suspenders insisted against him in a criminal action, raised with concurrence of the public prosecutor, concluding for the pains of law, damages and expenses; and the perjury of the first oath having been established *prout de jure,* the Court sentenced the pannel to six months' imprisonment, the pillory, and £150 of damages, besides expenses, which in effect corrected the iniquity of the false oath,

[1] Burnett, 206; Hume, i. 374.—[2] Burnett, 207; Hume, i. 374.—[3] Ibid.— [4] Burnett, 207.—[5] Ibid.

which was not directly reversible either in the civil or criminal court.

7. The oaths must not only be made before the proper officer, but in the due and accustomed form, in the department of business to which it relates.

Certain formalities are required in the administration of oaths; and it is indispensable that such as are fixed by law or custom should have been observed in the oath which is the subject of an indictment for perjury.[1]   Thus, if the oath is not reduced to writing in situations where by law or custom it should have been done; or if the oath of a witness or party has not been read over to him before signing; or if, after being read over, it has not been signed either by the deponent or the presiding commissioner or judge; or if the judge has refused to take down any explanation which the deponent requested to have added after hearing it read over; or if the oath has been emitted verbally, the pannel has modified or explained away his story;—in all these situations, the law considers the perjury as not having been committed.[2]   In some of them there is not the finished and deliberate intention to assert a falsehood on oath which law deems indispensable to the offence; in others, the deposition has not been duly authenticated, or proved to have been accurately taken down, and, therefore, the proper evidence is awanting on which the crime is to be substantiated.[3]

In inferior courts, where the oath is taken down at full length in writing, and then read over to the deponent, and signed by him and the judge, or, if he cannot write, by the judge in his presence, it is indispensable that the formalities should be observed, and appear *ex facie* of the oath produced in the indictment for perjury.[4]   In courts where the depositions of the witnesses are emitted *viva voce*, and their substance only taken down by the judge, as in the Justiciary Court, or in the courts which have recently acquired by act of Parliament the privilege of proceeding in this expeditious manner, it is indispensable that the deposition which is meant to be founded on as a perjury should be reduced to writing, read over to the

- [1] Hume, i. 371.—[2] Ibid.—[3] Ibid.; Mackenzie, No. 7, Perjury.—[4] Hume, i. 375.

deponent, and signed by him if he can write, and the judge in his presence; and it is very doubtful whether it is competent to found an indictment for perjury on what is merely taken down in the judge's notes, or has been heard by him or the bystanders.[1] In all cases, accordingly, where prosecutions for perjury have been instituted on account of what has been sworn in the Supreme Criminal Court, the foundation for it has been laid by the objectionable matter having been taken down with the formalities and security against error above set forth; and it is in the oath thus reduced to writing that the indictment has charged the perjury as consisting. Such was the course adopted in the cases of Robertson and Bachelor, 24th July 1806, John Skelton, March 2. 1812, and Mrs Mackinnon, March 14. 1823, in all of which cases the objectionable depositions were taken down, though no farther proceedings were instituted against the suspected party.[2] But in the case of William Edmond, January 24. 1810, and Mrs Muir, Glasgow, spring 1830, prosecutions for perjury were instituted against these parties, in consequence of their depositions, then reduced to writing, on previous occasions in the Justiciary Court; and though the first pannel was acquitted, the second was transported seven years.[3]

8. Perjury is not inferred by not acting up to the spirit or even letter of an oath, as to the regulation of the future conduct, nor even by expressly breaking it.

In common language, and *in foro conscientiæ*, one who takes an oath, as of fidelity to his sovereign, or *de fideli administratione* in an office, and afterwards violates it, as by engaging in treason or transgressing his duty, may be said to be guilty of perjury; but that is not the legal meaning of the word, which signifies a false oath contrary to the administration or course of justice. In such cases, accordingly, no indictment for perjury can lie.[4] Such violations of oaths are termed *consequential perjury,*[5] and differ from legal perjury in this, that the falsehood is not committed at the time of *taking the oath*; but it was rightly and innocently taken at the time, and the wrong consisted in a subsequent deviation from it; whereas, what law requires in the perjury which is to be the subject of trial and punishment, is

[1] Hume, i. 375.—[2] Ibid.—[3] Unreported.—[4] Hume, i. 371-2; Burnett, 208.
—[5] Mackenzie, Tit. Perjury.

the wilful affirmation of what is known to be false at the time of emitting the oath.[1]

There are instances, however, in which such subsequent deviations from an oath are punishable as perjury; but this is always by the force of special statute. An example of this occurs in the case of the breach of duty by clerks at elections in not returning the person chosen by the majority, which, by 7th Geo. II. c. 16, § 35, 37 and 39, is declared punishable as perjury, although the violation of the duty was of course subsequent to the oath.[2]

9. When contradictory and inconsistent oaths have been emitted, the mere contradiction is not decisive evidence of the existence of perjury in one or other of them; but the prosecutor must establish which was the true one, and libel on the other as containing the falsehood.

Where depositions contradictory to each other have been emitted by the same person on the same matter, it may with certainty be concluded that one or other of them is false But it is not relevant to infer perjury in so loose a manner; but the prosecutor must go a step farther, and specify distinctly which of the two contains the falsehood, and peril his case upon the means he possesses of proving perjury in that deposition.[3] To admit the opposite course, and allow the prosecutor to libel on both depositions, and make out his charge by comparing them together, without distinguishing which contains the truth and which the falsehood, would be directly contrary to the precision justly required in criminal proceedings.[4] In the older practice this distinction does not seem to have been distinctly recognised; but it is now justly considered indispensable that the perjury should be specified as existing in one, and the other deposition referred to *in modum probationis*, to make out, along with other circumstances, where the truth really lay.

10. Perjury may be committed equally by swearing falsely *super facto alieno*, or *super facto proprio*, with this difference, that the proof must be more pregnant and conclusive in the former case than the latter.

---

[1] Burnett, 208.—[2] Ibid.—[3] Hume, i 372; Burnett, 565.—[4] Ibid.—
[5] Hume, i. 372.

The most unfavourable case for the paunel, and that which admits the most decisive evidence against him, is, where he swears falsely as to any action of *his own;* as that he was at such a place on such a day, and there witnessed certain proceedings; whereas it can be proved that he was on that day at a different place, and differently engaged [1] Of this description is the assertion on oath that the deponent had received no bribe for giving his evidence, when in truth he had done so; or was no relation of the person who cited, when in reality he was so, and was aware of the fact.[2] But perjury may also relate, and generally does relate, to the acts of others; as where a witness swears that at such a time and place he saw John assault and wound James, when, in fact, nothing of the kind took place, as can be proved by those who had equal or better opportunities of observation. Of this last sort was the perjury in the case of Mrs Muir, Glasgow, April 1830, who deponed, on a former trial, that the police-officers who apprehended the prisoner then on trial got drunk, and misconducted themselves in various essential particulars in her presence, whereas there was not a word of truth in the whole story, as she afterwards admitted, by pleading guilty to the charge of perjury.[3]

But it is worthy of especial notice, in this species of perjury, that it is not to be inferred from the mere fact of there being a discrepancy, even of a very serious kind, between the story told by one witness and others in regard to the same transaction, unless the contradiction is of so gross and glaring a kind that it is quite impossible that both can be true. For a very slight acquaintance with criminal proceedings must be sufficient to convince every one, that such is the variety of lights in which even the same acts strike different observers in different situations, and such the different *media* through which they are viewed on a retrospect, according to their several passions and inclinations, that, without any positive intention to deceive, the story ultimately told comes to be essentially, and to appearance irreconcilably, different. This is more especially the case if the deposition relate to an affray or struggle in which the witness himself bore a part; for it is proverbial that the account given on the opposite sides are in such cases almost invariably different, and strongly tinged with the passions with which they

---

[1] Hume, i. 372.—[2] Ibid.; Burnett, 565.—[3] Unreported.

are respectively actuated at the period when it took place. The case is different, however, where the witness swears to a fact altogether false; as the presence of a party who was not there, the appearance of weapons when none were in the possession of those engaged in the scuffle; for, after making every allowance for the different lights on which witnesses on opposite sides view the same facts, there can be no excuse for the total invention of a fact which had no existence. After all, in considering the evidence in cases of perjury, it is always to be recollected, that it is merely the weighing of oath against oath; and, therefore, unless the evidence tending to prove the falsehood clearly preponderate, either in quantity, weight, or consistency, the pannel is *in dubio* entitled to the benefit of an acquittal.

11. In trials for perjury, the tenor of the oath must be established by the best evidence of which the case will admit, and its falsehood by such evidence *prout de jure* as is sufficient to convince a reasonable understanding.

The proof of the tenor of the oath is, in cases of perjury, a matter of very great importance, on account of the facility with which mistakes may occur in regard to the words uttered, and the omission of particulars by which apparent falsehoods or contradictions may be explained or accounted for. It is, accordingly, a rule, that in all those cases where regularly and in common course the oath should be reduced to writing, no other evidence of the tenor of the oath is admissible but a written record, signed by the party's own hand, and the Judge, or by the Judge alone, if he cannot write, and proved at the trial by that Judge's deposition.[1] But if the record has accidentally, and without the prosecutor's fault, perished, there seems to be no doubt that secondary evidence is admissible; but of course, in such a case, the caution of the jury, and the difficulty of conviction, must be proportionally greater.

As it is the invariable practice of the Court of Justiciary, when proceedings are intended to be founded on an oath emitted in its presence, to have the words taken down by the clerk read over to the deponent, and authenticated by his subscrip

[1] Hume, 1 376; Burnett, 367.

tion and that of the Judge, or, if he cannot write, by that of the Judge alone, and as such a course is always possible, and affords the best possible evidence of the tenor of the oath, it follows, that, unless in cases where that record has perished without the prosecutor's fault, no secondary or inferior evidence by parole proof can be admitted.[1] Mr Hume, indeed, inclines to an opposite opinion, and cites the cases of Archibald M'Killop, November 18. 1754, and James Wilson, August 15. 1768,[2] where it was found that perjury committed in the Justiciary Court may be proved by parole evidence: but it is to be observed, that in neither of these cases was a conviction obtained; and the question argued at the Bar was rather, whether the *ipsa verba* of an oath must be set forth in an indictment for perjury, than whether secondary evidence is admissible where the best could have been got, and has not been adduced.[3] If the party who is called upon to sign his deposition refuse either to sign or retract, there seems no doubt that it may be signed by the Judge in his presence, the doquet bearing, as in cases of declaration, that it was subscribed by a Judge, in respect the deponent had refused to subscribe the same; but if he retract before the last seal is put by his signature, or if the deposition as written vary materially from that which was verbally emitted, the proper foundation does not appear to be laid for a prosecution for perjury; but he may be summarily punished for wilful prevarication on oath before leaving the box.[4]

The oath itself is the best evidence of its own tenor, and, therefore, in cases where the Court before whom the trial for perjury is to proceed, is different from that where the oath libelled on as false was emitted, an extract should not be admitted, but the original deposition libelled on and produced.[5] In the case, accordingly, of Row, August 9. 1665, where the oath challenged had been emitted before the Commissary of Dunkeld, and, in proof of the tenor of the oath, an extract of the proceeding was tendered, the Court refused to admit the evidence.[6] The Judge before whom the oath is taken should also be cited to prove that the prisoner is the person who emitted the deposition; or, if he is not able to attend by reason of illness or absence, the clerk, or other officer of court, must be adduced to supply his place.[7]

[1] Burnett, 562.—[2] Hume, i. 376.—[3] Burnett, 562.—[4] Ibid.—[5] Ibid.—[6] Ibid. 563.—[7] Ibid.

5

Whether or not the *notes* taken by the Judge in those courts, where such a practice is usual or legal, is sufficient evidence of the tenor of the oath, without having it formally reduced to writing, is a more doubtful question, upon which no decision has yet been given. Certainly such evidence is incomparably stronger than that of persons who merely speak from memory as to what they heard the parties declare, and is the best that can be adduced where the formality of reducing it to writing has not been adopted. Still it wants the additional guard against error, which arises from the slow process of dictation, and the reading over the oath before signature; but, whether the absence of these would be deemed a sufficient objection to the trial proceeding on such evidence, is a question upon which no decision has yet been given; though it may perhaps be anticipated that, as it is held sufficient to the effect of convicting the prisoner and possibly forfeiting his life, it would probably be held adequate to the inferior matter of establishing what one of the witnesses said on the trial.

With regard to the falsehood of the oath, it is established in modern practice that this may be made out *prout de jure*, or by evidence of any sort, either written or parole; and that too indiscriminately, whether the oath be that of a party on reference, or of a witness on a trial, or in the course of any judicial proceeding.[1] Indeed it is evident, that unless this were the rule, perjury, in its worst cases, would frequently go unpunished; for persons who are guilty of this offence hardly ever have so far committed themselves before as to furnish written evidence of the falsehood of what they have said. In admitting, however, the testimony of others to disprove the oath of the party accused, to the effect of subjecting him to punishment, the law justly requires that the proof of the fact on which the perjury is charged, shall be pregnant and conclusive, and made out by witnesses or circumstances above all suspicion.[2] The guilt of the accused is not to be made out by the testimony of the pannel one way, and of others to the contrary; but, from a proof of opposite and inconsistent facts, equally known to the pannel as to them, and by him wilfully dissembled or denied, and this corrupt state of his mind is to be collected from the whole circumstances of the case.[3] It is not

[1] Hume, i. 376; Burnett, 564.—[2] Burnett, 564.—[3] Hume, i. 377.

sufficient, therefore, to make out perjury; to establish that the pannel has sworn one way, and others of greater credibility another; the prosecutor must go a step farther, and shew that what these last deponed to was known to the pannel when he emitted his deposition, and the reverse nevertheless asserted For example, if the pannel is charged with perjury, in respect of his having sworn that John did not fire at James on a certain occasion; evidence must here be given not only of the firing, but also of the pannel's having been so situated at the time, that he must have heard the shot, which may be farther confirmed by his conduct at the time, and what he said or did afterwards.[1]

A party cannot be convicted of perjury upon the evidence merely of previous or subsequent declarations emitted by him, inconsistent with what he has sworn; because, *in dubio*, it must be presumed that what was said under the sanction of an oath was the truth, and the other an error or falsehood; but both such declarations and written evidence under his hand, inconsistent with what he has sworn, form important articles, which, with others, will be sufficient to make the scales of evidence preponderate against him.[2] Accordingly, in the case of Maitland of Hatton, July 1681, who was accused of perjury before the Lords of the Articles, the chief mean of proof adduced against him were certain holograph letters which had been recovered at variance with what he had sworn; but it was justly held that such letters, which might have been written in error or in haste, were not sufficient proof *per se* that what was subsequently sworn was false.[3]

In cases where the perjury consists in a false narrative of conversations, there is a material distinction to be observed. If the discrepancy lies merely in the *import* of what was said, much allowance must be made for the mistakes of language, and the different meaning attached to expressions, according to the different passions of the hearers; but the case will be totally different, if the oath challenged either assert that a conversation took place, where it can be proved it did not, or deny that it took place, where it can be established it did. In such a case no such allowance for error can be made; and, if the reverse of the oath, in either case, be established by sufficient

---

[1] Hume, l. 377.—[2] Burnett, 565.—[3] State Trials, viii. 435

evidence, there seems no means of avoiding the conclusion that the perjury was committed.

11. The punishment of perjury is arbitrary, varying, according to the magnitude of the offence, from a few months' imprisonment to transportation.

The punishment of this offence has not been entirely left to the common law, but is the subject of several enactments. The most precise is the act 1551, c. 19, which prescribes "confiscation of all their gudes moveable, warding of their persons for year and day, and langer, during the Queen's will, and, as infame persons, never to brook office, honour, dignitie, nor benefice in time to come." The subject is also touched on by 1551, c. 22, and 1555, c 47, and 1540, c. 80. All these statutes speak of farther and indefinite pains; and, in construing the powers conferred by these enactments, the Court have held that the pains of perjury are arbitrary, and may be carried to any thing short of life and limb.[1]

In the older practice, indeed, instances are not awanting of capital pain having been inflicted for this offence;[2] and, indeed, in cases where the perjury has led to a capital conviction and execution of an innocent person, there seems much justice in such severity. But, should such a case occur, the proper course seems to be, to charge it under the name of conspiracy and murder, under which denomination it unquestionably warrants a capital punishment.[3]

It was also for long the practice to inflict severe corporal pains for this offence. Thus, on 10th July 1605, William Galbraith was ordered to be pilloried and banished; June 13. 1581, Mungo Stevenson to have his tongue bored, have his moveables escheated, and be declared incapable of office; January 30. 1650, John Wilson and John Sinclair to have their ears nailed to the Tron, and their moveables escheated; January 8. 1736, John Blackadder to be exposed on the Cross, with his ear nailed to a post, his moveables escheated, and be declared infamous; July 15. 1762, John Bell to be pilloried and declared infamous.[4]

But since more humane ideas have become prevalent, these

[1] Hume, i. 378; Burnett, 208.—[2] Hume, i. 378.—[3] Ibid 370.—[4] Ibid 378.

corporal severities have been generally exchanged for transportation. Thus, in the case of John Lees, February 20. 1772,
the pannel was declared infamous, and transported seven
years; and Alexander Menzies, February 12. 1790, was transported seven years, and banished Scotland for life.[1] The like
sentence of transportation for seven years was inflicted on
John Baillie, 19th May 1823; William Hay, 16th July 1824;[2]
and John Carter, July 20. 1831, all of whom were convicted
of perjury, in taking the oaths prescribed by the sequestration
act.[3] Much milder punishments, however, are sometimes inflicted. Thus in the case of Ker, Glasgow, April 1788, Lord
Braxfield only sentenced an imprisonment of three months, on
a pannel convicted of taking a false custom-house oath.[4]

12. The cognizance of perjury, as an original and independent offence, is peculiar to the Court of Session;
but if it has emerged, in the course of any proceeding in
an inferior court, the judge of that Court seems competent
to take cognizance of it.

It is stated by Mr Hume, that cognizance of perjury is only
peculiar to the Court of Justiciary, if pursued in the form of
an original and proper libel.[5] No authority, however, is quoted
by him for this opinion, and it is to be understood of those
cases only in which the falsehood on oath has not taken place
before an inferior court; for, if this be the case, there seems
no ground on which the jurisdiction of the Sheriff, at least as the
judge-ordinary of the bounds, should be excluded in the cognizance of this offence, any more than any other, not excluded by
statute or custom, which has originated within his jurisdiction.
The libel may be insisted in either by the Lord Advocate, or the
private party with his concourse, if he has been injured by the
oath libelled on as false; as if, in consequence of it, he has
been convicted of a crime, or been imprisoned on a *meditatione
fugæ* warrant, or has been worsted in a competition for a seat
in Parliament. This title last mentioned was sustained in the
case of Cumming of Altyre, 27th June 1785.[6] Such an interest
as this will be sustained as a sufficient title to prosecute, even
although the perjury has not had the desired effect upon the

[1] Hume, i. 378.—[2] Ibid. 374.—[3] Unreported.—[4] Burnett, 208.—[5] Hume,
i. 379.—[6] Ibid

party intended to be injured; just as one who has been assaulted, or attempted to be robbed, is entitled to insist for the punishment of the offender, though the intended violence did not produce the anticipated result.[1]  In the case of James Fife, December 5. 1796, the Court were of opinion, that the title of freeholder, on the roll of a county, is a sufficient title to prosecute for perjury, committed by taking the oath of trust and possession; a decision which proceeded on the principle not of such a prosecution being open *cuivis e populo*, which is entirely foreign to the principles of our law, but on the peculiar and vested interest which every freeholder has in guarding the purity of the roll of electors.[2]

13. Prevarication, or wilful contradiction on oath, is an offence, punishable summarily by the pillory or imprisonment at the moment the offence is committed.

The usual manner in which falsehood on oath appears, is by prevarication or contradiction upon oath; and this, as a high offence, and both indicating a contempt of Court, and as tending directly to the obstruction of justice, may be summarily punished on the spot by the Court before which it has occurred.[3]  Numerous instances accordingly are to be found on record, in which pillory or imprisonment have been inflicted on a witness who has manifestly contradicted himself, or prevaricated upon oath.  Thus in the case of Robert Logan, August 6. 1767, the witness who had prevaricated upon oath was instanter declared infamous, and sentenced to the pillory;[4] the like with Christian Craufurd, December 24. 1760; and James Laing, February 14. 1767, Archibald Maclachlan, November 22. 1738, and John Russell, August 30. 1793, and Robert Currie, 10th December 1799, and Margaret Morrison, Glasgow, 24th April 1811, in the trial of Allan, Black, and Gillies.[5] ·

More lately, since the punishment of the pillory has fallen, comparatively speaking, into disuse, the usual course has been, when a witness has clearly prevaricated upon oath, to sentence him summarily, *de plano*, to imprisonment or hard labour in Bridewell, for a limited period, generally from six weeks to three months.  Of this practice, unhappily too frequently ren-

[1] Hume, i. 379.—[2] Ibid.—[3] Hume, i. 380, Burnett, 209.—[4] Hume, i. 380.—
[5] Ibid

dered necessary by the corrupt habits of witnesses in later times, the following may be given as examples :—Ayr, autumn 1828, Robert Logan, on the trial of George Buchanan and others, for housebreaking and theft, was summarily sentenced, by Lord Alloway, to three months' imprisonment, for evident falsehood and contradiction on oath ;[1] at Glasgow, on the trial of James Devlin, spring 1828, George Muir was sentenced to imprisonment for six weeks, for prevarication on oath ;[2] in the trial of John Stewart, George Buckley, and others, Glasgow, spring 1825, George Harley, a *socius*, was sentenced to two months' imprisonment for the same offence ;[3] and, in the High Court, November 14. 1831, in the trial of T. Beveridge, for murder, James Gray was sentenced to three months' imprisonment for evident prevarication during the course of his evidence.[4] The same course has now become so frequent at Glasgow, that hardly a circuit is concluded without one or two instances being made of witnesses, who have behaved in this disgraceful manner during examination.

Mere falsehood on oath, how gross or apparent soever, is not a sufficient ground for the infliction of these summary pains, if it appears only on a comparison of what the witness has said with what has been sworn to by others. It is incompetent to punish a witness in this way, because what he has said is at variance with previous testimony ; that must be done by a regular indictment for perjury. It is his contradiction of *himself* on oath which warrants this summary procedure.

It is seldom, by threats or intimidation, that witnesses, who are evidently speaking what is false, can be brought either to contradict themselves, or to retract what they have said. Against intimidation of that kind, they are generally sufficiently steeled by the previous dissolute habits of their lives. It is by a rapid course of questions, on *details* not directly connected with the subject of examination, that they are in general led into contradictions ; because they are, in this way, brought upon topics on which their previous preparation and foresight will not avail them ; and it is rare, when such a course is skilfully adopted, that the perjured witness is not led into such contradictions with himself or others, as is sufficient with any intelligent jury to overthrow his whole testimony.

[1] Unreported.—[2] Unreported.—[3] Unreported.—[4] Unreported

# CHAPTER XXI.

## OF SUBORNATION OF PERJURY.

SUBORNATION of Perjury consists in the inducing others to give false testimony. It is ranked in our statutes 1540, c 80, and 1555, c. 47, in the same rank as actual perjury; and indeed is perhaps a more base, cowardly, and detestable crime than the other.

1. Subornation of perjury is only completed when the witness yields to the seduction, and swears to the concerted falsehood; if this be not done it amounts to an attempt only.

Towards the completion of the crime of subornation, three things are necessary: 1. The inducement must have been to swear falsely; 2. A false oath must have been actually taken; 3. The oath must have been taken as a witness, in consequence of the inducement then held forth.[1] If these requisites concur, it is of no moment what the unlawful means are by which the corrupter has prevailed, whether bribe or good deed, or the promise of such, or the use of violence, or threats of mischief, or the insinuation of mischief, if the opposite course be adopted. So it was found in the cases of Charles Hay, January 31. 1710, and Macdonell of Barrisdale, January 1736.[2] As little does it alter the case, though the suborner have not, in direct terms, covenanted with the witness for a false story, but in other and more artful ways accomplishes the same end; as, for example, by putting into his hands a written story, instructing him how to depone. Such a practice was found a relevant point of dittay in the case of Charles Hay, July 1710.[5]

[1] Burnett, 209; Hume, i. 381.—[2] Hume, i. 381.—[3] Ibid.

2. Attempt at subornation is a point of criminal dittay, and is completed as soon as the corrupt inducements to swear falsely have been offered to the witness, though he has immediately rejected them, and nothing has followed on the attempt.

If the witness has once engaged to swear falsely, the guilt on the part of the suborner is complete; and the crime of attempt is completed, though no oath has actually been emitted, whether owing to the timidity or repentance of the witness, or any other cause.[1] Nay, the same shall hold, though the person practised on should have steadily resisted the solicitations, and never even made the semblance of complying, provided only that the solicitation or inducement has been tendered in such a manner as clearly manifests the guilty intention of their author.[2] Accordingly, in the case of Charles Hay, July 31. 1710, a libel was sustained, which charged the pannel with having practised upon sundry persons, though without success, except in one instance, in which the declaration was not produced, in order to induce them to emit false affidavits[3]. Again, in the case of Macdonell, January 19. 1736, the libel was sustained, though it did not state that any of the persons practised upon had either made oath or engaged, or even intended to have complied.[4] So also, in the case of James Souter and James Hog, July 30. 1738, the attempt to suborn witnesses on a charge of wilful fire-raising, was sustained, though the libel itself stated that, in almost every article, the persons to whom the inducements were held forth had resisted; and though the matter related not to a depending but a future and contemplated process.[5] In all these instances, the prosecution was at the instance of the private parties whose title was without hesitation sustained; although, in the later case of Jardine v. De la Motte, June 15. 1795, the title of the private prosecutor was, in such circumstances, but apparently without sufficient consideration, repelled.[6] The attempt to suborn was also sustained as a relevant point of dittay in the case of Robert Stuart and others, July 1713.[7] More lately, in the case of Robert Stirling, February 27. 1821, a summary complaint, at the Lord Advocate's instance, was sustained against the pannel,

---

[1] Hume, i. 382.—[2] Ibid i. 382; Burnett, 210.—[3] Burnett, 210.—[4] Hume, i. 382.—[5] Ibid. 383.—[6] Ibid.—[7] Ibid.

for certain improper instructions given by him to a witness how
to depone, although she was so far from having complied, that
she disclosed the whole circumstances in her examination *in
initialibus*, which led to the detection and punishment of the
offender.[1]  In many of the older cases, such attempts were prosecuted under the name of subornation; but they are, strictly
speaking, instances of attempt only, and should be prosecuted
under that designation [2]

3  All practices tending to procure false evidence are
punishable, though not falling exactly under the description of subornation or attempt at subornation.

Many cases may be figured in which, though there may be
some doubt as to the propriety of charging subornation or attempt at that crime, there can be none as to the propriety of
punishing the offender.   Offences of this sort consist in with-
drawing or suppressing evidence, soliciting or inducing others
to concur in a false and malicious prosecution of others, or the
like.  One noted instance of this occurred in the case of Campbell of Burnbank, March 31. 1721, who had sentence of infamy and transportation for a conspiracy to destroy the fame
of a married woman, and induce her divorce, by contriving
deceitful evidence against her.[3]   In like manner, in the case of
Charles Isackson, Robert Forrest, and Mary Hamilton, July 17.
1710, it was found a relevant subject of accusation, that the
latter of these parties, having born a child to Isackson, at his
instigation, and that of Forrest, signed a written declaration
fastening the child on Sir Alexander Rigby, a married man.[4]
So also, in the case of the Reverend James Dun, 11th March
1793, who, in the course of the precognition which was going
on against Thomas Muir for sedition, tore out several leaves
from a book containing the names of the members of an association, with a view to destroy the evidence thence arising, the
Court, on advising a complaint, with answers, sentenced the
offender to three months imprisonment.[5]  But if an offence of
this description has not arisen during a precognition, or some
other step of criminal procedure, so as to entitle the Lord Advocate to interfere by summary application, the regular course

[1] Hume, ii 140 —[2] Burnett, 210.—[3] Ibid. i. 383.—[4] Ibid —[5] Burnett, 217.

of procedure is by indictment, and a summary complaint will be dismissed as incompetent. So it was found in the case of A. Ritchie, 21st October 1797.[1] Such a petition, complaining of proceedings as derogatory to the dignity of the Court, is competent only to the public prosecutor, or to the Court *ex proprio motu*, but not to a private party.[2]

The same principle extends to the punishment of all those attempts to prejudice either the public prosecutor or the accused in those trials concerning which a strong public feeling has been excited. It is fit that, on all such occasions, the jurymen should, as much as possible, come into Court with their minds unbiassed; and though this, with the general diffusion of newspapers, is by no means easy, yet, whenever a direct and palpable attempt at prejudging the question is detected, the Court will, on a summary application, visit it with condign punishment. For a misdemeanour of this kind, John Gilkie, a writer, was sent to prison for a month, and ordered to find caution for his good conduct. He had been private agent in a case of murder; and, after the pannels were committed, had published memorials, advertisements, and addresses, tending to prejudice the public against the accused.[3] In the case of Thomas Mitchell and Robert Morrison, Perth, May 6. 1785, the delinquents, in a similar case, were more leniently dealt with. They had, after the service of the indictment against the prisoners, composed and published a sort of narrative and vindication on his part. This the Court held a palpable infringement on the course of justice; but, in consideration of the confession and penitence of the offenders, visited them only with a fine.[4] More lately, the Court expressed their determination to proceed in a similar manner on occasion of the trial of Robert Emond, February 6. 1830. Bills were circulated through the streets previous to this man's trial, giving an exaggerated and highly inflammatory account of the evidence against him; and, on this being brought under the notice of the Court, by summary motion on the part of the prisoner, they interdicted such proceedings, and declared they would summarily punish any one who should continue them.[5]

4. Every indictment for subornation of perjury, or at-

[1] Burnett, 211.—[2] A. Ritchie's Case, 29th January 1798; Burnett, 212.—[3] Hume, i. 384.—[4] Ibid. i. 385.—[5] Unreported.

tempt to commit that crime, should give a distinct and specific account of the crime, and the time, place, and manner of its committal.

In all charges of subornation, the indictment should state the fact or crime to which the subornation applied, the manner and species of the indictment offered; whether the person practised on consented or not; if he did, what followed in pursuance of the criminal design, and the time and place at which these different steps took place. For want of a due specification of this kind, the libel was found not relevant in the case of Procurator-fiscal of Ayrshire *v.* Guthrie and others, 20th June 1810.[1]

5. The punishment of subornation is an arbitrary pain, varying according to the magnitude of the case, from a few months imprisonment to transportation.

In former times, the highest pains were frequently applied to this offence as well as to perjury, as in the case of Alexander Cheyne, March 15. 1605, and Graham of Long Boddon, March 8. 1615.[2] But, for more than a century and a half, the punishment has been held to be an arbitrary pain only. In the case of James Hog and Thomas Souter, August 1. 1730, the pannels, convicted of repeated attempts to suborn, were fined £250, declared infamous, and banished Scotland for life.[3] The like sentence was passed on Neil Macvicar, February 23. 1739, and James Orr, February 21. 1745.[4] In modern times, there can be no doubt that, in suitable cases, transportation might be awarded.[5] Accordingly, in the case of William Hutchinson, July 20. 1831, who pleaded guilty to an extensive series of acts of subornation, transportation for seven years was awarded, being the same pain inflicted on the principal parties convicted of perjury.[6]

[1] Burnett, 211.—[2] Hume, i. 384.—[3] Ibid.—[4] Ibid.—[5] Ibid.—[6] Unreported.

# CHAPTER XXII.

## OF DEFORCEMENT

THE crime of deforcement, one of the best known in the law, consists in the resistance to the officers of justice in the execution of their duty. It is frequently applied, both in ordinary and legal language, to every species of resistance, whether ultimately successful in preventing the execution of the warrant or not; but, since correct phraseology became more usual in drawing indictments, it is usually applied to such instances of resistance as defeat the warrant, while the previous and unsuccessful attempts to defeat it, are charged under the name of resisting and obstructing officers of the law, in the execution of their duty.

1. The person resisted must be a lawful officer, or a person aiding and assisting a lawful officer

It is not *cuivis e populo* that the law communicates the high privilege of not being resisted without incurring the serious penalties of deforcement. The person deforced must be a *lawful officer*, one of the regular and proper executors of that sort of diligence which is hindered.[1] If he be an ordinary individual who has arrogated to himself the character of servant of the law, or if he be *in cursu* only of being appointed, or if he has been deposed or suspended, or, though a lawful officer, if he be meddling with a business which does not belong to his official duty, as if a sheriff-officer be executing letters under the Signet, or a constable executing the sheriff's precept, or either acting beyond their own bounds; in all these situations the crime of deforcement, or obstructing and resisting, is not committed.[2] Even if a warrant be addressed to a private in-

---

[1] Hume, ι. 386.——[2] Ibid. 387.

dividual, it would rather appear that the man does not by such a course become an officer; but if a regular officer be on the spot, and proceeding in a lawful manner, the protection of the law extends to his concurrents or assistants, because they are considered as the hands by which he acts, and any opposition offered to them is considered in the same light as opposition to himself.[1] By the uniform style of indictment, accordingly, the resisting, obstructing or deforcing officers of the law, is followed by " or those employed by them in the execution of their duty." But though these concurrents, acting with and under the officer, are considered in the same light as the officer himself, yet it is not to be imagined that they become, merely by having been called to his assistance, independent persons in the execution of the warrant, or entitled to act in the same way of their own authority, as he is in its execution. On the contrary, they can only aid and assist *him* in the execution of the duty, and therefore, if he is absent, or has declined or failed to discharge his duty, they cannot, merely upon the pretence of having been summoned to his assistance, pretend to act as officers *pro hac vice*. But, on the other hand, if he has taken them with him, and is *in cursu* of carrying the warrant into execution, the assistants are all protected though he is not at the moment present, being perhaps engaged in another part of the premises, or conducting another part of the duty. It is not necessary, nor is it usual, to libel on the officer's appointment; and his oath, that he is an officer of the law, is good evidence of the fact without production of his commission, as every day's practice demonstrates; but if the commission be libelled on and produced, any error or informality in it will be fatal to the charge of deforcement. So it was found by Lord Justice-Clerk Boyle, at Dumfries, spring 1824, in the case of Hugh Graham and others. The *species facti* there was, that a water-bailie with his assistants had seized a net, employed in illegal fishing on the River Annan, and the prisoners were indicted for breaking into his house and carrying away the net. The indictment libelled on the act appointing the water-bailie, and set forth that he had been regularly appointed; but, as it turned out upon examination of the document that the appointment was by one instead of two justices,

---

[1] Hume, i. 387.

which the act required, it was held that the whole charge, based on that alleged regular appointment, must fall to the ground.[1]

2. The officer must not only be possessed of a lawful commission, but at the time of the resistance he must be executing something to which he is bound by that commission.

The principle on which the law in regard to deforcement rests is, that it is the authority of the law which is set at nought by the resistance which is offered. The officer, therefore, must not only be vested with a lawful commission, but he must, at the time he is obstructed, be in the execution of something to which he is bound by that commission, and in which he cannot be repulsed, without bringing the authority of the law itself into contempt.[2] Thus, a constable or sheriff-officer has not the benefit of this high protection in any accidental broil or quarrel in which he may be engaged; on all such occasions, *utitur jure communi*, he is in no better situation than an ordinary individual. Then only is he protected when he is in the execution of one of those *acts legitimi*, or formal and solemn proceedings, which take place under regular and written authorities, and he alone can perform.[3] It follows that a sheriff-officer or constable has not the protection of the law more than an ordinary individual, if he is only acting *tanquam quilibet*, in the execution even of official duty; as, for example, if he is carrying a packet of letters from the sheriff, or has been sent to a certain quarter of the country to make private inquiries or commence a precognition about a crime.[4]

Nay, the same principle goes the length of excluding the officer's high privilege, in situations which approach much more nearly to his protected duties. Thus suppose he is attacked in his own house, and has the letters of caption or warrant taken from him; or that he is met half way on the road, and there waylaid and robbed of his warrant; such proceedings, though undoubtedly an aggravated species of assault, are not deforcement. In short, to be within the protection of this law, he must be either engaged in executing a warrant or *in actu*

---

[1] Unreported.—[2] Hume, i. 387.—[3] Ibid.—[4] Ibid.

*proximo* to its execution. Accordingly, in the case of John Wallace, January 26. 1789, it appeared that John Young, a tide-waiter, had taken his station in a field of corn to watch a smuggling vessel which was approaching the shore; and, being discovered there, was assaulted and beaten by the prisoner. This was considered only as an aggravated species of assault.[1]

As little is the officer under any peculiar safeguard, if the acts of violence take place after the *actus legitimus* has been concluded, and in revenge for its performance, or to deter from its repetition; as, for example, if, after having desisted from, or concluded, his diligence, he is met on his way home by another set of persons, who assail him on account of what was then done or attempted. In the case, accordingly, of Janet Hay, December 16. 1728, this principle was applied. She was charged with deforcing a messenger in the execution of a warrant in the town of Tranent, and afterwards instigating a rabble to beat him, on his return, at Prestonpans. The first act was found relevant as a deforcement, the last as a riot and beating only.[2]

The correct way to libel all such cases of assault, connected with the execution of legal diligence, but not occurring at or near the time of the execution of the warrant, is as " assault, especially when committed with intent to deter an officer of the law from acting in the execution of his duty, or in revenge for his having performed or attempted to perform it." In a great variety of cases, this mode of libelling the offence has been sustained as relevant of late years by the Court, particularly in the cases of Thomas Leslie and Alexander Lindsay, Aberdeen, autumn 1824, and Donald Maccallum and others, Inverary, April 1825.[3]

It is not, however, to be understood that it is indispensable that the first formalities of the execution should be actually commenced, if he be in near and immediate preparation, *in actu proximo* to proceed to them if he shall be allowed.[4] Thus it is unquestionably a deforcement if, when the messenger bearing letters of caption has come near the debtor's house, he is met by a host of people, who drive him off on notice or suspicion of his errand; or if instantly, on entering the debtor's field, with a view to poind his cattle, he is assailed and driven

[1] Hume, i. 888.—[2] Ibid.—[3] Both unreported.—[4] Hume i 388.

off before he can even begin to read the letters.[1] In the case, accordingly, of Rorie Macneil and others, June 2. 1715, it was sustained as a sufficient deforcement that the pannels had garrisoned the house or fortalice, and fired on the messenger as he approached the building, so that he could not affix a copy of the summons to the door.[2] In like manner, in the case of William Sutherland and others, July 22. 1722, it was held deforcement, that, upon the messenger's approach to the house to execute a caption, a body of armed men sallied out and hindered his approach :[3] and, in the case of Sir James Campbell and others, August 6. 1722, the same law was laid down, after a formal debate upon the charge that the messenger advanced to the house with his blazon displayed, with a caption to take a prisoner, and that he was opposed by armed men, who threatened him with death if he persisted. The objection was here repelled that the libel did not specify circumstances amounting to the *actus proximus* of actual apprehension of the prisoner.[4] These precedents were lately confirmed by Lord Gillies, at Ayr, April 1830, in the case of Michael Wallace. It there appeared that the prisoner, proceeding on the idea that some furniture which had been poinded from a debtor was not the property of the debtor, but of himself, by reason of a prior transfer to him, instead of petitioning the Sheriff to have them struck out of the schedule of the debtor's goods, proceeded *brevi manu* with several of his friends to the house where they were on the morning when they were to be removed from the debtor's custody, in order to prevent their removal. The officer and his party were never permitted to get at the goods, but joistled, threatened, and driven out of the house the moment they approached the threshold. The Court held the proceeding altogether illegal, and the deforcement completed; and the prisoner was convicted, and sentenced to three months' imprisonment.[5]

3. The officer must not only have entered, or be about to enter, on the discharge of his duty, but he must have proceeded therein up to the moment of interruption in a formal and legal manner.

This head includes several important articles of duty. And in the first place, it lies with the officer to notify his quality as a servant of the law, and that he is about to proceed to the execution of his official duty.[1]  As to what shall be esteemed a sufficient compliance with the law in this particular, it is settled that, in the case of messengers and constables, whose blazon and baton are the well known badges of their commission,—the display of these is a sufficient proclamation of the authority of the officer[2]  And if the messenger is acting in a quarter of the country where he is not known, this seems indispensable towards putting the lieges *in mala fide* to resist authority.[3]  But the display of the blazon is not an indispensable part of the ceremony.  Certainly, if the officer be well known, or the behaviour of the prisoner at the time shews that he was aware what he came about, there seems to be no need of any farther notification than that the messenger is about to proceed to the execution of his duty.[4]  In the cases, accordingly, of Margaret Yule, June 21. 1680, Anne Elphinston, February 14. 1687, and Macneil of Barra, July 28. 1679, libels were found relevant without any mention of the display of the blazon[5]  It was also found in the Court of Session, January 18 1699, that a messenger executing a caption need not shew his blazon till he has apprehended the debtor.[6]

In the numerous class of cases where excise-officers attempt to make a seizure of smuggled goods, and are deforced in so doing, there is no necessity for any display of the symbols of authority.  In truth, officers of that description have no blazon or baton which they carry about with them, and they are in general perfectly well known to the smugglers without any official symbol.  All that is usually practised in such cases is, that the officer announces aloud that he is a King's officer, and that he makes seizure of the goods in the King's name.  In the cases, accordingly, of Robert Clark and Alexander Inglis, Aberdeen, September 1824; and James Simpson and William Skene, Perth, 1825, and many others,[7] the deforcement was sustained without any other than this announcement of the quality and errand of the officer.  Nay, the rule is the same although the officers had not called out that they made seizure of the goods in the King's name, if the libel assert that the prisoners knew that they were excise-officers proceeding to the execution of their duty, a species of knowledge which is to

---

[1] Hume, l. 389.—[2] Ibid.—[3] Ibid.—[4] Ibid.—[5] Ibid. l. 391.—[6] Ibid.—[7] Unreported.

be inferred from their words and general behaviour.  So the Court held in the cases of Alexander Gordon and Donald Macpherson, Perth, spring 1826, and Charles Lamont and John Smith, July 17. 1826; in neither of which did the libel make any mention of a seizure of the goods in the King's name, but merely stated that the resistance was offered when the pannels well knew that the officers were proceeding to the discharge of their duty.[1]

4. It is part of a messenger's duty to notify that he is acting officially; but this is not indispensable if it appear that the parties resisting him were aware of the errand on which he came.

Though the pannels well know that the person is a messenger, they may not be aware that he is acting in his official character at the time.  It therefore lies with him, before proceeding, duly to warn them in this particular also, if he have reason to think that they have any doubt whatever as to the character in which he acts.[2]  It cannot therefore be laid down absolutely that there can be no deforcement, unless this precaution be observed, but only that it will not be committed unless either from previous knowledge, present circumstances, or actual information at the time, the pannel was made aware that it was the authority of the law itself which he was withstanding.  In regard to a messenger-at-arms, it has been settled by a long course of decisions, that the display of the blazon is of itself a sufficient warning to put the party *in mala fide* to resist the diligence.  The objection of the officer's omission to exhibit his diligence, accordingly, has been repelled in the following cases of deforcement of a caption, Gordon of Braco, February 26. 1672, and Campbell of Lawers, August 6. 1722; and the following of deforcement of a poinding, William Sutherland, 20th June 1715, and James Hamilton, January 3. 1726.[3]  In Campbell's case it was pleaded in defence, " that the messenger did not tell Sawers that he had a caption, and was going to apprehend him;" but to this it was sustained as a sufficient reply, " it is sufficient that it is libelled that the messenger, with his blazon displayed, was proceeding to do his duty; it is

[1] Unreported.—[2] Hume, i 390.—[3] Ibid

I I

not pretended that the pannel called for the caption and was refused."

5. The messenger is bound to shew his warrant, if required, and it is no deforcement if he be resisted in consequence of refusing to do so; but he is not bound either to part with the warrant, or shew it to any other than the person to whom it applies.

A messenger or officer possessed of a warrant either of caption or poinding, is bound to exhibit it if required by the party, and if, on being so required, he refuse, the party is entitled to believe that he is acting without a warrant, and may be lawfully resisted.[1] In the case, accordingly, of James Edmonston and others, August 7. 1695, and George and John Sinclair, November 20. 1699, it was found a sufficient defence " that the messenger was not known to be a Sheriff-officer, and that no warrant was produced by him from the Sheriff *when required* for seizing his prisoner."

But it is to be observed, on the other hand, that though the messenger must shew, he is not bound to *part with* his diligence, a proceeding which might put it in the power of the party interested to destroy it; and that, though bound to shew the warrant to the party himself or his family, or immediate connexions, he is not bound to do so to any of the bystanders, whose interference is presumed to have been prompted rather by curios y than any real desire to examine into the accuracy of the proceedings. The objection on the ground of a refusal to shew the letters was repelled in the case of Hamilton, December 1725, where the resistance was on the part of a disorderly multitude long after the apprizing was over, and at some miles distant.[2] Wherever, also, it is manifest from the proceedings of the prisoner or his friends that the real object of the officer was well known, and that they were determined, at all hazards, to resist him, the charge of deforcement will be held good, although the warrant was never either asked for or exhibited, provided the officer had it, and it was liable to no objection[3] So it was held by Lord Gillies, Dumfries, 1830, in the case of Jean Steel and others.[4] It need hardly be observed,

---

[1] Hume, i 390 —[2] Ibid i. 391 —[3] Ibid.—[4] Unreported.

that this defence of the warrant having been called for and refused, has no application to the case of custom-house or excise officers, who have in general no special warrant for the seizure of any particular goods, but a general commission to seize smuggled goods wherever they can be found within their district.

6. The officer, if he have commenced his diligence, must act in a legal manner, and give the party against whom it is directed the benefit of all the defences or advantages allowed by law.

In the discharge of so high and important a duty as the execution of legal diligence, the officer is bound to attend with scrupulous attention to the legal rights of the parties against whom it is directed. If, therefore, he shall execute letters of caption on a Sunday,[1] or after seeing a sist or suspension of them;[2] or if he shall attempt to poind plough goods in time of labour,[3] or any goods at all between sunset and sunrise;[4] or if he shall carry off corn in prejudice of the landlord, who objects his prior and preferable right of hypothec;[5] or if he shall attempt to break open doors to poind, without the authority either of letters of caption or letters of open doors;[6] or if he shall insist upon poinding goods in defiance of a written conveyance of them, and refuse to take the disponee's oath that he is the true proprietor:[7] in all these cases the officer may be lawfully resisted, and the establishment of such a legal defence will be fatal to the prosecution.[8]

These principles were lately applied in the case of William and Catharine Forgan, February 20. 1811. It there appeared that the pannels were charged with deforcement of constables in the execution of a poinding, proceeding on a warrant of Justices of the Peace in a revenue matter, under a special statute. It was objected that the officer proceeded to attach plough-horses before attaching the pannel's other goods, and that the diligence of poinding was used instead of distress,

[1] Edmiston's Case, August 7. 1695; Hume, i. 392.—[2] Burnett's Case, August 4. 1697; Ibid.—[3] Dick v. Sands, December 1630, and Graham's Case, December 17. 1700.—[4] Porteous's Case, July 8. 1700.—[5] Stewart's Case, July 28. 1701, and Thomas Ross and others, June 7. 1706; Hume, i. 392.—[6] Hume, i. 392.—[7] Purves v. Craw, March 20 1676, and Magdalene Grahame, December 17 1703, Hume, i. 392.—[8] Hume, i. 392.

which alone was authorised by the statute on which the warrant was founded. These objections were both sustained, and
the pannel dismissed from the bar.[5] But if the goods have
once been poinded, and the schedule left with the debtor, any
person claiming them is bound to make an application to the
Sheriff for a warrant to have the poinded goods delivered to
him, or to have the sale delayed until the question of right
shall be determined; or if, instead of doing this, he shall come
with a party of his friends and resist the removal of the goods
under the Sheriff's warrant, he is guilty of deforcement. So it
was held by Lord Gillies in the case of Michael Wallace, Ayr,
spring 1830.

The officer, however, is not in the general case authorised
to receive payment of the debt, and therefore it will be no defence against a deforcement that the debtor offered payment to
the officer; his remedy is to go with the messenger and con-
sign the sum contained in the diligence in the hands of the
jailor, who will be liable in wrongous imprisonment if he in-
carcerate him after such offer.[3] But the case is different if the
officer have received a special power from the creditor to receive payment of the debt, and acts not *qua* messenger only
but *qua* agent;[4] but, in that case, the debtor, to authorise his
resistance, must shew that he was made aware that the messenger held this novel character, and therefore was justified in
holding him bound to accept payment. Nay, it has been more
than once decided that he is not bound to desist, even on production of evidence of previous payment, compensation, discharge or compromise, nor any thing short of a regular written discharge of the debt and *diligence* in the officer's hands;
for the officer is not a fit judge of such matters, and is bound
to look to nothing but either a sist or suspension, or a regular
discharge of the diligence with which he is intrusted.[5] In the
case, accordingly, of David Simpson, March 6. 1662, the defence of previous payment was repelled; and in that of Francis
Duguid, December 1. 1673, that of an offer of payment to the
messenger.[6] It is also not competent in defence against a deforcement, to found upon any alleged practice of particular
sheriffdoms or districts not sanctioned or supported by the ge-

---

[1] Hume, i. 392.—[2] Unreported.—[3] Hume, i. 393.—[4] Ibid.—[5] Ibid.—[6] Both
in Hume, i. 393.

neral law or custom of the land. So it was found in the case of John Davidson and others, Inverness, April 28. 1821.[1]

7. The messenger must be possessed of a warrant *ex facie* fair and regular; but he is neither bound to be possessed of or look into the previous proceedings, nor answerable for any irregularity they may contain.

It is not the whole legal process terminating in the warrant which is the subject of dispute that is put into the messenger's hands, but only the last step, containing the deliverance of the judge, which he is directed to carry into effect. Of course, as he has no access to see, so he is nowise answerable for any errors or irregularities which may exist in any previous part of the proceedings, and may not be lawfully resisted on the ground of the existence of such previous informalities.[2] The officer loses his privilege in the case only of such vices as appear in the immediate frame or texture of the warrant which is put into his hands, and is not affected by those remote and extrinsic, and to him undiscoverable irregularities, which may have occurred in the application for the warrant or the process in which it terminated.[3] If fatal objections occur to the process or proceedings which have terminated in this warrant, the party against whom it is directed shall only be held the more inexcusable, that, instead of applying for the legal remedy by sist or suspension, which arises from such objection, he *brevi manu* proceeds to deforce the officer, to whom it is in all probability unknown, or by whom, if known, it cannot be corrected.[4]

But, on the other hand, the officer is held bound to know so much of the law as relates to the legality or formality of the warrant itself, or petition praying for it, which is put into his hand, and the regular manner in which an extract of the deliverance of the judge should be authenticated; and the charge of deforcing him will be elided if an informality appear in his warrant in either of these respects.[5] If, therefore, the warrant is not signed, or not dated, or if it is subscribed by a judge who has no jurisdiction in the place where it is to be enforced, or if it does not bear the offender's name, or proceeds upon an application for the apprehension of a person for an act which is

[1] Shaw, No. 24.—[2] Hume, i. 200.—[3] Ibid.—[4] Ibid.—[5] Ibid

notoriously not a crime; in all these and the like situations, the charge of deforcement will be elided.[1] Nay, so far is this strictness carried, that in the case of Whitelaw and Bisset, July 15. 1831, it was considered a good defence against a deforcement, that the warrant, which was an extract, did not bear the addition of the word " clerk" to the Sheriff-clerk's name who wrote the extract, when that was required by the act of Parliament under which the decree was given, and the deforcement in consequence was not insisted in.[2]

7. But although the officer, where he has proceeded irregularly, or is the bearer of a warrant *ex facie* defective, may be lawfully resisted ; yet the pannel is bound to exercise the due moderation in his conduct in so doing, and will be liable under an indictment for assaulting, rioting or mobbing, for any improper excess.

Though the diligence may be liable to some fatal defect, or the officer in the execution of it may have acted illegally, still the person against whom it is directed does not thereby acquire the right to exercise every sort of excess or outrage against him. He is entitled to exert that degree of resistance which is necessary to prevent the irregular or illegal design upon his person or property, but no more; and if, instead of confining himself to this, he shall indulge in acts of rage or cruelty against the officer, he may be punished for the assault and injury. Nay, if the officer shall be killed in the course of such a malicious or intemperate pursuit, it will depend upon the *excessus moderaminis* whether it will not even amount to murder.[5]

8. The violence used in the case of deforcement must be done with the design of resisting the process of the law, and be so considerable as with a person of ordinary firmness of character to have that effect.

The essence of the crime of deforcement consists in the design of obstructing the process of the law; and, therefore, though the violence done to the messenger may substantially have the effect of preventing the execution of the warrant, yet if it was

[1] Hume, i. 200.—[2] Unreported —[3] Hume, i. 393.

not done with that design, the defender, however amenable to
punishment for riot, mobbing or assault, is not liable to a prosecution for deforcement. For example, if, in the course of
executing a warrant, an accidental quarrel arises between him
or any of his assistants and the bystanders, or that they are
waylaid and assaulted in pursuance of an old grudge; these acts
of violence, though they may have the effect of staying or preventing the execution of the diligence, do not properly fall under deforcement, because they were not committed with the
design of resisting the authority of the law. In the case accordingly of Alexander Innes, November 1723, which was just
such a case, the libel was drawn for assault only; and in that
of David Simpson, March 6. 1662, it was sustained as a relevant defence that the assault was an incidental quarrel, nowise
connected with the poinding.[1]

Farther, the opposition must have been of such a kind as afforded a reasonable impediment to the officer's proceeding.
Not that there is any foundation for the idea, which receives
some countenance from the older authorities,[2] that it is necessary that the officer should be assaulted to the effusion of his
blood; on the contrary, it has been always held the rule, that
it is a deforcement, if, by any sort of actual violence, or the
shew and preparation of mischief, or the wilful opposing of real
impediments, the officer is hindered from proceeding to the discharge of his duty.[3] Thus, in the case of Macneil, July 1679;
of Sutherland, June 1715; and of Forbes of Tolquhon, July
25. 1719, it was held to be a deforcement where the officer or
his party were fired at with loaded fire-arms, though they
escaped unhurt;[4] and the same was considered as fixed law in
the case of Donald Stewart, Aberdeen, autumn 1829, where, although a great number of shots were fired from a distance at
the officer's party, none of them took effect.[5] The same is law
if he is assailed and beat off with stones or other missiles, intended, no matter how ineffectually, to injure his body; as was
held by Lord Justice-Clerk Boyle, Inverness, spring 1826, in
the case of Donald Macpherson and others, where the objection
taken on this very ground was overruled, that the deforcement,
which took place in the Highland village of Kingussie, consisted merely of boys and women throwing stones, none of which

---

[1] Hume, i. 394.—[2] 1592, c. 152.—[3] Hume, i. 394.—[4] Ibid.—[5] Unreported.

did any serious injury to the officer, was an obstruction only,
and not a deforcement.[1]   In like manner, if a tumultuous crowd
take the poinded goods out of the officer's possession;[2] or he has
got into the house and began to poind, and is pushed out again
and the door barred in his face;[3] or he is opposed by an armed
posse, who shew their arms and forbid him access;[4] or if the
opposers forcibly lock up the debtor, and lay hold of and master the officer so that he cannot get at him;[5] or if they shall
pull the debtor out of the messenger's hands after he has been
taken into custody,[6] and so give him the means of escaping;
or shall break up the door of the room where the prisoner is,
and so compel his surrender:[7]—in all these and the like cases
the opposer is guilty of deforcement, though the officer escape
without any bodily harm.   And this is evidently a wholesome
and necessary rule; for bloodshed and murder would be of con-
tinual occurrence, if the officer was in every case compelled to
persist till his life was brought into actual danger.[8]

2. It is indispensable to the crime of deforcement that
the diligence shall have been hindered being put in execution ; but if this has once been done, it cannot be got
quit of by the submission of the refractory parties.

If the officer, notwithstanding the most violent opposition,
has succeeded in making good his point, the pannel cannot be
indicted for deforcement, which his resistance has prevented
from being carried into effect.   The proper designation of such
an offence is assault with intent to deforce, or with intent to
revenge or prevent the execution of legal diligence.[9]   Numerous instances of such indictments have occurred of late years.
On the other hand, it is no less clear, that, if the resistance has
once compelled the officer to abandon his purpose, no subsequent submission of the accused, or obedience to the law, will
purge the offence, any more than a defence of subsequent restitution will elide a charge of theft.   Such a defence accordingly was overruled in the case of Hamilton, January 1726.[10]

[1] Unreported.—[2] Hamilton's Case, December 1725.—[3] M'Wallace's Case,
Ayr, April 1830; unreported.—[4] Campbell's Case, July 1722, Hume, i. 395
—[5] Duguid's Case, December 1. 1673.—[6] Jean Steel and others, Dumfries,
spring 1830; unreported.—[7] Ramsay's Case, 23d November 1724; Hume, i.
395.—[8] Hume, i. 395.—[9] Ibid.—[10] Ibid. i 396

10. Every solemn act of an officer of the law, if resisted, will implicate the refractory party, or those aiding and assisting him, in the pains of deforcement.

It is of no importance in the estimation of law, what is the nature of the legal diligence which is prevented being carried into effect, whether letters of poinding, caption, or ejection, or the mere execution of a summons,[1] or of a summary warrant to apprehend and imprison.[2] The words of the act 1592 are quite general of " all persons whatsoever," and of the precepts of all judges within the realm.[3] On this principle the pains of deforcement have been found to have been incurred, even in the case of successful resistance to the precept of a baron court.[4] As little does it make any difference what is the dignity of the court from which the warrant has emanated, whether letters under the King's Signet, or the precept of any inferior court, so as the warrant was not carried into execution beyond its proper territory.[5] One numerous and important class of cases arises from the resistance of smugglers to the seizure of smuggled goods, or goods suspected to be smuggled, by officers of the customs or excise. In the case of John Costine, 7th January 1712, the statutes against deforcement were found to apply to the hindering of a steward officer from levying the mart-cow, or the cow which he was entitled to levy from each parish in his district.[6] In the case of James Little and others, Jedburgh, spring 1815, the Court had no doubt that the pains of deforcement might be incurred by resisting the water bailies on the river Tweed, if acting legally; though in that particular case the indictment was dismissed as irrelevant, in respect that the local statute founded on required a written warrant, and gave no power to act without such warrant, except in the case of obstructions or illegal practices on the water, and that the officers in that particular case had no such warrant, and the matter of their interference did not fall within the exception specified in the statute.[7]

All persons, of whatever description, or without exception, even of the highest, may be involved in the pains of deforcement; and the degree of accession which shall be held sufficient to implicate them, does not depend on any peculiar rule, but

[1] Macneil's Case, July 1719.—[2] Sinclair's Case, July 6. 1699.—[3] 1592, c. 152.—[4] Dict. of Decisions, i. 231.—[5] Hume, i. 396.—[6] Ibid.—[7] Ibid.

on the general principles of art and part applicable to all offences. In the case of Hugh Fraser, July 20. 1675, the commanding the pannel's natural son to come up and relieve him
from the messenger's hands, was found to render him art and
part in the deforcement which followed.[1] Nay, in the case of
Thomas Mitchell, December 26. 1698, it was found relevant as
a charge of deforcement, that the pannel, being a magistrate
within his jurisdiction, twice refused to assist the messenger
against the rabble who were obstructing him in the execution
of his duty; but such tacit declining to support the authority of
the law, would not be construed into an act of deforcement in
the case of an ordinary individual.[2]

10. In modern practice, the pains of law for deforcement is imprisonment or fine; but in serious cases, or
where the resistance has been attended with mobbing and
rioting, or serious wounding of the messenger or his assistants, or the discharge of loaded fire-arms, transportation
is not unfrequently inflicted.

In former times, and by the statutes 1581, c. 118, and 1587,
c. 85, persons convicted of deforcement were directed to be
punished with confiscation of moveables, and the placing of
their persons at the King's will. But even in ancient times,
when the unsettled state of the country rendered it necessary
to chastise this crime with great severity, it does not appear
that any farther corporal pains were inflicted than imprisonment, accompanied with the pecuniary penalties.[3] These patrimonial pains are escheats of moveables, the one-half to go to
the King, the other half to the party whose diligence was hindered. To secure this, the sentence usually taxed the debt,
and declared that the King's half shall be burdened with the
balance, in case the private party's debt was not satisfied by his
half.[4] This was done in the case of Ramsay, November 27.
1724, and Macleod, July 1659.[5]

In other cases, the Court have at once, instead of confiscating
moveables, decerned at once for a certain sum in name of fine
or damages. This was done in particular in the case of James
Macneil, July 1679, who was sentenced to pay 1000 merks

---

[1] Hume, 1. 397.—[2] Duguid's Case, December 1. 1673; Hume, 1. 397.—
[3] Hume, 1. 398.—[4] Ibid.—[5] Ibid.

Scots; and Joseph Watson, July 28. 1707, where the sentence was for payment of the debt, and a fine of 500 merks.[1]

More lately the practice seems to have gone entirely into disuse of decerning for the escheat of moveables, which would be no punishment at all in most cases, and a most severe one in others, and instead, sentencing the pannel to a certain period of imprisonment. In the case of William Calderwood, Ayr, April 1823, the case of the pannel, convicted of deforcing a messenger-at-arms, without any very aggravated circumstances, was certified to the High Court, for the purpose of fixing the sentence which should follow on the verdict, and the Court fixed on six months' imprisonment and caution to keep the peace.[2] In the numerous cases of convictions for this offence which have taken place of late years, the sentence has usually been imprisonment for various periods, according to the magnitude of the crime; but where it has been coupled with a very aggravated assault, or mobbing or rioting of a dangerous character, or the discharging of loaded fire-arms, transportation has in general been the punishment. Of the more lenient course, the following instances may be given. At Inverness, spring 1823, on a confession of a charge of deforcement without any aggravation, John Fraser was sentenced to three months' imprisonment.[3] At the same Circuit, Donald Macpherson, convicted of deforcing a revenue officer, without any aggravation, escaped with imprisonment for one month.[4] At Aberdeen, spring 1823, John Gordon and others, for a simple deforcement, were sentenced to six weeks' imprisonment.[5] At Inverness, September 1824, Robert Clark and others were sentenced to three months' imprisonment for a deforcement, accompanied with a slight assault to the effusion of blood.[6]

In more serious cases of assault with the deforcement the punishment has been much more severe. Alexander Gordon and others, Perth, spring 1826, were sentenced to twelve months' imprisonment for a deforcement of excise officers, accompanied by severe wounding of the revenue officers with sticks and stones.[7] At Inverary, spring 1825, Donald Mac-Callum and others, convicted of deforcing officers of the revenue, accompanied with mobbing and rioting, were imprisoned for the like period.[9] George Young, Perth, autumn 1824, re-

[1] Hume, i. 399.—[2] Shaw's Cases.—[3] Unreported.—[4] Unreported.—[5] Unreported.—[6] Unreported.—[7] Unreported.—[8] Unreported.—[9] Unreported.

ceived nine months' imprisonment for a violent assault and deforcement of a revenue officer in the streets of Forfar.[1] At Dumfries, spring 1827, William Anderson received twelve months' imprisonment for a violent deforcement of a messenger-at-arms and constables in the execution of a warrant of caption.[2] And in the case of David Morrison and Alexander Wardlaw, June 2. 1823, the prisoners, convicted of mobbing and rioting, with intent to prevent the execution of legal diligence, were sentenced to nine months' imprisonment.[3]

But where the deforcement has been accompanied, as it has too often been of late years, by discharging of loaded fire-arms at the revenue officers by bodies of armed men, a very different punishment has been deemed necessary, and certainly not without good reason. In the case of Charles Lamond, July 17. 1826, the pannel, convicted of deforcement, accompanied by a violent assault and discharging loaded fire-arms, though none of the officers were struck by the shot, was sentenced to fourteen years' transportation.[4] And in the case of James Garden and William Garden, July 16. 1827, where the deforcement was committed by a large party of armed men in a Highland district, and one of the officers was shot through the body, though he recovered, the pannels were transported for life.[5]

12. Either the Lord Advocate, the messenger deforced, or the private party, owner of the diligence, may prosecute for deforcement; but the only Court competent to try a deforcement of the King's officers, is either the Court of Justiciary or Session, though inferior judges are all competent to take cognizance of any resistance to their own officers.

The interest of the private party, in a prosecution for deforcement, is obvious, as he has a right, in the event of a pecuniary penalty being awarded, to part of the fine or damages. In addition to these prosecutors, the title of the messenger and lord-lyon, even without the concurrence of the private party, was sustained in the case of Duguid, December 1. 1673. The Lord Advocate, of course, may prosecute for this, as every other offence.

[1] Unreported.—[2] Unreported.—[3] Unreported.—[4] Unreported.—[5] Unreported.

It is stated by Hume, that the only competent court for the trial of the deforcement of any of the King's officers, is either the Court of Session or Justiciary.[1] It does not very distinctly appear on what ground the Sheriff, in virtue of his general commission to keep the King's peace, is not competent to try for this as well as any other offence not excluded by statute or custom; but till the reverse is established by a decision of the Supreme Court, it is safest to follow this course; and, where it is not thought advisable to bring such deforcements to the Justiciary Court, to try these before the Sheriff for assault, aggravated by the intention to deforce, to which there seems no doubt that that judge is competent.

In prosecutions at the instance of the Lord Advocate, the messenger and his assistants, if he has any, are not only competent but necessary witnesses.[2] It is no sufficient objection to an assistant giving his testimony, in a prosecution by the messenger, that he is a near relation of the messenger.[3] Hume lays it down, that the party, who is the employer of the messenger, cannot give his evidence even in the Lord Advocate's process, unless he discharge his interest in the escheat;[4] but this is not supported by any authority, and it seems contrary to the analogy of law, in the case of witnesses whose subscriptions have been forged, or goods stolen; but, without doubt, the existence of that interest should make the jury cautious in receiving his testimony.

# CHAPTER XXIII.

## OF MOBBING AND RIOTING

THE general term Mobbing and Rioting includes all those convocations of the lieges for violent and unlawful purposes, which are attended with injury to the persons or property of the lieges, or terror and alarm to the neighbourhood in which it takes place. The two phrases are usually placed together; but nevertheless they have distinct meanings, and are some-

[1] Hume, i 399.—[2] Ibid —[3] Sword v. Franks, July 13. 1669.—[4] Hume, i. 400

times used separately in legal language; the word Mobbing being peculiarly applicable to the unlawful assemblage and violence of a number of persons, and that of Rioting to the outrageous behaviour of a single individual.

1. It is indispensable that a considerable host or number of persons shall have been assembled for some unlawful purpose.

It is in the appearance of power, as well as in the disposition to execute their unlawful purposes, of their own will and authority, and without regard to legal authority, that the crime of mobbing chiefly consists. Of course it is indispensable that a considerable number of persons shall have been assembled; such a number as threatens the peace of the neighbourhood, and is calculated to excite alarm and terror among the lieges. No specific rule can be laid down as to the number of persons who must be assembled together in order to constitute a mob; and truly this is a matter which is better left to be decided by the circumstances of each particular case, and the degree of excess to which the meeting have proceeded; for, without doubt, the higher these are, the less number will be sufficient to bring the convocation under the description of a mob; and, on the other hand, inferior outrages may raise it to that character, if they proceed from so great a number as to be on that account the subjects of terror and alarm.[1] In many cases assemblages of seventy, fifty, and forty persons have been libelled on as amounting to a mob, and the indictments sustained without hesitation by the Court. The Riot act fixes the number at *twelve* or more, a principle which seems decisive of the law on this subject. In England it is held that in every riot there must be some such circumstances either of force or violence, or of an apparent tendency thereto, as is apt to strike terror into the people; but it is not necessary that actual violence should have been committed to constitute the crime.[2]

2. The assembly must be to the fear of the lieges, and the disturbance of the public peace; and it may be committed even in the execution of a legal object, if done in a violent and outrageous way.

[1] Hume i. 416.—[2] Hawk i. c. 65 § 5; and Camp ii. 369.

It does not affix the character of mobbing upon an assembly, that it is one which is intended for a wrong or unlawful purpose, even such an one as is forbidden under pain of death, if the business is conducted regularly and quietly, and no preparation or intention of commotion exists[1]. Even the assembling to compass the king's death, which is an overt act of high treason, for which the offenders may be arrested on the spot, is not an act of mobbing, so as it is done secretly, and after the manner of a conspiracy rather than a tumultuous assembly.[2] Of course, assemblages for purposes nowise illegal, though sometimes contrary to morals, as foot-ball, racing, cock-fighting, or the like, where the purposes of the meeting are not public disturbances, or the accomplishment of any violent and illegal objects, do not fall under this offence.[3]

On the other hand, acts of mobbing may be committed by the lieges, in the prosecution even of a legal object, if it be set about after a tumultuous and disorderly manner. Thus a sheriff, a justice of the peace, and, in some cases of extremity, a messenger, constable, or revenue officer, has a right to command the assistance of the neighbourhood; but if, instead of employing only the requisite and necessary degree of force, the assembly shall proceed to acts of unnecessary violence or outrage, they are undoubtedly amenable to the law of mobbing. Thus in the case of George Robertson, sheriff-substitute, David Beatson, messenger, and a number of gentlemen of the county of Ross, 26th February 1722, a libel was sustained against these parties for acts of violence and outrage committed by them, in the execution of a caption against certain councillors of the burgh of Dingwall; and the same view was taken by the Court of Session, in the case of a great number of persons who, in November 1790, under authority of a decree of that Court for removing a dam-dike on the river Leven, proceeded to acts of unnecessary violence.[4]

Farther, it is not to be supposed that acts of mobbing can be committed with impunity, even in the vindication of the supposed rights of the lieges, and which ultimately, when investigated by the proper tribunal, turn out to be well founded. If, instead of presenting a bill of suspension, or adopting other legal measures for preventing the encroachment, the injured parties shall proceed to take the law into their own hand, with circumstances of tumult and violence, their offence will amount to mobbing, and the alleged illegality of the proceedings against which their violence was directed, will furnish no defence. Accordingly, in the case of Alexander Macphie and others, Glasgow, autumn 1823, the pannels were indicted for riotously assembling, and in a tumultuous manner pulling down certain walls which had been erected across a foot-path at or near the eastern and western boundaries of Mr Harvie's estate, at Glenthorn, on the river Clyde, and which obstructed a foot-path which had long been frequented by the public along the banks of the river. It was objected to the libel, that it did not aver that the walls pulled down were Mr Harvie's property: but this was repelled, on the ground that, whether they were on his property or not, the violent and tumultuous proceedings libelled amounted to the crime of mobbing; and that, if the lieges had a right to the walk, they should proceed to establish their right by the proper proceedings in the civil courts, instead of violently taking the law into their own hands　They were convicted; and, in consideration of good character, and of their having proceeded on a mistaken idea of right, sentenced only to six months' imprisonment. Afterwards, in a trial in the Jury Court, affirmed in the House of Lords, the question of right was determined in favour of the inhabitants, and the obnoxious bulwarks ordered to be removed.[1] In like manner, in the case of Hugh Macdonald and others, June 9. 1823, it appeared that the pannels, who were inhabitants of the parish of Croy, near Inverness, conceived that their legal rights, as parishioners, had been invaded by the appointment of a minister by the patron of the parish; and, in order to get quit of him, they violently resisted his entrance into the church on the day on which he had been appointed by the presbytery to officiate. For this offence they were sentenced to the mitigated punishment of two months' imprisonment each, in consideration of their good character, and of their having proceeded on a mistaken idea of right.[2] In England it is held, that, if there be violence and tumult, it is immaterial whether the act intended to be done be of itself legal or not; for the law will not suffer persons to seek redress of their private grievances by such dangerous disturbances of

---

[1] Unreported.—[2] Unreported.

the public peace; but the legality of the object is a good ground for mitigation of punishment.[1] If three or more persons, in a violent and tumultuous manner, join together in removing an illegal nuisance, they are as much guilty of a riot as if the act intended by them were unlawful [2]

3. The assembly must not only have proceeded to acts of violence, but they must have done so in pursuance of a common design, either previously formed or taken up at the moment in pursuance of a common feeling.

It is in the convocation of a number of persons for some common purpose that the essence of mobbing consists And it is in this particular that it differs from a common or casual affray, which, although it may be as numerous or violent, is not properly a mob if no common object actuated its members. But, on the other hand, it is not indispensable that this common object be formed, though usually it is so, previous to the time of meeting; it is sufficient if a sudden and tumultuous consent is given at the moment to some common proceeding, for the attainment of a common object.[3] And wherever this sort of tacit confederacy is evident in the behaviour and proceedings of the multitude who direct their efforts to one common end, the crime will amount to mobbing, though the idea was suggested only at the moment by some occurrence which could not have been foreseen.[4]

In England the law is the same. There must be a common object, but it may be taken up at the moment, and though the parties assemble in the first instance for an innocent purpose, they may be afterwards guilty of a riot, if they suddenly take up the design of tumultuous proceedings.[5]

4. The common object in mobbing must be some local or private matter, and not the attainment of any general or national object, in which case it merges in treason.

When mobbing is carried on on a great scale it is very nearly allied to treason, and the same offence may frequently be prosecuted either under that formidable name, or under the lower

---

[1] Hawkins, c. 65, § 7.—[2] Mod. xii. 648, Russell, i. 249.—[3] Hume, i. 418. —[4] Ibid.—[5] Hawkins, i. c 65. § 3, Russell, i. 250.

denomination. But the true distinction between them consists
in this, that treason contemplates some violent opposition to the
government, or forcible revolution or reform in the affairs of the
state, or threatens the security of the crown; whereas mobbing contemplates some minor and subordinate violence, directed not against the national but some subordinate authority, and
intended to accomplish, not a general, but some local object,
either of a public or a private nature.   Thus, to take up arms
against the King's government, and openly resist the royal
forces, for the sake of effecting a reformation in the state, or
the repeal of taxes or corn-laws, or the abrogation of the House
of Peers, the annihilation of the National Debt, or the like objects of popular ambition, is undoubtedly high treason; while
resistance to soldiers, even if done in pursuance of a minor or
local object, or in resistance only to a subordinate authority, as
to reduce the price of grain in a particular market, to rescue a
criminal from justice, hinder the division of a common, enforce
an illumination against certain unwilling inhabitants, carry off
a bailie at an election, tear down the door of a prison and liberate the prisoners, or the like, are more properly acts of
mobbing and rioting.   Thus, the great acts of violence which
occurred at Glasgow in 1725, known under the name of the
Shawfield Mob, and the still more serious tumult which took
place at Edinburgh on occasion of the Porteous Mob, though
both almost amounted to insurrection, and the last in particular was attended by the violent murder of a condemned individual for whom it was feared a pardon would be obtained,
were prosecuted under the name of mobbing, though they undoubtedly were on the frontiers of high treason.[1]   If the same
things had been done by a convocation of persons from all
quarters of the country, and with the declared purpose of compelling the repeal of the malt-tax, or to hinder generally the
execution of royal pardons, certainly such acts of violence, in
pursuance of such *general* objects, would have amounted to
high treason.[2]

These principles have been recently exemplified on occasion of
the serious riots which occurred in Scotland on the subject of the
Reform Bill.   Though amounting in many cases to a local and
temporary insurrection, and accompanied with excessive and

---

[1] Hume, i. 418.—[2] Ibid. i. 419.

4

disgraceful acts of violence, and directed to objects of general government; yet, being done in violation only of local authorities, and in local tumults, without any general ramification or connexion with each other, they were very properly prosecuted under the denomination of mobbing and rioting only. Thus, William Lithgow and John Robb, July 18. 1831, received twelve and nine months' imprisonment respectively, the former for having thrown a piece of glass at Colonel Douglas, when sitting as preses of the freeholders at the Lanark election, which cut him on the head; the latter for aiding and abetting him in that violent act.[1] On June 12. 1831, Thomas Kettle, James Barnett, and others, were brought to trial for a most serious riot on the streets of Dundee, on occasion of the illumination for the second reading of the Reform Bill. It appeared that some rioters having been imprisoned in the police-office of Dundee, on account of disturbances in the streets during the illumination, the mob brought a boat full of combustible materials to the door of the jail where the rioters were confined, forced it open, burnt and destroyed the contents of the police-office, which was under the same roof with the jail, assailed and beat off the police-officers, broke their windows by showers of stones, burnt the furniture and books of the police-office, and liberated all the prisoners. For these aggravated offences the two principal offenders were sentenced to fourteen years' transportation; and two inferior ones, in consideration of good character and other alleviating circumstances, to seven and eighteen months in Bridewell only.[2] So also in the case of the Haddington rioters, July 16. 1831, it appeared that a mob surrounded the Court-House at Haddington, where two prisoners, apprehended for an outrage at the Greenlaw election, were under examination before the Sheriff-depute of the county, broke open the door with a great beam used as a battering-ram, and carried off the culprits in triumph. This, too, was most properly prosecuted as mobbing, and the prisoners were sentenced to eighteen months' imprisonment.[3] In these instances the offences were committed in pursuance of the common design of securing the return of reforming members to the House of Commons, and that, too, by the most violent and unlawful measures; but as the violence was directed to local

[1] Unreported.—[2] Unreported.—[3] Unreported.

objects, and the authority set at nought was that of local judges, it was properly considered as mobbing only.

5. The degree of violence requisite to constitute the crime of mobbing is either the invasion of the person or properties of the lieges by a tumultuous assembly, or such a preparation and shew of violence as evinces a determination to set legal authority at defiance, and carries terror and intimidation into the neighbourhood.

Any violence to property, whether by damaging, destroying, rifling, or forcibly carrying off; or to persons, as by assaulting, pursuing, seizing, or constraining them; or to inclination, as by intimidating any one to act contrary to his interest, or compelling him to sell grain at a particular price, or to vote for a particular candidate at an election; if committed by an united and tumultuous assembly, constitute acts of mobbing.[1]   Thus, in the case of William Paton and David Black, May 25. 1720, it was found, that the entering into warehouses by a tumultuous body, and making search there for oats, constituted acts of mobbing.[2]   So also the assembling in a menacing manner in a market-place, and threatening the magistrates, in order to compel the lowering the price of provisions;[3] threatening to force the guard, and burn the houses in a town;[4] throwing stones at the windows of a distillery, and staving some casks on the outside of the building, on occasion of an assembly produced by the high price of meal;[5] carrying off a bailie by a lawless multitude, in order to influence an election;[6] have all been found to be acts of mobbing, and, in some cases, particularly that of Peter Macgregor, August 3. 1784, visited with transportation for fourteen years.  It is needless to say, that any acts of actual violence or outrage, whether to persons or property, as by breaking windows, seizing and rifling carts, intruding into vessels, breaking open or pillaging shops, warehouses, or private houses, or assaulting and injuring individuals, if committed by large assemblages, undoubtedly fall under this offence.

[1] Hume, i. 419 ——[2] Ibid.——[3] Alexander Barry's Case, 27th May 1720, Hume, i 419 ——[4] James Geddes's Case, 26th May 1720, Hume, i. 419.—— [5] Peter Macgregor's Case, August 3. 1784, Hume, i. 419.—[6] Lauder Rioters, November 21 1831.

Nay, it is by no means essential that the mob should have proceeded to acts of actual violence, in order to implicate them in the pains of this offence. It is quite the same thing in point of law, as it plainly is in point of reason, if they have once plainly discovered their intention to engage in some violent enterprise, and made a movement, or taken some step towards its execution.[1] Thus, if a multitude assemble in the streets of a borough in time of scarcity, and take the road, in a body, to a certain mill or granary, with a declared intention of dispersing on the way, they are unquestionably guilty of a riot, though they never reach the place of their destination, either from change of purpose, previous dispersion, or any other cause;[2] or if a great host of people assemble on the streets of any city, with standards or other ensigns, and continue to parade there for a length of time, armed with stones, bludgeons, or offensive weapons, and if they refuse to disperse when warned by the peace-officers or magistrates, and evince, by angry gestures and words, their determination to repel all interference, this of itself, independent of any ulterior acts of violence, constitutes an act of mobbing.[3] In the cases, accordingly, of Peter Macgregor, August 3. 1784; John Fraser, July 26 1784; and Paul and Anderson, August 23. 1784, the convocation of a tumultuous rabble, is made an article of charge, and sustained at common law, independent of the subsequent acts of violence.[4] Any convocation of the lieges, in short, in a tumultuous and menacing manner, without lawful authority, in defiance of the constituted authorities, for a common purpose, and with the declared or understood intention of committing violence, or constraining will, or intimidating others, is of itself an act of mobbing, even though they have not proceeded to carry their illegal intentions into effect.

6. A person becomes art and part in mobbing, not only by aiding, instigating, advising, or encouraging the guilty, but even without participating in any of their acts of violence, or sharing in their intention, by remaining with them after their illegal purpose has been declared or be-

---

[1] Hume, i. 420.—[2] Fraser's Case, 26th July 1784, Hume, i. 420 —[3] Hume, i. 420.—[4] Ibid.

come known, and, still more, in disobedience to orders to disperse.

The subject of the degree of accession which constitutes the crime of art and part in mobbing, deserves particular attention, from the facility with which persons, without any guilty intention, may be involved in serious pains from mere misapprehension of the law, and the general ignorance on the subject which prevails even among those who should be better informed.

The circumstance which renders a mob so dangerous is, that it implies a large convocation of disorderly persons, and of course not only accumulates a force generally irresistible and always formidable to individuals, but puts them in a situation where the passions are most strongly excited, and the contagion of violence becomes most difficult to be withstood. For this reason all are held to be art and part in the enterprise, who, by their mere presence, add to the terror and intimidation which the acts of the more violent are calculated to inspire[1] But the different degrees of accession which an recognised by law, require more particular attention.

In the first place, every one who, by previous counsel, assistance, or preparation, furthers the object of the enterprise, is held as art and part, though he were not present with the mob in any of their proceedings.[2] He, therefore, who beats a drum, or distributes placards or handbills to convocate the rioters, or is a member of a committee who fix the time or place of their assemblage; or prints or throws off the handbills which lead to its becoming known, is justly held an accessary to all that follows, being, in truth, the nerve and sinew of the enterprise in which the others are, comparatively speaking, mere passive instruments.[3] Paul and Anderson, August 24. 1784, were convicted as art and part of mobbing, the former " by beating a drum," the latter "by exciting the mob in a less degree." The former received fourteen years' transportation as the ringleader, the latter six months' imprisonment as a mere follower.[4] In like manner, Captain Walter Hamilton, July 27. 1722, was convicted of mobbing, by having uttered words of exhortation to the mob to perpetrate acts of violence.[5] The giving orders

[1] Hume, 1. 421.—[2] Ibid.—[3] Ibid.—[4] Ibid.—[5] Ibid.

to a refractory body of parishioners to resist the settlement of
a minister, or the exhorting them to act in the actual tumult,
standing at a small distance and looking on during the time
the violence was committed by the rabble, have been found relevant to infer the pains of rioting.[1] The riotously and tumultuously assembling or convocating a mob by beat of drum or
otherwise, as also the exciting, instigating, encouraging, or fo-
menting it, was found relevant in the case of John Taylor,
July 12. 1792.[2]

By still nearer proximity to the mob, though without actually joining them in their excesses, a pannel may clearly be
implicated as art and part in all they do; as by sending money
or liquor to them from some short distance, furnishing them
with stones or staves to break doors or windows, promising
spirits to those who would go out and join them; providing
them with guns, powder, or ball; directing or regulating their
movements.[3] Alexander Keith, accordingly, 26th February
1686, was found guilty of mobbing, in respect of his having in
an alehouse drunk success to a riot then going on in the adjoining streets, and promised liquor and money to all who
would go and assist them.[4] This decision would have been
correct if it had also found it proven, that, in virtue of the
counsel thus given, any persons had actually joined the mob;
but the mere uttering wishes for the success of a cause, without in some shape co-operating with it, is no legal ground *per
se* for a conviction as art and part with those actually engaged.[5]

Mere presence in a mob, if accompanied by any evidence of
an intention to join in their proceedings, affords an indubitable
ground for a conviction as art and part. Though a person may
be in a mob from an innocent, or at least not a guilty, intention for a short time; yet, if he remain there for any considerable period, or go about with them from place to place, his
continued presence can be accounted for on no rational motive
but a desire to aid these proceedings.[6] And how short soever
the time, yet, if the circumstances or conduct of the prisoner
were such as to indicate clearly a design to abet these proceedings, as, if he be found in the throng with his face blackened,
or in woman's apparel, or with a shirt over his coat, or with

[1] Burnett, Scott, and others, 12th February 1711, Hume, i. 421; Croy
Rioters, June 9. 1823, unreported.—[2] Hume, i. 420.—[3] Ibid.—[4] Ibid. i. 422.
—[5] Ibid.—[6] Ibid. i. 423.

arms in his hands, or handbills in his pockets, or the badge of
the rioters in his hat, he may justly be convicted, though he
neither, by word, deed, or gesture, encouraged their proceedings.[1]   Of course there can be as little doubt if, without such
external marks of concert, the prisoner's conduct has evinced
it, as by joining in their cries, pursuing the police-officers, or
the like, though without the use of any actual violence.[2]

Farther still, mere presence is of itself a lawful ground of
conviction, if continuing in circumstances when it is the duty
of every good citizen to separate and go home, in order to prevent his presence from aiding the apparent strength, or encou-
rage the hardihood of the ringleaders of the tumult, or for such
a length of time as plainly demonstrates a desire that the outrage should continue.  If, therefore, any one remain with a mob
after they have begun to commit guilty excesses, as throwing
stones at windows, pelting the military, assaulting constables
or police-officers, breaking into shops, pillaging carts, assaulting individuals, or the like, he is justly held amenable to punishment, though he take no hand in these excesses himself, and
if his presence be proved, it will be no defence that he individually did no mischief.[3]   The like must hold, if the pannel be
proved to have continued with the mob after they were ordered to disperse by the proper authorities, whether magistrates,
constables, or military, from the dread of an approaching
breach of the peace, though no violence has yet been committed.  In short, to use the words of Mr Solicitor-General
Cockburn, on occasion of the trial of the Edinburgh rioters,
July 16 1831, it is quite clear, that, if a man find himself in
a mob, which is engaged in, or commencing a contest with, any
legal authorities, or doing mischief, he can only avoid a conviction by straightway joining the authorities, or going home.

Numerous decisions, in every period of our history, prove
this to be the fixed law of Scotland.  Thus, in the case of Thomas Gilkie, 5th August 1720, the jury found it proven, " that
the pannel was in the mob at the time libelled, but *not proven*
that he was seen breaking shops or taking away victual ;" upon which he was ordered to be scourged.[4]   In like manner, on
May 12. 1741, William Gilchrist had sentence of transportation for seven years, on a verdict which found it proven, that

[1] Hume, i. 422 —[2] Ibid.—[3] Ibid. i. 423.—[4] Ibid

at the time when Bells' Mills were broken open, and the meal carried away, the pannel was present in the mob, and that he was not compelled to go thither by force.[1]  In like manner, on 16th March 1773, Richard Robertson was transported for life, on a verdict which finds it proven, " that he was engaged in the riot in the house of Millfield; but do not find it proven that he had any hand in demolishing or pulling down the said house."[2]   In like manner, in the case of Walter Buchanan and others, 14th October 1725, on a verdict finding that Buchanan was " in the mob that threw stones at the soldiers, and in the mob at Shawfield's house, and in the mob which brought back the soldiers prisoners, with a gun, and that Macfarlane was in the mob in Shawfield's house; and that Mitchell was in the mob in ⌐field's house; and that Ballony was in the mob that drew the chariot along the street towards the Gorbals; and that Hamilton was in the mob both in the street and in Shawfield's house:" the prisoners were all adjudged to very severe punishments; Buchanan, Macfarlane and Mitchell, were transported for life, and scourged; Mitchell transported, and Ballony twice pilloried.[3]  In like manner, in the case of Murison, Nicol and others, Aberdeen, 27th April 1813, Murison pleaded guilty to being in the mob at the time libelled, and helping to promote its object, but without being guilty of any acts of violence, and was sentenced to imprisonment for one month.[4]  More lately still, mere presence in a mob was found a sufficient ground of conviction against two of the prisoners, in the case of Robert M'Callum and others, Inverary, spring 1825; and of Ralph Forrester, July 12. 1831.[5]  This last pannel was indicted both with mobbing and rioting, on the North Bridge of Edinburgh, and assaulting the Lord Provost there, and trying to throw him over the parapet of the bridge.  It was proved that he was in the mob which made the tumult, but his accession to the assault was not established; and so the jury found: he was sentenced to nine months' confinement in Bridewell. Mere presence was also sustained as a sufficient ground of conviction, with regard to some of the pannels, in the case of Thomas Kettle, James Barnett, and others, June 12. 1831, convicted of the great riot on occasion of the reform bill at Dundee.[6]

[1] Hume, 1. 423.—[2] Ibid.—[3] Ibid. 1. 424.—[4] Ibid.—[5] Unreported.—[6] Unreported

In England the law is settled on the same footing. If any person, seeing others actually engaged in a riot, joins himself to them, he is considered as much a rioter as if he had been there from the beginning;[1] and any person who encourages, promotes, or takes part in riots, whether by words, signs, or gestures, or wearing the badge or ensign of the rioters, is to be considered as himself a rioter.[2] Where great numbers of people, complaining of a common grievance, meet together in such a fashion as, from its general appearance and accompanying circumstances, is calculated to excite terror and alarm, it is considered as a rout or unlawful assembly;[3] and all    sons who join an assembly of that kind, disregarding its probable effect, and the alarm which is likely to ensue, and all who give countenance and support to it, are criminal parties.[4]

7. One who joins himself to a mob becomes art and part in all their criminal proceedings, done in pursuance of the common design of the assemblage ; but not of such as are taken up at the moment by detached parties with which he was not present.

If a great multitude separate into a number of small bodies, who proceed to different places, and commit different acts of mischief   re, though all be done in pursuance of a common design, yet the violence of the one party cannot be charged against the individuals of another.[5] But, on the other hand, if any one meets a mob on their passage, after     have done some outrageous act, and, knowing this, proceeds with them to other places, where the like acts are committed, he becomes implicated in the whole illegal proceedings of his party; and this will be true even although the tumult has continued for days ; for by so doing he ratifies and connects himself not only with the future but the past violence.[6] In the case, accordingly, of John Baird, Stirling, 14th July 1820, who were arraigned for high treason, it appeared that Baird and Hardie were in arms together, and very active in the combat with the King's troopers at Bonnymuir; and it was offered to be proved, that, on

[1] Hawkins, c. 15. § 3.—[2] Per Lord Mansfield; Campbell, ii. 370; Hale, i. 463.—[3] Per Judge Bayley, Hunt's Case, York, spring 1820; Russell, i. 524.—[4] Per Holroyd, Stark, iii. c. 76; Russell, i. 251.—[5] Hume, i. 424.—[6] Ibid. i. 424-5.

the same morning, about two hours before, Hardie, when on the road to Bonnymuir, with a party of insurgents, stopped a sergeant of the 10th Hussars, and delivered to him a treasonable address, inciting the soldiers to revolt against the government. This was objected to as evidence against Baird; but the Court, including the Chief Baron Shepherd, were clear that, as the evidence had already connected Baird and Hardie in a treasonable conspiracy and act of rebellion, any thing previously done by Hardie in the same conspiracy and rebellion was evidence against Baird, though absent at the time.[1] The law is fixed on the same principles in England, of which indeed that decision, proceeding on the English treason law, is evidence. In the case of Brandreth, Turner and others, Derby, October 1817, it was held that, when once the prisoners were proved to be engaged in the conspiracy, the acts of any other members of the conspiracy, though done at the distance of miles or days from any proceedings of the prisoners, were good evidence against them as proof of the common design by which they were actuated.[2]

In ordinary cases of riot, which do not form part of an extensive commotion, it is seldom necessary to consider the different degrees of activity of the prisoners in its proceedings; but it is sufficient to prove, in the first place, what the mob upon the whole did, and then that the prisoners were present, and taking a share in the disturbance, without specifying the individual share which they had in any particular acts of violence. Law holds, and that too upon reasonable and necessary grounds, that every member of the riotous assembly is art and part in what is done by the whole while he continues with it, in so far as they are the natural consequences of their common design, or what was contemplated as the original object of their assemblage; and that upon the clear and invincible ground, that by their presence they both add to the audacity of the actual perpetrators of the mischief, and diminish the chance of their being checked by the proper authorities.[3] In the case, therefore, of an ordinary mob, all insults offered to passengers, magistrates, or law officers, all threats of mischief to persons or property, all violence or damage naturally incidental to such tumults, are chargeable alike on all who are present. In the case of Bertram and Lockie, July 17. 1792, accordingly, who were tried as accessaries to a tumult in which several violent things were done, upon a verdict finding " that Lockie was seen in the mob libelled, and threw *one stone* towards the soldiers," the pannel was sentenced to fourteen years' transportation, though that would have been far too severe a punishment for that single outrage standing alone.[1] In like manner, in the case of the Dundee rioters, June 12. 1831, it was deemed perfectly sufficient to prove the general acts of the mob, and that the pannels were engaged in it, without specifying the acts of violence perpetrated by each individual.[2] In like manner, if a mob set out with a declared intention to burn a certain house, or kill a certain person, and they carry this design into effect, all are guilty of the fire-raising or murder, though they are not the very persons who inflicted the wounds or applied the torch. In the case, for instance, of the Porteous Mob, the guilt of the murder was not peculiar to him who put the rope about the neck of the unfortunate victim, but extended to all who were active in breaking open the jail, or attending in arms at the place of execution, or in any other way co-operating in the enterprize.[3]

But, on the other hand, it is no less worthy of notice, that this holds only with such outrages as are the natural result of the common enterprize, and which all who engaged in it must have made up their minds to be indifferent to, when they once concurred in its adoption. It will not hold, therefore, with separate and independent acts of violence, as are not so much the object or natural and usual consequence of the undertaking, as the result of an accidental and casual ebullition of wickedness on the part of some of the actors, which went much beyond the common purpose of the assembly. Thus if a mob repair to a warehouse of grain, with intent to compel the dealer to sell at their own price, certainly all the measures calculated to constrain or intimidate his will are chargeable upon all those present, as throwing stones, breaking open his doors, threatening or maltreating his own or his servants' persons, or the like; but if, taking advantage of the opportunity thus afforded, some individuals break into the building and commit theft, or set it on fire, or murder the inmates, these ulterior and undesigned

[1] Hume, i. 425.—[2] Unreported —[3] Hume, i 425

acts of violence can be stated only against the actual perpetrators.[1]   So the law was laid down by Lord Justice-Clerk Boyle, Perth, autumn 1824, in the case of Thomas Marshall, George Scott, and James White, who were charged with mobbing and rioting and murder.   It appeared on the proof that a mob of lads from Dundee collected near the tollbar of Stobsmuir, near Dundee, and attacked some country masons, one of whom was killed, and several severely wounded.   It did not appear that there was any intention here on the prisoners' part, either of committing murder or of assaulting the masons-in a reckless and outrageous manner; and the proof failed to fix the fatal blow on any one prisoner present, while it clearly shewed that one blow in particular had occasioned death, and that the prisoners were present and active in the mob.   In these circumstances, it was laid down by the Court, that the acts of mobbing and rioting and assault were fairly chargeable on all the prisoners, without distinguishing who actually committed them; but that the murder, which was the result of one blow, and not of a succession of smaller injuries, and which did not appear to have been part of the general design, could be fixed only on the person who struck the fatal blow.   They were convicted accordingly, and sentenced according to their degrees of guilt; Marshall to fourteen years transportation, Scott to seven, and White to twelve months' imprisonment.[2]

8. The pains of law, independent of special statute for mobbing and rioting, are arbitrary, varying, according to the magnitude of the offence, from a few months' imprisonment to transportation for life.

Mobbing and rioting, to whatever excess they may have led, are not punishable with a capital punishment at common law.[3] Not but what, where stouthrief, murder, fire-raising, or housebreaking, are committed by a mob, they may afford materials for a capital charge and conviction; but, where this is the case, they should be charged separately against the pannels, under the name and in the form required in regard to these crimes, in the same indictment in which the minor charge of mobbing is preferred.   Murder, accordingly, was combined with mobbing and rioting in the case of Maclachlan, one of the Por-

[1] Hume, i. 425.—[2] Unreported.—[3] Hume, i. 427.

teous Mob, June 1737;[1] and in that of Marshall, Scott and
White, Perth, autumn 1824.[2]    Fire-raising was combined
with mobbing in the case of William Spence, December 13.
1784, where the libel charged the pannel with " being active
in exciting and encouraging the said mob, and with having
with his own hands set fire to the distillery."[3]   Theft and
housebreaking were combined with mobbing, and sustained as
relevant, in the cases of Allan Guthrie, 16th June 1716, and
William Gilchrist, March 1741;[4] and stouthrief, robbery and
housebreaking, with mobbing, in the case of John Innes, November 13. 1727.[5]   Assault or wounding are very generally
combined with mobbing, where the individual acts can be fixed
on any of the pannels.

But it is to be observed in all these cases, that, where
the libel is laid for a separate offence, combined with mobbing, that additional charge must be regulated by the rules
of the common law, and the principles of art and part applicable to such offences ; and the prosecutor cannot, on the proof
of such charges, resort to the latitude of the principle justly
admitted in the proof of violence committed under a charge of
mobbing.   He may unquestionably obtain a capital conviction
for murder or stouthrief, when combined with mobbing, as
well as when standing alone on the record ; but he cannot do
so by merely proving that murder or stouthrief were committed by the mob, and that the prisoner was present in the crowd,
and assisting their proceedings.   Under such a proof he may obtain a conviction of mobbing, warranting the infliction of the
highest arbitrary pains ; but, for a conviction of the capital
crimes, he must bring home the perpetration of that offence
individually to the pannel, just as if he stood charged with it
alone.

In ordinary cases the punishment of mobbing and rioting,
or rioting alone, is imprisonment, varying, according to the
magnitude of the offence, from one to eighteen months.   The
following examples will shew the recent practice in this particular :—Duncan Allanach, Aberdeen, September 1827, convicted of mobbing and rioting, in a slight degree, was sentenced
to three months, and William Milne to one month's imprisonment.[6]   David Mackay and William Corbet, convicted at In-

_____
[1] Maclaurin, No. 93.—[2] Unreported.—[3] Hume, i. 428.—[4] Ibid.—[5] Ibid.
429.—[6] Unreported.

verness, April 24. 1827, of a more serious riot, were imprisoned nine months.[1]  James Reid, on a conviction of mobbing and assault at Ayr, September 1826, was imprisoned six months.[2] Barnabas Taylor and others received nine months' confinement, for mobbing and rioting only, at Ayr, September 1826.[3]  The like sentence was passed, for a similar offence, at Ayr, September 1826, on James Humphry.[4]  For much more serious acts of mobbing, committed upon a sheriff-officer, when poinding for arrears of taxes, William O. Boyling and James Nielson were, at Glasgow, September 1824, imprisoned eighteen months.[5]  Mobbing and rioting, in opposition to an officer of the army acting in execution of his military duty, was visited with three months' imprisonment, at Inverness, autumn 1821.[6] Andrew Mackay, convicted at Glasgow, September 1819, of accession to a serious riot in the streets of Greenock, was sentenced to twelve months' imprisonment.[7]  James Silliers, for a conviction of mobbing and rioting, and deforcing revenue-officers, Ayr, May 1822, was sentenced to six months' imprisonment; as was Andrew Roxburgh, on a verdict finding him guilty of riot merely, at Ayr, spring 1824.[8]  Alexander Macphie, John Baird, and others, were sentenced to six months' imprisonment in jail, for accession to the mob which blew up Mr Harvie's walls at Glasgow, September 1823.  Ralph Forrester, one of the Reform rioters on the North Bridge of Edinburgh, where an attempt was made, though not by him, to throw the Lord Provost over the North Bridge, was sentenced to nine months' hard labour in Bridewell; as was William Lithgow, 18th July 1831, found guilty of throwing a piece of glass at Colonel Douglas, when sitting as preses of the Lanark election, on occasion of the same tumults.[9]

But, in more serious cases, the pains of transportation have, from a remote period, been inflicted on persons convicted of mobbing; and, in determining the degree of punishment, the Court have attended not only to the magnitude of the individual charge against the prisoner, but the spirit of the tumult of which he formed a part, and the unruly temper of the times, which rendered severe examples indispensable.  Thus, on occasion of the great mobs in 1720, on account of the high price of grain, numbers of persons were transported, particularly

[1] Unreported.—[2] Unreported.—[3] Unreported.—[4] Unreported.—[5] Unported.—[6] Unreported.—[7] Unreported.—[8] Unreported.—[9] Unreported.

Alexander and David Barry, 27th May 1720, and James Geddes, 26th May 1720.[1]   Again, on 14th October 1725, for an accession, though in regard to most of the pannels by presence merely, to the great tumult and disorders known by the name of the Shawfield ., Buchanan, Macfarlane, and Hamilton were scourged . transported for life, and Mitchell was transported for fourteen years.[2]   William Gilchrist, May 12. 1741, was transported seven years, for mere presence at a mob which broke into Bells' Mills, near Edinburgh.[3]   Richard Robertson, 16th March 1773, for presence in the mob which pulled down the house of Millfield, though without any farther accession, was transported for life.[4]   Bertram and Lockie, July 17. 1792, were transported fourteen years, for accession to a mob which assailed and threw stones at soldiers.[5]   More lately still, in the case of the Reform Riots at Dundee, when the police-office was forced open, and the prisoners liberated, on 12th June 1831, Thomas Kettle and James Barnett were transported for fourteen years, and an associate of inferior delinquency was sentenced to seven years' transportation; and, in the case of the Haddington rioters, July 16. 1831, who forced the police-office, and liberated two of the Greenlaw reformers, two of the pannels received eighteen months' and a third twelve months' confinement in Jail; the Judges, at the same time, expressing their opinion, that, but for the uncommonly good character of the accused, they could not have dispensed with transportation.[6]

9. By special statute, commotions within borough are punishable with confiscation of moveables, and the placing the life of the offender in the King's will, which, however, is not now held to warrant the pain of death.

By a statute of James II. 1457, c. 77, it is enacted, " That within the burrows throughout the realm, no leagues nor bandes be maid, nor zit na commotion nor rising of commounes, in hindering of the common law, but at the commandment of their head officiar.   And giff ony dois in the contrary, and knawledge and taint may be gotten thereof, their gudes that ar foundin guilty therein to be confiscat to the King, and their

---

[1] Hume, L 419.—[2] Ibid. L 424.—[3] Ibid. L 423.—[4] Ibid.—[5] Ibid. L 425.—
[6] Unreported.

2

lives at the King's will" This act is re-enacted by 1491, c. 34, and 1606, c. 17.

The commotions within burgh, " in hindering of the common law," spoken of in these statutes, have been held to include all attempts to obstruct the apprehending, imprisoning, or executing of criminals ; all attempts to break open jails, or set free prisoners ; all invasions of courts of justice in their sittings; all attempts to prevent the execution of their sentence; all attempts to resist the raising of the militia, or the levying of a supply ; and, in general, all enterprizes by mobs, in defiance of the order of law, or authority of the government or of the local magistracy.[1] For an accession to a tumult of this description, more than one prisoner has, in former times, been sentenced to suffer death, particularly, 8th February 1686, David Mowbray for accession to a tumult which rescued a criminal from the officers of justice; and Alexander Keith, 26th February 1686, for a more remote accession to the same offence.[2]

In later times, however, this rigorous construction has been abandoned ; and it has been settled, by a long series of decisions, that these statutes, even in the most aggravated cases, authorize the infliction of an arbitrary punishment only. This was settled in the cases of Charles Wen and others, July 22. 1700, the riots in 1720, and the Shawfield mob in 1725, where it was solemnly found, September 20. 1725, that even the great commotions there libelled on, amounting to all but open levying of war against the Sovereign, were relevant only to infer an arbitrary punishment.[3]

10. By the British Riot Act, if any person shall riotously pull down, or begin to pull down, any church or private dwelling, they become liable to the punishment of death; and if twelve or more persons shall continue together for an hour or upwards, after ordered, by proclamation from the lawful authorities, to disperse, they become liable, even without any farther acts of rioting, to the same pain.

The well known statute, known by the name of the *Riot Act*, passed on occasion of the many tumults and divisions that

---

[1] Hume, i. 431 —[2] Ibid.—[3] Ibid. i. 433

followed the accession of the House of Hanover to the throne, contains chiefly two enactments.[1]

The first declares, " That if any persons, unlawfully, riotously, and tumultuously assembled together, to the disturbance of the public peace, shall unlawfully, and with force, demolish and pull down, or begin to demolish and pull down, any church or chapel, or any building for religious worship, certified and registeied according to the statute made in the first year of William and Mary, or any dwelling-house, barn, stable, or other out-house, then, every such demolishing or pulling down, or beginning to demolish or pull down, shall be adjudged felony without benefit of clergy."  In the case of the Darrachs, September 1725, it was held that the tearing down the doors or window-sashes of a house, if done by those who were already in the building, was a beginning to demolish within the act; but that the same would-not hold with those acts if done by persons from without, in order to obtain entrance. It was held, in the same case, that to tear down the partition or the panneling of the apartments, or the slates or lead from the roof, was a beginning to demolish within the meaning of the act; but that the destroying statues, vases, or other exterior ornaments of the house and gardens, was not.[2]

It is only the tearing down or demolishing a house that falls within the sanction of the act; and it does not extend to burning, blowing up, or destroying houses in any other way.[3]  It has been decided in England, that where a prisoner aided and encouraged rioters beginning to pull down or demolish a house by shouting and using expressions to incite them, he was a principal in the second degree, and fell under the capital sanction.[4]  It is worthy of observation, that not only churches, but " dwelling-houses, barns, stables, or other out-houses," are under the protection of the act.  Women are punishable as rioters; but infants under the age of discretion are not, though above that age they are.[5]

By the 52d Geo. III. c. 130, it is enacted, that if any person or persons unlawfully, riotously and tumultuously assembled together, in disturbance of the public peace, shall unlawfully, and with force, demolish and pull down, or begin to demolish or pull down, any erection and building, or engine which

---

[1] Geo. I. c. 5, § 4.—[2] Hume, i 434.—[3] Ibid.—[4] Rex v. Royce, Burnett, iv. 2073; Russell, i. 251.—[5] Hawkins, c. 65, § 14 ; Russell, i. 253.

shall be used or employed in carrying on or conducting of any trade or manufactory, or any branch or department of any trade or manufactory, of goods, wares, or merchandize, of any kind or description whatsoever, or in which any goods, wares, or merchandize shall be warehoused or deposited; that then every such pulling down and demolishing, or beginning to pull down and demolish, shall be adjudged felony, without benefit of clergy."

But the most important enactment on this subject is the second branch of the Riot Act, which, proceeding on the narrative of the many riots and tumults in divers parts of the kingdom, proceeds to enact, for the preventing and suppressing such riots in future, " That if any persons, to the number of *twelve* or more, being unlawfully, tumultuously, and riotously assembled together, to the disturbance of the public peace, and being required or commanded by any one or more justice or justices of the peace, or by the sheriff of the county, or his under-sheriff, or by the mayor, bailiff, or bailiffs, or other head officer or justice of the peace, of any city or town corporate, where such assembly shall be, by proclamation to be made in the King's name in the form hereinafter directed, to disperse themselves, and peaceably to depart to their habitations, or their lawful business, shall, to the number of twelve or more, notwithstanding such proclamation being made, unlawfully, riotously, and tumultuously remain or continue together, by the space of one hour after such command or request made by proclamation; that then such continuing together to the number of twelve or more, after such command or request, made by proclamation, shall be adjudged felony, without benefit of clergy."

The proclamation appointed to be made is in these terms: " Our Sovereign Lord the King chargeth and commandeth all persons, being assembled, immediately to disperse themselves, and peaceably depart to their habitations, or to their lawful business, upon the pains contained in the act made in the first year of King George the First, for preventing tumults and riotous assemblies.—God save the King." And every justice, sheriff, &c., on notice of such unlawful assembly, are authorized and required straightway to resort to the place, and there make, or cause such proclamation to be made [1]

[1] § 2.

The third section enacts, " That if the persons so unlaw-fully, riotously, and tumultuously assembled, or twelve or more of them, after such proclamation, shall continue together, and not disperse themselves within an hour, that it shall be lawful for every justice, sheriff, or under-sheriff of the county, where such assembly shall be, and for every constable and peace-officer within such bounds, or for any person who shall be commanded to be assisting any such justice, sheriff, or un-der-sheriff, mayor, or bailiff, or other head officer, who are hereby authorized to command all his Majesty's subjects, of age and ability, to assist them therein, to seize and apprehend such persons so unlawfully, riotously, and tumultuously con-tinuing together, after proclamation made, and they are hereby required so to do." And it farther enacts, " That if any of the persons so assembled shall happen to be killed, maimed, or hurt in the dispersing, seizing, or apprehending them, or in the en-deavour to do so, by reason of their resisting, that then every such justice, sheriff, &c. constable, or other peace-officer, and all persons aiding and assisting them, shall be free, discharged, and indemnified concerning such killing, maiming, or hurt-ing."[1]

It is farther enacted, " That if any person or persons do or shall, with force and arms, wilfully and knowingly oppose, ob-struct, or in any manner wilfully and knowingly let, hinder, or hurt, any person or persons that begin to proclaim, or go on to proclaim, according to the proclamation hereby directed to be made, whereby such proclamation shall not be made, that then every such opposing, obstructing, letting, hindering, or hurting such person or persons, so beginning, or going to make such proclamation as aforesaid, shall be adjudged felony, with-out benefit of clergy; and that also, every such person or per-sons being so unlawfully, riotously, and tumultuously assem-bled, to the number of twelve or more, as aforesaid, to whom such proclamation should, or ought to have been made, if the same had not been hindered as aforesaid, shall likewise, in case they, or any of them, to the number of twelve or more, shall continue together, and not disperse themselves, within one hour after such let or hinderance so made, having knowledge of such let or hinderance so let or made, shall be adjudged felons, without benefit of clergy."[2]

[1] § 3.—[2] § 5.

By section 8th, it is provided, that no person shall be prosecuted by virtue of the act, for any offence committed contrary to it, unless the prosecution be commenced within twelve months after the offence committed. And, by the 9th section, sheriffs, sheriff's-substitute, justices of the peace, and magistrates, shall have the same powers in Scotland, as justices, &c. have in England, and offenders in Scotland against the act shall suffer death, and confiscation of moveables.[1]

To authorize the proclamation, it is not necessary that the meeting should have proceeded to any felonious attack on property or persons, such as wounding, fire-raising, or housebreaking. If the persons are unlawfully, riotously, and tumultuously assembled, that is with such circumstances of power, commotion, disorder, or threatened disorder, as are alarming to the lieges, and amount to a disturbance, or threatened disturbance, of the public peace, this *of itself* is a sufficient ground for the magistrate to interpose, and command all present to disperse.[2] If they despise this warning, and, at the end of an hour, are still found assembled together in the same tumultuous or menacing fashion, they are then, without any actual violence, guilty of the offence, which is punishable with death.[3]

On the other hand, it is in an especial manner worthy of observation, and it is not so generally known as it should be, that if the rioters proceed to injure property or person; here, though the hour has not expired, nay, though proclamation has not been made, the offenders are liable not only to be ultimately brought to trial for such offences, but forcibly resisted, suppressed, and apprehended on the spot, either by the magistrates and those assisting them, or the persons invaded, and those who may concur in their defence.[4] Nay, even private persons may interfere, without any magisterial authority, to suppress a riot, if either the disturbance is so serious as to savour of rebellion,[5] or a felony be evidently in contemplation, or about to be committed; for a private person may, *brevi manu*, and on the spot, do any thing to prevent the perpetration of a felony.[6] So the law was laid down by two of the greatest masters of the English law, Lord Loughborough, on occasion of the riots in London, in 1780,[7] and Lord Ellenborough, on

[1] § 8. & 9 —[2] Hume, i 435 —[3] Ibid —[4] Hume, i. 435, 438, Hawkins, i. c. 65, § 11; Russell, i 266 —[5] Russell, i. 266; Kil 76 —[6] Bos & Pul. ii. 265, Russell, i 266.—[7] Hume, i 446

the trial of James Ripley and others, March 1815, who were
accused of killing two persons, in defence of Mr Robinson's
house, against a formidable attack on occasion of the corn
bill.[1]

All those who were present when the proclamation was
made are presumed to have heard and understood it; and if
they are found in the assembly after the hour, this brings
them within the statute, without any proof of their having
been there during the intermediate time.[2]   Those who shall
join themselves to the multitude, however recently, and whether they know of the proclamation having been made or not,
must run the risk of any violence being used to suppress the
tumult, and this should be in an especial manner recollected
by all who, either from ignorance or curiosity, intermingle with
such perilous assemblies.[3]   But, on the other hand, one who
was not present when the proclamation was made, cannot be
convicted under the clause of the statute of the capital offence,
of obstinately remaining during the hour; because it is the
wilful holding together during that *whole* period which constitutes the crime.[4]   But if it can be proved that, after joining
the mob, he was informed of proclamation having been made
some time before, and he still continues with them till the
hour has expired; or if he joins after the hour, is then told, or
learns, that the hour had expired, and does not go home, he
contracts the same guilt as the others, and becomes liable to
the same penalty.[5]

The riot act was passed in aid, not in limitation, of the common law; and therefore every power originally inherent in the
magistrates for the preservation of the peace remains in them
notwithstanding its enactment.   Every magistrate has, both
by the Scotch and English law, an inherent power of checking
riotous or tumultuous proceedings, by whatever number of persons, the moment they are committed; and for his support in
this attempt, he is entitled on the spot to summon the aid of all
well disposed subjects, as well before as after proclamation, under the riot act.[7]   It is in the power of dispersing a tumultuous
or menacing assembly, *before they have proceeded to any excesses,* that the addition to his power by the riot act was made.[6]

[1] Hume, i. 436; Russell, i. 266.—[2] Hume, i. 436.—[3] Ibid.—[4] Ibid.—[5] Ibid.
—[6] Blackstone, b. iv. c. 11, Hume, i. 437.—[7] Hale, i. 53, 293, 495; Hawkins,
i. 158, 159; Foster, 270; Blackstone, b. iv. c. 11, Hume, i. 437.—[8] Hume, i.
435.

In an indictment for riot, it was held that resolutions passed at a former meeting assembled a short time before in a distant place, but at which the pannel presided, he having also presided at the one in question, was admissible evidence to shew the intent of assembling and attending the meeting in question. And that a copy of these resolutions, delivered by the pannel to the witness, and which corresponded with those which the witness heard read from a written paper, was admissible without producing the original.[1] It was also held in the same case, where large bodies of men came marching in regular order to the place of assemblage, that it was competent to prove that within two days of the time when it took place, a number of persons were seen drilling before day-break at a place from whence one of their bodies had come to the place of assemblage, and that they ill-treated the persons who saw them, and made them take an oath never to be a King's man again ; and that parole evidence of the inscriptions and devices on banners and flags was competent without producing the originals.[2] When the question is *quo animo* a number of persons assembled to drill, declarations made by those assembled and in the act of drilling, and farther declarations or solicitations made by them to others to accompany them, declaratory of their object, are admissible to prove the intent of the assemblage, and, in general, any evidence to shew that the meeting caused alarm and apprehension, and that in consequence thereof information was given to the proper authorities.

# CHAPTER XXIV

## OF BIGAMY

BIGAMY is the wilful contracting of a second marriage when the contracting party knows that the first is still subsisting ; and is justly regarded as a serious offence, from the disregard of the prior obligations of the married state which it infers, and the irremediable ruin to the deceived party which it occasions.

[1] Hunt's Case, Russell, i. 268.—[2] Ibid.—[3] Stark, iii. 1510, Redford v. Birley, 1822 ; Russell, i. 218.

1. By special statute, bigamy is declared punishable with the pains of perjury, and it is also an offence at common law.

The act 1551, c. 19, enacts, that " Whatsumever person marries twa sindrie wivis, or woman marries twa sindrie husbands, livand together, undivorced lawfully, contrair to the aith and promise maid at the solemnization and contracting of the matrimony, and swa are of the law perjured and infamous, therefore, that the pains of perjuring be execute upon them with all rigour." [1]  From these words it appears that it was chiefly the violation of the sacrament and solemn vow or oath contained in marriage which the statute had in view.  But it is also, independent of the act, an offence cognizable and punishable, like every other transgression of civil rights, by the common law. [2]

2. To authorize a charge of bigamy, it is necessary that both marriages shall have been formal and regular.

The most important question in the law of bigamy is, whether both marriages must be by formal celebration, or whether the charge lies though one of them or both has been contracted in that loose and unceremonious fashion which is sustained by the custom of Scotland.  In those cases where *both* the matrimonial connexions were of this ambiguous character, there seems to be no doubt that no prosecution for bigamy can lie; and that a second wife who marries either by promise and copula, courtship and acknowledgment, or habite and repute, takes her chance of a previous matrimonial connexion having been contracted in the same irregular manner. [3]  Where the first marriage has been regular, but the second clandestine, the offending party seems entitled to plead, that he truly never did intend to marry at all, but was bent upon a connexion of a different nature, and that the partner of his crime has herself to blame for not having taken those precautions, by proclamation of banns and otherwise, which the law has provided for that very case. [4]  But in the case of George Story, Dumfries, April 1824, Lord Justice-Clerk Boyle sustained as relevant a charge of bigamy, where the second marriage was a clandestine one, solemnized at Annan after the fashion of that place. [5]  In re-

---

[1] 1551, c. 19.—[2] Hume, 1. 459.—[3] Ibid. 1. 459, 460.—[4] Ibid. 1 400 —[5] Unreported.

gard to the most unfavourable case for the pannel, that of a regular marriage following a clandestine matrimonial connexion; still it deserves consideration, that possibly the man did not intend to marry in the first instance, and was entirely ignorant that he had involved himself in its bonds; a situation by no means unlikely to occur, when it is recollected how many men, under the present law of Scotland, do not know whether they are married or not · and how long an investigation is frequently required to enable others to determine the point. So that, as law cannot sustain a criminal prosecution where the criminal intent is not apparent, it rather appears, though there is no decided case expressly in point, that there are not the requisite materials for a prosecution for bigamy unless both marriages were formal.[1]

In the case of John Roger, Aberdeen, September 1813, it appeared that the pannel had had a connexion with Mary Innes, with whom he had cohabited many years, and had a family. The woman having been brought before the kirk-session, and rebuked for fornication, the prisoner, in presence of the minister, admitted that she had yielded in consequence of a promise of marriage on his part; upon which the minister, somewhat rashly, declared them married persons, much against the prisoner's will. They afterwards cohabited as man and wife in the house of the woman's father. In these circumstances there was a promise and *copula*, and marriage by habite and repute, but as the case was of an ambiguous character, the jury, under the direction of Lord Gillies, found the pannel not guilty; a verdict evidently implying that a charge of bigamy could not be supported where the first marriage was of this irregular and disputed description.[2]

If, however, the first marriage, though clandestine in the outset, has gradually assumed the character and consistence of a regular connexion, and the parties have lived together invariably in that way for a length of time, there seems to be little doubt that a second regular marriage, following such a permanent and acknowledged *status* with another woman, will expose to the pains of bigamy.[3]

3. The first marriage, to support a charge of bigamy, must be a lawful and subsisting connexion; but it is not

[1] Hume, i. 460.—[2] Ibid.—[3] Ibid. i. 461

necessary that the second should be the same, if it has been regularly solemnized.

Should the first marriage be null on account of any intrinsic or fatal defect, as near relationship, adultery, or the like, there can be no prosecution for bigamy; or the law will not employ its vengeance in defence of that which itself has forbidden.[1] The marriage also must have been not only lawful but subsisting; and, therefore, if before the second marriage, the first has been dissolved by decree of divorce in due course of law, the parties are free to contract anew.[2] Though the decree of divorce be afterwards set aside, yet it shall afford a good defence to the party who in the mean time, on its faith, has proceeded to form a new connection;[3] unless the reduction has taken place on such grounds as bribery, perjury, subornation, collusion, or the like, as imply fraud and deceit on the part of the parties obtaining the separation.[4]

To this just and necessary rule the proceedings of the English courts furnish a singular and anomalous exception. William Martin Lolly, an Englishman, married regularly at Liverpool, having been divorced at the suit of his wife for adultery by the Commissary Court in Edinburgh, Lolly was tried and convicted of bigamy at the Lancaster Assizes, autumn 1812; and, after a full argument before the Twelve Judges, the sentence was sustained, upon the ground that an English marriage is indissoluble all the world over, except by English act of Parliament.[5] The obvious hardship of this judgment, which appears, independent of its injustice, to be directly contrary to that *comitas* which the laws of all countries preserve towards the decisions of each other, has led to the statute 9th Geo IV. c. 31, § 22, by which it is provided that the pains of bigamy shall not extend to any person whose husband or wife shall have been continually absent for seven years, and not known by such person to be living; nor " to any person who, at the time of such second marriage, shall have been divorced from the bond of the first marriage, or to any person whose former marriage shall have been declared void by the sentence of any court of competent jurisdiction."

The crime of bigamy is clearly committed if a second mar-

[1] Hume, l. 461.—[2] Ibid.—[3] Mackenzie, tit. Bigamy; Hume, l. 461.—[4] Ibid.—[5] Russell, 190

riage is contracted before the first has been actually dissolved by decree of divorce by the Commissary Court, although legal proceedings may have been adopted for that purpose, and though the process was on the point of being brought to a conclusion by such decree being pronounced. So the Court held in the case of Janet Henderson, December 27. 1829, where the defence that a process of divorce was in dependence was repelled, and the pannel sentenced to six months' imprisonment.[1]

It seems a good defence that the former marriage was truly and on reasonable grounds believed to have been dissolved by death.[2] But it will not do for the pannel to allege merely that he believed his former wife to have been dead, for that is easily done, and seldom omitted by persons in this predicament: it is necessary that the proof on the prosecutor's part, in this particular, arising from the completion of the first marriage, shall be met by evidence on his part that he had reasonable grounds for believing that the former marriage was dissolved by death.[3]

It is of no consequence, provided the *second* marriage be formal and ceremonious, how vitious and exceptionable it may be in other respects. It is always null in consequence of the prior legal connexion; and if it be also incestuous, adulterous, or vitious in any other respect, this cannot wipe away the guilt, or shelter from the pains of bigamy.

4. The pains of bigamy may be incurred not only by the person who marries the second time, but by the one who becomes art and part with him in that offence, by marrying him pending his known legal connection with another.

The second wife, in general, is the innocent victim of the fraud or deceit of her seducer. But this is not always the case. If she was in the knowledge of the first impediment, and nevertheless knowingly and wittingly entered into the connexion, she becomes art and part of his offence, and may be prosecuted as such.[4] The same is true of the priest who marries, or the witnesses who are present at the second marriage, if they can be clearly shewn to have been aware of the prior subsisting impediment; for although bigamy, like rape, can only be ac-

[1] Unreported.—[2] Hume, L 461.—[3] Campbell's Case, March 9. 1680; Hume, L 461.—[4] Ibid. L 462

tually committed by one person, yet others may be implicated
as art and part of his offence.[1]

5. The best evidence of which the case will admit must
be adduced to prove both marriages; and though the first
wife is an _ competent, the second is a competent, witness
against the husband.

As both marriages must, in the general case, be formal and
regular, there should exist the regular evidence in proof of
each, arising from the extract of proclamation of banns and
the marriage-certificate of the clergyman, and that is the documentary evidence usually adduced on such occasions, coupled
with the testimony of the clergyman and witnesses who offi-
ciated or were present at the ceremony. And there seems to
be no reason to believe, that a marriage will be held as competently proved if such documentary evidence exists, and is not
laid before the jury, upon the general principle that the best
evidence of which the case admits must always be adduced
But if it be proved that the extract of proclamation or certificate has been either destroyed or lost, or never existed, then
the next best evidence of which the case will admit may be
received, and will be deemed sufficient, arising from the testimony of the persons present at the marriage; or, if these are
dead. of those who knew by report that the parties were married, and lived openly as man and wife. The clergyman, if he
be alive, must swear to his certificate; or, if he be dead, some
one who knows his handwriting must prove it, and also the
application of the certificate to the prisoner in question. The
extract of proclamation of banns, if it be regular, will prove
itself in the same way as the extract of a conviction, but the
application of it to the pannel and the first marriage must be
established by parole evidence.

As the second marriage is null, there can be no objection
to the admissibility of the second wife against the husband;
but, to render her unobjectionable, a foundation must be laid
by proving the first marriage in the first instance It has been
decided on the Circuit, by Lord Gillies, that the first wife is
inadmissible against her husband to prove the first connexion;[2]

[1] Hume, i 462.—[2] John Rodger's Case, Aberdeen, Sept. 1813; Hume ii. 349.

and this decision seems supported by the authority of Burnett;[1] but it deserves consideration whether it is not at variance with the rule, that a wife, though generally inadmissible against her husband, may be received in the special case of an injury inflicted on herself,[2] and whether there is any sufficient ground for holding that she may be received to prove the most trifling assault, and may not establish the greatest injury which she can receive at his hands.

In the law of England it is settled, that a marriage in Scotland, though between minors, is valid if good according to the *lex loci*, and that it is sufficient to shew that it was performed according to the rites and custom of the country where it was celebrated[3] In an indictment for bigamy, a marriage by a dissenting teacher in a private room in Ireland, was good.[4] On indictments for bigamy, it is not deemed sufficient to prove a marriage by reputation; but either some person present at the marriage must be called, or the original register, or an attested copy of it, be produced.[5] If the register or the copy of it be produced, any evidence which satisfies the jury as to the identity of the parties is sufficient;[6] and, on the other hand, if the marriages are each proved by a person present at the time, it is neither necessary to prove the registration, license, nor banns.[7] Acknowledgment by the pannel of his marriage, accompanied with any documentary evidence tending to substantiate it, will be deemed sufficient[8] After proof of the first marriage, the second wife may be a witness, but the first and true wife is inadmissible[9]

6. Having proved the first marriage, and that the first wife is still alive, and a second marriage contracted, the prosecutor has made out his case; and this it lies on the pannel to rebut, by shewing that he had reasonable ground to believe her dead.

In every charge of bigamy, the prosecutor undertakes to prove that the pannel contracted the second marriage, while he knew that the first one was still subsisting This, however,

---

[1] Burnett, 433.—[2] Ross's Case, May 11 1824; Hume II. 349.—[3] H Blackstone, 145, Russell, I. 201 ; Rex v. Brampton, East x. 282 —[4] Russell, I. 205. —[5] Burr. IV. 2057; Russell, I. 206.—[6] East. I. 472 —[7] Alison's Case, Russell, I 207.—[8] Thomson's Case, East I 470.—[9] Hale, I. 693, East. I. 469, Russell, I 207.

like every other kind of guilty knowledge, must be established by external conduct; and it is justly held sufficient to infer guilty knowledge, if the contracting of both marriages is proved, and the existence of the first wife at the contracting of the second. This being done, it is presumed that the pannel was aware of the impediment at the time of the second contract, as no man can be allowed, without evidence, to plead ignorance of the fate of his own wife; and, if he does so, he must elide the presumption, by shewing such circumstances as might, on reasonable grounds, warrant him in concluding that the first contract was dissolved, and a second might be lawfully contracted.

7. The punishment of bigamy, in modern practice, at common law, is imprisonment; but, by the statute, confiscation of moveables, and infamy, is superadded.

The act 1551, c. 19, declares the punishment of bigamy to be the same as those of perjury; that is to say, " confiscation of all their gudes moveable, warding of their persons for year and day, and longer during the Queen's will, and, as infamous persons, never able to bruick office, honour, dignity, nor benefice, in time to come." But these pains are not only unsuitable to modern ideas, but are founded on the notion of the perjury involved in bigamy,—a principle which is more founded on the statutory than the common law view of the offence. In modern practice, accordingly, it is usual to libel only on the common law, and limit the punishment to imprisonment   Indeed this is done whether the statute has been libelled on or not. Thus, at Inverness, September 1814, on a libel laid both at common law and on the statute, the prisoner was sentenced to six months' imprisonment [1]  Arthur O'Niel, Ayr, autumn 1816, received six months' imprisonment, even where the first marriage was according to the Catholic form, and thus the guilt of perjury had been incurred.[2]  On 17th July 1817, Andrew Craig, convicted of bigamy on his own confession, on a charge laid at common law and on the statute, was imprisoned twelve months.[3]  James Macadie, 13th March 1821, on an indictment limited to the common law, was imprisoned ten months [4]  James Sime, 24th March 1824, on an indictment at common law, was

[1] Hume 1. 460.—[2] Ibid.—[3] Ibid.—[4] Ibid.

imprisoned three months. Andrew Scott Wilson, 2d June 1828, on a confession of a charge of bigamy of a much more aggravated kind, was imprisoned twelve months; as was Alexander Cullen, 8th November 1827, on a conviction of a similar kind.[1] Charles Wilson, 3d March 1828, was imprisoned nine months; and John Macinnes, 12th March 1828, twelve months on the same charge.[2] At Glasgow, spring 1828, John Macewan was sentenced to eighteen months' confinement in Bridewell; he having been proved to have married two wives, and the circumstances of the case leaving no doubt, though not libelled on from defect of evidence, that he was in reality married to a third.[3] It is the extraordinary prevalence of this crime among the numerous Irish settlers in this country of late years, which has rendered necessary the increased severity in its punishments.

# CHAPTER XXV.

### OF CLANDESTINE MARRIAGE.

THE offence of celebrating clandestine marriages consists in the contracting or performing the marriage ceremony, without the forms which the law has prescribed for this important contract.[4] For though marriages of this irregular and clandestine fashion are sustained as sufficient *quoad civilem effectum*, yet the law does not approve them; but, on the contrary, subjects both the contracting parties and the celebrators to penalties. None are approved of but such as are celebrated by a priest duly ordained by some church, and after regular proclamation of banns.[5]

1. By special statute the parties to clandestine marriages are liable to imprisonment for three months, and certain fines, according to their rank; and the witnesses to certain fines.

By 1661, c. 34, the parties to a clandestine marriage are

---

[1] Syme's Cases.—[2] Hume i. 462.—[3] Unreported.—[4] Hume, i. 464.—[5] Ibid.

subjected to imprisonment for three months, and certain fines, according to their rank; which fines may be enforced by imprisonment; and, if the offenders cannot pay the fine, they are to be punished farther with stocks and irons.

By 1698, c. 6, the witnesses are liable to a fine of £100 Scots each; and the parties may be compelled, by certain specified forms, to declare who these witnesses are.

2. The celebrator of irregular marriages is by special statute liable to be banished the kingdom, never to return under pain of death.

The act 1661, c. 34, declares, that the celebrator of clandestine marriages be banished the kingdom, never to return therein under pain of death. And by 1698, c. 6, which ratifies the former act, it is farther declared, that he shall be liable to seizure and imprisonment for trial at the discretion of any ordinary magistrate, and to " such pecunial or corporal pains as the Lords of Privy Council may think fit to inflict" This power has expired with the extinction of the Privy Council in Scotland; at least there is no instance on record of the Lords of Justiciary having, in virtue of this enactment, exercised these additional powers.[1]

3. Any person becomes liable in these penalties who celebrates marriage, even in the most regular and formal way, without being either authorized by the Established Church, or in possession from some ecclesiastical authority of the sacerdotal office.

Be the marriage ever so regular in other respects, its celebrator becomes involved in these pains, if he is not regularly called to the exercise of the pastoral functions; or, in the words of the statute 1661, " authorized by the kirk." If, therefore, the celebrator be either a deposed minister of the Established Church,[2] or the pastor of an Episcopal meeting, who had been convicted and declared incapable of officiating as such for three years, under the 32d Geo. III. c. 63. § 4, he is legally incapable of officiating on such an occasion. At Inverary, accordingly, April 10. 1775, John Connacher was convicted,

---

[1] Hume i. 464.—[2] Kerr's Case, June 18. 1590, Hume, i. 461

5

and had sentence in terms of the statute, as being neither possessed of proper letters of orders, nor having taken the necessary oaths.[1] It need hardly be added, that these penalties do not apply to a member either of English or any other dissenting Church Establishment, if he be in orders, and subject to no disability, according to the forms of his own persuasion.

Much more does the same hold, where, as is generally the case, the person who takes upon himself to celebrate clandestine marriages has no pretensions to the character of priest or pastor, but is a mere impostor, who has audaciously assumed that sacred office.[2] Of this description are almost all the cases which have occurred of late years, the celebrators being persons in the lower ranks of life, who, for a gratuity to themselves, ply this irregular traffic.

There is nothing, however, illegal in a Magistrate, Justice of the Peace, or even a private individual, being called upon in a civil capacity to witness the exchange of the matrimonial consent; the irregularity begins if he goes a step farther, and officiates as a clergyman would, by praying on the occasion, pronouncing the nuptial benediction, reading the service of the Church of England, or the like.[3] On this principle it was held by Lord Justice-Clerk Boyle, at Aberdeen, September 1822, in the case of George Lyon, that when a bailie, without assuming the character or performing the functions of a clergyman, went through the form of having a fictitious petition prepared to himself, in which the parties were charged with celebrating a clandestine marriage, which they admitted to be true in his presence, and paid a fine of five shillings, which was his gratuity on the occasion, there was no violation of the statute, and the proceeding could not be made the subject of criminal proceedings.[4] This principle was carried still farther by Lord Gillies at Dumfries, spring 1830, in the case of Andrew Nicolson. This man, who was a publican at Annan, was charged with celebrating three different clandestine marriages at that place. On the proof, it appeared that, in all the instances, the couples came into his presence, and, upon his interrogatory, confessed themselves to be married persons; upon which he declared them married, and wrote out a certificate, which he delivered to the woman, signed by himself and two witnesses,

[1] Arnot, p 232.—[2] Hume, i 465.—[3] Ibid.—[4] Ibid

M m m

setting forth the fact, and declaring that they were married. The matrimonial consent was interchanged *de præsenti* in his presence, but without any prayer or religious ceremony whatever. Upon this *species facti*, the Court directed the jury to bring in a verdict of not proven, which was accordingly done, upon the ground that this was not " celebrating a marriage" in the sense of the statutes, which implied the assumption of some part of the ecclesiastical character.[1]   Should this decision be ultimately adhered to by the High Court, it enables any person to evade the whole pains of clandestine marriage, by merely avoiding any parts of the ceremony which are of a religious character.

4. Celebration of a marriage without proclamation of banns is clandestine, whatever may be the qualifications of the person officiating.

The proclamation of banns is one of the few relics of the Catholic and Canon law which has escaped the wreck of the Reformation.   It was *in viridi observantia* at the date of the act 1661, which therefore includes it as part of the laudable order and constitution of the kirk therein appointed to be maintained. It is specially mentioned and recognised as a necessary article of the order of marriage, by the 10th Anne, c. 7, which prohibits the episcopal ministers from marrying unless banns have been proclaimed, as well in the parish kirk where the parties reside as in the episcopal meeting, and this under the penalties of the Scottish acts against clandestine marriages.   Several old convictions were obtained against episcopal ministers for non-observance of those statutes which are mentioned in Hume.[2]

In the proof of a charge of this description, it is sufficient if the prosecutor proves the celebration of the marriage, and that no certificate of proclamation was exhibited to the person officiating on that occasion.   Having done this he has made out his case, because he cannot be required to prove the negative that no proclamation was made; and this it lies on the pannel to elide, by showing that there was.[3]   If a false or forged certificate of proclamation has been exhibited, it will liberate the person who celebrates the marriage, unless he can

[1] Unreported.—[2] Hume, i 466.—[3] Ibid

be implicated as accessary to the forgery; in which case, he may not only be prosecuted for the clandestine marriage, but as art and part in the more serious matter of the forgery.[1] It is no sufficient defence in point of law, however much it may alleviate it *in foro conscientiæ*, that the parties alleged to the minister that proclamation had been made, for this is a point on which he is not at liberty to receive any other evidence but that arising from production of the certificate itself[2]

5. The punishment of this offence is that prescribed the statute, viz. banishment from Scotland for life

Several prosecutions and convictions have taken place of late years against the celebration of clandestine marriages. Thus, at Jedburgh, 15th April 1812, Andrew Rutherford and James Hoggan were convicted of acting as clergymen in the celebration of clandestine marriages, and were banished for life in terms of the statutes.[3] At Perth, April 1818, John Macdiarmid was convicted of celebrating the irregular and clandestine marriage libelled, and received the same sentence.[4] On 18th March 1818, Joseph Robertson was found guilty of celebrating clandestine marriages, and he and William Pearson were found guilty of feloniously using certificates of proclamation of banns as genuine, knowing them to be forged. Both had sentence to be imprisoned for three months, and to be banished from Scotland, Robertson for life and Pearson for fourteen years.[5] At Jedburgh, spring 1827, John Forster was convicted on the statute and banished for life.[6] At Perth, autumn 1827, George Robertson and John Robertson were indicted for forging certificates of proclamation of banns, and the case having been remitted to the Sheriff, they were convicted and imprisoned.

In aggravated cases, the common law seems of itself to be adequate to the punishment of the offence A charge of celebrating clandestine marriages was accordingly sustained at common law, as well as on the statute, in the case of George Craighead, February 6. 1750.[7]

[1] Hume, i 466 —[2] Ibid.—[3] Ibid —[4] Ibid i 465 —[5] Ibid i 467 —[6] Unreported.—[7] Hume, i 467.

# CHAPTER XXVI.

## OF NIGHT POACHING.

THE statute 57th Geo. III. c. 90, on the narrative that idle and disorderly persons go frequently armed in the night time, for the purpose of protecting themselves, and aiding, abetting, and assisting each other, in the illegal destruction of game and rabbits, and that such practices were found to lead to the commission of felonies and murders, enacts, " That if any person or persons, having entered into any forest, chace, park, wood, plantation, close, or other open or enclosed ground, with the intent illegally to destroy, take or kill game or rabbits, or with the intent to aid, abet and assist any person or persons illegally to destroy, take or kill game or rabbits, shall be found at night, that is to say between the hours of six in the evening and seven in the morning from the 1st October to the 1st February, between seven in the evening and five in the morning from the 1st February to the 1st April, and between nine in the evening and four in the morning for the remainder of the year, armed with any gun, cross-bow, fire-arms, bludgeon, or other offensive weapon, every such person so offending, being thereof lawfully convicted, shall be adjudged guilty of a misdemeanour, and sentenced to transportation for seven years, or shall receive such other punishment as may by law be inflicted on persons guilty of a misdemeanour, and as the Court before whom such offenders may be tried and convicted shall adjudge; and if any such offender or offenders shall return into Great Britain before the expiration of the term for which he or they shall be so transported, contrary to the intent and meaning hereof, he or they so returning, and being thereof duly convicted, shall be adjudged guilty of felony, and shall be sentenced to transportation for his or their natural life." Great numbers of persons have been convicted in Scotland under this act, though in none

FOLLOWING
PAGE(S)
MUTILATED

as yet has it been thought necessary to inflict the punishment of transportation.

1. **If any one of the party is armed, all who are with him knowing the fact are within the act.**

It has been determined by the Twelve Judges, that if several are together, and any one of them is armed, the whole are liable to be convicted under this act. O. Flannagan and two others were in a park at night, and two of them had guns but the third not. Upon a point reserved, the Judges were clear that, if any one of the party was armed, the whole were within the act, and the conviction of the whole was held right.[1] But this holds only if they all know that one of their number was armed; for if one had arms unknown to the others, they are not liable to be convicted under the act.[2] If the discharge of a gun is seen, the person firing is held to be found, though his person was not seen at the time, and it is no answer to a charge under the act, that the parties laid down their arms and left them before they were seen, if it appear that some one was there armed before the discovery was made;[3] and this will hold although the poachers had abandoned their guns, and crept 200 yards away from them before they were discovered.[4]

2. **By the same statute, it is lawful for rangers, game-keepers, &c. to apprehend offenders and bring them to justice, whether armed or unarmed.**

By 57th Geo. III. c. 90, § 2, it is enacted, " That it shall be lawful for the rangers, owners and occupiers of any such forest, chace, park, wood, plantation, close, or other open or enclosed ground, and also for their servants, keepers, and for any other persons, to seize and apprehend, or assist in seizing and apprehending, offenders by virtue of this act, and to convey and deliver such offenders into the custody of a peace officer, who is hereby authorized and directed to convey them before a Justice of Peace for the county or place where such offence shall be alleged to have been committed," who shall commit them for trial.

[1] Rex v. Smith, Russell, L 418.—[2] Rex v. Southern, Russell, 1 418 —
[3] Nash's Case, Russell, 1 418.—[4] Russell, 1 418

Persons going *unarmed* at night for the destruction of game are not liable to such serious penalties  With respect to such persons unlawfully entering into or found in any forest, &c. or other open or enclosed ground, at night, in the sense of that act, having any net, engine, or other instruments, for the purpose and with intent to destroy, take or kill, or who shall wilfully destroy, take or kill game or rabbits, it enacts that the rangers, owners and occupiers of any such forest, &c. or other open or enclosed ground, and also their keepers, servants, &c. may seize and apprehend, or assist in seizing and apprehending, such offenders, and deliver them to a peace-officer, who is to convey them before a Justice of the Peace, there to be dealt with according to law.

Many convictions have taken place in Scotland under this act, but the Judges have with great propriety limited the punishment to much less than the statute allowed, and been severe in those cases only where the conduct of the accused has evinced a reckless or brutal disposition  In the case of William Forrester and William Mason, March 20. 1826, the pannels were sentenced, on a confession, to three months' imprisonment.[1]  The like sentence was passed on George Binnie and Robert Orrock, March 15. 1827 ; on Gideon Wood, 15th May 1827, who also confessed his guilt ;[2] and on Thomas Crichton, Dumfries, April 24 1827.[3]  James Ramsay, Stirling, April 5. 1828, received the same punishment.[4]  In the case of John Macdonald, March 1828, in respect of the good character of the accused, the sentence was still milder, being only one month's imprisonment and security to keep the peace [5]

In the case of James Ramsay, April 5. 1828, the Court sustained as relevant an indictment on this statute, which charged the pannel with being *found* in a wood armed with a gun, though he was only apprehended *coming out of it*, upon the ground that it is immaterial where he was seized, provided he was found, that is seen, in the forbidden limits  In the case of Thomas Crichton and John Lorimer, April 24. 1827, an indictment was sustained which charged the former of these parties with being in a plantation armed with a gun, and the latter " aiding and abetting the said Thomas Crichton, armed as aforesaid, in his said wicked and illegal intent "[6].  In the case

[1] Unreported.—[2] Unreported.—[3] Unreported.—[4] Unreported.—[5] Unreported.—[6] Unreported.

of William Maclean and Thomas M'Ilwraith, Ayr, April 1827, the indictment charged both pannels with being found armed with a gun; this was objected to, on the ground that, as the libel set forth that there was only one gun between the two, the libel was irrelevant *quoad* the other, and that it should have been specified which had the gun. The case was certified for the decision of the Supreme Court, but the flight of the pannel prevented any farther proceedings.

The statute directs that the offending party in Scotland " shall be dealt with as any person or persons charged with a trans-portable offence." Under this clause the question arose whether the Sheriff was competent to try offences of this description, he not having the power of transportation. The Sheriff of Linlithgow, in the case of John Russell, moved a doubt as to the competency of the case before him; and the Court, on March 17. 1827, held that, as the libel concluded for the pains mentioned in the statute, which the Sheriff was not competent to inflict in their full extent, the case could only be entertained by the Justiciary or Circuit Courts.[1] Under this decision, it remains doubtful whether he be not competent to entertain a libel where the pains of law are limited to fine or imprison-ment.

By a subsequent statute, 9th Geo. IV. c. 69, some alterations are made on these enactments. It provides—

1. " That, if any person shall, after the passing of this act, by night, unlawfully take or destroy any game or rabbits in *any land, whether open or enclosed ;* or shall, by night, unlawfully enter or be in any land, whether open or enclosed, with any gun, net, engine, or other instrument, for the purpose of taking or destroying game, such offenders shall, upon conviction thereof, before two Justices of the Peace, be committed, for the first offence, to the common jail or house of correction for any period not exceeding three calendar months, there to be kept at hard labour, and, at the expiration of such period, shall find surety, by recognizance, or, if in Scotland, by bond of caution, himself in ten pounds, and two sureties in five pounds each, for the space of one year next following; and, in case of not finding such sureties, shall be farther imprisoned, and kept to hard labour for the space of six calendar months, unless such sureties are sooner found

[1] Hume, ii 60

"And in case such person shall so offend a second time, and shall be thereof convicted before two Justices of the Peace, he shall be committed to the common jail or house of correction for any period not exceeding six calendar months, there to be kept at hard labour, and, at the expiration of such period, shall find security by recognizance or bond as aforesaid, himself in twenty pounds, and two sureties in ten pounds each, or one surety in twenty pounds, for his not so offending for the space of two years next following; and, in case of not finding such sureties, shall be farther imprisoned and kept to hard labour for the space of one year, unless such sureties are sooner found; and in case such person shall so offend a third time, he shall be guilty of a misdemeanour, and, being convicted thereof, shall be liable to be transported beyond seas for seven ye  , or to be imprisoned and kept to hard labour in the common jail or house of correction for any time not exceeding two years; and, in Scotland, if any person shall so offend a first, second, or third time, he shall be liable to be punished in like manner, as is hereby provided in each case."

2. " That, where any person shall be found upon any land committing any such offence as is herein before mentioned, it shall be lawful for the owner or occupier of such land, or for any person having a right or reputed right of free warren or free chace thereon, or for the lord of the manor or reputed manor wherein such land may be situate; and also for any gamekeeper or servant of any of the persons herein before mentioned, or any person assisting such gamekeeper or servant, to seize and apprehend such offender upon such land, or in case of pursuit being made in any other place to which he may have escaped therefrom, and to deliver him as soon as may be into the custody of a peace-officer, in order to his being conveyed before two Justices of the Peace; and in case such offender shall assault or offer any violence with any gun, cross-bow, fire-arms, bludgeon, stick, club, or any other offensive weapon whatever towards any person hereby authorised to apprehend or seize him, he shall, whether it be his first, second, or any other offence, be guilty of a misdemeanour, and be liable, at the discretion of the Court, to be transported beyond seas for seven years, or to be imprisoned and kept to hard labour in the common jail or house of correction for any term not exceeding two years; and, in Scotland, where any person shall so offend, he shall be liable to be punished in like manner."

3. By section 9. it is declared, " that if any persons, to the number of three or more together, shall, by night, unlawfully enter or be in any land, whether open or enclosed, for the purpose of taking or destroying game or rabbits; any of such persons being armed with any gun, cross-bow, fire-arms, bludgeon, or any other offensive weapon, each and every of such persons shall be guilty of a misdemeanour, and being convicted thereof before the Justices of Jail Delivery, or of the Court of Great Sessions of the county or place in which the offence shall be committed, shall be liable, at the discretion of the Court, to be transported beyond seas for any period not exceeding fourteen years nor less than seven years, or to be imprisoned and kept to hard labour for any term not exceeding three years; and, in Scotland, any person so offending, shall be punished in like manner."

By sect. 3. When any person shall be charged on the oath of a credible witness, or, in Scotland, on the application of the Procurator-Fiscal of Court, before any Justice of the Peace, with any offence punishable with summary conviction by this act, the Justice may issue his warrant for apprehending such person, and bringing him before two Justices of the Peace to be dealt with according to law.

By sect 4. Every prosecution for every such offence, punishable upon summary conviction by virtue of this act, shall be commenced within six calendar months after the commission of the offence; and the prosecution of every offence punishable by indictment, or otherwise than upon summary conviction, shall be commenced within twelve calendar months after the commission of such offence.

By sect. 6. An appeal from a conviction before the Justices may be brought by appeal to the Quarter-Sessions by notice given three days after the conviction, upon lodging a bond of caution to appear at the Quarter-Sessions and abide the issue of the appeal, and, upon such bond being lodged, the person convicted shall in the mean time be liberated.

By sect. 7. No such conviction or adjudication made on appeal therefrom shall be quashed for want of form, or be removed by *certiorari* or otherwise into any of his Majesty's superior courts of record, or, in Scotland, by advocation or suspension into any superior court; and no warrant of commitment shall be held void by reason of any defect therein,

provided it be therein alleged that the party has been convicted, and there be a good and valid conviction to sustain the
same.

By sect. 10. " In Scotland, the Sheriff of the county within
which the offence shall have been committed shall have a cu-
mulative jurisdiction with the Justices of the Peace in regard
to the same, and the conviction in Scotland may be proved in
the same manner as a conviction in any other case, according
to the law of Scotland.

By sect. 11. In all cases in Scotland of a third offence, or in
other cases in Scotland where a sentence of transportation may
be pronounced, the offender shall be tried before the High
Court, or Circuit Court of Justiciary.

By sect. 13. For the purposes of this act the word "game"
shall be deemed to include hares, pheasants, partridges, grouse,
heath or moor game, black game, and bustards.

4. By sect. 12. The night shall be considered, and is hereby
declared to commence, at the expiration of the first hour after
sunset, and to conclude at the beginning of the last hour before
sunrise.

Under this act many convictions have taken place in this
country.   In the case of Robert Henderson and James Blair,
February 26. 1830, twelve months' imprisonment was inflicted
on the pannels, who pleaded guilty to being in a plantation
three together, under the statute, and to an assault on the
gamekeepers; six months being inflicted for the one offence,
and six months for the other.[1]  Peter Taylor, John Young, and
Walter Omit, March 12. 1830, were convicted under the same
clause of being three together in a plantation in Linlithgow-
shire, under the statute.[2]  And at Dumfries, spring 1830, John
Little was convicted under the first clause of the act, and of
an assault under the second, and sentenced to nine months'
imprisonment; three for being armed on the ground at night,
and six for the assault.   The assault was there committed not
in the wood where the poaching was committed, but in a field
to which the pannel had run, on pursuit being given, across the
Water of Kirtle; but Lord Gillies was clear that, under the
words of the statute, this case was reached equally with that
of an assault committed on the ground entered at such untimely hours for the purpose of poaching.[3]

<hr />

[1] Unreported.—[2] Unreported.—[3] Unreported

# CHAPTER XXVII.

## OF PRISON-BREAKING.

THE act of *Prison-Breaking,* however natural to the inmates of those gloomy abodes, cannot be overlooked by the law, as being a violation of the order and course of justice, and a direct infringement of regulations essential to the peace and well-being of society. It has, accordingly, always been regarded as a point of dittay by our common law.

1. It is equally prison-breaking for any prisoner, civil or criminal, to make his escape from jail, and by whatever manner, provided he was confined on a legal warrant.

Whatever the quality of the prisoner may be, and whatever the cause of his committal, law holds him bound to remain there till legally liberated, and therefore equally guilty of prison-breaking if he escape without lawful authority.[1] This holds alike with a prisoner on a civil debt,[2] as one confined on a criminal or even a capital charge.[3]

In like manner, the guilt is held to be incurred in every instance of unlawful escape, whether by breaking through the building, violence to the jailor or turnkey, false keys, corrupting the jailor, or taking advantage of his supineness or negligence, or of the violence or invasion of others.[4] Accordingly, in the case of James Ratcliff or Walker, June 25 1739, the Court found a libel relevant, which charged a prisoner with having escaped out of the jail of Edinburgh when the doors were forced open by the Porteous Mob, and that, too, after a full debate on the relevancy.[5] Nay, this holds even though the prisoner be confined for debt, and he only escape by avail-

---

[1] Hume, i. 461.—[2] Irvine's Case, July 3 1673, Hume, i. 461.—[3] Inglis's Case, August 1720, Hume, i. 461.—[4] Hume, i. 462.—[5] Ibid.

ing himself of the effraction of the building by his more desperate criminal associates.[1]

But it is indispensable to the relevancy of such a charge that
the pannel has been in a *lawful* state of custody, that is to say,
that he was imprisoned on a warrant *ex facie* regular and truly
applying to him.[2]   If, therefore, the pannel have been laid hold
of instead of some other person, or if his name be different
from that contained in the warrant, or if there were no written
warrant in circumstances where the ordinary course of practice
requires it, or if the warrant have proceeded from a person
who had no jurisdiction within those bounds; in any of these
cases the man is not a prisoner in the legal sense of the word,
and is nowise blameable, if he endeavour to escape from such
an illegal state of confinement.   Accordingly, in the case of
James Inglis, August 1720, where the libel charged three acts
of prison-breaking, two of which were escapes from the jail of
Tranent, to which he had been committed by a constable, and
the third an escape from the jail of Edinburgh, to which he had
been committed by a warrant from one of the Lords of Justiciary; this last charge alone was sustained as relevant, in respect a constable has no title to imprison.[3]

But, on the other hand, if the warrant is apparently good,
and *ex facie* regular, truly applicable to the pannel, and subject to no blot or flaw over its face, the prisoner is then in a
state of legal custody, and is not entitled to break prison on
account of any remote and less palpable irregularities, which
have happened in the proceedings anterior to the warrant, or
in the immediate process to obtain it.[4]   Thus, if a *meditatio
fugæ* warrant has been granted on an irregular oath, or letters
of horning have issued on a decree of Justices of the Peace, or
a criminal warrant has been granted without any signed information, the debtor is still a prisoner, and must seek his relief
by legal proceedings.   The jailor must look only to the warrant put into his hands, and, if it is regular, he is bound to detain the prisoner, till by legal means a different warrant is delivered.[5]   It would be otherwise if the prisoners were committed on a warrant which did not express the crime for which
the incarceration is ordered; for such a warrant is illegal, and
neither is the prisoner bound, nor the jailor entitled to give it

[1] Mackenzie, tit. Prison-breaking, Irvine of Hilton's Case, July 3. 1673.—
[2] Hume. i. 402.—[3] Ibid 403.—[4] Ibid.—[5] Ibid

any legal effect;[1] but, at the same time, it is to be observed, that, in all the cases in which it is lawful for a prisoner to escape from prison, it can only be done with impunity when accomplished without violence or bloodshed, for any assault on the jailor, or other outrage, would unquestionably subject the offender to punishment, be his warrant of committal ever so illegal; and still less are any of the lieges entitled to raise a mob and tumult, and break open a public jail, and liberate prisoners, upon the pretence that there were fatal defects in their warrants of incarceration.[2] Accordingly, in the case of John and George Sinclair, November 26. 1690, the defence of the prisoners, who had tumultuously broken into the Jail of Thurso, was repelled, that they had been unlawfully confined.[3]

2. The place of confinement, from which the prisoner escapes, must be a proper public and established jail, and not a temporary or occasional place of confinement.

It is not every place of confinement, even though in some degree sanctioned by public authority, which is in legal language denominated a Prison. Those only come under this denomination which are sanctioned by the Supreme Court, or general usage, and attached to a particular district, as the legal jail of the jurisdiction. To escape from a lock-up-house, or mere temporary place of confinement, if done with violence, and attended with tumult, may indeed be an offence, but it is not prison-breaking.[4] If, however, it be an established jail, it is of no importance whether it be a county jail, or that of a borough, or even a barony.[5] In the case of Sinclair, accordingly, November 20. 1699, it was objected that the prisoners had not been confined in the proper tolbooth, but in another and private place of keeping, and the interlocutor of the Court, in allusion to this defence, required that the breaking be that of the *public* prison.[6] A bridewell, or house of correction, would unquestionably be considered as a prison in this matter; and, by the act for the erection of the Edinburgh Jail, the lock-up-house there is specially declared part of the Tolbooth of Edinburgh, and, of course, any escape from that place

---

[1] Hume, i. 403.—[2] Ibid. i. 403-4.—[3] Ibid.—[4] Ibid.—[5] Ibid.—[6] Ibid.

5

of confinement would fall under the description of prison-breaking.

3. The pains of prison-breaking, in modern practice, are imprisonment, unless it is accomplished by mobbing or external violence, in which case a higher punishment may be inflicted.

The punishment of prison-breaking is not determined by any statute, and therefore it must be proportioned to the circumstances of each individual case. Imprisonment is the natural penalty of the offence; and, in consideration of the strong temptation under which a prisoner lies, to free himself from an irksome state of duress, it is usually limited, when no mobbing or tumult has accompanied the escape, to a short period.[1] If, however, it is accomplished by means of housebreaking from without, or fire-raising, it becomes a capital offence; for these crimes are equally committed by breaking into, or setting fire to, a jail as an ordinary dwelling;[2] and, if accomplished by accession to a tumult or mob, it may be visited with the highest arbitrary pains;[3] but it is only by being accessary to such violent proceedings, and not merely by taking advantage of the means of escape which they afford, that the pannel becomes implicated in these serious pains. If, therefore, a prisoner escapes, upon the jail being broken open from without, as in the case of the Porteous Mob at Edinburgh, or the late election riots at Dundee, without any connexion with these outrageous proceedings, he is not liable to a severer punishment than for ordinary prison-breaking; and, if he was art and part with the more guilty parties, the proper course is to indict him not only for the prison-breaking, but for the mobbing, rioting, or housebreaking, by which it was effected.

---

[1] Hume, i. 404.—[2] Henderson's Case, Stirling, autumn 1826, and Hume, i. 404.—[3] Hume, i. 404, and i. 423.

# CHAPTER XXVIII.

## OF RETURNING FROM TRANSPORTATION.

The offence of Returning from Transportation bears a close affinity to that of prison-breaking; with this difference, that being a violation of an order for a severe punishment, it is chastized with far greater severity.

1. By special statute the returning from transportation is punishable with death.

By 5th Geo. IV. c. 84, which regulates the transportation of offenders, it is enacted, " That if any offender who shall have been or shall be sentenced or ordered to be transported or banished, or who shall have agreed or shall agree to transport or banish himself or herself, on certain conditions, either for life or any number of years, under the provisions of this or any former act, shall be afterwards at large within any part of his Majesty's dominions, without some lawful cause, before the expiration of the term for which such offender shall have been sentenced or ordered to be transported or banished, or shall have so agreed to transport or banish himself or herself; every such offender, so being at large, being thereof lawfully convicted, shall suffer death, as in cases of felony, without benefit of clergy; and such offender may be tried either in the county or place where he or she shall be apprehended, or in that from whence he or she was ordered to be transported or banished." Several trials have taken place in Scotland of late years, but in none of these has it been deemed necessary to inflict the extreme penalty of the law.

Thus, in the case of Walter Middleton, June 2. 1828, the pannel, convicted of returning from transportation under this act, was sentenced to be transported for fourteen years.[1] The

---

[1] Unreported

3

like sentence was inflicted on David Craig, 8th January 1828, for a similar offence.[1]  In both cases the libel was restricted.[2] In the case of Angus Maclean, March 14. 1830, the prisoner stood his trial, and was transported for life.[3]

2. In proof of this offence, it is sufficient to prove the first conviction, and the fact of the pannel being found at large in Scotland, before the expiry of the period of his transportation.

The prosecutor, in proving his case, must of course com-mence with establishing the first conviction, and its application to the prisoner.  This is to be done by production of the ex-tract of the conviction, which proves itself, and proof by two persons who saw him convicted, or in jail, under warrant of the sentence, and can prove its application to him.  Having done this much, and proved that the pannel was found at large in this country, before the term of transportation expired, he has done enough to obtain a conviction.  It is of no conse-quence whether the pannel was actually sent to New South Wales, or to the Hulks, or the Penitentiary, or never removed from a jail in Scotland.  In all these cases he is equally under sentence of transportation, and, if found at large, is liable to the penalties which it has prescribed.  It is no less clear, that if the pannel has any lawful excuse, as liberation for good con-duct, or the like, which is sometimes the case, it lies upon him to prove it in defence, and remove thereby the presumption which his appearance at large, before the expiration of his time, is fitted to produce.

3. The regular course for the trial of this offence, is by an indictment before a jury, and the Supreme or Circuit Court.

Doubts were formerly entertained whether a person sen-tenced to transportation, and found at large before his sentence expired, might not be summarily tried without the intervention of a jury, and, upon his identity being established, transported of new, in terms of his former sentence;[4] but, in the end, it came to be considered as the more regular course to indict the

---

[1] Unreported.—[2] Unreported.—[3] Unreported.—[4] Hume, ii. 146.

offender of new before the Court and a jury.    Accordingly, in
the case of James Baillie, March 1773, where the pannel had
obtained a pardon on condition of transporting himself, and
being found at large, pleaded that ill health had disabled him
from carrying the sentence into execution, the Court found
that the subject-matter, and conclusions of the said petition,
with the defence of the prisoner, is proper for a jury trial." [1]
And, as it never can be anticipated what defence the prisoner
has to offer for this new offence which he has committed, it is
certainly proper that, like every other serious crime, it should
be made the subject of consideration before an assize.

This rule, however, suffers two exceptions.   One who is banished forth of Scotland, or from a particular sheriffdom or jurisdiction within its bounds, may, if discovered within the forbidden district, before his period expires, be summarily, and
without any regular trial, subjected to the penalty contained
in his sentence, without any other formality than a petition
from the public prosecutor of the bounds, setting forth the fact
and proof of the identity of the prisoner.   This is matter of
daily practice, in the case of banishment from, and return to,
particular sheriffdoms, where it is very usual, especially at
Glasgow, to inflict whipping, in terms of the certification contained in the sentence, without any challenge or suspension
ever being moved as to the illegality of the proceedings; and
the reason is, that the sentence of banishment not only contains, as in cases of transportation, a warning to the pannel of
the pains he is to suffer, in the event of his return, but also a
warrant to the proper magistrates, to inflict those pains whenever the exile shall be found within the forbidden bounds. [2]
In the event, too, of a convict, sentenced to transportation by
the sentence of an English Court, being found at large in this
country, it is competent to apply for a Secretary of State's warrant to have him transmitted at once to the Hulks, where the
formalities of identification are gone through.   This accordingly was the course adopted in the case of J. Murray, February 1825, who had been transported for life to New South
Wales at the Old Bailey, and returned to this country, where
he was engaged in a great robbery of the Stirling coach; but,
having been acquitted of that charge, he was transmitted, by

[1] Hume, ii 146.—[2] Ibid. ii. 147

a Secretary of State's warrant, to the Hulks at Woolwich, from whence he was sent, after being identified, to the same place of banishment, to undergo the remainder of his sentence.[1]

In England it has been determined, that where a prisoner, convicted of a capital crime, who had received a pardon on condition of transportation for life, was afterwards found at large without lawful excuse, he should be remanded to suffer his original sentence.[2] In a subsequent case, where a prisoner, having been sentenced to seven years' transportation, had been pardoned on condition of *transporting himself* beyond seas for the same period, within fourteen days of the period of his discharge, and he was found at large in Great Britain after that period, it was much doubted whether he should be remitted to his former sentence, or convicted of the capital felony, as being found at large without lawful excuse. But it was clearly held, that if the prisoner had a clear intention of leaving the kingdom, and was prevented by ill health, these impediments amounted to a lawful excuse.[3]

# CHAPTER XXIX.

## OF INCEST AND UNNATURAL OFFENCES.

INCEST is the carnal knowledge between persons in the forbidden degree of affinity; an offence acknowledged by the law of all nations in the case of those near relations, such as parent and child, brother and sister, where Nature herself inspires an abhorrence of the act; but founded on positive regulation in the remoter degrees of affinity.

1. Incest is committed by carnal knowledge between all those persons who are forbidden to marry in the Divine law.

In Catholic times, the prohibition of marriage was extended

---

[1] Unreported.—[2] Madan's Case, Leach, i. 223; Russell, i. 404.—[3] Aikle's Case, Leach, i. 396; Russell, i. 404, 5.

to the fourth degree of affinity, by the canonical computation, which corresponds to the eighth by our method of counting, up one side and down the other;[1] but, at the Reformation, the forbidden degrees were reduced to those mentioned in the Jewish law. By 1567, c 14, the offence is limited to those " that abuses their bodie with sik personis in degrie, as God in his word hes expresslie forbidden, as is contained in the 18th chapter of Leviticus." But, in pursuance of the severe and rigid spirit of the times, the punishment was raised from the spiritual censures which were inflicted in Catholic times, to death.

According to the Jewish law, as laid down in Leviticus, the only relations expressly forbidden in the direct line are parent and child, and grandfather and granddaughter, and in the collateral sister and brother, whether by the full or the half blood, or uterine or consanguinean. Accordingly, in the case of James and Agnes Bonnar, 2d February 1570, a brother and sister were convicted of incest and adultery, and had sentence to be burnt. On 28th January 1642, Andrew Bannock had sentence of death for incest with his sister; as had Jean Weir, sister to the noted Major Weir, April 1670.[2]

A nephew is forbidden to know his aunt (v. 12, 13), whether on the father's or mother's side. Nothing is expressly said as to uncle and niece; but our Judges, considering that the relationship is the same, have extended the prohibition to them also, and that alike in the full as the half blood. On 8th February 1638, John Baxter, and Helen Sheviz his niece, by a sister uterine, had sentence of death; and in the case of George Johnston and Janet Johnston, where the crime was with a brother's daughter, the defence that it was not incest by the law of Leviticus, was repelled. The like decision was given in the case of Elizabeth Hunter, indicted for incest with John Brown, her uncle by the mother's side;[3] but the prohibition and crime extends no farther with the collateral relations.[4]

As to relations *in affinity*, a brother is indeed expressly forbidden to know his brother's wife; and, for an infringement of this command, sentence of death passed in the well known case of Catherine Nairne and Patrick Ogilvie, August 1765.[5]

[1] Canons of Scots Prov. Councils, Act 65.—[2] Hume, i 448.—[3] Ibid. i 448, 449.—[4] Ibid i. 449.—[5] Ibid.

But whether the term *wife* extends also to *widow*, and the prohibition extends to connexion with the widow, is much more doubtful, and forms the well known point on which all the theologians of Europe were engaged in the case of Henry VIII. and Catherine of Arragon. Judgment was once given with us in the case of Jeffray Irvine, September 1764, on the rigorous side; and again, in the case of James Drysdale and Barbara Tannadyce, March 12. 1705, to a connexion with a wife's sister after the wife's death; [1] but these are precedents drawn from morose times, on which no reliance can be placed in modern practice.

There are numerous instances of a capital conviction in the case of connexion with a sister by affinity, during the lifetime of the wife of the man, and that too on libels laid for incest only; [2] but here again it is very doubtful whether such extreme severity would be followed, on a matter admitted by theologians to be involved in so much doubt.

It is stated to be incest in Leviticus (v. 14.) for a woman to know her husband's nephew by his brother; and this was applied by the Court in the case of Elizabeth Smith and Thomas Hardie, 12th November 1705, though the libel was afterwards deserted. Nay, in the case of John Weir, April 25. 1629, this was extended to the marriage of a grandaunt in affinity, and the pannel had sentence of death. [3]

Nay, so strong did the current of the times run against these connexions, that the pains of incest were applied in a great variety of cases for which the text of Leviticus makes no sort of provision. Thus, on 9th September 1630, Alexander Blair was sentenced to be beheaded for incest, committed after his wife's death, with the daughter of his wife's brother by the half blood; [4] as was Alexander Gourlay, July 26. 1626, for incest with the sister of his wife's mother. [5] It is difficult to see on what ground these judgments were founded, as they are neither supported by Leviticus nor by the statute; and, accordingly, in the subsequent case of Alison Beatson, who was accused of incest with John Nicol, the husband of her mother's sister, the libel on that charge was found only relevant to infer an arbitrary punishment [6]

Nay, what is still stronger, in the first fervour of the Refor-

1 Hume, i 449.—2 Ibid. i 450.—3 Ibid —4 Ibid.—5 Ibid.—6 Ibid.

mation, the capital pains of incest were repeatedly applied to *illicit* connexion with two brothers or two sisters.[1] That such acts are highly indecent and immoral is quite clear; but it is not less obvious that they are not *incest*, which means connection with persons in the forbidden degrees of blood or *legal affinity* by marriage. Accordingly, in the later case of Margaret Paterson, February 1. 1692, who had been found in bed with two brothers, the capital conclusions of the libel were abandoned by the prosecutor.[2]

A case of incest recently occurred at Glasgow, in the case of Knox and Whyte, September 1829, who was charged with committing the crime with his sister consanguinean. They were convicted, and transported on a restriction for fourteen years.[5]

**2. Incest is not committed by connexion with bastard relations, how near soever.**

That the guilt of incest, in a moral point of view, is incurred by connexion with a bastard relation of the nearest kind, as a daughter, mother, or sister, cannot be doubted; but there is no authority for holding that it is incest, which is confined to relations by blood or legal affinity. In the only case, accordingly, where this point occurred, that of George and his niece Janet Johnston, June 18. 1705, the Court pronounced an interlocutor finding the libel relevant only between " uncle and niece," which implies that, if the relationship was natural, the charge fell to the ground; and, accordingly, the libel was found not proven.[4]

**3. If either party was ignorant of the relationship in which he stood to the other, the crime is not committed.**

In this, as all other offences, it is indispensable to the guilt of the person accused that he erred knowingly If either of the parties was ignorant of the situation in which he stood to the other, he is an object of commiseration, but not of criminal prosecution;[5] but the other party, who erred in knowledge of the relation, has no protection. This ignorance, however, it lies on the pannel who alleges it to prove; for, *in dubio*, it is not to be presumed that any one was ignorant of his connexion with relations who stand in the forbidden degrees.

¹ Hume, i. 451.—² Ibid.—³ Unreported.—⁴ Hume, i 452.—⁵ Ibid.

4. Proof of actual connexion, either directly or by circumstances, is indispensable to a conviction for incest.

The proof of connexion must be as clear and pregnant in cases of incest as rape; and the crime must have been completed by penetration of the privy parts and entry of the body.[1] A mere *conatus* is not sufficient, though it may be prosecuted as an attempt to commit incest. The guilty paramour may be adduced as a witness, as in any other case of a *socius criminis*, but such testimony is to be looked on with a most suspicious eye. Actual emission does not seem to be indispensable any more than in rape; but the proof of penetration must be clear.

5. Sodomy and Bestiality are the unnatural connexion of a man with a man, or an animal, after the manner and in the place where that crime is usually committed.

The crime of sodomy, or the unnatural connexion of one man with another, is to be proved after the same manner, and with the same scrupulous attention, as rape.[2] Proof of the completion of the offence by penetration is equally indispensable in both.[3] The act must be in the part where it is usually committed in the victim or associate of the crime, and if done elsewhere it is not sodomy.[4] If the party on whom the offence is committed is a boy under fourteen, he is not guilty of felony, but the actual agent only is exposed to its pains.[5] The guilty associate is a competent witness against the pannel. Two old cases, John Swan and John Litster, 1st September 1570, and Michael Erskine, April 2 1630, occurred for this crime, in both of which the accused were executed. to which we must add that of James Leckie, Jedburgh, autumn 1827, who was charged with no less than nine acts, and on a confession of two, and, on restriction of the libel, was transported for life.[6]

The convictions for bestiality are more numerous, and have been followed invariably with death. On March 1. 1675, James Mitchell was ordered to be drowned for this crime; and Andrew Love, 17th April 1672; Major Weir, April 1670; Thomas Fotheringham, November 11. 1702; George Robert-

---

[1] Hume, i. 452.—[2] Hale, i. 669, Blackstone, iv. 215.—[3] *Ante.*—[4] Jacob's Case, Russell, i 568.—[5] Hale, i 670, Inst. iii. 39, East i. c. 14, § 2.— [6] Unreported.

son, December 14. 1710, were severally condemned to be strangled at the stake.[1] The attempt to commit this offence was found to be indictable in the case of David Oliphant, February 4. 1734;[2] and the attempt to seduce others to commit sodomy in the above case of James Leckie; and in England it is likewise punishable, as well as attempts to commit sodomy.[3] In the general case it is not advisable to proceed criminally against such offenders; experience having proved that the exposure and publicity consequent on their trial is much more hurtful than the punishment is beneficial in deterring from their commission.

# CHAPTER XXX.

### OF FRAUDULENT BANKRUPTCY.

FRAUDULENT BANKRUPTCY, or the wilful cheating of his creditors by an insolvent person, is a crime which has arisen of course since the bankrupt statutes have provided a code of regulations for persons in that situation. But where once these statutes vested rights of a certain description in creditors of a bankrupt, there seems no doubt that the common law, of its own native vigour, is competent to repress any fraudulent invasion of these rights, upon the principle that all rights which are successively created by statute, or originate in the change of manners, naturally fall under its protection. Fraudulent bankruptcy has been, accordingly, more than once sustained as a relevant charge at common law, particularly in the cases of David Morrison, 6th March 1817, and of John Carter, July 20. 1831.[4] But, besides this, various statutory enactments have been passed in regard to this offence.

1. By special statute, fraudulent bankruptcy is punishable by infamy, and any pain short of death.

The act 1621, c. 18, which introduced the first elements of a system of bankruptcy, declares, " That all such bankrupts

---

[1] Hume, i. 470.—[2] Ibid.—[3] Russell, i. 568, Chitty, 50.—[4] Unreported.

and interposed persons, and all who hold counsel and assist them in their fraudulent practices, shall be reputed and holden dishonest, false, and infamous persons, incapable of all honours, dignities, benefices and offices, or to pass upon inquests or assizes, or bear witness in judgment or outwith the same in all time coming." By the next bankrupt act, 1696, c. 5, the cognizance of this sort of iniquity is remitted to the Supreme Civil Court, who are empowered not only to declare the offender infamous, but to punish him " by banishment or otherwise, death excepted, as they shall see cause, according to the measure of his fault." Lastly, the sequestration act, 54th Geo. III. c. 137, § 33, declares, with respect to any bankrupt sequestrated under it, " That, if he shall wilfully fail to exhibit a fair state of his affairs, or to make oath, as appointed by the act, to the fairness or fulness of his disclosure of his means and funds, or to make a complete surrender of his effects and estate, he shall be considered as a fraudulent bankrupt, and punished accordingly with infamy and other pains." The same declaration is made, and pains announced, for any one who shall falsely take the oath therein prescribed.

2. Either the Court of Justiciary, or the Court of Session, are competent to the trial of this offence; but if it is prosecuted in the former Court, it must be by indictment, in the latter by petition and complaint.

The jurisdiction of the Court of Session, in fraudulent bankruptcy, could not be doubted, after the express declaration of the act 1696, c. 5. But it was very much questioned whether the Court of Justiciary was also competent to the trial of this offence; and, in the case of James Duncan v. Lord Advocate, the Court here determined, 21st January 1823, by a majority of three to two, that the Justiciary Court was not competent.[1] The case went to the House of Peers, and that supreme tribunal decided it upon other grounds, waving the question of jurisdiction altogether.[2] But all these doubts are now removed by the act 7th and 8th Geo. IV. c. 20, introduced by Mr Home Drummond, which declares, " That it shall and may be lawful to prosecute all persons accused of fraudulent bank-

---

[1] Hume, i. 509.—[2] Ibid. ii. 110.

ruptcy in Scotland, before the High Court, or any of the Circuit Courts of Justiciary, by indictment or criminal letters, and according to the same form and course of proceeding as is used in regard to other offences prosecuted before the said Courts; and all the Judges of the said High Court and Circuit Courts are hereby empowered and authorized to try all cases of fraudulent bankruptcy, and to inflict such punishment on persons convicted thereof, as is now competent for the Lords of Session to award against persons convicted of the said crime : Provided always that it shall and may be lawful for the trustee appointed for the management of the sequestrated estates of any bankrupt in Scotland, or any creditor whose claim has been received, and has been duly ranked upon any such sequestrated estate in the sederunt-book kept by the trustee, with the concourse of his Majesty's Advocate for Scotland, to prosecute any such offence before the High Court, or any Circuit Court of Justiciary, without prejudice always to the title of the Public Prosecutor to insist in all such prosecutions." If the proceeding is before the Court of Session, it must be by petition and complaint, that being the mode of proceeding adapted to its forms; if before the Justiciary, by indictment, that being the only method recognised by that tribunal of bringing crimes before the knowledge of an assize; and this course, accordingly, was adopted in the case of John Carter, July 20. 1831.[1] When raised in the Civil Court, it must be with the concourse of the Lord Advocate, August 10. 1765, Syme *v.* Steele; February 9. 1796, Darby *v.* Love.[2] In the case of Macalister *v.* Orr and others, 21st February 1822, the Court sustained a summary petition and complaint, brought at the instance of a landlord, with concourse of the Lord Advocate, against some of his tenants, charged with fraudulent bankruptcy, and clandestinely carrying off their stock, in prejudice of his hypothec, and concluding for the pains of the act 1696.[3]

3. The evidence of fraudulent bankruptcy is to be found in the fraudulent alienation to the prejudice of creditors; secret disposal of funds or moveables so as to be beyond the reach of the trustee; and, in general, all acts which tend fraudulently and illegally to diminish the

[1] Unreported.—[2] Hume, i 510.—[3] Ibid. i 500

funds belonging to the bankrupt at the time when they
are put away, and which his creditors have a legal right
to have transferred or secured to them.

The devices of traders and others, in contemplation of bankruptcy, are so various, that it is impossible to attempt any
thing approaching to their enumeration. Suffice it to say,
therefore, that the points which must be established to a jury
in every case of fraudulent bankruptcy are these,—1. That,
by some alienation, abstraction, or concealment of property
belonging to the bankrupt, the estate divisible among his creditors has been diminished; 2. That it has been diminished
contrary to law, that is, either contrary to the provisions of the
acts 1621, 1696, or the sequestration act, or by such fraudulent
alienations as are reducible from their enormity at common
law. 3. That the bankrupt has been accessary to this dilapi-
dation, either directly or through the agency of others whom
he instigated to join him in the design; 4. That these acts were
done with a fraudulent intent, and in the knowledge that the
legal rights of creditors were thereby unjustly invaded.

If these requisites concur the crime is completed, whatever
species of bankruptcy has been incurred; whether the passive
species established by the acts 1621 or 1696, or the more active and general one which is introduced by the sequestration
act. In either case, if the bankrupt has wilfully infringed the
regulations of the statutes, and prejudice has thereby accrued
to his creditors, he falls under the pains of fraudulent bankruptcy, which indeed were enacted in the case of the two first
of these statutes, long before the sequestration act was in contemplation. The cases of James Wauchope, February 4. 1757,
and Syme, August 10. 1765, occurred prior to the first sequestration act.[1]

At present, cases of fraudulent bankruptcy usually occur in
bankrupts who have been sequestrated; and it is in fraudulent
embezzlement of the funds in contemplation of, or subsequent
to, that event that the crime consists. The evidence of such
abstractions, and of the guilty design with which they were done,
must be satisfactory; but it is in general so pregnant and manifold as to leave no doubt whatever on either point. Conceal-

---

[1] Hume, i. 509.

ment of goods in the houses of neighbours or associates, or under the floor, or in the roof of the bankrupt's own house or shop; sending them clandestinely away under cloud of night to places of concealment; indorsing away bills or bonds to favourite creditors on the eve of bankruptcy, and after insolvency was known to the bankrupt; alienations to conjunct and confident persons in a state of insolvency, contrary to the act 1621; setting off for America or the Continent after bankruptcy, with funds covertly realized out of property which legally belonged to his creditors, constitute the usual *indiciæ* on which guilt is fixed to pannels in cases of this description. In the case of Robert Noble, 27th November 1716, the principal circumstance was, that he was taken at Liverpool with goods and money in his hands to the amount of £430, with which he was about to embark for America.[1] David Morrison, seized at the same part, and on the eve of a similar voyage, with bills and money to the amount of £650, was convicted on these facts. In the recent case of John Carter, on July 20. 1831, no less than fourteen charges of fraudulent abstraction of goods, worth in all £800, some before, some after, his sequestration, were confessed by the pannel, supported by a fraudulent oath in a sequestration, for which he was separately indicted.[2]

4. The punishment of fraudulent bankruptcy varies from imprisonment to transportation, according to the magnitude of the offence; but infamy, and ineligibility for office, or to be received as a witness or juryman, forms in every case a proper addition.

In inconsiderable cases, fraudulent bankruptcy has been punished with imprisonment, infamy, and all its disqualifications; to which occasionally banishment from Scotland has been superadded. The pillory, also, was frequently inflicted in former times, particularly in the cases of James Wauchope, February 4. 1757, and James and George Kellie, February 14. 1776.[3] On 27th November 1816, Robert Noble was declared infamous, and sent to goal for eight months, having already suffered sixteen months' imprisonment; and David Morrison, 6th March 1817, having been twelve months in jail, was im-

---

[1] Hume, i 510.—[2] Unreported.—[3] Hume, i. 509

prisoned for the farther period of three months, and banished from Scotland for seven years.[1]   But in more serious cases, and especially where the fraudulent bankruptcy had been in fraud of a statutory sequestration, transportation has been inflicted.   This was done long ago in the case of George and Robert Forresters, July 26. 1748, who were transported for seven years; and the same punishment was more lately inflicted, besides infamy, on John Carter, July 20. 1831.

5. It is competent, either instead of, or in addition to, a charge of fraudulent bankruptcy in cases of sequestration, to indict the bankrupt for the perjury contained in his statutory oaths, and the punishment in such a case is generally transportation.

Wherever a sequestration has been awarded, and the bankrupt has been examined under the statute, his oath, if the bankruptcy has been fraudulent, will contain much falsehood, and it was accordingly the practice, where such cases occurred prior to the late statute, which settled the jurisdiction of the Justiciary Court in this matter, to indict for the perjury contained in the statutory oath.   For perjury on such an occasion, William Haig, on July 16. 1824, was transported seven years[2] But it is also competent to indict for the fraudulent bankruptcy, separately from the perjury; the one crime being an addition to, not involved in, the other; and accordingly, John Carter, July 20. 1831, in addition to seven years' transportation for his fraudulent bankruptcy, received seven years more for the perjury contained in his statutory oath.[3]

---

[1] Hume, i. 509.—[2] Unreported.—[3] Unreported.

# CHAPTER XXXI.

## OF INVADING OR SLANDERING JUDGES, AND SENDING THREATENING LETTERS OR CHALLENGES.

As the situation and duties of Judges expose them in an especial manner to the obloquy or violence of the populace, the law has been careful, on the one hand, to protect them from injury or defamation for the conscientious, and, on the other, to expose them to summary chastisement for the corrupt, discharge of their duty. The exposition of the law on this head being more in these times a subject of curiosity than practical use will not require any lengthened detail.

1. It is a capital offence, by several statutes, to strike or hurt any judge when sitting in judgment.

By 1593, c. 177, it is declared a capital offence to strike or hurt any judge whatever when sitting in judgment. To kill any of the Lords of Justiciary or Session sitting in judgment is treason by 7th Anne, c. 21. To invade or pursue any of " His Highness's Session," on account of service done to the King in that capacity, is, by 1600, c. 4, declared a capital crime.

2. By the common law, any act of violence, insult, or disorder offered to judges, either when in judgment or in ordinary life, on account of any thing by them done judicially, is liable to punishment.

The bare preparation and shew of violence, as, by clenching the fist or shaking a stick; the use of contumelious, reproachful, or slanderous words; the challenging to fight; or the insinuating of mischief or revenge; or exciting others to their commission, if offered to a judge, either in or out of Court, on

1

account of his judicial proceedings, is a violation of the respect due to his character, and as such punishable, either on the spot, if done in court, by summary imprisonment without any trial, or subsequently by indictment or complaint. Our practice contains numerous instances of both modes of proceeding.

In the case of Sinclair of Stobo *v.* Murray, December 15. 1724, it appeared that the pannel Sinclair had come up to Murray, who was sheriff of Peeblesshire, when attending as bailie at the fair of Linton, had shaken a stick over his head, and other threatening gestures, as well as loading him with reproaches, but without any blow. The Court found the libel relevant to infer an arbitrary pain, but the pannel escaped with a verdict of not proven.[1] In like manner, in the case of John Brown, 6th July 1829, which was an advocation from the Sheriff-Court of Ayrshire of a complaint at the instance of the Procurator-Fiscal: it was stated in the libel that the pannel had " assaulted, insulted, and slandered," a Judge in Kilmarnock, who had recently before pronounced a deliverance on his case; but the assault was merely verbal, having amounted only to calling the bailie a damned liar, and similar expressions, on the street. The pannel had been convicted in the inferior court, and sentenced to pay a fine; and the case having been brought under review by advocation, it was objected that the slandering and insulting a judge was not an indictable offence, unless expressly set forth as having been done on account of a judgment pronounced by him as a magistrate; but the Court repelled the objection, and subjected the pannel in expenses.[2]

It has been already noticed, that if the pannel, instead of confining himself to verbal abuse, or threatening gestures or menaces, shall so far forget himself as to strike the magistrate, or offer him any other violence, on account of any thing done by him in his judicial capacity, he is guilty of an assault, which law considers as of a very aggravated kind[3] Robert Duncan, 3d December 1827, for a blow struck to a magistrate of Edinburgh, on account of a judicial proceeding, was sentenced to six months' imprisonment;[4] and Robert Laughlan, convicted of an assault on Mr Cunningham of Lainshaw, a Justice of the Peace in Ayrshire, for the same cause received twelve months' imprisonment[5]

---

[1] Hume, i. 406.—[2] Unreported.—[3] *Ante,* p 194.—[4] Syme, 280 —[5] Hume, i. 339.

2

3. Slandering of Judges, or speaking or writing of them in abusive or libellous terms, on account of any thing done by them in their judicial capacity, is an indictable offence.

The necessity of protecting judges in the exercise of their legal functions was so strongly felt that it was long ago enacted by 1540, c. 104, that if any person should slander or accuse a judge, " if the offender proovis not the samin sufficientlie, he sall be punished in semblable maner and sorte as the saide judge or person whom he murmuris, and sall pay ane paine-arbitral at the will of the King's grace, or his Councel, for the infaming of sic persones." Accordingly, in the case of J. Macmillan, June 14. 1831, the charge against the pannel, of having written calumnious letters to the Sheriff-substitute of Fort-William, in relation to a process depending before him, was unanimously found to be relevant by the Supreme Court.[1]

Offences of this sort, if relative to any proceeding which is at the time or has lately been depending in the Supreme Court, may be instantly punished on the spot, or by summary complaint, without the intervention of a jury.[2] This was the case accordingly adopted in the case of Donald Campbell, 24th February 1673, who was sentenced to have his tongue bored for accusing, in open Court, one of the Judges of partiality to one, and injustice to another prisoner[3] In like manner the Court, in respect of some reflections cast by certain printers on them for the trial of Nairne and Ogilvie, on November 25. 1765, inflicted a rebuke on the delinquents, in consideration of their contrite acknowledgments[4] Johnstone and Drummond were not so fortunate, for on February 23. 1793, on summary conviction, they received three months' imprisonment, for a publication libellous on the proceedings of the Justiciary Court. The same course was adopted, on January 13. 1820, with Gilbert Macleod, who had published a false and calumnious account of certain proceedings of the same Court, and was sentenced to four months' imprisonment. On this occasion the objection to the competency of proceeding without a jury in cases of that description was expressly overruled.[5]

---

[1] Unreported.—[2] Hume, i. 406.—[3] Ibid i 407.—[4] Ibid. i. 406.—[5] Shaw, No 4 , Hume, ii. 139

4. The sending of a threatening or incendiary letter, whether signed or anonymous, is an offence at common law, punishable with an arbitrary pain.

Not only does the law take cognizance of fire-raising, or other acts of real mischief, but it chastises also with exemplary severity any threats to inflict such damage, more especially if contained in the form of a written menace; and that too indiscriminately, whether the letter be signed by the parties' name, or anonymous, or with a feigned signature.[1] On a charge of sending letters of this sort, signed by his name, John Shand, March 1759, was sentenced to seven years' transportation.[2]

Such attempts are usually made with feigned signatures, or altogether anonymously, and are justly regarded as a very heinous offence. It is settled in England that such acts, even when completely successful, cannot be prosecuted either as theft or robbing;[3] but they form the subject of two different acts, 9th Geo. I. c. 22, and 27th Geo. II. c. 15, by which the sending of any letters anonymously, or with a feigned name, demanding money or other valuable thing, is declared felony, without benefit of clergy. And by 30th Geo. II. c. 24, sending an anonymous letter, threatening to accuse of any crime punishable with an infamous punishment, or with an intent to extort money, goods, wares, or merchandize, is an indictable offence, and felony. It appears from the decision in the case of James Gray, July 11. 1737,[4] that this first statute does not extend to Scotland; nor is this of any consequence, as the powers of the common law are amply sufficient and much better adapted for the punishment of the offence. Accordingly, James Gray was convicted of writing anonymous letters to various persons, and threatening every sort of violence if a purse were not laid for him in a certain place full of money.[5] The question occurred in the case of Thomas Gemmel, January 29. 1781, whether the second of these statutes, which bears to have been passed to explain and amend the first, extends to Scotland; and it may be presumed that the Court hesitated on the point, as the prosecutor abandoned the statutory charge, and restricted the case to the charge at common law[6] In many other cases, charges of this description were sustained, though the pannels had the good fortune to escape

[1] Hume, i. 439.—[2] Ibid.—[3] Leach, ii. 678.—[4] Hume, i. 441.—[5] Ibid.—
[6] Ibid.

with a verdict of not proven, owing to the difficulty of proof in so occult a crime, particularly William Gilchrist, March 9. 1741, John Edwards, March 18. 1761, and William Rennie, February 5. 1781.[1] But, at Jedburgh, spring 1815, where John Jaffray was indicted for wilful fire-raising, and for writing an incendiary letter, the result was different. The letter was there addressed James Cairns, and dropped *near* the door of his house in Kelso, and it contained a threat to burn the houses of some persons there named, but not Cairns's own house. It was objected that there was no threat to burn Cairns' house, and that the letter was neither addressed nor communicated to the persons whose property was threatened. The Court repelled the objection, and the pannel was convicted chiefly on the evidence arising *comparatione literarum*, and from the identity of the paper on which the letter was written with that of a sheet which he had bought that day in Kelso, and of the disposal of which he could give no account. The fire-raising was not insisted in, and the prisoner for sending the threatening letter received sentence of seven years' transportation [2] More lately still, in the case of James Stewart, March 14. 1831, an indictment was raised which charged the pannel with sending an anonymous letter threatening to burn the house and farm-yard of a gentleman in the county of Stirling, but the case was not prosecuted to a conviction, owing to the absence of the pannel at the trial.[3]

5. It makes no difference though the demand for money is couched under the form of a request for charity, or an appeal to benevolence, or under the threat to accuse of an infamous crime, if substantially it is intended to extort money by such fear as a person of ordinary firmness cannot be expected to withstand.

Though the demand is made in the most artful or cautious terms, or the charity or benevolence instead of the fears of the person addressed are appealed to, or though no threat of personal violence, but of bringing about some calamity or accusing of some infamous crime are used, the case is the same, and law equally considers the offender as liable to punishment, if sub-

---

[1] Hume, i. 441.—[2] Ibid.—[3] Unreported.

stantially and at bottom the object is to be gained by fear of some sort or other, of such a kind as a person of ordinary firmness is not likely to withstand. Thus, in the case of Michael Robinson, an anonymous letter was sent requesting a banknote to be sent to a particular address, by initials, as a matter of benevolence, and stating that the writer was in possession of a manuscript which it was of importance to the person to whom the letter was sent should be destroyed. The prisoner was convicted, chiefly by some ulterior correspondence between him and the prosecutor being allowed to be given in evidence, which shewed that the manuscript was a libel, accusing the prosecutor of having, while an apprentice, murdered his master and married his widow, an accomplice in the crime. It was objected to the conviction, that the letter *per se* did not contain a threat or demand, and that the ulterior evidence which explained it was improperly received; but the objection was unanimously overruled, upon the ground, that though a mere request, such as asking charity, would not come under the word " demand," yet a request under a threat, that, if not complied with, a libel charging an infamous crime would be published, most certainly does [1]

But though to obtain money under a threat of any kind is an immoral action, it is only indictable when the threat is of such a nature as is calculated to overcome a firm and prudent man;[2] and, on this principle, it was held that, where the menace was to charge a party with penalties for selling without a stamp medicines which required one, the prosecution could not be supported.[3] A letter signed with initials only, is held to be a letter without a name.[4] It was held by all the Judges, that where the prisoner had given the letter to a woman at the grate of Newgate, with instructions to put it into the post-office, which was accordingly done, and it reached its destination, there was sufficient ground for leaving it to the jury to say, whether he delivered it knowing its contents, and that their verdict finding him guilty was a right conviction.[5] Where the prisoners were indicted for sending a letter, the proof was held sufficient as to both, that it was in the handwriting of one, and

[1] Robinson's Case, 1796, Leach, ii. 749; Russell, ii. 581.—[2] See Lord Ellenborough in Rex v. Southerton, East. vi. 126.—[3] Southerton's Case, Russell, ii. 575.—[4] Robinson's Case, Russell, ii. 584.—[5] Girdwood's Case, Leach, i. 142; Russell, ii. 585.

was thrown by the other prisoner into the yard of the prosecutor, where it was taken up by him.[1]   So also dropping a letter in a person's way in order that he might pick it up,[2] or putting it in a vestry room which he was in the habit of entering every Sunday,[3] or delivering it to a third person in order that he may convey it to the prosecutor, if it was really so delivered, have all been held sufficient sendings of the letters to bring the case within the statutes.   Prior and subsequent letters from the prisoner to the party threatened may be given in evidence, as explanatory of the intent of the particular letter on which the indictment was founded.[4]

6. Verbal threatenings, if serious, and sufficient to intimidate a man of ordinary resolution, are also the fit subjects of punishment.

By the Scotch law, even verbal threatenings of personal mischief, if violent and pointed, form a point of criminal dittay, and that independent altogether of the peculiar and statutory remedy of lawburrows for that offence.[5]   Caution, on a conviction for uttering such threats, may be made as high as to the Court shall seem necessary to restrain the offence, which gives this mode of proceeding a manifest superiority over the civil remedy of lawburrows, where the penalties are limited by the statute itself.[6]   So the Court found in the case of Captain Andrew Nairn, November 24 1712.[7]

7. The sending a challenge to fight a duel is an indictable offence at common law, and exposes all concerned in the giving, sending or accepting thereof, to an arbitrary punishment.

To restrain the fervid disposition of the Scottish people has long been a favourite object with our Legislature.   By 1600, c. 12, the bare act of *engaging in a duel* is made a capital crime, whether or not any harm has ensued to either of the parties.[8] And by 1696, c. 35, the giving, sending, or accepting of a chal-

---

[1] Jepson and Springell's Case, East. ii. 1215; Russell, ii. 585.—[2] Wagstaff's Case, Russell, ii. 585.—[3] Lloyd's Case, Ibid.—[4] Robinson's Case, Russell, ii. 578, 587.—[5] Hume, i. 442.—[6] 1593, c. 170, Mackenzie on the Statutes, 59; Hume, i. 442.—[7] Hume i 442.—[8] Ibid.

lenge is declared to be punishable in all concerned with banishment and confiscation of moveables.[1]  Several convictions took place on this statute in former times, particularly James Macall, April 5. 1714, and David Cairns, 2d May 1712.[2]  It must, however, have been a serious and formal challenge which is to be attended with these serious consequences to all concerned, and not any hasty or intemperate expressions, or passionate words of defiance, even though importing a design to fight, if not followed up with more deliberate proceedings.[3]

But these old acts are now repealed by a recent statute, 59th Geo. III. c. 70, which, after reciting the acts 1600, c. 12, and 1696, c. 35, declares, that, " from and after the passing of this act, the said recited acts shall be and hereby are repealed " The offence of sending a challenge, or posting a person as a coward for not fighting, now rest on the footing of the common law only, which is amply sufficient to reach and punish all such breaches, or attempted breaches, of the peace, and all such near approaches to the crime of murder.

# CHAPTER XXXII.

## OF SEDITION.

SEDITION is in the strictest sense a public crime, being directed against the peace of the State, and leading to the unutterable miseries of civil war.  The distinction between it and Treason consists in this, that though its ultimate object is the violation of the public peace, or at least such a course of measures as evidently endangers it, yet it does not aim at direct and open violence either against the laws or the life of the Sovereign, but at the dissemination of such a turbulent spirit as is calculated ultimately to produce it.[4]

It is extremely difficult to define with precision in what sedition consists, because it is evident that the same language or

[1] Hume, i. 442.—[2] Ibid. i. 443.—[3] Ibid.—[4] Burnett, 239; Hume, i. 553.

publications which are calculated at one period to stir up immediate dissension, may be diffused at another without the slightest danger; and the language which in one age is stigmatized as highly inflammatory, is to be found at another in every newspaper or pamphlet of the day. It is utterly vain, therefore, to select any particular expressions which shall at all times be deemed seditious; but it is more safe to lay it down in general, that all language or publications are seditious which stimulate the subjects of the realm to attempt the alteration of the laws and existing institutions by violent and illegal methods, and not in the ordinary course prescribed by the constitution for their modification.

1. Every publication or speech is seditious which prompts either to the subversion of the constitution by illegal authority, or the attainment of legitimate objects by violent and illegal means.

It is the undoubted right of every subject of the realm to argue, that the power of the Crown, of the Lords, or of the people, has become overgrown; but if, instead of confining himself to this position, or recommending the legal means for its remedy, the writer proceeds to recommend that they should at all hazards, and by illegal means, be retrenched, he becomes guilty of sedition.[1] In like manner, all attempts to induce the people to compel the Legislature to adopt certain measures by illegal means, as by refusing to pay taxes, or by assembling and meeting together to elect a new Parliament, or forming a convocation to intimidate or overawe the existing Legislature, unquestionably fall under the same rule.[2] The same is true of all such reviling or scoffing, either at the Royal Person or either branch of the Legislature, as evidently goes beyond the bounds of fair and free discussion, and is calculated not to awaken the reason to measures of redress, but to rouse the passions to unmeasured discontent and ultimate rebellion.[3] It is not less sedition to exhort the people to attempt to take the redress of their real or supposed grievances into their own hands, by resisting or disobeying any of the laws, by forming associations to intimidate or overawe the Legislature, or pre-

[1] Hume, i. 553, Burnett, 239.—[2] Hume, i 554.—[3] Burnett, 259; Hume, L 553.

venting that free and unbiassed exercise of judgment in Parliament which they claim for themselves.[1]

2. Real sedition consists in such a course of conduct as tends to defeat the execution of the laws, disturb the public peace on a great scale, or excite the people to acts of violence and disorder.

Sedition is either verbal or real;—the first consisting in such words, whether written or spoken, as prompt men to attempt, by illegal means, the subversion of the established institutions;—the latter in such acts as are calculated to disturb, or do disturb the peace, for the attainment of the same object. The last is carrying into effect, and beginning to execute, what the first recommended.[2]

Real sedition, therefore, bears a very close alliance to mobbing and rioting; and the distinction between them consists not so much in the act done, as in the object in view, or the extent of the association which is formed. Mobbing and rioting are, in general, exerted for partial objects, and in opposition to local authority only. Real sedition aims at a general reformation of the state by illegal means, and is connected with ramifications through all the disaffected districts. The same acts which, done in one city or county, merely from a partial turbulent spirit, or for a local purpose, and unconnected with similar mutinous proceedings in other quarters, are justly denominated mobbing only, become real sedition if done in pursuance of a general design to reform the state by illegal means, and in alliance with similar attempts in other quarters. If these efforts break out into open resistance to the king, or his government, they amount to high treason. Real sedition, then, holds a middle place between mobbing and high treason.[3] The riots produced by the embodying of the militia in 1797, were all charged as mobbing and rioting, aggravated by being connected with a design to prevent the execution of the public law,—a mode of proceeding which was unquestionably both competent and proper, though several of the mobs, particularly that organized by Cameron and Menzies, from the extent to which they were carried, and the general object at which they aimed, might have been brought under a charge of high treason.[4]

[1] Hume, 1 554.—[2] Burnett, 240.—[3] Ibid.—[4] Ibid.

3. Sedition, whether real or verbal, is a point of dittay by the common law of Scotland, punishable with an arbitrary punishment, independent of any statutory enactment.

Considering the evident peril of seditious publications, and the obvious danger to the stability of government and the peace of society from their prevalence, it is not surprising that the common law of Scotland has, from the most remote period, recognized it as an indictable offence.[1]   Indeed it is impossible that any law, professing, as the Scotch does, to embrace every act criminal in itself, or obviously subversive of the peace of society, could permit acts of this description to go unpunished; tending as they do to the most frightful disorders, and likely to produce, if completely successful, a mass of suffering, in comparison of which that produced by the fire-raiser or the murderer, is utterly insignificant.   At the same time, our practice, justly mindful of the mistaken or virtuous intentions from which such dangerous ebullitions frequently proceed, proportions the punishment to the magnitude of the offence, and the obvious peril with which it is attended; and, while it cannot permit the subjects of the state to throw about firebrands, and say it is in sport, has a great regard to the deluded but not wicked intentions from which such practices too often emanate; proceeding, in this respect, in a more humane and enlightened course than the laws of some other states, which, by affixing a fixed and statutory punishment to such offences, render it excessively severe in some cases, and unreasonably light in others.

The law on this subject underwent a thorough and anxious discussion in the year 1793, when the contagion of the French Revolution had infected a large proportion of our manufacturing classes, and the evident peril of the country induced the Court to inflict some punishments which are now justly regarded as too severe;—another proof, among the many which might be adduced, of the wisdom of entrusting the punishment of this offence to the common rather than the statute law: for, while the former moulds itself to the increasing humanity or liberality of succeeding times, the latter remains rigid and

[1] Hume i, 555, Burnett, 211

unbending through all the changes it has endured. How long ago would the horrid severity of the English punishment for treason have been softened, but for the undeviating enactments of its statutory code?

The first case on this subject, in recent times, was that of Morton, Anderson and Craig, 8th January 1793, who were indicted for " uttering seditious speeches, tending to excite a spirit of disloyalty and dissatisfaction to the king and established government; more especially when such speeches are addressed to soldiers, and intended to corrupt and withdraw them from their duty and allegiance." They had gone to the Barracks in the Castle, and proposed as a toast, George the Third, and death and damnation to all crowned heads; at the same time endeavouring to seduce them from their duty, by promising them higher pay if they would join the Friends of the People. They were convicted, and sentenced to eleven months' imprisonment,—a sentence which no reasonable man can consider as too severe.[1]

Again, in the case of Berry and Robertson, 18th February 1793, it appeared that the pannels had printed and published a pamphlet, entitled the " Political Progress of Britain," in which the constitution was described as a conspiracy of the rich against the poor, and parliament as a phalanx of mercenaries embattled against the reason, happiness, and liberties of mankind. It was strongly objected that these words were not necessarily seditious, and that the times could not be taken into view in judging of the intent; but this the Court repelled, and Berry was sentenced to three, and Robertson to six months' imprisonment.[2] For a similar offence, J. Jaffray, who had given as a toast, " Destruction to the King, Queen, and Royal Family," was sentenced at Stirling, September 1793, to three months' imprisonment.[3] Lastly, in April 1817, Alexander Maclaren and Thomas Baird, were sentenced to six months' imprisonment on a libel laid at common law, for delivering and publishing, at Kilmarnock, speeches on reform in Parliament, tending to bring Government into contempt, and to infuse jealously and dissatisfaction into the minds of the people.[4]

But, in more serious cases, where sedition of a deeper die, and more extensive ramifications, has come before them, the Court have felt themselves called upon to pronounce very dif-

[1] Burnett, 241.—[2] Ibid. 243.—[3] Ibid. 260.—[4] Hume, i. 557.

ferent sentences. In the case of Thomas Muir, 30th August 1793, the pannel was brought to trial, charged with various seditious harangues, addressed by him to meetings called together for the purpose, and with circulating various pamphlets, particularly Paine's Rights of Man, the object of which was, to represent the constitution of Great Britain, and especially the monarchical part of it, as a system of injustice, tyranny, and oppression, and to procure an alteration of government by *clamour and constraint*. He was found guilty, and sentenced to fourteen years' transportation.[1] Again, in the case of Fysche Palmer, Perth, September 1793, the prisoner was indicted for writing, printing, and distributing a seditious handbill, in which he represented the people of the country as groaning under despotism and slavery, and called on them to vindicate their rights as men, and unite in obtaining universal suffrage. In addressing the jury, the Court laid it down, that there is an essential distinction between canvassing freely and fairly the measures of government, a right inherent in the citizens of every free country, and publishing speeches or writings which, under pretence of discussing particular measures, level their strictures against the general frame and system of the constitution, call on the people to resist, and employ language calculated to excite to acts of *violence and outrage*. The pannel was convicted, and transported fourteen years.[2]

Such severity has appeared in an especial manner called for, in cases where the proceedings of the pannels has indicated, not merely a wish to stir up others to acts of rebellion, but an actual organization and arrangement preparatory to that event. Thus in 1794, the club entitled, " The British Convention of the Delegates of the People, associated to obtain Universal Suffrage and Annual Parliaments," proceeded to acts not only seditious, but bordering on high treason. They assumed the language, and imitated the organization, of the French Convention, called each other citizen, appointed committees of organization, finance, and secrecy, and in every particular copied the proceedings of the French Assembly. Their speeches were all published in the Edinburgh Gazette; and all evinced that their object was not reform, but a total change and subversion of the whole frame and system of government. William Skir-

---

[1] Burnett, 244; Hume, l. 556.—[2] Burnett, 246.

ving, the secretary to the association, was brought to trial, on 6th January 1794, for circulating the seditious handbill for which Palmer had been convicted, and for being a member of the British Convention, in which seditious speeches, motions, and resolutions were made: he was convicted, and sentenced to fourteen years' transportation. In commenting on this case, Mr Solicitor-General Blair observed, that " the very name assumed by this association of ' The British Convention of the Delegates of the People,' had a seditious tendency, as it was holding out falsely to the people that they were the representatives of the people of Great Britain, and that such representatives called for universal suffrage, and annual parliaments, the former of which never did or could exist in this country, without a complete subversion of the fundamental principles of the constitution." [1] This case was followed by that of Charles Sinclair, February 17. 1794, in which it was objected that sedition was not a crime at common law, and that it amounted only to verbal leasing-making, the punishment of which, by the act 1703, c. 4, was alleged to be not transportation, but banishment from Scotland only. The Court, however, were clearly and unanimously of opinion that, by the constitution of the Court, they had an inherent jurisdiction in the punishment of all crimes, without the aid of any statute; that the crime here charged was not leasing-making, but sedition; that this latter crime may be committed without any overt act of violence, provided something is done clearly manifesting the intent, and that transportation was only a peculiar and more severe mode of executing the sentence of banishment. The pannel was not brought up for sentence, not being deemed a leading offender; but, on 13th January 1794, Maurice Margarot, another member of the convention, and one of the English delegates, was transported fourteen years This was followed by the trial of Joseph Gerald, 10th March 1794, who was also transported fourteen years. There can be no doubt whatever that he had been guilty of sedition, and was meditating high treason; for he had proposed and enforced a resolution, in which it was declared that the convention " should pay no regard to any act of the Legislature abolishing their meetings, and that the event of an *invasion* should be the signal for the delegates repairing to the

[1] Burnett, 240.

places which the secret committee shall appoint, and that the first seven members shall have power to declare their sittings permanent, and twenty-one shall constitute a convention, and proceed to business." In Solicitor-General Blair's speech, it was justly observed, that the facts here charged were not verbal but real sedition, and therefore all argument as to the punishment of leasing-making is out of the case; that the charge is not of being a member of an association to obtain reform, but to procure it by *illegal means*, and the subversion of the constitution; that the very act of holding themselves out as delegates of the people at large, is seditious, when a Parliament exists, composed of the real representatives; and that the whole language of the convention breathes an air of defiance to the legitimate authority of the state, and is little short of high treason. He was convicted and sentenced to fourteen years' transportation.[1] More lately, and at a period farther removed from the vehement faction of that unhappy period, Gilbert Macleod was, on 21st February 1820, brought to trial for sedition, contained in a Glasgow paper, entitled The Spirit of the Union, of which he was the editor. He was convicted of publishing a composition " calculated and intended to degrade and bring into contempt and detestation the Government, Legislature, and Constitution of this realm, and to withdraw therefrom the confidence, affection, and allegiance of the people, and fill the realm with trouble, dissension, and insubordination." He was convicted, but recommended to lenity, in consideration of his good character; and, after hearing a full and able argument on the incompetence of pronouncing a sentence of transportation on such a sentence, he was transported five years.[2]

There can be no question, therefore, that sedition constitutes an offence cognizable by the common law of Scotland; a decision founded not only on an invincible train of precedents, but the plainest principles of expedience and justice, and which never could have been questioned but during the vehemence of party strife.

It is no answer to this to observe, as has since been repeatedly done, that the objects for which these unhappy men contended in 1793 were the same with those which a large part of the nation advocated not forty years after; and that a plan of Reform which was brought forward by Government in 1831

---

[1] Burnett, 250, 255.—[2] Hume, 1 557

could not have been sedition in 1793. Supposing the objects had been the same, which they were not, for annual parliaments and universal suffrage formed no part of the Reform Bill of 1831, still every thing depends on the *mode* of bringing forward the measure, the *means* proposed to be adopted, and the temper of the times when it is broached. It is not seditious to advocate universal suffrage and annual parliaments, but it is seditious to do so in a way calculated to excite rebellion, or effect the objects by the weapons of actual violence. It is not unlawful, in the ordinary case, to fire a gun, but it is unlawful to do so in a crowded street, where imminent peril to the lieges must be anticipated; the dose which may be safely prescribed to a full grown person cannot be given to a child without the hazard of murder. As little can there be any doubt that, by the law as it then stood, transportation was a *competent* punishment for that offence; for this reason, of itself decisive, if none other existed, that sedition, being a crime at common law, and one, in aggravated cases, of the most perilous nature, it is just as competent to inflict transportation on such offenders as on those convicted of culpable homicide, fraud, or embezzlement.[1] But in regard to the *expedience* or *equity* of inflicting such a punishment, especially on men such as Muir or Gerald, described by their friends as of fine talents and amiable, though mistaken, dispositions,[2] a very different opinion may be formed. Had the Court found the punishment of transportation competent, but, in consideration of the character of the accused, inflicted only a milder pain, the law would have been saved, the constitution protected, and the breath of calumny silenced. Experience of civil dissension, and of the blindness which it induces even on the clearest minds, should render all parties charitable in judging of the intentions of their opponents, when arraigned before a criminal tribunal; and the only fault, for which both sides should have no pardon, is want of humanity on either.

4. By special statute the punishment of sedition is now, for the first offence, fine and imprisonment, or both; and for the second, fine or imprisonment, or both, or banishment from his Majesty's dominions for such time as the Court shall appoint.

[1] Burnett, 255; Hume, i. 360, 365.—[2] Burnett, 251.

All disputes concerning the punishment of sedition are now at an end, by the enactment of the 6th Geo. IV. c. 47, which, proceeding on the narrative of its being expedient that this offence should be punished in Scotland as it is in England, enacts, " that a person convicted of this offence shall, for the first offence, be punished with fine or imprisonment, or both, at the discretion of the Court: for the second offence the offender is liable, at the discretion of the Court, to be fined or imprisoned, or both; or to be banished from his Majesty's dominions for such a term of years as the Court shall order." Having been so banished, the offender, if he shall not depart from the United Kingdom within thirty days after his sentence, for the purpose of going into banishment, may be conveyed by his Majesty to such part out of his dominions as his Majesty, by the advice of his Privy Council, shall direct. And having been banished as aforesaid, the offender, if he shall be found, and without some lawful cause, within any part of his Majesty's dominions after the end of forty days from the date of his sentence, and if he shall be lawfully convicted thereof, shall be liable to be transported to such place as shall be appointed by his Majesty for any term not exceeding fourteen years. No conviction for sedition has taken place in this country since the pains of the common law were restricted by this enactment.

5. By special statute the establishment of seditious societies, or the administering of unlawful oaths or engagements towards any seditious or mutinous object, is punishable with transportation for seven years.

The 37th Geo. III. c. 123, upon the narrative that wicked and evil-disposed persons had attempted to seduce his Majesty's forces into acts of mutiny and sedition, and had attempted to give effect to their wicked proceedings, by oaths unlawfully administered, enacts, " That any person or persons who shall, in any manner or form whatsoever, administer, or cause to be administered, or be aiding or assisting at, or present at, or consenting to, the administering or taking of any unlawful oath or engagement, purporting or intended to bind the person taking the same to engage in any mutinous or seditious purpose, or to disturb the public peace, or to be of any association, society, or confederacy formed for any such purpose, or to obey the orders or commands of any committee or body of men not lawfully constituted, or of any leader or commander, or other person not having authority by law for that purpose, or not to inform or give evidence against any associate, confederate, or other person; or not to reveal or discover any unlawful combination or confederacy; or not to reveal or discover any illegal act done or to be done; or not to reveal or discover any legal oath or engagement which may have been administered or tendered to, or taken by such person or persons, or to or by any other person or persons, or the import of such oath or engagement, shall, on conviction, be adjudged guilty of felony, and be transported for any term not exceeding seven years; and every person who shall *take* any such oath or engagement, not being compelled thereto, shall, on conviction, be adjudged guilty of felony, and transported for any term not exceeding seven years." On this statute, which authorises transportation for seven years; and, on the common law against sedition, which authorises transportation also, Mealmaker, a weaver in Dundee, was indicted at Perth, September 1798. The indictment charged that he was a member of the society called the United Scotsmen, the object of which was, under pretence of reform, " to create in the minds of the people a spirit of disloyalty to the king and disaffection to the established government, and, ultimately, to excite and stir them up to acts of violence and opposition to the laws and constitution of the country;" and the oath of secrecy was stated as having been, " that neither hopes, fears, rewards, or punishments, should ever induce them, directly or indirectly, to inform on, or give any evidence against, any member or members of this or similar societies, for any act or expression of theirs done or made, collectively or individually, in or out of this society, in pursuance of the spirit of this obligation." The pannel was charged with administering this oath, and with distributing seditious publications in forwarding the purposes of this association. He was convicted both of the common law and the statutory charge, and transported fourteen years, seven on the one and seven on the other.[1] The same punishment was inflicted on J. Paterson, Perth, September 1799, on a conviction for the same offence, and on a similar indictment.[2] And again, on 23d June 1800, Ser-

---

[1] Burnett, 259.—[2] Ibid. 260.

jeant William Maxwell, another member of the Society of United Scotsmen, was convicted and transported seven years on an indictment which charged both sedition at common law, and also that he had administered oaths to entrant members, instructed them in the private signs and watchwords of the society, distributed pamphlets containing their oaths, rules, and constitution, and had composed and circulated a seditious song.[1]  It has been determined in the Court of King's Bench, upon this statute, that it is not confined to oaths administered for seditious or mutinous purposes, but extended to an oath not to reveal an act done by an association, the object of which was to raise wages and make regulations in a certain trade, without reference to any political object whatever.   Judge Lawrence observed, " It is true that the preamble and the first part of the enacting clause are confined in their object to cases of mutiny and sedition, but it is nothing unusual in acts of Parliament for the enacting part to go beyond the preamble; the remedy often extends beyond the particular evil which first suggested the law."[2]

6. By special statute it is felony, without benefit of clergy, to administer any oath or engagement purporting or intended to bind the person taking the same, to commit treason, murder, or any felony punishable by law with death.

By the 52d Geo. III. c. 104, § 1, it is enacted, " That every person who shall, in any manner or form whatsoever, administer, or cause to be administered, or be aiding or assisting at the administering of any oath or engagement purporting or intending to bind the person taking the same to commit any treason or murder, or any felony punishable by law with death, he shall, on conviction, be adjudged guilty of felony, without benefit of clergy; and that every person who shall *take* any such oath or engagement, not being compelled thereto, shall, on conviction, be transported for life, or for such term of years as the Court shall adjudge."

But, by both this statute and the preceding statute, the information must be given within a limited time to obtain the

---

[1] Hume, i. 357.—[2] Rex v. Marks, East iii. 157; Russell. i. 130.

defence of compulsion. By 37th Geo. III. c. 123, it is enacted, " That compulsion shall not justify or excuse any person taking such oath or engagement, unless he or she shall, within *four* days after the taking thereof, if not prevented by actual force or sickness, and then, within four days after the hinderance produced by such force or sickness shall have ceased, declare the same, together with the whole of what he or she know touching the same, and the person and persons by whom and in whose presence, and when and where such oath or engagement was administered or taken, by information or oath before one of his Majesty's Justices of the Peace, or one of his Majesty's Privy Council, or one of his Majesty's Principal Secretaries of State; or in case the person taking such oath or engagement shall be in actual service in his Majesty's service, by sea or land, then by such information on oath as aforesaid, or by information to his commanding officer." The 52d Geo. III. c. 104, contains a similar enactment, with this difference only, that the period is, by that statute, extended from four to fourteen days.

By the first statute, any engagement or obligation whatever in the form of an oath, and, by the second, any obligation or engagement whatever in the form of an oath binding to the commission of any treason or capital felony, shall be deemed an oath within the meaning of the acts, and whether the same shall be administered by some person or persons, or taken by others without any administration.

All persons aiding or assisting at, or present or consenting to, the administering or taking of such unlawful oaths, or aiding or assisting, or present at, or consenting to, the taking of such unlawful oaths, shall be deemed principals, and tried as such. And it is declared sufficient to set forth in the indictment the purpose of the oath or engagement, without specifying its actual words. It has been decided by all other Judges on this last clause, that the act intended that it should be sufficient to allege and prove what the object of the oath and engagement was, without setting forth any words at all.[1] It is sufficient, where the oath was read from a paper, to give parole evidence of its contents, without giving notice to produce such paper;[2] and where the oath, on the face of it, did not purport

[1] Rex v. Moors, East. vi. 419; Russell, i. 132.—[2] Rex v. Moors, East. vi. 421.

5

to be for a seditious purpose, it was held that declarations made
at the time by the party administering such an oath, were admissible to prove that such was its real tendency.[1]

In the noted case of Andrew Mackinlay, 18th July 1817, an
indictment laid on this statute was found relevant. It charged
him with administering an oath which engaged the persons
taking it " to commit treason by obtaining Annual Parliaments
and Universal Suffrage by physical strength or force." The
evidence failed, and the pannel was acquitted.[2]

7. By special statute, societies, the members of which
shall take unlawful oaths or engagements, or where the
names of some of the persons or members forming committees shall be kept secret, or where there are divisions or
branch societies, are to be deemed unlawful combinations
and confederacies.

The 39th Geo. III. c. 79, proceeding on the narrative that
many dangerous societies, inconsistent with the public tranquillity, had sprung up in various parts of the empire, enacts, " That
all the said societies of United Englishmen, United Scotsmen,
and United Irishmen and United Britons, and the society called
the London Corresponding Society, and all other societies called
corresponding societies of any other city, town, or place, shall
be, and the same are hereby, utterly suppressed and prohibited
as being unlawful combinations and confederacies against the
Government of Our Sovereign Lord the King, and the peace
and security of his Majesty's subjects." [3]

It is farther enacted by the same statute, that " the said societies, and every other society then established, or hereafter
to be established, the members whereof shall, according to the
rules thereof, or to any provision or agreement for that purpose, be required or admitted to take any oath or engagement
which shall be an unlawful oath or engagement within the intent or meaning of the 37th Geo. III. c. 123, or to take any
oath not required or authorised by law; and every society, the
members whereof, or any of them, shall take, or in any manner bind themselves by any such oath or engagement on becoming, or in consequence of being, members of such society;

[1] Rex v. Moors, East vı. 421.—[2] Hume, L 557.—[3] 39th Geo. III. c. 79
§ 1.

and every society, the members whereof shall take, subscribe, or assent to any test or declaration not required by law, or not authorized in manner hereinafter mentioned; and every society, the names of the members of which, or any of them, shall be kept secret from the society at large, or which shall have any committee or select body so chosen or appointed, that the members constituting the same shall not be known by the society at large to be members of such committee or select body, or which shall have any president, secretary, treasurer, or other officer so chosen or appointed, that the election or appointment shall not be known to the society at large, or of which the names of all the members and of all presidents, treasurers, secretaries, or other office-bearers, shall not be entered in a book kept for that purpose, and open to the inspection of all the members; and every society which shall be composed of different divisions or branches, or of different parts, acting in any manner separate or distinct from each other, or of which any part shall have any separate or distinct president, treasurer, secretary, or other officer, elected or appointed by or for such part, or to act as an officer for any such part, shall be deemed and taken to be unlawful combinations and confederacies." These enactments are so extremely broad that they strike at all societies having branches or corresponding divisions; and, therefore, by 59th Geo. III. c. 19. § 27, it is declared that this enactment is not to extend to the meetings of Quakers, or to any meeting or society for purposes of a religious or charitable nature only, and in which no other matter shall be discussed.

It is farther enacted, That every person who shall, directly or indirectly, maintain correspondence or intercourse with any such society, or with any division, branch, committee, or other select body, president, &c., or other officer or member thereof as such, or who shall, by contribution of money or otherwise, aid, abet, or support such society, or any members or officers thereof, shall be deemed guilty of an unlawful combination and confederacy.[1] The act is declared not to extend to declarations approved by two Justices of the Peace, and registered with the Clerk of the Peace, nor to Lodges of Freemasons existing at the passing of the act, " provided that there be a certificate of two of the members, upon oath, that such society or

---

[1] 39th Geo. III. c 79, § 2.

lodge had been usually held under such denomination, and in conformity to the rules of such societies, the certificate, duly attested, being, within two months after the passing of the act, deposited with the Clerk of the Peace, with whom also the name and denomination of the society or lodge, and the usual time and place of meeting, and the names and descriptions of the members, are to be registered yearly."[1]  The Clerk of the Peace is required to enrol such certificate, and regularly to lay the same once every year before the general session of the Justices; and the Justices may, on complaint upon oath that the continuance of the meetings of any such lodge or society is likely to be injurious to the public peace and good order, direct them to be discontinued; and any such meeting held notwithstanding such order and discontinuance, and before the same shall by the like authority be revoked, shall be deemed an unlawful combination and confederacy under the act.[2]  Proceedings may be instituted either before the Justices, or by indictment before the Justiciary or Circuit Courts.  The offenders are liable to be convicted by the oath of one or more credible witnesses, and a fine of £20, or imprisonment for three months, may be awarded; and, if the proceeding is by indictment, the offender may be imprisoned two months, or transported seven years.[3]  In the case of the Procurator-fiscal of Wigtonshire v. the Mason Lodge of Newton-Stewart, June 2. 1825, the Court were clear that this act struck at an *Orange Lodge* established in that place, although, in consequence of an informality in the original application before the Justices, they dismissed the complaint.[4]

Some farther enactments regarding societies taking unlawful oaths, or electing committees or delegates, are contained in 57th Geo. III. c. 25, which imposes the same penalties as are contained in the 39th Geo. III. c. 79   This act also extends to Scotland[5]  And, by 60th Geo. III., and 1st Geo. IV. c. 1, meetings for the purpose of military exercise, without legal authority, are prohibited; and persons attending such meetings for the purpose of training others, or aiding therein, are liable to be transported seven years, or imprisoned two years.  Prosecutions must be commenced within six months, and the persons so assembled may be dispersed, detained, and held to bail.[6]

[1] 39th Geo. III. c. 79, § 3.—[2] Ibid. § 7 —[3] Ibid § 8.—[4] Unreported —
[5] 57th Geo. III. c. 57, § 37.—[6] Ibid § 2, 7

# CHAPTER XXXIII.

## OF HIGH TREASON.

The old law of Scotland regarding high treason, now abolished by the Articles of Union, was more complicated and extensive in its application, and in many respects more severe in its tendency, than that of England, which is now substituted in its stead. All commentary, however, on its provisions is now rendered superfluous by the express declaration of the Treaty of Union, and the statute of Anne[1] The first of these declares, "That the laws which concern public right, policy and civil government, may be made the same throughout the United Kingdom." And, in pursuance of this, it is provided by the 7th Anne, c. 21, "That such crimes and offences as are high treason, or misprision of high treason, within England, shall be construed, adjudged, and taken to be high treason and misprision of high treason within Scotland; and that from henceforth no crimes or offences shall be high treason or misprision of high treason within Scotland, but those that are high treason and misprision of high treason in England." In considering the doctrine of treason, therefore, the English law is now exclusively the object of consideration, with those cases upon it which have subsequently arisen in this country.

1. It is high treason " where a man doth compass the death of our lord the king, or of our lady the queen, or of their eldest son and heir."[2]

The great basis of the English treason law is the well known statute 25th Edward III c. 2, passed for the great purpose of settling the nature and limit of this offence, and correcting the

---

[1] Art. 18th Union.—[2] 25th Edward III. c. 2.

undue latitude which had arisen in extending it in the courts of the common law.[1]

Under the words " compassing or imagining the death of the king, queen, or heir-apparent," it is held, that not merely the actual perpetrating, but the conceiving or designing the death of these persons, provided it be evinced by sufficient and unequivocal actions. " The law," says Foster, " tendereth the safety of the king with an anxious, and, if I may use the expression, a concern bordering upon jealousy: it considereth the wicked imaginations of the heart, in the same degree of guilt as if carried into actual execution, from the moment that measures appear to have been taken to render them effectual [2]

But it is justly settled in their law, that this hidden design, to come within the treason law, must be manifested by *overt acts*, which must be made out by proper evidence. No stronger proof of this can be given than that which occurred in the case of the regicides who were tried for the death of Charles I. At a meeting of the Judges preparatory to this trial, it was agreed, " that the actual murder of the king should be precisely laid in the indictments, with the special circumstances as it was done, and should be made use of as one of the *overt acts* to prove the compassing of his death."[3] These overt acts are regarded not only as the evidence, and the only admissible evidence, of the intent, but also as the means devised to carry it into execution.[4]

To remove all doubts as to the degree of violence which shall be held necessary to establish a purpose against the *life* of the king, it is declared by 36th Geo. III. c. 7, made perpetual by 57th Geo. III. c. 6, a statute first passed on occasion of an outrage offered on the king's person, " that it is treason to compass, imagine, invent, devise, or intend death or destruction, *or any bodily harm tending to death or destruction*, maim or wounding, imprisonment or restraint, of the body of our sovereign lord the king."

It is settled, that any overt acts tending *directly* to the king's death, as lying in wait in order to attempt it; providing arms or preparing poison in order to effect it; sending letters tending to induce its perpetration; assembling and consulting as to the means of carrying it into execution, though no specific place

---

[1] Hale, 1 80; Hawkins, 1 c 17, No 1.—[2] Foster, 193, 195, Blackstone, iv c. 6.—[3] State Trials, ii 303.—[4] Foster, 203, 204.

be adopted for that purpose; even the mere presence at the consultation, though without taking any active part in the deliberation, if by a person who knew previously of the intention, and took no subsequent measures to divulge it to the proper authorities; offering money or any other consideration to any one to kill the king, though the money be not taken, or the consideration be declined; or in any other way instigating or encouraging any one to a course of action tending plainly to take away the life of the king, queen, or heir-apparent, are clear overt acts of treason.[1]

Farther, it is equally settled, that all acts and measures which in their consequences naturally tend to endanger the king's life, and cannot be carried into effect without manifest peril to it, fall under the same rule.[2]   On this principle, it is held an overt act under the statute to march with an array, however small, against the king;[3]  to fortify a house or castle to resist his forces; to enlist men to depose him; or by bond of association, gathering of company, writing of letters, or otherwise to take measures to imprison him, or forcibly gain possession of his person; experience having shewn, as Foster observes, that between the prisons and the graves of princes the distance is but small.[4]   The same rule is held to apply to the mere conspiracy or consultation to levy war, or the holding of deliberations and the taking of measures towards insurrection, if the object be such as law construes to be against the person or government of the king, as to *compel* him to alter his measures, or dismiss his ministers or counsellors, or submit to general measures for the reformation of the state, or in general to *constrain* him in any acts in which he has a right to exercise his own discretion by the prerogative of the crown:[5]  for such purposes, it is evident, cannot be enforced by numbers and open force, without manifest danger to his person; and it is held a kind of natural and necessary consequence, that he that attempts to conquer and subdue the king cannot intend less than to take away his life.[6]

These principles have been applied in a great variety of cases, both in England and Scotland.   Thus, in the case of Christo-

[1] Blackstone, iv. 79 , Foster, 195 ; Hale. i. 109, 119, 122, Hawkins, i. 38.— [2] Hume, i. 514 —[3] Hale, i. 142, 138, 139.—[4] Hawkins, i. 38 , Foster, 195; Hale, i. 109, 110.—[5] Foster, 211 , Hale, i. 148, 122, 123; Hawkins, i. 35, State Trials, i. 209.—[6] Hale, i 148.

pher Layer, November 1722, it was held a settled point, that to plan and consult to levy war, in order to seize and depose the king, was a compassing his death.[1] In like manner, in the case of Watt and Downie, August 1794, the pannels were convicted of high treason for holding consultations and providing arms towards an insurrection, for the purpose of taking the government into the hands of a great association, and compelling the king to submit to their demands.[2] Even the mere act of soliciting a foreign power, though not an open enemy, to invade the kingdom, has been held to fall under the same rule; or the mere act of going into a foreign country with such an intention, if duly proved.[3]

2. By special statute, the compassing to depose the king, or to levy war within the realm, in order to compel a change of measures, or intimidate or constrain either House of Parliament, or to move any foreign power to invade the realm, are substantive acts of treason.

The attempts already enumerated, and held to amount to a compassing of the king's death, embrace the doctrine of *constructive* treason, so much the subject of obloquy from various writers in England, and which clearly went beyond, in some instances, the intention of the statute of Edward  To prevent any farther extension of a similar kind, and also to facilitate the proof of such treasons, it is enacted, by the 36th Geo. III. c. 7, made perpetual by the 57th Geo. III. c. 6, that it is treason, 1st, " To compass, imagine, invent, devise, or intend to deprive or depose the king from the style, honour, or kingly name of the imperial crown of this realm." 2d, " To compass, imagine, invent, devise, or intend, to *levy war* against the king within the realm, in order to compel him to change his measures or councils, or in order to intimidate or put any constraint upon either House of Parliament." 3d, " To compass, imagine, invent, devise, or intend, to move any foreign power to invade the realm." These are now not *constructive* treasons, as formerly under the act of Edward, but open and *substantive* acts of treason under the act of George.[4] The words of the statute are, " That if, during the natural life of the king, any

[1] State Trials, vi. 328.—[2] Hume, i. 516.—[3] Lord Preston's Case, State Trials, vi. 448.—[4] Hume, i. 516.

person shall within the realm, or without, compass, imagine, invent, devise, or intend, death or destruction, or any bodily harm tending to death or destruction, maim or wounding, imprisonment or restraint, of the person of our lord the King, his heirs and successors, or to deprive or depose him or them from the style, honour, or kingly name of the imperial crown of this realm, or of any other of his majesty's dominions or countries, or to levy war against his majesty, his heirs and successors within this realm, in order by force or constraint to compel him or them to change his or their measures or councils, or in order to put any force or constraint upon, or to intimidate and overawe both or either House of Parliament, or to move or stir any foreigner or stranger with force to invade this realm, or any of his majesty's dominions or countries under the obeisance of his majesty, his heirs and successors, and such compassings, imaginings, inventions, devices, or intentions, or any of them, shall express, utter, or declare, by publishing any printing or writing, or by any overt act or deed, being legally convicted thereof upon the oath of two lawful lords or witnesses, or otherwise convicted or attainted by due course of law, then every such person and persons so, as aforesaid, offending, shall be deemed, declared, and adjudged to be a traitor "

At Paisley, August 1. 1820, James Speirs was brought to trial under an indictment of which the first charge or *count*, in the language of English law, was for compassing and imagining the death of the king, and the fourth, for compassing to levy war against the king, in order to compel him to change his measures. The same overt acts were enumerated, as tending to support both counts. The third overt act was " for printing, publishing, and posting, on the 1st April, an address to the inhabitants of Great Britain, which bore to be issued, " By order of the Committee of Organization for forming a Provisional Government." In this proclamation, under the name of recovering the people's rights, and freeing the king and country from thraldom, they declared that they had been " induced to *take up arms* for the redress of our common grievances," and would treat as enemies to their king and country all who should be found carrying arms to oppose them, and they called on the lieges in general, and especially the soldiers of the king's army, to join and assist them in the prosecution

of these public purposes, and declaring that equality of rights
was their object, that Liberty or Death was their motto, and
that they had sworn to return home in triumph or return no
more. It closed with an earnest address to all the lieges " to
desist from their labour from and after this 1st April, and to
attend wholly to the recovery of their rights," and recommended the proprietors of public works, and all others, to stop the
one and shut up the other

It appeared in evidence, that on Sunday, April 2, copies of
this address were posted on the porch of the chapel, and on the
corners of several streets in Johnstone, near Paisley, and circulated there; that on Monday, April 3, it was read to a numerous meeting of mechanics, held in the school-green, who
chose a preses, and resolved, by a shew of hands, to stop the
cotton-mills, of which there were several in and near the village; that, in the course of the morning and forenoon, noisy
and tumultuous assemblages of people took place in the village,
who proceeded in great numbers to the several mills, and there
compelled the owners and managers to stop working, in which
state they continued several days. And it was proved that the
prisoner had struck work himself, and took an active part in
persuading and compelling others to do the same. On this
state of the case, it was laid down by Lord Justice-Clerk Boyle,
with the concurrence of Chief-Baron Shepherd and the whole
Special Commissioners, that this proclamation was clearly treasonable; that all persons engaged in putting it up, or in carrying it into effect, by compelling or inducing others to yield
obedience to it, were involved in the treason; and that the prisoners at the bar seemed to be involved, by the evidence, in
this accession. The jury, however, declined to find him guilty
generally, but found him guilty of striking work, and compelling others to strike work, on the day libelled, and maliciously
and illegally hindering and obstructing divers manufactures
from being proceeded in on that day. As they did not find
him guilty of doing these acts with the treasonable intent
charged in the indictment, their verdict led to the pannel's acquittal.[1]

A similar case occurred at Dunbarton, 26th July 1820, Robert Monro. He was not only proved to have yielded obedience to this proclamation by striking work himself and com-

[1] Treason Trials, III. 5-469.

pelling others to do the same, but had actually taken possession of an iron-forge, where the conspirators were actively engaged in making pikes. The jury found the prisoner not
guilty, it being doubtful how far he was brought in contact
with these unquestionably treasonable acts.[1]

The result, however, was different in the case of Andrew
Hardie, July 13. 1820, Stirling, who was indicted for levying
war and compassing to levy war, in order to compel the king
to change his measures. He was charged with publishing and
posting near Stirling the treasonable address already noticed,
and with various overt acts for the purpose of carrying the designs and injunctions of that proclamation into effect. He was
convicted of this charge, as well as of the levying of war
against the king, and executed.[2]

It was laid down by Chief-Justice Dallas, in the case of the
Derby Rioters, " that if there be an insurrection, by which is
meant a large rising of the people, in order by force and violence to accomplish and revenge, not any private object of their
own, not any private quarrels of their own, but any general
purpose, that is considered by the law as a levying of war, and
this you may take to be clearly the law of the land." [3]　Every
insurrection which, in the judgment of law, is intended against
the person of the king, whether it be to imprison or to dethrone
him, or oblige him to alter his measures of government, or remove counsellors from about him, amounts to a levying of war
within the statute, whether attended with the pomp and circumstance of open war or not.[4]　At the Old Bailey, April
1820, Thistlewood, Ings, and others, were convicted of high
treason of this sort, for compassing to levy war against the
king, to compel him to change his measures.[5]

3. No writings, how wicked soever, amount to an overt
act of treason, if unconnected with a treasonable design,
actually on foot at the time; but if so connected, they
amount to it, though unpublished, and much more if uttered to any third party.

A treatise, branding all kingly government as a usurpation,

---

[1] Treason Trials, ii. 407, 699.—[2] Ibid. i. 1-230.—[3] Trial of Derby Rioters,
Treason Trials, iii. 303.—[4] Per Lord Justice-Clerk, Treason Trials, iii. 394;
Foster, 211.—[5] Hume, i. 516.

advocating a perfect republic, or even maintaining that it is right to dethrone or kill a sovereign, will not amount, if unpublished, to high treason. On this account, the judgment in the case of Algernon Sidney was clearly illegal; for not only were unpublished essays found in his repositories, founded on as overt acts of high treason, but they were so considered, though unconnected by legal evidence, with an actual treasonable measure [1]

But, on the other hand, it is no less clear that writings, though unpublished, and much more if uttered and delivered, may amount to proper overt acts, if they are written in relation to and in connexion with, and furtherance of, any treasonable design actually on foot at the time.[2] Accordingly, in the case of Lord Preston and Mr Ashton, January 19. 1690, it was held that papers and memorials by these persons, containing the plan of an invasion, intended for the French king or his ministers, though not as yet communicated to them, were overt acts of treason, being written in the prosecution of an existing treasonable design.[3] The same was held in the case of Francis Francia, where the overt act chiefly insisted in in the indictment was the writing certain letters to persons in France, declaring his intention of joining in a rebellion, and soliciting assistance.[4] And the same doctrine prevailed in the case of Mr Layer, November 1722, where the paper was published, and had reference to a design of seizing on the Tower, and some of the leading persons about the King.[5]

4. Writings published, which contain an exhortation to kill the king, or levy war against him, amount to high treason; but if they contain only general declamation against kingly government, to a misdemeanour.

If words be written and published which, without actually recommending or relating to any specific attempt against the king's life, are yet obviously dangerous to it, from the principles they contain, there is room for a distinction. If they distinctly recommend an attack upon the sovereign's life, and maintain the right of putting him to death as a tyrant, this is

[1] Foster, 198, Blackstone, iv. 80, 81 —[2] Hume, i. 517 —[3] Blackstone, iv 80.—[4] State Trials, vi. 100, 102.—[5] Foster, 198, 218, Blackstone, iv. 80.

a direct overt act of compassing his death; [1] and, accordingly,
John Twyn, printer, February 22. 1663, arraigned for printing
and publishing a book, which not only exhorted the people to
throw off their allegiance, but in direct terms urged them to
put the king to death, was held clearly guilty of high treason.[2]
But, on the other hand, if any one publish a book, or utter a
writing, not specifically levelled at the existing sovereign of
these realms, but containing general declamations against mo-
narchy, or teaching that it is lawful to kill kings in general,
this is not treason but sedition, and punishable as a misdemeanour.[3]

5. Words spoken, though ever so wicked and abominable, in relation to the king, will not amount to high
treason, unless they relate to a specific design against his
life.

Words, how atrocious or abominable soever, do not amount
to treason, unless they indicate an actual and existing design
against the King's person; for words are liable to be mistaken,
misconstrued, and misconceived, whereas writing is a deliberate act, indicating a more settled purpose of mind, and concerning which there can be no misconception.[4] But, on the
other hand, words become overt acts if they are spoken in relation to, and to be taken in connexion with, such acts as are
in themselves treasonable.[5] All consultation and debates,
therefore, though purely verbal, how to kill the king, or how
to levy war to depose him, or to force him to change his measures or counsellors, is an undoubted overt act of treason; for
these are not only words spoken but measures in preparation.[6]
By stronger reason, if there be any treasonable act also charged
against the pannel with which they are connected, such words
and act together become an overt act. Thus, if money be
given on condition of killing the King, or as a reward of that
stipulated service, and this is proved by the words which passed
on the occasion, no one can doubt that the acts and words together amount to treason.[7]

---

[1] Hale, i. 118.—[2] State Trials, iii. 287.—[3] Hume, i. 518.—[4] Hale, i. 111;
Blackstone, iv. 80, Foster 204, Coke, 38.—[5] Hale, i. 115, Foster, 202, 203.—
[6] Hume, i. 519.—[7] Hale, i. 116.

6. The statute applies to the king *de facto*, though he be not the king *de jure*, and to the queen-consort and heir-apparent ; but the treason must be directed against the life of these latter persons, and not against their liberty or rank.

Though the queen and the king's eldest son are within the statute of Edward, yet they are so in a much inferior sense from the reigning monarch of the realm, in whom the power and authority of government is immediately centered.[1] There are, in consequence, many overt acts of compassing the King's death, which will not apply to the queen or prince. Thus it is not treason to compass to depose the queen, or to constrain or imprison the prince; for there are many situations in which these personages may be necessarily subjected to such coercion[2] With respect to them, therefore, the compassing is to be understood of those acts which go directly to threaten their lives;[3] and the queen enjoys the protection only as long as she is queen-consort, or wife of a reigning king, and during the subsistence of the marriage.[4] Farther, no heir to the crown enjoys it, with the exception of the king's son; it does not extend to a collateral heir, nor to the eldest daughter of the king, when there is no son, unless by the force of special statutes applicable to her particular case.[5]

The statute applies to a queen-regnant, but not her husband, as also to the true heir of the king, though not yet crowned, from the moment of his predecessor's death.[6] By a wise provision also of the English, introduced after the disputed succession in the time of York and Lancaster, the statute applies to the king *de facto*, the person in possession of the crown, though not the king *de jure ;* and, on the other hand, the rightful heir of the crown, while an usurper is in possession, is not protected by the law of treason.[7] In pursuance of this principle, the statute 11th Henry VII. c. 1, declares, that all persons shall be freed from any penalties or disabilities, on account of any assistance in the field, or otherwise, by them rendered to the king for the time; a statute which is truly declaratory of the common law on the subject.[8] It would rather appear, however, that though this is undoubted law, where the rightful

---

[1] Hume, 1 520 —[2] Hale, 1 127, 128.—[3] Ibid 1 521 —[4] Ibid 1. 124.—[5] Ibid 1. 125, 126.—[6] Ibid 1. 101, Hawkins, i 36.—[7] Hume, 1. 520 —[8] Ibid

1

heir has never been at all in possession, the same will not hold
if he has once been in possession, has been expelled by an
usurper, and again regains the throne;[1] unless it appear that
the assistance rendered was in compliance with the usurper's
power and authority for the time, and not of the free will of
the subject.[2]

7. The next treason in the statute of Edward is, if a
man do violate " the king's companion, or his eldest daughter unmarried, or the wife of the king's eldest son and
heir."

The purposes of this provision is mainly for the preservation
of the blood-royal pure and uncontaminated by foreign admix-
ture; and therefore it is equally treason to have carnal knowledge of these personages by force or consent, and in the woman consenting not less than the man.[3]   Only the consort of
the king or prince still in life is within the act; but the eldest
daughter is included, though there be sons before her in existence, who of course are called before her to the throne.[4]

8. By the statute of Edward it is treason " if a man
do levy war against our lord the king within his realm."

Under this provision it is held, that there must be an *actual
levying* of war; whereby are excluded all consultations, conspi-
racies, and projects to levy war, how complete soever in themselves, and how serious the objects in view, if no war has actually been levied.[5]   And herein lies the great improvement
made on the treason law by the 36th Geo. III. c. 7, already
considered, which makes the " compassing, imagining, invent-
ing, devizing, or intending to levy war against the king, in order to compel him to change his measures or counsels, or to
put any restraints upon either House of Parliament," in itself
treason, though no levying of war has followed.  These things
had been *constructively* held as treason before that time, as involving, by legal implication, the king's death; but they are
now made substantive acts of treason, without any implication

In construing what shall be held a levying of war under this

---

[1] Hale, L 104.—[2] Hume, i. 520.—[3] Hale, L 128, 129; Hawkins, i. 37;
Blackst. iv. 81.—[4] Hume, i. 521.—[5] Hawkins, i 38, Foster, 211; Hale, i.
131; Blackst iv. 82.

2

act, it is held that any attack on the king's forces, how inconsiderable soever, so as it be made not for any private or personal object, but for a public reason or enmity to them, as the military power and instruments of the state, and for the purpose of effecting a forcible change in the government, institutions, or legislature of the country, is high treason.[1] The same holds with any forcible holding out of any castle or fort against the king's troops; or the fortifying one's own house, so as to make head against the king's troops; or even the bare raising and assembling a force, arrayed in manner of war, and with warlike weapons, though no actual fighting has ensued, if done with the same design. The same holds with a mere detainer of the king's fort or castle from him, and the refusal to admit his forces, if done in connexion with other acts of rebellion.[2] So it was held by Hale, in regard to the Earl of Essex, when the queen sent the keeper of the great seal to him, commanding him to dismiss the armed persons in his house; and he refused to come, and continued the armed persons in his house, and fortified it against the queen's officers: this he considers as treason.[3]

In the case of John Baird, Stirling, 14th July 1820, these principles were applied in Scotland. This man had joined a party of forty persons, who, on Tuesday 5th April 1820, assembled near Glasgow, some armed with fire-arms, and some with pikes, and with which they proceeded to the height of Bonnymuir in Stirlingshire. On their way thither they marched occasionally in military order, and on one occasion stopped a serjeant of the 10th Hussars, in order to take his arms, in which, however, they did not persist. Having halted for half an hour on the hill of Bonnymuir, a party of the 10th Hussars and of the Kilsyth Yeomanry came upon them, upon which they gave three cheers, and advanced to a wall three or four feet high, which they lined, prepared there to receive the charge of the horse. From this post they kept up an irregular fire on the troops as they advanced, and Baird took post at an opening in the wall; and, on the officer of the 10th Hussars approaching, deliberately pulled the trigger of his blunderbuss within a few yards of his side, though it missed fire, and thrust a pike through a serjeant's arm. The insurgents were quickly

[1] Hume, i. 522.—[2] Hale, i 141-152, Foster, 218, 219; Hawkins, i. 36.—[3] Hale, i. 136-152

dispersed, and nineteen prisoners taken. All this was proved to have been done in pursuance of an organized project of insurrection at Glasgow, and in the neighbouring counties, and in furtherance of the treasonable proclamation already noticed, calling upon the people to rise in rebellion, and bearing to be issued by " order of the committee of organization performing a provisional government." In these circumstances, there could be no doubt either of the levying of war, or the treasonable intent with which it was done, and the pannel was convicted and executed." [1]

Andrew Hardie was tried at Stirling, July 13. 1820, for levying war, by being engaged in the fight at Bonnymuir, and also for circulating the treasonable proclamation, already so often mentioned. The party had a bundle of those proclamations with them, and the pannel was proved to have taken an active share in their circulation. He was convicted both of actually levying war under the statute of Edward, and of compassing so as to come under the statute of George III , and also suffered death.[1] Sixteen other persons pleaded guilty to the same charges, and were transported for life.[2]

9. A meeting of persons irregularly armed, if in pursuance of a treasonable purpose, will constitute a levying of war, though no fighting has actually occurred with the king's forces.

In the cases hitherto considered, war was held to be levied by an assembly, how small soever in regular array; but what shall be said of those cases when the array was more tumultuous, and armed with ruder implements, as pitchforks, crowbars, and scythes ? It was settled in the case of Damarie and Purchase, April 21. 1710, that a tumultuous body so armed, which proceeded to pull down all dissenting meeting-houses, was a treasonable assembly,[3] and this decision was approved of by Foster.[4]

The same doctrine has since that time been applied in this country. In the case of James Wilson, Glasgow, July 20. 1820, it was applied to military preparations and organization, in furtherance of a treasonable design, though no fighting had actually occurred. The *species facti* there was,

---

[1] Treason Trials, i. 308, *et seq* —[2] Ibid. i. 299 —[3] State Trials, vi. 332.— [4] Foster, 208, 212

that, on Sunday 2d April, the treasonable proclamation was generally posted in the town of Strathaven, and, in obedience to it, the men all struck work on the Monday. On the evening of the 5th there was a great concourse of radicals coming and going from Wilson's house, and a great noise of voices and splitting of wood heard within the house, and pike poles were seen standing against the wall in the kitchen. Soon after dark, intelligence reached them that the friends of the cause were " all up" in Glasgow; upon which a party, among whom was the pannel's son-in-law, set out from the pannel's, visited various houses in Strathaven, and by threats of death and fire-raising, compelled many to join them, or deliver up their fire-arms; and, in one instance, forced a shopkeeper to furnish them with gunpowder, shot, and flints, which were set down " to the radical account." Next morning a party of these persons, from fourteen to twenty, set out from Wilson's house, all armed with guns or pikes, and carrying a flag, bearing on one side the words, " Strathaven Union Society, 1819," and on the other, " Scotland free, or a desert." In the rear came Wilson, bearing a sword, which had been sharpened on the Wednesday before. They advanced in a loose marching order, eight miles on the road to Glasgow, when, finding that the intelligence of an insurrection in that town was false, they gradually fell off, and Wilson returned home in the evening without his sword. On this evidence the Lord President Hope, in concurrence with Chief-Baron Shepherd and Lord Justice-Clerk Boyle, delivered it as undoubted law, that, to make a levying of war under the statute, it was not necessary that there should be battles, or a regular trained force, or an array of battalions clothed and armed like regular soldiers, but " that the smallest body which *rises in arms to effect a general purpose* (they may have more or less hopes of success according to their numbers), is treasonable, and constitutes a levying of war.[1] No doubt, small bodies will not succeed till they assemble in a great body, but how are they to assemble in a great body, unless they march in individual detachments, and by so marching, each party is doing all that it can in furtherance of the conspiracy; it lends its individual force and influence, if it has any influence, to the furtherance of that object, which cannot be carried into effect till all the bodies are joined. That is the undoubted law of the land."[2]

[1] Treason Trials, ii. 335 —[2] Ibid ii 339

10. The war must be levied against the king; but under this head are included all insurrections, which have for their object to effect by force and numbers any innovation of a public and general nature, or redress any public grievance, real or imaginary, which can only be legally accomplished by the king's authority, or that of the whole legislature.

The raising and employing the most formidable military force in rapine and bloodshed is not treason, if it be done on a private quarrel, or from family feuds, or the desire of plunder and revenge, and not from any hostile motive to the authority of the king or the government of the land. So it was determined in England in the reign of Edward I., on occasion of the contests between the Lords Hereford and Gloucester, Marchers of the Western Counties, who brought out a great array against each other.[1]

On the other hand, it is no less clear, and has been decided by our greatest authorities, that the levying of war against the king is not limited to those insurrections which are immediately directed against his person, as with a view to dethrone or imprison him, or compel a change of measures or of counsellors, but embrace also those commotions directed to objects of a more general character, and which are rather intended for the forcible reformation of the state or of the constitution of Parliament.[2] Insurrections, therefore, which have it in view to throw open all enclosures, to pull down all prisons or courts of justice, to resist all revenue-officers in the collection of the revenue; in short, all risings to accomplish a general purpose, or to hinder a general measure, which can only be legally attained or prohibited by authority of the king or parliament, amount to a levying of war against the king, and have always been tried and punished as treason.[3] To reform the established law, religious or political institutions of the land, or to obtain redress of grievances, real or imaginary, by force and coercion, applied either to the king or either house of parliament, is unquestionably a treasonable intent; and if this be manifested by overt acts, though small and despicable compared to the magnitude of the object in view, yet indicating a settled and deliberate

[1] Hume, i. 524.—[2] Ibid.—[3] Per Lord President Hope, Treason Trials, i. 23; Hale, i. 132; Foster, 211; Blackst. iv. 82.

purpose, this will constitute high treason.[1]  So the law has been laid down by the greatest sages and ornaments of the English bench; by Lord Loughborough, in July 1780, on the trial of the insurgents against popery; by Lord Mansfield, February 1781, on the trial of Lord George Gordon for inciting those rioters; by Lord Ellenborough, in June 1817, on the trial of Dr Watson for treason; and again by the same great authority at Derby, October 1817, on the commission for the trial of Brandreth and others for the same crime; and by Lord Chief-Justice Abbot, March 1820, on occasion of the opening of the commission for the trial of Thistlewood and others.[2]

Nay, this constructive levying of war against the king is held to go farther than this, and to embrace all systematic and extensive opposition to the laws or executive authority of the realm in matters of general interest.  Thus, all projects to abate *all* rents, to raise *all* wages, to lower the prices of *all* provisions, to hinder the payment of *all* taxes, are clearly treasonable.[3]  This was exemplified in the case of Peter Massinger and others, 4th April 1668, who had assembled armed, with a captain and ensign, and proceeded to pull down all bawdy-houses, which was adjudged high treason.[4]  In like manner, in the well known case of Damaree and Purchase, April 21. 1710, an enterprise, the object of which was to pull down all dissenting meeting-houses, was adjudged treason.[5]  And in the case of Burton and others, a conspiracy to rise in arms, and set out on a general enterprise to pull down all enclosures, was held to be the same crime.[6]

Insurrections for these general and formidable objects, are distinguished from others of a somewhat similar character, formerly considered under the head of riots, in this, that they relate to objects of general policy, institution, or law, which require to be accomplished by the authority of *Parliament;* whereas the others are for the attainment of an individual and local object, which is to be attained or coerced by a court of *justice.*  Insurrections of the first character are deemed treason, because they are the forcible attempts to do what belongs to the legislature or the sovereign authority; those of the last, mobbing and riot-

---

[1] Hume, i. 524.—[2] See the Reports of these trials, State Trials, and Hume, i. 524.—[3] Hawk. i. 37; Fost. 211-12.—[4] State Trials, ii. 587. But this was against Hale's opinion; Hale, i. 134.—[5] Foster, 214-15.—[6] Hale, i. 144.

ing, because they are more private crimes, interfering not with
the sovereignty of government, but the due administration of
justice.[1]    On this ground the Porteous mob in Edinburgh, being
a violent interference with the administration of *justice* by the
crown, was, after due consideration, proceeded against as a riot
only;[2] and on a similar ground, it was held, on a consultation
of all the Judges, that where there was a great rising of weavers
in many counties at the same time to destroy the engine-looms
for weaving ribbons, this, though a very general movement, yet
being directed against individuals or master manufacturers, and
not the state, was a riot only.[3]    Upon the same ground, the
Luddites, in 1811, who proceeded to such extrem·· in burning machines in the manufacturing districts, ar     e frame
breakers, who committed such devastation in .      southern
counties of England in the winter of 1830, were indicted on
the statutes against machine breaking, or for riot, but not for
treason.

The levying of war must be within the king's realm; but
not only all the British dominions but the narrow seas are held
the realm, so that to assail any of the king's ships, which are
deemed floating castles on these seas, if done by a subject of
the realm for a treasonable purpose, is a levying of war under
the statute.[4]

Those constructive ways of levying war which have no immediate relation to the king's life or government, can be committed only by some overt acts, and not by a *mere conspiracy*
to engage in them; whereas, where the object is to imprison,
dethrone, kill, or constrain him, the mere entering into such a
conspiracy is of itself an overt act.[5]

11. It is treason by the statute of Edward, " if a man
be adherent to the king's enemies within this realm, giving to them aid or comfort within the realm or elsewhere."

It is clearly treason to join and march with the enemy in
warlike array, or to cruise under his command or commission,
even though no fighting with the king's ships has ensued, or to
remain in his service and take his pay, though without actual

---

[1] Hume, i. 526.—[2] Per President Hope, Treason Trials, i. 23.—[3] Hale, i.
143; Foster, 210 —[4] Hume, i. 527.—[5] Foster, 213; Hallam, Const Hist.
II. 505.

collision with Great Britain, or anyhow to accompany and be attached to the enemy's force, provided these acts be done not from the effect of fear and compulsion to the *life* of the pannel, for threats to his property are no excuse.[1]  The same is true of all voluntary sending of intelligence to the enemy, or arms, provisions, warlike stores, or surrendering any of the king's fortresses or ships of war for bribe or reward and not cowardice, and in general any sort of combination with the enemy.[2]  On the same principle, any one who shall fairly and voluntarily take an oath of fealty and allegiance to an enemy is guilty of treason.[3]  But the mere fact of remaining abroad in an enemy's country after war has broke out, even though after a proclamation to all British subjects to return home, is not deemed an act of adherence to the king's enemies; and an invitation to a foreign power *at peace* with Great Britain is not treason, because there is no enemy at the time of the solicitation to whom it can be construed an adherence.[4]

The term *enemy* in this question is applied not only to a king or state in open hostility with Great Britain, even though no proclamation of war may have been made, but to every alien who comes into Great Britain in a state of hostility;[5] so that if even the subject of a foreign state at peace with Great Britain, shall, without a commission from his sovereign, invade this country in a hostile manner, any aid lent to such a belligerent subject is treason.[6]  It is also the same in open war, whether the adherence be given to the enemy in combating the king's forces or those of his allies, and whether within or without the realm; and so it was held by Holt in the case of Thomas Vaughan, November 6. 1696.[7]  But there is this distinction between a levying war and an adherence to the king's enemies in the statute; that the former must be within the realm or on the narrow seas, whereas the latter may be by assistance rendered to the enemy either within the realm or elsewhere [8]

12. It is treason " to counterfeit the king's great or privy seal," or any of the " seals appointed by the 24th article of the Union to be kept, used, and continued in Scotland."

---

[1] Foster, 216–17; Hale, i. 167–68.—[2] Hawk, i 30; Blackst. iv. 83.—[3] Hale, i. 165.—[4] Ibid i. 165, 167 —[5] Hume, i. 529.—[6] Hale, i. 163; Foster, 219–20.—[7] State Trials, v. 34, Hale, i. 165–66 —[8] Hale, i. 165–66.

It is treason by the act of Edward, " if any man counterfeit the king's Great or Privy Seal;" and by the 7th Anne, c. 21, " if any person counterfeit her majesty's seals appointed by the 24th article of the Union to be kept, used, and continued in Scotland," that the doing thereof shall be construed and adjudged to be treason.　No adjudged cases have occurred on this branch of the statute.

13. It is treason by the statute of Edward, " if a man counterfeit t⋯ king's money, or bring false money into the realm κnⁿwing it to be false, to make payment in deceit of our lord the king and of his people."

Under these words it is held, that the guilt of treason attaches to those who import counterfeit British money, *with intent* to make merchandise or payment therewith, though none such have actually been made.[1]　Coining the king's money is treason, without uttering, but uttering without coining is not.[2] None but gold and silver coin is placed under this high protection, or considered as " king's money," much less any thing that is counterfeited after the similitude of a foreign coin, even though it be current here by proclamation.[3]

14. It is treason by the act of Edward to " slay the Chancellor, Treasurer, or the King's Justices of the one ⋯ ⋯, or the other Justices in Eyre or Justices of Assize, and all other Justices assigned to hear and determine, being in their places doing their offices."

By 7th Anne, c. 21, the Supreme Judges of the Scotch Courts are placed on the same footing as their English brethren; it being provided, " that if any person shall slay any of the Lords of Session or Lords of Justiciary, sitting in judgment in the exercise of their office, within Scotland, the doing thereof shall be construed, adjudged, and taken to be high treason."
For the statutory treasons relating to the Protestant order of succession against the Pretender, and relative to the Protestant religion, being now, from the change of times, the subjects of

---

[1] Hale, i. 227; Hawk, i. 42.—[2] Blackst. iv. 84; Hume, i. 530.—[3] Hume, i. 530; Hale, i. 227.

curiosity rather than use, it is sufficient to refer to Hume, vol. i. p. 531-2.

15. By various late statutes, offences against the king's money, or gold and silver coin, are declared treason.

The multifarious offences against the coin have occasioned a large addition to the treason law, since the days of Edward III.

1. By 1st William and Mary, § 2. c. 6, it is treason to counterfeit any foreign coin of gold or silver that is current within the realm, by consent of the Crown, or to forge the sign-manual, privy signet, or privy seal.

2. By 1st and 2d Philip and Mary, c. 11, it is treason to bring into the realm any such false or counterfeit foreign money, with the intent to utter or make payment therewith; and, under these words, the importing with that intent, without actual uttering is treason.[1]

3. By 5th Elizabeth, c. 11, whoever shall wash, clip round, or file; and, by 18th Elizabeth, c. 1, whoever shall impair, diminish, falsify, scale, or lighten the proper coin of the realm, or that of other realms, current here by proclamation, is guilty of high treason.

4. By 8th and 9th William III. c. 26, made perpetual by 7th Anne, c. 25, whoever shall knowingly make or mend, buy or sell, or have in his possession any instruments proper for the coinage of money, or shall convey such instruments out of the King's Mint, is guilty of treason.

5. The same statute makes it also treason to colour, case, or gild over any coin resembling the current coin of the realm, or even round blanks of base metal.

6. By 15th and 16th Geo. III c. 28, it is not less treason to colour or alter any current silver coin of the realm, so as to make it resemble a gold coin, or any copper coin, so as to resemble a silver one.[2]

It would rather appear that all the offences against the coin which are made treason by these enactments, must now be prosecuted in Scotland, under that denomination, and cannot be indicted under the old Scotch law on the subject.[3] In the case, accordingly, of John Smith, July 1749, the trial for false coining of gold coin was conducted and concluded under the trea-

---

[1] Hale, l. 229.—[2] Hume, l. 532, 3 —[3] Ibid. 533

son forms.[1] But, on the other hand, all offences against the coin, which are not treason by the English law, remain here on their former footing; and, accordingly, the trial of William Deane, September 1729, for falsehood and coining of halfpence, which is not treason by the English law, as they hold the " king's money" to be gold or silver only, was conducted according to the Scotch forms, and he had sentence of pillory and transportation.[2]

16. In treason there are no accessaries either before or after the fact, but all are principal.

The law of treason has this peculiarity, which distinguishes it from the other crimes recognised in the English law, that there are no accessaries in it either before or after the fact, but all are principals.[3] All who become partakers in the traitorous project, whether at an early or late stage of it, whether as leaders or followers, whether they engage in the whole plot or in part of it only, are equally guilty of treason, provided that the part which they do take, relates strictly and properly to the forwarding and accomplishing the grand object in view by the rest of the conspirators.[4] The same acts which render a man accessary in other offences, render him principal in this. By incitement, therefore, or aid towards the doing of an act of treason; by comforting or harbouring the treator after the deed; by rescuing him from the officers of justice, assisting him to break jail, or even conniving at his escape, if intrusted with his custody, the guilt of treason is incurred.[5] The reason is, that the mere preparation, conspiracy, or advice to do the thing itself, amounts to a principal treason, or overt act of compassing, even though the deeds contemplated should never have been carried into execution.[6]

17. All persons may be guilty of treason who owe allegiance to the king; and under that description are included all natural born British subjects, and all aliens who have become naturalized.

Allegiance is derived from two sources, that which springs

[1] Hume, i. 533.—[2] Ibid.—[3] Ibid.—[4] Per President Hope, Treason Trials, i. 25.—[5] Hume i. 533.—[6] Hale, 223, Hawl. ii. 310, Blackst iv. 35; Foster, 341.

from birth, and that which is acquired by those not naturally subjects of the realm.

1. Every person is deemed a British subject who is born within the realm, of whatever parents he may have sprung,[1] or even out of it, if of a British subject. This natural and primitive obligation of allegiance, *inhæret ossibus*, cannot be cast off or lost by any length of residence in a foreign state. Go where he will, remain as long as he choose, he still remains a British subject, and is guilty of treason if he engage in any design against its government.[2] This was strongly exemplified in the case of Angus Masdonald, 10th December 1747, who was born in Britain, and of British parents, but carried in early infancy to France, where he had lived all his life, and was engaged in a profession. He was held amenable to our treason law, and convicted; but most properly pardoned by the Crown.[3]

2. An alien who comes to this country, and resides here, if he be an alien *ami*, as the English lawyers term it; that is, the natural born subject of a state in amity with Great Britain, shall be held guilty of treason, if he commit any treasonable offence in this country.[4] Nor does it make any difference though his sovereign, originally in amity with Great Britain, should declare war against it. If such an event occurs, he may withdraw to his original state, and so be free of his British allegiance; but, if he remain here, he is held to have made his election in favour of this realm, and must be held bound by his acquiescence to its sovereign. Nay, it has been held by all the Judges, that the same holds with an alien *ami* if, though he go abroad himself on the breaking out of a war, he leave his family and effects behind him in this country.[5]

3. An alien who comes into Britain for the first time after the commencement of war with his prince, is to be regarded as a spy, and seized and dealt with as such.[6]

17. Legal evidence in treason consists in the concurring testimony of two witnesses to each overt act, or of one witness to each overt act, if there are several overt acts of the same kind, unless in cases of attempts to kill the king, when the ordinary rules of murder by the English law prevail.

[1] Hume, i. 534.—[2] Hale, i. 96; Hawk. i. 35; Foster, 183.—[3] Foster, 183, 184.—[4] Hale, i 59, 60; Foster, 185.—[5] Foster, 185, Tracey Price's Case.—[6] Hale, i. 94; Foster, 187

It was enacted in the English law, by repeated statutes, that two witnesses are indispensable to prove an overt act of treason;[1] but it was solemnly held and settled by all the Judges in the trial of the regicides, " That there need not be two witnesses to prove *every act* tending to the compassing of the king's death, but one witness to prove one overt act tending to the compassing of the king's death, and another witness to another act tending to the same end, are sufficient.[2] And the law was laid down in the same manner by all the Judges, in the trial of Lord Stafford.[3] This is farther confirmed by the statute 7th William III. c. 3, where it is enacted, that there must be two witnesses to the same overt act of treason; or, if they swear to different acts, these must be acts of the same sort of treason, so as to cohere, in some measure, and strengthen each other.[4]

In the interpretation of this act, it is held that if the treason is to be made out against the prisoner, by his accession to two or more overt acts, it is not necessary that each overt act should be made out by two witnesses; but it is sufficient if there is one good witness to each overt act.[5] This, therefore, brings the English law of treason to precisely the same standard as the Scotch law, in regard to ordinary crimes, where, if the case rests upon direct evidence alone, two witnesses to the fact are indispensable; but if it is to be made out by a chain of circumstantial evidence, one witness to each link in the chain is sufficient.[6]

The overt acts, however, which are thus adequately proved by the evidence of one witness, must be of the same kind of treason. Thus if one witness swear that a letter was written to provide arms for an attempt on the king's life, and another that the prisoner lay in wait to assassinate him, this is sufficient evidence to justify his conviction on the count of compassing the king's death.[7] But, on the other hand, if one witness swear that the prisoner lay in wait to kill the king, and another that he cruized at sea under the enemy's commission, or committed an act of levying war against the king, this is not sufficient evidence, because the acts do not conspire to fasten the *same charge* upon the prisoner.[8] In short, by considering each count in the treason indictment as a separate charge, the

[1] State Trials, ii. 714 —[2] Ibid. iii. 303.—[3] Ibid. ii. 204.—[4] Hume, i. 541. —[5] Per President Hope, Treason Trials, i. 26; Hume, i. 541.—[6] Ibid. 27.— [7] Foster, 235; Hawk. ii. 326; State Trials, v. 38.—[8] Hume, i. 541; Treason Trials, i. 27.

ordinary law of Scotland becomes applicable to treason, viz. that each charge must be substantiated either by two direct witnesses, or by a chain of circumstances, each link of which is substantiated by a single credible testimony.[1]

Farther, it is only one of the overt acts laid in the indictment, if taken *per se* as a proof of guilt, which is held to require the evidence of two witnesses. Minor and collateral facts, by the common law both of England and Scotland, may be proved by a single witness, how important soever to the case; as, for example, that the prisoner was a native-born subject, and not an alien; that he was at a particular place, at a particular time; that he was dressed or disguised in a particular manner. All these articles of proof, though decisive of the case, may be proved by a single testimony.[2]

Lastly, an alteration was made on the law in this particular, and the common law of England restored by 39th and 40th Geo. III. c 93, in relation to all *direct* attempts at the assassination of the king. It enacts, that where the overt acts alleged in the indictment are, " the assassination or killing of the king, or any direct attempt against his life, or any direct attempt against his person, whereby his life may be endangered, or his person may suffer bodily harm, the person or persons charged with such offence shall and may be indicted, arraigned, tried, and attainted in the same manner, and according to the same course and order of trial, in every respect, and upon the like evidence, as if such person or persons stood charged with murder;" and the person so indicted shall not be entitled to the benefit of the provisions of the 7th of King William or the 7th Anne. In such a case, therefore, the conviction may proceed on the evidence, if credible, of a single witness.[3]

18. Proof by confession, if made in open Court, is competent; and the declarations of the prisoner, though not sufficient *per se* to convict the prisoner, are an article of evidence against him, as in ordinary cases of Scotch law.

By the act of William, it is declared that the confession of the prisoner, on which he is to be convicted, must be in " open

---

[1] Per Lord President Hope, Treason Trials, i. 27.—[2] Foster, 240; President Hope's Charge, i. 28 , Hume, i. 541.—[3] Philips, i. 150, 151, fifth edition; Hume, ii. 541.

Court;" and, under these words, it is held that no confession is sufficient, if not made on arraignment and in presence of the Court.[1] This, however, is only to be understood of such confession as is relied on as *per se* sufficient proof of guilt, for, most unquestionably, regular declarations taken before a magistrate, and even verbal statements or admissions overheard and proved by witnesses, are to be taken as articles of evidence to make up along with others the legal measure.[2] This point underwent a very deliberate consideration in the case of James Spears, Paisley, August 1. 1820. His declarations were there objected to as not receivable in a trial for treason, and also as having been taken on questions put; but both objections were overruled by the Court. Chief Baron Shepherd, who delivered the opinion of the Court, observed, " that the question is not whether the declaration be evidence of a confession, but whether, receivable in evidence, it may not more or less corroborate the evidence that has been already given; and if the statement of the prisoner, either in declaration or examination, have been voluntary, and not produced under the influence of fear, arising from threat, or the influence of promise or expectation of mercy held out, such statement is admissible." On the second objection, he observed " that the examination of the prisoner does not lay him under any necessity of answering; but if he choose to speak, the Judge is not only entitled, but bound, to put the questions to him." [3] The result of this is, that the declarations of the prisoner stands on exactly the same footing in trials for treason as in ordinary offences, by the Scottish law.

19. No evidence is receivable of any overt act of treason not specified in the indictment; but, if it tend to establish such overt acts as are laid, it may be received to that effect.

The act of William declares, " that no evidence shall be admitted or given of any overt act not expressly laid in the indictment." This means that the proof must be confined to the charges and heads set forth in the indictment, on which alone the prisoner comes prepared for his defence. One, for example, is indicted for compassing the king's death, and an overt

act set forth in the indictment is lying in wait for the king, it
is not competent to prove that he gave money to another to induce him to lie in wait; for such an overt act, if intended to
be proved, should have been set forth in the indictment.[1]  But
the rule must be received with the proper limitations.  It certainly excludes the proof of any overt acts not laid, but not of
facts and circumstances tending to establish such overt acts as
are laid.[2]  With this view, the declaration of the prisoner, and
seditious language used by him, are clearly admissible in evidence as explaining his conduct in respect to any of the overt
acts specially laid.[3]  Thus, in the case of Ambrose Rockwood,
April 21. 1696, two of the overt acts laid in the indictment
were, 1st, That he had consulted on the means of waylaying
the king; and, 2d, Provided forty men for that purpose.  In
evidence of these it was offered, and on full consultation allowed, to be proved, that Rockwood shewed to one of the conspirators a list of a certain number who were to join in the attempt, at the head of which his own name appeared as leader.
This was held admissible evidence of both the overt acts laid,
though not specified in the indictment.[4]  Thus, the true import of the statute is, that an overt act not laid in the statute,
and which has no relation to an overt act that is laid, cannot
be given in evidence; and that, if the circumstances, when admitted, do not go to establish the overt acts laid, but other
overt acts not laid, they must be thrown out of view altogether.[5]

20. The punishment of treason is death, accompanied
with beheading and quartering, the forfeiture of the whole
estate of the traitor, heritable and moveable, and the corruption of his blood, so as to render all succession through
him impossible to any future persons.

Peculiar severity has been deemed necessary in the punishment of this great offence.

The cruel circumstances of the ancient law have been, however, to a certain extent, altered by 54th Geo. III. c. 146,
which declares " That the traitor shall be drawn on a hurdle
to the place of execution, and be there hanged by the neck till

---

[1] Hume, i. 543.——[2] Philips, i. 170.——[3] Philips, i. 179; Hume, i. 543.——
[4] Foster, 245, 246; Hawkins, ii. 436; State Trials, iv. 432.——[5] Hume, i. 544.

he be dead; and that, afterwards, the head shall be severed from the body of such person, and the body, divided into four quarters, shall be disposed of as his Majesty and his successors shall think fit." In the case of a female prisoner, the 30th Geo. III. c. 48, orders, that the execution shall be by drawing on a hurdle to the place of execution, and hanging by the neck. And, in every case, his Majesty may, by the 54th Geo. III., alter the mode of execution after sentence pronounced, by ordering the traitor to be conveyed in a different manner to the place of execution, there beheaded, and his body disposed of according as the Royal order shall direct.

2. In regard to the estate of the traitor, the consequences are confiscation of all his moveables, as in other cases of felony; and the forfeiture of all honours and landed estate to the Crown for ever.[1]

This absolute forfeiture, however, now extends only to an estate held in fee-simple, or what law regards as equivalent to that tenure. By the act 1690, c. 33, it is enacted that no heir of entail should be prejudged by the forfeiture of his predecessor, except in so far as the traitor had power to contract debt, or affect the lands, by the quality of his right, provided the tailzie were duly completed in terms of the act.

In England, it is held that a tenant in tail forfeits for himself and *his heirs*; but the remainder-man and his heirs are safe from the consequences of the forfeiture.[2] In the case of Gordon of Park, November 16. 1750, it was decided by the House of Lords, that the *substitutes* of the Scotch law are to be put *in pari casu* in this respect with the remainder-man of the English law; so that, if the entail be strict, and all the statutory requisites observed upon John and his heirs, whom failing, James and his heirs, and John is attainted, he forfeits for himself and his heirs; but James and his heirs, who come in under a new stock *specially named in the entail*, and not as heirs of John, succeed to the estate.[3] But this applies only to such tailzies as are duly completed in terms of the act 1681.[4] Any attempt to elude this law by restrictions in the entail is nugatory;[5] and if the traitor have contravened the tailzie before the treason was committed, this will not avail his successors, unless the irritancy had also been declared before that event,

---

[1] Hume, i. 546.—[2] Ibid. i. 547.—[3] Ibid.—[4] Kinloch's Case, Jan. 10. 1751, Morrison, *voce* Tailzie.—[5] Kilk. No. 8. Tailzie.

3

for, till declarator, the contravener's infeftment still subsists.[1]
By the common law, the forfeiture relates backward to the
time of the treason, so that all previous alienations, if duly
completed, are effectual against the Crown, but none subsequent to that period.[2] The act 1690, c 39, secures the right
of all creditors, whether personal or real, against the property
in the hands of the Crown    'ly as in those of the attainted
person, so that the rights o₁   a and courtesy, jointures fixed
by marriage-contracts, the interests of vassals and tenants, if
clothed with possession, and of creditors of every description
in the estate of the traitor, remain secure, notwithstanding the
attainder.[3]

3 The blood of the attainted person is, by the English law,
communicated to us by the statute of Anne,[4] completely corrupted, which has the effect not only of preventing him from
succeeding to any property from his ancestors, but any of his
descendants and relations from inheriting through him. By
this taint, the channel which conveyed the hereditary blood
from his ancestors to him is not only exhausted for the present,
but totally dammed up and rendered impervious for the future.[5]
This severe penalty extends not to his own immediate descendants only, but to all, either upwards or collaterally, who have
occasion to trace their connexion through him.[6] But if the
attainted person be not necessary to be mentioned in tracing
the descent from the deceased to the person claiming, then the
corruption of the blood is no obstacle.[7] This taint is not removed by a royal pardon, nor can any thing guard against its
effects but an act of the legislature.[8]

It is remarkable, and highly to the honour of Scottish jurisprudence, that this terrible penalty, which punishes the innocent with the guilty, and extends to the remotest generations,
and the most distant blood, the pains of treason, was never
known as a matter of ordinary law in Scotland.[9] Forfeiture
with us never inferred corruption of blood, except in those
cases where the sentence specially inflicted it; and, even in the
days of Lord Stair, the descendants of a traitor might succeed
to their grandfather or other predecessor through him.[10]

---

[1] Hume, 1 548; Gordon of Park's Case, November 16, 1750.—[2] Hume, 1.
549.—[3] 1690, c 33; Hume, i. 549.—[4] 7th Anne, c. 21.—[5] Blackstone, ii. 254.
—[6] Hawkins, b ii. c 49.—[7] Ibid.—[8] Blackstone, b. ii. c. 15, Hume, 1 550.—
[9] Stair, iii. 3, 37, 38, Hume, i. 550.—[10] Ibid.

# CHAPTER XXXIV.

## OF INNOMINATE OFFENCES.

THE crimes hitherto considered are those which, from their frequency and serious consequences, have acquired separate names or *nomina juris*, by which they are known and distinguished, both in legal language and ordinary life. But besides this, there are a great variety of offences constantly emerging in the progress of society, which were altogether unknown in former times, but have arisen from the altered manners, more extended opulence, or increasing commerce of the present age. How, then, are such crimes to be dealt with? Must they remain unpunished until their frequency and enormity have introduced separate statutes applicable to each, or is there an inherent principle in the common law which renders legislative enactments for each particular case unnecessary, and embraces every successive delinquency, as the changes of time brings it into existence?

1. By the common law every new crime, as it successively arises, becomes the object of punishment, provided it be in itself wrong, and hurtful to the persons or property of others.

In the particulars above stated, the great and ruling distinction between the Scotch and English law is to be found, and from it the superior mildness and humanity of our practice has arisen. In England the powers of the common law do not extend in the general case beyond a misdemeanour, and all the serious crimes, and almost all the modern offences, are the subject of legislative enactments. The consequence is, that their statutes, made on the spur of the moment, and frequently at the suggestion of interested or suffering parties, are, in general, characterized by excessive severity; and the judges, having no power to modify the penalties, find themselves constrained to pronounce the pain of death on numerous offenders wholly unworthy of so extreme a punishment, and who, as a matter of course, are afterwards pardoned. In Scotland, on the other hand, where the powers of the common law are more extensive, and we have been less afflicted, till recent times, with the fever of legislation, new delinquencies, as they have successively arisen, have fallen under the coercion of the common law, and thence they have been not only visited at first with a milder punishment than those ordained in the sister kingdom by the supreme authority of the legislature, but the criminal practice has been softened by the increasing humanity of successive times, and accommodated itself to the ideas and necessities of more civilized ages. Hence, while the capital crimes of England are still, notwithstanding the enlightened efforts of recent legislation, nearly 300, those of Scotland are not yet 50, of which more than a half have originated with the British Parliament.

Illustrations of this legal principle may be drawn from most of the multifarious crimes which have been already considered, which are almost all treated with more or less severity by the common law. But in the following instances the common law has interposed in regard to delinquencies which have not yet become so frequent as to have acquired a distinct legal designation.

2. Furious or improper driving along the high road is in itself a police offence; and if it leads to injury to the persons or property of others, becomes the fit object of higher criminal punishment.

It has been already noticed, in treating of Culpable Homicide, that where furious or improper driving leads to the death of any person, it becomes punishable under that name, and as such, is the subject of daily trial in the criminal courts. But, besides this, furious driving is itself an indictable offence if it lead to the overturning or injury of carriages, the maiming or hurting of individuals, or the fracture or injury of property.[1]

[1] Hume, i 193

R R

This was first settled in the case of James Bartholomew, William Sommerville, and James Watson, 21st November 1825. The major proposition sustained in that case, was " The culpable and furious driving of carts along the King's highway, to the terror and danger of the lieges, and where the carts of the lieges driving peaceably along the said highway are thereby overturned, and the persons in the said carts seriously injured, and the effects which the said carts contain broken or destroyed," and the *species facti* was, that the pannels had driven three horses and carts, containing empty barrels, at a furious rate along the high road from Edinburgh to Mid-Calder, and when so driving, they passed two carts loaded with furniture, which were going on the proper side of the road, one of which, from the shock received in passing, was overturned, a considerable quantity of the furniture damaged, and a servant on the cart had her leg broke. They were convicted and sentenced to twelve months' imprisonment each.[1] This precedent was since followed in the case of Peter Johnston and Alexander Lawson, July 16. 1829. It there appeared that the pannels had recklessly driven their carts along the Dalkeith Road at a gallop, and in passing another carter knocked him down, and broke several of his ribs. Johnston was found guilty, and sentenced to six months' imprisonment, and Lawson acquitted, as *his* cart was not the one which struck the man; but the Court were of opinion that *both* were guilty, as the one knocked down the man, and the other, by coming up at the same instant at the gallop, prevented his getting away, and was thus art and part in the consequences which followed.[2] So also in the case of Benjamin Davidson and William Train, Jedburgh, September 1829, the pannels were convicted of furious driving, whereby a woman on the road was knocked down, and the wheels passed over her body and legs.[3] Thomas Bolton, Jedburgh, April 1828, was convicted of reckless riding in the High Street of Kelso, at a time when a cattle-market was held there, and knocking down and wounding a man in the streets, and sentenced to four months' imprisonment. Lastly, in the case of James Grant, May 14. 1830, besides a charge of culpable homicide, the charge was sustained of " Riding along the highroad on any horse or mare at a furious and dangerous rate, so

---

[1] Hume    193.—[2] Unreported.—[3] Unreported.

as to ride over and wound any of the lieges, to the effusion of their blood, and danger of their lives." He had galloped along the road from Stockbridge to Comely Bank, and near Moray Place rode over two old women on the footpath, on the north side of the road; one of whom was killed and the other was severely wounded. He escaped with a verdict of not proven, in consequence of some evidence which rendered it probable that 'h horse had taken fright at the noise made by some boys on the road-side, and that it was running with him against his will when the accident occurred.[1]

3. Culpable and negligent steering of any steam-boat or sailing-vessel, so as to bring it into collision with, and run down, break, or injure, any other vessel, and damage the property it contains, is an indictable offence though no life be lost in consequence.

On the same grounds, and for much stronger reasons, which have led to the establishment of furious driving at land as an indictable offence, a similar offence, committed at sea, either in a steam or sailing vessel, may be made the subject of trial and punishment. In the case of Ezekiel Machaffie, November 26. 1827, besides culpable homicide, the charge was sustained of " Culpably, negligently, and recklessly managing or directing any vessel or steam-packet, so as to bring it in collision with, and cause it to run down, sink, or destroy any other boat or vessel, and thereby seriously wound and injure the persons, and endanger the lives, of any of the lieges sailing in such other boat or vessel." The facts appeared to have been, that the prisoner, who was the master of the Dunbarton Castle Steam-boat, had neglected to station any person on the look-out, but had intrusted that important duty to all the crew indiscriminately who happened to be on deck at the time; the consequence of which was, that on passing the quay of Gourock, the boat ran down a fishing-boat in the Frith of Clyde, whereby one person was drowned and the boat destroyed. The pannel was convicted in the Court of Admiralty, and sentenced to six months' imprisonment; and the case having come by suspension before the Supreme Court, the indictment was

[1] Unreported

sustained as relevant in all its parts : a decision which establishes this as a relevant point of dittay in our practice.[1]

By the recent statute 9th Geo. IV. c. 29, offences of this sort can be competently tried before the Justiciary Court, which, indeed, since the abolition of the Admiralty, is the only place where such offences can be made the subject of investigation.

4. Administering drugs to procure abortion is an offence at common law, punishable with an arbitrary pain, and that equally whether the desired effects be produced or not.

In the case of Catherine Robertson and George Bachelor, 28th June 1806, it was sustained as a relevant point of dittay, " the wilfully causing or procuring a pregnant woman to abort, or part in an untimely manner with the fœtus or child in her womb." In that case the nefarious object was accomplished by the application of an instrument to the womb, and it brought on premature labour in the fifth or sixth month of pregnancy. They were convicted, and sentenced to seven years' transportation ;[2] a punishment certainly not too severe when it is recollected that the life of one human being is by such practices seriously endangered, and an incipient existence stifled in another.

This crime is equally committed by the woman who submits to the operation, or the taking the noxious medicines, as the man who administers; though her offence is of an inferior degree, and she is often the object rather of commiseration than punishment; and the surgeon or apothecary who should lend himself to such a transaction, or furnish medicines for the purpose, knowing the end to which they were to be applied, or give advice as to the mode of its commission, would unquestionably render himself liable as ait and part.[3] The " wilfully causing or procuring a pregnant woman to abort or part in an untimely manner with the fœtus or child in her womb," was again sustained as relevant at Perth, September 1823, in the case of Alexander Aitken, surgeon. He was charged with having, for the sum of twenty-five shillings, agreed to induce abortion on a pregnant young woman, and actually performed

[1] Syme, Appen No. 3.—[2] Hume, 1 187.—[3] Ibid 1 279

the operation by means of an external instrument. He was convicted, and sentenced to seven years' transportation.[1] So also in the case of Charles Munn, Inverary, April 20. 1824, the pannel, who had administered arsenic to a woman to procure abortion, and nearly killed her in consequence, besides producing premature labour, was sentenced to fourteen years' transportation.

If the crime is attempted but not completed by getting away the child, the proper description of the offence is, " attempt to procure abortion," and there seems no doubt that it is a relevant point of dittay, though of inferior magnitude to the completed offence.

5. The felonious administering of laudanum or other narcotic or deleterious drugs, with intent to produce stupefaction, whether in malice or to facilitate the commission of any crime, is a relevant point of dittay at common law.

Akin to the administration of drugs to procure abortion, is the administering laudanum or other narcotic drugs, to occasion stupefaction, either from a malicious or a theftuous intention ; and, as a most dangerous and atrocious crime, nearly allied to murder, it has always been visited with an exemplary punishment. In the case of David Wilson, William Wilson, and Charles Parker, 22d December 1828, " the wickedly and feloniously administering laudanum, or other narcotic and deleterious substance, to any of the lieges, to the serious injury of the person, with intent to produce stupefaction, and thereafter to steal the property of the persons stupified," was sustained as a relevant charge. The prisoners were charged with having administered a quantity of laudanum to a man and his wife, in a change-house near Leith, and, after occasioning stupefaction, broken open their locked drawers, and stolen £3 from them, and £5 from the persons of their victims, but they were acquitted of the theft. They were all sentenced to seven years' transportation.[2] And, in the case of John Stuart and Catherine Wright, July 14. 1829, besides the charge of murder, it was stated and sustained as a relevant charge, " The

---

[1] Unreported —[2] Unreported

wickedly and feloniously administering laudanum, or other narcotic or noxious substance, to any of the lieges, to the injury of
the person, especially with intent to murder, or to produce stupefaction, and thereafter steal the property of the persons murdered or stupified," and the pannels were convicted of that
charge, as well as the more serious one of murder.[1]

6. The wickedly and feloniously enticing or inducing
an infant child to leave its parents or guardians, without
their knowledge or consent, is a crime at common law.

It has been already noticed, that the act of *stealing* a child,
or *plagium*, is a capital crime;[2] but what if the child is not
stolen, but *enticed away*, for the purposes of lucre, or any other
motive, in the person committing so wicked and heartless an
act. This point occurred, but was not decided, in the case of
Richard Smith, July 16. 1829. The major proposition there
set forth was " manstealing or *plagium*, as also the wickedly,
fraudulently, and feloniously enticing or inducing any infant
child of tender years, and while still within the years of pupilarity, to desert its parents, guardians, or other legal protectors,
without the knowledge or consent of the said parents, guardians, or legal protectors of the said child, especially when committed with the wicked and felonious intent of rendering the
child a source of profit or lucre." The *species facti*, as set
forth in the libel was, that the pannel, who was a teacher of elo-
cution, and was desirous to get a little child to recite poetry to
his audience, applied to a girl of the name of Elizabeth Shanks,
an infant of nine years of age, in the Orphan Hospital, and
prevailed on her, by promises of fine clothes, and making a lady
of her, to leave the Hospital, and come to him, where she was
soon after found in his custody. This was done at clandestine
interviews with the child, and without the knowledge or concurrence of her relations, who had placed her in the Hospital.
The Court, as this charge was new, ordered informations; but
the only difficulty they seemed to have was, whether the second
charge was not virtually the same as the first, in consideration
of the legal incapacity of an infant of such tender years to consent to leave the place where it had been placed by its natural

_____
[1] Unreported.—[2] Unreported.

protectors; but they were unanimous that, under the one designation or the other, the offence was cognizable at common law; and that if the child could legally adhibit its consent, the second charge became relevant. The flight of the pannel, who was on bail, prevented farther proceedings in the case beyond his outlawry.[1]

7. Wilfully destroying a bill, or other voucher of debt, in the possession of the holder or creditor, with intent to prevent its being used as a voucher of debt by the proprietor against the pannel, or any other person, is an offence at common law.

A case of this description occurred at Aberdeen, autumn 1830, in the case of Alexander Murray. The *species facti* there was, that the pannel, who had signed an accommodation-bill, along with several other persons, from which they had all derived some benefit, upon the bank clerk calling to demand payment, asked him to let him see the bill for a moment to examine his signature; and, having got it into his hands, he instantly tore it in pieces, and told the clerk he defied them all. The offence was charged under the name of " the wickedly and feloniously seizing and destroying a bill, or other voucher of debt, subscribed by the party so seizing and destroying, when presented to him for payment, with intent to destroy the evidence of the debt vouched by the said bill or voucher, and of defrauding the holder thereof, and freeing the person so seizing and destroying from payment of the sum therein contained;" and the prisoner having confessed, was sentenced to three months' imprisonment.[2]

8. Using threats of death to any person, or attempting or pretending to carry them into execution, in order to compel a confession of a real or supposed crime, is punishable at common law.

At Inverary, spring 1828, in the case of Andrew Macgregor, a curious case of this description occurred. A pack-boy came by a steam-boat to Argyleshire, and passed near the pannel's house;

[1] Unreported.—[2] Unreported

a theft was discovered about the same time, and he and all the
family immediately concluded that he was the thief. He was
seized accordingly, and brought tothe premises, where preparations were soon after made for his being suspended by the neck,
which was carried into effect, without any design of really killing him, but in order to extort a confession of the crime This
the boy refused to make, and accordingly a rope was put about
his neck, and he was suspended for a few seconds in the air,
and then taken down and locked up in a hay-loft, from whence,
during the course of the night, he made his escape For this
offence the pannel was brought to trial, on the charge of "Laying hold of any of the lieges, without legal authority, and
threatening him with immediate death, if he did not confess a
supposed crime laid to his charge, and thereafter binding the
arms of the said person, and forcibly putting a rope about his
neck, and threatening him with immediate hanging, if he did
not confess the said supposed crive, and thereafter suspending
him by the neck till he is reduced to a state of insensibility, and
put in imminent danger of his life, especially when committed
with intent to extort a confession of a supposed crime, which
the injured person has not committed." He was convicted,
but, in consideration of a remarkably good character, and as
the danger of life was not proved, received only three months'
imprisonment; a punishment which, had the motive been more
oppressive, or the injury more serious, would have been totally
incommensurate to the offence.[1]

9. Violence or oppression, more especially when committed by persons in authority, or intrusted with legal
power, is cognizable and punishable with an arbitrary
pain at common law.

Any acts of oppression or partiality on the part of judges,
magistrates, law-officers, or others, intrusted with legal authority, are directly punishable by the common law[2] Many instances occurred in former times of such prosecutions against
sheriffs even, and other superiors, which the improved state of
public manners has since not rendered necessary. Thus frequent and causeless acts of imprisonment by a judge were

---

[1] Unreported.—[2] Hume, 1 408.

found relevant to infer an arbitrary punishment.[1] Raising of repeated and frivolous prosecutions on false pretences, which were never brought to trial, and holding unlawful courts, were found relevant as an article of charge against a bailie-depute and his fiscal[2]· libel for oppression was raised against the Sheriff-depute, Sheriff-clerk, and Fiscal of the Shire of Caithness, for irregular poindings for fines, the refusal of extracts, and exacting unlawful dues, and only found irrelevant from the defective mode of drawing the libel.[3] Various other cases of summary punishment of judges, sheriff-clerks, and other officers for malversation in office, are given by Mr Hume.[4] And in the case of Alexander Waddell senior, Alexander Waddell junior, and James Strathern, January 19. 1829, the Court pronounced a very severe sentence upon two messengers and a sheriff-officer in Lanarkshire, for malversation in their respective offices. It there appeared that the pannels, under pretence and colour of legal diligence, had seized hold of a weaver near Airdrie, of infirm mind, compelled him to abandon his work, carried him a prisoner with much violence to Airdrie, where they incarcerated him in a lock-up-house, and stripped and searched his person, all in order to extort money. The libel which narrated the offence nearly in these terms, was sustained as relevant, and Alexander Waddell junior and James Strathern sentenced to seven years' transportation each, by the High Court, for whose consideration the punishment to follow on the verdict had been certified from the Glasgow Winter Circuit, and Alexander Waddell senior, in consideration of a severe crural hernia, which rendered him incapable of undergoing the hard labour of the Hulks, to twelve months' imprisonment[5]

10. Any violent invasion of personal freedom, or of the security of private houses, though not done for the purposes of theft or spoliation, is in itself an indictable offence.

The principle of law is, that the personal freedom of every individual, and the sanctity of private houses, is, in an especial manner, under its protection; and, therefore, any acts infring-

---

[1] August 1687, Case of Fife, Hume, 1 409.—[2] Kennedy's Case, July 23. 1722, Hume, ibid.—[3] Hume, 1. 409, November 22. 1714.—[4] Hume, 1. 409-411.—[5] Unreported

ing upon either, contrary to the will of the individual or owner who suffers, especially if accompanied with violence, are the fit objects of punishment. A curious case of this description occurred at Inverness, May 1826, in the case of James Watson, collector of excise, and John Humphreys and Alexander Macewan, surgeons in Tain. The *species facti* there was, that James Maclean, an excise-officer, had a quarrel with a smuggler, and discharged a gun, which wounded him severely in the knee, in consequence of which the excise-officer was apprehended, and the smuggler was confined to bed in great pain, and in danger of his life. Maclean was imprisoned, and bail had been refused by the sheriff, till the wounded man was declared out of danger; and, in order to secure his liberation, the pannels, without any legal authority or warrant, entered his house, took the wounded man out of bed, undid his bandages, examined the wound, to his great pain and vexation, in order to make a report to the sheriff that he was out of danger. The libel, which charged " the violently, culpably, and recklessly entering and invading the house of any of the lieges, and assaulting the inhabitants thereof, especially when they are confined to bed, in danger of their lives, and the violently, and culpably, and recklessly, removing the bandages from the limbs of the said inhabitants against their will, and against legal authority," was sustained as relevant, and the pannels convicted; though, in consideration of their excellent character, and of no wicked intention having prompted their actions, the prosecutor declined to move for sentence.[1] William Turner, William Graham, James Pettigrew, and Thomas Allan, convicted at Glasgow, spring 1828, of violently invading the house of a weaver there, and assaulting the inmates in an outrageous manner, in order to deter them from working at a low rate of wages, were sentenced to seven years transportation.[2]

11. Wilful neglect of duty, especially when committed by persons intrusted with official situations of trust, is a point of dittay at common law.

Wilful neglect of duty in persons intrusted with official situations is undoubtedly cognizable at common law, indepen-

[1] Unreported.—[2] Unreported.

dent of the act 1457, c. 76, which confirms the common law in that particular.   For neglect of duty in not having adequately provided the city of Edinburgh with the means of defence against the rebels, in 1745, a libel was sustained against Archibald Stewart, Provost of Edinburgh, but the pannel was acquitted.[1]   In like manner, in the case of Donald Smith, June 4. 1827, the " wilful neglect of duty and violation of the duty and trust of his office, by a public officer, in the course of his employment as such, particularly the wickedly and illegally removing or breaking open the seal or wafer of a letter, and opening such letter by any letter-carrier, or other person intrusted in the post-office," was sustained as a relevant charge at common law, after a full objection from the pannel.[2]   In the case of William Cunningham, 18th May 1820, " Wilful neglect of duty and violation of the trust and duty of his office, by a public officer, in the course of his employment as such, particularly the detaining, secreting, and failing to deliver any letters which had come officially into the custody of any person in the employment of the General Post-Office," was sustained as relevant by the sheriff of Edinburgh, and the pannel convicted and sentenced to six months' imprisonment, without any suspension being moved in the Supreme Court, though he was ably defended.[3]   A similar charge, that of " wilful neglect of duty, and violation of the trust and duty of his office by a public officer in the course of his employment as such, particularly the wilfully and illegally detaining, secreting, and failing to deliver, by any person in the employment of the post-office, any letters which had come officially into his possession," was sustained by the High Court in the case of John Graham, March 1. 1830, and the prisoner convicted and sentenced to nine months' imprisonment.   He had secreted, or at least failed to deliver, nine different letters, none containing any money, which had been put into his hands, as a letter-carrier, for immediate delivery. The knowingly secreting any letter containing money, is capital by 52d Geo. III. c. 143; but, though there was such a charge in the indictment, it was departed from, as the pannel did not seem to have known the contents of that letter when he secreted it.

9. At common law, and by the force of statute, the

[1] Hume, i 411 —[2] Unreported.—[3] Unreported.

buying and selling of offices of public trust and importance, is punishable with fine and imprisonment, except in
those cases where it is sanctioned by statutory exemption,
or consuetudinary usage.

The buying and selling offices of a public nature is considered as a *malum ad se*, and indictable by the English common
law;[1] and, as the provisions of their statutory law are extended
by a recent act of Parliament to this country,[2] the points decided by them are worthy of consideration in a treatise on
Scotch law.

It is settled in England, at common law, that a conspiracy
to obtain money, by procuring from the Lords of the Treasury
the appointment of a person to an office in the customs, is a
misdemeanour, without the aid of any statute;[3] and an attempt
merely to bribe a cabinet minister and a member of the Privy
Council to give the dependant an office in the colonies, was
held to fall under the same rule;[4] and, where the defendant
who was clerk to the agent of the French prisoners at Por-
chester Castle, took bribes to procure the exchange of some of
them, out of their turn, it was considered as the fit subject of
an indictment.[5]

By 5th and 6th Edward VI. c 16, extended to Scotland by
49th Geo III. c 126, it is enacted, for the avoiding corruption,
which might hereafter happen in the officers in place, where
there is requisite to be had the true administration of justice,
or services of trust, and to the intent that persons worthy and
meet to be advanced, should thereafter be preferred, enacts,
that if any person bargain or sell any office, or deputation of
office, or take any money or profit, directly or indirectly, or
any promise, bond, or assurance to receive any money for any
office, or deputation of office, which office, or any part or parcel thereof shall in anyways concern the administration or execution of justice, or the receipt, payment, or controulment of
the king's treasure, rent, or revenue, &c. or any of the king's
customs, or the keeping the king's towns, castles, &c. used for
defence, or which shall concern any clerkship in any court of

[1] Hawk 1. c. 67, § 3; Russell, 1  48.—[2] 49th Geo. III. c. 126.—[3] Rex v
Pollman and others; Camp 11. 229 —[4] Rex v  Vaughan, Burnett, iv 2494,
Russell, l 149.—[5] Rex v. Beale, East 1 183

record where justice is administered, the offender shall not only forfeit all his right to such office, or deputation of office, but also shall be adjudged a person disabled to have, occupy, or enjoy such office or deputation. The statute farther enacts, that such bargains, sales, bonds, agreements, &c. shall be void; and that the act shall not extend to any office whereof any person shall be seized of any estate of inheritance, nor to any office of the keeping of any park, house, manor, garden, chase, or forest. The act excepts the Chief-Justices of the King's Bench, and Common Pleas, and the Justices of Assize.

Under this act it has been decided, that the officers of Chancellor, Registrar, and Commissary in the Ecclesiastical Courts, fall under it purview;[1] that of Surveyor of Customs, of Collector and Supervisor of Excise,[2] and the offices of Clerk of the Crown and Clerk of the Peace in Ireland.[3] But it does not reach to offices in fee,[4] nor to the sale of a bailiwick in a hundred, nor to military officers,[5] nor to the plantations.[6] And where an office is within the statute, and the salary certain, if the principal make a deputation, reserving a less sum out of the salary, it is good, but if the agreement is to pay a certain sum whether it is made good or not, it is void.[7]

By 49th Geo. III. c 126, it is enacted, " That all the provisions of the 5th and 6th Edward VI. c. 16, shall extend to Scotland and Ireland, and to all offices in the gift of the Crown, or of any office appointed by the Crown; and all commissions, civil, naval, or military, and to all places and employments, and all deputations to any such offices, commissions, places, or employments, in the respective departments or offices, or under the appointment or superintendence and contiol of the Lord High Treasurer, or Commissioners of the Treasury, the Secretary of State, the Lords Commissioners foi executing the office of Lord High Admiral, the Master General, and principal officers of his Majesty's Ordnance, the Commander in Chief, the Secretary at War, the Paymaster-General of his Majesty's Forces, the Commissioners for India, the Commissioners of Excise, the Treasurer of the Navy, the Commissioners of Victualling, the Commissioners of Transports, the Commissary-General, the Storekeeper-General, and also the

[1] Hawk 1 c 67, § 4 — [2] Law's Case, Williams, iii 391.— [3] Russell, 1. 150. — [4] Ellis v Reid & Co, I iv. u. 151, Russell, 1. 150 — [5] Vern 1. 98.— [6] Mod 222, Russell, 1 150.— [7] V Bacon, Abridgment, 195.

principal officers of any other public department or office of his
Majesty's government, in any part of the United Kingdom, or
in any of his Majesty's dominions, colonies, or plantations, and
to all offices, commissions, places, and employments belonging
to, or under the controul of, the East India Company."

All persons buying or selling, or receiving, or paying money,
or rewards for offices included within this act, are guilty of a
misdemeanour.[1] All persons receiving or paying money for
soliciting or obtaining offices, and any negociations, or pretended negociations, relating thereto, are guilty of the same offence[2]
There are several exceptions in the act; and, in particular, it
does not extend to purchases or exchanges in the army at the
regulated prices, nor to any thing done in that behalf; but
officers paying or receiving, or agreeing to pay or receive, more
than the regulated prices, or paying agents for negociating
such transactions, are liable to be cashiered, and have their
commissions forfeited.[3] The act does not extend to deputations, where it is lawful to appoint a deputy, nor to any agreement, in such a case, in regard to any allowance to such principal where it is lawful to make them. Offenders against this
act, in Scotland, are liable to be punished by fine and imprisonment, or the one or the other, as the judges shall direct.[4]
This statute is well worthy of attention by all those who adventure on the perilous and doubtful course of taking or offering money for any office connected, however remotely, with
the administration of justice, or the discharge of any public
duty

10 Piracy is an offence at common law, punishable
with death.

Piracy, or the crime of roving and robbing on the high seas,
is a point of dittay by the criminal law of Scotland,[5] as well as
that of England,[6] and of all other civilized states.[7] The true
characteristic, and that wherein a pirate differs from a regular
enemy, is, that he has no license or commission of hostility from
any acknowledged state or government, but acts predoniously,
and carries on a private and indiscriminate war privily of his
own authority;[8] for it is a maxim of all civil societies that all

[1] § 3.—[2] § 4.—[3] § 8.—[4] § 13.—[5] Hume, 1 480.—[6] State Trials, vol. 11 —
[7] Moller, ii. 4 No 9-15.—[8] State Trials, 1 No. 169, Hume, 1. 481.

employment of force, save in resistance against injuries, must be by public authority, and that any adventurer who sails on a private and unlicensed warfare, even against the enemies of his country, as a matter of profit, and condemns, distributes, or disposes of prizes taken at sea, or elsewhere, by his own authority, is no other than a pirate, and may be treated as such by the laws of all civilized states [1]

Even though a privateer, that is a private individual holding a commission or letters of marque from his own government, have the requisite authority for cruizing against the enemies of his country; yet if, under the pretence of this commission, he proceed to plunder ships of his own or friendly states, he shall not be less held a pirate, that he so far abuses the authority he has received.[2] Piracy is committed either by taking the ship, its cargo, or crew; and equally whether the violence is perpetrated by strangers who invade, or the mariners on board who seize upon the vessel.[3] In the case, accordingly, of Joseph Dawson and others, October 19. 1696, it was adjudged piracy for a part of the crew, with the assistance of certain strangers who came from another ship, to seize and run away with a vessel.[4] Of the same description was the case of Peter Heaman, an Englishman, and Francis Gautier, a Frenchman, who were convicted of piracy in the High Court of Admiralty, on a charge of murder and piracy, and had sentence of death, which was carried into execution within flood-mark on the Sands of Leith. The pannels, and some others of the crew, had murdered one of the seamen whom they deemed hostile to their purpose, fastened down the hatches, and seized the master and mate, got possession of the vessel, and divided £13,000 worth of dollars, with which they landed on the beach near Stornoway, where they were soon discovered and apprehended.[5]

The crew, though *socii criminis*, are competent witnesses in this matter; and accordingly, in the case of Heaman and Gautier, they were held not only to be admissible, but credible and good witnesses for the Crown, in consideration of their having taken the earliest opportunity of giving information of the crime.[6] Compulsion, if made out on reasonable evidence, is a

[1] Hume, 1 481, Bank. 11 2. 3; Stair, 11 2 1 —[2] Kidd's Case, May 8. 1701, State Trials, v No 169, Pott's Case, December 10. 1781, Hume 1 184.—[3] Hume, 1. 483.—[4] State Trials, v. 521.—[5] Hume, 1. 483.—[6] Ibid.

3

better defence in this than any other crime, there being no situation in which constraint can so easily be imposed on unwilling associates as where they are confined within a ship.[1] On this ground, out of 165 persons, tried on special commission at Cabo Corso Castle, on the coast of Africa, 74 were acquitted. But, on the other hand, if the unwilling associate con'inue with the pirates after the constraint had ceased, and share in the spoil, or take a command in the ship, his conduct affords a reply to the defence of original constraint.[2]

The punishment of piracy, as of all violent depredations, is death, and the competent court for its trial, in any part of the world, is now, since the abolition of the Admiralty Court, and by the late act, 9th Geo. IV. c. 29, the High Court of Justiciary.

11. Plundering wrecks is an offence at common law, punishable with the highest arbitrary pains, though no living creature be found on board; and if any one survive, and the goods are taken by force, it is stouthrief.

By the modern law of Scotland, differing in that respect from our former practice, the plundering of wrecks, even though all on board have perished, and the owner is utterly unknown, is punishable with the highest arbitrary pains.[3] By 12th Anne, sect. 2. c. 18, 4th Geo. I. c. 12, and 26th Geo. II. c. 19, offences of this sort are rendered felony without benefit of clergy, but the last of these statutes, by its express provision, does not extend to Scotland, and the like has been found in the other articles of their enactment, as to the two former.[4]

But the vessel is not a wreck so long as any human being in it is alive, and therefore, if any violent plundering goes on in such circumstances, it is to be regarded as stouthrief or robbery.[5] Law regards the right of custody and possession of the vessel, and all it contains, as vested in the survivors or survivor of the crew; and if, during their or his life, any articles are forcibly taken away, it can be considered in no other light but as violent depredation. If no violence has been used in the plundering, theft is the proper name of the offence. In the case, accordingly, of Robert Graham and others, March 1792,

[1] Hume, i 484.—[2] Ibid.—[3] Ibid. i. 485.—[4] Case of Maciver and Maccallum, July 14 1784, Hume, i. 485.—[5] Hume, i. 486.

5

who had pillaged a stranded vessel, the indictment, charging the crime under the name of theft and robbery, was sustained as relevant; and in the case of John Macrorie and others, August 1625, the offenders were prosecuted and charged as pirates, they having forcibly invaded and plundered a stranded Flemish vessel, and killed several of the crew [1]

12. Wilful sinking or destroying ships, to defraud insurers, is a fraud at common law, punishable with the highest arbitrary pains, to which, by special statute, the punishment of death is superadded.

The act of sinking or destroying ships for the purpose of defrauding insurers, as a most dangerous fraud, is an offence punishable at common law with the highest arbitrary pains [2] James Herdman, January 29. 1784, convicted in the Court of Admiralty of sinking a vessel with this intent, was sentenced to stand in the pillory, and banished Scotland for life [3] Nay, in the case of Macivor, January 29. 1784, the attempt even to engage in such a villanous project was sustained as a relevant point of dittay [4]; and, in the case of James Macnair, March 14. 1751, the completed crime was sustained as relevant to infer an arbitrary pain in the Admiralty Court [5]

By 29th Geo III. c. 46, this crime is declared capital in Scotland It enacts, " That if any owner of, or captain, or master, officer, or mariner, belonging to any ship or vessel, shall, after the 1st September 1789, wilfully cast away, burn, or otherwise destroy, the ship or vessel of which he is owner, or to which he belongeth, or in anywise direct or procure the same to be done, with intent or design to prejudice any person or persons that hath, or shall underwrite any policy or policies of insurance thereon, or of any merchant or merchants that shall load goods therein, or of any owner or owners of such ship or vessel, the person or persons offending therein being thereof lawfully convicted before any court competent to the trial of such crimes in that part of Great Britain called Scotland, shall suffer death, as in other cases of capital crimes " And it is enacted, in more clear and extensive terms than in the former act, by 43d Geo. III. c. 113. § 2, " That if any

---

[1] Hume, i 186 — [2] Arnot 279 — [3] Hume, i 486 — [4] Arnot, 279 — [5] Ibid

person or persons shall wilfully cast away, burn, or otherwise
destroy, any ship or vessel, or in anywise counsel, direct, or
procure the same to be done, and the same be accordingly done,
with intent or design thereby wilfully and maliciously to
prejudice any owner or owners of such ship or vessel, or any
owner or owners of any goods laden on board the same, or any
person or persons, body politic or corporate, that hath or have
underwritten, or shall underwrite, any policy or policies of insurance upon such ship or vessel, or upon any goods loaden on
board the same, the person or persons offending therein being
thereof lawfully convicted, shall be deemed a principal felon
⁓ felons, and shall suffer death, as in cases of felony, without
benefit of clergy." This statute extends to Scotland.[1]

Under the first of these statutes, as well as at common law,
James Menzies was indicted before the High Court of Admiralty, July 14 1823, but the trial was postponed and never afterwards resumed, on account of the absence of the principal
witness.[2] John Macdougall pleaded guilty to an indictment at
common law and on both these statutes, on 14th June 1821, in
the same court, and received, upon a restriction, seven years'
transportation.[3] The proper court for the trial of all such cases,
since the abolition of the Admiralty, is the High Court of Justiciary.

13. Forcible carrying off, or detaining any delegate
authorized to vote at the election of a Member of Parliament, or interfering in any way with the freedom of
election of a Member of Parliament, is an offence at common law, punishable with an arbitrary pain.

As it is of the very highest importance to the purity of elections, that the choice of the electors and the delegates should
be free and unrestrained, any attempt to intimidate or overawe
them in the exercise of their political functions, or to procure
by fraud or violence a return contrary to the sense of the real
majority, is an offence at common law. Several cases of this
description have been made the subject of trial and punishment
at different times. In the case of Lindsay, Lockerbie and
others, 31st January 1791, for carrying off a bailie at Loch-

---

[1] Hume, i. 487.—[2] Unreported.—[3] Unreported

maben, to influence the election, the charge was sustained as
relevant, and the pannels received three months' imprisonment, besides three of them a public whipping.[1]   Again, at
Inverness, in the case of J. Taylor, autumn 1826, a libel was
found relevant on a similar charge, for carrying a bailie at
Elgin out to sea on the day of election, but the case was not
prosecuted to a conviction, owing to the absence of a witness.[2]
Lastly, in the case of Maclachlan, Badger, and Brown, November 20. 1831, the matter underwent a thorough discussion
These parties were charged, the two former with being accessary to the violent tumult and riot at Greenlaw, April 1831,
when the Sheriff was knocked down, the civil force overpowered, and the delegate carried off, which gave the majority
to the reforming party,—and the latter with driving the chaise
in which the delegate was removed   The two former stood
their trial, and the case was completely established so far as
the *corpus delicti* went, but the identification not being made
out to the satisfaction of the jury, they escaped with a verdict
of not proven; the latter pleaded guilty, and was sentenced to
nine months' imprisonment, and to find caution to the extent
of 300 merks.   The Court at the same time expressed an opinion, that if the case had been proved against the principal
delinquents, who had seized upon the delegate, and borne him
with such circumstances of violence from the protection of the
civil power, nothing less than transportation could have been
the punishment.[3]

14. Publishing a blasphemous work is a relevant point
of dittay at common law, inferring an arbitrary punishment; but it is now restricted to fine and imprisonment.

The publication of a blasphemous work undoubtedly falls under the cognizance of the common law.[4]   Several severe statutes existed in Scotland during the rigid time of the Reformation, against this offence; but they are repealed by 53d Geo.
III c. 160, § 3, and by 6th Geo. IV. c. 47, the punishment of
this offence is declared to be fine A imprisonment, or both,
for the first offence, and for the second banishment from his
Majesty's dominions   Matthew Shiels, 21st December 1819,
was outlawed for this offence; as were Andrew Marshall and

Margaret Wright, 17th January 1820, for the same crime, and
that of vending seditious publications. Lastly, on 30th May
1824, James Affleck pleaded guilty to a charge of blasphemous
publications, tending to bring the Christian religion and the
Holy Scriptures into contempt, and was sentenced to three
months' imprisonment, and to find caution for his good behaviour for five years.[1]

# CHAPTER XXXV.

## OF THE EXCUSES FOR CRIMES ARISING FROM THE STATE OF THE PANNEL.

How clearly soever a crime may be proved to have been
committed, there may be circumstances in the situation of the
pannel which prevent him from being the fit object of punishment. He may be insane at the time of the trial, or he may
have been so at the time of the acts in question He may
have been a pupil too young to have been capable of distinguishing right from wrong, or to be the object of the severity
of criminal law; or he may have acted under such constraint
as alleviates, or totally exculpates him. Hence the defences
against a libel, founded on the state of the pannel, may be divided into those arising from insanity, from pupilage, or from
constraint to the will.

### SECT. I.——INSANITY AND IDIOCY.

IF insanity be of that complete and perfect kind which entirely overpowers the reason, and takes away from the pannel
the power of distinguishing right from wrong, or knowing
what he is doing, it forms a complete bar to any criminal prosecution; and the pannel is ordered to be disposed of in such a

---

[1] Hume, I. 573

way as to prevent his being hurtful to others in time to come. But several nice and delicate questions arise as to the degree of insanity which in law have this effect.

1. To amount to a complete bar to punishment, the insanity, either at the time of committing the crime, or of the trial, must have been of such a kind as entirely deprived him of the use of reason, as applied to the act in question, and the knowledge that he was doing wrong in committing it.

Though law requires, as a complete defence against a criminal prosecution, on the ground of insanity, that the pannel should have laboured, at the time of committing the act, under a complete alienation of reason,[1] yet it is not to be understood that this means either that he was altogether furious, or did not understand the distinction of right or wrong.[2] Cases of that extreme kind very seldom occur, and certainly much more unfrequently than the instances in which the pannel's state of mind has been such as to render him not a fit object of punishment. It is very seldom that a mad person is either deprived of the power of knowing what he is doing, or of reasoning and conversing on its different subjects, or of understanding the distinction between right and wrong, in the *general* case, and with reference to other persons. The great characteristic of insanity, which originates in the general case, is an excessive turning of the mind to its own affairs, consists in an alienation of reason with reference to itself, and in the illusions under which it labours, and the chimeras it has nourished in regard to its own concerns. Few men are mad about others, or things in general; many about themselves  Although, therefore, the pannel understands perf. tly the distinction of right and wrong; yet if he labours, as is generally the case, under an illusion and deception, as to his own particular case, and is thereby disabled from applying it correctly to his own conduct, he is in that state of mental alienation which renders him not criminally answerable for his actions. For example, a mad person may be perfectly aware that murder is a crime, and will admit that, if pressed on the subject; but still he may conceive that a ho-

[1] Hume, i. 37–37 —[2] Ibid i. 37,

micide he had committed, was nowise blameable, because the deceased had engaged in a conspiracy with others against his own life; or was his mortal enemy, who had wounded him in his dearest interests, or was the devil incarnate, whom it was the duty of every good Christian to meet with the weapons of carnal warfare  If, therefore, the accused is in such a situation that, though possessing a sense of the distinction between right and wrong, he cannot apply it correctly to his own case, and labours under an illusion which completely misleads his judgment, as mistaking one person for another, or fastening a dreadful charge, entirely groundless, on a friend, he is entitled to the benefit of the plea of insanity in defence against a criminal charge.[1]

This principle was well expressed by Dr Monro senior, in the case of David Hunter, 13th March 1801, charged with murder.  Dr Monro deponed, " that he was incapable of judging of the *propriety of his actions*, or of reasoning with propriety upon them; and, in particular, he gave the deponent a strong indication of this, by leading the deponent to believe that he had been led to commit the crime of which he stood accused, by the circumstance of the woman whom he was accused of shooting, having *smothered his own mother*, in the presence of a number of persons who had made it up among them; and that the pannel did not seem to have any remorse at what had happened, saying repeatedly that the woman had shed innocent blood."[2]  " It is the condition of very many," says Lord Hale, " especially melancholy persons, who, for the most part, discover their defect in excessive fears and griefs, and yet are not wholly destitute of the use of reason; but this partial insanity seems not to excuse them in the committal of any capital offence.  Doubtless mad persons that kill themselves, are under a partial degree of insanity when they commit these offences; and it is very difficult to define the invisible line that divides perfect from partial insanity; but it must rest upon circumstances, to be duly weighed by the Judge and jury, lest, on the one hand, there be an inhumanity towards the defects of human nature; or, on the other, too great an indulgence shewn to great crimes."[3]

In the case of Robert Spence, June 30. 1747, it appeared

---

[1] Hume, i 37-38.—[2] Ibid. 38.—[3] Hale, i. 30

that the pannel and the deceased, who was a schoolmistress, were occupiers of separate floors in the same building. The pannel having risen from bed in his shirt in the dusk of the evening, knocked at her door, and upon its being opened rushed in, uttering some strange and incoherent expressions, and struck the woman with a hatchet on the head, which killed her. He then ran off to his own house, and escaped from a *posse* who assembled to seize him. On returning to his own house, he violently clove through a *wig-block* which stood there, and was found besmeared with the woman's brains and gore. Great restlessness, disordered behaviour and a wandering disposition, had been observed in him for some days preceding, but without any actual outrage · and some years before he had shewn symptoms of derangement on board a ship, and had been in consequence confined occasionally for ten days at a time. The jury " found it proven that the pannel was furious at the time he committed the said murder, but to what degree they could not determine;" and, in pursuance of this verdict, he was ordered to be confined for life.[1] It was plain that, though not insane on every subject, he laboured under some hallucination with reference to the object of his violence.

Jean Blair, 14th March 1781, was charged with murdering her mistress. It appeared in evidence, that, in a sudden fit of frenzy, she had seized a hatchet and murdered her mistress, with whom she had lived as a confidential servant, set fire to the house, and ran out stark naked into the street, and herself gave the alarm to the guard. She had shewn symptoms of insanity ten years before. She was of course acquitted of the murder, and ordered into confinement for the remainder of her life.[2]

A more difficult case, and which well illustrates the delusions under which insane persons labour, was that of Robert Thomson, June 1739. He was accused of the murder of George Forrester, on the Moor of Ballincrief, between Haddington and Aberlady, at noonday. The pannel had been employed in his trade as a blacksmith as usual that morning, and those who saw him a little before the commission of the fatal act saw nothing remarkable in his appearance; but, when taken into custody, he used many expressions clearly indicating that he was

---

[1] Hume, v 39.—[2] Ibid. i 40

labouring under a mental delusion at the time he committed the act; saying that the deceased had many times cried for mercy when he was striking him on the ground, but that he had no mercy on him, for he believed it was the devil which he had killed. He added, that, before meeting Forrester, he had chased the devil through the moor, and that he had suddenly vanished. He was proved also to have been subject to fits of melancholy, and frequently started from his bed, saying he was grappling with the devil; and he had been in one of these fits a few days before the murder. The jury found no insanity proved till after the murder; but he received a transportation pardon, and there seems little doubt that he was insane at the time of committing it.[1]

A similar case was that of Ann Sparrow, Glasgow, autumn 1829. It there appeared that she had poured vitriolic acid in considerable quantities down the throat of her own child, a girl of seven years of age, and nearly killed it. After committing the horrid act, she ran into the neighbours' houses in a state of evident derangement, saying that she had killed the devil; and before that she had frequently threatened her own life, and expressed to the neighbours her resolution to commit suicide. The case was proved, as well as the insanity, and she was ordered to be confined for life. So also, in a case related by Sir M. Hale, a woman, married, and of good character, not having slept for some nights after her delivery, and being otherwise evidently disordered in her intellects, being left alone, killed her own child. Shortly after she shewed the body to some persons, and told what she had done. She was instantly carried to jail, where she soon fell into a deep sleep, and wakened quite sane, and wondered how she came there. She was found not guilty of the murder.[2] Similar to that was the case of Agnes Crocket, 23d July 1756, who also had killed her own child. She was unmarried, but had nursed her child; and she was somewhat strange in her conduct, and, being left alone with the infant, destroyed it. She made, however, no attempt to conceal the body, but shewed it to the people of the house, saying the devil had tempted her. The evidence of insanity was very weak, and the jury rightly found the pannel guilty; but the Royal mercy prevented her execution.[3] Ano-

---

[1] Hume, i. 40 —[2] Hale, i. 36 —[3] Hume, i. 42.

ther case of a similar character was that of Robert Coalston, Jedburgh, April 1785. The pannel, in this case, had some years before been struck by lightning, and had ever since been subject to depression of spirits. Shortly before the event he became much more restless, and left his master's house for twenty-four hours, roaming about the country without any object. In the evening of the next day he returned to his master's house, and having now become outrageous, he abused his fellow servants and assaulted his mistress, snatched a child out of her arms, with which he ran out of the house, and soon after the child and the man were found together in an outhouse, the child dead and dashed to pieces, and the man sitting quietly beside it, unconscious of what he had done. On being taken to jail, he fell into a stupor, and on wakening had no recollection of what had happened, and expressed the greatest sorrow for it.[1] He was justly acquitted, and ordered to be confined for life. The plea of insanity was also successful in the case of John Somerville, December 8. 1704, who had shot a soldier of the Town Guard sent to apprehend him, on his becoming outrageous. It was proved that, three or four months before the fatal act, the Magistrates, observing a strangeness in his manner, had ordered him into confinement, and awarded him a safe conduct, which he had applied for, under the idea that there was a conspiracy against his life; that, four months before the slaughter, he had called for a sword to kill his own brother; that he had become strange and slovenly in his dress, and uttered hideous cries in church; that, on the morning in question, he ran into the street with a drawn sword, and after his committal behaved in so outrageous a manner, both in jail and to the magistrate who examined him, that he required to be confined in the cage of the prison. The jury brought in such a verdict as amounted to sustaining the defence of insanity, and saved the pannel's life.[2] A similar case occurred at Edinburgh, November 9. 1831, in the trial of George Waters for the murder of his son. It there appeared that the pannel, in a rude and strange manner, had taken his son by the hand, who was playing near the Water of Leith at Bonnington, and had a fork in his possession. As he got nearer

---

[1] Hume i. 42.—[2] Ibid. i 43.

the place where the fatal deed was perpetrated, his look appeared to the witnesses who saw him wilder and more frantic. He was seen looking into the water where the body was thrown after it was committed in a raised and insane manner. He was seen near the spot, in a subsequent part of the same day, moving about like a deranged person, and declared he was Sir William Wallace, and an honour to his country. When apprehended, he admitted having killed his son, made no resistance, spoke incoherently, and prayed aloud. The evening before he had spoke very insanely about having been at Inchkeith on a raft. In November 1829 he had been committed for disturbing his neighbours; he then had the appearance of *delirium tremens*, and was confined in a strait-waistcoat; and his relations had subsequently written to the Leith Police to look after the pannel, as he could not take care of himself. In these circumstances, the insanity was clearly proved, and so the jury held, with the approbation of the Court; and he was ordered to be confined for life.

It is by no means unusual to find instances of persons committing crime under the influence of insanity, who yet give no indications of it when conversing in jail with a medical man. An instance of this occurred in the case of Janet M‘Callum, Stirling, September 11. 1829. She was charged with having stolen a child belonging to her mistress, as well as a quantity of clothes from her house. Insanity was pleaded in bar of trial; but, after the examination of a single witness, who said he saw nothing insane about her, it was withdrawn, and she pleaded guilty. The case, however, was certified to the High Court, to give time to investigate the state of the woman's mind, which was very suspicious from the style of her declaration, and from most of the stolen articles having been found torn to pieces in the wood near her master's house. It ultimately turned out that she had been insane, and escaped some months before from a Lunatic Asylum near Greenock, and had been considered insane all her life. Still the medical men who examined her in Edinburgh declared they did not regard her as void of reason; but, as the crime had evidently been committed in a state of mental alienation, the prosecutor did not move for sentence, and she was confined till her sanity was restored.[1] Somewhat of the same description was the case of James Cummings, 12th January 1810, charged with murder. It came out in evidence that this man had met some years before with a severe injury on the head, but had recovered, enlisted, and was not considered by his fellow soldiers as insane; but he was silent, solitary, and quarrelsome when in liquor. One morning, when on guard as a sentinel, being teased by a fellow soldier, he became suddenly outrageous, and pursued him into the barracks. Having arrived there, he pushed at a woman with his bayonet, and missed her, but immediately after struck at a fellow soldier coming out of a door, and killed him on the spot. The jury, by a plurality of voices, found the pannel insane at the time of committing the murder; but there seems good grounds for Baron Hume's opinion, that it would have been more agreeable to law to have found him guilty, but recommended him, on account of a constitutional irritability, arising from his wound, over which he had no control, to the Royal mercy.[2]

Insanity was clearly proved in the case of William Douglas, May 28. 1827, who had set fire to the furniture of the lodgings which he occupied at Peebles, and nearly burned the house. He was convicted of attempt at fire-raising, but, in consequence of his state of mind, ordered to be confined for life.[3]

The law of England is founded on the same principles. Thus, in the noted case of James Hadfield, 1800, who was indicted for shooting at the King in Drury Lane Theatre, it was proved that he had been a private soldier, and severely wounded on the head, and that he had been dismissed from the army on account of insanity; and since his return to the country he had been confined as a lunatic. When affected by his disorder, he generally imagined that he held intercourse with God, and was Jesus Christ; but at other times he was blasphemous and irreligious, and sometimes quite sober and quiet. Three days before committing the act he was more than usually disturbed, and uttered many blasphemous expressions, rose and attempted to murder his child, an infant eight months old, of which he was uncommonly fond, ran into a cupboard, overthrew a jug, and declared that the water was his own blood. In the two days he was still worse, declaring that he had seen God in the

---

[1] Unreported.—[2] Hume, i. 41.—[3] Unreported.

night; that the coach was waiting, and that he had been to dine with the King, of whom he spoke very favourably, as well as of the whole royal family. Two hours before committing the act he drank tea, and after repeating his irreligious expressions went to the theatre. On the other hand, it appeared that he was noways disturbed in the theatre, where he had been nearly three quarters of an hour before the King appeared; that he rose when the King entered, and fired deliberately and with a good aim. When apprehended, he said he did not mean to kill the King; that he was glad he had not done so; that his life was forfeited, and he only meant by the attempt to get quit of his life of which he was weary. It was quite clear that this man was mad, and his case was eloquently pleaded by Lord Erskine. Lord Kenyon held, that, as the prisoner was insane immediately before the offence was committed, that it was probable that he had not recovered his senses at the time he fired, and that, as there was no reason to believe that he had recovered his sanity in the interval between the two events, he was entitled to an acquittal, which he accordingly received, and was ordered to be confined for life.[1]

2. If it appear from the evidence that the pannel, though partially deranged, was not so much so as to relieve him entirely from punishment, the proper course is to find him guilty; but, on account of the period of infirmity of mind, which he could not control, recommend him to the royal mercy.

Cases frequently occur in the highest degree perplexing both to the Court and jury, which can only be justly resolved by an application of the principle and mode of proceeding above set forth. They are those in which the accused was to a great degree to blame, but would not probably have committed the fatal act but for some constitutional or supervening derangement which rendered him not *so far responsible* as those who, by enjoying their reason unclouded, have no defence whatever against atrocious actions. In such cases there is a mixture of guilt and misfortune; for the former he should be severely punished, for the latter the extreme penalty of the law should

---

[1] Collis. 480, Russell L 11, 12.

be remitted. This can only be effected by adopting the course above pointed out.

Thus, in the case of William Gates, 21st November 1811, who was tried for shooting his wife with a musket, insanity was pleaded in bar of trial, but failed. On the evidence it appeared that whisky and consequent irritability of temper had a large share in the deed; but that, even when sober, he was of a melancholic temperament, and not like other men. The jury found that the act was committed in a state of insanity; But Baron Hume's opinion is obviously well founded, that they should have convicted, and recommended to the royal mercy.[1] In like manner, in the case of Pierce Hoskins, 23d April 1812, who was tried for the murder of his own child of four years' old, in a fit of drunken insanity, it appeared that the pannel, when intoxicated, was perfectly mad for days together, and in that state he committed the fatal deed. He was acquitted by the jury, but Baron Hume declares that it is questionable " whether an assize do right when they sustain the plea of this lower degree of infirmity of mind, exasperated only into a short fit of outrage and fury by excess of liquor; or where they receive as evidence of madness the atrocity or brutality of the act itself that has been done, though there have been no previous symptom of the disease."[2] The latter course was followed in the case of Alexander Campbell, 18th December 1809, who was found guilty of robbery, but recommended to mercy " on account of a certain degree of weakness of intellect to which he appears to be subject," and received in consequence a transportation pardon. In like manner, in the case of Susan Tilly, 11th March 1816, a more rational verdict was returned. It there appeared, from the testimony of two physicians and a surgeon, who had visited the pannel in jail, that she was of a weak mind, laboured under religious dreams, spoke of her interviews with the devil, said he had tempted her to burn the barn, and that God had reproved her by scorching her hands on the occasion. On other subjects, however, she reasoned correctly, and knew the distinction between right and wrong. She was convicted, but recommended to mercy; and received in consequence a pardon from the crown.[3] The same course was followed at Jedburgh, autumn 1831, in the case of Samuel Ro-

[1] Hume, 1 41 — [2] Ibid — [3] Ibid.

gors. He was accused of murdering an Irish reaper, in the course of harvest, whom he pursued into the river Tweed, and a considerable degree of insanity was proved at the trial. The jury found the pannel guilty; " but, in respect of the *alleged insanity*, recommend him to mercy." This way of wording the verdict was incorrect; but their meaning evidently was that a *certain degree* of *insanity* only was proved, insufficient to liberate the pannel from punishment altogether, but sufficient to excuse him from the extreme penalty of the law. The case, however, was not so viewed in the proper quarter, for he was executed in pursuance of his sentence.[1]

This seems the proper way of resolving those cases, unhappily too numerous, in which a fatal act has been committed in the course of a temporary fit of insanity, arising from excessive drinking. In all such cases, there is room for a distinction. If the pannel, naturally sane, has been rendered mad *solely by drink*, and this infirmity was known to him, he seems to have no defence whatever against the legal punishment of his actions, committed during the temporary alienation of reason; for it is the duty of every man to abstain from indulgences which lead to perilous consequences; and as intoxication is, as we shall presently see, no defence, so the insanity consequent upon its excessive and criminal indulgence seems to be as little.[2] But, on the other hand, if either the insanity has supervened from drinking, without the pannel's having been aware that such an indulgence in his case leads to such a consequence, or if it has arisen from the combination of drinking with a half crazy or infirm state of mind, or a previous wound, or illness, which rendered spirits fatal to his intellect, to a degree unusual in other men, or which could not have been anticipated, it seems inhuman to visit him with the extreme punishment which was suitable in the other case. In such a case, the proper course is to convict; but, in consideration of the degree of infirmity proved, recommend to the royal mercy.

3. If the pannel, though somewhat deranged, is yet able to distinguish right from wrong, in his own case, and to know he was doing wrong in the act which he com-

---

[1] Unreported.—[2] Hume, i. 41, Note.

mitted, he is liable to the full punishment of his criminal acts.

It has been already noticed, that the true test of insanity is to be found, not in the ability to distinguish between right and wrong in the general case, but with reference to the particular case of the pannel; and that he is amenable to the same punishment as other men, when his conscience tells him, or is in a situation to have told him, that what he did was wrong.[1]  But any thing short of this complete alienation of reason will be no defence; and mere oddity of manner, or half craziness of disposition, if unaccompanied by such an obscuring of the conscience, will not avail the prisoner.[2]  This is proved by a multitude of cases both in the Scottish and English practice.

Thus in the case of Thomas Gray, July 27. 1773, who was indicted for murder, by stabbing, it appeared that he was of a very weak intellect, subject to sudden gusts of passion, and excessive drinking, and in that state half crazy.  All this, however, being plainly short of madness, in the sense of the law, he was found guilty of the murder.[3]  In like manner, in the case of Robert Bonthorn, Dec. 12. 1763, charged with having pushed a revenue officer over a precipice into the sea, and broken his thigh, in revenge for some contraband goods seized in his possession, it was found by the jury that " the pannel's intellects were weak, irregular, and confused," and therefore they recommended him to the leniency of the Court.  He was sentenced, nevertheless, to a punishment adequate to his offence.[4]  It is not, however, indispensable that the madness should be continued in respect of time, so as it be clearly established at the date of the crime.  In the case, accordingly, of Sir Archibald Kinloch, June 29. 1795, who had had his senses injured by the acute delirium of a West India fever, and was afterwards subject to occasional fits of derangement, in one of which he killed his own brother; the jury justly found the insanity proven, though he regained his senses completely a short time after the melancholy event.[5]

The plea of insanity must be received with much more diffidence in cases proceeding from the desire of gain, as theft, swindling, or forgery, and which generally requires some art

---

[1] *Ante,* p 645.—[2] Hume, 1. 38.—[3] Ibid.—[4] Ibid.—[5] Ibid.

1

and skill for their completion, and argue a sense of the advantage of acquiring other people's property.[1]  It was pleaded for Thomas Henderson, March 9. 1731, that he was subject to occasional fits of insanity ; but, as it appeared that he had stolen the horse in the night, conducted himself prudently in the adventure, and rode straight by an unfrequented road to a distance, sold it, and taken a bill for the price, this defence was justly overruled.[2]  Such a defence has been very frequently attempted in subsequent cases, but hardly ever with success. Indeed it is difficult to figure that state of mental alienation which leads pannels to lay their hands on other people's property ; or, if they labour under such an illusion as made them mistake it for their own, which induces them to adopt the art, skill, and concealment necessary for its effectual perpetration. Such cases, however, do sometimes occur, one of which was that of John Smith, Dumfries, spring 1827, who was charged with horse-stealing, but was evidently insane, and treated as such ; and the other that of Alexander Duff, Aberdeen, spring 1829.  He had stole a horse, near Fyvie, out of a stable in the night ; and, with some art, having untied the door, which was fastened with a string, but he had afterwards abandoned it on the road-side, where it was found next morning among some corn, at the distance of five miles from the place of the theft. The whole circumstances evinced a disordered mind, and the charge, in consequence, was not insisted in by the prosecutor In all cases where such a defence is pleaded, the great thing to attend to is the subsequent conduct of the panuel, and whether he evinced any symptoms of conscious guilt, or a desire to conceal what had been done subsequent to its commission ; for, if he did, it is difficult to see how the plea can be well founded, that he knew not the criminal nature of his actions.

The same principles are fully established in the English practice.  In the case of Lord Ferrers, tried before the House of Lords for murder, it was proved that he was occasionally insane, and incapable of knowing what he was doing ; but the murder was deliberate, and, when he committed the crime, he had capacity sufficient to form a design and know its consequences.  He was found guilty and executed.[3]  Again, in Arnold's case, charged with shooting at Lord Onslow, it clearly

[1] Hume, 1 39.—[2] Ibid.—[3] State Trials, xix 947

appeared that the prisoner was, to a certain extent, deranged, and that he had greatly misconceived Lord Onslow's conduct, but formed a regular design, and prepared the proper means for carrying it into effect. Mr Justice Tracy laid it down to the jury, that the defence of insanity pleaded against a great offence, must be clearly established: that it is not every idle and frantic humour of a man which will exempt him from being accountable for his actions, but such a deprivation of reason as renders him as an infant, a brute, or a wild beast, incapable of knowing what he was doing. He was convicted, but, at Lord Onslow's intercession, reprieved, and confined for life.[1]

In Parker's case, who was indicted for entering the service of France, during its war with this country, the defence of the prisoner was rested on insanity. He was proved to have been weak from childhood, and that it excited surprize his being received in the army; but that he had deliberately entered the foreign service, and knew what he was doing when he did so, and stated as a reason that it was more agreeable to be at liberty, and have plenty of money, than be at want in a dungeon. He was convicted, under the direction of the Court that insanity was not established.[2]

Bowler's case, 2d July 1812, accused of shooting Mr Burrowes, was one of considerable difficulty. Insanity, occasioned by epilepsy, was the defence pleaded  It appeared that he had an epileptic fit in July 1811, and, since that time, had been very strange in his demeanour, eating his meat almost raw, and lying on the grass exposed to the rain, and so dejected, that it was necessary to watch him lest he should destroy himself. A commission of lunacy was produced, dated 17th June 1812, on which the prisoner was found insane from 30th March last. Mr Warburton, the keeper of a lunatic asylum, had no doubt of the insanity of the prisoner, and stated, that persons subject to that species of madness often took strong antipathies, founded on illusions totally destitute of foundation. Mr Justice Le Blanc laid it down to the jury, that they had to determine whether the prisoner, when he committed the offence, was incapable of distinguishing right from wrong, or under the influence of *an illusion*, in respect to the prosecutor, which rendered his mind at the moment insensible to the nature of

[1] Collison, 475; State Trials, xvi. 764 —[2] Russell, i. 9, Collison, 477.

the act he was about to commit, since in that case he would not
be legally responsible for his actions; but that, if he was not under such an illusion, or not incapable of understanding the distinction between right and wrong, he was amenable to punishment. This appears the true view of the subject. The jury,
after much deliberation, found the prisoner guilty.[1]

In Bellingham's case, 2d July 1812, accused of shooting Mr
Percival, insanity was pleaded to the jury, and many strong
facts brought out in support of the plea, tending to shew that
the prisoner falsely imagined himself subject to a long series of
injuries from that minister. But Lord Chief-Justice Mansfield
laid it down to the jury, that, in cases of murder, it must be
proved beyond all doubt that the prisoner, at the time of committing the act, did not consider that murder was a sin by the
laws of God and nature; that lunatics, as long as they can distinguish right from wrong, are answerable for their conduct;
and that the mere fancying of a series of injuries which did not
exist, was no defence against the charge of murder, if the prisoner were in other respects capable of distinguishing right
from wrong.[2] On this case it may be observed, that unquestionably the mere fancying a series of injuries to have been received will not serve as an excuse for murder, for this plain
reason, that supposing it true that such injuries had been received, they would have furnished no excuse for the shedding
of blood; but, on the other hand, such an illusion as deprives
the pannel of the sense that *what he did was wrong* amounts to
legal insanity, though he was perfectly aware that murder in
general was a crime; and, therefore, the law appears to have
been more correctly *laid down* in the cases of Hadfield and
Bowler than in this instance, though no injustice may have
been committed in the actual result

4. The proof of insanity it lies upon the pannel to establish; and in the case of an insane person having lucid intervals, it lies upon him to shew that the criminal act was
committed during the continuance of the disease, unless
those intervals were of short duration.

It is universally agreed that the proof of madness rests upon

[1] Collison, 673; Russell, i. 10.—[2] Collison, *Addenda*, 636; Russell, i. 11.

the pannel, and that if he fail in establishing that defence, he must suffer the ordinary punishment of his actions.[1] But in the case of an insane person having lucid intervals, the question occurs, upon whom does it lie to establish the state of the prisoner's mind at the commission of the deed?[2] There can be no room for any such dispute, except in those cases, which must be extremely rare, where there is evidence of previous madness with lucid intervals, but none of the pannel's situation at the time of committing the crime. And the general rule seems to be, that the pannel must substantiate his defence in this as well as in other cases, if the lucid intervals were long, and he was recently before in one of them; but that it is otherwise if they were extremely short, and he was apprehended shortly after the act in a state of furiosity.[3] Upon the whole, however, the remark of Mr Hume appears well founded, that the point should be left for the consideration of the jury, rather than made the subject of any unbending presumptions, which must in many instances be unsuitable to the justice of the particular case with which they are entrusted.[4]

5. Insanity may be pleaded in bar of trial, if the pannel be then insane, and the Court, *ex proprio motu*, will take cognizance of the state of a prisoner's mind, if he appear incapable of conducting his defence

Wherever a prisoner, whether he was insane or not at the time of committing an offence, is, or appears to be, insane at the time of the trial, it is the duty of his counsel to state the objection in bar of trial; and, if not stated by him, the Court are not only entitled, but bound, to take up the matter, if the appearance or circumstances of the pannel seem to indicate serious disorder of mind. Proof may competently be brought forward by any one capable of speaking to the point, whether contained in the list of witnesses or not; and this proof is taken by the Court itself, without the intervention of an assize.[5] This mode of proceeding was first fixed in the case of David Hunter, February 16. 1801, and has since been followed in various cases since that time, where the Court, either on the objection taken, or *ex proprio motu*, proceed to take evidence and

[1] Hume, i. 40.—[2] See Math&aelig;us, Tit. Qui Crim Adm. Poss No 6.—
[3] Hume, i. 41.—[4] Ibid.—[5] Ibid.

pronounce a deliverance themselves on the state of the pannel's mind. This was done, in particular, at Aberdeen, September 1815, in the case of James Essen, charged with murder. Again, in the cases of Donald Mackilliken, Inverness, April 1816, charged with hamesucken and assault; John Warrand, 17th January 1825, charged with a murder committed on a turn-key in a lunatic asylum, where this objection was not pleaded by counsel, but taken up voluntarily by the Court; and of John Smith, 25th June 1827, accused of horse-stealing.[1] The proper interlocutor to be pronounced in all such cases is, that the pannel is not at present a fit object of trial, and therefore order him to be confined, subject to the future orders of the Justiciary Court. If his health amends, he may apply, by petition, to the Court, praying to have his trial brought on; and if, on taking evidence, this appears well founded, the Court will fix a diet for his trial; or the Lord Advocate may serve him with a new indictment; and, on his sanity being established, and when he is prepared for the trial, it will proceed as in common cases.

6. Where the trial goes on, and insanity is found proven by the jury, the Court orders the prisoner to be confined for life, or until caution is found by his friends to put him in a place of safe custody during the remainder of his days.

If it be proved that a prisoner, in a fit of insanity, has committed a serious crime; and, most of all, if he has taken away a life, it is the duty of the Court to take care that so dangerous a character shall not again be let loose on society. Provision is accordingly always made in the sentence, acquitting him of the crime, for his confinement, either until his complete and final restitution to health is certified to the Court, or until his friends find caution to their satisfaction, to place him, for the remainder of his life, in a state of safe custody. In the case of Somerville, December 8. 1704, the Court ordered the prisoner to be confined in the house of correction, " never to be liberated therefrom, but upon a certificate under the hand of the magistrates, and two known physicians, that he has con-

---

[1] Hume, ii 144.

talesced and become sound in his judgment.' " In modern practice, the usual course is to order him to be confined till his relations shall become bound, under a sufficient penalty, to detain him in safe custody for the future. This was done in the following cases· Robert Spence, June 3. 1747; Jean Blair, March 14. 1781; Gordon Kinloch, June 29 1795; James Cummings, February 7. 1810; William Gates, November 21. 1811; Peter Lawrie, May 22. 1820;[2] John Warrand, January 17. 1825; Lieutenant William Douglas, May 28. 1827; and Ann Sparrow, Glasgow, autumn 1829.[3] Where the accused is in the rank of a gentleman, the penalty is proportionally greater. In the case of Gordon Kinloch it was L.10,000.

SECT. II.—INTOXICATION.

Nothing is better established in our law than that intoxication, so far from being an alleviation, is an aggravation of a criminal charge; and indeed such is the tendency to this brutalizing vice, among the lower orders in this country, that if it were sustained as a defence, three-fourths of the whole crimes in the country would go unpunished; for the slightest experience must be sufficient to convince every one, that almost every crime that is committed, is directly or indirectly connected with whisky. For these reasons, our law utterly disowns any such defence, and that without any regard to the distinction between those who are occasionally and habitually drunk, *inter ebrios et ebriosos*, known in the civil law.[4] But this important doctrine requires to be received with the due degree of caution.

1. The defence of intoxication cannot be received against any criminal charge, for an offence in itself perilous or hurtful.

In cases innumerable, the defence of intoxication has been overruled in our practice; as, for example, in that of Joseph Hume, February 1732, for murder; Hamilton and Grieve, August 1716, for murder; Maclachlan, March 1737, for murder

---

[1] Hume, i. 44.—[2] Ibid. 45.—[3] Unreported —[4] Hume, i. 46.

and riot; and Patrick Kinninmount, December 13. 1697, for blasphemy.[1]

In two late cases, the same just and necessary rule has been strongly exemplified. Peter Bowers was indicted 14th June 1819, for murdering a brother workman with an axe. It clearly appeared that he was not an habitual drunkard, but intoxicated when he committed the fatal act, and, some hours after, when brought before the sheriff for examination. He was nevertheless found guilty, and sentenced to death, with a recommendation to mercy, which procured him a transportation pardon.[2] In like manner, on 13th March 1827, Mysie Brown was brought to trial for attempting to murder her husband by strangling. It appeared that she had assaulted him when lying in bed and asleep, and had succeeded in putting a cord round his neck, and suspending him from a beam, where he was accidentally discovered by a neighbour, and cut down before quite dead. The woman was so infuriated with drink at the time, that she continued to vent execrations upon the body when lying apparently lifeless before her. The husband declared he had no reason to believe she would have committed such an act, when sober, and that he had no objection to live with her again. She was found guilty, but recommended to mercy, on account of her age, and sentenced to eighteen months' confinement in Bridewell, with no stronger drink than water.[3]

The law of England is founded on the same principles. If drunkenness with them be voluntary, it cannot excuse a man from the commission of any crime, but is held as an aggravation of whatever he does;[4] but if by constraint, or the prescription of a physician, a man is involuntarily reduced to madness by intoxication, he has the same defence as in any other case of insanity, and the same will hold if he be *permanently* and clearly mad, even though a long course of previous intoxication may have been its original cause.[5] And, though voluntary drunkenness is held no excuse for the commission of a crime, yet where, as in a charge of murder, it is material to inquire whether the thing was done *ex proposito*, or in hot blood, the fact of the person being intoxicated is a point to be taken into consideration.[6]

[1] Hume, i. 46, 47.—[2] Ibid i. 46.—[3] Syme, No. 43.—[4] Hale, i. 32; Hawkins, 1 c. 1. § 6.—[5] Blackstone, iv. 26; Plowd. 19; Russell, i. 8.—[6] Per Holroyd, Russell, i. 8

2. The plea of intoxication is relevant to diminish the punishment of such offences, as are not so much *mala in se* as proscribed for the good order of society.

The unbending but necessary rule now laid down, applies to such crimes as murder, assault, theft, robbery, or the like, as are contrary to good conscience, and fatal to the peace and good order of society; but a more indulgent rule may be followed in regard to such crimes, as blasphemy, uttering seditious expressions, cursing of parents, or the like; which are serious offences, when uttered in good and sober earnest, as expressing a wicked disposition; but are to be considered rather as *verba jactantia*, when flowing from the effects of intoxication, and scarcely deserving of serious notice, unless when they appear the indications of hidden designs.[1]

### SECTION III.—OF MINORITY AND PUPILAGE.

THE vast increase in juvenile delinquency. arising from the corrupted manners, temptations to vice, and incessant drunkenness, of a large proportion of the lower orders, in all our great cities, has unfortunately fixed the law on too well known a footing in regard to minority and infancy, to render any lengthened discussion necessary.

1. Minors, whether male or female, who have attained the age of fourteen years, are liable to any punishment, not excepting death itself, for grave offences.

Nothing is better fixed in our practice, than that for such offences as murder, robbery, housebreaking, fire-raising, or the like, which are forbidden, under the highest penalties, by God himself, and contrary to the conscience even of inveterate offenders, the highest punishment may be inflicted.[2] Without quoting other examples, it may be sufficient to refer to the case of Samuel Pirrie, post-boy, Ayr, April 21. 1786, who was sentenced to be hanged for stealing from the mail, and recommended to mercy, though the verdict bore that he was " under, or little above fourteen years, and of weak understanding." He

---

[1] Hume, i. 47.—[2] Ibid. i 31, 32

received, with great propriety, a transportation pardon from the Crown.[1] In like manner David Urquhart, aged sixteen, was sentenced to death, but pardoned by the Crown, and transported for the same offence of stealing from the mail, on 4th September 1797. So also Macdonald, aged eighteen, and Macintosh, aged sixteen, were sentenced to death, and executed for murder and robbery, in March 1812; as were Black and Macdonald, 17th June 1813, for shooting a man near Coltbridge, the one being eighteen, the other nineteen years old.[2] Again, on 25th March 1818, Main and Aitchison, two boys of fifteen years each, were sentenced to death, but received a transportation pardon; on 11th January 1823, Charles Maclaren, Thomas Grierson, and James Macewan, convicted of theft by housebreaking, were sentenced to death, though Macewan declared he was fourteen, and Grierson thirteen years of age.[3] Lastly, at Glasgow, autumn 1823, Edward Maccaffie was condemned to death for highway robbery, though only sixteen years old, but he received a transportation pardon;[4] and on 23d December 1824, Alexander Mackay, aged fifteen, was sentenced to death; James Stevenson, Glasgow, autumn 1826, convicted of robbery, aged eighteen, was condemned and executed. But of all such cases of extreme youth it may be observed, that though the law is rightly allowed to take its course in pronouncing sentence; yet the royal clemency generally interposes to commute it to transportation; and, certainly, unless in extreme cases, such as murder or fire-raising, or atrocious rape, this practice should not be departed from.

But very different has been the practice in regard to the *transportation* of such juvenile offenders. Our Judges have most justly considered, that the transportation of such youthful depredators is the only means not only of ridding society of their crimes, but of giving them that chance of amendment in another country which they have lost in their own. In cases innumerable, accordingly, transportation has been inflicted on minors just turned fourteen years. Thus, on 21st December 1818, Gun and Chisholm, two boys of fourteen years of age, were transported fourteen years, as was Robert Thomson, Glasgow, 14th April 1821, though aged only thirteen years. The like sentence, passed at Glasgow, September 1826, on Wil-

<hr>

[1] Hume, i. 33.—[2] Ibid. i. 32.—[3] Ibid.—[4] Unreported.

liam Weir, aged fourteen, and at Edinburgh, July 7. 1828, on Daniel Cormie, a boy of fifteen[1]; but it is superfluous to quote farther examples of a matter of daily practice.

2. Pupils, though below fourteen years of age, nay though only nine, ten, or eleven years of age, may be subjected to an arbitrary punishment, if they appear qualified to distinguish right from wrong, but not to the pain of death.

The same salutary principle of our law, in transporting juvenile delinquents, has been rigorously applied, of late years, to boys and girls of much younger years, if either from their conduct or appearance they seem capable of understanding the nature of a crime. It has not been unusual to transport children of eleven and twelve years, where their character seemed hardened, and to imprison them where they did not appear so completely depraved.[2] Thus at Glasgow, spring 1818, Robert Turnbull, a boy of *ten*, and Boyd Hay, a boy of *nine* years of age, were convicted of theft by housebreaking, and sentenced to twelve months' confinement in Bridewell. At the same place, April 1817, James Gracie, a boy between *thirteen* and *fourteen*, convicted of theft, was sentenced to twelve months in Bridewell. At Jedburgh, April 1817, Rutherford and Watson, two boys of *thirteen* years of age, were sentenced to eighteen months in Bridewell.[3] In the High Court, 6th November 1827, William Campbell, aged *nine* years, was sentenced to eighteen months' hard labour in Bridewell; and at Glasgow, April 1828, Mary Anne Macleish and Elizabeth Stewart, aged respectively *thirteen* and *eleven* years, received the same punishment.[4]

But, in cases of more hardened delinquency, transportation is constantly inflicted on pupils of this tender age. Thus Alexander Livingston, 1749, a boy of twelve years of age, convicted of stabbing another boy, so as to occasion his death, was held, on a full argument, to be *doli capax*, and transported for life.[5] John Brand, June 30. 1789, a boy of *thirteen* and eight months, was tried for stealing letters from the post-office,

---

[1] Unreported.—[2] Hume, i. 32, 33.—[3] Unreported.—[4] Unreported.—[5] Maclaurin, No. 55.

by a contrivance of his own, and sentenced to transportation.[1]
On 13th November 1493, at Lauder, Thomas Gothraston, a
boy eight years old, charged with murder, was ordered to be
sharply scourged.[2]  And, in the cases of Maxwell, January 11.
1605, who was *eight* years of age, and William Menzies, Perth,
May 10. 1800, who was also *eight* years old, the plea of nonage
was proposed and repelled.[3]  So also James Alexander, Perth,
18th April 1801, convicted of wilful fire-raising, aged *thirteen*
and four months, was sentenced, on a restriction of the libel,
to fourteen years transportation, after the case had been certified to all the Judges, on the point of the punishment which
should be inflicted.[4]  John Maclean, Glasgow, April 1817,
aged *fourteen*, was transported fourteen years.[5]  At Aberdeen,
autumn 1827, John Milier, Patrick Quin, and others, convicted of theft by housebreaking, received fourteen years transportation, though only thirteen years of age each.

On a due consideration of these precedents, many of which
were for the most atrocious crimes, inferring death in a grown
person, there seems no sufficient authority for inflicting that
punishment on any pannel under fourteen years of age;[6] and
certainly there is good reason for confining that extreme penalty
to the case of more advanced delinquents, and not cutting off
life in infancy, and at a period when, whatever may have been
the depravity of the acts committed, complete corruption of
the heart can hardly have taken place, and the influence of
guilty parents, or elder associates, is the general cause of their
having been perpetrated.

3. Children under *seven* years of age are held to be
incapable of crime, and not the object of any punishment.

No authority has ever yet maintained that an infant under
*seven* years of age is liable to any punishment; and certainly
at that tender age, whatever vice exists, must be ascribed to
improper tuition, or bad example, and the child cannot be considered as answerable for a violation of what he could not understand.[7]

In the law of England it is held that a child below seven
years of age can be visited with no punishment; that between
seven and fourteen an infant shall *prima facie* be presumed to

[1] Hume, i. 34.—[2] Ibid. i. 35.—[3] Ibid.—[4] Ibid.—[5] Unreported.—[6] Hume,
i. 34.—[7] Ibid. i. 35.

be *doli incapax*, yet so that this presumption weakens as the prisoner's age approaches puberty, and may at any period between these years be overcome by evidence of a capacity for crime, *si malitia supplet ætatem*.[1] The evidence of malice in such cases must be pregnant if the crime be serious; but, if sufficient proof of a malignant disposition exists, they hold that an infant of ten years of age may be hanged;[2] and, in one case, a child of that age, was actually hanged for the crime of murder;[3] but it is probable that this precedent would not now be followed, for the matter underwent great consideration, and terminated in the child's life being saved, in similar circumstances, in the case of William York, Bury Assizes, 1748. This boy was ten years of age, and had murdered a little girl, a companion of his own, of five years, for which he was sentenced, by Chief Justice Willis, to be hanged. He was reprieved, however, for the opinion of the Twelve Judges, as to whether sentence should be carried into execution. The Judges held unanimously, 1st, That the declarations which the boy had emitted before the Justice, and other persons who examined him, were rightly left to the jury; 2d, That the circumstances of the case indicated so much of what Lord Hale calls a *mischievous discretion*, that he was amenable to the highest punishment. A second reprieve, however, was granted to give time for farther investigation, and in the end, many years after, the boy got a pardon, upon condition of his entering the Royal Navy.[4] A boy under fourteen is held incapable, from defect of power, of committing a rape; but he may be art and part in a rape committed by one of maturer years, if it appears, from other circumstances, he had a mischievous discretion.[5]

Nearly akin to pupilarity is that state of mental imbecility which arises from the pannel's being deaf and dumb. It was solemnly decided by the Court, in the case of Jane Campbell, 17th July 1817, that a person in this situation may be tried and punished, if it appear that he is capable of understanding that what he did was wrong.[6] But a previous proof by the prosecutor that this is the case is indispensable where the defect has existed from infancy; and in all cases it is a difficulty which will be found no easy matter to surmount.[7]

[1] Hale, i 25–27; Blackstone, iv. 23.—[2] Russell, i 3.—[3] Spiguonal's Case, Hale, i. 26.—[4] York's Case, Fost. 70; Russell, i 5.—[5] Hale, i. 630.—[6] Hume, i. 45.—[7] Ibid.

SECT. III.—OF SUBJECTION TO OTHERS.

As crime consists in the intentional violations of the rights of others, it follows that it cannot be visited with punishment where it has arisen not from intention or voluntary depravity, but such a coercion as has deprived the party of the free exercise of his will. The consideration, therefore, of the restraints on the will forms an important subject of inquiry.

1. A wife is not excusable in the commission of any crime by the influence or power of her husband, if she has taken any part in its commission along with him.

Nothing is better established in our practice, than that the authority or coercion of the husband is no palliation for the commission of crimes by the wife, who is presumed to have at least such freedom of action left as to be capable of resisting the temptations to crime, of whatever sort they may be.[1] And this holds not only in regard to the more atrocious crimes, such as murder, robbery, or fire-raising, but the smaller, such as theft, assault, reset, forgery, or the like, which are not so perilous by the danger and alarm with which they are attended.[2] Nothing is more common, accordingly, than to have a husband and wife put to the bar and tried together on the same libel for the same offence. Witness among other instances, if any were necessary, the recent cases of John Stewart and Catherine Wright, his wife, convicted of murder, July 14. 1829, and James Byres and Mary Steele, his wife, Glasgow, autumn 1831, both executed for murder, and William Heath and Elizabeth Crowder, his wife, Glasgow, same circuit, tried for breaking into one of the Glasgow Banks.[5] Some argument on this head took place in the case of James Hyslop and Jessie Hyslop, his wife, accused of assisting French prisoners to make their escape from prison. It was pleaded that she was married to a French prisoner, and had by his command assisted the others to make their escape; but, upon the reply, that the law could not recognise any marriage between a British subject and an alien prisoner of war, and that this was not one of the *leviora*

---

[1] Hume, i. 47, 48.—[2] Ibi t. i. 48.—[5] Unreported.

3

*delicti* where alone, if at all, our law can admit the command of the husband to exculpate the wife, the libel was found relevant.[1]

On this point the law of England is more favourable than that of Scotland to the wife of a prisoner. According to them, she shall not suffer any punishment for committing a theft, or even a housebreaking, by the coercion of her husband, or in his company, which law deems a coercion.[2] This, however, only holds if the husband be *present*,[3] and, therefore, where a woman, by the incitements of a husband, but *out of his presence*, uttered a forged order for the receipt of a seaman's prize-money, for this she was held by the Twelve Judges answerable in her own person, and the husband was held an accessary before the fact.[4] And, in a subsequent case, it was laid down as clear law on the Bench, " that the coercion must be at the time of the *act done*, and then the law out of tenderness refers it *prima facie* to the coercion of the husband ;" but, where the crime has been completed in his absence, no subsequent act of his, though it might make him an accessary to the felony of the wife, can influence what was done in his absence."[5] But the privilege of the wife does not extend to the greater crimes, as treason, murder, or robbery, though performed in presence of her husband, and by his express command ;[6] nor to any cases in which she is either the principal actor, or was the original promoter of it.[7]

2. A wife shall not be held answerable for harbouring, concealing, or comforting, her husband, even after the commission of the greatest crimes ; and if any crime with which she is charged appears to have flowed from such a motive, she shall be absolved for its commission.

By the first principles of Nature, a wife is bound to protect, defend, and cherish her husband in all circumstances, and not the less so because he has been involved in crime and has no refuge but in her affection and fidelity.[8] She cannot, therefore, be involved in any prosecution for any act done by her from such motives, even though it should in itself savour of a

---

[1] Hume, ι. 49 —[2] Hale, ι 45 ; Blackstone, ιv 29.—[3] Hale, ι 45.—[4] Russell, ιι. 18 ; Leach, ι 1096.—[5] Hughes' Case, Russell, ι. 18.—[6] Hale, ι. 45.—[7] Russell, ι. 16, 17.—[8] Hume, ι. 49

criminal nature.[1] " Uxor alicujus non tenetur virum suum ac-
cusare, nec furtum suum nec feloniam detegere, cum ipsa sui
ipsius potestatem non habeat." [2]

But what shall be said of cases such as reset of theft, where
the act of the wife, in harbouring or concealing her husband,
or the goods he has stolen, is not only yielding to the natural
and excusable feelings which she must entertain towards him
in every situation, but commencing in her own person a separate offence, to which law has attached an appropriate punishment? This question is to be resolved by a distinction. Where
the wife appears to have plied the trade of reset along with
her husband for a length of time, and to have taken an active
part in carrying it on, he furnishing the stolen goods and she
taking charge of the selling and disposing of them, certainly it
is not to be supposed that in such a case she has any exemption from her connexion with him, or that a partnership in iniquity, in which she has been so active an agent, can be carried
on with impunity to any of its members. On the other hand,
if her accession was confined merely to a few acts: if she appear to have done nothing to instigate him to the commission
of crime, and, above all, if she has *merely concealed*, and not
disposed, or attempted to dispose, of the stolen goods, her conduct will not be considered as the proper object of punishment,
but ascribed rather to her design to screen him from detection
and punishment. Authorities exist on both sides of the rule.
Thus, on the one hand, in the case of Robert Stewart and Catherine Stewart, his wife, 8th June 1818, convicted of no less
than *seven* different acts of reset, committed for a considerable
period of time, the libel was found relevant against both, and
they were transported for life.[3] So also in the case of William
Mackie, mariner, Boyd Maccormick, and Mary Maccormick
his wife, Aberdeen, September 1827, a charge of theft, by
housebreaking and theft, was sustained against the two male
prisoners, and of reset against the female one, and they all received seven years transportation, as it appeared that the wife
had taken an active part in plying the trade, and had offered
some of the stolen articles for sale.[4] On the other hand, in
the case of Thomas Mallach and Margaret Rennie his wife,
Glasgow, spring 1828, where the husband was charged with two

[1] Hume, i. 49.—[2] Stat. William, c. 19, No. 1.—[3] Hume, i. 48.—[4] Unreported.

2

acts of housebreaking, and the wife with resetting the articles stolen by him in her own house; the Lord Justice-Clerk Boyle recommended to the prosecutor not to insist in the case against the wife, which was accordingly done, and she was acquitted, as it appeared that she was not concerned in the actual depredation, and merely received the stolen articles into their common house, and hid them there, without having had any hand in vending them to the public, or realizing a profit from the offence.[1]

3. The commands or influence of the father afford a just ground for mitigation of punishment to children under puberty, but amounts to no legal defence, unless the offence be trivial and the youth extreme.

Such is the depravity of many of the lower orders in our great cities, from the irregular lives which they lead, and the incessant habits of intoxication in which they indulge, that, if it were once established that the commands or exhortations of the parent are a protection to the child, there would be no end to the commission of crimes. Multitudes of persons in great towns send their children out regularly in the morning to the streets or highways to beg, and steal as opportunity may occur; and not only scold, but sometimes punish them severely, if they return at night without something picked up in one or other of these ways. It is settled law, accordingly, that the commands of the parent will not *absolve* the child in the commission of crime, however much, in particular circumstances, it may alleviate the punishment.[2] In the case of John Rae, indeed, January 21. 1662, the pannel was assoilzied in respect of his nonage, and of what he did being by the command of his father; but this was mainly on account of the *age* of the boy.[3] And, in no other case has the command of the parent been sustained as a *defence* to the minor culprit, though doubtless it must always operate as an alleviation of punishment. In the case, accordingly, of Thomas and David Urquhart, 4th September 1797, accused of stealing from the mail, the son, a boy of sixteen years, was condemned to death, with a recommendation to mercy, though it appeared clearly that he acted

[1] Unreported.—[2] Hume, 1. 50.—[3] Ibid

at the instigation of his father.[1]   Miserable cases occur every
day of children being instigated to the commission of crimes
by their parents, without such a circumstance ever being
thought of as any legal defence.   Such a case occurred at
Glasgow, autumn 1829, in that of Patrick Finnie.[2]   In awarding the punishment, in such a case, the Judges justly follow a distinction: if the child who has committed an offence
worthy of transportation can in any way be separated from,
or rendered independent of, the parents who have urged him to
the commission of the offence, they try the effect of hard labour
in Bridewell; but, if he cannot be separated from such guilty
protectors, or has acquired the character of an habitual thief,
or is evidently incorrigible in this country, they at once transport him, as his only chance of amendment, and generally for
such a period as will ensure his being sent to New South
Wales.

4. The commands, however express, of the master, furnish no excuse to the servant or apprentice in the commission of crimes.

Whatever may have been the case formerly, during violent
and arbitrary times, the law, as above stated, has now been
settled for a very long period, both by the Scotch[3] and English
law.[4]

5. The excuse of compulsion will only avail if the pannel was in such a situation that he could not resist without manifest peril to his life or property.

The plea of compulsion is admitted with much caution by
the law, and clear evidence justly required, if the inability of
the pannel to resist the forcible attempt said to have been made
to divert him from the path of right conduct.[5]   There are
some cases, however, in which it must plainly be sustained.
Such are those of a great rising or commotion in the country,
which overpower the civil force, and set at nought the authority of government.   A person, therefore, will not be held
guilty of treason if, being in a part of the country commanded
by the rebels, he yield them supplies of arms, money, or pro-

[1] Hume, i. 50.—[2] Unreported.—[3] Hume, i. 51.—[4] Hale, i. 41, Hawkins, i.
c. 1. § 14; Russell, i. 15.—[5] Hume, i. 51.

visions, nor even though he be with them for a time in arms, if it distinctly appear that all this was done under the threat of death or military execution, and continued no longer than that state of coercion endured.[1]  Nay, the same will hold without any treasonable insurrection if an ordinary mob, or any unlawful assembly of persons, compel any individual by threats and violence to accompany them on any unlawful expedition, provided he did not yield too easily to intimidation, but held out as long as in such circumstances can be expected from a man of ordinary resolution.[2]  Accordingly, in the cases of Andrew Fairney, July 25. 1726, William Gilchrist, March 12. 1741, and Robert Main and others, October 11. 1725, the defence of force and compulsion was sustained against charges of mobbing and rioting, if supported by sufficient evidence.  Such a defence seems in a peculiar manner applicable in a case of piracy, where the mutineers frequently gain the entire command of a vessel, and compel many within it, much against their will, to engage in that desperate and lawless mode of life.[3]  In the case, accordingly, of Roger Hews and sixteen others, November 15. 1720, charged with piracy, the jury found the " defence of force, and fear of death, and sickness, proven" in favour of seven of the pannels, and they were accordingly dismissed from the bar.[4]

6. The express command of a magistrate or officer will exonerate an inferior officer or soldier, unless the command be to do something plainly illegal, or beyond his known duty.

If through gross ignorance, or neglect, or design, a judge or magistrate pronounce an unlawful sentence, what shall be said of the officers or others who carry it into execution?  This question is to be resolved by a distinction similar to that already noticed when treating of homicide, by officers in striving to execute irregular or defective warrants.  If the order or warrant was plainly illegal, as, for example, to strangle a prisoner in jail, or to poison him, or the like, certainly the mere possession of such a warrant will not prevent the officer who

---

[1] Hume, i. 51.—[2] Ibid , State Trials, xviii. 393, Russell, i. 15.—[3] Ibid —
[4] Ibid.

wickedly yields it obedience from being held as art and part in the legal murder, and suffering for its commission. But, on the other hand, if the error was in such a part of the proceedings as the officer intrusted with its execution has no opportunity of seeing, and is not called upon in duty to examine, and if the warrant put into his hands be fair and in ordinary form, certainly he will not be answerable for any illegality or vice in the previous and to him inscrutable proceedings[1].

The same distinction is applicable to the case of a soldier acting in obedience to the orders of his superior officer, with this additional circumstance in his favour, that he is not only in a much humbler station, and trained to more implicit obedience, than a legal functionary, but subjected to a peculiar and peremptory code of laws, armed with powers of extraordinary severity, for the express purpose of enforcing on his part the most implicit obedience to command.[2] It will require, therefore, the very strongest case to subject a soldier to punishment for what he does in obedience to the distinct commands of his commanding officer. But still this privilege must have its limits; it is confined to what is commanded in the course of official duty, and which does not plainly and evidently transgress its limits.[3] For what if an officer command a private soldier to commit murder, or to steal, or to aid him in a rape, or if he order a file of soldiers to fire on an inoffensive multitude, certainly in none of these cases will the privates be exempt from punishment if they yield obedience to such criminal mandates.[4] Of this description was the case of William Ferguson and others, February 6. 1674, who had been sent out to poind for deficiencies in the quota of militiamen, upon the warrant of their officer alone, who had no right to give it, and who had been guilty of great excess in carrying it into execution. They were held answerable for the consequences.[5] But these cases are rare, and, in general, the express command of the magistrate is considered as liberating the military officer, and that of the officer the private soldier

7. The excuse of extreme distress or hunger is not admitted as a legal defence, though, when duly proved, it may be a just ground for extenuating punishment.

---

[1] Hume, i. 54.—[2] Ibid.—[3] Ibid.—[4] Ibid.—[5] Ibid.

The principle of our law in this respect is just and necessary, that no defence founded on alleged want or necessity can be admitted.[1] The law of *Burdensack*,[2] as it was called, did not amount to an absolute liberation from the punishment of theft, but only a mitigation of its pains.[3] Even under this limitation, however, the law has long ago been abandoned,[4] and the mitigation of the usual penalty in such cases wherein severe want has been really experienced, is left to the discretion of the judge; or, if the case be one of a capital nature, to the interposition of the royal mercy.[5]

[1] Burnett, 117; Hume, 1. 55 —[2] Reg Maj. iv. Act 16.—[3] Skene, c. 13. No. 9; Hume, l. 55.—[4] Burnett, 117 —[5] Hume, l. 56.

# INDEX.

# INDEX.

FINIS.

PRINTED BY NEILL & CO.
OLD FISHMARKET.

Lightning Source UK Ltd.
Milton Keynes UK
UKOW030029131011

180204UK00002B/134/P